Linux Essentials for Cybersecurity

William "Bo" Rothwell
Denise Kinsey

Pearson

Linux Essentials for Cybersecurity

ISBN-13: 978-0-7897-5935-1
ISBN-10: 0-7897-5935-7

Library of Congress Control Number: 2018941152

1 18

Trademarks

All terms mentioned in this book that are known to be trademarks or service marks have been appropriately capitalized. Pearson IT Certification cannot attest to the accuracy of this information. Use of a term in this book should not be regarded as affecting the validity of any trademark or service mark.

Warning and Disclaimer

Every effort has been made to make this book as complete and as accurate as possible, but no warranty or fitness is implied. The information provided is on an "as is" basis. The authors and the publisher shall have neither liability nor responsibility to any person or entity with respect to any loss or damages arising from the information contained in this book.

Special Sales

For information about buying this title in bulk quantities, or for special sales opportunities (which may include electronic versions; custom cover designs; and content particular to your business, training goals, marketing focus, or branding interests), please contact our corporate sales department at corpsales@pearsoned.com or (800) 382-3419.

For government sales inquiries, please contact governmentsales@pearsoned.com.

For questions about sales outside the U.S., please contact intlcs@pearson.com.

Editor-In-Chief: Mark Taub

Product Line Manager: Brett Bartow

Executive Editor: Mary Beth Ray

Development Editor: Eleanor Bru

Managing Editor: Sandra Schroeder

Project Editor: Mandie Frank

Copy Editor: Bart Reed

Indexer: Ken Johnson

Proofreader: Debbie Williams

Technical Editors: Casey Boyles, Andrew Hurd, Ph.D.

Publishing Coordinator: Vanessa Evans

Designer: Chuti Prasertsith

Composition: Studio Galou

Contents at a Glance

Table of Contents

About the Authors

William "Bo" Rothwell At the impressionable age of 14, William "Bo" Rothwell crossed paths with a TRS-80 Micro Computer System (affectionately known as a "Trash 80"). Soon after the adults responsible for Bo made the mistake of leaving him alone with the TRS-80, he immediately dismantled it and held his first computer class, showing his friends what made this "computer thing" work.

Since this experience, Bo's passion for understanding how computers work and sharing this knowledge with others has resulted in a rewarding career in IT training. His experience includes Linux, Unix, and programming languages such as Perl, Python, Tcl, and BASH. He is the founder and president of One Course Source, an IT training organization.

Denise Kinsey, Ph.D, CISSP, CISCO Dr. Denise Kinsey served as a Unix administrator (HP-UX) in the late 1990s and realized the power and flexibility of the operating system. This appreciation led to her home installation of different flavors of Linux and creation of several academic courses in Linux. With a strong background in cybersecurity, she works to share and implement best practices with her customers and students. Dr. Kinsey is an assistant professor at the University of Houston.

Dedications

For the last three books, I have thanked my wife and daughter for their patience, and my parents for all that they have done throughout my life. My gratitude continues, as always.

—William "Bo" Rothwell

May 2018

This book is dedicated to…

My family, who inspire and encourage me…

My students, whom I work to inspire and who inspire me…

Those who are interested in Linux and/or cybersecurity. I hope you find the information useful, valuable, and easily applicable.

—Denise Kinsey

Acknowledgments

Thanks to everyone who has put in a direct effort toward making this book a success:

- Denise, my co-author, for her extremely valuable insight and for dealing with the chaos around my creative process.
- Mary Beth, for putting her trust in me for yet another book.
- Eleanor and Mandie, for keeping me on track (with very gentle reminders) and all of the hard work and dedication.
- Casey and Andrew, for excellent feedback and for proving four brains are better than two.
- Bart Reed, for ~~painsteakingly~~ painstakingly reviewing every word, sentence, graphic, table, and punctuation character.
- And all the other folks at Pearson who have had an impact on this book.

I have always felt that I was fortunate because I had strong technical skills combined with the ability to impart my knowledge to others. This has allowed me to be an IT corporate instructor and courseware developer for almost 25 years now. It is the experiences I have had teaching others that have put me in a position to write a book like this. So, I would also like to acknowledge the following people:

- All of the students who have listened to me for countless hours (I have no idea how you do this). I teach to see the light bulbs go on in your heads. You have taught me patience and given me an understanding that everyone needs to start from some place. Thanks for making me a part of your journey.
- All of the excellent instructors I have observed. There have been so many of them, it would be impossible to list them all here. I'm a much better "knowledge facilitator" because of what I have learned from you.
- Lastly, I have no way to express my gratitude toward people like Linus Torvalds. Without pioneers like Linus (who is one of a great many), so much of the technology we now take for granted just wouldn't exist. These folks have given us all the opportunity to learn tools that we can use to make even more great inventions. I urge you to not think of Linux as just an operating system, but rather as a building block that allows you and others to create even more amazing things.

—William "Bo" Rothwell

May, 2018

Thank you to all who made this book a reality—from Mary Beth and everyone at Pearson Education, to the technical editors for their time and detailed reviews.

Also, thanks to the many wonderful faculty in cybersecurity who share their knowledge freely and offer their assistance—from the design of virtual networks to the design of curriculum. This includes the many wonderful people at the Colloquia for Information Systems Security Education (CISSE), the Center for System Security and Information Security (CSSIA), and the National CyberWatch Center. The resources provided by these organizations are wonderful and a great place to start for anyone looking to build cybersecurity programs.

Finally, I wish to thank my co-workers W. "Art" Conklin and R. "Chris" Bronk. I appreciate your guidance in the world of academia and suggestions for research.

—Denise Kinsey

About the Technical Reviewers

Casey Boyles developed a passion for computers at a young age, and started working in the IT field more than 25 years ago. He quickly moved on to distributed applications and database development. Casey later moved on to technical training and learning development, where he specializes in full stack Internet application development, database architecture, and systems security. Casey typically spends his time hiking, boxing, or smoking cigars while "reading stuff and writing stuff."

Andrew Hurd is the Technical Program Facilitator of Cybersecurity for Southern New Hampshire University. Andrew is responsible for curriculum development and cyber competition teams. He holds a dual Bachelor of Arts in computer science and mathematics, a masters in the science of teaching mathematics, and a Ph.D. in information sciences, specializing in information assurance and online learning. Andrew, the author of a Network Guide to Security+ lab manual and Cengage, has more than 17 years as a higher education professor.

We Want to Hear from You!

As the reader of this book, *you* are our most important critic and commentator. We value your opinion and want to know what we're doing right, what we could do better, what areas you'd like to see us publish in, and any other words of wisdom you're willing to pass our way.

We welcome your comments. You can email or write to let us know what you did or didn't like about this book—as well as what we can do to make our books better.

Please note that we cannot help you with technical problems related to the topic of this book.

When you write, please be sure to include this book's title and author as well as your name and email address. We will carefully review your comments and share them with the author and editors who worked on the book.

Email: feedback@pearsonitcertification.com

Reader Services

Register your copy of *Linux Essentials for Cybersecurity* at www.pearsonitcertification.com for convenient access to downloads, updates, and corrections as they become available. To start the registration process, go to www.pearsonitcertification.com/register and log in or create an account*. Enter the product ISBN 9780789759351 and click Submit. When the process is complete, you will find any available bonus content under Registered Products.

*Be sure to check the box that you would like to hear from us to receive exclusive discounts on future editions of this product.

Introduction

Introduced as a hobby project in 1991, Linux has become a dominant player in the IT market today. Although technically Linux refers to a specific software piece (the kernel), many people refer to Linux as a collection of software tools that make up a robust operating system.

Linux is a heavily used technology throughout the IT industry, and it is used as an alternative to more common platforms because of its security, low cost, and scalability. The Linux OS is used to power a larger variety of servers, including email and web servers. Additionally, it is often favored by software developers as the platform they code on.

As with any operating system, cybersecurity should be a major concern for any IT professional who works on a Linux system. Because of the large variety of software running on a Linux system, as well as several different versions of Linux (called distributions), cybersecurity can be a complicated process that involves both system users and system administrators.

Regretfully, cybersecurity is often overlooked in books and classes on Linux. Typically, these forms of learning tend to focus on how to use the Linux system, and cybersecurity is often mentioned as an afterthought or considered an advanced topic for highly experienced professionals. This could be because the authors of these books and classes feel that cybersecurity is a difficult topic to learn, but ignoring this topic when discussing Linux is a huge mistake.

Why is cybersecurity such an important topic when learning Linux? One reason is that Linux is a true multiuser operating system. This means that even regular users (end users) need to know how to keep their own data secure from other users.

Another reason why cybersecurity is critical is because most Linux operating systems provide a great number of network-based services that are often exposed to the Internet. The prying eyes of millions of people worldwide need to be considered when securing a personal Linux system or the Linux systems for an entire organization.

Our goal with this book is to provide you with the skills a Linux professional should have. The approach we take is a typical "ground-up" approach, but with the unique methodology of always keeping an eye on security. Throughout this book, you will find references to security issues. Entire sections are devoted to security, and a strong emphasis is placed on creating security policies.

Linux is a very large topic, and it is really impossible to cover it entirely in one book. The same is true regarding Linux security. We have made every effort to provide as much detail as possible, but we also encourage you to explore on your own to learn more about each topic introduced in this book.

Thank you, and enjoy your Linux cybersecurity journey.

Who Should Read This Book?

It might be easier to answer the question "who shouldn't read this book?" Linux distributions are used by a large variety of individuals, including:

- Software developers
- Database administrators
- Website administrators
- Security administrators

- System administrators
- System recovery experts
- "Big data" engineers
- Hackers
- Governmental organizations
- Mobile users and developers (Android is a Linux distribution)
- Chip vendors (Embedded Linux is found on many chip devices)
- Digital forensic experts
- Educators

The previous list isn't even a complete list! Linux is literally everywhere. It is the OS used on Android phones. A large number of web and email servers run on Linux. Many network devices, such as routers and firewalls, have a version of embedded Linux installed on them.

This book is for people who want to better use Linux systems and ensure that the Linux systems that they work on are as secure as possible.

How This Book Is Organized

Chapter 1, "Distributions and Key Components," dives into essential information related to understanding the various parts of Linux. You learn about the different components of the Linux operating system, as well as what a distribution is. You also learn how to install the Linux operating system.

Chapter 2, "Working on the Command Line," covers the essential commands needed to work within the Linux environment.

Chapter 3, "Getting Help," provides you with the means to get additional information on Linux topics. This includes documentation that is natively available on the operating system as well as important web-based resources.

Chapter 4, "Editing Files," focuses on utilities that you can use to edit text files. Editing text files is a critical Linux task because much of the configuration data is stored in text files.

Chapter 5, "When Things Go Wrong," reviews how to handle problems that may arise in Linux. This chapter provides details on how to troubleshoot system problems within a Linux environment.

Chapter 6, "Managing Group Accounts," focuses on group accounts, including how to add, modify, and delete groups. Special attention is placed on system (or special) groups as well as understanding the difference between primary and secondary groups.

Chapter 7, "Managing User Accounts," covers the details regarding user accounts. You learn how to create and secure these accounts, as well as how to teach users good security practices in regard to protecting their accounts.

Chapter 8, "Develop an Account Security Policy," provides you with the means to create a security policy using the knowledge you acquired in Chapters 6 and 7.

Chapter 9, "File Permissions," focuses on securing files using Linux permissions. This chapter also dives into more advanced topics, such as special permissions, the umask, access control lists (ACLs), and file attributes.

Chapter 10, "Manage Local Storage: Essentials," covers topics related to the concepts of local storage devices. This includes how to create partitions and filesystems, as well as some additional essential filesystem features.

Chapter 11, "Manage Local Storage: Advanced Features," covers topics related to advanced features of local storage devices. This includes how to use **autofs** and create encrypted filesystems. You also learn about logical volume management, an alternative way of managing local storage devices

Chapter 12, "Manage Network Storage," discusses making storage devices available across the network. Filesystem sharing techniques such as Network File System, Samba, and iSCSI are also included.

Chapter 13, "Develop a Storage Security Policy," provides you with the means to create a security policy using the knowledge you acquire in Chapters 9–12.

Chapter 14, "crontab and at," covers two sets of tools that allow you to automatically execute processes at future times. The **crontab** system allows users to execute programs at regular intervals, such as once a month or twice a week. The **at** system provides users with a way to execute a program at one specific time in the future.

Chapter 15, "Scripting," covers the basics of placing BASH commands into a file in order to create a more complex set of commands. Scripting is also useful for storing instructions that may be needed at a later time.

Chapter 16, "Common Automation Tasks," covers the sort of tasks that both regular users and system administrators routinely automate. The focus of this chapter is on security, but additional automation tasks are demonstrated, particularly those related to topics that were covered in previous chapters.

Chapter 17, "Develop an Automation Security Policy," provides you with the means to create a security policy using the knowledge you acquire in Chapters 14–16.

Chapter 18, "Networking Basics," covers the essentials you should know before configuring and securing your network connections.

Chapter 19, "Network Configuration," covers the process of configuring your system to connect to the network.

Chapter 20, "Network Service Configuration: Essential Services," covers the process of configuring several network-based tools, including DNS, DHCP, and email servers.

Chapter 21, "Network Service Configuration: Web Services," covers the process of configuring several network-based tools, including the Apache Web Server and Squid.

Chapter 22, "Connecting to Remote Systems," discusses how to connect to remote systems via the network.

Chapter 23, "Develop a Network Security Policy," provides you with the means to create a security policy using the knowledge you acquire in Chapters 18–22.

Chapter 24, "Process Control," covers how to start, view, and control processes (programs).

Chapter 25, "System Logging," covers how to view system logs as well as how to configure the system to create custom log entries.

Chapter 26, "Red Hat–Based Software Management," covers how to administer software on Red Hat–based systems such as Fedora and CentOS.

Chapter 27, "Debian-Based Software Management," covers how to administer software on Debian-based systems, such as Ubuntu.

Chapter 28, "System Booting," covers the process of configuring several network-based tools.

Chapter 29, "Develop a Software Management Security Policy," provides you with the means to create a security policy using the knowledge you acquire in Chapters 26–28.

Chapter 30, "Footprinting," covers the techniques that hackers use to discover information about systems. By learning about these techniques, you should be able to form a better security plan.

Chapter 31, "Firewalls," explores how to configure software that protects your systems from network-based attacks.

Chapter 32, "Intrusion Detection," provides you with an understanding of tools and techniques to determine if someone has successfully compromised the security of your systems.

Chapter 33, "Additional Security Tasks," covers a variety of additional Linux security features, including the fail2ban service, virtual private networks (VPNs), and file encryption.

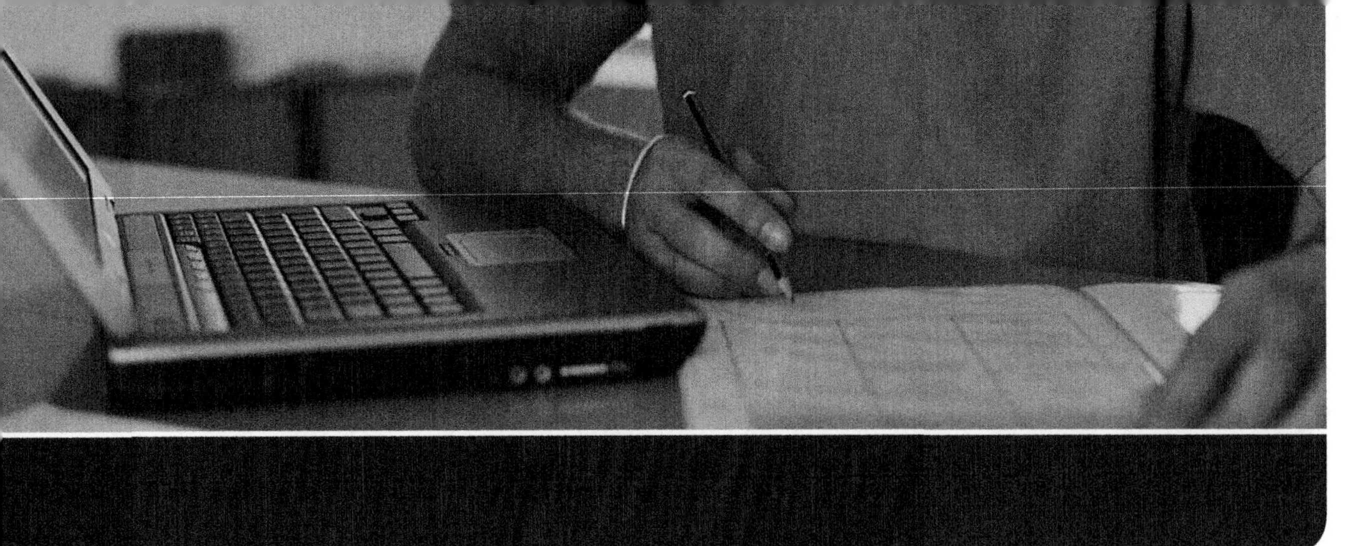

In 1991, University of Helsinki student Linus Benedict Torvalds was working in an operating system called Minix. Minix (from "mini-Unix") is a Unix-like operating system that was designed to be used in educational environments. While Linus liked many features of Minix, he found it lacking overall. So, on August 25, 1991, he made the following post online:

> "Hello everybody out there using Minix -
>
> I'm doing a (free) operating system (just a hobby, won't be big and professional like gnu) for 386(486) AT clones. This has been brewing since April, and is starting to get ready. I'd like any feedback on things people like/dislike in Minix, as my OS resembles it (same physical layout of the file-system (due to practical reasons) among other things)."

This "just a hobby" project was the start of what would eventually become Linux. Since that time, Linus's project has grown into a major component of the modern IT landscape. It has resulted in a robust operating system used by millions throughout the world. In fact, it is somewhat hard to avoid Linux because it powers many cell phones (Android is based on Linux) and is the operating system of choice for many web servers, email servers, and other Internet-based servers.

Part I

Introducing Linux

In Part I, "Introducing Linux," you will be introduced to some important Linux topics:

- Chapter 1, "Distributions and Key Components," dives into essential information related to understanding the various parts of Linux. You learn about the different components of the Linux operating system, as well as what a distribution is. You also learn how to install the Linux operating system.
- Chapter 2, "Working on the Command Line," covers essential commands needed to work within the Linux environment.
- Chapter 3, "Getting Help," provides you with the means to get additional information on Linux topics. This includes documentation that is natively available on the operating system as well as important web-based resources.
- Chapter 4, "Editing Files," focuses on utilities that you can use to edit text files. Editing text files is a critical Linux task because much of the configuration data is stored in text files.
- Chapter 5, "When Things Go Wrong," reviews how to handle problems that may arise in Linux. This chapter provides details on how to troubleshoot system problems within a Linux environment.

Distributions and Key Components

Before you start learning about all the features and capabilities of Linux, it would help to get a firm understanding of what Linux is, including what the major components are of a Linux operating system. In this first chapter, you learn about some of the essential concepts of Linux. You discover what a distribution is and how to pick a distribution that best suits your needs. You are also introduced to the process of installing Linux, both on a bare-metal system and in a virtual environment.

After reading this chapter and completing the exercises, you will be able to do the following:

Describe the various parts of Linux

Identify the major components that make up the Linux operating system

Describe different types of Linux distributions

Identify the steps for installing Linux

Introducing Linux

Linux is an operating system, much like Microsoft Windows. However, this is a very simplistic way of defining Linux. Technically, Linux is a software component called the *kernel*, and the kernel is the software that controls the operating system.

By itself, the kernel doesn't provide enough functionality to provide a full operating system. In reality, many different components are brought together to define what IT professionals refer to as the Linux operating system, as shown in Figure 1-1.

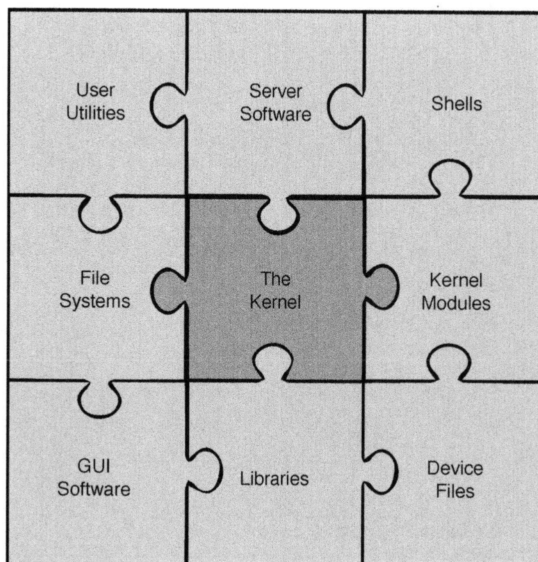

Figure 1-1 *The Components of the Linux Operating System*

It is important to note that not all the components described in Figure 1-1 are always required for a Linux operating system. For example, there is no need for a graphical user interface (GUI). In fact, on Linux server systems, the GUI is rarely installed because it requires additional hard drive space, CPU cycles, and random access memory (RAM) usage. Also, it could pose a security risk.

Security Highlight

You may wonder how GUI software could pose a security risk. In fact, any software component poses a security risk because it is yet another part of the operating system that can be compromised. When you set up a Linux system, always make sure you only install the software required for that particular use case.

The pieces of the Linux operating system shown in Figure 1-1 are described in the following list:

- **User utilities**: Software that is used by users. Linux has literally thousands of programs that either run within a command line or GUI environment. Many of these utilities will be covered throughout this book.
- **Server software**: Software that is used by the operating system to provide some sort of feature or access, typically across a network. Common examples include a file-sharing server, a web server that provides access to a website, and a mail server.
- **Shells**: To interact with a Linux operating system via the command line, you need to run a shell program. Several different shells are available, as discussed later in this chapter.
- **File systems**: As with an operating system, the files and directories (aka folders) are stored in a well-defined structure. This structure is called a *file system*. Several different file systems are available for Linux. Details on this topic are covered in Chapter 10, "Manage Local Storage: Essentials," and Chapter 11, "Manage Local Storage: Advanced Features."
- **The kernel**: The kernel is the component of Linux that controls the operating system. It is responsible for interacting with the system hardware as well as key functions of the operating system.
- **Kernel modules**: A kernel module is a program that provides more features to the kernel. You may hear that the Linux kernel is a modular kernel. As a modular kernel, the Linux kernel tends to be more extensible, secure, and less resource intensive (in other words, it's lightweight).
- **GUI software**: Graphical user interface (GUI) software provides "window-based" access to the Linux operating system. As with command-line shells, you have a lot of options when it comes to picking a GUI for a Linux operating system. GUI software is covered in more detail later in this chapter.
- **Libraries**: This is a collection of software used by other programs to perform specific tasks. Although libraries are an important component of the Linux operating system, they won't be a major focus of this book.
- **Device files**: On a Linux system, everything can be referred to as a file, including hardware devices. A device file is a file that is used by the system to interact with a device, such as a hard drive, keyboard, or network card.

Linux Distributions

The various bits of software that make up the Linux operating system are very flexible. Additionally, most of the software is licensed as "open source," which means the cost to use this software is often nothing. This combination of features (flexible and open source) has given rise to a large number of Linux distributions.

A Linux distribution (also called a *distro*) is a specific implementation of a Linux operating system. Each distro will share many common features with other distros, such as the core kernel, user utilities, and other components. Where distros most often differ is their overall goal or purpose. For example, the following list describes several common distribution types:

- **Commercial**: A distro that is designed to be used in a business setting. Often these distros will be bundled together with a support contract. So, although the operating system itself may be free, the support contract will add a yearly fee. Commercial releases normally have a slower release cycle (3–5 years), resulting in a more stable and secure platform. Typical examples of commercial distros include Red Hat Enterprise Linux and SUSE.
- **Home or amateur**: These distros are focused on providing a Linux operating system to individuals who want a choice that isn't either macOS or Microsoft Windows. Typically there is only community support for these distros, with very rapid release cycles (3–6 months), so all of the latest features are quickly available. Typical examples of amateur distros include Fedora, Linux Mint, and Ubuntu (although Ubuntu also has a release that is designed for commercial users).
- **Security enhanced**: Some distributions are designed around security. Either the distro itself has extra security features or it provides tools to enhance the security on other systems. Typical examples include Kali Linux and Alpine Linux.
- **Live distros:** Normally to use an operating system, you would first need to install it on a system. With a Live distribution, the system can boot directly from removable media, such as a CD-ROM, DVD, or USB disk. The advantage of Live distros is the ability to test out a distribution without having to make any changes to the contents of the system's hard drive. Additionally, some Live distros come with tools to fix issues with the installed operating system (including Microsoft Windows issues). Typical examples of Live distros include Manjaro Linux and Antegros. Most modern amateur distros, such as Fedora and Linux Mint, also have a Live version.

Security Highlight

Commercial distributions tend to be more secure than distributions designed for home use. This is because commercial distributions are often used for system-critical tasks in corporations or the government, so the organizations that support these distributions often make security a key component of the operating system.

It is important to realize that these are only a few of the types of Linux distributions. There are also distros designed for educational purposes, young learners, beginners, gaming, older computers, and many others. An excellent source to learn more about available distributions is https://distrowatch.com. This site provides the ability to search for and download the software required to install many different distributions.

Shells

A *shell* is a software program that allows a user to issue commands to the system. If you have worked in Microsoft Windows, you may have used the shell environment provided for that operating system: DOS. Like DOS, the shells in Linux provide a command-line interface (CLI) to the user.

CLI commands provide some advantages. They tend to be more powerful and have more functions than commands in GUI applications. This is partly because creating CLI programs is easier than creating GUI programs, but also because some of the CLI programs were created even before GUI programs existed.

Linux has several different shells available. Which shells you have on your system will depend on what software has been installed. Each shell has specific features, functions, and syntax that differentiate it from other shells, but they all essentially perform the same functionality.

Although multiple different shells are available for Linux, by far the most popular shell is the BASH shell. The BASH shell was developed from an older shell named the Bourne Shell (BASH stands for Bourne Again SHell). Because it is so widely popular, it will be the primary focus of the discussions in this book.

GUI Software

When you install a Linux operating system, you can decide if you only want to log in and interact with the system via the CLI or if you want to install a GUI. GUI software allows you to use a mouse and keyboard to interact with the system, much like you may be used to within Microsoft Windows.

For personal use, on laptop and desktop systems, having a GUI is normally a good choice. The ease of using a GUI environment often outweighs the disadvantages that this software creates. In general, GUI software tends to be a big hog of system resources, taking up a higher percentage of CPU cycles and RAM. As a result, it is often not installed on servers, where these resources should be reserved for critical server functions.

Security Highlight

Consider that every time you add more software to the system, you add a potential security risk. Each software component must be properly secured, and this is especially important for any software that provides the means for a user to access a system.

GUI-based software is a good example of an additional potential security risk. Users can log in via a GUI login screen, presenting yet another means for a hacker to exploit the system. For this reason, system administrators tend to not install GUI software on critical servers.

As with shells, a lot of options are available for GUI software. Many distributions have a "default" GUI, but you can always choose to install a different one. A brief list of GUI software includes GNOME, KDE, XFCE, LXDE, Unity, MATE, and Cinnamon.

GUIs will not be a major component of this book. Therefore, the authors suggest you try different GUIs and pick one that best meets your needs.

Installing Linux

Before installing Linux, you should answer the following questions:

- Which distribution will you choose? As previously mentioned, you have a large number of choices.
- What sort of installation should be performed? You have a couple of choices here because you can install Linux natively on a system or install the distro as a virtual machine (VM).
- If Linux is installed natively, is the hardware supported? In this case, you may want to shy away from newer hardware, particularly on newer laptops, as they may have components that are not yet supported by Linux.
- If Linux is installed as a VM, does the system have enough resources to support both a host OS and a virtual machine OS? Typically this comes down to a question of how much RAM the system has. In most cases, a system with at least 8GB of RAM should be able to support at least one VM.

Which Distro?

You might be asking yourself, "How hard can it be to pick a distribution? How many distros can there be?" The simple answer to the second question is "a lot." At any given time, there are about 250 active Linux distributions. However, don't let that number scare you off!

Although there are many distros, a large majority of them are quite esoteric, catering to very specific situations. While you are learning Linux, you shouldn't concern yourself with these sorts of distributions.

Conversational Learning™—Choosing a Linux Distribution

Gary: Hey, Julia.

Julia: You seem glum. What's wrong, Gary?

Gary: I am trying to decide which Linux distro to install for our new server and I'm feeling very much overwhelmed.

Julia: Ah, I know the feeling, having been there many times before. OK, so let's see if we can narrow it down. Do you feel you might need professional support for this system?

Gary: Probably not… well, not besides the help I get from you!

Julia: I sense more emails in my inbox soon. OK, that doesn't narrow it down too much. If you had said "yes," I would have suggested one of the commercial distros, like Red Hat Enterprise Linux or SUSE.

Gary: I'd like to pick one of the more popular distros because I feel they would have more community support.

Julia: That's a good thought. According to distrowatch.com, there are several community-supported distros that have a lot of recent downloads, including Mint, Debian, Ubuntu, and Fedora.

Gary: I've heard of those, but there are others listed on distrowatch.com that I've never heard of before.

Julia: Sometimes those other distros may have some features that you might find useful. How soon do you need to install the new server?

Gary: Deadline is in two weeks.

Julia: OK, I recommend doing some more research on distrowatch.com, pick three to four candidates and install them on a virtual machine. Spend some time testing them out, including using the software that you will place on the server. Also spend some time looking at the community support pages and ask yourself if you feel they will be useful.

Gary: That sounds like a good place to start.

Julia: One more thing: consider that there isn't just one possible solution. Several distros will likely fit your needs. Your goal is to eliminate the ones that won't fit your needs first and then try to determine the best of the rest. Good luck!

A handful of distributions are very popular and make up the bulk of the Linux installations in the world. However, a complete discussion of the pros and cons of each of these popular distros is beyond the scope of this book. For the purpose of learning Linux, the authors recommend you install one or more of the following distros:

- **Red Hat Enterprise Linux (RHEL), Fedora, or CentOS**: These distributions are called Red Hat–based distros because they all share a common set of base code from Red Hat's release of Linux. There are many others that share this code, but these are generally the most popular. Note that both Fedora and CentOS are completely free, while RHEL is a subscription-based distro. For Red Hat–based examples in this book, we will use Fedora.
- **Linux Mint, Ubuntu, or Debian**: These distributions are called Debian-based distros because they all share a common set of base code from Debian's release of Linux. There are many others that share this code, but these are generally the most popular. For Debian-based examples in this book, we will use Ubuntu.
- **Kali**: This is a security-based distribution that will be used in several chapters of this book. Consider this distribution to be a tool that enables you to determine what security holes are present in your environment.

Native or Virtual Machine?

If you have an old computer available, you can certainly use it to install Linux natively (this is called a *bare-metal* or *native* installation). However, given the fact that you probably want to test several distributions, virtual machine (VM) installs are likely a better choice.

A VM is an operating system that thinks it is installed natively, but it is actually sharing a system with a host operating system. (There is actually a form of virtualization in which the VM is aware it is virtualized, but that is beyond the scope of this book and not necessary for learning Linux.) The host operating system can be Linux, but it could also be macOS or Microsoft Windows.

In order to create VMs, you need a product that provides a hypervisor. A *hypervisor* is software that presents "virtual hardware" to a VM. This includes a virtual hard drive, a virtual network interface, a virtual CPU, and other components typically found on a physical system. There are many different hypervisor software programs, including VMware, Microsoft Hyper-V, Citrix XenServer, and Oracle VirtualBox. You could also make use of *hosted* hypervisors, which are cloud-based applications. With these solutions, you don't even have to install anything on your local system. Amazon Web Services is a good example of a cloud-based service that allows for hosted hypervisors.

Security Highlight

Much debate in the security industry revolves around whether virtual machines are more secure than bare-metal installations. There is no simple answer to this question because many aspects need to be considered. For example, although virtual machines may provide a level of abstraction, making it harder for a hacker to be aware of their existence, they also result in another software component that needs to be properly secured.

Typically, security isn't the primary reason why an organization uses virtual machines (better hardware utilization is usually the main reason). However, if you choose to use virtual machines in your environment, the security impact should be carefully considered and included in your security policies. For the purposes of learning Linux, we will use Oracle VirtualBox. It is freely available and works well on multiple platforms, including Microsoft Windows (which is most likely the operating system you already have installed on your own system). Oracle VirtualBox can be downloaded from https://www.virtualbox.org. The installation is fairly straightforward: just accept the default values or read the installation documentation (https://www.virtualbox.org/wiki/Downloads#manual).

After you have installed Oracle VirtualBox and have installed some virtual machines, the Oracle VM VirtualBox Manager will look similar to Figure 1-2.

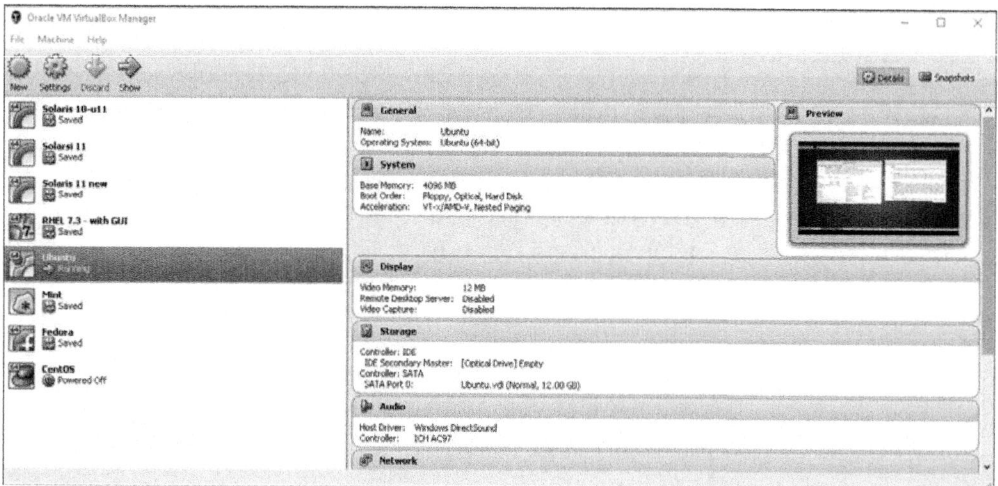

Figure 1-2 *The Oracle VirtualBox VM Manager*

Installing a Distro

If you are using Oracle VirtualBox, the first step to installing a distro is to add a new "machine." This is accomplished by taking the following steps in the Oracle VM VirtualBox Manager:

1. Click Machine and then New.
2. Provide a name for the VM; for example, enter **Fedora** in the Name: box. Note that the Type and Version boxes will likely change automatically. Type should be Linux. Check the install media you downloaded to see if it is a 32-bit or 64-bit operating system (typically this info will be included in the filename). Most modern versions are 64 bit.
3. Set the Memory Size value by using the sliding bar or typing the value in the MB box. Typically a value of 4196MB (about 4GB) of memory is needed for a full Linux installation to run smoothly.

   Leave the option "Create a virtual hard disk now" marked.
4. Click the Create button.
5. On the next dialog box, you will choose the size of the virtual hard disk. The default value will likely be 8.00GB, which is a bit small for a full installation. A recommended minimum value is 12GB.
6. Leave the "Hard disk file type" set to VDI (Virtual Hard Disk). Change "Storage on physical hard disk" to Fixed Size.
7. Click the Create button.

After a short period of time (a few minutes), you should see your new machine in the list on the left side of the Oracle VM VirtualBox Manager. Before continuing to the next step, make sure you know the location of your installation media (the *.iso file of the Linux distro you downloaded).

To start the installation process, click the new machine and then click the Start button. See Figure 1-3 for an example.

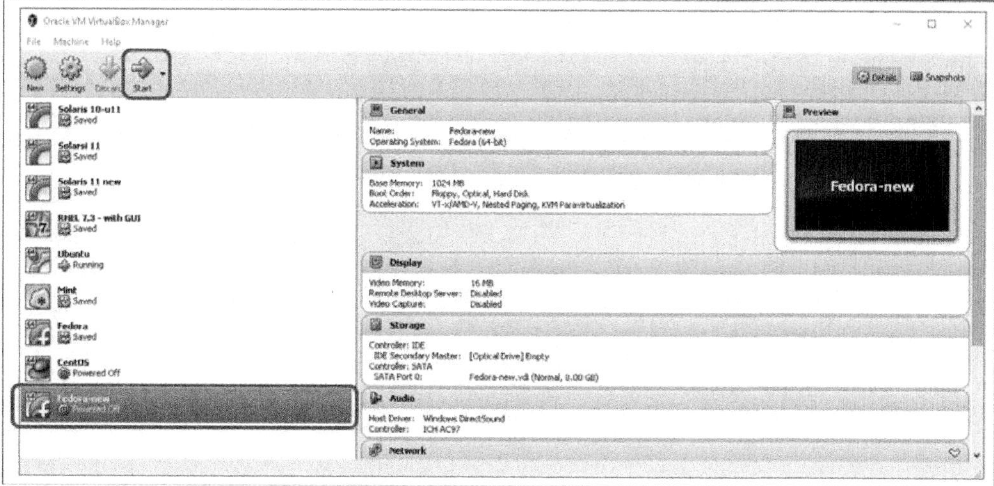

Figure 1-3 *Start the Installation Process*

In the next window that appears, you need to select the installation media. In the Select Start-up Disk dialog box, click the small icon that looks like a folder with a green "up arrow." Then navigate to the folder that contains the installation media, select it, and click the Open button. When you return to the dialog box, click the Start button.

Once the installation starts, the options and prompts really depend on which distribution you are installing. These can also change as newer versions of the distributions are released. As a result of how flexible these installation processes can be, we recommend you follow the installation guides provided by the organization that released the distribution.

Instead of providing specific instructions, we offer the following recommendations:

- **Accept the defaults.** Typically the default options work well for your initial installations. Keep in mind that you can always reinstall the operating system later.
- **Don't worry about specific software.** One option may require that you select which software to install. Again, select the default provided. You can always add more software later, and you will learn how to do this in Chapter 25, "System Logging."
- **Don't forget that password.** You will be asked to set a password for either the root account or a regular user account. On a production system, you should make sure you set a password that isn't easy to compromise. However, on these test systems, pick a password that is easy to remember, as password security isn't as big of a concern in this particular case. If you do forget your password, recovering passwords is covered in Chapter 28, "System Booting," (or you can reinstall the Linux OS).

Summary

After reading this chapter, you should have a better understanding of the major components of the Linux operating system. You should also know what a Linux distribution is and have an idea of the questions you should answer prior to installing Linux.

Key Terms

kernel, shell, file system, kernel modules, libraries, distribution, distro, CLI, GUI, virtual machine, VM

Review Questions

1. A _____ is a structure that is used to organize files and directories in an operating system.
2. Which of the following is not a common component of a Linux operating system?
   - **A.** kernel
   - **B.** libraries
   - **C.** disk drive
   - **D.** shells
3. Which of the following is a security-based Linux distribution?
   - **A.** Fedora
   - **B.** CentOS
   - **C.** Debian
   - **D.** Kali
4. A _____ program provides a command-line interface to the Linux operating system.
5. A _____ is an operating system that thinks it is installed natively, but it is actually sharing a system with a host operating system.

Working on the Command Line

One of the more amazing features of Linux is the vast number of command-line utilities. There are literally thousands of commands, each of which is designed to perform a specific task. Having so many commands provides a great deal of flexibility, but it also makes the process of learning Linux a bit more daunting.

The goal of this chapter is to introduce you to some of the more essential command-line utilities. You learn commands used to manage files and directories, including how to view, copy, and delete files. You also learn the basics of a powerful feature called *regular expressions*, which allows you to view and modify files using patterns. This chapter introduces some of the more commonly used file-compression utilities, such as the **tar** and **gzip** utilities.

After reading this chapter and completing the exercises, you will be able to do the following:

Manage files and directories

Use shell features such as shell variables

Be able to re-execute previous commands using the shell feature called history

Identify regular expressions and know how to use them with commands like find, grep, **and** sed

Manage file-compression utilities

File Management

The Linux operating system includes a large number of files and directories. As a result, a major component of working on a Linux system is knowing how to manage files. In this section, you learn some of the essential command-line tools for file management.

The Linux Filesystem

Most likely you are already familiar with Microsoft Windows. That operating system makes use of drives to organize the different storage devices. For example, the primary hard drive is typically designated the C: drive. Additional drives, such as CD-ROM drives, DVD drives, additional hard drives, and removable storage devices (USB drives) are assigned D:, E:, and so on. Even network drives are often assigned a "drive letter" in Microsoft Windows.

In Linux, a different method is used. Every storage location, including remote drives and removable media, is accessible under the top-level directory, named root. The root directory is symbolized by a single slash (/) character. See Figure 2-1 for a demonstration of a small portion of a Linux filesystem (a full Linux filesystem would contain hundreds, if not thousands, of directories).

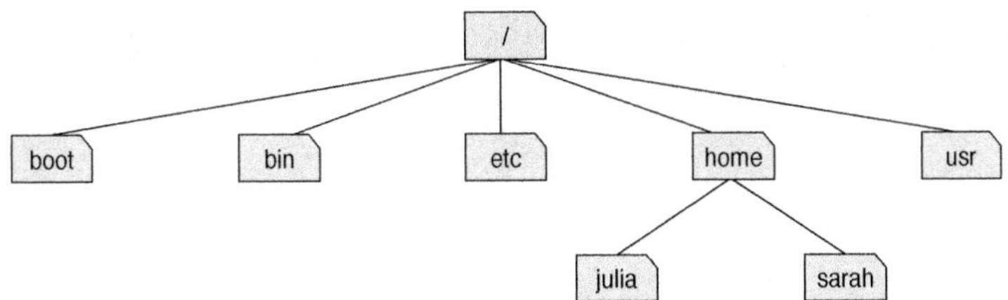

Figure 2-1 *Visual Example of a Small Portion of a Linux Filesystem*

Using the example in Figure 2-1, the **boot**, **bin**, **etc**, **home**, and **usr** directories are considered to be "under" the / directory. The **julia** and **sarah** directories are considered to be "under" the **home** directory. Often the term *subdirectory* or *child directory* is used to describe a directory that is under another directory. The term *parent directory* is used to describe a directory that contains subdirectories. Hence, the **home** directory is the parent directory of the **julia** subdirectory.

To describe the location of a directory, a full path is often used that includes all the directories up to the root directory. For example, the **julia** directory can be described by the /home/julia path. In this path, the first / represents the root directory and all further / characters are used to separate additional directories in the path.

You may be wondering what is stored in these different directories. That is a good question, but also a difficult one to answer at this point given that you are just starting to learn about the Linux operating system. So although the answer will be provided here, realize this isn't something you should worry about too much right now—these locations will make more sense as you explore Linux further.

The Filesystem Hierarchy Standard (FHS) is a definition of where files and directories are supposed to be placed on Unix and Linux operating systems. A summary of some of the more important locations is provided in Table 2-1.

Table 2-1 FHS Locations

Location	Description/Contents
/	The root or top-level directory.
/bin	Critical binary executables.
/boot	Files related to booting (starting) the system.
/etc	Configuration files for the system.
/home	Regular user home directories.
/lib	Critical system libraries.
/media	Location of mount points for removable media.
/mnt	Location for temporary mounts.
/opt	Optional software packages.
/proc	Information related to kernel data and process data. (This is a virtual filesystem, not a disk-based filesystem.)
/root	Home directory for the root user account.
/sbin	Critical system binary executables.
/tmp	Location for temporary files.
/usr	Location for many subdirectories that contain binary executables, libraries, and documentation.
/usr/bin	Nonessential binary executables.
/usr/lib	Libraries for the executables in the **/usr/bin** directory.

Location	Description/Contents
/usr/sbin	Nonessential system binary executables.
/usr/share	Data that is architecture independent.
/var	Data that is variable (changes in size regularly).
/var/mail	Mail logs.
/var/log	Spool data (such as print spools).
/var/tmp	Temporary files.

Command Execution

The standard way of executing a shell command is to type the command at a command prompt and then press the Enter key. Here's an example:

```
[student@localhost rc0.d]$ pwd
/etc/rc0.d
```

Commands also accept options and arguments:

- An option is a predefined value that changes the behavior of a command. How the option changes the behavior of the command depends on the specific command.
- Typically options are a single character value that follow a hyphen (-) character, as in **-a**, **-g**, and **-z**. Often these single-character options can be combined together (for example, -agz). Some newer commands accept "word" options, such as **--long** or **--time**. Word options start with two hyphens.
- Arguments are additional information, such as a filename or user account name, that is provided to determine which specific action to take. The type of argument that is permitted depends on the command itself. For example, the command to remove a file from the system would accept a filename as an argument, whereas the command to delete a user account from the system would accept a user name as an argument.
- Unlike options, arguments do not start with a hyphen (or hyphens).

To execute a sequence of commands, separate each command with a semicolon and press the Enter key after the last command has been entered. Here's an example:

```
[student@localhost ~]$ pwd ; date ; ls
/home/student
Fri Dec  2 00:25:03 PST 2016
book   Desktop    Downloads  Music     Public  Templates
class  Documents  hello.pl   Pictures  rpm     Videos
```

The pwd Command

The **pwd** (print working directory) command displays the shell's current directory:

```
[student@localhost rc0.d]$ pwd
/etc/rc0.d
```

The cd Command

To move the shell's current directory to another directory, use the **cd** (change directory) command. The **cd** command accepts a single argument: the location of the desired directory. For example, to move to the **/etc** directory, you can execute the following command:

```
[student@localhost ~]$ cd /etc
[student@localhost etc]$
```

The **cd** command is one of those "no news is good news" sort of commands. If the command succeeds, no output is displayed (however, note that the prompt has changed). If the command fails, an error will be displayed, as shown here:

```
[student@localhost ~]$ cd /etc
bash: cd: nodir: No such file or directory
[student@localhost ~]$
```

Security Highlight

For security reasons, users cannot **cd** into all directories. This will be covered in greater detail in Chapter 9, "File Permissions."

When the argument you provide starts with the root directory symbol, it is considered to be an absolute path. An absolute path is used when you provide directions to where you want to go from a fixed location (the root directory). For example, you could type the following command:

```
cd /etc/skel
```

You can also give directions based on your current location. For example, if you are already in the **/etc** directory and want to go down to the **skel** directory, you could execute the **cd skel** command. In this case, the **skel** directory must be directly beneath the **etc** directory. This form of entering the pathname is called using a relative pathname.

If you think about it, you have given directions in one of these ways many times in the past. For example, suppose you had a friend in Las Vegas and you wanted to provide directions to your house in San Diego. You wouldn't start providing directions from the friend's house, but rather from a fixed location that you both are familiar with (like a commonly used freeway). But, if that same friend was currently at your house and wanted directions to a local store, you would provide directions from your current location, not the previously mentioned fixed location.

In Linux, there are a few special characters that represent directories to commands like the **cd** command:

- Two "dot" (period) characters (**..**) represent one level above the current directory. So, if the current directory is **/etc/skel**, the command **cd ..** would change the current directory to the **/etc** directory.
- One dot (**.**) represents the current directory. This isn't very useful for the **cd** command, but it is handy for other commands when you want to say "the directory I am currently in."
- The tilde character (**~**) represents the user's home directory. Every user has a home directory (typically **/home/*username***) where the user can store their own files. The **cd ~** command will return you to your home directory.

The ls Command

The **ls** command is used to list files in a directory. By default, the current directory's files are listed, as shown in the following example:

```
[student@localhost ~]$ ls
Desktop   Downloads  Pictures  Templates
Documents Music      Public    Videos
```

As with the **cd** command, you can provide a directory argument using either an absolute or relative path to list files in another directory.

The **ls** command has many options. Some of the most important options are shown in Table 2-2.

Table 2-2 ls Command Options

Option	Description
-a	List all files, including hidden files.
-d	List the directory name, not the contents of the directory.
-F	Append a character to the end of the file to indicate its type; examples include * (executable file), / (directory), and @ (symbolic link file).
-h	When used with the **-l** option, file sizes are provided in human-readable format.
-l	Display long listing (see the example after this table).
-r	Reverse the output order of the file listing.
-S	Sort by file size.
-t	Sort by modification time (newest files are listed first).

WHAT COULD GO WRONG? In Linux, commands, options, filenames, and just about everything else is case sensitive. This means that if you try to execute the command **ls -L**, you will get different output (or an error message) than if you type the command **ls -l**.

The output of the **ls -l** command includes one line per file, as demonstrated in Figure 2-2.

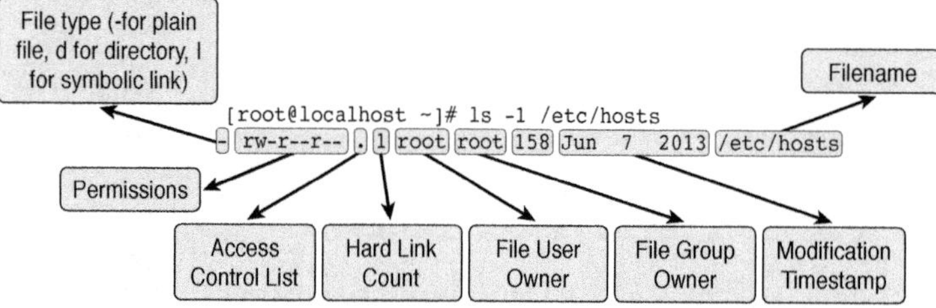

Figure 2-2 *The ls -l output*

File Globbing

A *file glob* (also called a *wildcard*) is any character provided on the command line that represents a portion of a filename. The following globs are supported:

Glob	Description
*	Matches zero or more characters in a filename
?	Matches any single character in a filename
[ ]	Matches a single character in a filename as long as that character is represented within the **[ ]** characters

This example displays all files in the current directory that begin with the letter *D*:

```
[student@localhost ~]$ ls -d D*
Desktop  Documents  Downloads
```

The next example displays all files in the current directory that are five characters long:

```
[student@localhost ~]$ ls -d ?????
Music
```

The file Command

The **file** command will report the type of contents in the file. The following commands provide some examples:

```
[student@localhost ~]$ file /etc/hosts
/etc/hosts: ASCII text
[student@localhost ~]$ file /usr/bin/ls
/usr/bin/ls: ELF 64-bit LSB executable, x86-64, version 1 (SYSV),
dynamically linked (uses shared libs), for GNU/Linux 2.6.32,
BuildID[sha1]=aa7ff68f13de25936a098016243ce57c3c982e06, stripped
[student@localhost ~]$ file /usr/share/doc/pam-1.1.8/html/sag-author.html
/usr/share/doc/pam-1.1.8/html/sag-author.html: HTML document,
UTF-8 Unicode text, with very long lines
```

Why use the **file** command? The next few commands in this chapter are designed to work only on text files, such as the **/etc/hosts** file in the previous example. Nontext files shouldn't be displayed with commands such as the **less**, **tail**, and **head** commands.

The less Command

The **less** command is used to display large chunks of text data, pausing after displaying the first page of information. Keys on the keyboard allow the user to scroll through the document. Table 2-3 highlights the more useful movement keys.

Table 2-3 Movement Keys

Movement Key	Description
h	Displays a help screen (summary of the **less** command movement keys).
SPACEBAR	Move forward one page in the current document.
b	Move back one page in the current document.
ENTER	Move down one line in the current document; the down-arrow key can also perform this operation.
UP ARROW	Move up one line in the current document.
/*term*	Search the document for *term*. (This can be a regular expression or just plain text.)
q	Quit viewing the document and return to the shell.

NOTE You may also see documentation regarding the **more** command. It uses many of the same movement options as the **less** command, but has fewer features.

The head Command

The **head** command displays the top part of text data. By default, the top ten lines are displayed. Use the **-n** option to display a different number of lines:

```
[student@localhost ~]$ head -n 3 /etc/group
root:x:0:
bin:x:1:student
daemon:x:2:
```

Security Highlight

The **/etc/group** file was purposefully chosen for this example. It is designed to hold group account information on the system and will be explored in detail in Chapter 6, "Managing Group Accounts." It was included in this example to start getting you used to looking at system files, even if right now the contents of these files might not be clear.

The tail Command

The **tail** command displays the bottom part of text data. By default, the last ten lines are displayed. Use the **-n** option to display a different number of lines:

```
[student@localhost ~]$ tail -n 3 /etc/group
slocate:x:21:
tss:x:59:
tcpdump:x:72:
```

Important options of the **tail** command include those shown in Table 2-4.

Table 2-4 Options of the **tail** Command

Option	Description
-f	Display the bottom part of a file and "follow" changes to the file. This is useful for a system administrator to dynamically view the contents of log files as they are written.
-n +x	Display from line number x to the end of the file. For example, the command **tail -n +25** file will display line 25 to the end of the file.

The mdkir Command

The **mkdir** command makes (creates) a directory.

Example:

```
mkdir test
```

Important options of the **mkdir** command are shown in Table 2-5.

Table 2-5 Options of the **mkdir** Command

Option	Description
-p	Create parent directories if necessary; for example, **mkdir /home/bob/data/january** would create all the directories in the path if the files did not exist.
-v	Display a message for every directory that is created. The **-v** option often means "verbose" in Linux. Verbose includes additional information about the action taken.

The cp Command

The **cp** command is used to copy files or directories. The syntax for this command is

```
cp [options] file|directory destination
```

where ***file*|*directory*** indicates which file or directory to copy. The ***destination*** is where you want the file or directory copied. The following example copies the **/etc/hosts** file into the current directory:

```
[student@localhost ~]$ cp /etc/hosts .
```

Note that the destination *must* be specified.

Table 2-6 provides some important options for the **cp** command.

Table 2-6 Options for the **cp** Command

Option	Description
-i	Provide an interactive prompt if the copy process results in overwriting an existing file.
-n	Never overwrite an existing file.
-r	Copy the entire directory structure (**r** stands for recursive).
-v	Be verbose (that is, describe actions taken when copying files and directories).

The mv Command

The **mv** command will move or rename a file.

Example:

```
mv /tmp/myfile ~
```

Important options include those shown in Table 2-7.

Table 2-7 Options for the **mv** Command

Option	Description
-i	Provide an interactive prompt if the move process would result in overwriting an existing file.
-n	Never overwrite an existing file.
-v	Be verbose (that is, describe actions taken when moving files and directories).

The rm Command

The **rm** command is used to remove (delete) files and directories.

Example:

```
rm file.txt
```

Important options include those shown in Table 2-8.

Table 2-8 Options for the ***rm*** Command

Option	Description
-i	Provide an interactive prompt before removing file.
-r	Delete entire directory structure. (**r** stands for recursive.)
-v	Be verbose (that is, describe actions taken when deleting files and directories).

The rmdir Command

The **rmdir** command is used to remove (delete) empty directories. This command will fail if the directory is not empty (use **rm -r** to delete a directory and all the files within the directory).

Example:

```
rmdir data
```

The touch Command

The **touch** command has two functions: to create an empty file and to update the modification and access timestamps of an existing file. To create a file or update an existing file's timestamps to the current time, use the following syntax:

```
touch filename
```

Important options include those shown in Table 2-9.

Table 2-9 Options for the **touch** Command

Option	Description
-a	Modify the access timestamp only, not the modification timestamp.
-d *date*	Set the timestamp to the specified *date* (for example, **touch -d "2018-01-01 14:00:00"**).
-m	Modify the modification timestamp only, not the access timestamp.
-r *file*	Use the timestamp of *file* as a reference to set the timestamps of the specified file (for example, **touch -r /etc/hosts /etc/passwd**).

Security Highlight

The **touch** command is very useful for updating the timestamps of critical files for inclusion in automated system backups. You will learn more about system backups in Chapter 10, "Manage Local Storage: Essentials."

Shell Features

The BASH shell provides many features that can be used to customize your working environment. This section focuses on these features.

Shell Variables

Shell variables are used to store information within the shell. This information is used to modify the behavior of the shell itself or external commands. Table 2-10 details some common useful shell variables.

Table 2-10 Shell Variables

Variable	Description
HOME	The current user's home directory.
ID	The current user's ID.
LOGNAME	The user name of the user who logged in to the current session.
OLDPWD	The previous directory location (before the last **cd** command).

Variable	Description
PATH	The location of where commands are found.
PS1	The primary prompt.
PWD	Print the working (current) directory.

NOTE There are many shell variables in addition to those listed in the previous table. More details regarding the **PATH** and **PS1** variables are provided later in this section of the chapter.

echo

The **echo** command is used to display information. Typically it is used to display the value of variables.

Example:

```
[student@localhost ~]$ echo $HISTSIZE
1000
```

The **echo** command has only a few options. The most useful one is the **-n** option, which doesn't print a newline character at the end of the output.

Some special character sequences can be incorporated within an argument to the **echo** command. For example, the command **echo "hello\nthere"** will send the following output:

```
hello
there
```

Table 2-11 describes some useful character sequences for the **echo** command.

Table 2-11 Character Sequences of the **echo** Command

Sequence	Description
\a	Ring terminal bell.
\n	Newline character.
\t	Tab character.
****	A single backslash character.

Security Highlight

The **echo** command can offer valuable troubleshooting information when attempting to debug a program or a script because the user can ring the terminal bell at various points as the program executes, to denote to the user that various points in the program were reached successfully.

set

The **set** command displays all shell variables and values when executed with no arguments. To see all shell variables, use the **set** command, as demonstrated here:

```
[student@localhost ~ 95]$ set | head -n 5
ABRT_DEBUG_LOG=/dev/null
AGE=25
BASH=/bin/bash
```

```
BASHOPTS=checkwinsize:cmdhist:expand_aliases:extglob:extquote:force_fignore:
histappend:interactive_comments:progcomp:promptvars:sourcepath
BASH_ALIASES=()
```

NOTE The **| head -n 5** part of the previous command means "send the output of the **set** command into the **head** command as input and only display the first five lines of this output." This is a process called redirection, which will be covered in detail in a later section of this chapter. It was included in the previous example because the output of the **set** command would end up taking several pages of this book.

The **set** command can also be used to modify the behavior of the shell. For example, using a variable that currently isn't assigned a value normally results in displaying a "null string" or no output. Executing the command **set -u** will result in an error message when undefined variables are used:

```
[student@localhost ~]$ echo $NOPE

[student@localhost ~]$ set -u
[student@localhost ~]$ echo $NOPE
bash: NOPE: unbound variable
```

Table 2-12 provides some additional useful **set** options.

Table 2-12 Options for the **set** Command

Option	Description
-b	When a background job terminates, report this immediately to the shell. A background job is a program running in the background (see Chapter 22, "Connecting to Remote Systems," for details). Use **+b** (the default) to have this report occur before the next primary prompt is displayed.
-n	A shell programming feature that reads commands in the script but does not execute the commands. Useful for syntax-error-checking a script.
-u	Issue an error message when an unset variable is used.
-C	Does not allow overwriting an existing file when using redirection operators, such as ***cmd* > *file***. See the discussions about redirection later in this chapter for more details on this feature.

unset

Use the **unset** command to remove a variable from the shell (for example, **unset VAR**).

The PS1 Variable

The PS1 variable defines the primary prompt, often using special character sequences (**\u** = current user's name, **\h** = host name, **\W** = current directory). Here's an example:

```
[student@localhost ~]$ echo $PS1
[\u@\h \W]\$
```

Note that variables are defined without a dollar sign character but are referenced using the dollar sign character:

```
[student@localhost ~]$ PS1="[\u@\h \W \!]\$ "
[student@localhost ~ 93]$ echo $PS1
[\u@\h \W \!]$
```

The PATH Variable

Most commands can be run by simply typing the command and pressing the Enter key:

```
[student@localhost ~]# date
Thu Dec  1 18:48:26 PST 2016
```

The command is "found" by using the **PATH** variable. This variable contains a comma-separated list of directory locations:

```
[student@localhost ~]$ echo $PATH
/usr/local/bin:/usr/local/sbin:/usr/bin:/usr/sbin:/bin:/sbin:
/home/student/.local/bin:/home/student/bin
```

This "defined path" is searched in order. So, when the previous **date** command was executed, the BASH shell first looked in the **/usr/local/bin** directory. If the **date** command is located in this directory, it is executed; otherwise, the next directory in the **PATH** variable is checked. If the command isn't found in any of these directories, an error is displayed:

```
[student@localhost ~]$ xeyes
bash: xeyes: command not found...
```

Security Highlight

In some cases when a command isn't found, you may see a message like the following:

```
Install package 'xorg-x11-apps' to provide command 'xeyes'? [N/y]
```

This is a result of when the command you are trying to run isn't on the system at all, but can be installed via a software package. For users who use Linux at home or in a noncommercial environment, this can be a useful feature, but if you are working on a production server, you should always carefully consider any software installation.

To execute a command that is not in the defined path, use a fully qualified path name, as shown here:

```
[student@localhost ~]$ /usr/xbin/xeyes
```

To add a directory to the **PATH** variable, use the following syntax:

```
[student@localhost ~]$ PATH="$PATH:/path/to/add"
```

The value to the right of **= sign ("$PATH:/path/to/add")** first will return the current value of the **PATH** variable and then append a colon and a new directory. So, if the **PATH** variable was set to **/usr/bin:/bin** and the **PATH="$PATH:/opt"** command was executed, then the result would be to assign the **PATH** variable to **/usr/bin:/bin:/opt**.

Security Highlight

Adding **"."** (the current directory) to the **PATH** variable poses a security risk. For example, suppose you occasionally mistype the **ls** command by typing **sl** instead. This could be exploited by someone who creates an **sl** shell script (program) in a common directory location (for example, the **/tmp** directory is a common place for all users to create files). With **"."** in your **PATH** variable, you could end up running the bogus **sl** "command," which could compromise your account or the operating system (depending on what commands the hacker placed in the script).

Environment Variables

When a variable is initially created, it is only available to the shell in which it was created. When another command is run within that shell, the variable is not "passed in to" that other command.

To pass variables and their values in to other commands, convert an existing local variable to an environment variable with the **export** command, like so:

```
[student@localhost ~]$ echo $NAME
Sarah
[student@localhost ~]$ export NAME
```

If the variable doesn't already exist, the **export** command can create it directly as an environment variable:

```
[student@localhost ~]$ export AGE=25
```

When a variable is converted into an environment variable, all subprocesses (commands or programs started by the shell) will have this variable set. This is useful when you want to change the behavior of a process by modifying a key variable.

For example, the **crontab -e** command allows you to edit your crontab file (a file that allows you to schedule programs to run sometime in the future; see Chapter 14, "crontab and at," for details). To choose the editor that the **crontab** command will use, create and export the **EDITOR** variable: **export EDITOR=gedit**.

See Figure 2-3 for a visual example of local versus environment variables.

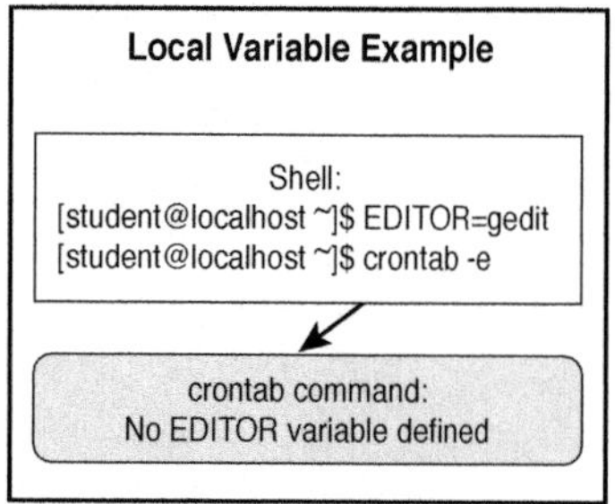

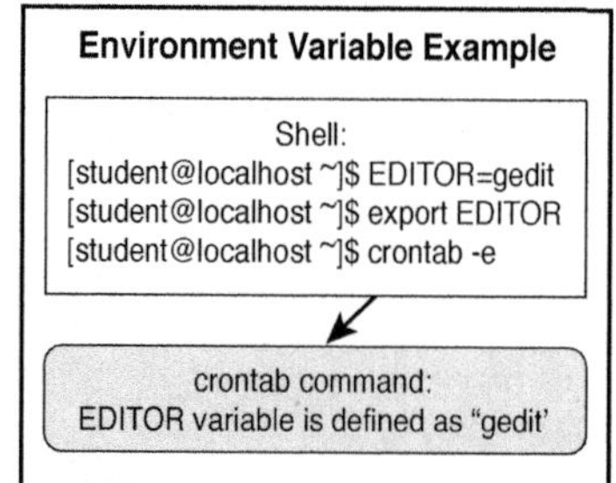

Figure 2-3 *Local versus Environment Variables*

The **export** command can also be used to display all environment variables, like so:

```
export -p
```

env

The **env** command displays environment variables in the current shell. Local variables are not displayed when the **env** command is executed.

Another use of the **env** command is to temporarily set a variable for the execution of a command.

For example, the **TZ** variable is used to set the timezone in a shell. There may be a case when you want to temporarily set this to a different value for a specific command, such as the **date** command shown here:

```
[student@localhost ~]# echo $TZ

[student@localhost ~]# date
Thu Dec  1 18:48:26 PST 2016
```

```
[student@localhost ~]# env TZ=MST7MDT date
Thu Dec  1 19:48:31 MST 2016
[student@localhost ~]# echo $TZ

[student@localhost ~]#
```

To unset a variable when executing a command, use the **--unset=VAR** option (for example, **env --unset=TZ date**).

Initialization Files

When a user logs in to the system, a login shell is started. When a user starts a new shell after login, it is referred to as a *non-login shell*. In each case, initialization files are used to set up the shell environment. Which initialization files are executed depends on whether the shell is a login shell or a non-login shell.

Figure 2-4 demonstrates which initialization files are executed when the user logs in to the system.

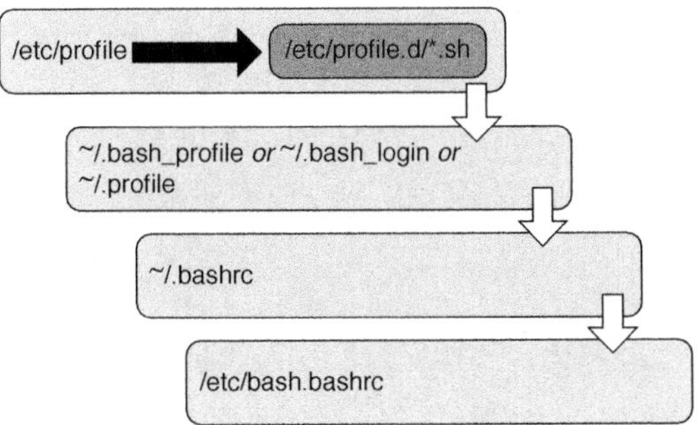

Figure 2-4 *Initialization Files Executed When the User Logs In to the System*

The following is an explanation of Figure 2-4:

- The first initialization file that is executed when a user logs in is the **/etc/profile** file. On most Linux platforms, this script includes code that executes all the initialization files in the **/etc/profile.d** directory that end in ".sh". *The purpose of the **/etc/profile** file is to serve as a place for system administrators to put code that will execute every time a BASH shell user logs in (typically login messages and environment variables definitions).*
- After the **/etc/profile** file is executed, the login shell looks in the user's home directory for a file named **~/.bash_profile**. If it's found, the login shell executes the code in this file. Otherwise, the login shell looks for a file named **~/.bash_login**. If it's found, the login shell executes the code in this file. Otherwise, the login shell looks for a file named **~/.profile** and executes the code in this file. *The purpose of these files is to serve as a place where each user can put code that will execute every time that specific user logs in (typically environment variables definitions).*
- The next initialization file executed is the **~/.bashrc** script. *The purpose of this file is to serve as a place where each user can put code that will execute every time the user opens a new shell (typically alias definitions).*
- The next initialization file executed is the **/etc/bash.bashrc** script. *The purpose of this file is to serve as a place where system administrators can put code that will execute every time the user opens a new shell (typically alias definitions).*

Figure 2-5 demonstrates which initialization files are executed when the user opens a new shell.

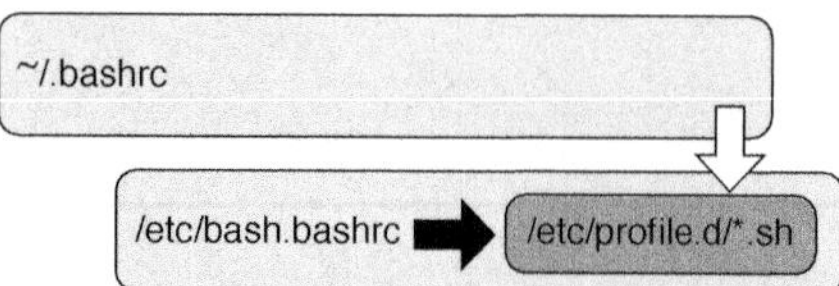

Figure 2-5 *Initialization Files Executed When the User Starts a Non-Login Shell*

The following is an explanation of Figure 2-5:

- The first initialization file that is executed when a user opens a non-login shell is the **~/.bashrc** script. *The purpose of this file is to serve as a place where each user can put code that will execute every time that user opens a new shell (typically alias definitions).*
- The next initialization file executed is the **/etc/bash.bashrc** script. On most Linux platforms, this script includes code that executes all the initialization files in the **/etc/profile.d** directory that end in ".sh". *The purpose of these initialization files is to serve as a place where system administrators can put code that will execute every time the user opens a new shell (typically alias definitions).*

Alias

An *alias* is a shell feature that allows a collection of commands to be executed by issuing a single "command." Here's how to create an alias:

```
[student @localhost ~]$ alias copy="cp"
```

And here's how to use an alias:

```
[student @localhost ~]$ ls
file.txt
[student @localhost ~]$ copy /etc/hosts .
[student @localhost ~]$ ls
file.txt  hosts
```

To display all aliases, execute the **alias** command with no arguments. To unset an alias, use the **unalias** command as shown in Example 2-1.

Example 2-1 *Using* ***unalias*** *Command to Unset an Alias*

```
[student @localhost ~]$ alias
alias copy='cp'
alias egrep='egrep --color=auto'
alias fgrep='fgrep --color=auto'
alias grep='grep --color=auto'
alias l='ls -CF'
alias la='ls -A'
alias ll='ls -alF'
[student @localhost ~]$ unalias copy
[student @localhost ~]$ alias
alias egrep='egrep --color=auto'
alias fgrep='fgrep --color=auto'
alias grep='grep --color=auto'
alias l='ls -CF'
alias la='ls -A'
alias ll='ls -alF'
```

Command History

Each shell keeps a list of previously executed commands in a memory-based history list. This list can be viewed by executing the **history** command.

The **history** command displays the contents of the history list. This output can be quite large, so often a numeric value is given to limit the number of commands displayed. For example, the following **history** command lists the last five commands in the history list:

```
[student@localhost ~]$ history 5
   83  ls
   84  pwd
   85  cat /etc/passwd
   86  clear
   87  history 5
```

Table 2-13 shows some useful options for the **history** command.

Table 2-13 Options for the **history** Command

Option	Description
-c	Clear the history list for the current BASH shell.
-r	Read the contents of the history file (see the section "The .bash_history File" in this chapter) and use those contents to replace the history list of the current BASH shell.
-w	Write the history list of the current BASH shell to the history file (see the section "The .bash_history File" in this chapter).

To execute a command in the history list, type **!** followed directly by the command you want to execute. For example, to execute command number 84 (the **pwd** command in the previous example), enter the following:

```
[student@localhost ~]$ !84
pwd
/home/student
```

Table 2-14 provides some additional techniques for executing previous commands.

Table 2-14 Techniques for Executing Commands

Technique	Description
!!	Execute the last command in the history list.
!-n	Execute the *n*th from the last command in the history list (for example, **!-2**).
!*string*	Execute the last command in the history list that begins with *string* (for example, **!ls**).
!?*string*	Execute the last command in the history list that has *string* anywhere in the command line (for example, **!?/etc**).
^str1^str2	Execute the previous command again, but replace **str1** with **str2**.

Here's an example of using **^str1^str2**:

```
[student@localhost ~]$ ls /usr/shara/dict
ls: cannot access /usr/shara/dict: No such file or directory
```

```
[student@localhost ~]$ ^ra^re
ls /usr/share/dict
linux.words  words
```

History Variables

Several variables can affect how information is stored in the history list, some of which are shown in Table 2-15.

Table 2-15 Variables Affecting Storage in the History List

Variable	Description
HISTIGNORE	A list of patterns, separated by colons, that indicates what commands to *not* place in the history list. For example, the following would have no **cd**, **pwd**, and **clear** commands placed in the history list: **HISTIGNORE="cd*:ls*;clear"**
HISTSIZE	Set to a numeric value that represents the maximum number of commands to keep in the history list.
HISTCONTROL	Limits the lines that are stored in the history list. This can be set to one of the following: ■ **ignorespace**: Any command executed with a space in front of it is not placed in the history list. ■ **ignoredups**: Duplicated commands result in only one occurrence placed in the history list. ■ **ignoreboth**: Combines **ignorespace** and **ignoredups**. ■ **erasedups**: The next write to the history list also removes all duplicate entries in the current history list.

The .bash_history File

When a user logs off the system, the current history list is written automatically to the user's **.bash_history** file. This is typically stored in the user's home directory (**~/.bash_history**), but the name and location can be changed by modifying the **HISTFILE** variable.

How many lines are stored in the **.bash_history** file is determined by the value of the **HISTFILESIZE** variable.

Security Highlight

The **history** command can pose a security risk because any Linux system that is not secured with a login screen and password-protected screensaver is susceptible to anyone having the credentials used to access the system and files simply by entering the **history** command and reading or copying the results to a file for later use. Always use a password-protected screensaver set for a short inactivity prompt to prevent this from happening. Clearing the history or using the **HISTIGNORE** variable to denote login information are additional security practices to prevent the use of authentication credentials found in past commands by others.

Redirecting Input and Output

Each command is able to send two streams of output (standard output and standard error) and can accept one stream of data (standard input). In documentation, these terms can also be described as follows:

- Standard output = stdout or STDOUT
- Standard error = stderr or STDERR
- Standard input = stdin or STDIN

By default, stdout and stderr are sent to the terminal window, whereas stdin comes from keyboard input. In some cases, you want to change these locations, and this is accomplished by a process called *redirection*.

Table 2-16 describes the methods used to perform redirection.

Table 2-16 Methods for Redirection

Method	Description
cmd < file	Override stdin so the input comes from the file specified.
cmd > file	Override stdout so the output goes into the file specified.
cmd 2> file	Override stderr so the output goes into the file specified.
cmd &> file	Override both stdout and stderr so the output goes into the file specified.
cmd1 | cmd2	Override stdout from **cmd1** so it goes into **cmd2** as stdin. See the section "Piping" for more details regarding this feature.

In the following example, stdout of the **cal** program is sent to a file named **month**:

```
[student@localhost ~]$ cal > month
```

It is common to redirect both stdout and stderr into separate files, as demonstrated in the next example:

```
[student@localhost ~]$ find /etc -name "*.cfg" -exec file {} \;
> output 2> error
```

Redirecting stdin is fairly rare because most commands will accept a filename as a regular argument; however, the **tr** command, which performs character translations, requires redirecting stdin:

```
[student@localhost ~]$ cat /etc/hostname
localhost
[student@localhost ~]$ tr 'a-z' 'A-Z' < /etc/hostname
LOCALHOST
```

Piping

The process of piping (so called because the | character is referred to as a "pipe") the output of one command to another command results in a more powerful command line. For example, the following takes the standard output of the **ls** command and sends it into the **grep** command to filter files that were changed on April 16th:

```
[student@localhost ~]$ ls -l /etc | grep "Apr 16"
-rw-r--r-- 1 root      321 Apr 16  2018 blkid.conf
drwxr-xr-x 2 root root    4096 Apr 16  2018 fstab.d
```

In Example 2-2, lines 41–50 of the copyright file are displayed.

Example 2-2 *Lines 41–50 of the Copyright File*

```
[student@localhost ~]$ head -50 copyright | tail
       b) If you have received a modified Vim that was distributed as
```

```
       mentioned under a) you are allowed to further distribute it
       unmodified, as mentioned at I). If you make additional changes
       the text under a) applies to those changes.
    c) Provide all the changes, including source code, with every
       copy of the modified Vim you distribute. This may be done in
       the form of a context diff. You can choose what license to use
       for new code you add. The changes and their license must not
       restrict others from making their own changes to the official
       version of Vim.
    d) When you have a modified Vim which includes changes as
       mentioned
```

You can add additional commands, as demonstrated in Example 2-3, where the output of the **tail** command is sent to the **nl** command (which numbers the lines of output).

Example 2-3 *Output of **tail** Command Is Sent to the **nl** Command*

```
[student@localhost ~]$ head -50 copyright | tail | nl
     1  b) If you have received a modified Vim that was distributed as
     2     mentioned under a) you are allowed to further distribute it
     3     unmodified, as mentioned at I). If you make additional changes
     4     the text under a) applies to those changes.
     5  c) Provide all the changes, including source code, with every
     6     copy of the modified Vim you distribute. This may be done in
     7     the form of a context diff. You can choose what license to use
     8     for new code you add. The changes and their license must not
     9     restrict others from making their own changes to the official
    10     version of Vim.
    11  d) When you have a modified Vim which includes changes as
    12     mentioned
```

Note that the order of execution makes a difference. In Example 2-3, the first 40 lines of the copyright file are sent to the **tail** command. Then the last ten lines of the first 40 lines are sent to the **nl** command for numbering. Notice the difference in output when the **nl** command is executed first, as shown in Example 2-4.

Example 2-4 *Executing the **nl** Command First*

```
[student@localhost ~]$ nl copyright | head -50 | tail
    36  b) If you have received a modified Vim that was distributed as
    37     mentioned under a) you are allowed to further distribute it
    38     unmodified, as mentioned at I). If you make additional changes
    39     the text under a) applies to those changes.
    40  c) Provide all the changes, including source code, with every
    41     copy of the modified Vim you distribute. This may be done in
    42     the form of a context diff. You can choose what license to use
    43     for new code you add. The changes and their license must not
    44     restrict others from making their own changes to the official
    45     version of Vim.
    46  d) When you have a modified Vim which includes changes as
    47     mentioned
```

Subcommands

To take the output of one command and use it as an argument to another command, place the command within the **$( )** characters. For example, the output of the **date** and **pwd** commands is sent to the **echo** command as arguments:

```
[student@localhost ~]$ echo "Today is $(date) and you are in the $(pwd) directory"
Today is Tue Jan 10 12:42:02 UTC 2018 and you are in the /home/student directory
```

Advanced Commands

As previously mentioned, there are thousands of Linux commands. The commands covered in this section are some of the more advanced commands you are likely to use on a regular basis.

The find Command

The **find** command will search the live filesystem for files and directories using different criteria. Here's the format of the command:

```
find [options] starting_point criteria action
```

The ***starting_point*** is the directory where the search will start. The ***criteria*** is what to search for, and the ***action*** is what to do with the results.

The options shown in Table 2-17 are designed to modify how the **find** command behaves.

Table 2-17 Options for the **find** Command

Option	Description
-maxdepth *n*	Limits how deep into subdirectories the search goes; for example, **find -maxdepth 3** will limit the search to three subdirectories deep.
-mount	Prevents searching directories that serve as mount points. This is useful when you're searching from the / directory. Mount points are used to access local or network-based filesystems. They are covered in greater detail in Chapter 10.
-regextype *type*	When regular expressions (RE) are used, this option specifies what type of RE will be used; ***type*** can be **emacs** (default), **posix-awk**, **posix-basic**, **posix-egrep**, or **posix-extended**. Note: the topic of regular expressions is covered in more detail later in this chapter.

Most criteria-based options allow you to specify a numeric value as an argument. This can be preceded by a - or + character to indicate "less than" or "greater than." For example, using **+5** would mean "more than five." Table 2-18 shows some important criteria-based options.

Table 2-18 Criteria-Based Options

Option	Description
-amin *n*	Matches files based on access time; for example, **-amin -3** would match files accessed within the past three minutes.
-group ***name***	Matches files that are owned by the ***name*** group.
-name ***pattern***	Matches a file or directory based on the ***pattern*** provided; the ***pattern*** can be a regular expression. Note: the topic of regular expressions is covered in more detail later in this chapter.
-mmin *n*	Matches files based on modification time; for example, **-mmin -3** would match files modified within the past three minutes.

Option	Description
-nogroup	Matches files not owned by a group.
-nouser	Matches files not owned by a user.
-size *n*	Match files based on file size; the value *n* can be preceded by a + (more than) or – (less than) and anteceded by a unit modified: **c** for bytes, **k** for kilobytes, **M** for megabytes, or **G** for gigabytes
-type *fstype*	Match all files that are the file type indicated by ***fstype***; ***fstype*** **d** for directories, **p** for named pipes, **f** for regular files, or other characters that represent more advanced file types.
-user *username*	Match all files owned by the ***username*** user (for example, **find /home -user bob**).

Once a file is found, an action can be taken on the file. Table 2-19 shows some important action-based options.

Table 2-19 Action-Based Options

Option	Description
-delete	Delete all matched files (for example, **find /tmp -name "*.tmp" -delete**).
-exec *command*	Execute a command on each matched file (see the examples following this table).
-ls	List details about each matched file.
-ok	Execute a command on each matched file, but prompt the user before each match; the prompt is a yes/no question to determine if the user wants to execute the command.
-print	Print the filename of each matched file; this is the default action option.

Here's an example of the **-exec** option:

```
[root@localhost ~]# find /etc -name "*.cfg" -exec file {} \;
/etc/grub2.cfg: symbolic link to '../boot/grub2/grub.cfg'
/etc/enscript.cfg: ASCII text
/etc/python/cert-verification.cfg: ASCII text
```

The **\;** is used to build a command line. For example, the command that was executed for the previous **find** example was **file /etc/grub2.cfg; file /etc/enscript.cfg; file /etc/python/cert-verification.cfg**. The **** before the **;** is required to escape the meaning of the **;** character for the BASH shell, so the **;** character is passed to the **find** command as a regular argument.

The **{}** characters represent where in the command the matching filename is placed. This can be used more than once, as demonstrated in the next example, which makes a copy of each matched file:

```
find /etc -name "*.cfg" -exec cp {} /tmp/{}.bak \;
```

Security Highlight

Use of the **find** command aids in identification of files recently accessed or files accessed immediately before a negative network event because those files (or entered commands) are likely the cause of the negative event (such as a corrupted file, the loss of system access, or incorrect information written to a file).

Additionally, using the **–nogroup** or **–nouser** option aids in finding files that may have been installed by a hacker or that have become orphaned in updates of operating systems and applications, so these files may be investigated and removed.

Regular Expressions

The term *regex* stands for regular expression (RE), which is a character or set of characters designed to match other characters. For example, in utilities that support REs, a dot (.) will match a single character of any type, whereas **[a-z]** would match any single lowercase character.

There are two types of REs: basic and extended. Basic REs are the "original," and extended REs are the newer additions. Utilities that use REs normally support basic REs by default and have some option or feature to enable extended REs. Although documentation may refer to basic REs as obsolete, they are still used by most modern utilities.

Commonly used basic REs are described in Table 2-20.

Table 2-20 Basic REs

RE	Description
^	Match the beginning of a line.
$	Match the end of a line.
*	Match zero or more characters.
.	Match exactly one character.
[ ]	Match exactly one character that is within the **[ ]** characters; a list of characters (**[abc]**) or a range of characters **([a-c]**) is permitted.
[^]	Match exactly one character that is *not* within the **[ ]** characters; a list of characters (**[^abc]**) or a range of characters (**[^a-c]**) is permitted.
\	Escape the special meaning of a regular expression; for example, the pattern **\.*** would match the value **".*"**.

Commonly used extended REs are described in Table 2-21.

Table 2-21 Extended REs

RE	Description
( )	Group sets of characters together to form an expression; for example, **(abc)**.
X|*Y*	Match either *X* or *Y*.
+	Match the preceding character or expression one or more times.
{*X*}	Match the preceding character or expression *X* times.
{*X*,}	Match the preceding character or expression *X* or more times.
{*X*,*Y*}	Match the preceding character or expression *X* to *Y* times.
?	The previous character or expression is optional.

The **find** command supports the **-regexp** option, which allows you to use regular expressions to perform pattern matching of the filename.

For example, the following command would search for all files that have "chpasswd" somewhere in the filename and an "8" somewhere in the filename after "chpasswd":

```
[student@localhost ~]$ find / -regex ".*chpasswd.*8.*" 2> /dev/null
/usr/share/man/zh_CN/man8/chpasswd.8.gz
/usr/share/man/ja/man8/chpasswd.8.gz
/usr/share/man/zh_TW/man8/chpasswd.8.gz
/usr/share/man/ru/man8/chpasswd.8.gz
/usr/share/man/de/man8/chpasswd.8.gz
/usr/share/man/fr/man8/chpasswd.8.gz
/usr/share/man/man8/chpasswd.8.gz
/usr/share/man/it/man8/chpasswd.8.gz
```

The grep Command

Use the **grep** command to search files for lines that contain a specific pattern. By default, the **grep** command will display the entire line when it finds a matching pattern.

Example:

```
[student@localhost ~]$ grep "the" /etc/rsyslog.conf
# To enable high precision timestamps, comment out the following line.
# Set the default permissions for all log files.
```

NOTE The pattern used to perform the search uses basic regular expressions.

Important options for the **grep** command include those shown in Table 2-22.

Table 2-22 Options for the **grep** Command

Option	Description
-c	Display a count of the number of matching lines rather than displaying each line that matches.
--color	The text that matches is displayed in a different color than the rest of the text.
-E	Use extended regular expressions in addition to basic regular expressions.
-f	Fixed strings; all characters in the pattern are treated as regular characters, not regular expression characters.
-e	Used to specify multiple patterns in one **grep** command (for example, **grep -e pattern1 -e** ***pattern2 file***).
-f ***file***	Use patterns found within the specified ***file***.
-i	Ignore case.
-l	Display filenames that match the pattern, rather than displaying every line in the file that matches. This is useful when you're searching multiple files (for example, **grep "the" /etc/***).
-n	Display the line number before displaying the line.
-r	Recursively search all the files in a directory structure. In this case, the term *recursively* means "throughout all subdirectories."
-v	Inverse match; return all lines that don't contain the pattern specified.

Option	Description
-w	Match whole words only; for example, the command **grep "the" file** will match the letters *the*, even when part of a larger word, such as *then* or *there*, but the command **grep -w "the" file** will only match *the* as a separate word.

For example, to search the filesystem based on file content, use the **grep** command with the **-r** option:

```
[student@localhost ~]$ grep -r ":[0-9][0-9]:games:" /etc 2> /dev/null
/etc/passwd:games:x:5:60:games:/usr/games:/usr/sbin/nologin
```

The sed Command

The **sed** command is designed to edit file data in a non-interactive method. Unlike most editors (such as the **vi** editor discussed in Chapter 4, "Editing Files"), which require human interaction to perform modification to files, the **sed** command can make changes automatically.

In the following example, the **sed** command will replace "localhost" with "myhost" in the **/etc/hosts** file:

```
[student@localhost ~]$ cat /etc/hosts
127.0.0.1 localhost
[student@localhost ~]$ sed 's/localhost/myhost/' /etc/hosts
127.0.0.1 myhost
```

Only the first occurrence on each line is replaced by default. To have all occurrences replaced, used the **/g** modifier, as shown in the next example:

```
[student@localhost ~]$ sed 's/0/X/' /etc/hosts
127.X.0.1 localhost
[student@localhost ~]$ sed 's/0/X/g' /etc/hosts
127.X.X.1 localhost
```

Note that a search pattern can be a regular expression (basic only; by default, use the **-r** option to include extended regular expressions).

The **sed** command does not replace the original file. Redirect output into another file, like so:

```
[student@localhost ~]$ sed 's/0/X/' /etc/hosts > myhosts
```

Important operations for the **sed** command include those shown in Table 2-23.

Table 2-23 Operations for the **sed** Command

Operation	Description
s/	Substitute all instances of a character or expression with the new value provided.
d	Delete; for example, the following would delete any line that contained "enemy": **sed '/enemy/d' filename**.
a\	Append data after the matching line (for example**, sed '/localhost/ a**). This adds a new line to **add/' /etc/hosts**.
i\	Insert data before the matching line.

Important options for the **sed** command include those shown in Table 2-24.

Table 2-24 Options for the **sed** Command

Option	Description
-f *file*	Use **sed** commands that are located in ***file***.
-i	Edit the file in place; be careful, this will replace the original file with the modifications.
-r	Use extended regular expressions in addition to basic regular expressions.

Compression Commands

A common task on most modern operating systems is to combine and compress multiple files into a single file. This could be in order to store files on a smaller device, to make it easy to download files from a website, or to merge and compress files for email transport. This section focuses on some of the more common Linux utilities that merge and compress files.

The tar Command

The purpose of the **tar** command, which stands for *tape archive*, is to merge multiple files into a single file. To create a tar file named **sample.tar**, execute the following:

```
tar -cf sample.tar files_to_merge
```

To list the contents of a **.tar** file:

```
tar -tf sample.tar
```

To extract the contents of a **.tar** file:

```
tar -xf sample.tar
```

Important options include those shown in Table 2-25.

Table 2-25 Options for the **tar** Command

Option	Description
-c	Create a **.tar** file.
-t	List the contents of a **.tar** file.
-x	Extract the contents of a **.tar** file.
-f	Specify the name of the **.tar** file.
-v	Be verbose (provide more details as to what the command is doing).
-A	Append new files to the existing **.tar** file.
-d	Compare the differences between a **.tar** file and the files in a directory.
-u	Update; only append newer files into an existing **.tar** file.
-j	Compress/uncompress the **.tar** file using the bzip2 utility. See more details regarding this utility later in this chapter.
-J	Compress/uncompress the **.tar** file using the xz utility. See more details regarding this utility later in this chapter.
-z	Compress/uncompress the **.tar** file using the gzip utility. See more details regarding this utility later in this chapter.

The gzip Command

Use the **gzip** command to compress files:

```
[student@localhost ~]$ ls -lh juju
-rwxr-xr-x 1 vagrant vagrant 109M Jan 10 09:20 juju
[student@localhost ~]$ gzip juju
[student@localhost ~]$ ls -lh juju.gz
-rwxr-xr-x 1 vagrant vagrant 17M Jan 10 09:20 juju.gz
```

Note that the **gzip** command replaces the original file with the smaller compressed file.

Important options include those shown in Table 2-26.

Table 2-26 Options for the **gzip** Command

Option	Description
-c	Write output to STDOUT and do not replace original file. Use redirection to place output data into a new file (for example, **gzip -c juju > juju.gz**). This is useful to keep the original file while also creating a compressed file.
-d	Decompress the file (you can also use the **gunzip** command).
-r	Recursive: Used when a directory argument is given to compress all files in the directory (and its subdirectories). Note that this does not merge the files together but rather creates multiple compressed files.
-v	Verbose: Display percentage of compression.

The gunzip Command

Use the **gunzip** command to decompress gzipped files:

```
[student@localhost ~]$ ls -lh juju.gz
-rwxr-xr-x 1 vagrant vagrant 17M Jan 10 09:20 juju.gz
[student@localhost ~]$ gunzip juju
[student@localhost ~]$ ls -lh juju
-rwxr-xr-x 1 vagrant vagrant 109M Jan 10 09:20 juju
```

The bzip2 Command

Use the **bzip2** command to compress files:

```
[student@localhost ~]$ ls -lh juju
-rwxr-xr-x 1 vagrant vagrant 109M Jan 10 09:20 juju
[student@localhost ~]$ bzip2 juju
[student@localhost ~]$ ls -lh juju.bz2
-rwxr-xr-x 1 vagrant vagrant 14M Jan 10 09:20 juju.bz2
```

Note that the **bzip2** command replaces the original file with the compressed file.

Important options include those shown in Table 2-27.

Table 2-27 Options for the **bzip2** Command

Option	Description
-c	Write output to STDOUT and do not replace the original file. Use redirection to place output data into a new file (for example, **bzip2 -c juju > juju.bz**).

Option	Description
-d	Decompress the file (you can also use the **bunzip2** command).
-v	Verbose: Display percentage of compression.

The xz Command

Use the **xz** command to compress files:

```
[student@localhost ~]$ ls -lh juju
-rwxr-xr-x 1 vagrant vagrant 109M Jan 10 09:20 juju
[student@localhost ~]$ xz juju
[student@localhost ~]$ ls -lh juju.xz
-rwxr-xr-x 1 vagrant vagrant 11M Jan 10 09:20 juju.xz
```

Important options include those shown in Table 2-28.

Table 2-28 Options for the **xz** Command

Option	Description
-c	Write output to STDOUT and do not replace the original file. Use redirection to place output data into a new file (for example, **xz -c juju > juju.xz**).
-d	Decompress the file (you can also use the **unxz** command).
-l	List information about an existing compressed file (for example, **xz –l juju.xz**).
-v	Verbose: Display percentage of compression.

The **gzip, xz,** and **bzip2** commands are very similar. The biggest difference is the technique used to compress files. The **gzip** command uses the Lempel-Ziv (LZ77) coding method, whereas the **bzip2** command uses the Burrows-Wheeler (BWT) block-sorting text-compression algorithm and Huffman coding. The **xz** command uses the LZMA and LZMA2 compression methods.

Summary

This chapter focused on essential commands that all Linux users should know. These commands allow you to navigate the Linux operating system, manipulate files and directories, and perform advanced end-user operations. Consider these topics as "must know" in order to learn more advanced security and advanced system administration topics.

Key Terms

current directory, root directory, parent directory, subdirectory, child directory, Filesystem Hierarchy Standard, option, argument, absolute path, relative path, file glob, wildcard, variable, local variable, environment variable, login shell, non-login shell, initialization file, alias, redirection, piping, subcommand, regular expression

Review Questions

1. The _____ command can be used to delete a directory and all its contents.
2. Which of the following is a valid path type? (Choose all that apply.)
   - **A.** absolute
   - **B.** full
   - **C.** complete
   - **D.** relative
3. Which of the following represents the current directory?
   - **A.** .
   - **B.** ..
   - **C.** -
   - **D.** ~
4. The _____ option to the **ls** command will display a file's permissions.
5. The _____ command will tell you what type of contents are contained in a file.

Getting Help

Because you are likely just beginning to learn Linux, the operating system will seem huge. Thousands of commands and hundreds of features are at your disposal… if you know how to use them. In fact, learning how to operate in Linux is going to put a tax on the grey matter between your ears. Fortunately, you don't need to memorize everything.

Linux comes with a great help system. Almost every command, feature, configuration file, and service has enough documentation to help you when your brain refuses to recall that important option, setting, or value. In this chapter, you learn how to make use of this documentation.

After reading this chapter and completing the exercises, you will be able to do the following:

Discover information about commands by using specific command-line options

Get help about a command, feature, or configuration file by using man **or** info **pages**

Use additional documentation on the system to solve problems

Man Pages

To discover additional information about a command or configuration file, you can use the man (short for manual) page. For example, to learn more about the **ls** command, execute **man ls**.

You can use the keyboard keys to navigate when viewing the content on a man page. Table 3-1 highlights the more useful movement commands.

Table 3-1 Movement Commands

Movement Command	Description
h	Used to display a help screen (summary of man page movement commands)
SPACEBAR	Move forward one page in the current document
b	Move back one page in the current document
ENTER	Move down one line in the current document; the down-arrow key can also perform this operation
UP ARROW	Move up one line in the current document
/term	Search the document for *term* (this can be a regular expression or just plain text)
q	Quit the man page and return to the shell

Man Page Components

Each man page is broken into many different components. See Figure 3-1 for a demonstration of some of the components of the man page for the **ls** command.

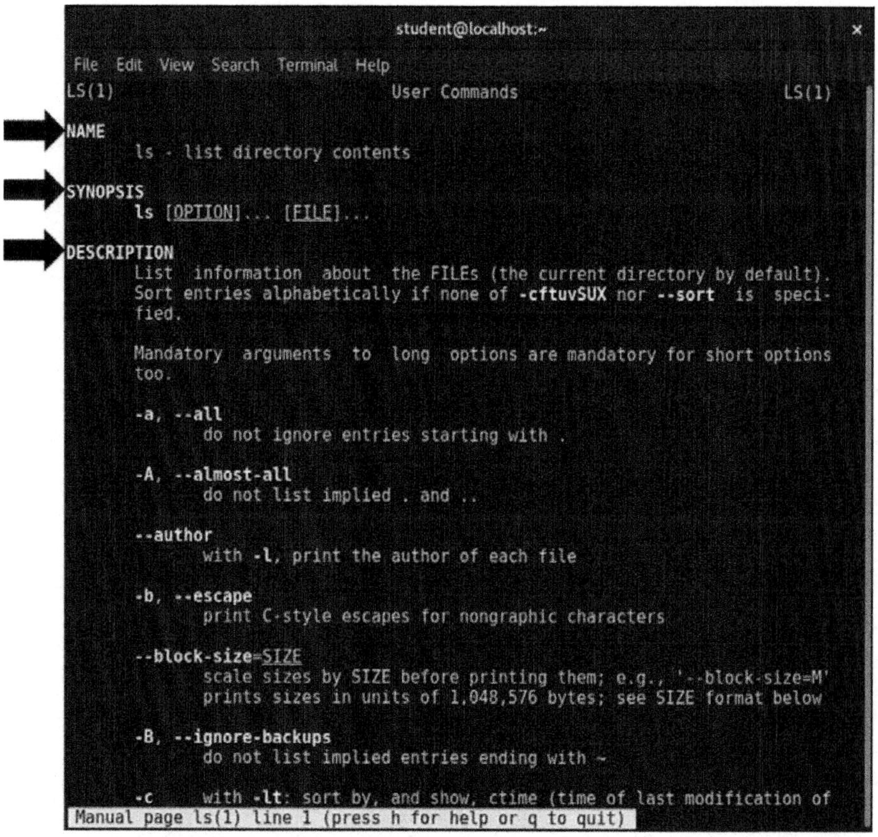

```
student@localhost:~
File  Edit  View  Search  Terminal  Help
LS(1)                          User Commands                          LS(1)

NAME
       ls - list directory contents

SYNOPSIS
       ls [OPTION]... [FILE]...

DESCRIPTION
       List  information  about  the FILEs (the current directory by default).
       Sort entries alphabetically if none of -cftuvSUX nor --sort  is  speci-
       fied.

       Mandatory  arguments  to  long  options are mandatory for short options
       too.

       -a, --all
              do not ignore entries starting with .

       -A, --almost-all
              do not list implied . and ..

       --author
              with -l, print the author of each file

       -b, --escape
              print C-style escapes for nongraphic characters

       --block-size=SIZE
              scale sizes by SIZE before printing them; e.g., '--block-size=M'
              prints sizes in units of 1,048,576 bytes; see SIZE format below

       -B, --ignore-backups
              do not list implied entries ending with ~

       -c     with -lt: sort by, and show, ctime (time of last modification of
 Manual page ls(1) line 1 (press h for help or q to quit)
```

Figure 3-1 *Components of the* ***ls*** *Command Man Page*

Table 3-2 describes the most common components.

Table 3-2 Common Components of **ls** Command

Component	Description
NAME	The name of the command
SYNOPSIS	A brief description of the command
DESCRIPTION	A detailed description of the command, including its options
AUTHOR	The persons who wrote the command
REPORTING BUGS	Where to send information about problems with the command
SEE ALSO	Additional commands or documentation related to the topic of this man page
EXAMPLES	Examples of the command in action

Man Page Sections

Because of the large number of man pages (remember, there are thousands of commands, utilities, and configuration files), they are broken into categories called "sections." In some cases, the section will need to be included as an argument. For example, **man passwd** (the man page for the **passwd** command) will produce a different document than **man 5 passwd** (the man page for the **/etc/passwd** file).

When you view a man page, the section is indicated in parentheses in the upper-left corner of the screen, as shown in Figure 3-2.

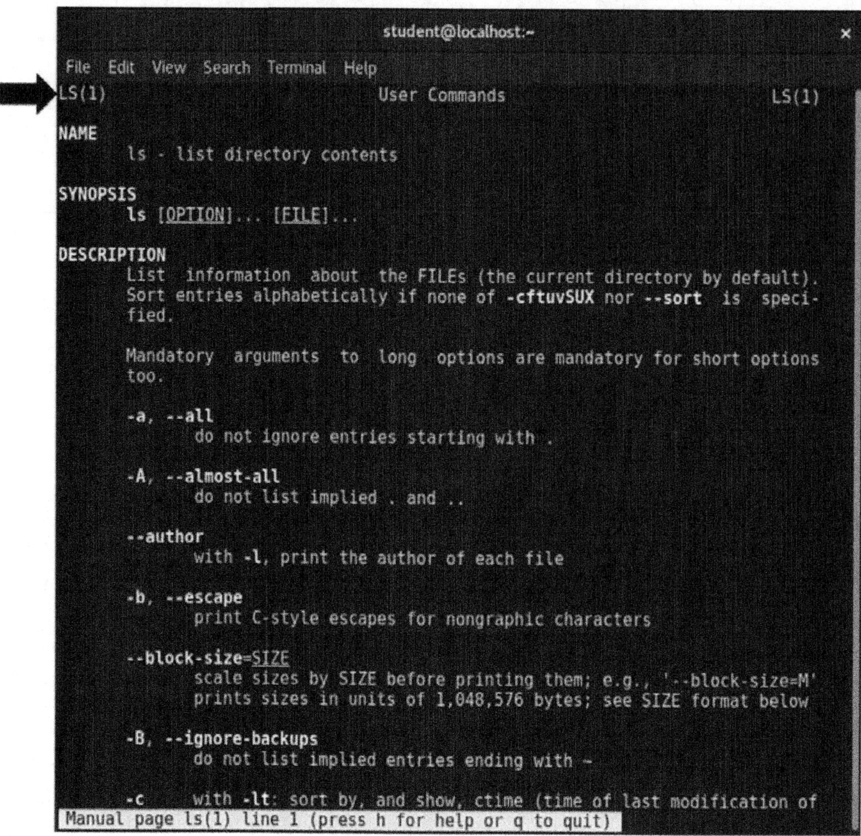

Figure 3-2 *Man Page Section for the **ls** Command*

The primary sections are detailed in Table 3-3.

Table 3-3 Primary Sections for the **ls** Command

Section	Description
1	Executable commands and shell commands
2	System calls
3	Library calls
4	Special files (aka device files in **/dev**)
5	File formats
6	Games
7	Miscellaneous
8	System administrator-based commands
9	Kernel routines

You may wonder how you are supposed to know the specific man page sections. You can see this information by using the **man -f** command:

```
[student@onecoursesource.com ~]$ man -f passwd
passwd (1)           - change user password
passwd (1ssl)        - compute password hashes
passwd (5)           - the password file
```


NOTE The **man -f** command is the same as the **whatis** command:

```
[student@onecoursesource.com ~]$ whatis passwd
passwd (1)           - change user password
passwd (1ssl)        - compute password hashes
passwd (5)           - the password file
```

The **man -f** command will list all the sections in a command or configuration file for any existing man page. If you do not know the exact name of the command or configuration file, you can use the **-k** option to the **man** command and have it search for a "keyword," as shown in Example 3-1.

Example 3-1 *The **man -k** Command*

```
student@onecoursesource.com:~$ man -k password | head -n 5
chage (1)            - change user password expiry information
chgpasswd (8)        - update group passwords in batch mode
chpasswd (8)         - update passwords in batch mode
cpgr (8)             - copy with locking the given file to the password ...
cppw (8)             - copy with locking the given file to the password ...
```

NOTE The **man -k** command is the same as the **apropos** command.

In some cases you might not get a response back when you use the **man -f** or **man -k** command. For example, you might get something like the following:

```
[student@onecoursesource.com ~]$ man -k passwd
passwd: nothing appropriate.
```

This could be because the database that holds a list of man pages and descriptions has not been built or updated. To build this database, run the **mandb** command as the root user, as shown in Example 3-2.

Example 3-2 *The **mandb** Command*

```
root@onecoursesource.com:~# mandb
Purging old database entries in /usr/share/man...
Processing manual pages under /usr/share/man...
…
Processing manual pages under /usr/share/man/pt_BR...
Processing manual pages under /usr/local/man...
0 man subdirectories contained newer manual pages.
456 manual pages were added.
0 stray cats were added.
7 old database entries were purged.
```

Man Page Locations

In some cases, a **man** command might not be in a standard location. This may happen when you install third-party software and the software developer chooses to place man pages in a location where they are not typically installed.

In these situations, you should specify an alternate location for the man page. To specify an alternate man page location, you can use the **-M** option:

```
[student@onecoursesource.com ~]$ man -M /opt/man testcmd
```

Alternatively, you can create a **MANPATH** variable:

```
[student@ onecoursesource.com ~]$ MANPATH=/opt/man
[student@ onecoursesource.com ~]$ man testcmd
```

NOTE The previous examples are purely for demonstration and will not function on your system unless you have a man page for **testcmd** in the **/opt/man** directory.

Command Help Options

Some commands support an option that provides some basic help features. In most cases, help is displayed by using the **--help** option, as shown in Example 3-3.

Example 3-3 *The First Few Lines of the Output of the **date --help** Command*

```
student@onecoursesource.com:~$ date --help | head -n 3
Usage: date [OPTION]... [+FORMAT]
  or:  date [-u|--utc|--universal] [MMDDhhmm[[CC]YY][.ss]]
Display the current time in the given FORMAT, or set the system date.
```

This output is useful to remind yourself of options and features of the command without having to read through the entire man page for the command.

NOTE A few commands use **-h** instead of **--help** to display basic help features.

The help Command

The **help** command provides information only for built-in shell commands, as these commands don't have separate man pages. For example, you might expect that the **cd** command has a man page because it is a valid command, but because it is a built-in shell command, there is no man page for it, as shown here:

```
student@localhost:~$ man cd
No manual entry for cd
```

There is a help page for the **cd** command that can be viewed by running the command **help cd**.

Helpful hint: Do not try to memorize which commands are built-in shell commands. If you get a "No manual entry..." error when trying to view a man page, just try to use the **help** command instead. Alternatively, you can get a list of all the built-in commands by running the **help -s** command, as shown in Example 3-4.

Example 3-4 *The Last Ten Lines of the Output of the* ***help -s*** *Command*

```
student@onecoursesource.com:~$ help -s | tail
export [-fn] [name[=va>  typeset [-aAfFgilrtux>
 false                    ulimit [-SHabcdefilmn>
 fc [-e ename] [-lnr] [>  umask [-p] [-S] [mode>
 fg [job_spec]            unalias [-a] name [na>
 for NAME [in WORDS ...>  unset [-f] [-v] [-n] >
 for (( exp1; exp2; exp>  until COMMANDS; do CO>
 function name { COMMAN>  variables - Names and>
 getopts optstring name>  wait [-n] [id ...]
 hash [-lr] [-p pathnam>  while COMMANDS; do CO>
 help [-dms] [pattern .>  { COMMANDS ; }
```

The info Command

Almost every command and configuration file has a man page because this is the technique for documenting these features. Somewhat new are info pages. Whereas each man page is simply a single text document, info pages are more like reading content from a website that has hyperlinks to provide more structure.

For example, type the command **info ls** and use the arrow keys to move down to the "* Menu:" section. You will see a "table of contents" that looks like Figure 3-3.

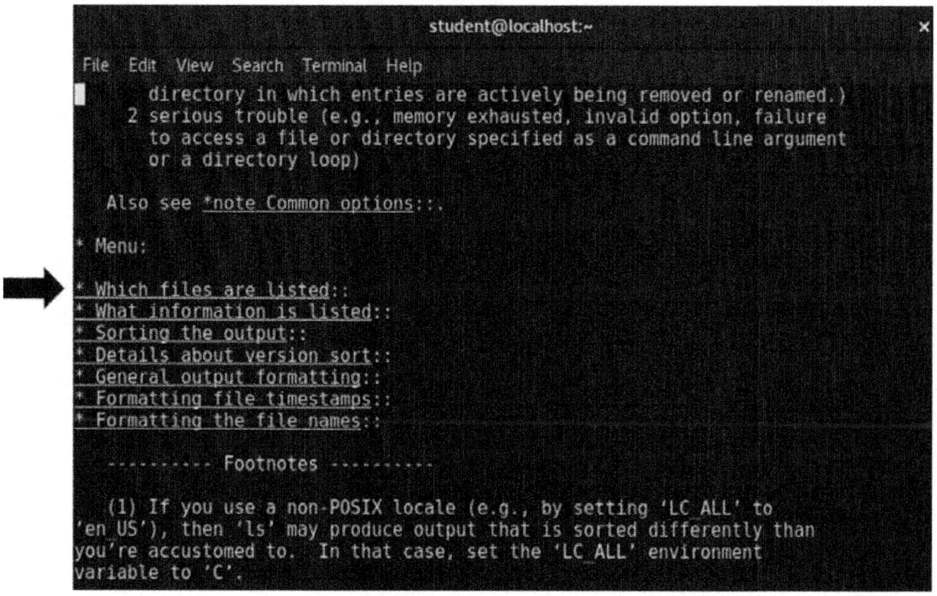

Figure 3-3 *Hyperlinks in the* ***ls*** *Info Page*

If you move your cursor to the "* Sorting the output::" line and then press the Enter key, you will be moved to a document that describes how you can sort the output of the **ls** command. You have moved into a sub-node ("10.1.3 Sorting the output", for example). To move back to the higher-level node, press the **u** key (**u** for up).

The Table 3-4 describes additional movement commands for the **info** command.

Table 3-4 Movement Commands for the **info** Command

Command	Description
n	Move to the next node (for example, if you are in 10.2.3, this would move you to 10.2.4)
p	Move to the previous node (for example, if you are in 10.2.3, this would move you to 10.2.2)
u	Move up to the parent node
l	Move to the last node (the node you were last in)
b	Move to the beginning location of the current node (top of the current screen)
t	Move to the top level of all nodes (the top-level table of contents is displayed)
q	Quit the **info** command

You may be wondering why there are both info and man pages and which one you should use. The following are some answers to these questions:

- Man pages have been around for a very long time (since the early days of Unix in the early 1970s). Although they might not be as easy to read, they offer a standard way for developers to provide documentation.
- Info pages are more user friendly, but also require more work for developers to create.
- Often a command will have a man page but not an info page. In these cases, the **info** command will display the man page.
- Info pages often read more like a tutorial; man pages read more like documentation.
- Man pages have the advantage in that they are easier to print than info pages.
- Overall, having both provides flexibility. Use the method that you like best.

The /usr/share/doc Directory

Additional documentation may also be provided in the **/usr/share/doc** directory. Which documentation is available in this directory depends on what software has been installed. Example 3-5 provides some typical output.

Example 3-5 *Typical Contents of the **/usr/share/doc** Directory*

```
student@onecoursesource.com:~$ ls /usr/share/doc
aufs-tools          libstdc++-5-dev
cgroupfs-mount      libxml2
gcc-5-base          libxml2-dev
icu-devtools        libxslt1.1
libexpat1-dev       libxslt1-dev
libffi6             linux-headers-4.4.0-51
libffi-dev          linux-headers-4.4.0-51-generic
libicu55            lxc-docker-1.9.1
libicu-dev          python-apt
libpython2.7        unzip
libpython2.7-dev    zip
libpython-dev
```

The contents of the **/usr/share/doc** directory are a collection of subdirectories that provide additional documentation for specific software packages. For example, Example 3-5 includes a subdirectory named **zip**. This directory contains documentation about the zip software package, as shown here:

```
student@onecoursesource.com$ ls /usr/share/doc/zip
changelog.Debian.gz  copyright  WHATSNEW
changelog.gz         TODO
```

There are no predefined requirements for the contents of these documentation subdirectories; the software vendor decides what content is added. Most commonly you will find copyright notifications, a changelog (changes made to the software over time), a README file that describes the software package, and other useful information.

Internet Resources

One great source of information is the website of the distribution you are using. All the major distributions provide additional documentation in the form of guides. For example, Figure 3-4 demonstrates a few of the guides provided on the website for Red Hat Enterprise Linux (https://access.redhat.com/documentation/en-us/red_hat_enterprise_linux).

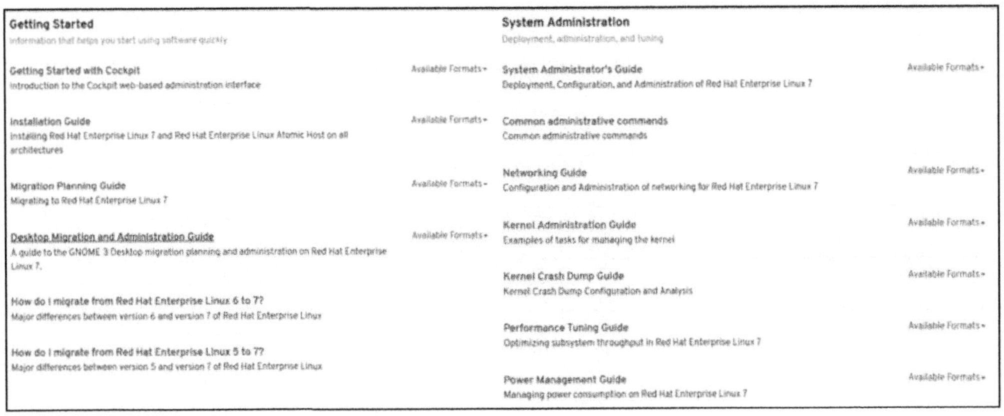

Figure 3-4 *Documentation Available for Red Hat Enterprise Linux*

In addition to the documentation provided by the distributions, you should also consider that Linux includes many open source projects. Each of these projects typically has some documentation that might provide you with additional information or user guides.

For example, in Chapter 2, "Working on the Command Line," the **gzip** utility was introduced. This utility is one of many projects from the GNUSoftware Foundation. It has an excellent user guide available on the site https://www.gnu.org/software/gzip/manual/gzip.html.

Because there are so many of these projects, it is not feasible to provide a complete list of all the documentation pages. Typically, the man or info page for the corresponding command will provide a URL, but you can also find these websites with a simple Internet search.

There are also many websites devoted to additional Linux documentation, blogs, news, and forums. There are too many to list in this book, but a few of the more useful ones are provided in the following list:

- **The Linux Documentation Project**: http://www.tldp.org/. Note that some content on this site is outdated, but the Advanced Bash Shell Scripting guide is a diamond in the rough.
- **Linux Today**: www.linuxtoday.com.
- **Linux Forums**: http://www.linuxforums.org.

Security Highlight

The authors do not want to discount the value of an Internet or "Google" search. However, the assumption is that you already possess the skill of searching the Internet. One caveat, which you likely already know: not everything you find on the Internet is accurate, so always try to find multiple sources of information when using the Internet as a source. Using bad information can pose a security risk in addition to frustrating you.

Conversational Learning™ — Where Should I Start?

Gary: Hi, Julia. I'm a bit overwhelmed. Can you give me some advice?

Julia: Of course, Gary. Always happy to help.

Gary: I just learned about all these great places to find useful information about Linux, but now I have no idea in what order I should start searching!

Julia: Ah, yes, information overload… or information sources in this case.

Gary: And I thought options were always a good thing!

Julia: Ha, not always. OK, so suppose you already know a command and you just can't remember how an option works. I'd suggest running the command with the **--help** option or maybe looking at the man page for the command.

Gary: Sounds like a good idea.

Julia: If you don't know anything about the command, then the info page might be better because it is easier to read.

Gary: Got it.

Julia: If there is a feature that seems specific to a distribution, I would go seek information on the documentation website for that feature.

Gary: OK, any other suggestions?

Julia: When all else fails, forums are a great place to ask questions. And, of course, you can always ask me!

Gary: Thanks, Julia!

Summary

Knowing where to turn for help is important when dealing with a massive operating system like Linux. In this chapter, you learned how to use command options to see helpful information about a specific command. You also learned how to use man pages and info pages to see detailed information about how commands and configuration files work. You also learned how to find additional documentation in the **/usr/share/doc** directory.

Key terms

man page, info page

Review Questions

1. The _____ character can be used while viewing a man page in order to search for a term in the document.
2. Which man page section is for file formats?
   - A. 1
   - B. 3
   - C. 5
   - D. 7
3. Which the following will display a list of man pages that match a keyword?
   - A. **man -keyword**
   - B. **man -k**
   - C. **whereis**
   - D. **whatis**
4. The _____ command will provide information about built-in shell commands.
5. The _____ key will move you to the previous node while viewing an info page.

Editing Files

You might wonder why there is an entire chapter devoted to editing files. The Linux operating system is configured largely by hundreds of text files. User and group accounts, system services, utilities, and many other features rely on text files to hold critical information.

Chapter 2, "Working on the Command Line," introduced several examples of critical files, including initialization files such as **/etc/profile** and **~/.bashrc**. These initialization files are used to modify the shell environment when a user logs in or opens a new shell process. Each one of these files is a text file that needs to be edited at some point.

In this chapter, you learn how to use text editors. The primary focus will be on the vi/vim editor, but additional editors are also introduced.

After reading this chapter and completing the exercises, you will be able to do the following:

Edit text files using the vi editor

Become familiar with additional text editors, such as Emacs, joe, and gedit

The vi Editor

Consider the early days of Unix, the precursor to Linux: A user would sit down at a keyboard, ready to edit a program that she is working on. She stares at the printer (yes, printer, not monitor) considering what commands to execute. Monitors were very rare in the early 1970s, and even if a user had one, it was primarily designed to display the output of executed code, not to interactively edit files.

Instead, the user would use a simple command-based editor, like the ed editor. With this editor a user could perform operations such as list the contents of a file (that is, print the file), modify specific characters of a file, or save the contents of a file. However, this was all accomplished in a way that may seem cumbersome today. The user would not see what she was editing, but rather just assumed the commands were successful (or she could print the file to verify).

When monitors became more commonplace, the ed editor seemed like a clumsy way to edit a text file. In the mid-1970s, a replacement editor named vi (short for visual) was introduced to Unix. It was a great improvement over the ed editor because you could actually see your document and move around the document as you edited it.

The vi editor is now a standard text editor for both Linux and Unix environments. Although it may not be as user friendly as other editors, it has a few important advantages:

- The vi editor (or vim, an improved version of the vi editor) is on every Linux distribution. This means if you know how to edit files with the vi editor, you can always edit a file regardless of which distribution you are working on.
- Because the vi editor is a command-line only editor, it does not require a graphical user interface (GUI). This is important because many Linux servers do not have a GUI installed, which means you cannot use GUI-based text editors.
- Once you understand vi, you will find it is an efficient editor, allowing you to edit files quickly compared to most other editors. This is because all commands are short and keyboard-based, so you do not waste time taking your hands off of the keyboard to use the mouse.

- The vi editor is very stable and has not changed much in the last 40+ years. You could take a cryogenically frozen user from the 1970s who used the vi editor, unfreeze her today, and she could edit files using a modern vi editor. Certainly features have been added to the vi editor since the 1970s, but the core functionality of vi does not change, making it very easy for you (or that cryogenically frozen user from the 1970s) to use throughout your career without having to "relearn" how newer versions work.

To edit a new file with the vi editor, you can just type the command with no arguments or type **vi** ***filename***.

4

What Is vim?

The vim editor was released in 1991 as a clone of the vi editor. The vim editor has the same base functionality as the vi editor, but it has several additional features. Some of these features can be useful for software developers.

It is possible that your distribution only has the vi editor. Many distributions have both the vi and vim editors. On some distributions, the command **vi** is actually a link to the vim editor.

There is an easy way to tell if you are using the vi or vim editor. See the Text Support™ dialog in Figure 4-1 to learn more.

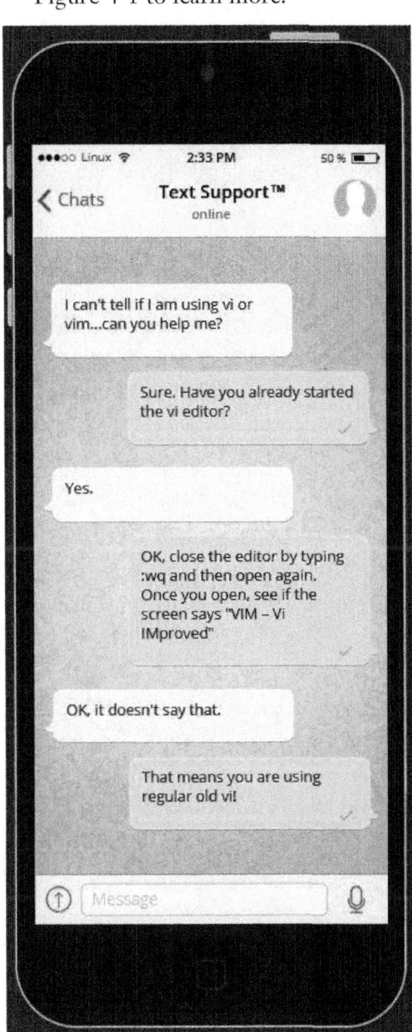

Figure 4-1 *Text Support™: Which Mode?*

NOTE Unless stated otherwise, the commands shown in this chapter will work both in the vi and vim editors. Any command that only works in vim will be denoted as such.

Security Highlight

Directly modifying system files can compromise the operating system if you make mistakes while editing the files. As a result, some utilities are designed to edit these files in a safer manner.

For example, in Chapter 6, "Managing Group Accounts," and Chapter 7, "Managing User Accounts," you will be introduced to user and group accounts. Information about these accounts is stored in a variety of text-based system files (such as **/etc/passwd**) that can be edited directly. However, it is safer to use commands like **useradd** and **usermod** to modify user accounts or **groupadd** and **groupmod** to modify group accounts. These tools will perform error-checking operations before modifying files, and they also often back up the previous version of the file.

Essential vi Commands

Becoming an expert vi user can take a lot of practice, but being able to effectively edit files requires the knowledge of a subset of the large amount of vi commands.

It helps to have a large file to edit. All Linux distributions should come with the **/etc/services** file, which is typically thousands of lines long. You can start by first copying this file to your home directory and then you can edit the copy with the **vi** command:

```
[student@onecoursesource.com ~]$ cp /etc/services .

[student@onecoursesource.com ~]$ vi services
```

Use Basic vi Modes

Because vi was designed to only use a keyboard, this poses a challenge because sometimes a specific key on the keyboard should execute a command and other times a key should represent a character to insert into the document. To allow the keys to perform different tasks, vi has three modes of operation:

- **Command mode**: This mode is the default mode. When you open vi, you are placed in the command mode. Within this mode you can perform commands that can move around the screen, delete text, and paste text.
- **Insert mode**: While you're in insert mode, any key typed will appear in your document as new text. When you are finished adding new text, you can return to the default mode (the command mode) by pressing the Escape key. See the "Entering the Insert Mode" section in this chapter for details regarding how to get into the insert mode.
- **Last line mode**: The last line mode, also called *ex mode*, allows you to perform more complex operations, such as saving a document to a file with a different name. To enter into last line mode from the command mode, press the : key. After you enter your command and press Enter, the command is executed and you are normally returned to the command mode. In some cases, you may need to press the Escape key to return to the command mode. Later sections will explore this mode in more detail.

NOTE You cannot move from the insert mode to the last line mode, or vice versa. To move to the insert mode or the last line mode, you first must be in the command mode. Pressing the Escape key places you in the command mode.

See Figure 4-2 for a graphical representation of the three modes of vi.

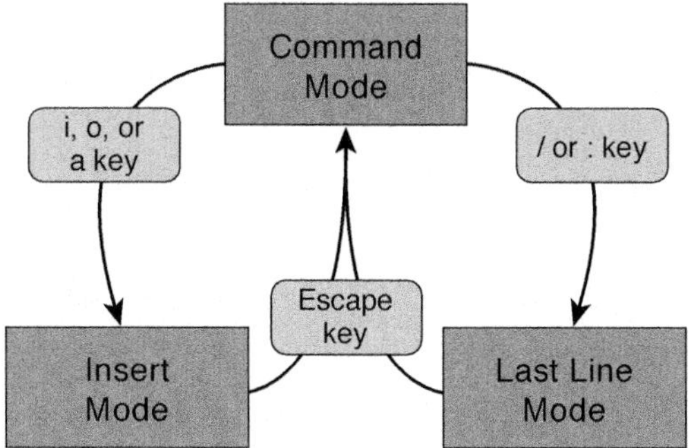

Figure 4-2 *The Three Modes of the vi Editor*

Entering the Insert Mode

When you first start the vi editor, you are placed in the command mode. This mode is designed to allow you to perform commands, such as navigating the text shown, copying text, and deleting text.

While in the command mode, you cannot insert new text into your document because all of the keyboard keys are assigned to command tasks. To insert new text, you must use the **s** command to move from command mode to insert mode. These commands include the following:

i	New text will appear before the cursor position.
a	New text will appear after the cursor position.
I	New text will appear at the beginning of the line.
A	New text will appear at the end of the line.
o	Opens a new line below the line that contains the cursor; new text will be placed on this line.
O	Opens a new line above the line that contains the cursor; new text will be placed on this line.

See Figure 4-3 for a visual depiction of how these vi commands work.

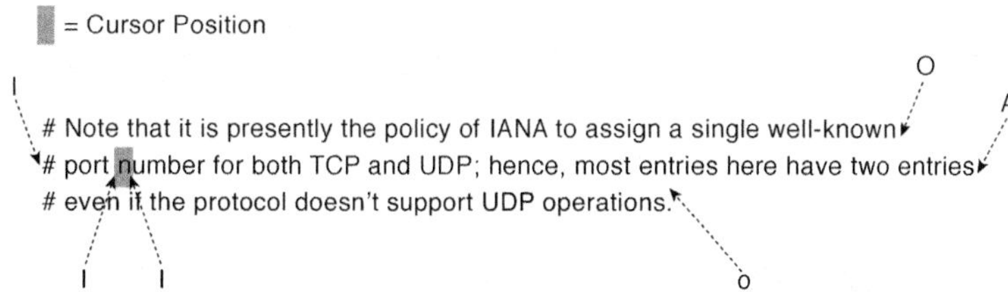

Figure 4-3 *vi Commands to Enter Insert Mode*

If you are working in a standard vi editor, then "-- INSERT --" does not appear at the bottom of the screen by default. To enable this feature in a standard vi editor, type the following command while in command mode:

```
:set showmode
```

When you want to return to the command mode, just press the Escape key. This is normally denoted in documentation as <ESC>. If you return to the command mode, then the "-- INSERT --" should disappear from the bottom of the screen.

Movement Commands

While you are in the command mode, you can move the cursor in your document by using a variety of keys. One of the common methods is to move the cursor one character to the left or right, or one line up or down. This can be done either using the arrow keys on your keyboard or using the h, j, k, and l keys, as shown in Figure 4-4.

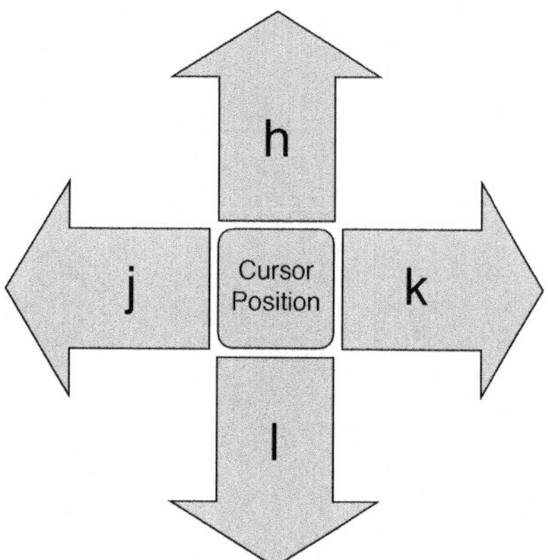

Figure 4-4 *vi Movement Commands*

There are many additional movement commands, including the following:

$	Move to the last column (character) on the current line.
0	Move to the first column (character) on the current line.
w	Move to the beginning of the next word or punctuation mark.
W	Move to past the next space.
b	Move to the beginning of the previous word's punctuation mark.
B	Move to the beginning of the previous word, ignoring punctuation.
e	Move to the end of the next word or punctuation mark.
E	Move to the end of the next word, ignoring punctuation.
)	Move forward one sentence.
(	Move back one sentence.
}	Move forward one paragraph.
{	Move back one paragraph.
H	Move to the top of the screen.
M	Move to the middle of the screen.
L	Move to the bottom of the screen.
[[	Move to the beginning of the document.
]]	Move to the end of the document.
G	Move to the end of the document (same as]]).
***x*G**	Move to line *x* (you can also use the technique of **:*x***).

Note that these are just some of the movement commands. Spend some time trying out these movement commands and then create a "cheat sheet" of the commands you feel will be most useful when you edit. Make this a cheat sheet that you can add more commands to as you learn additional useful commands by making it a text document you save in your Linux system. You can also visit the "Vi lovers" page (http://thomer.com/vi/vi.html) and download one of the "reference cards" under the "Vi pages/manuals/tutorials" section.

Repeater Modifiers

In the previous section, you discovered that you can jump to a specific line in a document by typing a number followed by a **G** while you are in the command mode. For example, the command **7G** will take you to line number 7 in the document.

Placing a number before a command acts as a modifier. Modifiers can be used on many different command-mode commands. Here are some examples:

3w	Move forward three words.
5i	Insert something five times.
4(	Move back three paragraphs.

You can also use repeat modifiers on commands like deleting, copying, and pasting. Typically if there is a command-mode command that you would logically want to execute multiple times, then repeat modifiers should work with that command.

Are You Trying These Commands?

Recall that we suggested you copy the **/etc/services** file to your home directory so you can try out the commands. Remember, if you get stuck in the insert mode, just press the <ESC> key to return to the command mode.

Don't worry if you end up with an unreadable file. It is just a practice file, and you are about to learn how to correct mistakes.

Undoing

You can undo whatever change has been made to the document by tying the **u** character in the command mode. In the standard vi editor, you can only undo a single action; in fact, the **u** command acts as an undo/redo key.

If you are using the vim editor, you can undo several actions. Just keep pressing the **u** character and older modifications will be "undone." You can perform a "redo," which undoes the changes performed by the undo command, by using the **^r** command (the Control key plus the r key).

Conversational Learning™—Clearing Out Mistakes Quickly

Gary: Hi, Julia. I'm really stuck here. I think I typed a number before going into the insert mode in vi and when I pressed Escape to return to the command mode, a huge amount of text was duplicated in my document!

Julia: OK, there are a few possible solutions here. If you press the **u** character in the command mode, then it will undo the last operation.

Gary: But, then I lose all of my work.

Julia: Right, and I'm guessing you don't want to input all of it again?

Gary: No way!

Julia: OK, so that means the second option won't work either.

Gary: What was the second option?

Julia: Quit without saving anything. Let's try another method. Scroll through your document. Let me know if there is any duplicate information.

Gary: OK... let's see... yes! It looks like the same five pages or so are repeated over and over.

Julia: OK, can you get to where the first set of five pages ends? Then go down to the first line of the second set of five pages.

Gary: OK, I'm there.

Julia: Great, now to delete from the current line to the end of the document, type **G$**.

Gary: Oh, yes, that worked!

Julia: Excellent. Keep the other two techniques in your back pocket, as they may come in handy some other time.

Gary: Thanks again, Julia. You saved me a ton of work.

Julia: Any time, Gary.

Suppose you made a large number of changes since you opened the document and you want to discard all of them. In this case, you probably want to close the document without saving and then open it again. To close the document without saving changes, type the command **:q!** (: key, q key, and ! key). More on this command and other ways to quit the vi editor are presented later in this chapter.

Copying, Deleting, and Pasting

The following is a summary of commonly used copying commands. Keep in mind, these should be executed while in command mode:

yw	Copy word; actually copies from the current character in the word until the end of the word (including punctuation) and the white space after the word. So, if your cursor was on the *h* in "this is fun", the **cw** command would copy "his " into memory.
yy	Copy the current line.
y$	Copy from the current character to end of the line.
yG	Copy the current line to the end of the document.

You may be wondering, why use the **y** character? This is because the process of copying text into the memory buffer used to be called "yanking."

The following is a summary of commonly used commands for deleting. Keep in mind, these should be executed while in command mode.

dw	Delete word; actually deletes from the current character in the word until the end of the word (including punctuation) and the white space after the word. So, if your cursor was on the *h* in "this is fun", the **dw** command would delete "his ", resulting in "tis fun".
dd	Delete the current line.
d$	Delete from the current character to the end of the line.
dG	Delete the current line to the end of the document.
x	Delete the character the cursor is currently on (functions like the Delete key).
X	Delete the character before the character the cursor is currently on (functions like the Backspace key).

Pasting commands can be a bit trickier because how they work depends on what you are pasting. For example, suppose you had copied a word into the buffer. In this case, the following describes how the paste commands would work:

p	Pastes the buffer contents before the cursor
P	Pastes the buffer contents after the cursor

The behavior is a bit different if you copy an entire line (or multiple lines) into the buffer:

p	Pastes the buffer contents in the line above the cursor
P	Pastes the buffer contents in the line below the cursor

If you are wondering where the cut commands are, read the Text Support™ dialog in Figure 4-5.

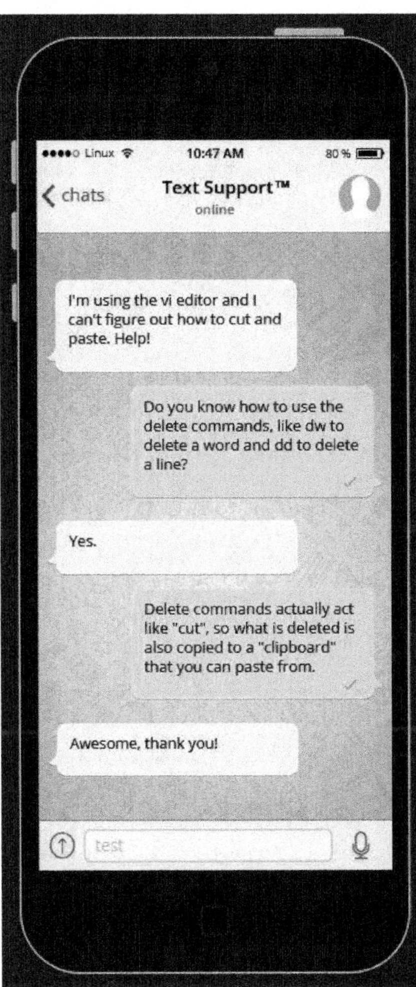

Figure 4-5 *Text Support™ Cutting Text in vi*

Finding Text

Finding text is a critical function for a software developer who is using the vi editor because often error messages that appear when code is executed include bits of code from where the error occurred. You can find text by using one of the following methods:

- While in the command mode, type the **/** (slash) key and you will see this character appear in the bottom-left corner of the terminal window. Now type what you want to search for and then press **<ENTER>**. The vi editor will search *forward* in the document for the text you asked it to look for.
- While in the command mode, type the **?** key and you will see this character appear in the bottom-left corner of the terminal window. Now type what you want to search for and then press **<ENTER>**. The vi editor will search *backward* in the document for the text you asked it to look for.

Suppose your search didn't find the specific match you were looking for. You can use the **n** command to find the next match. The **n** command will search forward when your last search started with the **/** key and will search backward when your last search started with the **?** key.

What if you searched for "/one" and realize you will need to press the **n** key many times to find what you are looking for. After furiously typing **n** repeatedly, you realize you went past the match that you wanted. To reverse the current search, use the **N** character. When you're searching forward, **N** will reverse the direction and search backward in the document. When you're searching backward, **N** will reverse the direction and search forward in the document.

Case Sensitive

As with just about everything you use in Linux, the search function is case sensitive. In other words, a search of "/the" will not match the following line:

The end is near.

Find and Replace

To search for text and replace it with other text, use the following format:

```
:x,ys/pattern/replace/
```

The values of **x** and **y** represent the lines in the document upon which you will perform the search. For example, to perform a search and replace on only the first ten lines of the document, use the following syntax:

```
:1,10s/I/we/
```

You can use the $ character to represent the last line in the document:

```
:300,$s/I/we/
```

So, to perform the substitution on the entire document, use the following:

```
:1,$s/I/we/
```

By default, only the first match on each line is replaced. Imagine if the line you are searching for and replacing looks like the following:

```
The dog ate the dog food from the dog bowl
```

If the command **:s/dog/cat/** was executed on the previous line, then the result would be the following:

```
The cat ate the dog food from the dog bowl
```

To replace all occurrences on a line, add a **g** at the end of the search command:

```
:s/dog/cat/g
```

You can think of **g** as standing for "get them all." It actually stands for "global."

Searching and replacing is case sensitive. Imagine if the line you are searching and replacing looks like the following:

```
The Dog ate the dog food from the dog bowl
```

If the command **:s/dog/cat/** was executed on the previous line, then the result would be the following:

```
The Dog ate the cat food from the dog bowl
```

The result matched the second "dog" because the first one has a capital *D*. To perform a case-insensitive search-and-replace operation, add an **i** at the end of the search command:

```
:s/dog/cat/i
```

Saving and Quitting

In the previous section, you typed a colon (**:**) character to perform a search-and-replace operation. Complex commands are performed in the last line mode, also called the *ex mode* in honor of the ex editor. The **:** character takes you to the bottom of the screen where the command will be displayed as you type it.

Another operation you can perform in this mode is "save and quit" your document:

```
:wq
```

NOTE You must save before quitting, so you cannot execute the command **:qw**, as that will attempt to quit and then save.

Security Highlight

Often users who are logged in as root will use **:wq!** to save and quit. This is sometimes necessary when directly modifying a system file that the root user doesn't currently have the permissions to change. The **!** character after **:wq** will force write changes to the file, effectively changing the permissions temporarily to writable, saving the changes, and then setting the permissions back to the original (see Chapter 9, "File Permissions," for more details about permissions).

Unfortunately, **:wq!** becomes a bad habit for a lot of system administrators. By using this as your default save method, you may end up accidently modifying a key system file, potentially modifying a file that could cause the system to not function properly or make the system vulnerable. Avoid picking up this bad habit and use **:wq** by default and **:wq!** only as needed—and after thinking about it carefully.

You may want to just save but continue working:

```
:w
```

You can also save to a different document, but there's a little "gotcha" to this operation. Suppose you want to save changes made to your **services** file into a file called **myservices**. Execute the following:

```
:s myservices
```

The changes will be placed into this file; however, any further changes will be saved by default into the original **services** file. Most modern editors "switch" the default save document to whatever the last saved document was, but vi doesn't do this. To see your current document, type **^G** (Control+g).

So, if you want to edit the new file, you should quit the vi editor and open the new file.

If you make changes to a file and then try to quit without saving (**:q**), you will receive an error message like the following:

```
E37: No write since last change (add ! to override)
```

To force-quit (quit without saving changes), execute the following command:

```
:q!
```

Expand Your vi Knowledge

Although we have covered many vi commands, we have only really just scratched the surface. The vi editor is a powerful tool with hundreds of commands. In addition, it provides some very advanced features, such as syntax highlighting, the ability to create macros, the ability to edit multiple files at the same time, and much more.

The vim editor has some useful built-in documentation, but you must have a specific software package installed in order to access this documentation. Installing software will be covered in greater detail in Chapter 26, "Red Hat-Based Software Management," and Chapter 27, "Debian-Based Software Management." For now, just make sure you are logged in as the root user and execute one of the following commands:

- On Red Hat, Fedora, and CentOS distributions, execute **yum install vim-enhanced**.
- On Debian, Ubuntu, and Mint distributions, execute **apt-get install vim-enhanced**.

NOTE On Ubuntu and Mint, you could log in to the regular user account that was created during the installation and run the **sudo apt-get install vim-enhanced** command.

If the vim-enhanced package is installed, you can execute the command **:help** while in the vim editor and you will see a help document appear. See Figure 4-6 for an example.

```
student@localhost:~
File  Edit  View  Search  Terminal  Help
help.txt        For Vim version 7.4.  Last change: 2012 Dec 06

                     VIM - main help file
                                                                   k
      Move around:  Use the cursor keys, or "h" to go left,        h   l
                    "j" to go down, "k" to go up, "l" to go right.   j
Close this window:  Use ":q<Enter>".
   Get out of Vim:  Use ":qa!<Enter>" (careful, all changes are lost!).

Jump to a subject:  Position the cursor on a tag (e.g. bars) and hit CTRL-].
   With the mouse:  ":set mouse=a" to enable the mouse (in xterm or GUI).
                    Double-click the left mouse button on a tag, e.g. bars.
        Jump back:  Type CTRL-T or CTRL-O (repeat to go further back).

Get specific help:  It is possible to go directly to whatever you want help
                    on, by giving an argument to the :help command.
                    It is possible to further specify the context:
                                                        help-context
                          WHAT                  PREPEND    EXAMPLE
                      Normal mode command       (nothing)   :help x
help.txt [Help][RO]                                     1,1            Top
# /etc/services:
services [RO]                                           1,1            Top
```

Figure 4-6 *vim Help Output*

Use your arrow keys (or h, j, k, and l) to scroll through the document. About 20 lines down, you will start to see some subtopics, as shown in Figure 4-7.

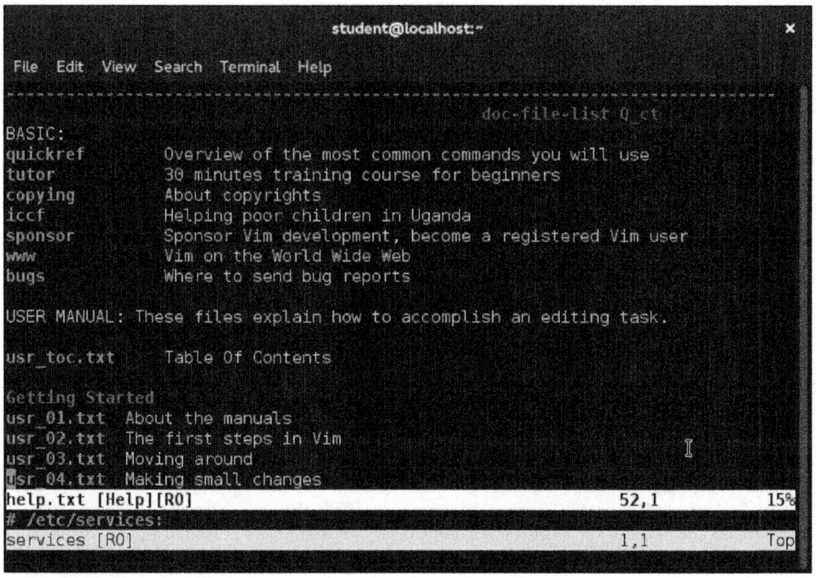

Figure 4-7 *vim Help Topics*

Each of these topics, such as quickref or usr_01.txt, is a separate help topic. To view these topics, first exit from the current help document by typing the **:q** command. Then type a command like the following, replacing ***topic*** with the full name of the topic you want to view:

```
:help topic
```

For example, to see help on "Using syntax highlighting," type the following command:

```
:help usr_06.txt
```

Additional Editors

There are a large number of editors that you can use in Linux. The focus of this section is to make you aware of these editors, not to teach you how to use each one. Note that it is likely not all of these editors will be installed on your distribution. You may need to install additional software packages to have access to additional editors.

Emacs

Like the vi editor, the Emacs editor was developed in the mid 1970s. Linux users who like Emacs will praise its ease of use and customization capability. If you launch Emacs (just run the **emacs** command) while in a GUI-based terminal, a GUI-based version of the program should open, as shown in Figure 4-8. As you can see, the GUI-based version has menus in addition to the commands that can be executed via the keyboard.

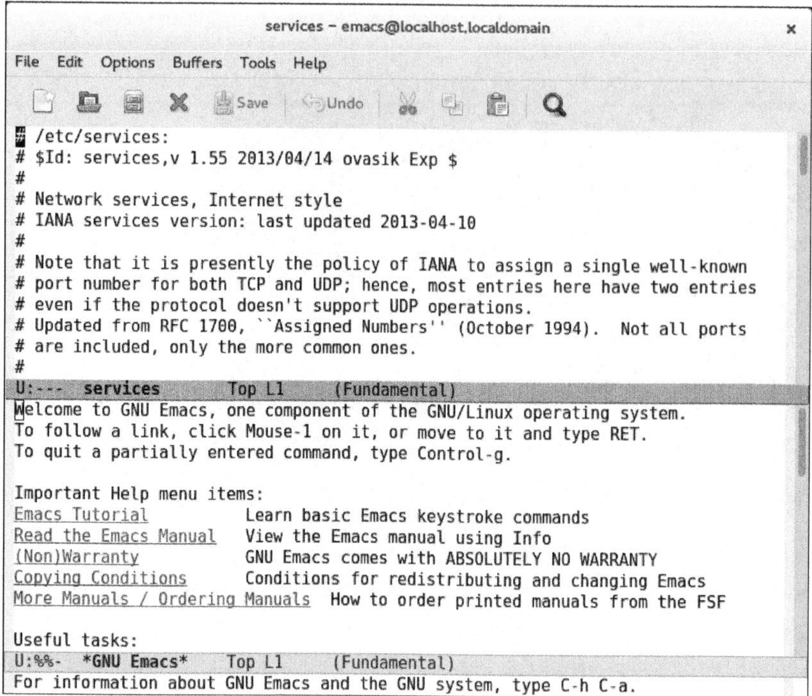

Figure 4-8 *GUI-Based Emacs*

If you execute the Emacs editor in a command line-only environment, the editor will look like Figure 4-9.

```
student@localhost:/home/student
File Edit Options Buffers Tools Help
# /etc/services:
# $Id: services,v 1.55 2013/04/14 ovasik Exp $
#
# Network services, Internet style
# IANA services version: last updated 2013-04-10
#
# Note that it is presently the policy of IANA to assign a single well-known
# port number for both TCP and UDP; hence, most entries here have two entries
# even if the protocol doesn't support UDP operations.
# Updated from RFC 1700, ``Assigned Numbers'' (October 1994). Not all ports
# are included, only the more common ones.
#
# The latest IANA port assignments can be gotten from
#       http://www.iana.org/assignments/port-numbers
# The Well Known Ports are those from 0 through 1023.
# The Registered Ports are those from 1024 through 49151
# The Dynamic and/or Private Ports are those from 49152 through 65535
#
# Each line describes one service, and is of the form:
#
# service-name  port/protocol  [aliases ...]   [# comment]

tcpmux          1/tcp                           # TCP port service multiplexer
tcpmux          1/udp                           # TCP port service multiplexer
rje             5/tcp                           # Remote Job Entry
-UUU:----F1  services       Top L1     (Fundamental) ---------------------------
For information about GNU Emacs and the GNU system, type C-h C-a.
```

Figure 4-9 *Text-Based Emacs*

> **GUI VIM?** If you install the vim-X11 software package, you will have access to a GUI-based version of the vim editor. Just execute **gvim** or **vim -g**.

gedit and kwrite

These editors are fairly standard GUI-based editors. If you are used to Notepad on Microsoft Windows, then you will find these editors fairly easy to use (although somewhat limited).

The gedit editor typically is installed on distributions that use the GNOME desktop by default. The kwrite (or KATE) editor typically is installed on distributions that use the KDE desktop by default. However, you can easily install gedit on a system that uses the KDE desktop or install kwrite on a GNOME desktop system.

nano and joe

The vi and Emacs editors are extremely powerful. In some cases, you may find that you want to use a simple editor in a command-line environment. The gedit and kwrite editors only work in GUI-based environments.

The nano and joe editors provide a simple interface for editing text files. These are command-line-only editors, so no GUI is required. See Figure 4-10 for an example of the nano editor.

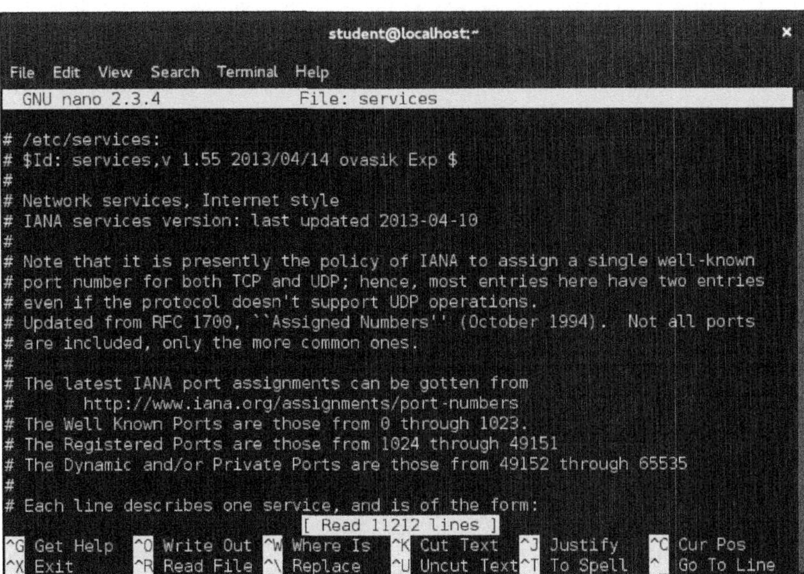

Figure 4-10 *The nano Editor*

lime and bluefish

The lime and bluefish editors take the process of editing a text file to the next level by providing tools and features that are really designed to help a developer create code. These tools provide features like syntax highlighting, insertion of code (by clicking a button), and automatic formatting (like automatically indenting code).

If you are going to make a career of coding on Linux, you should start to explore these tools (or many of the other similar editing tools). See Figure 4-11 for an example of the bluefish editor.

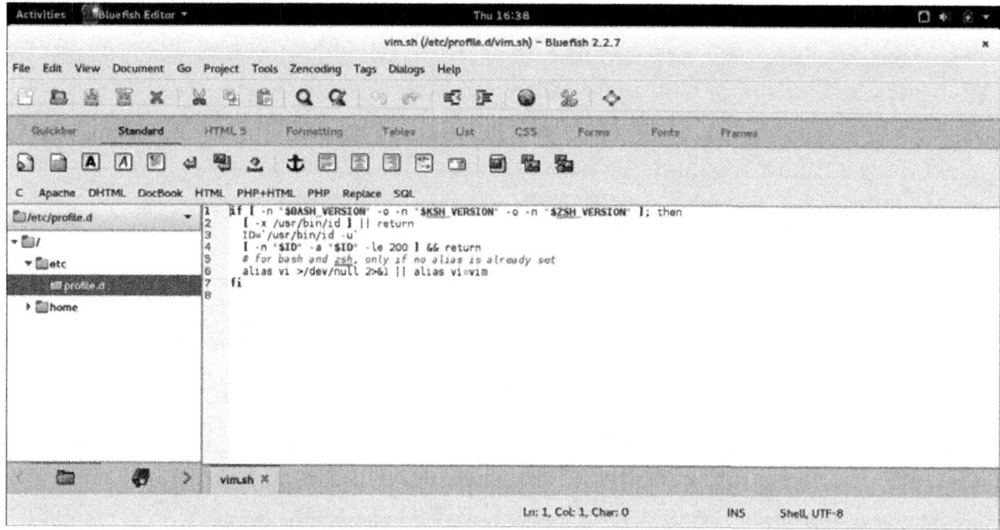

Figure 4-11 *The bluefish Editor*

Summary

With the large number of text files on a Linux system, it is important to know how to edit such files. In this chapter, you explored a variety of techniques to edit text files, including the vi editor, Emacs, gedit, and kwrite.

Key Terms

vi mode

Review Questions

1. The _____ mode allows you to enter complex operations while working in the vi editor.
2. Which of the following command-mode commands does not place you in the inset mode?
   A. a
   B. e
   C. i
   D. 0
3. To use a repeat modifier, type a _____ before a vi command.
   A. letter
   B. space
   C. number
   D. special character
4. The _____ command will copy an entire line in the vi editor.
5. The _____ command will allow you to search for text forward from the current position while using the vi editor.

When Things Go Wrong

First, the bad news: Something is going to go wrong. Commands will fail, programs will crash, and configurations will have errors.

Now the good news: There are techniques to handle these problems. Troubleshooting is not just taking a "stab in the dark." You should take specific steps when things go wrong in order to determine the problem and identify the best solution.

In this chapter, you learn the techniques and practices you should follow when things do not work out quite the way you were hoping. You also discover techniques that you can use as an administrator to inform users about system issues.

After reading this chapter and completing the exercises, you will be able to do the following:

Correctly use troubleshooting skills to diagnose system problems

Notify users of system issues during login or while a user is logged in to the system

The Science of Troubleshooting

Although troubleshooting may seem like some mystical art known only to those who agree to a code of secrecy, it is more a science for those who are routinely successful at solving problems. This science is not limited to Linux, as you can apply the methods provided here to problems on other operating systems and other areas of Information Technology, as well as to problems you face in life.

To begin with, here are the general steps you should take to troubleshoot a problem:

1. Gather all relevant information related to the problem. This is an important step because we tend to want to solve problems quickly without researching them completely. This can easily result in a faulty conclusion, which in turn can further complicate the problem.
2. Determine what is the most likely cause of the problem. Again, avoid jumping to a conclusion about the first possible cause. Really consider what other conditions may have caused the problem and make an educated guess at the most likely cause.
3. Document the actions you plan to perform to solve the problem before taking any action. This is perhaps the most commonly overlooked step in this process, but it's a critical one. If you document the actions you plan to take, it will be easier to undo anything that did not work correctly. Part of this step could also include making backup copies of critical files before modification.
4. Perform *only* the documented actions to solve the problem. Note the emphasis on the word *only*. Do not decide halfway through solving the problem to go off on a different tangent. If you decide your plan is not going to work, back track out of the solution (undo the steps to that point) and form a new plan of attack.
5. Determine if the problem has been correctly solved. This step may seem unnecessary to mention, but you will find that often you think you've solved a problem only to discover

sometime in the future that you really did not. This is fairly common when you solve problems for others; for example, if you are a system administrator and attempt to solve a problem for another user.

6. If the problem is not correctly solved, use the documentation from Step 3 to get back to the state the system was in when you started this process. Then go back to Step 2 and perform Steps 2–5 again.
7. If the problem is solved, determine if any additional problems now exist as a result of the actions you took. This is a commonly overlooked step. For example, you may have modified a user account to provide specific access to a directory, but this modification results in the user not having access to other directories that the user previously had access to. You obviously cannot check everything, but think to yourself "what problems could this solution create?" before going on to the next step.
8. Store the documentation that you created, including the actions that did not solve the problem, using a technique that will be easy for you to retrieve in the future. We find that some problems crop up again and again, and our brains just are not adept at remembering the solutions we previously worked so hard at discovering. Create a troubleshooting log or handbook for yourself or your organization to make solving problems easier in the future. Also, keep in mind that your solution could cause more problems, which might not surface until sometime in the future. Having a log of what you did can make life a lot easier in the future.
9. Consider what you can do to prevent this problem from happening in the future. Be proactive, as it can save you time, increase productivity, and protect you (and others) from big headaches down the road.

Step 1: Gathering Information

To explore how you can gather information, consider this scenario. Suppose you tried to copy a file using the **cp** command, as was described in Chapter 2, "Working on the Command Line."

```
student@onecoursesource:~$ cp /etc/hosts
cp: missing destination file operand after '/etc/hosts'
Try 'cp --help' for more information.
```

Clearly the previous command failed, and you might be able to determine the reason fairly quickly. However, this is a demonstration of how to gather information when you encounter a problem. One technique is to read the actual message that appears after you attempt to execute the command: **cp: missing destination file operand after '/etc/hosts'**.

You could also try the suggestion for getting more information:

```
student@onecoursesource:~$ cp --help
Usage: cp [OPTION]... [-T] SOURCE DEST
  or:  cp [OPTION]... SOURCE... DIRECTORY
  or:  cp [OPTION]... -t DIRECTORY SOURCE...
Copy SOURCE to DEST, or multiple SOURCE(s) to DIRECTORY.

Mandatory arguments to long options are mandatory for short options too.
  -a, --archive                same as -dR --preserve=all
...
```

We shortened the output of this **cp --help** command because of its size, but the point is that this command provides more useful information. But, what if this is not enough information? Maybe you could try other commands on the file in question:

```
student@onecoursesource:~$ ls /etc/hosts
/etc/hosts
```

Although this was not the case in the previous example, additional errors could result and lead you to the problem.

As you read though this book, you will gather more tools to add to your troubleshooting toolkit. Be ready to develop a "cheat sheet" of commands and techniques that you can use to make troubleshooting easier.

Step 2: Determine the Likely Cause

For this step, if the cause is not clear, you should consider using other sources to point you in the right direction, including the following sources:

- Reading documentation, such as man and info pages
- Asking a coworker for their opinion
- Contacting your system administrator and asking for advice
- Researching your problem on Linux forum sites, like those mentioned in Chapter 3, "Getting Help"
- Perform Internet searches using information you have gathered, as demonstrated in Figure 5-1

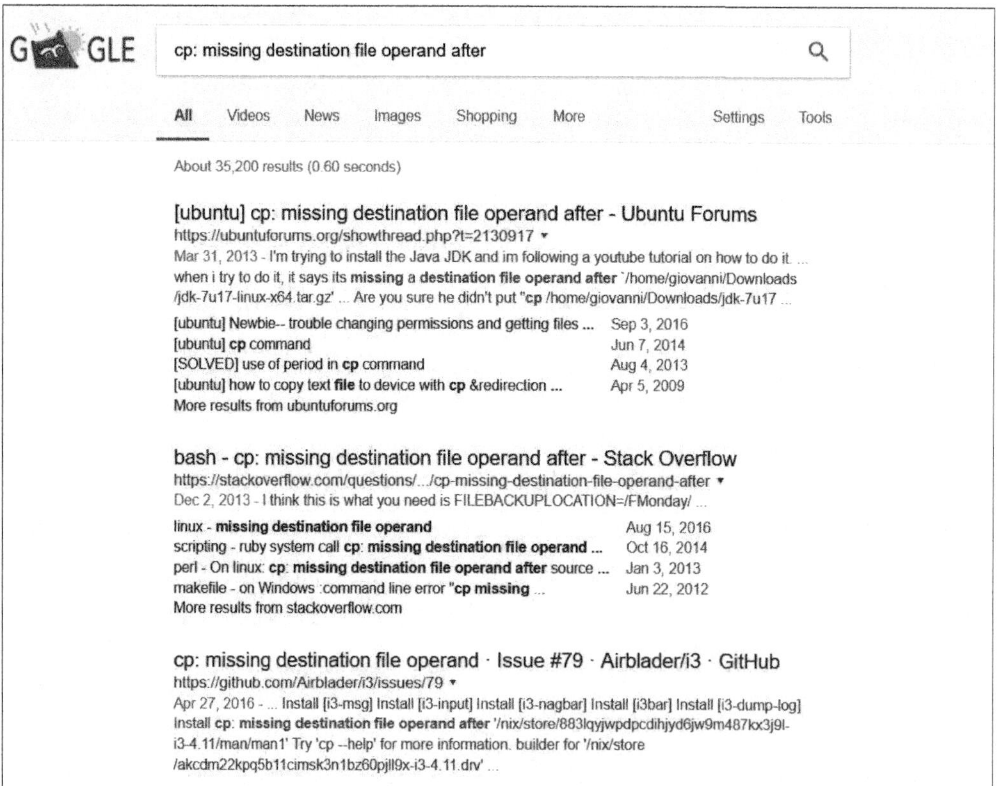

Figure 5-1 *Performing an Internet Search*

> **NOTE** If you plan on asking a coworker or system administrator for assistance, be ready to provide all the information you gathered in the first step so they can understand the problem and its context. Going to your system administrator or IT support staff and saying "I can't copy a file" is not going to provide enough information to help solve your problem. The more details you gather, the more likely your problem will be solved quickly.

Step 3: Document Your Plan of Attack (POA)

Granted, many problems will not require detailed documentation, but as you learn more complex topics in Linux, you will discover the solutions themselves become more complex. Get in the habit of documenting a POA now because it will be more difficult to pick up this habit in the future.

Consider the following when planning how you will perform the documentation step:

- How can I make the process easy?
- How can I ensure the documentation will be easy to retrieve and reference? (Scrap pieces of paper are a very bad idea.)
- What tools are available? Consider file sharing tools like Google Docs and Dropbox. For an organization, you might consider a tool designed specifically for tracking issues, like Bugzilla (www.bugzilla.org).

Step 4: Perform the Actions

This may seem like an easy step, but you should take into account a few things. First, do not just perform the actions to solve the problem blindly. If you are performing 10 steps, for example, stop after every step and evaluate. Ask yourself the following questions:

- Did that work correctly?
- Did I make any typos?
- Did I get the output that I expected?
- Does something else seem amiss?

This should not require a long, complicated, soul-searching observation on your part—just a momentary sanity check to make sure your solution is on the right track.

Steps 5 and 6: Is the Problem Solved?

Identifying whether the issue is solved is perhaps the easiest step in most cases. Is the problem you were having still an issue? Remember, if it is, you need to undo what you did in the previous step because those actions could further confuse the situation or create even more problems.

Step 7: Are There Other Problems?

In some cases, this step is not required. Recall the issue in a previous example:

```
student@onecoursesource:~$ cp /etc/hosts
cp: missing destination file operand after '/etc/hosts'
Try 'cp --help' for more information.
```

The problem was that the **cp** command requires two arguments—a file to copy and where to put the copy:

```
student@onecoursesource:~$ cp /etc/hosts /tmp
student@onecoursesource:~$
```

This solution is unlikely to cause any other problems (unless, of course, you copied the file to the wrong directory). However, as problems and solutions become more complex, you should take more time to ensure no other problems arise as a result of your solution. It is hard to provide an actual example so early in this book, but consider the following scenario: Years ago one of the authors of this book was a young system administrator who was approached by a user who could not log in to a system. This system admin quickly determined the problem was a setting in one of the configuration files for users (the **/etc/shadow** file, to be precise, which will be covered later in Chapter 7, "Managing User Accounts"). A quick edit of this file solved the problem.

However, this quick solution had an unintended side effect: All of the other users who had accounts on the system could no longer log in to the system. The quick fix ended up causing a much bigger problem. To make matters worse, this young, brash administrator did not document the actions that he took, so other administrators had no idea what caused this problem.

It is not always possible to anticipate all potential problems that a solution may create, but it does not hurt to probe around the edges of the solution, looking for other potential problems that may have cropped up.

Step 8: Store the Documentation

This step is very similar to Step 3 and was covered previously.

Step 9: Prevent Future Problems

It is highly likely that the same problems are going to occur multiple times, possibly to multiple people. One way to prevent future problems is to be proactive in notifying others. This is typically the job of the system administrator, who can either send messages (email, text, and so on) or display messages when users log in to the system. This is the focus of the next topic of this chapter.

Notifying Users

It is important to ensure that users are kept up to date regarding changes in the network or system. Linux has several methods to automate notifying users of this sort of information.

Pre- and Post-login Messages

You may have hundreds of systems in your environment, making it difficult to tell every user useful information such as what each system is designed for, the distribution on each system, and what system they should use. This sort of information can be provided on a system-by-system basis by creating messages that appear either prior to the login process or after the login process.

Consider carefully what information you want to display. Too much information and you risk users only reading a small portion. Too little, and you risk not providing enough information.

The /etc/issue File

Suppose that one day you decide to work on your web server, a system that has no GUI interface. You sit down at the server and are presented with a login screen similar to the one in Figure 5-2.

Figure 5-2 *Typical Command-Line Login Screen*

You begin to wonder why it says the OS name and the kernel version before the prompt. Or, perhaps more important, you wonder how you can change that.

The message that you see comes from the **/etc/issue** file:

```
[root@onecoursesource ~]# more /etc/issue
\S
Kernel \r on an \m
```

As you can probably guess, the values of **\S**, **\r**, and **\m** are translated into something else before being displayed on the login screen. The special values you can place in this file are described in Table 5-1.

Table 5-1 Special Values for the **/etc/issue** File

Value	Meaning
\b	Displays the baud rate, which is the speed of the connection. If you are connected via a serial port terminal, this can be useful information.
\d	Use this to display the current date.
\s	Displays the system name.
\S	Similar to **\s**, **\S** reads the system name from the **/etc/os-release** file. This provides some flexibility on the system's name that **\s** does not provide.
\l	Inserts the name of the TTY device. Each command-line login is associated with a device name from the **/dev** directory. For local logins, names like **/dev/tty1** and **/dev/tty2** are normally used.
\m	Displays the value of the output of the **uname -m** command (the architecture of the system).
\n	Displays the nodename (also known as hostname) of the system (same as the output of the **uname -n** command).
\o	Displays the Network Information Service (NIS) domain name (same as the output of the **uname -d** command). NIS is a service that provides network account information to client systems.
\r	Displays the OS release number (same as the output of the **uname -r** command).
\t	Displays the current time.
\u	Displays the number of users logged in at the time that the **/etc/issue** file is printed to the screen.
\U	Similar to **\u**.
\v	Displays the version of the OS.

Note that these special values are actually used by a process called **agetty**. The **agetty** command is what provides the login prompt.

The **/etc/issue** file can also be used to provide additional information, such as warning messages regarding the use of the system. Note the changes made to the following **/etc/issue** file and then look at Figure 5-3 to see the result of these changes.

```
[root@onecoursesource ~]# more /etc/issue
\S
Kernel \r on an \m


Running on terminal \l


Platform: \m


Note: Secure system - No unauthorized access!  All activity is closely monitored
```

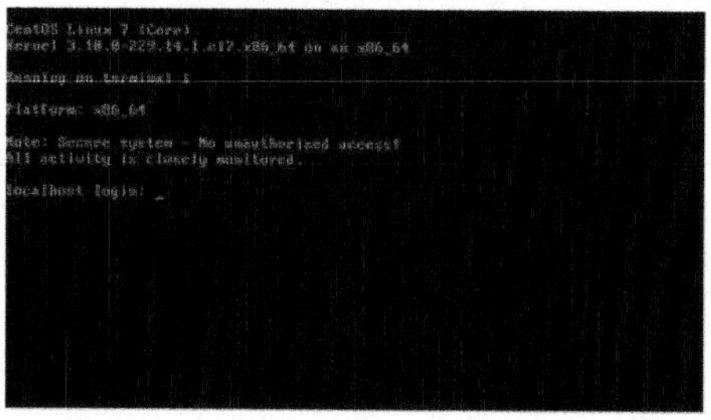

Figure 5-3 *Customized Command-Line Login Screen*

To test changes in the **/etc/issue** file, you need to be able to log in via the command line. Most likely you have been logging in via a GUI on your practice system. You should be able to access a command-line login by holding down the Ctrl and Alt keys on your keyboard and pressing the F2 key (or F3, F4, and so on).

To see changes in the **/etc/issue** file, log in via the command line and then log off. The new **/etc/issue** display should appear when the login screen is displayed.

To return to the GUI, either use Ctrl+Alt+F1 or Ctrl+Alt+F7 (one of those should work). Typically F2 through F5 are command-line logins. Either F1 or F7 is normally a GUI display (the one that is not the GUI should be another command-line login).

The /etc/issue.net File

The **/etc/issue** file is only displayed when a user logs in via a local command-line login. If a user logs in from a remote system, you can display a message by placing information in the **/etc/issue.net** file. Originally this was designed to display a message to a user logging in via telnet, but telnet is largely a dinosaur, having been replaced by the more secure SSH service.

However, you should know that SSH servers do not display the contents of the **/etc/issue.net** file by default. To make the contents of this file appear when an SSH connection starts, you should modify the **Banner** setting in the **/etc/ssh/sshd_config** file. By default this setting looks like this:

```
[root@onecoursesource ~]# grep Banner /etc/ssh/sshd_config
#Banner none
```

Display the contents of the **/etc/issue.net** file by making the following change (be certain to restart the sshd daemon after you modify this file; this is covered in Chapter 28, "System Booting," and can vary based on distribution):

```
[root@onecoursesource ~]# grep Banner /etc/ssh/sshd_config
Banner /etc/issue.net
```

The contents of the **/etc/issue.net** file are similar to the **/etc/issue** file:

```
[root@onecoursesource ~]# more /etc/issue.net
\S
Kernel \r on an \m
```

The special character sequences work well when connecting via telnet (except for **\S**, it appears):

```
[root@onecoursesource ~]# telnet onecoursesource
Trying ::1...
Connected to onecoursesource .
Escape character is '^]'.

Kernel 3.10.0-229.14.1.el7.x86_64 on an x86_64
onecoursesource  login:
```

However, these character sequences have no special meaning to the Secure Shell server:

```
[root@onecoursesource ~]# ssh onecoursesource
\S
Kernel \r on an \m
root@onecoursesource 's password:
```

Unless you are actually allowing telnet connections, you probably want to change the **/etc/issue.net** file so it contains no special character sequences. If you are allowing both telnet and SSH connections, keep the special character sequences in the **/etc/issue.net** file and change the **Banner** setting in **/etc/ssh/sshd_config** to point to another location:

```
[root@onecoursesource ~]# grep Banner /etc/ssh/sshd_config
Banner /etc/ssh.banner
```


Security Highlight

It is actually considered a bad idea to provide system information via a pre-login message on remote connections. Someone probing your system might be able to use that information to gain unauthorized access.

For example, suppose your banner includes information about the kernel version or the distribution. Someone attempting to gain unauthorized access to your system might know of some exploits that work on that kernel version or that specific distribution.

Ask yourself why providing this information before login is important. If you do not have a good reason, do not display the information.

Some administrators have a serious-sounding warning with the intent to scare someone off. Such a warning is likely to backfire because it is like saying "something really good is on this system"—not the sort of message you want to send out to potential bad guys.

Noting that the system is proprietary and contains confidential information is usually sufficient.

You should also consider not allowing telnet connections because of security issues. All telnet-related data is sent in plain text, including the user's name and password.

Additional Pre-login Messages

Administrators often use the **/etc/issue** and **/etc/issue.net** files to display pre-login messages. These files are useful to display pre-login messages when the user is logging in via the local command line, via telnet, and (if configured correctly) via SSH. However, there are other ways that you can access the system, such as via FTP (File Transfer Protocol) and GUI-based login:

- **FTP**: This can depend on your FTP server. Many distributions use the vsftpd server; its configuration file is the **/etc/vsftpd/vsftpd.conf** file. You can change the **ftpd_banner** setting to specify a banner (just provide the banner as a value: **ftpd_banner=<*insert_message_here*>**) or have a file displayed by changing the **banner_file** setting.
- **GUI (gdm)**: If you are using GDM as your GUI login manager (GDM=Gnome display manager), then either modify the **/etc/gdm/custom.conf** file (for Red Hat–based systems) or the **/etc/gdm/gdm.conf-custom** file (for Debian-based systems). For Red Hat–based systems, you may need to add the line **Greeter=/usr/libexec/gdmlogin** in the **[daemon]** section. For all distributions, search for the **[greeter]** section and make the following changes:

```
DefaultWelcome=false
Welcome=Message for local users
RemoteWelcome=Message for remote login users
```

NOTE Additional GUI display managers (also known as login managers) have similar approaches to GDM. It is just a matter of finding the configuration file and determining the correct settings. Often this feature is called a *banner* or a *greeter*, so use those terms when searching documentation.

The /etc/motd File

The techniques discussed in this chapter so far are all designed to display a message prior to the login process. However, after a user has properly logged in, you may want to display a different sort of message. This can be accomplished by editing the **/etc/motd** file. (The **motd** stands for "message of the day.")

The following gives you some ideas of what you might want to place in the **/etc/motd** file:

- **A friendly welcome message**: Let users know you are happy they are here. Seriously, you have no idea how many regular users, especially newbies, are intimidated by logging in to a Linux machine. Offer some friendly advice, provide some helpful resources (like the tech support or help desk information), and let users know they are not alone.
- **A "don't you dare" warning message**: Okay, we know this sounds like the opposite of the previous suggestion. However, on your mission-critical servers, you do not want to be all nice and happy. Make sure users know how closely this server is monitored. Let them know that if they break the rules, the results will be severe.
- **Upcoming changes**: If you are planning on bringing down this system for maintenance next Tuesday, make note of it in the **/etc/motd** file. If you are adding new software in the coming weeks, indicate that with a notice in the **/etc/motd** file.
- **Purpose of the system**: If this is your web server, why not make that clear when the user logs in? Users should know what sort of system they are working on or logging on to, and the **/etc/motd** file is a great place to make this clear. You can only imagine how many times system administrators have heard "Oh, I didn't know that was our mail server!" when the user is asked "Why did you run this CPU-intensive program on that system?"

These are just a few ideas of what you can place in the **/etc/motd** file. You can pass on many other useful bits of information to users by placing this information in the **/etc/motd** file. (Note: The **/etc/motd** file is empty by default on most distributions.)

To see an example of the **/etc/motd** file, first look at the output of the following command and then look at the output shown in Figure 5-4:

```
[root@onecoursesource ssh]# more /etc/motd
Note: This system will be down for maintenance on Friday from 10PM to 10:30PM.
During this time you will not be able to log in and any cron jobs that you
have will not be executed. See Julia if you have any questions.
```

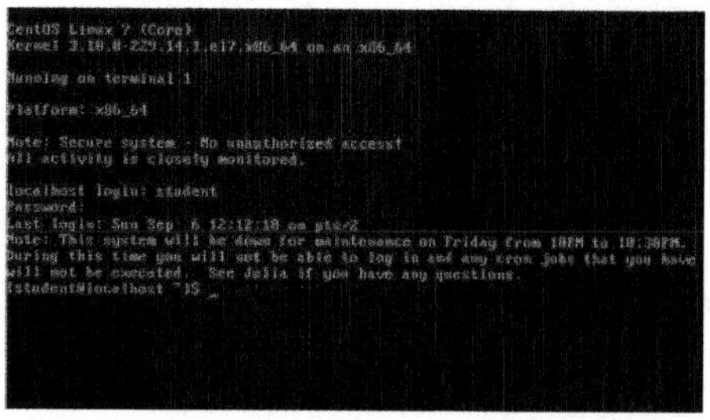

Figure 5-4 *Customized Command-Line Login Screen*

Broadcasting Messages

The **/etc/issue**, **/etc/issue.net**, and **/etc/motd** files are great for providing useful information during the login process. But what if you have 10 users on the system right now and you need to send them an urgent message? This section focuses on techniques to communicate with users who are currently logged in to the system.

The wall Command

Sometimes you may need to send a message to all users who are currently logged in to the system. The **wall** command provides you with the ability to broadcast a message to every user's terminal. An example of the **wall** command follows:

```
[root@onecoursesource ~]# wall shutting down in five minutes
Broadcast message from root@onecoursesource (pts/3) (Sun Oct 25 12:44:33 2019):

shutting down in five minutes
```

5

NOTE The **wall** message is limited to a total of 20 lines.

To avoid displaying the banner at the top of the message, use the **-n** option when executing the **wall** command. The banner is the following part of the message:

```
Broadcast message from root@onecoursesource (pts/3) (Sun Oct 25 12:44:33 2019):
```

On many distributions, regular users are also allowed to use the **wall** command. In some cases this can become annoying:

```
[student@onecoursesource ~]$ wall today is my birthday!
Broadcast message from student@onecoursesource (pts/3) (Sun Oct 25 12:52:36 2019):

today is my birthday!
```

All users can use the **wall** command because it is an SGID program. This is a permission set that will be covered in detail in Chapter 9, "File Permissions." The "s" character in the following output indicates this is an SGID program:

```
[root@onecoursesource ~]# ls -l /usr/bin/wall
-r-xr-sr-x. 1 root tty 15344 Jun  9  2019 /usr/bin/wall
```

All the terminal devices (**/dev/tty1**, **/dev/tty2**, **/dev/pts/0**, and so on) are group-owned by the tty group. The tty group has write access to these files, so when the **wall** command runs as the tty group, it can write information to these terminal devices directly. To disable regular users' ability to send **wall** messages, just take away the SGID permission set:

```
[root@onecoursesource ~]# ls -l /usr/bin/wall
-r-xr-sr-x. 1 root tty 15344 Jun  9  2019 /usr/bin/wall
[root@onecoursesource ~]# chmod g-s /usr/bin/wall
[root@onecoursesource ~]# ls -l /usr/bin/wall
-r-xr-xr-x. 1 root tty 15344 Jun  9  2019 /usr/bin/wall
[root@onecoursesource ~]# su - student
Last login: Sun Oct 25 12:51:36 PDT 2018 on pts/3
[student@onecoursesource  ~]$ wall today is my birthday!
```

No error message is displayed to the regular user, but the **wall** command does not send messages to any user accounts.

It is possible for a user to disable **wall** messages to a specific terminal. This is something that you may want to do if you are editing a file, reading a man page, or performing some critical task. The **wall** message will not mess up your work, but it does cause confusion to have a bunch of text appear on your screen when you are trying to edit a file (see Figure 5-5 for an example).

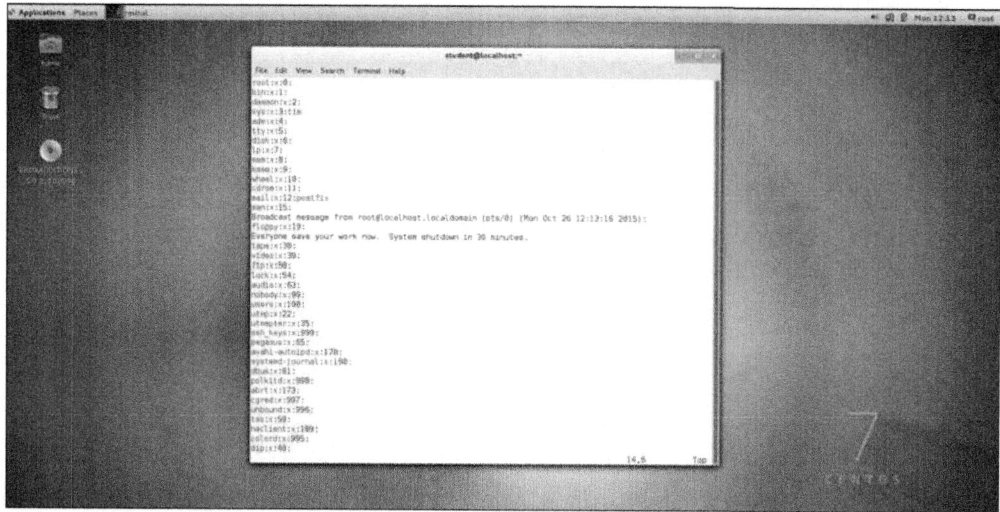

Figure 5-5 *Annoying **wall** Message*

To ignore a **wall** message in a specific terminal, set your **mesg** value to "no" by executing the following command:

```
[root@onecoursesource ~]# mesg n
[root@onecoursesource ~]# mesg
is n
```

You can always change the value back to "yes" at a later point. Remember to do so because critical information about forced shutdowns or reboots will be missed:

```
[root@onecoursesource ~]# mesg y
[root@onecoursesource ~]# mesg
is y
```

The shutdown Command

If the purpose for sending users a broadcast message is that you need to bring the system down, consider using the **shutdown** command. The syntax of the **shutdown** command is

```
shutdown [OPTIONS...] [TIME] [WALL...]
```

The **[WALL...]** is the broadcast message that you want to send to everyone. Of course, you want to provide the users time to save their work and log off the system, so you can use the **[TIME]** value to specify how long to wait before actually shutting down the system:

```
shutdown +5 "system shutdown
```

The value of **+5** tells the **shutdown** command to wait 5 minutes before actually shutting down. The message displayed to all users is similar to the following:

```
Broadcast message from root@onecoursesource (Sun 2019-02-11 13:20:09 PDT):

shutting down
The system is going down for power-off at Sun 2019-02-1113:25:09 PDT!
```

This message will be continuously displayed at regular intervals (5 minutes before shutdown, 3 minutes before, and so on). If you start the shutdown earlier (for example, **shutdown +60**), then users can continue to log in. However, 5 minutes before the shutdown is to occur, user logins are disabled because the **shutdown** command creates the **/run/nologin** file, which prevents additional login attempts.

As the administrator, you can cancel a pending shutdown by using the **shutdown -c** command:

```
[student@onecoursesource ~]$ shutdown -c

Broadcast message from root@onecoursesource (Sun 2019-02-1113:23:32 PDT):

The system shutdown has been cancelled at 2019-02-1113:24:32 PDT!
```


Here are a few additional useful options:

- **-r**: Reboot rather than shut down.
- **-h**: Halt the system (may be the same as a shutdown, depending on your distribution).
- **-k**: Do not actually shut down; just send a **wall** message saying the system is shutting down.

Summary

The focus of this chapter was to learn techniques to troubleshoot problems that can arise while working on a Linux distribution. You also learned how to send messages to users, either as they log in or while they are logged in, in order to provide them with important information about the system.

Review Questions

1. The **/etc/**_____ file is displayed prior to local command-line login attempts.
2. The **/etc/**_____ file is displayed prior to telnet login attempts.
3. The **/etc/**_____ file is displayed after a successful login.
4. The _____ command will display a message to all users currently logged in to the system.
   - A. **wall**
   - B. **mesg**
   - C. **send**
   - D. **shutdown**
5. The _____ option to the **shutdown** command is used to cancel a shutdown operation.

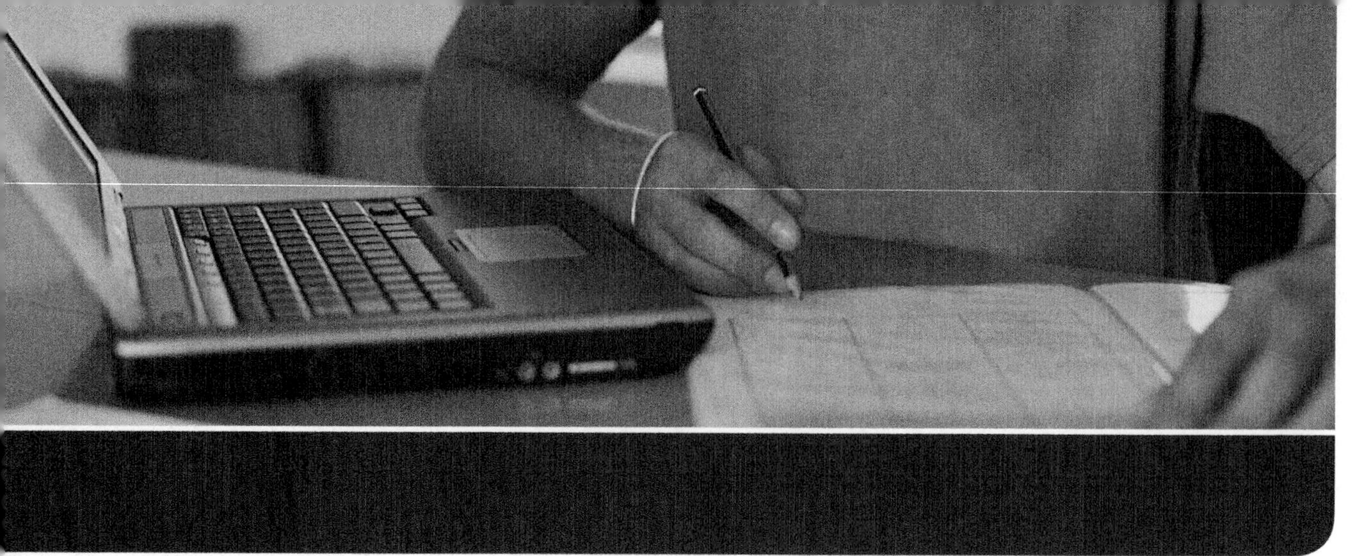

The importance of user and group accounts in terms of system security cannot be emphasized enough. If someone can gain access to the system using even a regular user account, this provides a foothold that allows this person to launch further attacks. Securing group and user accounts starts with understanding what these accounts are used for.

Part II

User and Group Accounts

In Part II, "User and Group Accounts," you will explore the following chapters:

- Chapter 6, "Managing Group Accounts," focuses on group accounts, including how to add, modify, and delete groups. Special attention is placed on system (or special) groups as well as understanding the difference between primary and secondary groups.
- Chapter 7, "Managing User Accounts," covers the details regarding user accounts. You learn how to create and secure these accounts as well as how to teach users good security practices in regard to protecting their accounts.
- Chapter 8, "Develop an Account Security Policy," provides you with the means to create a security policy using the knowledge you acquire in Chapters 6 and 7.

Managing Group Accounts

Because Linux is a multiuser operating system, security is often based on accounts. Each person is provided a user account (see Chapter 7, "Managing User Accounts," for details), and each user account is a member of one or more group accounts.

The group accounts are used to provide access or apply restrictions to user accounts that are members of a group. This access/restriction can be applied to files, directories, or other operating system features. By using group accounts, you can easily apply a security policy to multiple user accounts.

In this chapter, you learn more about the concept of group accounts. You also explore how to create, modify, and delete group accounts.

After reading this chapter and completing the exercises, you will be able to do the following:

Understand the concept of Linux groups

Manage groups, including creating, modifying, and deleting group accounts

Understand the security feature called User Private Groups (UPGs)

Learn how to create group administrators

What Are Groups Used For?

Each person who has access to a Linux system is provided a user account. This user account offers several different features, including a user name and a password. Additionally, each user is a member of one or more group accounts.

Being a member of a group allows a user special access to system resources, such as files, directories, or processes (programs) that are running on the system. This group membership can also be used to prevent access to system resources because several security features in Linux make use of groups to impose security restrictions. These security features are covered in later chapters of this book.

Primary versus Secondary Groups

Every user is a member of at least one group. This first group is called the user's *primary* group. Any additional groups a user is a member of are called the user's *secondary* groups.

Group membership can be displayed by executing either the **id** or **groups** command:

```
student@onecoursesource:~$ id
uid=1002(student) gid=1002(student)
groups=1002(student),60(games),1001(ocs)
student@onecoursesource:~$ groups
student games ocs
```

The output of the **id** command is described in Table 6-1.

Table 6-1 Output of the **id** Command

Value	Description
uid=1002(student)	The user ID and username for the current user
gid=1002(student)	The primary group ID and group name for the current user
groups=1002(student),60(games),1001(ocs)	The secondary group IDs and group names for the current user

The output of the **groups** command includes every group the current user is a member of. The primary group is always listed first.

6

Security Highlight

Both the **id** and **groups** commands display information about the current user by default. Both commands also accept an argument of another user account name:

```
student@onecoursesource:~$ id root
uid=0(root) gid=0(root) groups=0(root)
student@onecoursesource:~$ groups root
root : root
```

The most important difference between primary and secondary group membership relates to when a user creates a new file. Each file is owned by a user ID and a group ID. When a user creates a file, the user's primary group membership is used for the group ownership of the file:

```
student@onecoursesource:~$ groups
student games ocs
student@onecoursesource:~$ touch sample.txt
student@onecoursesource:~$ ls -l sample.txt
-rw-rw-r-- 1 student student 0 Sep 15 11:39 sample.txt
```

After a file has been created, a user can change the group ownership of the file to another group by using the **chgrp** command:

```
student@onecoursesource:~$ ls -l sample.txt
-rw-rw-r-- 1 student student 0 Sep 15 11:39 sample.txt
student@onecoursesource:~$ chgrp games sample.txt
student@onecoursesource:~$ ls -l sample.txt
-rw-rw-r-- 1 student games 0 Sep 15 11:39 sample.txt
```

WHAT COULD GO WRONG? Although users can change group membership of their own files to a group they are a member of, they cannot change the group membership of files owned by other users because this poses a security risk. The following commands demonstrate a typical error message when a user attempts to change another user's file group ownership:

```
student@onecoursesource:~$ ls -l /etc/hosts
-rw-r--r-- 2 root root 199 Sep 15 11:24 /etc/hosts
student@onecoursesource:~$ chgrp games /etc/hosts
chgrp: changing group of '/etc/hosts': Operation not permitted
```

Another potential issue is when a user tries to change the group ownership of one of their own files to a group that the user isn't a member of. A similar error message will appear:

```
student@onecoursesource:~$ ls -l sample.txt
-rw-rw-r-- 1 student games 0 Sep 15 11:39 sample.txt
student@onecoursesource:~$ id
uid=1002(student) gid=1002(student)
groups=1002(student),60(games),1001(ocs)
student@onecoursesource:~$ chgrp users sample.txt
chgrp: changing group of 'sample.txt': Operation not permitted
```

A user might be able to temporarily change their primary group to another group, but this depends on a security feature known as the **/etc/group** file, covered next.

The /etc/group File

Group information is stored in several files:

- The **/etc/passwd** file contains user account information, including the primary group membership for each user. Details regarding the contents of this file are discussed in Chapter 7. For the purpose of discussing groups in this chapter, this primary group membership is stored using the GID of the group, as shown in the following example:

  ```
  student@onecoursesource:~$ grep student /etc/passwd
  student:x:1002:1002::/home/student:
  ```

- The **/etc/group** file stores information about each group, including the group name, group ID (GID) and secondary user membership.
- The **/etc/gshadow** file stores additional information for the group, including group administrators and the group password. Details regarding the contents of this file are discussed later in this chapter in the section titled "The /etc/gshadow File."

Example 6-1 demonstrates part of a typical **/etc/group** file.

Example 6-1 *The /etc/group File*

```
student@onecoursesource:~$ head /etc/group
root:x:0:
daemon:x:1:
bin:x:2:
sys:x:3:
adm:x:4:syslog,bo
tty:x:5:
disk:x:6:
lp:x:7:
mail:x:8:
news:x:9:
```

Security Highlight

As demonstrated in Example 6-1, regular (non-administrator) users can view the **/etc/group** file. This highlights the need to prevent unauthorized access to the system because even a regular user can gain valuable information about the system by viewing the **/etc/group** file. Note that administrators should not change file permissions for the **/etc/group** file because this will cause some programs to not work correctly.

Keep in mind, this is not uncommon for operating systems, as regular users can see basic group information on other operating systems, including Unix, macOS and Microsoft Windows.

Each line in the **/etc/group** file describes one group. Each line is separated into fields of data, with the colon (:) character as the field separator. Table 6-2 describes these fields using the **adm:x:4:syslog,bo** line as an example.

Table 6-2 Fields of the **/etc/group** File

Field	Description
adm	The group name. The group name must be unique for the current system to avoid issues related to file ownership.
x	The password placeholder. Group passwords used to be placed in the **/etc/group** file, but have been moved to the **/etc/gshadow** file for security purposes. This is because the **/etc/group** file is viewable by all users, but the **/etc/gshadow** file is only viewable by the root user. Details regarding group passwords are discussed later in this chapter in the section titled "The /etc/gshadow File."
4	This is a numeric value that represents the group's ID (GID). The GID must be unique for the current system to avoid issues related to file ownership.
syslog,bo	This is the member list for the group. To add a user to a group as a secondary member, administrators add the user name to this field. This is typically accomplished by either the **usermod** or **gpasswd** command (see the "Adding Users to Groups" and "Group Administrators" sections later in this chapter).

Security Highlight

Normally the **/etc/group** file isn't manually modified. Administrators use commands like **groupadd**, **groupdel**, and **groupmod** to change the contents of the **/etc/group** file. However, the **/etc/group** file can be changed manually; as a result, errors in the file can occur. To see if there are any errors in the **/etc/group** file, execute the **grpck** command while logged in as the root user.

Special Groups

A typical Linux system will have many default group accounts. These default group accounts typically have GID values under 1000, making it easy for an administrator to recognize these as special accounts.

Additionally, if you add new software to the system, more groups may be added as software vendors make use of both user and group accounts to provide controlled access to files that are part of the software.

Administrators who are focused on security should be aware of these special group accounts because these accounts can provide either security features or pose security threats. Table 6-3 highlights the more important special group accounts (it is beyond the scope of this book to cover every special group).

Table 6-3 Special Group Accounts

Group	Description
root	This group account is reserved for the system administrator. Do not add a regular user to this group because it will provide the regular user with elevated access to system files.
adm	Members of this group typically have access to files related to system monitoring (such as log files). Being able to see the contents of these files can provide more information about the system than a regular user would typically have.
lp	This is one of many groups (including tty, mail, and cdrom) used by the operating system to provide access to specific files. Typically regular users are not added to these groups because they are used by background processes called *daemons*.
sudo	This group is used in conjunction with the **sudo** command. The **sudo** command is discussed in detail in Chapter 7.
staff	A default group that was traditionally used on Unix systems but is rarely used in modern Linux distributions.
users	A default group that is rarely used in modern Linux distributions.
operators	A group that was traditionally used on Unix systems for users who required elevated privileges for specific system tasks. This group is rarely used in modern Linux distributions.

Security Highlight

As an administrator, you should be aware of what each group is designed to do. Take the time to explore all the groups listed in your **/etc/group** file and carefully consider the impact of adding a user to a special group. Also, after adding software to the system, review the contents of the **/etc/group** file to determine if new groups were added. If new accounts were added, explore the purpose of these new groups.

User Private Groups

Typically when a user account is created, a group for that user is also created. This is designed to overcome a scenario that was common in the early days of Linux where system administrators would routinely add all users to one group (typically called "users" or "staff").

This practice resulted in a situation where users were provided access to files that they shouldn't have access to. By placing everyone in a single group, every new file that every user created was owned by that group, which meant that either everyone in the organization had access to the file via the group permissions or the user had to remember to remove all permissions for the group for each new file created. Figure 6-1 demonstrates the problems that this scenario creates (**file1.txt** demonstrates the security risk, and **file2.txt** demonstrates when a user remembers to remove all permissions for the group).

The concept of creating a group for each user is called User Private Groups (UPGs), where each user has their own group as their private group, meaning the security risk of all users being able to access the files of all other users is limited.

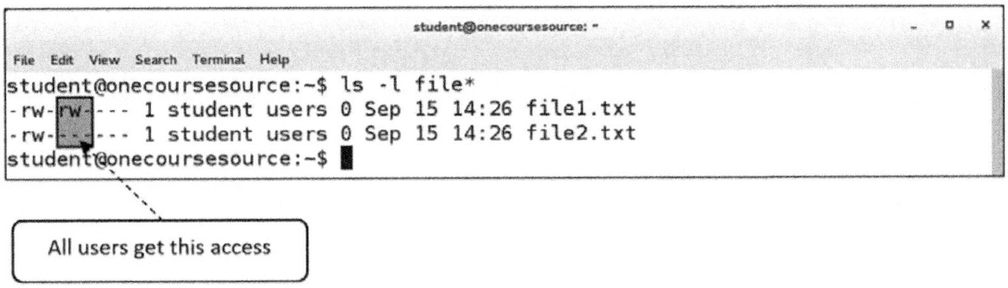
student@onecoursesource: ~
File Edit View Search Terminal Help
student@onecoursesource:~$ ls -l file*
-rw-rw---- 1 student users 0 Sep 15 14:26 file1.txt
-rw------- 1 student users 0 Sep 15 14:26 file2.txt
student@onecoursesource:~$
All users get this access

Figure 6-1 *The Issue with Having a Global Group for Everyone*

Unfortunately, this approach also poses security risks if the system administrator doesn't handle group membership correctly. UPG essentially makes the user's primary group worthless (at least by default) because the user is the only member of this private group. If the user isn't a member of additional groups, then to give access to a file for a specific user, the others permission set is often used. This ends up giving access to everyone on the system, which is the very problem that UPG was designed to avoid. Figure 6-2 demonstrates the problems that this scenario creates.

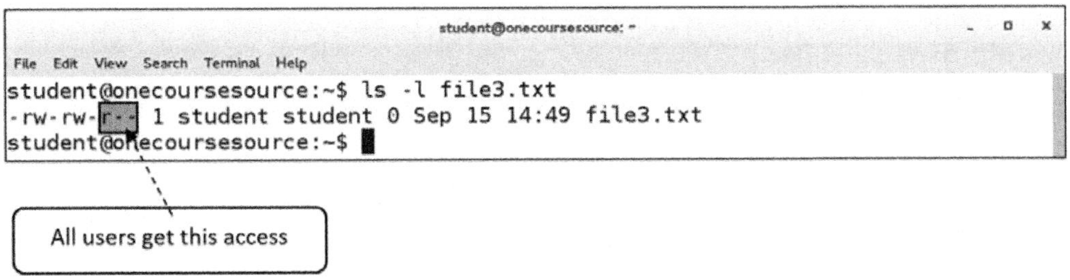
student@onecoursesource: ~
File Edit View Search Terminal Help
student@onecoursesource:~$ ls -l file3.txt
-rw-rw-r-- 1 student student 0 Sep 15 14:49 file3.txt
student@onecoursesource:~$
All users get this access

Figure 6-2 *Potential Issue with UPG*

UPG does provide a solution, but only a partial one. The administrator must also implement a security policy to include one or more of the following:

- A procedure to place users into additional groups to make it easier for people who work together to share access to files.
- A plan to teach proper use of permissions to all users. A detailed discussion of this topic can be found in Chapter 9, "File Permissions."
- The administrator should consider allowing users the ability to add new users to their own private group. A detailed discussion of this topic is provided in the next section, "The /etc/gshadow File."
- A plan to teach users how to use access control lists (ACLs), a method of assigning permissions to specific users or groups. A detailed discussion of this topic can be found in Chapter 9.

Conversational Learning™—Planning Groups

Gary: Hi, Julia. Do you have a moment so I can pick your brain?

Julia: Sure, what do you need?

Gary: I'm trying to make a plan to create the Linux groups that our organization needs, but I'm not really sure where to start.

Julia: Typically Linux groups are created so users can share files between each other using group permissions. For example, each department in your organization should probably have its own group.

Gary: That's it? Just make a group for each department?

Julia: No, there are other factors to consider. For example, two people from different departments might need to share files. If they are in different groups, this presents a challenge. If they are working on a project together, it makes sense to create a group for that specific project.

Gary: OK, so create groups for each department and also for projects that need shared file access. Anything else?

Julia: Even if a project doesn't involve people from different departments, you may want to create a group for it. So, instead of the files being shared with everyone in the department, only a select few within the department can access the files.

Gary: Any other common reason to create groups?

Julia: You also may want to consider job titles when creating groups. Companies often have different groups for managers, engineers, contractors, and so forth.

Gary: OK, great. This gives me a good idea of where to start. Thanks for your help!

Julia: Anytime!

The /etc/gshadow File

The **/etc/group** file contains some of the group account information, but more can be found in the **/etc/gshadow** file. This file is only viewable by the root user, so more sensitive data is stored in the **/etc/gshadow** file.

Example 6-2 demonstrates part of a typical **/etc/gshadow** file.

Example 6-2 *The /etc/gshadow File*

```
root@onecoursesource:~# head /etc/gshadow
root:*::
daemon:*::
bin:*::
sys:*::
adm:*:student:syslog,bo,student
tty:*::
disk:*::
lp:*::
mail:*::
news:*::
```

Each line in the **/etc/gshadow** file describes one group. Each line is separated into fields of data, with the colon (:) character as the field separator. Table 6-4 describes these fields using the **adm:*:student:syslog,bo,student** line as an example.

Table 6-4 Fields of the **/etc/gshadow** File

Field	Description
adm	The group name. This matches up with the group name in the **/etc/group** file.
*	The group password. A value of * or **!** means "no valid password set." This password is used with the **newgrp** command and set by the **gpasswd** command. See more about this password in the discussion following this table.

Field	Description
student	The group administrator for the group. Group administrators can add and remove users from the group. See the section titled "Group Administrators," later in this chapter.
syslog,bo,student	This is the member list for the group. This should match up with the corresponding field in the **/etc/group** file.

The purpose of the password field in the **/etc/gshadow** file is to allow users to temporarily change their primary group by using the **newgrp** command. By default, any user who is a member of a group can switch their primary group:

```
student@onecoursesource:~$ groups
student adm games ocs
student@onecoursesource:~$ newgrp games
student@onecoursesource:~$ groups
games adm ocs student
```

6

Users cannot switch their primary group membership to a group they don't belong to, unless they know the password for that group. This password is set by the administrator using the **gpasswd** command:

```
root@onecoursesource:~# gpasswd staff
Changing the password for group staff
New Password:
Re-enter new password:
root@onecoursesource:~# grep staff /etc/gshadow
staff:$6$iv.gICgaA$iWGw611b/ZqKhu4WnMfA9qpNQvAQcljBFGuB1iXdWBhMWqgr2yQn7hn6Nu8BTrtErn734
  wLDhWzS6tNtJmkV/::
```

Once the password has been set, a user can change their primary group by entering the group password at the prompt when running the **newgrp** command:

```
student@onecoursesource:~$ groups
student adm games ocs
student@onecoursesource:~$ newgrp staff
Password:
student@onecoursesource:~$ groups
staff adm games ocs student
```

Although you can use the group password method, consider this: If you want to allow a user to switch to a new primary group, why not just add them to that group? Because of this logic, group passwords are not very often used on Linux systems.

See Figure 6-3 for additional information.

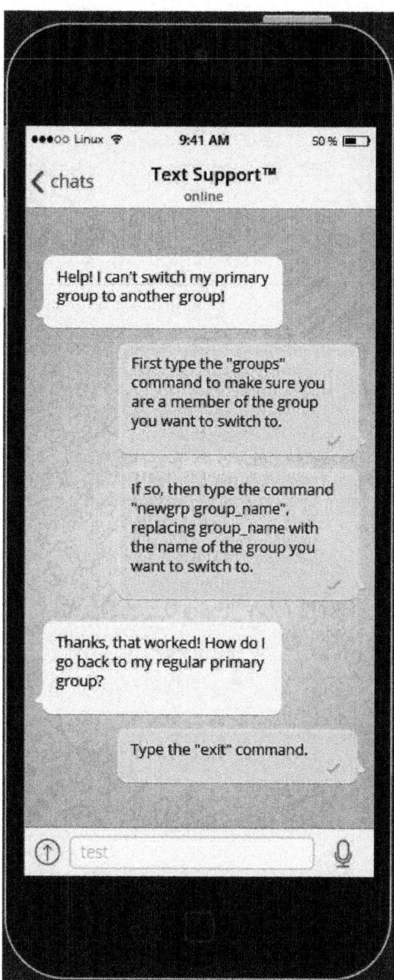

Figure 6-3 *Text Support™—Changing Primary Groups*

Managing Groups

The process of managing groups includes creating new groups, modifying existing groups, and deleting groups. These operations require the privilege provided by the root account.

Managing groups can also include the process of adding a user to a group or removing a user from a group. Typically, these operations require the privilege provided by the root account, but if group administrators are created, then a group administrator can also perform these tasks for specific groups.

Creating Groups

Create a new group by using the **groupadd** command, like so:

```
root@onecoursesource:~# groupadd -g 5000 payroll
root@onecoursesource:~# tail -1 /etc/group
payroll:x:5000:
```

NOTE The **-g** option is used to assign a GID to the group. If the **-g** option is omitted, then the next available GID above 1000 will be used (on some systems, the next available above 500 may be used). Best practice is to use the **-g** option and use a higher value (5000 or above) so this won't impact the GIDs used for User Private Groups.

WHAT COULD GO WRONG? When creating a group, you must use a GID and name that is not currently used or you will get errors:

```
root@onecoursesource:~# groupadd -g 4000 payroll
groupadd: group 'payroll' already exists
root@onecoursesource:~# groupadd -g 5000 test
groupadd: GID '5000' already exists
```


Modifying Groups

The most typical change an administrator would make to a group, besides adding and removing members, is to change the group name. The reason for this change may be because the original name isn't descriptive enough, so another name would be better.

To change a group's name, use the **groupmod** command with the **-n** option, as shown here:

```
root@onecoursesource:~# tail -1 /etc/group
payroll:x:5000:
root@onecoursesource:~# groupmod -n payables payroll
root@onecoursesource:~# tail -1 /etc/group
payables:x:5000:
```

Deleting Groups

Deleting a group is accomplished by executing the **groupdel** command. However, before deleting a group, the administrator should search the filesystem for all files owned by the group and change the ownership to another group. If this step isn't taken, then files owned by that group end up being owned just by the GID of the group, making group permissions worthless. Here's an example:

```
root@onecoursesource:~# ls -l /tmp/example
-rw-r--r-- 1 root payables 0 Sep 15 16:07 /tmp/example
root@onecoursesource:~# groupdel payables
root@onecoursesource:~# ls -l /tmp/example
-rw-r--r-- 1 root 5000 0 Sep 15 16:07 /tmp/example
```

See Figure 6-4 for information on how to search for files by group ownership.

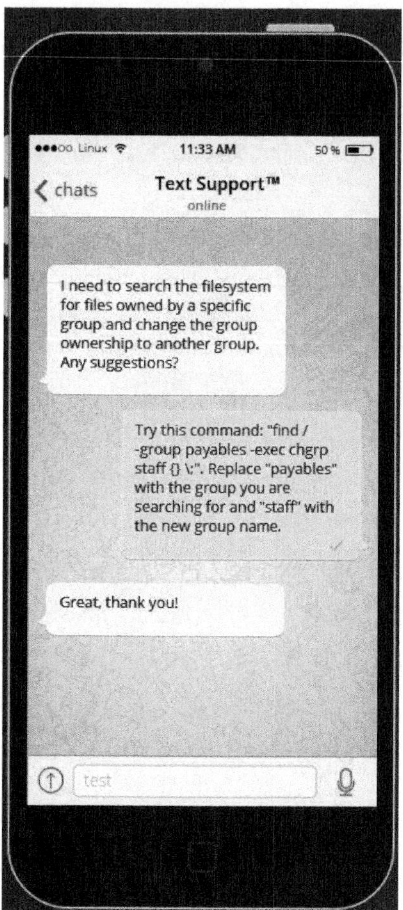

Figure 6-4 *Text Support™—How to Find a File by Group Ownership and Change the Ownership*

Adding Users to Groups

The **-G** option to the **usermod** command is used to add a user to a group. However, be careful because by default this option will override existing group membership. Here's an example:

```
root@onecoursesource:~# id student
uid=1002(student) gid=1002(student)
groups=1002(student),60(games),1001(ocs)
root@onecoursesource:~# usermod -G adm student
root@onecoursesource:~# id student
uid=1002(student) gid=1002(student) groups=1002(student),4(adm)
```

To add a user to a group while maintaining the user's current group membership, use the **-a** option in conjunction with the **-G** option:

```
root@onecoursesource:~# id student
uid=1002(student) gid=1002(student)
groups=1002(student),60(games),1001(ocs)
root@onecoursesource:~# usermod -G adm -a student
root@onecoursesource:~# id student
uid=1002(student) gid=1002(student)
groups=1002(student),4(adm),60(games),1001(ocs)
```

Security Highlight

Don't add a user to a group unless there is a valid need because this would provide the user with unnecessary escalated privileges.

Group Administrators

By default, the only person who can add or remove users from a group is the person who is logged in as the root user. To allow a user to manage a group, you need to add them as a group administrator by using the **-A** option to the **gpasswd** command:

```
root@onecoursesource:~# grep games /etc/gshadow
games:::student
root@onecoursesource:~# gpasswd -A student games
root@onecoursesource:~# grep games /etc/gshadow
games::student:student
```

6

Now the student user can add users to the games group by using the **-a** option to the **gpasswd** command:

```
student@onecoursesource:~$ gpasswd -a bo games
Adding user bo to group games
student@onecoursesource:~$ grep games /etc/group
games:x:60:student,bo
```

Using the **-d** option to the **gpasswd** command, the student user can remove users from the games group:

```
student@onecoursesource:~$ grep games /etc/group
games:x:60:student,bo
student@onecoursesource:~$ gpasswd -d bo games
Removing user bo from group games
student@onecoursesource:~$ grep games /etc/group
games:x:60:student
```

NOTE Group administrators can use the **gpasswd** command to administer groups that they are an administrator for only. They also can't use the **groupadd**, **groupmod**, and **groupdel** commands.

Summary

The Linux operating system makes use of group accounts to control access to key components, including files and directories. In this chapter, you learned how to manage these group accounts. This included how to create, modify, and delete group accounts, as well as how to use special group account features such as User Private Groups and group administrators.

Key Terms

group account, primary group, secondary group, UID, user ID, GID, group ID, special groups, UPG, User Private Group

Review Questions

1. Every user is a member of at least _____ group(s).
2. Which of the following commands will display the groups that the user nick is a member of?
   - A. **id**
   - B. **groupinfo**
   - C. **info groups**
   - D. **groups**
3. Which files are used to store group information?
   - A. **/etc/groupoinfo**
   - B. **/etc/shadow**
   - C. **/etc/groups**
   - D. **/etc/gshadow**
4. Special groups are groups with GID numbers typically under the numeric value of _____.
5. If the system is using UPG, the group name of the user account named jake should be _____.

Managing User Accounts

Because Linux is a multiuser operating system, security is often based on accounts. Each person is provided a user account that allows the user access to the system.

As an administrator, it is important to know the basics of creating and managing user accounts. In regard to security, you should consider user accounts as one of the biggest potential risks to the system. As a result, properly securing user accounts is a critical system administration task.

In this chapter, you learn more about the concepts of user accounts. You also explore how to create, modify, secure, and delete user accounts.

After reading this chapter and completing the exercises, you will be able to do the following:

Understand the concept of Linux user accounts

Manage users, including creating, modifying, and deleting user accounts

Understand network-based user accounts

Use su **and** sudo **to gain privileged system access**

Restrict user accounts using PAM

The Importance of User Accounts

User accounts play a critical role on Linux operating systems, including the following:

- **Granting system access**: User accounts provide a means for users to log in and gain controlled access to the system.
- **Securing files and directories**: Each file (and directory) is owned by a user account. The user account owner of the file can access the file based on the file permissions.
- **Security processes**: Each process (program) that is running is owned by a user account. This user account has the right to stop or modify the running process, while other users do not have this access.
- **Additional privileges**: System administrators can provide special privileges to a user account. This can include the ability to run specific processes or perform specific system operations that other users don't have the ability to perform.
- **Additional authentication**: Some software programs verify user accounts for authentication. This means that to run the software programs, the user account and user password (or some other authentication method) is used.

User Account Information

Account data for local users is stored in several different files:

- **/etc/passwd**: Primary account data.
- **/etc/shadow**: User passwords and password-related data.

- **/etc/group**: Group account data, which includes information related to user accounts. Details regarding this file are found in Chapter 6, "Managing Group Accounts."
- **/etc/gshadow**: Group account data, which includes information related to user accounts. Details regarding this file are found in Chapter 6.

Note that these files are only used to store local user account information. User accounts can also be provided by network servers, allowing a user to log in to several different systems using the same user name and password.

Network-based user accounts are covered in more detail later in this chapter.

The /etc/passwd File

The **/etc/passwd** file contains basic user account information. However, despite its name, this file doesn't contain any information related to the users' passwords.

Example 7-1 demonstrates part of a typical **/etc/passwd** file.

Example 7-1 *The /etc/passwd File*

```
student@onecoursesource:~$ head /etc/passwd
root:x:0:0:root:/root:/bin/bash
daemon:x:1:1:daemon:/usr/sbin:/usr/sbin/nologin
bin:x:2:2:bin:/bin:/usr/sbin/nologin
sys:x:3:3:sys:/dev:/usr/sbin/nologin
sync:x:4:65534:sync:/bin:/bin/sync
games:x:5:60:games:/usr/games:/usr/sbin/nologin
man:x:6:12:man:/var/cache/man:/usr/sbin/nologin
lp:x:7:7:lp:/var/spool/lpd:/usr/sbin/nologin
mail:x:8:8:mail:/var/mail:/usr/sbin/nologin
news:x:9:9:news:/var/spool/news:/usr/sbin/nologin
```

Security Highlight

As demonstrated in Example 7-1, regular (non-administrator) users can view the **/etc/passwd** file. This highlights the need to prevent unauthorized access to the system because even a regular user can gain valuable information about the system by viewing the **/etc/passwd** file. Keep in mind, this is not uncommon for operating systems—regular users can see basic user account information on other operating systems, including Unix, macOS, and Microsoft Windows.

Note that administrators should not change file permissions for the **/etc/passwd** file because this will cause some programs to not work correctly.

Each line in the **/etc/passwd** file describes one group. Each line is separated into fields of data, with the colon (:) character as the field separator. Table 7-1 describes these fields using the **root:x:0:0:root:/root:/bin/bash** line as an example.

Table 7-1 Fields of the **/etc/passwd** File

Field	Description
root	The user name. The user name must be unique for the current system to avoid issues related to file ownership.

Field	Description
x	The password placeholder. User passwords used to be placed in the **/etc/passwd** file but have been moved to the **/etc/shadow** file for security purposes. This is because the **/etc/passwd** file is viewable by all users, but the **/etc/shadow** file is only viewable by the root user. Details regarding user passwords are discussed later in this chapter in the section titled "The /etc/shadow File."
0	This is a numeric value that represents the user's ID (UID). The UID must be unique for the current system to avoid issues related to file ownership.
0	This is a numeric value that represents the user's primary group. Recall from Chapter 6 that users can be members of multiple groups, but the primary group is used to set initial group ownership on new files and directories.
root	This is a comment field, commonly called the GECOS (General Comprehensive Operating System) field. On most systems, the administrator will use this field to place the name of the person who the account has been assigned to, but it can include other useful information, such as phone extension or office location. GECOS is a feature that makes use of specific commands to populate and view this field (see the "Managing GECOS" section later in this chapter).
/root	This is the user's home directory. Typically this will be a directory under the **/home** directory (for example, **/home/bob**), but the root user has a special home directory of **/root**.
/bin/bash	This is the user's login shell. The value of **/bin/bash** indicates the user has a typical BASH shell provided when logging in to the system via the command line or remotely across the network. Other commonly used values include the following: ■ **/usr/sbin/nologin**: For daemon accounts (accounts used by the system that are not intended for regular users to log in with). ■ **/bin/false**: Also sometimes used for daemon accounts. ■ **/bin/tcsh**: For TCSH to (T shell, an enhanced version of the C shell) accounts. ■ **/bin/dash**: For DASH (Debian Almquist Shell) accounts. ■ **/bin/rbash**: For restricted shell accounts. See the "Restricted Shell Accounts" section later in this chapter for more details.

Security Highlight

Normally the **/etc/passwd** file isn't manually modified. Administrators use commands like **useradd**, **userdel**, and **usermod** to change the contents of the **/etc/passwd** file. However, administrators can choose to modify the **/etc/passwd** file manually; as a result, errors in the file can occur. To see if there are any errors in the **/etc/passwd** file, execute the **pwck** command while logged in as the root user.

Special Users

A typical Linux system will have many default user accounts. These default user accounts typically have UID values under 1000, making it easy for an administrator to recognize these as special accounts.

Some of these default accounts are often referred to as "daemon accounts" because they are used by daemon-based software. *Daemons* are programs that run in the background, performing specific system tasks.

Other default accounts may exist to provide features for the operating system. For example, the nobody account is used to apply permissions for files that are shared via NFS (Network File System).

Additionally, if you add new software to the system, more users might be added because software vendors make use of both user and group accounts to provide controlled access to files that are part of the software.

Administrators who are focused on security should be aware of these default user accounts because these accounts can provide either security features or pose security threats. Table 7-2 highlights the more important special group accounts (it is beyond the scope of this book to cover every default user).

Table 7-2 Default User Accounts

Group	Description
root	This account is the system administrator account. It is important to note that what makes the root account special is the UID of 0. Any user with a UID of 0 is a full system administrator. As a security note, when you're performing audits, look for any user with a UID of 0, as this is a common hacking technique.
syslog	This account is used by the system logging daemon to access files.
lp	This is one of many users (including mysql, mail, postfix, and dovecot) used by the operating system to provide access to specific files by background processes called daemons.
bind	This user is used by the software that provides DNS (Domain Name System) functions.

7

Security Highlight

As an administrator, you should be aware of what each user account is designed to do. Take the time to explore all the users listed in your **/etc/passwd** file and carefully consider the impact of each account. Also, after adding software to the system, review the contents of the **/etc/passwd** file to determine if new user accounts were added. If new accounts were added, explore the purpose of these new accounts.

The /etc/shadow File

The **/etc/passwd** file contains some of the user account information, but none of the password information. Ironically, this password data is stored in the **/etc/shadow** file. This file is only viewable by the root user, which is why more sensitive data regarding passwords is stored in the **/etc/shadow** file.

Example 7-2 demonstrates part of a typical **/etc/shadow** file.

Example 7-2 *The /etc/shadow File*

```
root@onecoursesource:~# head /etc/shadow
root:$6$5rU9Z/H5$sZM3MRyHS24SR/ySv80ViqIrzfhh.p1EWfOic7NzA2zvSjquFKi
➥PgIVJy8/ba.X/mEQ9DUwtQQb2zdSPsEwb8.:17320:0:99999:7:::
daemon:*:16484:0:99999:7:::
bin:*:16484:0:99999:7:::
sys:*:16484:0:99999:7:::
```

```
sync:*:16484:0:99999:7:::
games:*:16484:0:99999:7:::
man:*:16484:0:99999:7:::
lp:*:16484:0:99999:7:::
mail:*:16484:0:99999:7:::
news:*:16484:0:99999:7:::
```

Each line in the **/etc/shadow** file describes one user account's password information. Each line is separated into fields of data, with the colon (:) character as the field separator. Table 7-3 describes these fields using the **news:*:16484:0:99999:7:::** line as an example.

Table 7-3 Fields of the **/etc/shadow** File

Field	Description
news	**The user account name field**: This matches up with the user name in the **/etc/passwd** file.
*	**The user password field**: A value of * or ! means "no valid password set." Note the value for the root account in Example 7-2 (the very long collection of characters) is an example of an encrypted password. Encrypted passwords are one-way hashed encrypted, which means there is no method to decrypt the password. When a user logs in, the password they provide during the login process is encrypted, and that value is compared to the value in the **/etc/shadow** file. If the values match, the user can log in. Security note: If this field is completely blank, then the corresponding user can log in by simply pressing <ENTER> when prompted for a password. This poses a considerable security risk, so when you're auditing your systems, look for accounts that have no password set.
16484	**The date of last password change field**: This number represents the number of days since January 1, 1970 and the date that the user's password was last changed. January 1, 1970 is referred to as the *epoch* (beginning of time) of Unix, as that was when Unix was released. This numeric value is used in conjunction with the other fields on this line to provide basic password-aging functionality. See the next two fields for more information.
0	**The minimum password age field**: This number represents how many days must pass after a user has changed the account's password before the password can be changed again. For example, if this field was set to a value of **5**, then the user would have to wait five days before changing the account password again. This field is necessary because of the function of the next field.
99999	**The maximum password age field**: This field represents how many days can pass before the user must change the account's password. For example, if this field was set to the value of **60**, then the user would have to change the account password every 60 days. The value of the previous field can be used to prevent the user from changing the password back to the original immediately after being forced to change the password.
7	**The password warning period field**: If the user does not change the password within the timeframe specified by the previous field, the account is locked out. To provide a warning for the user, this field is used. This numeric value represents the number of days a warning is displayed as they log in to the system, alerting the user to change their password before the account is locked.

Field	Description
[Not set in example]	**The password inactivity period field**: Imagine if the user ignores the warnings and doesn't change the password before the maximum password age date. The account is locked and, to unlock it, the user would need to contact the system administrator. However, if the value of this field is set, then a grace period is provided in which the user can log in for a specific period of time (in days after the maximum password age value has been exceeded). This does require the user to change the account password during the login process.
[Not set in example]	**The expiration date field**: This value represents the number of days since January 1, 1970 and the date the account will expire. When the expiration date occurs, the account password is locked. This field is useful for contractor accounts or accounts that are used by individuals who are temporarily assigned to work within a specific company group.
[Not set in example]	**The unused field**: Currently the last field is not used, but is reserved for future use.

The **/etc/shadow** file, with password-aging features of minimum password aging, maximum password aging, password inactivity, and other features, tends to cause confusion for beginning Linux users. It is essential for system administrators to understand this account because it provides important user account security features. The example displayed in Figure 7-1 is designed to provide a better understanding of the fields of the **/etc/shadow** file.

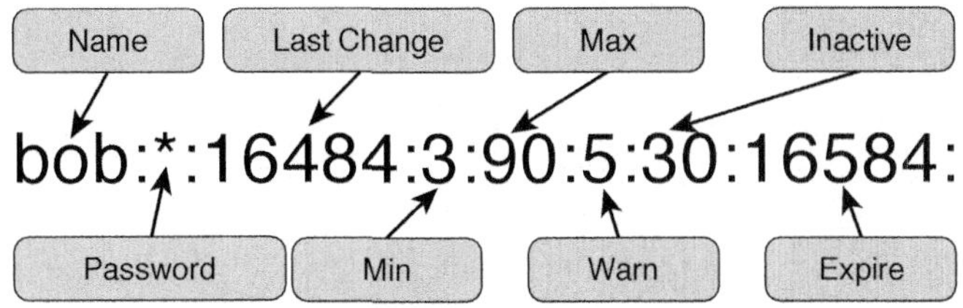

Figure 7-1 *The Fields of the **/etc/shadow** File*

Using the values of the sample record displayed in Figure 7-1, we can determine the following about the **bob** user account:

- It currently has a locked password (* = locked).
- It has been 16,484 days since January 1, 1970 and the last time the account password was changed (or locked in this case). Note that there are tools that we will cover in this chapter to convert standard dates into epoch dates.
- The user must change the account password every 90 days and must keep that new password for at least three days.
- The user is warned during the login process if the account password must be changed within five days.
- If the user exceeds the maximum password-aging value of 90 days, there is a grace period of 30 days. Within the next 30 days, the user can change the account password during the login process.
- The account will expire (be locked) 16,584 days from January 1, 1970.

Conversational Learning™—Understanding Password Aging

Gary: Hi, Julia. I'm stuck on something related to user passwords.

Julia: What's the problem, Gary?

Gary: I have a user trying to change his password, but he keeps getting a weird error message.

Julia: Is he using the **passwd** command to change his password?

Gary: Yep.

Julia: What error message does he get?

Gary: "You must wait longer to change your password."

Julia: Ah, I assume that he probably has recently changed his password and is now trying to change it again to something else?

Gary: Right. Yesterday the command worked, but today it gives him that error message.

Julia: OK, look at the **/etc/shadow** file, specifically the line that contains this person's account data. Look at the fourth field of the line. What value is there?

Gary: 10.

Julia: That means the user must wait ten days after he changes his password before he can change it again. This prevents people from reverting to their previous password right after the system forces them to change to a new password.

Gary: But what if he really needs to have this changed?

Julia: No problem. An administrator can make the change for the user.

Gary: OK, great. Thanks for the info!

Julia: You are welcome!

Managing Users

The process of managing users includes creating new users, modifying existing users, and deleting users. These operations require the privilege provided by the root account.

Creating Users

Create a new group by using the **useradd** command:

```
root@onecoursesource:~# useradd timmy
root@onecoursesource:~# tail -1 /etc/passwd
timmy:x:1003:1003::/home/timmy:
root@onecoursesource:~# tail -1 /etc/shadow
timmy:!:17456:0:99999:7:::
```

Some important notes regarding the **useradd** command:

- The **-u** option can be used to assign a UID to the user. If the **-u** option is omitted, then the next available UID above 1000 is used (on some systems, the next available UID above 500 may be used).
- Notice that although the user's home directory in the **/etc/passwd** file was set to **/home/timmy**, this directory was not created by default. To create this directory, you must use the **-m** option when issuing the **useradd** command. Creating the home directory can also be set as the default; see the "Using Defaults" section later in this chapter for more details.
- The new user's account is locked by default (hence the **!** in the second field of the **/etc/shadow** file). Use the **passwd** command to set the account password after it has been created.

Table 7-4 describes additional useful options for the **useradd** command.

Table 7-4 Useful **useradd** Options

Option	Description
-c	Set the comment field of the **/etc/passwd** file.
-d	Specify the home directory for the user instead of defaulting to **/home/username**.
-e	Set the expiration date for the account; use an argument in the format of YYYY-MM-DD (for example, **-e 2020-12-31**).
-f	Set the inactive field of the **/etc/shadow** file.
-g	Set the user's primary group. Note that on systems that use User Private Groups (UPGs), this overrides the UPG features. See Chapter 6 for details regarding UPG.
-G	Set the user's secondary groups. Use a comma to separate each group (for example, **-G games,staff,bin**).
-k	Use a skeleton directory. See the "Using Skel Directories" section later in this chapter for more details.
-D	Display or set defaults. See the "Using Defaults" section later in this chapter for more details.
-p	Set the user password. Note that this option should not be used due to security issues. It does not normally encrypt the password correctly. Additionally, the command itself contains the password in plain text, which could be visible by someone viewing the screen while it is typed, viewing running processes as this process is executed, or viewing the root user's history list.
-s	Specify the user's login shell (for example, **-s /bin/tcsh**).
-u	Specify the user's UID.

7

WHAT COULD GO WRONG? When creating a user, you must use a UID and name that is not currently used; otherwise, you will get errors, as shown next:

```
root@onecoursesource:~# useradd -u 1002 bob
useradd: UID 1002 is not unique
root@onecoursesource:~# useradd nick
useradd: user 'nick' already exists
```

Setting the Account Password

After creating the user account, you need to set a password for the user. This is accomplished by using the **passwd** command:

```
root@onecoursesource:~# tail -1 /etc/shadow
timmy:!:17456:0:99999:7:::
root@onecoursesource:~# passwd timmy
Enter new UNIX password:
Retype new UNIX password:
passwd: password updated successfully
root@onecoursesource:~# tail -1 /etc/shadow
timmy:$6$29m4A.mk$WK/qVgQeJPrUn8qvVqnrbS2m9OCa2A0fxON3keWM1BsZ9Ft
➥vfFtfMMREeX22Hp9wYYUZ.0DXSLmIIJQuarFGv0:17456:0:99999:7:::
```

Using Defaults

You can use options to change how a user is created, but if you don't use these options, then default values are normally used. Some of these default values can be viewed by using the **-D** option to the **useradd** command:

```
root@onecoursesource:~# useradd -D
GROUP=100
HOME=/home
INACTIVE=-1
EXPIRE=
SHELL=/bin/sh
SKEL=/etc/skel
CREATE_MAIL_SPOOL=no
```

Some of these values are not exactly accurate. For example, the value **GROUP=100** is supposed to mean "place users in the group with the GID of 100 by default"; however, most modern Linux distributions use User Private Groups, so this value is not really used. However, some of these values, like the **EXPIRE** value, which indicates the default account-expiration date, are used.

These settings can be changed by editing the values found in the **/etc/default/useradd** file. Several additional default settings can be viewed and modified in the **/etc/logins.def** file. For example, Example 7-3 shows settings related to default password-aging policies.

Example 7-3 *Default Password-Aging Policies*

```
root@onecoursesource:~# grep PASS /etc/login.defs
#     PASS_MAX_DAYS    Maximum number of days a password may be used.
#     PASS_MIN_DAYS    Minimum number of days allowed between password changes.
#     PASS_WARN_AGE    Number of days warning given before a password expires.
PASS_MAX_DAYS     99999
PASS_MIN_DAYS     0
PASS_WARN_AGE     7
#PASS_CHANGE_TRIES
#PASS_ALWAYS_WARN
#PASS_MIN_LEN
#PASS_MAX_LEN
# NO_PASSWORD_CONSOLE
```

Using Skel Directories

Creating a user account is only part of the process. In many cases it would benefit the user to have specific default files placed in the user's home directory. This can be accomplished by using skeleton directories.

When a skeleton directory is used, the entire contents of the specified directory are copied to the new user's home directory. The files that are copied are also automatically owned by the new user, as Example 7-4 demonstrates.

Example 7-4 *Files Are Owned by the New User*

```
root@onecoursesource:~# ls -lA /etc/skel
total 12
-rw-r--r--   1 root root   220 Apr  8  2014 .bash_logout
-rw-r--r--   1 root root  3637 Apr  8  2014 .bashrc
```

```
-rw-r--r--   1 root root   675 Apr  8  2014 .profile
root@onecoursesource:~# useradd -m -k /etc/skel steve
root@onecoursesource:~# ls -lA /home/steve
total 12
-rw-r--r-- 1 steve steve  220 Apr  8  2014 .bash_logout
-rw-r--r-- 1 steve steve 3637 Apr  8  2014 .bashrc
-rw-r--r-- 1 steve steve  675 Apr  8  2014 .profile
```

Different directories can be used for different types of users. For example, you could create a directory structure named **/etc/skel_eng** that has a **.bashrc** file containing aliases designed to be used by software engineers. Then you could create another directory named **/etc/skel_sales** that has a **.bashrc** file containing aliases designed to be used by sales engineers. Use the **-k /etc/skel_eng** option when creating an account for software engineers and the **-k /etc/skel_sales** option when creating an account for sales engineers.

NOTE If you don't use the **-k** option, the **useradd** command will automatically copy the contents of the **/etc/skel** directory into the new user account.

7

Modifying Users

As an administrator, you can modify user accounts using the **usermod** command and the same type of options used by the **useradd** command. For example, if you want to change a user's name, use the **usermod** command with the **-c** option:

```
root@onecoursesource:~# grep timmy /etc/passwd
timmy:x:1003:1003::/home/timmy:
root@onecoursesource:~# usermod -c "Timmy Smith" timmy
root@onecoursesource:~# grep timmy /etc/passwd
timmy:x:1003:1003:Timmy Smith:/home/timmy:
```

Whereas the **usermod** command can be used to change the expiration date and inactive fields of the **/etc/shadow** file, the **chage** command can change additional fields with the options shown:

-m	Change the min days field.
-M	Change the max days field.
-d	Change the "date since last password change" field (YYYY-MM-DD format).
-I	Change the inactive field.
-E	Change the expiration date field (YYYY-MM-DD format).
-W	Change the warning days field.

Managing GECOS

Recall from earlier in the chapter the comment field in the **/etc/passwd** file that is commonly called the GECOS (General Comprehensive Operating System) field. Although not used very often on modern Linux systems, there is a feature that allows regular users to modify the comment field of the **/etc/passwd** file, at least for their own account. By default, users can make these changes by using the **chfn** command, as shown in Example 7-5.

Example 7-5 *The chfn Command*

```
student@onecoursesource:~$ chfn
Password:
Changing the user information for student
Enter the new value, or press ENTER for the default
    Full Name:
    Room Number []: 101
    Work Phone []: 999
    Home Phone []: 1-555-555-5555
student@onecoursesource:~$ grep student /etc/passwd
student:x:1002:1002:,101,999,1-555-555-5555:/home/student:
```

Some regular users like this feature because this data can be easily displayed using the **finger** command:

```
student@onecoursesource:~$ finger student
Login: student                    Name:
Directory: /home/student                Shell: /bin/sh
Office: 101, 999            Home Phone: 1-555-555-5555
Never logged in.
No mail.
No Plan.
```

However, this feature can result in a security risk because it provides regular users with the ability to modify the **/etc/passwd** file. Granted, it should only modify the comment field, but it is always possible that a security hole in the **chfn** program could result in an exploit, so you might consider turning off this feature. An easy way to remove this feature is to change the permission of the **chfn** program:

```
root@onecoursesource:~# ls -l /usr/bin/chfn
-rwsr-xr-x 1 root root 46424 Feb 16  2014 /usr/bin/chfn
root@onecoursesource:~# chmod u-s /usr/bin/chfn
root@onecoursesource:~# ls -l /usr/bin/chfn
-rwxr-xr-x 1 root root 46424 Feb 16  2014 /usr/bin/chfn
```

This results in the following error:

```
student@onecoursesource:~$ chfn
Password:
Changing the user information for student
Enter the new value, or press ENTER for the default
    Full Name:
    Room Number [101]: 222
    Work Phone [999]: 222
    Home Phone [1-555-555-5555]: 222
Cannot change ID to root.
```

NOTE Permissions and the **chmod** command are covered in detail in Chapter 8, "Develop an Account Security Policy."

Deleting Users

Deleting a user account is accomplished by executing the **userdel** command. However, before you delete a user, you need to make a decision: Do you want to delete just the account from the **/etc/passwd** and **/etc/shadow** files or do you also want to delete the user's home directory and mail spool?

In some cases, keeping the user's home directory can be useful for the person who is replacing the user. The mail spool, which contains inbound mail messages, may be necessary for audits or liability reasons.

To remove a user and keep the user's home directory and mail spool, use the **userdel** command without any additional arguments:

```
root@onecoursesource:~# userdel steve
```

To remove a user and their home directory and mail spool, include the **-r** option to the **userdel** command.

Restricted Shell Accounts

In certain cases you will want to provide very limited access to a system for specific users. For example, suppose you have a guest user who only needs very limited access to a system (for example, for assisting in a hardware repair that requires testing on the network). Or perhaps you have created a kiosk-based system and you only want users to perform very specific tasks, such as booking a car rental or viewing their student schedule.

In these cases, you should consider creating a restricted shell account. This sort of account makes use of the BASH shell, but has many important restrictions, including the following:

- The user cannot change directories using the **cd** command.
- The user cannot change the values of the following variables: **SHELL**, **PATH**, **ENV**, and **BASH_ENV**.
- The user cannot run any commands that have a pathname that starts with the / character (such as **/bin/bash**).
- The user cannot redirect output to a file.

There are additional restrictions that can be viewed in the man page for **rbash**. However, the point is that a restricted shell account is very limited and will only have access to built-in commands and commands that are available via the **PATH** variable.

To create a restricted shell account, use the **-s** option to the **useradd** command and provide an argument of **/bin/rbash**:

```
root@onecoursesource:~# useradd -m -s /bin/rbash limited
```

Next, modify the account so the user has limited access to commands. For example, if you only want the user to run commands from the **/bin** directory, add the following to the end of the user's **.bashrc** file:

```
PATH=/bin
```

This could also be set to a directory where you have copied specific commands, rather than the entire **/bin** directory. Once the user logs in, they are limited in the commands they can execute. For example, the **ls** command is in the **/bin** directory, so that is allowed. However, the **vi** command is in the **/usr/bin** directory, not the **/bin** directory, so it will fail:

```
limited@onecoursesource:~$ ls
limited@onecoursesource:~$ vi
-rbash: /usr/lib/command-not-found: restricted: cannot specify
➥'/' in command names
```

Security Highlight

It takes practice and some experience to fine-tune the restricted account to provide just the right access. As a recommendation, start with a limited amount of commands and add more as needed.

Network-Based User Accounts

At this point in the book, a full discussion regarding network-based accounts is a bit premature. The topics of networking in general and services that provide network-based accounts haven't been covered yet. As a result, the discussion in this chapter is more theory based. Several later chapters—most notably Chapter 19, "Network Configuration"—cover these topics in more detail.

Using network-based accounts to log users in to different systems requires setting up a client-server relationship between the system you want the user to log in to and a server that provides login information. Linux platforms have several different login servers, including the following:

- **LDAP (Lightweight Directory Access Protocol)**: An LDAP server can provide both user and group account data, as well as other data defined by the LDAP administrator. It is a commonly used server for network-based accounts on Linux distributions.
- **NIS (Network Information Service)**: Although not as flexible as LDAP, NIS provides the advantage of being an easy service to set up and administer. However, administrators who are concerned about security will often avoid NIS due to its security issues.
- **Active Directory and Samba**: Active Directory is a Microsoft product and Samba is a Linux-based service that can make use of Active Directory to allow users to log in to Linux systems using the Active Directory server. This can be a complex configuration due to changes made to Active Directory that do not take the Linux system structure into consideration.

When a system can use a server for network-based accounts, local accounts are still available. However, given that there could be conflicts, there is a method to indicate which location account information is accessed first. This is accomplished by settings in the /etc/nsswitch.conf file, which is the configuration file for a local service called NSS (Name Service Switch). For example, the following settings in the **/etc/nsswitch.conf** file would have the local database files (**/etc/passwd**, **/etc/shadow**, and **/etc/group**) referenced first when a user attempts to log in:

```
passwd:         files ldap
group:          files ldap
shadow:         files ldap
```

If the user's account information is not found in the local files, the LDAP server would be used. More details on network-based user accounts can be found in Chapter 19 where network services are discussed.

Using su and sudo

As an administrator, you often will want to test user accounts by logging in as a specific user. Unfortunately, even the administrator does not know the password for regular user accounts. However, the root user can "switch user" (**su**) to another user account, as demonstrated here:

```
root@onecoursesource:~# id
uid=0(root) gid=0(root) groups=0(root)
root@onecoursesource:~# su - student
student@onecoursesource:~$ id
uid=1002(student) gid=1002(student)
➥groups=1002(student),4(adm),60(games),1001(ocs)
```

The **su** command opens a new shell in which the identity has been switched to a new user (in this case, the student user). To return to the original account, use the **exit** command to close the shell, as demonstrated next:

```
student@onecoursesource:~$ id
uid=1002(student) gid=1002(student)
➥groups=1002(student),4(adm),60(games),1001(ocs)
student@onecoursesource:~$ exit
logout
root@onecoursesource:~# id
uid=0(root) gid=0(root) groups=0(root)
```

The **-** option used with the **su** command has a special purpose. It allows you to switch to the other user account as if you were logging in to it directly. This results in all of that user's initialization files being executed before the new shell is provided. Typically this is the most desired behavior, but if you have a reason to not run all the initialization files, omit the **-** option to the **su** command.

7

The root user is not the only one who can use the **su** command, but it is the only account that does not require knowledge of the password for the account being switched to. For example, suppose you are logged in as a regular user and you want to execute commands as the root user. You can use the **su** command to gain access to the root account, but you will be prompted for the root password, as shown here:

```
student@onecoursesource:~$ su - root
Password:
root@onecoursesource:~#
```

Security Highlight

It is a bad habit to log in as the root user to perform tasks. The more often you do this, the more likely your system can be compromised. For example, suppose you log in as the root user every day, and then one day you take a coffee break, leaving your terminal exposed. As you might imagine, it is much better to log in as a regular user and then use the **su** command to execute specific administrative commands. Also, you should immediately exit from the privileged shell once the task is complete.

In some cases you may want to provide some users with the ability to execute specific tasks as the administrator. This is the purpose of the **sudo** command. With the **sudo** command, authorized users can execute specific commands as the administrator, as demonstrated in Example 7-6.

Example 7-6 *Using the **sudo** Command*

```
student@onecoursesource:~$ apt-get install joe
E: Could not open lock file /var/lib/dpkg/lock - open (13:Permission denied)
E: Unable to lock the administration directory (/var/lib/dpkg/), are you root?
student@onecoursesource:~$ sudo apt-get install joe
[sudo] password for student:
Reading package lists... Done
```

```
Building dependency tree
Reading state information... Done
The following NEW packages will be installed:
  joe
0 upgraded, 1 newly installed, 0 to remove and 575 not upgraded.
Need to get 351 kB of archives.
After this operation, 1,345 kB of additional disk space will be used.
Get:1 http://us.archive.ubuntu.com/ubuntu/ trusty/universe joe amd64 3.7-2.3ubuntu1
➥[351 kB]
Fetched 351 kB in 0s (418 kB/s)
Selecting previously unselected package joe. (Reading database ... 172002 files and
➥directories currently installed.)
Preparing to unpack .../joe_3.7-2.3ubuntu1_amd64.deb ...
Unpacking joe (3.7-2.3ubuntu1) ...
Processing triggers for man-db (2.6.7.1-1ubuntu1) ...
Setting up joe (3.7-2.3ubuntu1) ...
update-alternatives: using /usr/bin/joe to provide /usr/bin/editor (editor) in auto mode
student@onecoursesource:~$
```

Note that in Example 7-6, the student user could not run the **apt-get** command initially. This command, which is used to install software on the system, requires administrative privileges. The **sudo** command was used to temporarily elevate the student user's privileges to allow execution of the **apt-get** command as the root user.

Also note the highlighted areas in Example 7-6 where the student user is asked for a password. This is the password for the student account, not the root account. The student user does not need to know the root password if the **sudo** access has been set up prior to executing this command.

This access is configured in a file called the **/etc/sudoers** file. To provide access to the student account, the following entry was made in this file:

```
root@onecoursesource:~# grep student /etc/sudoers
student ALL=/usr/bin/apt-get
```

The format for this line is ***account_name SYSTEM=command***. Both ***account_name*** and ***command*** are self-explanatory, but the ***SYSTEM*** value requires a bit of explanation. This could be the host name of the system where this configuration line is valid. In this case, it could have been set to "onecoursesource" because that is the current system's host name. However, if this /etc/sudoers file were copied to another system, the file would have to be updated. Using **ALL** as a value here means "no matter what system this file is on, this line applies."

Note that the **/etc/sudoers** file should not be modified directly, but rather with the **visudo** command. This command performs basic syntax checking and issues an error message if there is a problem:

```
>>> /etc/sudoers: syntax error near line 22 <<<
What now?
Options are: ?
  (e)dit sudoers file again
  e(x)it without saving changes to sudoers file
  (Q)uit and save changes to sudoers file (DANGER!)

What now? x
root@onecoursesource:~#
```

Also note that only the root user can edit the **/etc/sudoers** file.

Security Highlight

A complete discussion of **sudo** is beyond the scope of this book. It is a powerful tool with many configurable options and features. Consider investigating this topic on your own by exploring the documentation (man and info pages) for the **sudo** and **visudo** commands as well as the **sudoers** file.

Most importantly, only provide **sudo** access when necessary. Too much access can result in a serious security risk.

Restricting User Accounts

Several methods can be used to limit user accounts, including file permissions and SELinux. These topics are discussed in later chapters, but it makes sense to cover one method now: Pluggable Authentication Modules (PAM).

PAM is a powerful tool that allows an administrator to provide many restrictions to user accounts. For example:

- PAM can be used to limit access to a system by time or date.
- PAM can limit system resource utilization after the user logs in, including limiting how many processes a user can run or how much RAM the user's processes can use.
- PAM can be applied to specific login commands. This allows for different rules for when a user logs in locally versus when they log in remotely.
- PAM can be used to create additional log entries for specific login events.

The preceding list details just a few features that PAM can provide. PAM is a set of libraries that is called by authentication-based software such as local command-line login, SSH (Secure Shell), and FTP (File Transfer Protocol). Essentially, every time a user account needs to be authenticated, PAM libraries are used to verify and validate the user.

PAM has a primary configuration file (**/etc/pam.conf**), but it is rarely used. Instead, each authentication-based software program has a separate configuration file under the **/etc/pam.d** directory, as shown in Example 7-7.

Example 7-7 *The /etc/pam.d Directory*

```
root@onecoursesource:~# ls /etc/pam.d
accountsservice                   cups-daemon               login
atd                               dovecot                   newusers
chfn                              gdm                       other
chpasswd                          gdm-autologin             passwd
chsh                              gdm-launch-environment    polkit-1
common-account                    gdm-password              pop3
common-auth                       gnome-screensaver         ppp
common-password                   imap                      samba
common-session                    lightdm                   sshd
common-session-noninteractive     lightdm-autologin         su
cron                              lightdm-greeter           sudo
```

7

The files you see in this directory will depend on what software is installed. For example, the **ls** command was executed prior to installing an FTP server. Example 7-8 highlights a new file that appears after the vsftpd software is installed.

Example 7-8 *New File After vsftpd Installation*

```
root@onecoursesource:~# ls /etc/pam.d
accountsservice                dovecot                    other
atd                            gdm                        passwd
chfn                           gdm-autologin              polkit-1
chpasswd                       gdm-launch-environment     pop3
chsh                           gdm-password               ppp
common-account                 gnome-screensaver          samba
common-auth                    imap                       sshd
common-password                lightdm                    su
common-session                 lightdm-autologin          sudo
common-session-noninteractive  lightdm-greeter            vsftpd
cron                           login
cups-daemon                    newusers
```

To understand how PAM works, we will focus on a single service: Secure Shell. An example of a PAM configuration file (without comment lines and blank lines) for Secure Shell is shown in Example 7-9.

Example 7-9 *Sample PAM Configuration File for SSH*

```
root@onecoursesource:~# grep -v "^#" /etc/pam.d/sshd | grep -v "^$"
@include common-auth
account    required    pam_nologin.so
@include common-account
session [success=ok ignore=ignore module_unknown=ignore default=bad]
➥pam_selinux.so close
session    required    pam_loginuid.so
session    optional    pam_keyinit.so force revoke
@include common-session
session    optional    pam_motd.so  motd=/run/motd.dynamic noupdate
session    optional    pam_motd.so # [1]
session    optional    pam_mail.so standard noenv # [1]
session    required    pam_limits.so
session    required    pam_env.so # [1]
session    required    pam_env.so user_readenv=1 envfile=/etc/default/locale
session [success=ok ignore=ignore module_unknown=ignore default=bad]
➥pam_selinux.so open
@include common-password
```

Each line represents a PAM rule. There are two types of lines: standard lines that have three or four values (like **account required pam_nologin.so**) and **@include** lines that are used to pull in more rules from another file.

For standard lines, the three possible values are described in Table 7-5.

Table 7-5 PAM Values

Value	Description
Category	Can be either **account, auth, password**, or **session**. See Table 7-6 for details.
Control	Used to determine what action to take if the module value returns "failure." See Table 7-7 for details.
Module	This is a library (technically called a *module* in PAM) that performs a specific task and returns either "success" or "failure." Many modules are available, and each one is designed to perform a specific task related to authenticating users.
Argument(s)	Arguments to the module that are used to change the module's behavior. Some modules do not use arguments, while others may require arguments. In a sense, this is much like the arguments you send to a command that you execute within the shell.

PAM Categories

A category is essentially one of the four primary operations that PAM can perform. These are described in more detail in Table 7-6.

Table 7-6 PAM Categories

Category	Description
account	Used to verify that a user account has the rights to use a service. This could include checking if a user can log in via the network or at a specific time of day.
auth	Used to authenticate (that is, verify) that the user is who they claim to be, normally by having the user provide a password for the account that they are attempting to use.
password	Used to update authentication methods, such as providing a new password for an account.
session	Used to perform actions prior to and after a service has been provided to a user. For example, this could be used to limit a user account access.

It is important to note that when an authentication request is made by an authentication program, the program will ask for the modules of a specific category to be executed. For example, if the user is logging in via SSH, then the SSH utility will attempt to validate the user account name first. This is accomplished by asking PAM to run the modules in the **account** category. If all of these modules run successfully, then the SSH utility will attempt to authenticate the user, perhaps by verifying that the user provided the correct password for the account (there are other methods available for SSH). This is accomplished by asking PAM to run the modules in the **auth** category.

Assuming these modules return "success," the SSH utility may run the **session** modules to set up the user's session. The term "may" is used because it is up to the developers who wrote the SSH utility as to which of these PAM categories it calls and when the call is made. It is up to you as the administrator to fine-tune which modules are called to customize how users are granted access to the system.

Figure 7-2 provides a visual demonstration of how this process works. The "S" arrows in this figure indicate the action that is taken if PAM returns "success" when the modules are run. The "F" arrows in this figure indicate the action that is taken if PAM returns "failure" when the modules are run.

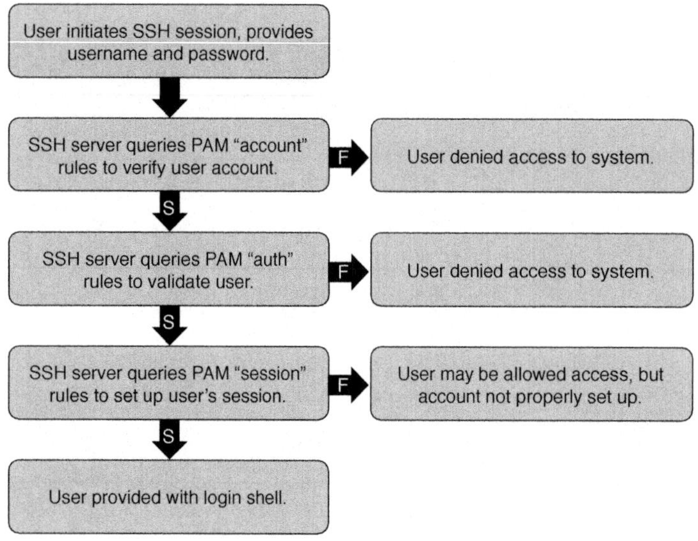

Figure 7-2 *SSH Using PAM Categories*

PAM Control Values

What determines whether or not a category is successful is largely dependent on the control values. These values are described in more detail in Table 7-7.

Table 7-7 PAM Controls

Control	Description
requisite	If the corresponding module returns a "failure," the rest of the category's modules are not executed and the category returns an overall result of "failure."
required	If the corresponding module returns a "failure," the overall result of the category will be "failure." However, additional modules will be executed (their return values are not used for the overall return value of the category).
sufficient	If the corresponding module returns a "success," the overall result of the category will be "success," without any additional modules executed. If, however, a previous module returned "failure" when a "required" control was specified, then this result is ignored.
optional	The outcome of the corresponding module is not relevant unless it is the only module for the service. Typically this value is used for performing an action during the authentication process that does not have to be tested for success or failure.

Note that you will likely encounter a more complex control type, which you can see an example of in the following output:

```
root@onecoursesource:~# grep ^auth /etc/pam.d/common-auth
auth     [success=1 default=ignore]     pam_unix.so nullok_secure
auth     requisite                pam_deny.so
auth     required               pam_permit.so
auth     optional               pam_cap.so
```

The **[success=1 default=ignore]** control type allows an administrator to further fine-tune the behavior of the PAM, but this is very complex and largely outside the scope of this book. If you review the man page for **pam.conf**, you will find there are dozens of these complex control values.

For this book, we focus on the four primary control types.

PAM Modules

The PAM modules are the actual code that is executed. Each module performs a specific task and should return a value of success or failure. Some of the more useful PAM modules are described in Table 7-8.

Table 7-8 Useful PAM Modules

Module	Description
pam_access	Used for "location-based" access control
pam_cracklib	Used to modify password policies
pam_deny	Always returns a "failure" result
pam_env	Used to set environment variables
pam_mkhomedir	Used to create home directories
pam_nologin	Used to determine if a user's login shell is **/etc/nologin**
pam_tally	Used to count login attempts
pam_time	Used for "time-based" access control
pam_timestamp	Used to control access based on last login
pam_unix	Used for standard user authentication

Security Highlight

The PAM configuration files already contain several PAM modules that are used by authentication software. You will likely be tempted to learn what these modules do, and you are encouraged to explore them. However, do not make changes or remove these modules from the configuration files unless you understand the modules and realize the impact such changes will have on authentication software.

This book focuses on how to make specific changes to some of these PAM modules and on adding key PAM modules to the configuration files. Not every PAM module will be explored in detail.

Using PAM to Alter the Password Policy

A common use of PAM is to modify the default password policy. As Table 7-9 illustrates, you can provide arguments to the pam_cracklib module to modify many password settings.

Table 7-9 Password Settings for pam_cracklib

Argument	Description
difok=N	How many characters must be different in the new password.
difignore=N	How many characters need to be in new password before ignoring the restriction of **difok** setting.
minlen=N	The minimum number of characters allowed in the password.

Argument	Description
retry=N	How many times to prompt user before displaying an error message (default is 1).
type=name	Changes the message displayed to the user when changing their password (default is Unix).

The **minlen** argument works in conjunction with four additional arguments: **dcredit** (digit credit), **lcredit** (lowercase credit), **ocredit** (other character credit) and **ucredit** (uppercase credit). Each of these items may be assigned a value that "goes toward" fulfilling the number of minimum characters in the password.

For example, the following requires a minimum password length of 12 characters, but using an uppercase character counts for three of the 12 character minimum (using more than one uppercase character does not provide any additional credits):

```
password     required     pam_cracklib.so minlen=12 ucredit=3
```

NOTE Not all Linux distributions have the cracklib module installed by default. When using Debian-based systems, execute the following command as the root user to install this module (if needed): **apt-get install libpam-cracklib**. On Red Hat–based systems, run this command: **yum install libpam-cracklib**.

WHAT COULD GO WRONG? Be very careful when changing PAM configuration files. You can easily lock the root account. As a suggestion, after changing a PAM configuration file, you should stay logged in to the system and attempt a separate login as the root user to confirm you can still gain access to the system. Also, be sure to always back up a configuration file before making any changes to make it easier to change the file back to its original values.

In addition to the pam_cracklib library, you can use the pam_unix library to modify password policies. For example, you can use the **remember=N** argument to have PAM remember *N* number of passwords (so users cannot just reuse the same passwords). The old passwords are stored in **/etc/security/opasswd** in encrypted format.

Here's an example of password settings in the **/etc/pam.d/common-password** file:

```
Password     required     pam_cracklib.so minlength=12 ucredit=3
type=Linux
password     [success=1 default=ignore]     pam_unix.so obscure
use_authtok try_first_pass sha512 remember=7
```

Summary

The Linux operating system uses user accounts to control access to key components, including files and directories. In this chapter, you learned how to manage these user accounts. This included how to create, modify, secure, and delete user accounts, as well as how to use special group account features, including restricted user accounts.

Key Terms

daemon, NFS, skel directory, GECOS, LDAP, NIS, Active Directory, Samba, NSS, PAM

Review Questions

1. User passwords and password-aging data are stored in the **/etc/_____** file.
2. Which UID makes the root account the administrator on the system?
   - **A.** 0
   - **B.** 1
   - **C.** 10
   - **D.** 125
3. What does the value **7** represent in the following line from the **/etc/shadow** file?

   ```
   sync:*:16484:0:99999:7:::
   ```

   - **A.** The date of last password change field
   - **B.** The minimum password age field
   - **C.** The maximum password age field
   - **D.** The password warning period field
4. The **/etc/default/_____** file contains default values used by the useradd command.
5. PAM configuration files are stored in the **/etc/_____** directory.

Develop an Account Security Policy

An important component of this book is the focus on making systems more secure. In modern IT environments, security is a very important topic, and learning how to secure a system early will help you strengthen your Linux skill set.

Most of the parts in this book end with a chapter that focuses just on security. In these chapters, you learn how to secure a particular component of Linux. The focus of this chapter is on securing your group and user accounts.

You have a large number of tools and features available to you to help you secure Linux. Although not all of these can be covered in this book, you will be exposed to a good variety of them.

After reading this chapter and completing the exercises, you will be able to do the following:

Use Kali Linux to perform security probes on systems

Create a security policy for user accounts

Introducing Kali Linux

Previously we discussed different Linux distributions, including how some distributions are very focused on a specific feature. There are many security-based distributions, some of which are natively more secure by default. Others provide tools and features designed for you to enhance security in your environment. Figure 8-1 displays the most popular security-based Linux distributions, according to distrowatch.com.

1. Kali Linux (15)
Kali Linux (formerly known as BackTrack) is a Debian-based distribution with a collection of security and forensics tools. It features timely security updates, support for the ARM architecture, a choice of four popular desktop environments, and seamless upgrades to newer versions.

2. Parrot Security OS (29)
Parrot Security OS is a Debian-based, security-oriented distribution featuring a collection of utilities designed for penetration testing, computer forensics, reverse engineering, hacking, privacy, anonymity and cryptography. The product, developed by Frozenbox, comes with MATE as the default desktop environment.

3. Tails (31)
The Amnesic Incognito Live System (Tails) is a Debian-based live DVD/USB with the goal of providing complete Internet anonymity for the user. The product ships with several Internet applications, including web browser, IRC client, mail client and instant messenger, all pre-configured with security in mind and with all traffic anonymised. To achieve this, Incognito uses the Tor network to make Internet traffic very hard to trace.

4. Qubes OS (57)
Qubes OS is a security-oriented, Fedora-based desktop Linux distribution whose main concept is "security by isolation" by using domains implemented as lightweight Xen virtual machines. It attempts to combine two contradictory goals: how to make the isolation between domains as strong as possible, mainly due to clever architecture that minimises the amount of trusted code, and how to make this isolation as seamless and easy as possible.

5. BlackArch Linux (61)
BlackArch Linux is an Arch Linux-based distribution designed for penetration testers and security researchers. It is supplied as a live DVD image that comes with several lightweight window managers, including Fluxbox, Openbox, Awesome and spectrwm. It ships with over a thousand specialist tools for penetration testing and forensic analysis.

6. ClearOS (65)
ClearOS is a small business server operating system with server, networking, and gateway functions. It is designed primarily for homes, small, medium, and distributed environments. It is managed from a web based user interface, but can also be completely managed and tuned from the command line. ClearOS is available in a free Community Edition, which includes available open source updates and patches from its upstream sources. ClearOS is also offered in a Home and Business Edition which receives additional testing of updates and only uses tested code for updates. Professional tech-support is also available. Currently ClearOS offers around 100+ different features which can be installed through the onboard ClearOS Marketplace.

7. Alpine Linux (69)
Alpine Linux is a community developed operating system designed for x86 routers, firewalls, VPNs, VoIP boxes and servers. It was designed with security in mind; it has proactive security features like PaX and SSP that prevent security holes in the software to be exploited. The C library used is musl and the base tools are all in BusyBox. Those are normally found in embedded systems and are smaller than the tools found in GNU/Linux systems.

Figure 8-1 *Popular Security-Based Distributions*

One of the more popular distributions is Kali Linux, a distro designed to provide you with tools to test security. We will make use of this distribution throughout this book. After you install Kali Linux, you can access the tools by clicking **Applications**, as demonstrated in Figure 8-2.

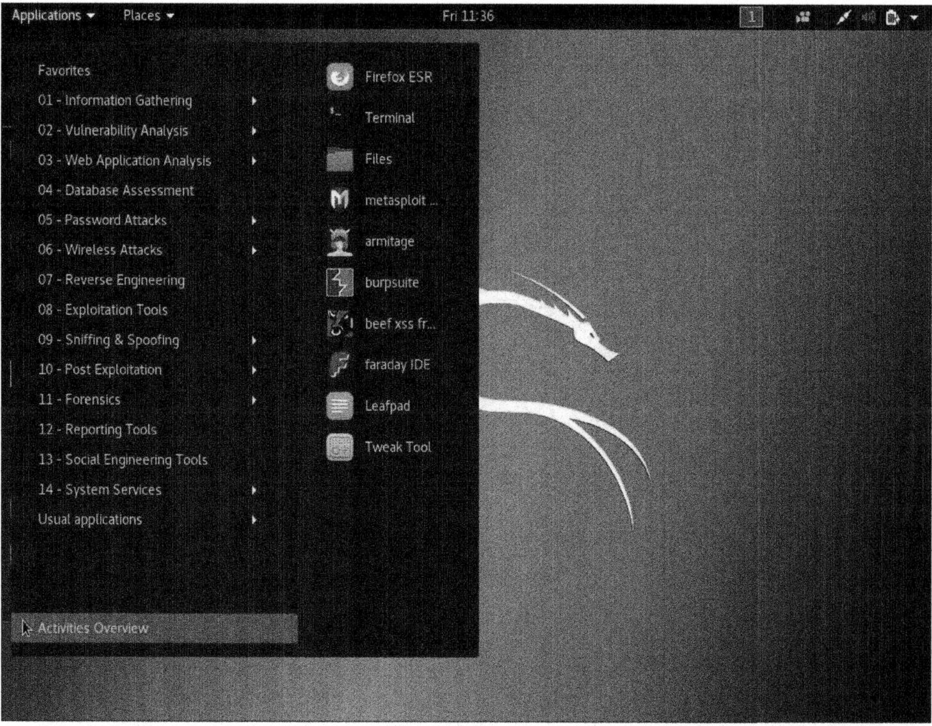

Figure 8-2 *Kali Linux Applications*

The tools are broken into different categories. For example, the "Password Attacks" category includes tools to test the strength of the passwords for user accounts. We will not cover all the tools available on Kali Linux, but each part of this book does include a discussion about some of the more important tools, and you can explore the others on your own.

Security Principles

The term *security* should be better defined before we continue any further. Although it may seem like a simple term, it is rather complex.

Most people think of "security" as something designed to keep hackers from getting into a system, but it really encompasses much more than that. Your goal in terms of security is to make systems, services, and data available to the correct entities while denying access to these resources by unauthorized entities.

We use the term *entities* because we are not just referring to people. For example, you may have a service that provides user account information to other systems. This information should not be provided to systems that are not supposed to have access. So, providing access to the service and the data provided by the service is done for specific systems, not specific people.

You also have to find the right balance between making a system secure and making it available. In other words, if you lock a system down so tightly that authorized entities cannot get the required access, you have essentially made the system less secure.

You also have to keep an eye on authorized users who may attempt to gain unauthorized access. Internal users have an edge because they already are past one level of security since they have access using their own accounts. They also tend to be trusted by default, so security personnel and administrators often overlook them as a source of unauthorized access.

External hackers may also try to compromise your security by making a system deny access to authorized entities (actually, internal hackers may also do this). Some people take great delight in making key servers (like your web server) inaccessible, or in posting embarrassing messages to harm the company's reputation.

Obviously there is a lot to consider when putting together a plan to secure your Linux systems, and you will find that no single book is going to address everything. But, just suppose for a moment that there was such a book and suppose that you followed every suggestion provided by this magical book. Even then, your systems would not be 100% secure. There is always a way to compromise a system if someone has enough time, resources, and knowledge. Securing a system is a job that is never complete, and a security plan should go through consistent revision as you learn more and discover new techniques.

Consider securing a Linux system or network similar to securing a bank. You have likely seen movies or TV shows where a complicated bank security system is compromised by very clever and determined thieves. It is your goal to make your system so secure that it requires very clever and determined hackers in order to have a chance to compromise it.

Creating a Security Policy

A good security policy is one that provides a blueprint for administrators and users to follow. It should include, at the very least, the following:

- A set of rules that determines what is and is not allowed on systems. For example, this set of rules could describe the password policy that all users must follow.
- A means to ensure that all rules are being followed. This could include actively running programs that probe system security as well as viewing system log files for suspicious activity.
- A well-defined plan to handle when a system is compromised: Who is notified, what actions should be taken, and so on. This is often referred to as an *incident response plan*.
- A way to actively change the policy as new information becomes available. This information should be actively sought out. For example, most distributions have a way to learn about new vulnerabilities and tools such as patches and updates, as well as techniques to address those vulnerabilities.

Securing Accounts

You must consider several components when securing user accounts. These include the following:

- Physical security of the system or network
- Education of users
- Ensuring accounts are not susceptible to attack

Physical Security

Often IT security personnel will neglect to consider physical security as part of the security policy. This is sometimes the result of thinking "physical security is not a responsibility of the IT department," as many companies have a separate department that is in charge of physical security. If this is the case, the two departments should work together to ensure the best overall security policy. If this is not the case, then physical security may be entirely the responsibility of the IT department.

When crafting a policy that includes physical security, you should consider the following:

- Secure physical access to the systems in your organization, particularly the mission-critical servers, such as mail and web servers. Be sure to consider which systems have the necessary access and authority to make changes on other systems.

- Secure physical access to the network. Unauthorized people should not have physical access to any network assets.
- Prevent unauthorized people from viewing your systems, particularly the terminal windows. Hackers can use information gathered from viewing keyboard input and data displayed on terminal windows. This information can be used to compromise security.
- Password-protect the BIOS of mission-critical systems, especially if these systems cannot be 100% physically secured.
- Protect systems from theft and hardware errors.

There are many other aspects to physical security that you should consider. The purpose of this section is to encourage you to think about including physical security as part of how you secure your systems. Consider this the first line of defense of a multilayer security policy.

Educating Users

Years ago one of the authors of this book was teaching a Linux security class and he said (mostly as a joke) "whatever you do, don't write down your password and tape it under your keyboard." After a good chuckle by the class, one student said "no one really does that, do they?" During the lunch break, some of the students took a trip around their office, flipping over keyboards and discovering three passwords. Actually, a fourth password was found taped to the monitor of the employee.

Clearly, users play a critical role in the security policy. Often they are unaware of how their actions can compromise security. When creating the security policy, you should consider how to encourage users to make your system more secure, rather than less secure. For example, consider the following:

- Encourage users to use strong passwords.
- Warn users about installing software that is not approved or supported by your organization.
- Encourage users to report any suspicious activity immediately.
- Ask users to be careful about accessing system-critical systems when logged into unsecure locations (like a public Wi-Fi spot). If users must access system-critical systems from unsecure locations, consider implementing a VPN (virtual private network) technology.
- Warn users that they should never share their accounts or passwords with anyone.
- Educate users about clicking links from emails or opening attachments from unknown sources. These often contain viruses or worms, or they may be a spoofing attempt (an attempt to gain account information by pretending to be a valid resource). Even if the sender is known or trusted, if their email account is compromised, the messages may contain malware.

Educating users is a fairly large topic by itself, but one that you should spend considerable time and effort on when putting together a security policy. We encourage you to explore this topic more, as further discussion is beyond the scope of this book.

Account Security

You can take specific actions on the system in order to make accounts more secure. Some of these actions will be covered later in this book. For example, you can make user accounts more secure by using the features of PAM (Pluggable Authentication Modules), a topic that was covered in detail in Chapter 7, "Managing User Accounts." Another example: Chapter 25, "System Logging," discusses using system logs—a topic that is important when it comes to securing user accounts. System logs are used to determine if someone is trying to gain unauthorized access to a system.

This section covers a collection of user account security topics. Each topic is briefly explained, and then we provide an idea of how you would incorporate the topic within a security policy.

User Account Names

Consider that for a hacker to gain unauthorized access to a system, they would need two pieces of information: a user name and a user password. Preventing a hacker from being able to figure out a user name would make the process of hacking into your systems more difficult. Consider using account names that are not easy to guess.

For example, do not create an account named "bsmith" for Bob Smith. This would be easy for a hacker to guess if the hacker knows that Bob Smith works for the company. Consider something like "b67smith" instead for a user account name. Remember, your employees may be named on the company website or in news that identifies their relationship to the company.

Incorporate this into a security policy: Create a rule that all user accounts must be something that is not easy to guess by knowing the person's real name. Also use mail aliases (see Chapter 20, "Network Service Configuration: Essential Services") to hide user names from the outside world.

Users with No Password

As you can probably guess, a user with no password poses a considerable security risk. With no password at all in the **/etc/shadow** file, only the user's name is required to log into the system.

Incorporate this into a security policy: Create a crontab entry (see Chapter 14, "crontab and at," for information about crontab entries) to execute the following command on a regular basis: **grep "^[^:]*::" /etc/shadow**. Alternately, you can use one of the security tools covered later in this chapter.

Preventing a User from Changing a Password

In certain use cases, you do not want a user to change the account password. For example, suppose you have a guest account, designed for restricted system access for non-employees. You do not want whoever uses this account to change the password because that would prevent the next guest from using the account.

If you make the **min** field of the **/etc/shadow** file a higher value than the **max** field, then the user cannot change the account password (note: on some distributions, like Kali, the options are **-n** for the **min** field and **-x** for the **max** field):

```
passwd -m 99999 -M 99998 guest
```

Incorporate this into a security policy: Determine which accounts should have this restriction and apply the restriction as needed. Remember to change the password regularly so past "guests" may not access the system later simply because they know the password.

Application Accounts

The guest account that was described in the previous example could also be an application account. For an application account, only command-line login should be permitted (no GUI should be displayed on the system). Then, change the last field of the **/etc/passwd** file for the user to an application, like the following:

```
guest:x:9000:9000:Guest account:/bin/guest_app
```

The **/bin/guest_app** would run a program that provides limited access to the system. You could also consider using a restricted shell, as described in Chapter 7, if you want the account to have access to more than one application.

Incorporate this into a security policy: Determine which accounts should have this restriction and apply the restriction as needed.

Enabling Process Accounting

A software tool called psacct can be used to keep track of all commands executed by users. This is very important on systems where you suspect hacking attempts might be successful. This tool needs to be downloaded and then installed using the following steps:

1. Download the tool from http://ftp.gnu.org/gnu/acct/.
2. Execute the **gunzip acct*** command to unzip the downloaded file.
3. Execute the **tar -xvf acct*** command to extract the file contents.
4. Execute the **cd** command to change into the directory that was created by the **tar** command.
5. Execute the **./configure; make; make install** command to install the software.

After the software has been installed, you can start the service by first creating the log file where the service will store data:

```
mkdir /var/log/account
touch /var/log/account/pact
```

Then start the service with the following command:

```
accton on
```

After the service has been started, you can view commands executed by using the **lastcomm** command:

```
root@onecoursesource:~# lastcomm
more                 root     pts/0       0.00 secs Sun Feb 25 15:42
bash              F  root     pts/0       0.00 secs Sun Feb 25 15:42
kworker/dying     F  root     __          0.00 secs Sun Feb 25 15:31
cron             SF  root     __          0.00 secs Sun Feb 25 15:39
sh                S  root     __          0.00 secs Sun Feb 25 15:39
lastcomm             root     pts/0       0.00 secs Sun Feb 25 15:37
accton            S  root     pts/0       0.00 secs Sun Feb 25 15:37
```

Useful information is also provided by the **ac** command. For example, to see a summary of all login times for each user in the last 24 hours, use the **ac -p --individual-totals** command.

Incorporate this into a security policy: On critical systems that may be vulnerable (such as web and mail servers), incorporate this software package and use a crontab entry (see Chapter 14 for information about crontab entries) to generate regular reports (hourly or daily).

Avoiding Commands Being Run as the Superuser

A large number of anecdotal stories involve system administrators creating destruction and wreaking havoc on systems because of commands that were run as the root user accidently. Consider a situation in which you run the **rm -r /*** command. As a regular user, you may end up deleting your own files, but permissions (discussed in Chapter 9, "File Permissions") prevent you from deleting any files on the system that you don't own. However, if that command is run by someone logged in as the root user, then all files could be destroyed.

Incorporate this into a security policy: Always log in as a regular user and use the **sudo** or **su** command's permission (see Chapter 9 for details about **sudo** and **su**) to gain temporary root access. When you're finished running the command that required root access, return to the regular account.

8

Security Tools

Many security tools can be used to search for security weaknesses. This section describes and demonstrates several of these tools using Kali Linux, but these tools can be installed and used on other distributions as well. The advantage of Kali Linux is that these tools are installed and configured by default.

On Kali Linux, most of these tools can be accessed by clicking **Applications** and then **05 – Password Attacks**, as demonstrated in Figure 8-3.

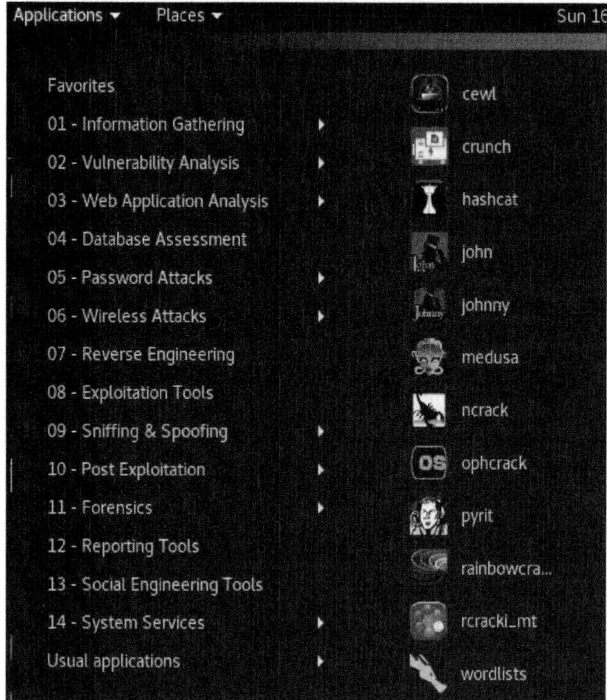

Figure 8-3 *Password Attacks*

You might also consider exploring "13 – Social Engineering Tools." Social engineering is a technique for gathering system information from users by using nontechnical methods. For example, a hacker might call an employee pretending to be a member of the company's IT support team and attempt to gather information from the employee (like their user name, password, and so on).

The john and Johnny Tools

The john utility (full name: John the Ripper) is a command-line password hacking tool. The advantage of a command-line tool is that it is something that you can automate via a crontab entry (see Chapter 14 for information about crontab entries), allowing you to schedule this tool to run on a regular basis.

The Johnny utility is a GUI-based version of the john utility. The advantage of this GUI tool is that it allows you to run **john** commands without having to memorize all of the command options.

In both cases, you need to have a file that contains both **/etc/passwd** and **/etc/shadow** entries. You can make this file by running the following command:

```
cat /etc/passwd /etc/shadow > file_to_store
```

When running Johnny, you can load this file into the utility by clicking the **Open password file** option. Next, select the accounts you want to try to crack and then click the **Start new attack** button. Each account appears as it is cracked, as shown in Figure 8-4.

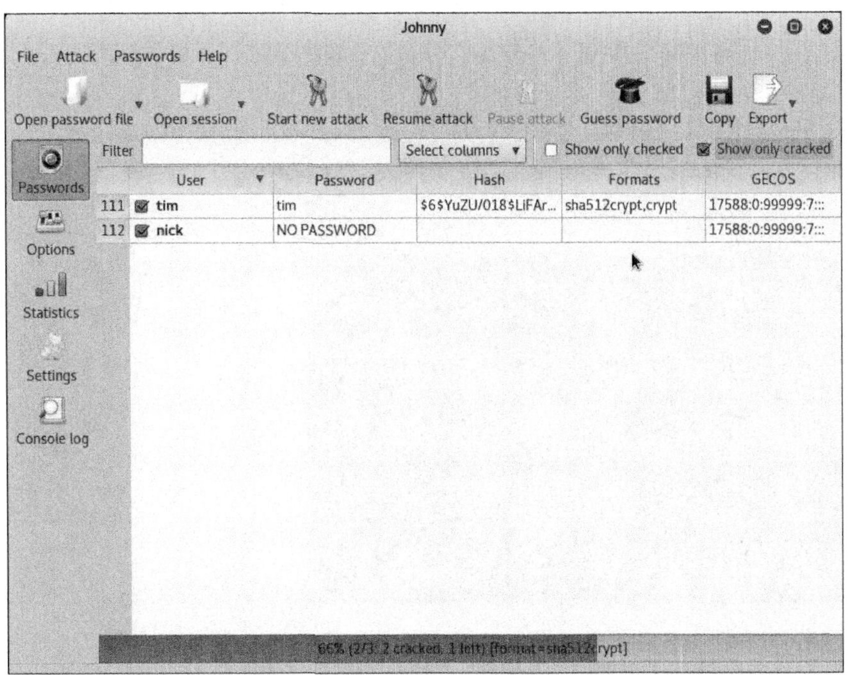

Figure 8-4 *Cracked Passwords*

To see what **john** command was executed, click the **Console log** button, as shown in Figure 8-5.

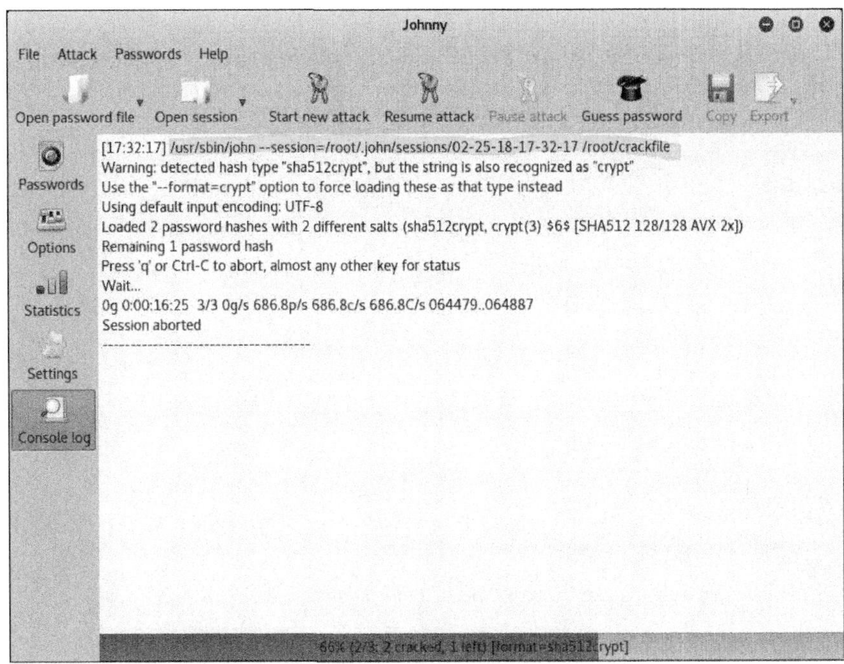

Figure 8-5 *The **john** Command*

The hydra tool

Whereas the john utility makes use of a file of user accounts and passwords, the hydra tool actively probes a system via a specific protocol. For example, the following command would use the hydra tool to attack the local system via FTP (File Transfer Protocol):

```
hydra -l user -P /usr/share/set/src/fasttrack/wordlist.txt ftp://127.0.0.1
```

Note that you should not run a command like this on any system for which you do not have written authorization to perform security analysis. Attempts to run this command on another organization's system can be considered an illegal hacking attempt.

The wordlist file is one of many available on the system. Click **Applications, 05 – Password Attacks, wordlists** to display a list of word files, as shown in Figure 8-6.

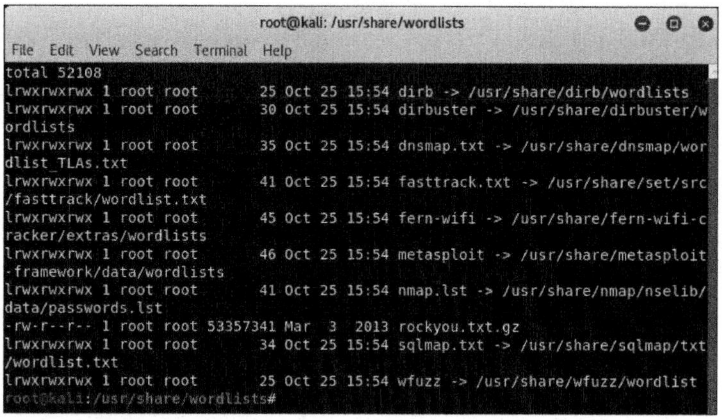

```
root@kali: /usr/share/wordlists
File  Edit  View  Search  Terminal  Help
total 52108
lrwxrwxrwx 1 root root       25 Oct 25 15:54 dirb -> /usr/share/dirb/wordlists
lrwxrwxrwx 1 root root       30 Oct 25 15:54 dirbuster -> /usr/share/dirbuster/w
ordlists
lrwxrwxrwx 1 root root       35 Oct 25 15:54 dnsmap.txt -> /usr/share/dnsmap/wor
dlist_TLAs.txt
lrwxrwxrwx 1 root root       41 Oct 25 15:54 fasttrack.txt -> /usr/share/set/src
/fasttrack/wordlist.txt
lrwxrwxrwx 1 root root       45 Oct 25 15:54 fern-wifi -> /usr/share/fern-wifi-c
racker/extras/wordlists
lrwxrwxrwx 1 root root       46 Oct 25 15:54 metasploit -> /usr/share/metasploit
-framework/data/wordlists
lrwxrwxrwx 1 root root       41 Oct 25 15:54 nmap.lst -> /usr/share/nmap/nselib/
data/passwords.lst
-rw-r--r-- 1 root root 53357341 Mar  3  2013 rockyou.txt.gz
lrwxrwxrwx 1 root root       34 Oct 25 15:54 sqlmap.txt -> /usr/share/sqlmap/txt
/wordlist.txt
lrwxrwxrwx 1 root root       25 Oct 25 15:54 wfuzz -> /usr/share/wfuzz/wordlist
root@kali:/usr/share/wordlists#
```

Figure 8-6 *Displaying Wordlists*

You can also find many wordlists online.

Summary

You have started the process of learning how to create a security policy. At the end of the five main parts of this book, you will expand on this knowledge. Based on what you learned in this chapter, you should have the information you need to create a security policy for user accounts, including using tools provided by Kali Linux to perform security scans.

Review Questions

1. Fill in the missing option so the user of the bob account can't change his password: **passwd _____ 99999 -M 99998 bob**

2. Which command can be used to find users who have no password?

   A. **find**

   B. **grep**

   C. **passwd**

   D. **search**

3. The _____ package provides process accounting.

4. Which of the following utilities can be used to perform password-cracking operations?

   A. john

   B. nick

   C. jill

   D. jim

5. Which command can be used to switch from a regular user to the root user?

A. switch

B. sed

C. du

D. su

One of the more critical elements of any operating system is the data. This data is stored on media devices, such as hard drives, DVDs, and USB drives. In order to organize and secure the data, Linux makes use of filesystems.

Understanding the features of filesystems and how to make use of tools to secure the data stored on the filesystems are important tasks for all users who work on the operating system. Regular users, for example, must learn how to protect their own files using permissions; whereas the system administrator must use a variety of skills to secure system files.

Part III

File and Data Storage

In Part III, "File and Data Storage," you will explore the following chapters:

- Chapter 9, "File Permissions," focuses on securing files using Linux permissions. This chapter also dives into more advanced topics, such as special permissions, the **umask**, access control lists, and file attributes.
- Chapter 10, "Manage Local Storage: Essentials," covers topics related to the concepts of local storage devices. This includes how to create partitions and filesystems, as well as some additional essential filesystem features.
- Chapter 11, "Manage Local Storage: Advanced Features," covers topics related to advanced features of local storage devices. This includes how to use autofs and create encrypted filesystems. You also learn about logical volume management, an alternative way of managing local storage devices
- Chapter 12, "Manage Network Storage," discusses making storage devices available across the network. Filesystem-sharing techniques such as Network File System, Samba, and iSCSI are included.
- Chapter 13, "Develop a Storage Security Policy," provides you with the means to create a security policy using the knowledge you acquire in Chapters 9, 10, 11, and 12.

File Permissions

Understanding file and directory permissions is critical for Linux security because Linux is a multiuser environment, and permissions are designed to protect your work from others. To understand permissions, you first need to know the types of permissions available in Linux and how they differ when applied to files versus to directories.

Once you understand the different permissions, you need to know how to set them. Linux provides two methods: the symbolic method and the octal (or numeric) method.

You also learn about special permissions in this chapter, including SUID, SGID, and sticky bit. These permissions provide special access to files and directories and are typically managed by the system administrator.

Several permission-related topics will also be introduced, including default permissions, access control lists (ACLs), and changing the user and group ownership of files and directories.

After reading this chapter and completing the exercises, you will be able to do the following:

Display and set standard Linux permissions

Use special Linux permissions to accomplish advanced security operations

Create a umask value for setting default permissions

Use access control lists to fine-tune the permissions on files and directories

Use file attributes to limit access to system files

Perform basic SELinux operations

Standard Permissions

Every file and directory has standard permissions (also called "read, write, and execute" permissions) that either allow or disallow a user access. Using these standard permissions is something that every Linux user should understand how to do, as this is the primary way a user will protect their files from other users.

Viewing Permissions

To view the permissions of a file or directory, use the **ls -l** command:

```
[student@localhost ~]$ ls -l /etc/chrony.keys
-rw-r-----. 1 root chrony 62 May  9  2018 /etc/chrony.keys
```

The first 10 characters of the output denote the file type (recall that if the character in the first position is a hyphen [–], it denotes a plain file, and **d** denotes a directory) and the permissions for the file. Permissions are broken into three sets: the user owner of the file (root in the previous example), the group owner (chrony), and all other users (referred to as "others").

Each set has three possible permissions: read (symbolized by **r**), write (**w**) and execute (**x**). If the permission is set, the character that symbolizes the permission is displayed. Otherwise, a hyphen (–) character is displayed to indicate that permission is not set. Thus, **r-x** means "read and execute are set, but write is not set."

Files Versus Directories

What read, write, and execute permissions really mean depends on whether the object is a file or directory. For files, these permissions mean the following:

- **Read**: Can view or copy file contents.
- **Write**: Can modify file contents.
- **Execute**: Can run the file like a program. After you create a program, you must make it executable before you can run it.

For directories, they mean the following:

- **Read**: Can list files in the directory.
- **Write**: Can add and delete files in the directory (requires execute permission).
- **Execute**: Can "**cd**" into the directory or use it in a pathname.

Security Highlight

The write permission on directories is potentially the most dangerous. If a user has write and execute permissions on one of your directories, then that user can delete every file in that directory.

Changing Permissions

The **chmod** command is used to change permissions on files. It can be used in two ways: symbolic method and octal method. With the octal method, the permissions are assigned numeric values:

- Read = 4
- Write = 2
- Execute = 1

With these numeric values, one number can be used to describe an entire permission set:

- 7 = **rwx**
- 6 = **rw-**
- 5 = **r-x**
- 4 = **r--**
- 3 = **-wx**
- 2 = **-w-**
- 1 = **--x**
- 0 = **---**

So, to change the permissions of a file to **rwxr-xr--**, you would execute the following command:

```
chmod 754 filename
```

With octal permissions, you should always provide three numbers, which will change all the permissions. But, what if you only want to change a single permission of the set? For that, use the symbolic method by passing three values to the **chmod** command, as shown in Table 9-1.

Table 9-1 Symbolic Method Values

Who	What	Permission
u = user owner	+	r
g = group owner	-	w
o = other	=	x
a= all sets		

The following demonstrates adding execute permission to all three sets (user owner, group owner, and others) using the symbolic method:

```
[student@localhost ~]$ ls -l display.sh
-rw-rw-r--. 1 student student 291 Apr 30 20:09 display.sh
[student@localhost ~]$ chmod a+x display.sh
[student@localhost ~]$ ls -l display.sh
-rwxrwxr-x. 1 student student 291 Apr 30 20:09 display.sh
```

Conversational Learning™ — Octal and Symbolic Permissions

Gary: Hi, Julia. I'm confused about something. Why do we have two methods that can be used to change permissions?

Julia: Hi, Gary. Do you mean octal and symbolic permissions?

Gary: Yes! It seems like only one is really needed.

Julia: Technically, yes. You can always use octal or always use symbolic if you want to. However, knowing both is going to make life easier for you.

Gary: What do you mean?

Julia: Let's say you just want to add read permission for the group owners and you choose to use the octal method. In that case, before you even run the **chmod** command, what would you need to do first?

Gary: Well, I'd have to list the current permissions to determine what values to use to add the new permission.

Julia: Exactly. Wouldn't it be easier to just use **g+r** in this case?

Gary: OK, so making small permission changes like that would be easier using the symbolic method. But why use the octal method then?

Julia: Well, what if you wanted to completely change the permission, or even just change a few? It would probably be easier to just determine the octal value and use that rather than doing something complicated like **u+wx,g-xo-wx**.

Gary: Oh, yeah, symbolic could get ugly in that situation. Got it. Thanks for the advice!

Julia: You are welcome!

Default Permissions

When a user creates a file or directory, the shell automatically sets default permissions. The default permissions are a configurable option. The **umask** command sets a value that is used to determine the default permissions for files and directories. Note that these default permissions are applied only when the file or directory is initially created.

The **umask** command is used to specify which default permissions to mask (not include) when creating a new file or directory.

The **umask** command accepts one argument: the mask value. The mask value is an octal value that is applied against the maximum possible permissions for new files or new directories, as shown in Table 9-2.

Table 9-2 Maximum Possible Permissions

Type	Maximum Possible Permission for New Item
File	**rw-rw-rw-**
Directory	**rwxrwxrwx**

As Table 9-2 demonstrates, new files are never given execute permissions. This permission set must always be added after the new file is created.

Figure 9-1 describes how a **umask** value of 027 would apply to new files versus how it would apply to new directories.

Description	File	Directories
Maximum	rw- rw- rw-	rwx rwx rwx
Umask Applied	--- -M- MM-	--- -M- MM-
Result	rw- r-- ---	rwx r-x --x

Figure 9-1 *Applying a **umask** value of 027 to Files and Directories*

While any octal value can be used to determine the permission mask, there are values that are more commonly used. Table 9-3 demonstrates the effect these commonly used **umask** values have on new files and directories.

Table 9-3 Commonly Used **umask** Values

Value	Files	Directories
002	**rw-rw-r--**	**rwxrwxr-x**
022	**rw-r--r--**	**rwxr-xr-x**
027	**rw-r-----**	**rwxr-x---**
077	**rw-------**	**rwx------**

Note that you can also use symbolic methods of specifying a **umask**. For example, the **umask rw-rwr---** command is the same as the **umask 002** command.

Each shell has its own **umask** value. If you change the **umask** in one shell, it will not affect the **umask** value in any other shell. To make a persistent change to your **umask** across logins, add the **umask** command to the **~/.bash_profile** file.

It is important that you understand that the **umask** value is only to provide an easy way to specify default permissions for files and directories. After a file or directory has been created, the **chmod** command can be used to adjust the permissions to meet a specific situation.

What Could Go Wrong?

Sometimes it can be really frustrating to determine why you cannot access a file or directory. For example, consider the following command:

```
bob@onecoursesource:~# cp sample /etc/skel
cp: cannot create regular file '/etc/skel/sample1': Permission denied
```

What is the problem? Keep in mind that several permissions are checked, like the read permission on the **sample** file, the execute permissions on the **/**, **etc**, and **skel** directories, as well as the write permissions on the **skel** directory.

To discover the error, first look closely at the output of the error message. In this case, the problem seems to be with creating the file in the **/etc/skel** directory, not with the **sample** file itself (which would have resulted in an error like "cannot open 'sample1' for reading").

Next, determine if you can get into all of the directories by either looking at the permissions for each one or using the **cd** command to move into each directory. Lastly, look for the write permission on the destination directory

Special Permissions

Whereas regular (non-administrative) users typically focus on standard permissions (read, write, and execute), system administrators must also be well aware of special permission sets. These special permissions are only used in very specific situations, and you should carefully monitor the system for these permission sets. An example of how to monitor the system is provided at the end of the "SUID" section.

SUID

To understand the SUID (also called "Set User ID"), consider the following situation. Suppose you are logged in to a Linux system as a regular user, such as the "student" user, and you run the **passwd** command to change your password:

```
student@onecoursesource:~$ passwd
Changing password for user student.
Changing password for student.
Current password:
New password:
Retype new password:
passwd: all authentication tokens updated successfully.
```

The fancy "all authentication tokens updated successfully" message indicates that the password for the "student" user was changed. But, if you think about it logically, this command should have failed. To understand why, look at the permissions for the **/etc/shadow** file:

```
student@onecoursesource:~$ ls -l /etc/shadow
----------. 1 root root 1726 Jan 23 14:02 /etc/shadow
```

According to these permissions, no user should be able to see the contents of this file, much less modify it:

```
student@onecoursesource:~$ more /etc/shadow
more: cannot open /etc/shadow: Permission denied
```

This seems odd, because as you learned in Chapter 7, "Managing User Accounts," user account passwords are stored in the **/etc/shadow** file. In order to modify the contents of this file, a user would need read and write permission. However, when a user runs a command, the access they would get to files is based on their account (UID and GIDs). So, how was the student user able to modify a file that he normally cannot even view?

The answer lies with the permissions of the **passwd** command itself:

```
student@onecoursesource:~$ which passwd
/usr/bin/passwd
student@onecoursesource:~$ ls -l /usr/bin/passwd
-rwsr-xr-x. root root 27768 Nov 25 06:22 /usr/bin/passwd
```

The "**s**" character in place of the owner's execute permission means that SUID permission has been placed on this file. With SUID permission, the command performs a "run as" feature, which allows the **passwd** command to access files as if it is either the student user account or the user account that owns the **/usr/bin/passwd** file (the root user in this case). Because the **passwd** command has "root access," it is able to modify the permissions of the **/etc/shadow** file temporarily in order to modify the contents.

Security Highlight

The SUID permission is often applied to files that are owned by the root user. For security reasons, it is important to be aware of SUID programs on your system.

You can use the **find** command shown in Example 9-1 to discover these programs (note: the **head** command is used to limit the output because this command could produce dozens of SUID programs).

Example 9-1 *Using **find** to Discover Programs*

```
student@onecoursesource:~$ find / -perm -4000 -ls | head
    13972      40 -rws--x--x   1  root       root         40248 Feb 11   2018 /usr/sb
in/userhelper
    13964      36 -rwsr-xr-x   1  root       root         36176 Mar 10   2018 /usr/sb
in/unix_chkpwd
    13802      92 -rwsr-xr-x   1  root       root         89472 Mar  2   2018 /usr/sb
in/mtr
    13830      12 -rwsr-xr-x   1  root       root         11152 Mar 10   2018 /usr/sb
in/pam_timestamp_check
    13974      12 -rwsr-xr-x   1  root       root         11192 May 26   2018 /usr/sbin/usernetctl
```

Security Highlight

When should you run the **find** command to discover SUID programs? Initially after installation of the OS is the first time. Take notice of each SUID program and determine which ones do not really need to be SUID. For instance, the **newgrp** command that was discussed in Chapter 6, "Managing Group Accounts," is an SUID program. If you do not have the need for users to use this command, consider disabling the SUID feature because it would result in a more secure system.

Also run the **find** command when new software is installed. Software vendors like to add SUID programs to the system that might not really be needed. This results in a false escalation of privilege and a vulnerability within the software.

Lastly, run the **find** command whenever you suspect the system has been compromised. Hackers like to create SUID programs to create "back doors" for future access to the system.

To set the SUID permission, use one of the following methods (note that **xxx** refers to the standard read, write, and execute permissions):

```
chmod u+s file
```

or

```
chmod 4xxx file
```

To unset the SUID permission, use one of the following methods:

```
chmod u-s file
```

or

```
chmod 0xxx file
```

SGID

Similar to the SUID permission, the SGID permission can be used to execute a command that has access to files and directories using the group ownership of the command. For example, consider the following:

```
student@onecoursesource:~$ ls -l /usr/bin/write
-rwxr-sr-x 1 root tty 19544 Nov 27  2018 /usr/bin/write
```

The **write** command has the SGID permission set (notice the **s** in the execute permission location for the group), which means when it is executed, it can use the group permissions of the "tty" group. This permission is important for this particular command because it sends data to terminal windows, which are represented by files that are group owned by the tty group.

In addition to SGID allowing group permission access, this special permission set has a different purpose when set on a directory. To understand this purpose, consider the following scenario:

Your company has three users who are part of different groups: bob (a member of the "staff" group), susan (a member of the "payroll" group), and julia (a member of the "admin" group). They approach you (the system administrator) because they need to be able to have a shared directory where they, and only they, can share files for a joint project they are working on. Your solution is to take the following steps:

Step 1. Create a group called "project" and add all these users to this group.

Step 2. Create a directory named **/home/groups/project**.

Step 3. Change the **/home/groups/project** directory to be owned by the project group.

Step 4. Change the permissions of the **/home/groups/project** directory to "**rwxrwx---**" so that only members of the project group have access to this directory.

Example 9-2 is an example of these steps in action (note that the **chgrp** command is covered later in this chapter).

Example 9-2 *Creating a Private Project Group*

```
root@onecoursesource:~# groupadd project
root@onecoursesource:~# usermod -G project -a bob
root@onecoursesource:~# usermod -G project -a susan
root@onecoursesource:~# usermod -G project -a julia
root@onecoursesource:~# mkdir -p /home/groups/project
root@onecoursesource:~# chgrp project /home/groups/project
```

```
root@onecoursesource:~# chmod 660 /home/groups/project
root@onecoursesource:~# ls -ld /home/groups/project
drwxrwx--- 2 root project 40 Dec 23 14:05 /home/groups/project
```

This may appear to be a good solution to the problem, but it is missing one component. Consider what happens when the user bob creates a file in the **/home/groups/project** directory by copying a file from his home directory:

```
bob@onecoursesource:~$ cd /home/groups/project
bob@onecoursesource:project$ cp ~/bob_report .
bob@onecoursesource:project$ ls -l bob_report
-rw-r----- 1 bob staff 1230 Dec 23 14:25 bob_report
```

It looks like everything worked just fine, until either the susan or julia user attempts to view the **bob_report** file:

```
julia@onecoursesource:project$ more bob_report
bob_report: Permission denied
```

The problem is that when the bob user copied the file into the **/home/groups/project** directory, his **umask** setting resulted in no permissions for the "others" permission set. This means that no one else can view this file. This problem could be fixed by the bob user by either changing the permission or group ownership of the file, but this would have to be done every time a file is created.

The solution would be to add SGID permission to the **/home/groups/projects** directory. When applied to a directory, the SGID permission will give the group ownership of all new files and directories to the group that owns the SGID directory. Here's an example:

```
root@onecoursesource:~# chmod g+s /home/groups/project
root@onecoursesource:~# ls -ld /home/groups/project
drwxrws--- 2 root project 40 Dec 23 14:05 /home/groups/project
root@onecoursesource:~# su - bob
bob@onecoursesource:~$ cd /home/groups/project
bob@onecoursesource:project$ cp ~/bob_report2 .
bob@onecoursesource:project$ ls -l bob_report2
-rw-r----- 1 bob project 1230 Dec 23 14:25 bob_report2
```

Now any new file created within the **/home/groups/project** directory will be group-owned by the project group.

To set the SGID permission, use one of the following methods (where **xxx** refers to the standard read, write, and execute permissions):

```
chmod g+s file
```

or

```
chmod 2xxx file
```

To unset the SUID permission, use one of the following methods:

```
chmod g-s file
```

or

```
chmod 0xxx file
```

Sticky Bit

To understand the "sticky bit" permission, consider a situation where you need a directory in which all users are able to share files. In other words, all users should be able to get into the directory (execute permission), see all files in the directory (read permission), and add new files into the directory (write permission):

```
root@onecoursesource:~# mkdir /home/shareall
root@onecoursesource:~# chmod 777 /home/shareall
root@onecoursesource:~# ls -ld /home/shareall
drwxrwxrwx 2 root project 40 Dec 23 14:05 /home/shareall
```

The problem with these permissions lies in the write permission for the directory. This permission allows the user to add new files to the directory, but it also allows a user to delete any file in the directory (regardless of whether or not they own the file). Clearly this poses a problem (and a potential security risk) if users start deleting each other's files.

There is a solution to the sticky bit permission. When applied to a directory, this permission changes the behavior of the write permission. A user can still add a file to the directory (assuming that would not overwrite an existing file owned by another user), but for the user to delete a file from a directory would require one of the following:

- The user would have to own the file, *OR*
- The user would have to own the directory, *OR*
- The user would have to be the system administrator.

The sticky bit permission should already be placed on at least one directory on your system: the **/tmp** directory. This directory is a place where users (or software programs) can place a file temporarily:

```
root@onecoursesource:~# ls -ld /tmp
drwxrwxrwt 16 root root 320 Dec 23 16:35 /tmp
```

To set the sticky bit permission, use one of the following methods (where **xxx** refers to the standard read, write, and execute permissions):

```
chmod o+t file
```

or

```
chmod 1xxx file
```

(Note that the number 1 is used here, not the lowercase letter *l*.)

To unset the SUID permission, use one of the following methods:

```
chmod o-t file
```

or

```
chmod 0xxx file
```

Table 9-4 summarizes the special permission sets of **SUID**, **SGID**, and sticky bit.

Table 9-4 Special Permission Sets of SUID, SGID, and Sticky Bit

	SUID	SGID	Sticky Bit
Description	When set on executable files, **SUID** allows a program to access files using the permissions of the user owner of the executable file.	When set on executable files, **SGID** allows a program to access files using the permissions of the group owner of the executable file. When it's set on directories, all new files in the directory inherit the group ownership of the directory.	When the sticky bit is set on directories, files in the directory can only be removed by the user owner of the file, the owner of the directory, or the root user.
Set	**chmod u+s file** or **chmod 4xxx file** (**xxx** refers to regular read, write, and execute permissions.)	**chmod g+s file** or **chmod 2xxx file** (**xxx** refers to regular read, write, and execute permissions.)	**chmod o+t file** or **chmod 1xxx file** (**xxx** refers to regular read, write, and execute permissions.) Note: Sticky bit permissions are almost always set to the octal value of 1777.
Remove	**chmod u-s file** or **chmod 0xxx file**	**chmod g-s file** or **chmod 0xxx file**	**chmod o-t file** or **chmod 0xxx file**

Access Control Lists (ACLs)

There is a fundamental problem with traditional read, write, and execute permissions. Consider the scenario in which an organization has 1000 users. One of the user accounts is the sarah user, who is a member of the "sales" group. There are 29 other members of the sales group besides the sarah user.

Now suppose the sarah user creates a new file that has permissions like the following:

```
sarah@onecoursesource:~$ ls -l sales_report
-rw-r----- 1 sarah sales 98970 Dec 27 16:45 sales_report
```

Based on the output of the previous command, you should be able to tell that the sarah user has read and write access to the file while the members of the sales group only have read access to the file. That means the rest of the organization (970 users) has the access provided by the last permission set (others). In other words, they have no access at all.

Suppose Sarah's boss (user account william) needs to be able to view the contents of this file, but his account isn't a member of the sales group. How would the sarah user grant this access?

The sarah user could give read access to the last permission set, like so:

```
sarah@onecoursesource:~$ chmod o+r sales_report
sarah@onecoursesource:~$ ls -l sales_report
-rw-r--r-- 1 sarah sales 98970 Dec 27 16:45 sales_report
```

The problem with this solution is that now *everyone* in the organization can view the contents of this file.

There is a better solution. If the sarah user was a group administrator of the sales group, she could add the william user to the sales group (or, she could ask an administrator to perform this task). However, this solution also has flaws, because now the william user would have access to all files that are group-owned by the sales group. So, this solution isn't really ideal either.

The best solution is to use access control lists (ACLs), which allow the owner of a file to give permissions for specific users and groups. The **setfacl** command is used to create an ACL on a file or directory:

```
sarah@onecoursesource:~$ setfacl -m user:dane:r-- sales_report
```

The **-m** option is used to make a new ACL for the file. The format of the argument to the **-m** option is *what:who:permission*. The value for *what* can be one of the following:

- **user** or **u** when applying an ACL for a specific user.
- **group** or **g** when applying an ACL for a specific group.
- **others** or **o** when applying an ACL for "others."
- **mask** or **m** when setting the mask for the ACL. (The mask will be explained later in this section.)

The value for *who* will be the user or group to which the permission will be applied. The permission can either be provided as a symbolic value (**r--**) or octal value (**4**).

Once an ACL has been applied on a file or directory, a plus sign (+) character will appear after the permissions when the **ls -l** command is executed, as shown here:

```
sarah@onecoursesource:~$ ls -l sales_report
-rw-rw-r--+ 1 sarah sales 98970 Dec 27 16:45 sales_report
```

To view the ACL, use the **getfacl** command:

```
sarah@onecoursesource:~$ getfacl sales_report
# file: sales_report
# owner: sarah
# group: sarah
user::rw-
user:william:r--
group::rw-
mask::rw-
other::r--
```

See Example 9-3 for an example of setting an ACL for a group.

Example 9-3 *Setting an ACL for a Group*

```
student@onecoursesource:~$ setfacl -m g:games:6 sales_report
student@onecoursesource:~$ getfacl sales_report
# file: sales_report
# owner: sarah
# group: sarah
user::rw-
user:william:r--
group::rw-
group:games:rw-
```

```
mask::rw-
other::r--
```

The mask Value

Note the **mask** value (**rw-**) in the output of Example 9-3. The **mask** is used to temporarily disable or restrict ACLs. Consider a situation in which you want the ACL value to not apply for a short period of time. If there were many ACLs, it would be difficult to remove every instance and then later reapply each one again. Instead, just change the **mask** value, as shown in Example 9-4.

Example 9-4 *Changing the **mask** Value*

```
sarah@onecoursesource:~$ setfacl -m mask:0 sales_report
sarah@onecoursesource:~$ getfacl sales_report
# file: sales_report
# owner: sarah
# group: sarah
user::rw-
user:william:r--                #effective:---
group::rw-                      #effective:---
group:games:rw-                 #effective:---
mask::---
other::r--
```

The **mask** specifies the maximum permissions that anyone besides the user owner and "others" have on the file. Notice the "effective" part of the previous output that demonstrates the effect that the **mask** value has on the permissions for the william user, the "games" group, and the group that owns the file ("group::").

To undo these restrictions, set the **mask** to what it was previously (**rw-** in this case), as shown in Example 9-5.

Example 9-5 *Resetting the **mask** Value*

```
sarah@onecoursesource:~$ setfacl -m mask:rw- sales_report
sarah@onecoursesource:~$ getfacl sales_report
# file: sales_report
# owner: sarah
# group: sarah
user::rw-
user:william:r--
group::rw-
group:games:rw-
mask::rw-
other::r--
```

Default ACLs

For regular permissions, the **umask** value is used to determine the default permissions applied for new files and directories. For ACLs, you can define a default ACL set for all new files and directories that are created within a shell by using the **-m** option with the **setfacl** command. In this case, the following syntax is used for the argument: **default:*what*:*who*:*permission***.

Example 9-6 will create a default ACL for the **reports** directory.

9

Example 9-6 *Setting a Default ACL for a Directory*

```
sarah@onecoursesource:~$ mkdir reports
sarah@onecoursesource:~$ setfacl -m default:g:games:r-x reports
sarah@onecoursesource:~$ setfacl -m default:u:bin:rwx reports
sarah@onecoursesource:~$ getfacl reports
# file: reports
# owner: sarah
# group: sarah
user::rwx
group::rwx
other::r-x
default:user::rwx
default:user:bin:rwx
default:group::rwx
default:group:games:r-x
default:mask::rwx
default:other::r-x
```

Example 9-7 demonstrates how new files and directories will inherit the ACLs that were created in the commands executed in Example 9-6.

Example 9-7 *ACL Inheritance*

```
sarah@onecoursesource:~$ mkdir reports/test
sarah@onecoursesource:~$ getfacl reports/test
# file: reports/test
# owner: sarah
# group: sarah
user::rwx
user:bin:rwx
group::rwx
group:games:r-x
mask::rwx
other::r-x
default:user::rwx
default:user:bin:rwx
default:group::rwx
default:group:games:r-x
default:mask::rwx
default:other::r-x
sarah@onecoursesource:~$ touch reports/sample1
sarah@onecoursesource:~$ getfacl reports/sample1
# file: reports/sample1
# owner: bo
# group: bo
user::rw-
user:bin:rwx                    #effective:rw-
group::rwx                      #effective:rw-
group:games:r-x                 #effective:r--
mask::rw-
other::r--
```

Security Highlight

Note that the **mask** value for the **reports/sample1** file in Example 9-7 is set to **rw-**, effectively disabling the execute permission for the "bin" group. This is because the maximum permissions that are ever placed on a new file are **rw-**. You will always need to manually set execute permissions on any new file.

Changing Ownership

Permissions are based on file and directory ownership, so it is important to know how to change the user and group owner. This section introduces the **chown** and **chgrp** commands to perform these tasks.

chown

The **chown** command is used to change the user owner or group owner of a file or directory. Table 9-5 demonstrates different ways to use this command.

Table 9-5 Using the **chown** Command

Example	Description
chown tim abc.txt	Changes the user owner of the **abc.txt** file to the "tim" user
chown tim:staff abc.txt	Changes the user owner of the **abc.txt** file to the "tim" user and the group owner to the "staff" group
chown :staff abc.txt	Changes the group owner of the **abc.txt** file to the "staff" group

NOTE Only the root user can change the user owner of a file. To change the group owner of a file, the user who executes the command must own the file and be a member of the new group receiving ownership of the file.

Important options for the **chown** command include those shown in Table 9-6.

Table 9-6 Options for the **chown** Command

Option	Description
-R	Recursively apply changes to an entire directory structure.
--reference=*file*	Change the user and group owner to the ownership of *file*.
-v	Verbose. Produce output demonstrating the changes that are made.

It is not possible for a user to give a file that they own to another user—but why? See Figure 9-2 for the answer.

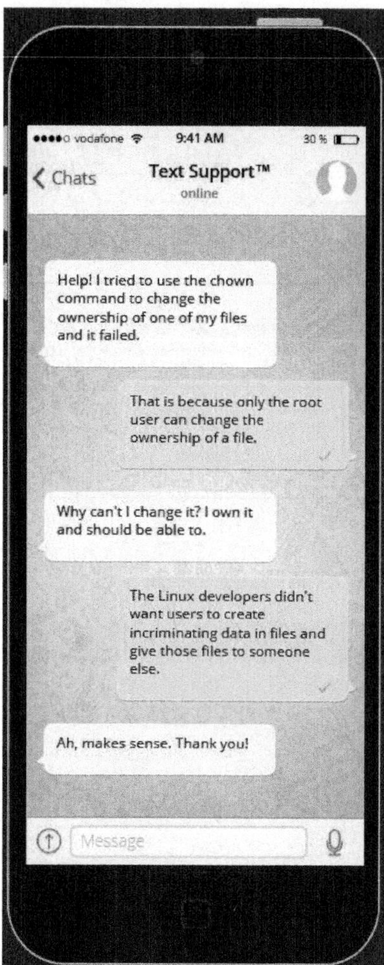

Figure 9-2 *Text Support™—Changing File Ownership*

chgrp

The **chgrp** command is designed to change the group ownership of a file. The syntax of this command is **chgrp [options]** ***group_name*** **file**. In the following example, the group ownership of the **abc.txt** file is changed to the "staff" group:

```
root@onecoursesource:~# chgrp staff abc.txt
```

To change the group owner of a file, the user who executes the command must own the file and be a member of the group receiving ownership of the file. (One exception is that the "root" user can always change the group ownership of any file.)

Important options for the **chgrp** command include those shown in Table 9-7.

Table 9-7 Options for the **chgrp** Command

Option	Description
-R	Recursively apply changes to an entire directory structure.
--reference=*file*	Change the user and group owner to the ownership of *file*.
-v	Verbose. Produce output demonstrating the changes that are made.

File Attributes

Although not technically permissions, file attributes do affect how users access files and directories, so they logically belong in any discussion regarding permissions. With file attributes, the system administrator can modify key features of file access.

For example, a useful file attribute is one that will make a file "immutable." An immutable file is completely unchangeable; it cannot be deleted or modified by anyone, including the root user. To make a file immutable, use the **chattr** command:

```
root@onecoursesource:~# chattr +i /etc/passwd
```

Note that now no user can change the **/etc/passwd** file, which means no new users can be added to the system (and existing users cannot be removed). This may seem like an odd thing to do, but imagine a situation in which a system is publicly available (like a kiosk in a mall). There is no need for new users, and you do not want anyone to remove users either.

Security Highlight

In the situation where we applied the immutable attribute to the **/etc/passwd** file, you may be asking yourself, "isn't this file already protected by permissions?" Although it is, adding the immutable attribute provides an additional layer of security, making the system overall more secure.

To see the attributes for a file, use the **lsattr** command:

```
root@onecoursesource:~# lsattr /etc/passwd
----i--------e-- /etc/passwd
```


The hyphen (-) characters indicate file attributes that are not set. A complete list of attributes can be found in the man page for the **chattr** command. Table 9-8 describes the file attributes that are important for system security.

Table 9-8 File Attributes for System Security

Attribute	Description
a	Append only mode; only allow new data to be placed in the file.
A	Disable modifying the access timestamp. This timestamp can be important for security reasons to determine when key system files have been accessed. However, for noncritical files, disabling the access time can make the system faster because it results in less hard drive writes.
e	Extent format, which allows for key features such as SELinux (discussed later in this chapter).
i	Immutable; file cannot be deleted or modified.
u	Undeletable; file cannot be deleted, but contents can be modified.

To remote the immutable file attribute, use the following command:

```
root@onecoursesource:~# chattr -i /etc/passwd
root@onecoursesource:~# lsattr /etc/passwd
-------------e-- /etc/passwd
```

Important options for the **chattr** command include those shown in Table 9-9.

Table 9-9 Options for the **chattr** Command

Option	Description
-R	Recursively apply changes to an entire directory structure.
-V	Verbose. Produce output demonstrating the changes that are made.

Introduction to SELinux

Like file attributes, SELinux (Security Enhanced Linux) is not a "file permission," but the topic belongs in this chapter because SELinux can also have a major impact on access to files and directories. It is important to note that SELinux is a potentially huge topic, and a full discussion of SELinux is well beyond the scope of this book (and, in fact, should be an entire book by itself). The purpose of this section is to introduce you to the concepts of SELinux and demonstrate how it works.

To understand SELinux, you'll first want to learn about some potential flaws to Linux's traditional method of securing files using permissions.

Users Create Security Holes

Files and directories may be compromised by users who either do not understand permissions or accidently provide more access than intended. This is a reflection of an old system administration saying: "If we didn't have users, nothing would break and the system would be more secure." Of course the response to this saying is, "Without users, we wouldn't have a job!" Users' mistakes often do provide unintended access to the data that is stored in files.

SELinux can be configured to accommodate for this flaw by providing an additional level of security when processes (programs) are used to access files. An SELinux security policy can be applied that will require processes to be a part of an SELinux security context (think "security group") in order to be able to access files and directories. Regular permissions will still be used to further define access, but for accessing the file/directory, this SELinux policy would be applied first.

However, although an SELinux policy can be configured to limit access to files and directories when regular users run processes, this is considered to be a very restrictive policy and is not nearly as common as the scenario we will discuss next. When a very secure filesystem is paramount, consider this more restrictive policy, but also consider that regular users may find the system much less useable and much more complex.

Daemon Processes Create Security Holes

A bigger concern, and one that most SELinux policies are designed to address, is how daemon (or system) processes present a security risk. Consider a situation where you have many active processes that provide a variety of services. For example, one of these processes may be a web server, like the Apache Web Server displayed in Example 9-8.

Example 9-8 *Apache Web Server Processes*

```
root@onecoursesource:~# ps -fe | grep httpd
root       1109     1  0  2018 ?        00:51:56 /usr/sbin/httpd
apache     1412  1109  0 Dec24 ?        00:00:09 /usr/sbin/httpd
apache     4085  1109  0 05:40 ?        00:00:12 /usr/sbin/httpd
apache     8868  1109  0 08:41 ?        00:00:06 /usr/sbin/httpd
apache     9263  1109  0 08:57 ?        00:00:04 /usr/sbin/httpd
apache    12388  1109  0 Dec26 ?        00:00:47 /usr/sbin/httpd
```

```
apache    18707  1109  0 14:41 ?        00:00:00 /usr/sbin/httpd
apache    18708  1109  0 14:41 ?        00:00:00 /usr/sbin/httpd
apache    19769  1109  0 Dec27 ?        00:00:15 /usr/sbin/httpd
apache    29802  1109  0 01:43 ?        00:00:17 /usr/sbin/httpd
apache    29811  1109  0 01:43 ?        00:00:11 /usr/sbin/httpd
apache    29898  1109  0 01:44 ?        00:00:10 /usr/sbin/httpd
```

Note that in the preceding output, each line describes one Apache Web Server process (**/usr/sbin/httpd**) that is running on the system. The first part of the line is the user who initiated the process. The process that runs as root is only used to spawn additional **/usr/sbin/httpd** processes. The others, however, respond to incoming web page requests from client utilities (web browsers).

Imagine for a moment that a security flaw is discovered in the software for the Apache Web Server that allows a client utility to gain control of one of the **/usr/sbin/httpd** processes and issue custom commands or operations to that process. One of those operations could be to view the content of the **/etc/passwd** file, which would be successful because of the permissions placed on this file:

```
root@onecoursesource:~# ls -l /etc/passwd
-rw-r--r-- 1 root root 2690 Dec 11  2018 /etc/passwd
```

As you can see from the output of the preceding command, all users have the ability to view the contents of the **/etc/passwd** file. Ask yourself this: Do you want some random person (usually called a hacker) to have the ability to view the contents of the file that stores user account data?

Security Highlight

Do not think of this problem as just related to the Apache Web Server. Any process running on your system can potentially be compromised and provide unintended access to someone who has bad intentions. Run the **ps -fe** command on your system to get an idea of how many processes are operational at any time.

With an SELinux policy, the **/usr/sbin/httpd** processes can be "locked down" so each can only access a certain set of files. This is what most administrators use SELinux for: to secure processes that may be compromised by hackers making use of known (or, perhaps, unknown) exploits.

SELinux Essentials

Not all Linux distributions have SELinux installed. One way you can tell if it is available (and actively being used) is to use the **getenforce** command:

```
root@onecoursesource:~# getenforce
Enforcing
```

The result "Enforcing" means SELinux is installed and the security policy is currently active. You can disable the security policy (useful when testing a new policy or troubleshooting SELinux problems) with the **setenforce** command:

```
root@onecoursesource:~# setenforce 0
root@onecoursesource:~# getenforce
Permissive
```

While in "Permissive" mode, SELinux will not block any access to files and directories, but warnings will be issued and viewable in the system log files.

Security Context

Each process runs with a security context. To see this, use the **-Z** option to the **ps** command (the **head** command is used here simply to limit the output of the command):

```
root@onecoursesource:~# ps -fe | grep httpd | head -2
system_u:system_r:httpd_t:s0 root      1109      1  0  2018 ?       00:51:56 /usr/sbin/httpd
system_u:system_r:httpd_t:s0 apache    1412   1109  0 Dec24 ?       00:00:09 /usr/sbin/httpd
```

The security context (**system_u:system_r:httpd_t:s0**) is complicated, but for understanding the basics of SELinux, the important part is **httpd_t**, which is like a security group or domain. As part of this security domain, the **/usr/sbin/httpd** process can only access files that are allowed by the security policy for **httpd_t**. This policy is typically written by someone who is an SELinux expert, and that expert should have proven experience regarding which processes should be able to access specific files and directories on the system.

Files and directories also have an SELinux security context that is also defined by the policy. To see a security context for a specific file, use the **-Z** option to the **ls** command (note that the SELinux context contains so much data that the filename cannot fit on the same line):

```
root@onecoursesource:~# ls -Z /var/www/html/index.html
unconfined_u:object_r:httpd_sys_content_t:s0 /var/www/html/index.html
```

Again, there are many pieces to a full SELinux security context, but the most important part for this book is **httpd_sys_content_t**. A process running with the **httpd_t** security context can access files that are part of the **httpd_sys_content_t** security context, according to the rules of the security policy.

To see an example of this access in action, first look at Figure 9-3, which demonstrates the Apache Web Server's ability to access the **/var/www/html/index.html** file.

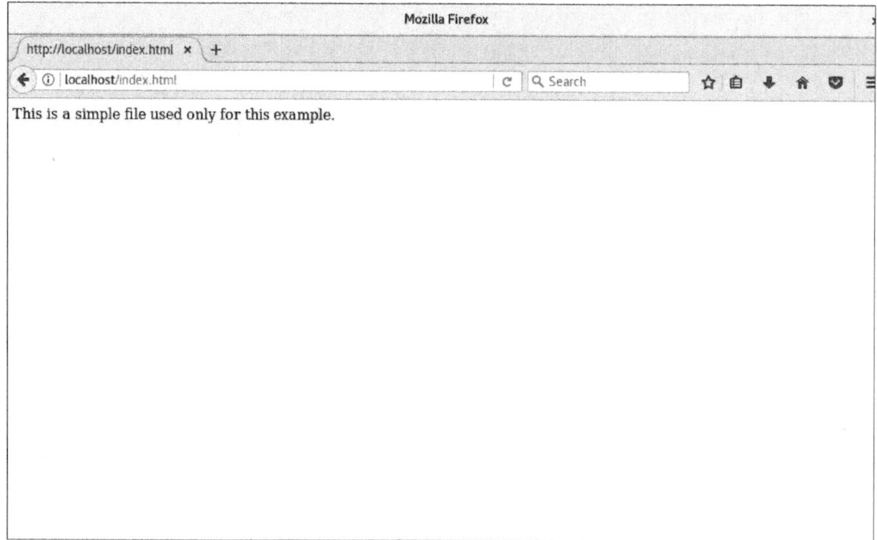

Figure 9-3 *Successful Display of the **index.html** File*

Next, the following command is used to change the SELinux security context to a different type:

```
root@onecoursesource:~# semanage fcontext -a -t user_home_t
➥/var/www/html/index.html
root@onecoursesource:~# restorecon -v /var/www/html/index.html
Relabeled /var/www/html/index.html from unconfined_u:object_r:httpd_sys_content_t:s0 to
unconfined_u:object_r:user_home_t:s0
```

Some notes about the previous commands:

- Typically you would not apply this security context to this particular file, as this security context is reserved for files found in users' home directories. However, the purpose of this is to demonstrate how SELinux protects files, so it makes sense to use a context like this.
- The **semanage** command applies the context of the file to the security policy, but to make this a permanent change on the file itself, the **restorecon** command must be executed.

Now look at Figure 9-4, which demonstrates how the Apache Web Server can no longer access the **index.html** file.

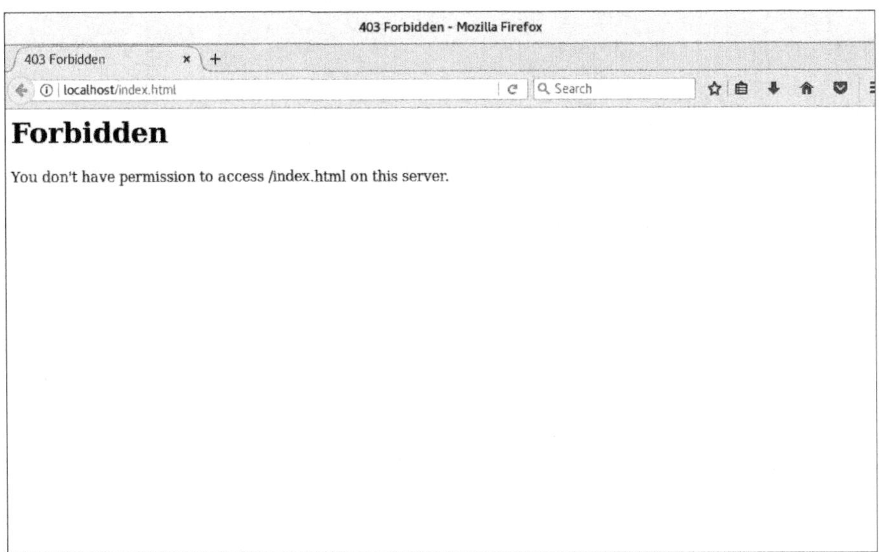

Figure 9-4 *Failure to Display the* ***index.html*** *File*

You can see why this failure happened by looking at the log entry:

```
root@onecoursesource:~# journalctl | grep index.html | tail -1
Dec 11 13:41:46 localhost.localdomain setroubleshoot[13444]: SELinux is preventing httpd
from read access on the file index.html. For complete SELinux messages run: sealert -l
afac171c-27bb-4dbc-9bec-994f44275fd3
```

Note that the **sealert** command mentioned in the output of the previous command is useful in providing additional information as to why the failure occurred.

SELinux Conclusion

The discussion in this book of SELinux provides a quick introduction to this powerful security tool. There is much more you can learn, including details regarding security policies and a host of commands that allow you to administer SELinux. With this introduction you should have an idea of what SELinux is, an understanding of what contexts are and how to view and set them, as well as how to use log entries to perform basic troubleshooting of SELinux.

Summary

In this chapter, you learned how to view and set standard permissions, the **umask** value, access control lists (ACLs), and special permissions. You also learned how to use file attributes to enhance the security of key system files. Lastly, you were introduced to the concepts behind SELinux, an advanced method for securing files and directories on a Linux operating system.

Key Terms

Permission, mask, SUID, SGID, sticky bit, access control lists, SELinux

Review Questions

1. The _____ option to the **ls** command will display basic file permissions.
2. Which permission would allow a user to delete a file in a directory?
   - **A.** Execute permission on the file
   - **B.** Write permission on the file
   - **C.** Write permission on the directory
   - **D.** Read permission on the directory
3. Which permission is used to modify the behavior of the write permission on a directory?
   - **A.** SUID
   - **B.** SGID
   - **C.** Sticky bit
   - **D.** None of these
4. The _____ command is used to specify which default permissions to mask (not include) when creating a new file or directory.
5. Fill in the blank to set the SGID permission set for the **/data directory**:
   chmod _____ /data.

Manage Local Storage: Essentials

The focus of this chapter is the key concepts and essential management of local storage devices.

You start by learning some key concepts, including what partitions and filesystems are and how they play an essential role on a Linux operating system. You then learn how to create partitions and filesystems, followed by how to make these new storage devices available to the operating system.

We complete this chapter by diving into the topic of swap devices, which are devices used to provide virtual memory space.

After reading this chapter and completing the exercises, you will be able to do the following:

Create partitions and filesystems

Perform advanced filesystem manipulation tasks

Mount partitions manually and automatically

Create and activate swap devices

Filesystem Essentials

The process of mounting makes a filesystem available by placing it under a directory location. Before you learn how to accomplish this, you should know some basics regarding filesystems.

Partitions

Partitions are used to separate a hard disk into smaller components. Each component can then be treated as a different storage device. On each partition, a separate filesystem (btrfs, xfs, etx4, and so on) can be created.

Traditional PC-based partitions have limitations regarding the number you can create. Originally only four partitions were permitted. These are referred to as *primary* partitions. As more partitions were needed, a technique was created that allows you to convert one of the primary partitions into an extended partition. Within an extended partition, you can create additional partitions called *logical* partitions.

In Figure 10-1, **/dev/sda1**, **/dev/sda2**, and **/dev/sda3** are primary partitions. The **/dev/sda4** partition is an extended partition that is used as a container for the **/dev/sda5**, **/dev/sda6**, and **/dev/sda7** logical partitions.

On most distributions that use traditional partitions, you will be limited to a total of 15 partitions, but a kernel tweak (modification) can increase this number to 63.

Traditional partition tables are stored on the Master Boot Record (MBR). A newer partition table, called the GUID partition table (GPT), does not have the same limitations or layout as an MBR partition table.

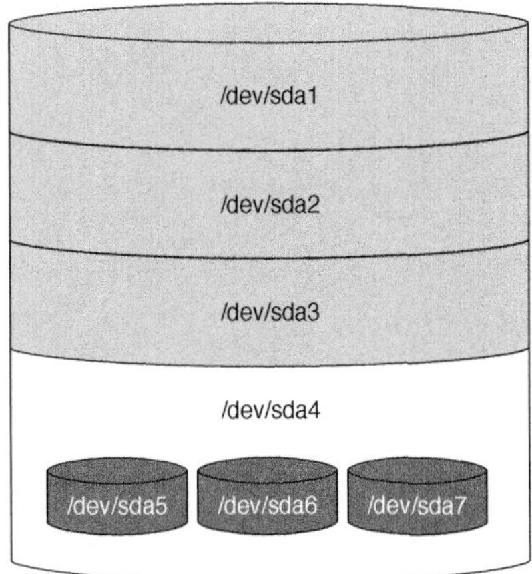

Figure 10-1 *Traditional Partition Structure*

Several different tools can be used to create or view partitions, including **fdisk**, **parted**, and a GUI-based tool provided by the installation program. The available GUI-based tools can vary based on the distribution.

Both **fdisk** and **parted** support command-line options, and both can be executed as an interactive tool. The **fdisk** and **parted** tools will be covered later in this chapter.

Filesystems

The term *filesystem* itself can be somewhat confusing. There are really two general types of filesystems: physical and virtual.

Physical filesystems are structures used to organize data on a device, such as a partition, logical volume, or RAID (redundant array of independent disks) device. Typically when the term *filesystem* is used, the reference is to a physical filesystem. There are many different types of physical filesystems, as described later in this chapter.

Virtual filesystems are what regular users see when they are looking at files and directories on the operating system. A virtual filesystem consists of several physical filesystems, merged together via the directory tree.

To understand this concept, first look at Figure 10-2.

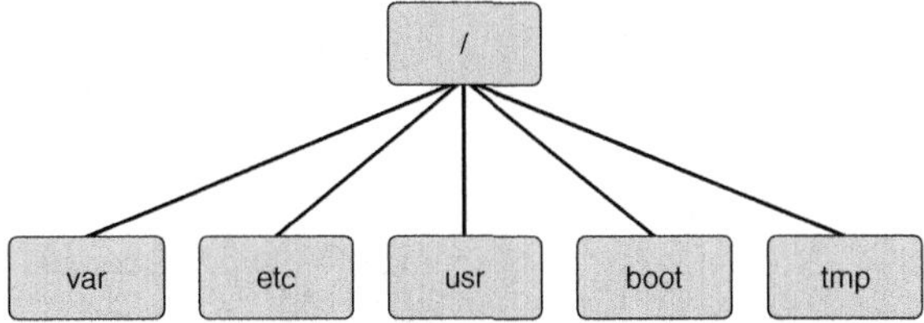

Figure 10-2 *A Virtual Filesystem*

Figure 10-2 shows a portion of a typical Linux virtual filesystem. This is how regular users view the filesystem, as a collection of directories that store data in a hierarchical manner. The top of the virtual filesystem structure is the **/** directory, and subdirectories and files are stored inside the **/** directory.

But as an administrator, you should know that there is more to this story. The **/** directory is a mount point for a physical filesystem. A mount point is how physical filesystems are merged together into the virtual filesystem, which is what the user sees as the directory structure. Other directories, such as **/var** and **/usr**, can also be mount points. In this case, you may want to consider the filesystem to be something like what is shown in Figure 10-3.

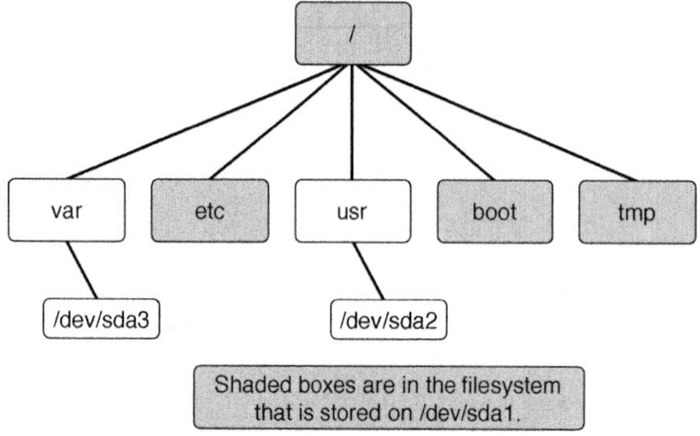

Figure 10-3 *A Virtual Filesystem with Mount Points Highlighted*

Figure 10-3 provides more insight about what is happening behind the scenes of the virtual filesystem. The directories highlighted in gray are in the filesystem stored on the **/dev/sda1** partition. Within the **var** directory is the filesystem that is stored on the **/dev/sda2** partition. Within the **usr** directory is the filesystem stored on the **/dev/sda3** partition.

Placing the filesystem under a directory is completed through a process called mounting. Mounting can be performed manually with the **mount** command or automatically by entries in the **/etc/fstab** file. The mounting process will be covered in more detail later in this chapter.

Why So Many Partitions/Filesystems?

You will discover that many Linux installations have several partitions—each, of course, with a separate filesystem. There are several reasons why you would want to create multiple partitions:

- **Mount options**: Each partition, when mounted, can have different mount options. This allows for more flexibility, as you may want to use a specific mount option for a specific situation. Later in this chapter we explore mount options and revisit this topic.
- **Filesystem types**: Each partition can have a different type of filesystem. Some filesystems are better for security, some are better for handling larger files, and some are better for performance. Picking the right filesystem for a given situation can result in a more secure system that performs its tasks more efficiently. Filesystem types are discussed later in this chapter.
- **Disk quotas**: This Linux feature allows you to limit how much space a user can use in a filesystem. The quota limit is per filesystem, so having multiple physical filesystems allows you the option of having different quota limits for different areas of the virtual filesystem.
- **Backup strategies**: Many backup utilities allow you to specify different frequencies when backups will occur on a filesystem-by-filesystem basis. For example, if the **/home** directory was the mount point of one filesystem and **/boot** was the mount point of another filesystem, you could create a strategy to back up the files in **/home** directory daily (files change often in this directory) while backing up the files in the **/boot** directory monthly (because files rarely change in this directory).
- **Limit possible full filesystems**: Consider a situation where the **/home** directory is a separate filesystem and a user generates a significant number of very large files. They could fill up the entire filesystem, making it impossible for other users to create files in their own home directories. However, if the **/home** directory wasn't a separate filesystem, but rather part of a single filesystem for the entire operating system, then this user could make the entire system unusable, as the entire hard drive would be full. This is one of the primary reasons why **/home**, **/var**, and **/tmp** are typically separate filesystems, as these are all directory structures where regular users have the rights to create files.

Security Highlight

Creating a virtual filesystem structure in which a single user can fill up the entire hard drive is considered a serious security risk. When the entire hard drive is full, the operating system can't function properly because many processes need the ability to write data to the hard drive.

Which Partitions/Filesystems Should Be Created?

The answer to this question really depends on several factors. You should consider the advantages of the different mount options, filesystem types, disk quotas, and backup strategies when determining which partitions you will create. Also take into consideration what these filesystems will contain. At the very least, consider making the following directories mount points for separate physical filesystems:

- **/ (root) filesystem**: The top level of the virtual filesystem. The size of this filesystem depends greatly on which other filesystems are created. This is a required partition.
- **/var filesystem**: The **/var** filesystem contains data that is variable in nature (that is, it changes often). This includes log files, mail files, and spools (such as the print spools). The size of this filesystem depends on many factors, including if this is a mail server, which log files are created on the system and if the system functions as a printer server. Consider making **/var** a separate filesystem for backup strategies and to limit the risk of the hard disk space becoming completely full.
- **/home filesystem**: The **/home** filesystem is where regular user home directories are stored. The size of this filesystem depends on many factors, including the number of users who work on the system and what functions these users perform. Consider making **/home** a separate filesystem for backup strategies and to limit the risk of the hard disk space becoming completely full.
- **/boot filesystem**: Location of where the boot files, including the **kernel**, **bootloader**, and **initramfs** files, are stored. When **/boot** is a separate filesystem, it is normally about 100–200MB in size. Because this filesystem must be easily accessible during the boot process, it is on a separate filesystem.

NOTE The preceding isn't a complete list of all possible filesystems. There are good arguments for making other directories, such as **/usr** and **/opt**, mount points for physical filesystems. Expect some trial and error until you find a good combination of physical filesystems that meets your needs.

Filesystem Types

Filesystems are used to organize the data (files and directories) on the system. Many different types of filesystems are available for Linux. Table 10-1 provides a brief summary of these filesystems.

Table 10-1 Filesystem Types

Option	Description
ext2	Ext2 is an improvement over the original ext, the extended filesystem.
ext3	Ext3 is an improvement over ext2 (added journal support, among other features).
ext4	Ext4 is an improvement over ext3 (allows for larger filesystems, among other features).
xfs	Xfs is a high-performance filesystem, often used in place of the ext2/ext3/ext4 family of filesystems.
btrfs	A filesystem designed to scale to large data devices.

Option	Description
UDF	The Universal Disk Format filesystem is primarily used as the filesystem on DVD discs.
ISO9660	A filesystem specifically designed to be used as the filesystem on CD-ROM discs.
HFS	A proprietary filesystem developed by Apple. More commonly used as the filesystem on CD-ROM discs on modern systems.

Conversational Learning™—Which Filesystem Type?

Gary: Hi, Julia. Can you provide me with some assistance? I'm trying to determine which filesystem to use on the new partition I created. There are so many that I just don't know which to pick.

Julia: Hey, Gary! I'm assuming you are talking about a traditional partition, like on a hard drive? Not something like a CD-ROM or DVD, right?

Gary: Correct.

Julia: OK, that rules out a bunch of filesystems, like UDF, ISO9660, and HFS. So, the first step is to determine what your distribution supports.

Gary: You mean not all distributions support all filesystems?

Julia: Nope. At least not by default. Often you can install additional software, but it may be better to choose one that is already part of the distro.

Gary: How can I figure this out?

Julia: Typically the documentation for the distribution will indicate this. You can also just try using some of the specific commands for creating the filesystem you are interested in.

Gary: Let's assume that I have a large choice of options. What do I choose? Ext4? Xfs?

Julia: There really isn't a simple answer to this question. You really need to consider what you want to use the filesystem for and do a bit of research to determine which filesystem best fits your needs.

Gary: Can you give me an example?

Julia: Sure. Suppose you will have very large files on your filesystem. In that case, you may find that xfs has better performance than other filesystems. Of course, you want to explore the other features, but that gives you an idea of what to look for.

Gary: OK, sounds like doing the "pre-work" is important here. Any other advice?

Julia: Yes, if it is a critical filesystem, consider creating several different types and performing benchmark testing to find which works best. Also, don't forget to consider key security features, especially if the filesystem will be accessible to the public, like a shared drive, or contain files for a web server.

Gary: Got it. Thanks again, Julia.

Managing Partitions

In order to create a filesystem, you first will want to create one or more partitions. Partitions are used to logically break up a hard disk or other storage media into smaller pieces. By creating partitions, you have more flexibility in features like mounting, backup, and filesystem security. The full collection of partitions on a single storage device is called the *partition table*.

Before using tools to create partitions, you should be aware that there are two different partition methods: MBR (Master Boot Record) and GPT (GUID partition table).

MBR

MBR partition tables are often referred to as "traditional" partitions as opposed to newer partition tables such as the GUID partition table. An MBR partition table has the restriction of only permitting four partitions by default. This is an extremely limiting factor for operating systems like Linux.

However, one of the primary partitions in an MBR partition table can be converted into an extended partition. Within this extended partition, additional partitions can be added. These additional partitions are called *logical partitions*. See Figure 10-4 for a visual example.

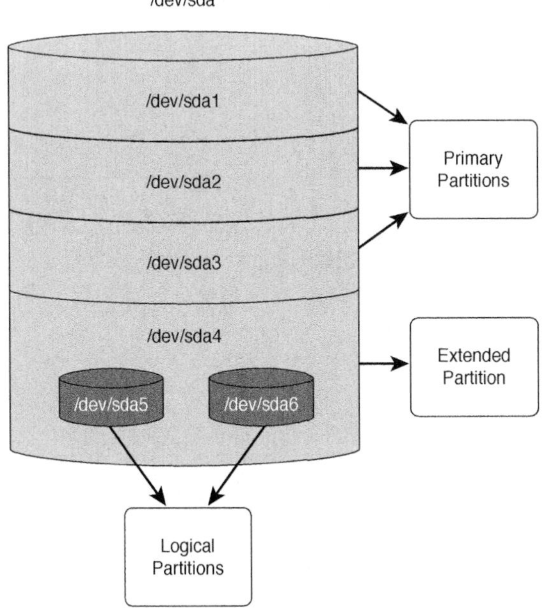

Figure 10-4 *Master Boot Record*

A note regarding hard disk device names: Hard disks are referred to via device names in the **/dev** directory. IDE-based devices have names that start with **/dev/hd**, whereas SETA, SCSI, and USB devices have names that start with **/dev/sd**. The first drive on the system is named "a," so the first SETA device would be **/dev/sda**. The second SETA device would be **/dev/sdb**, and so on. Partitions are numbered sequentially, starting from 1, as in **/dev/sda1**, **/dev/sda2**, and **/dev/sda3**.

GPT

There are several differences between GPT and MBR partitions. However, in this instance, the most important one you should be aware of is the structure of the partitions table. GPT supports creating many more partitions than MBR and doesn't have the "four primary, one extended, multiple logical" structure. All partitions in GPT are just simply partitions, and there is no need to overcome the legacy issues associated with MBR partitions.

Creating MBR Partitions

To create an MBR partition, you can use the **fdisk** command.

NOTE Normally the entire hard disk is used during the installation process, making it difficult to make partitions to practice creating filesystems. If you are using a virtual machine, you can add a new disk to the system fairly easily (consult the documentation for VirtualBox, VMware, or whatever virtualization software you are using). If that is not an option, you can always use a small thumb drive for practice—just make sure to remove all important data from the thumb drive first!

To display the current partition table for a device, use the **-l** option to the **fdisk** command, as shown in Example 10-1.

Example 10-1 *The fdisk -l Command*

```
[root@onecoursesource ~]# fdisk -l /dev/sdb

Disk /dev/sdb: 209 MB, 209715200 bytes
255 heads, 63 sectors/track, 25 cylinders
Units = cylinders of 16065 * 512 = 8225280 bytes
Sector size (logical/physical): 512 bytes / 512 bytes
I/O size (minimum/optimal): 512 bytes / 512 bytes
Disk identifier: 0xccd80ba5

   Device Boot      Start         End      Blocks   Id  System
```

The device in Example 10-1 currently has no partitions, so the data under the "Device Boot Start End…" line is empty. To add partitions to this device, use the **fdisk** command without the **-l** option:

```
[root@onecoursesource ~]# fdisk /dev/sdb
WARNING: DOS-compatible mode is deprecated. It's strongly recommended to
         switch off the mode (command 'c') and change display units to
         sectors (command 'u').
Command (m for help):
```

Note the warning that is displayed. Depending on your distribution, you might not receive this warning because the recommendations (switch off the mode and change display units to sectors) are sometimes the default for the **fdisk** command. If you do receive this warning, quit from the **fdisk** utility by entering **quit** at the command prompt and start the **fdisk** command again with the **-c** and **-u** options:

```
Command (m for help): quit
[root@onecoursesource ~]# fdisk -cu /dev/sdb
Command (m for help):
```

NOTE Instead of quitting the **fdisk** utility, consider using the **c** and **u** options at the command prompt to toggle to the correct mode.

To create a new partition, enter **n** at the command prompt:

```
Command (m for help): n
Command action
   e   extended
   p   primary partition (1-4)
p
Partition number (1-4): 1
First sector (2048-409599, default 2048):
Using default value 2048
Last sector, +sectors or +size{K,M,G} (2048-409599, default 409599):
Using default value 409599
```

To save these changes, enter the **w** command at the command prompt:

```
Command (m for help): w
The partition table has been altered!
Calling ioctl() to re-read partition table.
Syncing disks.
```

Creating MBR Partitions

The **parted** utility is an interactive tool that allows you to display and modify both traditional and GUID partition tables. It can also create a filesystem on a partition.

To display a partition table, use the **-l** option (run this command as the root user):

```
[root@onecoursesource ~]# parted -l /dev/sda
Model: ATA VBOX HARDDISK (scsi)
Disk /dev/sda: 42.9GB
Sector size (logical/physical): 512B/512B
Partition Table: msdos

Number  Start   End     Size    Type     File system  Flags
 1      1049kB  42.9GB  42.9GB  primary  ext4         boot


Model: Linux device-mapper (thin) (dm)
Disk /dev/mapper/docker-8:1-264916-f9bd50927a44b83330c036684911b54e494e4e48efbc2329262b-
6f0e909e3d7d: 107GB
Sector size (logical/physical): 512B/512B
Partition Table: loop

Number  Start  End    Size   File system  Flags
 1      0.00B  107GB  107GB  ext4


Model: Linux device-mapper (thin) (dm)
Disk /dev/mapper/docker-8:1-264916-77a4c5c2f607aa6b31a37280ac39a657bfd7e-
ce1d940e50507fb0c128c220f7a: 107GB
Sector size (logical/physical): 512B/512B
Partition Table: loop

Number  Start  End    Size   File system  Flags
 1      0.00B  107GB  107GB  ext4
```

To modify the partition table of a drive, run the **parted** command without the **-l** option:

```
[root@onecoursesource ~]# parted  /dev/sda
GNU Parted 2.3
Using /dev/sda
Welcome to GNU Parted! Type 'help' to view a list of commands.
(parted)
```

There are several useful commands you can type at the **parted** prompt, some of which are shown in Table 10-2.

Table 10-2 Useful Commands at the **parted** Prompt

Command	Description
rm	Delete a partition.
? or help	Print a menu of possible commands.
mkpart	Create a new partition.
mkpartfs	Create a new partition and filesystem.
print	Print the current partition table.
quit	Quit without saving any changes.
w	Write (save) changes to the partition table on the hard drive.

Creating Filesystems

Now that you have a partition, you can create a filesystem using the **mkfs** command. For example, to create an ext4 filesystem on the **/dev/sdb1** partition, execute the **mkfs** command as shown in Example 10-2.

Example 10-2 *The mkfs Command*

```
[root@onecoursesource ~]# mkfd -t ext4 /dev/sdb1
-bash: mkfd: command not found
[root@onecoursesource ~]# mkfs -t ext4 /dev/sdb1
mke2fs 1.41.12 (17-May-2010)
Filesystem label=
OS type: Linux
Block size=1024 (log=0)
Fragment size=1024 (log=0)
Stride=0 blocks, Stripe width=0 blocks
51000 inodes, 203776 blocks
10188 blocks (5.00%) reserved for the super user
First data block=1
Maximum filesystem blocks=67371008
25 block groups
8192 blocks per group, 8192 fragments per group
2040 inodes per group
Superblock backups stored on blocks:
    8193, 24577, 40961, 57345, 73729

Writing inode tables: done
Creating journal (4096 blocks): done
Writing superblocks and filesystem accounting information: done

This filesystem will be automatically checked every 38 mounts or
180 days, whichever comes first. Use tune2fs -c or -i to override.
```

The **mkfs** command is a front-end command to commands designed to make specific filesystems. For example, the **mkfs -t ext4** command runs the **mkfs.ext4** command. You can see what filesystems the **mkfs** command can create by typing **mkfs.** and then pressing the **<TAB>** key twice:

```
[root@onecoursesource ~]# mkfs.
mkfs.cramfs   mkfs.ext3   mkfs.ext4dev  mkfs.vfat
mkfs.ext2     mkfs.ext4   mkfs.msdos
```

You can run any of these commands directly, but often it is just easier to execute the **mkfs** command.

The **mkfs** command by itself has few options. However, each of the **mkfs.*** commands has several options that modify how the filesystem is created. When specifying options with the **mkfs** command, any option that isn't part of the **mkfs** command is passed to the **mkfs.*** command. For example, the **-m** option to the **mkfs.ext4** command specifies how much of the filesystem (percentage of filesystem) is reserved for the superuser (the default is 5%). The following command ends up executing the **mkfs.ext4** command and passing in the **-m** option to that command:

```
mkfs -t ext4 -m 10 /dev/sdb1
```

Security Highlight

Filesystems have many options, and we highly recommend you explore the options available for the filesystems on your systems. Which options are enabled can make a big difference for system performance and sometimes for security.

For instance, consider the **-m** option for ext-based filesystems, which is used to specify how much of the filesystem is reserved for the superuser. The purpose for this is so the root user (or daemons running as root) is able to store files on a filesystem, even if regular users "fill up" the filesystem.

Suppose you have a separate filesystem for **/home** and that it is a 500GB filesystem. The default reserved for the superuser is 5%, unless you use the **-m** option and specify a different value. If you don't use this option when this filesystem is created, that would mean that 25GB are reserved for the root user, a user who will likely never place a single file in the **/home** filesystem!

To learn more about these options, read the man page specific to your filesystem. For example, to learn more about ext4, you could execute the following command: **man mkfs.ext4**.

Ext-Based Filesystem Tools

Several tools allow you to change and view ext-based filesystems. These include the following:

- **fsck.***
- **dumpe2fs**
- **tune2fs**
- **debugfs**

fsck.*

The purpose of the **fsck** command (and related **fsck.*** commands) is to fix filesystem issues. A filesystem becomes corrupt or broken when the operating system is not properly shut down. This could be the result of a power outage or a careless employee who accidentally kicks the power cord.

The reason why this causes a problem is that changes to the filesystem metadata (data about the file such as its name, permissions, ownership, timestamp, and so on) are initially stored in memory. At regular intervals this data is written to the hard disk. However, if the system is improperly shut down while this data is still in memory, the data on the hard disk is out of date, resulting in a corrupted filesystem.

When the system is booted after an improper shutdown, a utility called **fsck** (filesystem check) checks all filesystems. In some cases it makes changes to the filesystem, but normally any error results in a failed boot (startup) process. You need to fix the filesystem errors manually.

The **fsck** utility is straightforward. For example, to execute it on the first partition of the first SATA (Serial Advanced Technology Attachment) drive, execute the following command:

```
fsck /dev/sda1
```

You might get a lot of questions that look like "blah, blah, blah is broken. Do you want to fix this problem?" The answer should always be "yes" (otherwise you won't be able to mount or use this filesystem). As a result, you probably always want to run the **fsck** utility with the **-y** option to answer yes to each question:

```
fsck -y /dev/sda1
```

Security Highlight

Do not run the **fsck** utility on live filesystems. Live filesystems do not have filesystem corruption; only filesystems that are not properly unmounted will have this issue. Running the **fsck** utility on a live filesystem can cause problems, rather than fix problems. Remember the saying "if it ain't broke, don't try to fix it!"

You should also know that the **fsck** utility, just like the **mkfs** utility, is really just a front-end utility for filesystem-specific **fsck** utilities. For example, if you execute **fsck** on an ext4 filesystem, the **fsck.ext4** utility is executed.

Note that there are different options for the different **fsck** utilities, so review the man pages to determine which options you can use.

dumpe2fs

The **dumpe2fs** command can display details regarding the ext* filesystem. The output of this command is huge and by default includes a great deal of information regarding block group descriptors, typically something that you don't need to see. To view this information while omitting the block group descriptors, use the **-h** option, as shown in Example 10-3.

Example 10-3 *The **dumpe2fs** Command*

```
[root@onecoursesource ~]# dumpe2fs -h /dev/sdb1
dumpe2fs 1.41.12 (17-May-2010)
Filesystem volume name:   <none>
Last mounted on:          <not available>
Filesystem UUID:          7d52c9b6-28a8-40dc-9fda-a090fa95d58f
Filesystem magic number:  0xEF53
Filesystem revision #:    1 (dynamic)
Filesystem features:      has_journal ext_attr resize_inode dir_index filetype extent
flex_bg sparse_super huge_file uninit_bg dir_nlink extra_isize
Filesystem flags:         signed_directory_hash
Default mount options:    (none)
Filesystem state:         clean
Errors behavior:          Continue
Filesystem OS type:       Linux
Inode count:              51000
Block count:              203776
Reserved block count:     10188
Free blocks:              191692
Free inodes:              50989
First block:              1
```

```
Block size:               1024
Fragment size:            1024
Reserved GDT blocks:      256
Blocks per group:         8192
Fragments per group:      8192
Inodes per group:         2040
Inode blocks per group:   255
Flex block group size:    16
Filesystem created:       Tue Sep 15 00:12:17 2017
Last mount time:          n/a
Last write time:          Tue Sep 15 00:12:18 2017
Mount count:              0
Maximum mount count:      38
Last checked:             Tue Sep 15 00:12:17 2017
Check interval:           15552000 (6 months)
Next check after:         Sat Mar 12 23:12:17 2017
Lifetime writes:          11 MB
Reserved blocks uid:      0 (user root)
Reserved blocks gid:      0 (group root)
First inode:              11
Inode size:               128
Journal inode:            8
Default directory hash:   half_md4
Directory Hash Seed:      a3bbea7e-f0c2-43b2-a5e2-9cd2d9d0eaad
Journal backup:           inode blocks
Journal features:         (none)
Journal size:             4096k
Journal length:           4096
Journal sequence:         0x00000001
Journal start:            0
```


As you can see from Example 10-3, a huge amount of information is provided by the **dumpe2fs** command. Table 10-3 describes some of the more important filesystem features.

Table 10-3 Filesystem Features

Option	Description
Filesystem features	This can be important to determine what the filesystem is capable of. For example, the output in Example 10-3 includes the **has_journal** feature, meaning that this filesystem is using journaling.
Default mount options	Although you can specify mount options in the **/etc/fstab** file (as you will see later in this chapter), you could also have default mount options embedded in the filesystem features. This portion of the output tells you the default mount options.
Inode count	Every file must have an inode. So, the inode count tells you the maximum number of files that can be placed on the filesystem.
Reserved block count	How many blocks are reserved for the superuser.
Block size	How large a block is for this filesystem.

In most cases, the block group descriptors information is not necessary, but there is one case in which you might want to display this information. When using the **fsck** utility to fix a filesystem, you might get a "bad superblock" error. The superblock is critical for filesystem health, so backups are made of this information in the block group descriptors. If you run the **dumpe2fs** command without the **-h** option, you see many sections of output like the following:

```
Group 1: (Blocks 8193-16384) [INODE_UNINIT, ITABLE_ZEROED]
  Checksum 0x12f5, unused inodes 2040
  Backup superblock at 8193, Group descriptors at 8194-8194
  Reserved GDT blocks at 8195-8450
  Block bitmap at 260, Inode bitmap at 276
  Inode table at 546-800
  7934 free blocks, 2040 free inodes, 0 directories, 2040 unused inodes
  Free blocks: 8451-16384
  Free inodes: 2041-4080
```

Note the "backup superblock" location of 8193. If your superblock contains an error, you can use this backup superblock, as shown here:

```
fsck -b 8193 /dev/sdb1
```

tune2fs

To make changes to a filesystem, use the **tune2fs** command. For example, to change the percentage of a filesystem reserved for the superuser, execute a command like the following:

```
 [root@onecoursesource ~]# tune2fs -m 0 /dev/sdb1
tune2fs 1.41.12 (17-May-2010)
Setting reserved blocks percentage to 0% (0 blocks)
```

It is important to realize that not all filesystem features can be changed by the **tune2fs** command. For example, the number of inodes (each file must have an inode, which is used to store information about a file) in the filesystem is set when the filesystem is created and cannot be changed. If you need more inodes, you have to back up the filesystem, create a new filesystem, and restore the data.

debugfs

The **debugfs** command is a useful tool that allows you to perform debugging operations in an interactive environment. The tool is designed to be executed on filesystems not currently active (mounted).

Start the tool by executing the command with the partition device name:

```
[root@onecoursesource ~]# debugfs /dev/sdb1
debugfs 1.41.12 (17-May-2010)
debugfs:
```

The **debugfs** tool provides many useful tools, including several that act similarly to regular Linux commands. Example 10-4 illustrates the feature of listing files in the current directory with the **ls** command.

Example 10-4 *The ls Command*

```
debugfs:  ls
 2  (12) .   2  (12) ..   11  (20) lost+found     12  (20) asound.conf
 13  (32) autofs_ldap_auth.conf    14  (24) cgconfig.conf
 15  (20) cgrules.conf    16  (36) cgsnapshot_blacklist.conf
```

```
17  (20) dnsmasq.conf    18  (20) dracut.conf    19  (20) fprintd.conf
20  (16) gai.conf    21  (20) grub.conf    22  (24) gssapi_mech.conf
23  (16) hba.conf    24  (20) host.conf    25  (20) idmapd.conf
26  (20) kdump.conf    27  (20) krb5.conf    28  (20) ld.so.conf
29  (24) libaudit.conf    30  (20) libuser.conf    31  (24) logrotate.conf
32  (20) mke2fs.conf    33  (20) mtools.conf    34  (20) named.conf
35  (24) nfsmount.conf    36  (24) nsswitch.conf    37  (16) ntp.conf
38  (20) openct.conf    39  (36) pm-utils-hd-apm-restore.conf
40  (20) prelink.conf    41  (24) readahead.conf    42  (20) reader.conf
43  (24) request-key.conf    44  (20) resolv.conf    45  (20) rsyslog.conf
46  (24) sestatus.conf    47  (20) smartd.conf    48  (16) sos.conf
49  (20) sudo.conf    50  (24) sudo-ldap.conf    51  (20) sysctl.conf
52  (24) Trolltech.conf    53  (24) updatedb.conf    54  (24) warnquota.conf
55  (20) xinetd.conf    56  (20) yum.conf
```

You can get information about this file by using the **stat** command, as shown in Example 10-5.

Example 10-5 *The **stat** Command*

```
debugfs:  stat yum.conf
Inode: 56   Type: regular    Mode:  0644   Flags: 0x80000
Generation: 1017195304    Version: 0x00000001
User:     0   Group:     0   Size: 969
File ACL: 4385    Directory ACL: 0
Links: 1   Blockcount: 4
Fragment:  Address: 0    Number: 0    Size: 0
ctime: 0x55f863e0 -- Tue Sep 15 11:30:56 2015
atime: 0x55f863e0 -- Tue Sep 15 11:30:56 2015
mtime: 0x55f863e0 -- Tue Sep 15 11:30:56 2015
EXTENTS:
(0): 8553
```

One of the most useful features of the **debugfs** command is the capability to undelete a file—if you act quickly! For example, consider the situation in Example 10-6, where a file is accidentally deleted.

Example 10-6 *Using **debugfs** to Undelete*

```
[root@onecoursesource ~]# ls /data
asound.conf                 host.conf        nfsmount.conf                smartd.conf
autofs_ldap_auth.conf       idmapd.conf      nsswitch.conf                sos.conf
cgconfig.conf               kdump.conf       ntp.conf                     sudo.conf
cgrules.conf                krb5.conf        openct.conf                  sudo-ldap.conf
cgsnapshot_blacklist.conf   ld.so.conf       pm-utils-hd-apm-restore.conf sysctl.conf
dnsmasq.conf                libaudit.conf    prelink.conf                 Trolltech.conf
dracut.conf                 libuser.conf     readahead.conf               updatedb.conf
fprintd.conf                logrotate.conf   reader.conf                  warnquota.conf
gai.conf                    lost+found       request-key.conf             xinetd.conf
grub.conf                   mke2fs.conf      resolv.conf                  yum.conf
gssapi_mech.conf            mtools.conf      rsyslog.conf
hba.conf                    named.conf       sestatus.conf
[root@onecoursesource ~]# rm /data/yum.conf
rm: remove regular file '/data/yum.conf'? y
```

10

To recover this file, first unmount the filesystem and start the **debugfs** command with the **-w** option (which opens the filesystem in read-write mode):

```
[root@onecoursesource ~]# umount /data
[root@onecoursesource ~]# debugfs /dev/sdb1
debugfs 1.41.12 (17-May-2010)
debugfs:
```

Now list deleted files with the **lsdel** command and recover the file with the **undel** command. Keep in mind you must do this soon after you delete the file; otherwise, the data blocks may be used by a new file.

Xfs-Based Filesystem Tools

Just as there are tools to help you view and modify ext-based filesystems, there are tools that allow you to perform these tasks on xfs-based filesystems. These include the following:

- **xfsdump**
- **xfsrestore**
- **xfs_info**
- **xfs_check**
- **xfs_repair**

> **NOTE** Not all Linux distributions have the xfs filesystem available. If you want to practice xfs commands, use CentOS 7 because xfs is the default filesystem for that distribution.

xfsdump and xfsrestore

The **xfsdump** command is used to back up a filesystem, either to a tape device or some other storage location. Assuming that it is unlikely you have access to tape devices, the examples provided in this section use a regular file as the storage location of the backup.

Example 10-7 demonstrates creating a full backup of the **/boot** directory (which is the mount point of **/dev/sda1** on this system) and placing the backup into the **/tmp/boot_back** file.

Example 10-7 *The **xfsdump** Command*

```
[root@onecoursesource ~]# xfsdump -f /tmp/boot_back /boot
xfsdump: using file dump (drive_simple) strategy
xfsdump: version 3.1.4 (dump format 3.0) - type ^C for status and control

 ============================= dump label dialog ==============================

please enter label for this dump session (timeout in 300 sec)
 -> /boot test
session label entered: "/boot test"

 --------------------------------- end dialog ---------------------------------

xfsdump: level 0 dump of onecoursesource.localdomain:/boot
xfsdump: dump date: Mon Oct 19 20:31:44 2017
xfsdump: session id: 5338bd39-2a6f-4c88-aeb8-04d469215767
xfsdump: session label: "/boot test"
xfsdump: ino map phase 1: constructing initial dump list
```

```
xfsdump: ino map phase 2: skipping (no pruning necessary)
xfsdump: ino map phase 3: skipping (only one dump stream)
xfsdump: ino map construction complete
xfsdump: estimated dump size: 191212416 bytes
xfsdump: /var/lib/xfsdump/inventory created

 ============================ media label dialog ============================

please enter label for media in drive 0 (timeout in 300 sec)
 ->
media label entered: ""

 -------------------------------- end dialog --------------------------------

xfsdump: WARNING: no media label specified
xfsdump: creating dump session media file 0 (media 0, file 0)
xfsdump: dumping ino map
xfsdump: dumping directories
xfsdump: dumping non-directory files
xfsdump: ending media file
xfsdump: media file size 190911592 bytes
xfsdump: dump size (non-dir files) : 190666096 bytes
xfsdump: dump complete: 17 seconds elapsed
xfsdump: Dump Summary:
xfsdump:   stream 0 /tmp/boot_back OK (success)
xfsdump: Dump Status: SUCCESS
```

Notice that in the execution of the **xfsdump** command in Example 10-7 the user was prompted to enter a label and a media label. The label is a name for the backup, whereas the media label is a name for the device (like a backup tape). If the backup spans multiple tapes, multiple medial labels can be provided.

By default, a full backup is made. This is referred to as a level 0 (full) backup. A level 1 backup (incremental backup) would back up all files that had changed since the last level 0 backup. A level 2 backup (differential backup) would back up all files that had changed since the last lower-level backup (either 0 or 1, whichever one is more recent). Use the **-l** option to specify the level of the backup (0 is the default if you don't specify the **-l** option).

The **xfsrestore** command can be used to restore files from a backup. In the following example, all the files from the backup would be restored in the current directory, designated by a dot (.) character in the following example:

```
xfsrestore -f /backup/location .
```

You can list the files in the backup by using the **-t** (for "table of contents") option (the **grep** command is to avoid displaying header information), as shown in Example 10-8.

Example 10-8 *The –t Option*

```
[root@onecoursesource ~]# xfsrestore -t -f /tmp/boot_back | grep -v "^xfsrestore" | head
.vmlinuz-3.10.0-229.11.1.el7.x86_64.hmac
.vmlinuz-3.10.0-229.el7.x86_64.hmac
System.map-3.10.0-229.el7.x86_64
config-3.10.0-229.el7.x86_64
symvers-3.10.0-229.el7.x86_64.gz
```

```
vmlinuz-3.10.0-229.el7.x86_64
initrd-plymouth.img
initramfs-3.10.0-229.el7.x86_64.img
initramfs-0-rescue-affb8edd5c9a4e829010852a180b0dc9.img
vmlinuz-0-rescue-affb8edd5c9a4e829010852a180b0dc9
```

Often you just want to restore a single file. One way of doing this is to use the interactive mode of the **xfsrestore** command. See a demonstration of this in Example 10-9 (note that for brevity, some output was omitted).

Example 10-9 *The xfsrestore Command*

```
[root@onecoursesource ~]# xfsrestore -i -f /tmp/boot_back /tmp

========================== subtree selection dialog ==========================

the following commands are available:
    pwd
    ls [ <path> ]
    cd [ <path> ]
    add [ <path> ]
    delete [ <path> ]
    extract
    quit
    help
-> ls
###Omitted###
             135 config-3.10.0-229.el7.x86_64
             134 System.map-3.10.0-229.el7.x86_64
             133 .vmlinuz-3.10.0-229.el7.x86_64.hmac
          524416 grub2/
             131 grub/
-> add config-3.10.0-229.el7.x86_64

-> extract

--------------------------------- end dialog ---------------------------------

xfsrestore: restoring non-directory files
xfsrestore: restore complete: 2807 seconds elapsed
xfsrestore: Restore Summary:
xfsrestore:   stream 0 /tmp/boot_back OK (success)
xfsrestore: Restore Status: SUCCESS
[root@onecoursesource ~]# ls /tmp/config*
/tmp/config-3.10.0-229.el7.x86_64
```

NOTE On some distributions, there are also commands designed to back up ext-based filesystems: the **dump** and **restore** commands. These commands work similarly to the **xfsdump** and **xfsrestore** commands.

xfs_info

The **xfs_info** command provides some basic filesystem information on xfs filesystems that are currently mounted, as seen in Example 10-10.

Example 10-10 *The xfs_info Command*

```
[root@onecoursesource ~]# xfs_info /dev/sda1
meta-data=/dev/sda1              isize=256    agcount=4, agsize=32000 blks
         =                       sectsz=512   attr=2, projid32bit=1
         =                       crc=0        finobt=0
data     =                       bsize=4096   blocks=128000, imaxpct=25
         =                       sunit=0      swidth=0 blks
naming   =version 2              bsize=4096   ascii-ci=0 ftype=0
log      =internal               bsize=4096   blocks=853, version=2
         =                       sectsz=512   sunit=0 blks, lazy-count=1
realtime =none                   extsz=4096   blocks=0, rtextents=0
```

xfs_check and xfs_repair

Similar to the **fsck** utility, the **xfs_repair** utility fixes unmounted xfs filesystems. See Example 10-11 for a demonstration.

Example 10-11 *The xfs_repair Command*

```
[root@onecoursesource ~]# xfs_repair /dev/sda1
Phase 1 - find and verify superblock...
Phase 2 - using internal log
        - zero log...
        - scan filesystem freespace and inode maps...
        - found root inode chunk
Phase 3 - for each AG...
        - scan and clear agi unlinked lists...
        - process known inodes and perform inode discovery...
        - agno = 0
        - agno = 1
        - agno = 2
        - agno = 3
        - process newly discovered inodes...
Phase 4 - check for duplicate blocks...
        - setting up duplicate extent list...
        - check for inodes claiming duplicate blocks...
        - agno = 0
        - agno = 1
        - agno = 2
        - agno = 3
Phase 5 - rebuild AG headers and trees...
        - reset superblock...
Phase 6 - check inode connectivity...
        - resetting contents of realtime bitmap and summary inodes
        - traversing filesystem ...
        - traversal finished ...
        - moving disconnected inodes to lost+found ...
Phase 7 - verify and correct link counts...
done
```

If you just want to check for filesystem problems, but not fix any problems, run the **xfs_check** command instead of the **xfs_repair** command.

You may find that your distribution does not include the **xfs_check** command, instead allowing the **-n** option (no repair) to the **xfs_repair** command, as it performs the same tasks that the **xfs_check** command performs. Regardless of which command you use, make sure the filesystem is unmounted before executing the command.

Additional Filesystem Tools

The **du** and **df** commands are designed to display information about filesystems. These tools are independent of the filesystem type.

du

The **du** command provides an estimated amount of disk space usage in a directory structure. For example, the following command displays the amount of space used in the **/usr/lib** directory:

```
[root@localhost ~]$ du -sh /usr/lib
791M    /usr/lib
```

Important options for the **/usr/lib** command include those shown in Table 10-4.

Table 10-4 Options for the **/usr/lib** Command

Option	Description
-h	Display values in human-readable size.
-s	Display a summary, rather than the size of each subdirectory.

df

The **df** command displays usage of partitions and logical devices:

```
[root@localhost ~]$ df
Filesystem          1K-blocks      Used Available Use% Mounted on
udev                  2019204        12   2019192   1% /dev
tmpfs                  404832       412    404420   1% /run
/dev/sda1            41251136   6992272  32522952  18% /
none                        4         0         4   0% /sys/fs/cgroup
none                     5120         0      5120   0% /run/lock
none                  2024144         0   2024144   0% /run/shm
none                   102400         0    102400   0% /run/user
```

Important options for the **df** command are shown in Table 10-5.

Table 10-5 Options for the **df** Command

Option	Description
-h	Display values in human-readable size.
-i	Display inode information.

Mounting Filesystems

In this section, you are introduced to the commands used to mount and unmount filesystems manually. You also learn how to modify the system to automatically mount filesystems during the boot process by creating entries in the **/etc/fstab** file.

The umount Command

Before discussing how to mount a filesystem, a brief demonstration of the **umount** command is in order. To unmount a filesystem, you can specify the **umount** command followed by either the mount point or the device name. For example, if the **/dev/sda1** device is mounted under the **/boot** directory, either of the following commands should unmount the filesystem:

```
umount /boot
umount /dev/sda1
```

More discussion regarding the **umount** command appears after the **mount** command is explored.

The mount Command

The **mount** command can be used to mount a filesystem as well as display which filesystems are currently mounted. When used with no arguments, the **mount** command displays mounted filesystems as well as some of the mount attributes (also called mount options), as shown in Example 10-12.

Example 10-12 *The **mount** Command*

```
[root@onecoursesource ~]# mount
/dev/mapper/vg_livecd-lv_root on / type ext4 (rw)
proc on /proc type proc (rw)
sysfs on /sys type sysfs (rw)
devpts on /dev/pts type devpts (rw,gid=5,mode=620)
tmpfs on /dev/shm type tmpfs (rw,rootcontext="system_u:object_r:tmpfs_t:s0")
/dev/sda1 on /boot type ext4 (rw,usrquota,grpquota)
none on /proc/sys/fs/binfmt_misc type binfmt_misc (rw)
sunrpc on /var/lib/nfs/rpc_pipefs type rpc_pipefs (rw)
/dev/sr0 on /media/VBOXADDITIONS_5.0.2_102096 type iso9660 ¿
    (ro,nosuid,nodev,uhelper=udisks,uid=500,gid=500,iocharset=utf8,mode=0400,dmode=0500
```

10

Each line describes one mounted device and is broken down into four fields, highlighted in bold:

```
device on mount_point type fs_type (mount_options)
```

Table 10-6 describes these fields in more detail.

Table 10-6 Fields of the **mount** Command Output

Option	Description
device	The device is the location of the filesystem that is mounted. This could be a Logical Volume Management (LVM is covered in Chapter 11, "Manage Local Storage: Advanced Features,") a device file (such as **/dev/mapper/vg_livecd-lv_root**), a partition device file (such as **/dev/sda1**), a CD-ROM (such as **/dev/sr0**), a pseudo filesystem (such as tmpfs), or other various device types (such as network drives, USB drives, RAID devices, and, if you hop back into that time machine, floppy drives). Pseudo filesystems (logical file groups) are filesystems that normally reside in memory and are a topic that is beyond the scope of this book.
mount_point	This is the directory where the filesystem is currently mounted. For example, the filesystem on the **/dev/sda1** device in Example 10-12 is mounted under the **/boot** directory.

Option	Description
fs_type	This is the type of filesystem. With the exception of pseudo filesystems, these are straightforward. Remember that filesystems are covered in more detail in future chapters.
mount_ options	The last field is critical because this is where you as an administrator can have impact on how a filesystem behaves. There are a large number of mount options that change the behavior of the filesystem. Each filesystem type has different mount options (although some mount options are valid for more than one filesystem). A good example is the **rw** option, which you can see for multiple types of filesystems in Example 10-12. This option makes the filesystem available for both reading and writing data.

Note that the **mount** command knows what is currently mounted on the system because this information is stored in the **/etc/mtab** file, as shown in Example 10-13.

Example 10-13 *The /etc/mtab File*

```
[root@onecoursesource ~]# more /etc/mtab
/dev/mapper/vg_livecd-lv_root / ext4 rw 0 0
proc /proc proc rw 0 0
sysfs /sys sysfs rw 0 0
devpts /dev/pts devpts rw,gid=5,mode=620 0 0
tmpfs /dev/shm tmpfs rw,rootcontext="system_u:object_r:tmpfs_t:s0" 0 0
none /proc/sys/fs/binfmt_misc binfmt_misc rw 0 0
sunrpc /var/lib/nfs/rpc_pipefs rpc_pipefs rw 0 0
/dev/sr0 /media/VBOXADDITIONS_5.0.2_102096 iso9660
➥ro,nosuid,nodev,uhelper=udisks,uid=500,gi
d=500,iocharset=utf8,mode=0400,dmode=0500 0 0
/dev/sda1 /boot ext4 rw,usrquota,grpquota 0 0
```

Whenever a filesystem is mounted or unmounted, the **/etc/mtab** file is updated. Another file that contains mounted filesystem information is the **/proc/mounts** file, shown in Example 10-14.

Example 10-14 *The /proc/mounts File*

```
[root@onecoursesource ~]# more /proc/mounts
rootfs / rootfs rw 0 0
proc /proc proc rw,relatime 0 0
sysfs /sys sysfs rw,seclabel,relatime 0 0
devtmpfs /dev devtmpfs rw,seclabel,relatime,size=247568k,nr_inodes=61892,mode=755 0 0
devpts /dev/pts devpts rw,seclabel,relatime,gid=5,mode=620,ptmxmode=000 0 0
tmpfs /dev/shm tmpfs rw,seclabel,relatime 0 0
/dev/mapper/vg_livecd-lv_root / ext4 rw,seclabel,relatime,barrier=1,data=ordered 0 0
none /selinux selinuxfs rw,relatime 0 0
devtmpfs /dev devtmpfs rw,seclabel,relatime,size=247568k,nr_inodes=61892,mode=755 0 0
/proc/bus/usb /proc/bus/usb usbfs rw,relatime 0 0
none /proc/sys/fs/binfmt_misc binfmt_misc rw,relatime 0 0
sunrpc /var/lib/nfs/rpc_pipefs rpc_pipefs rw,relatime 0 0
/etc/auto.misc /misc autofs
➥ rw,relatime,fd=7,pgrp=1822,timeout=300,minproto=5,maxproto=5,
➥indirect 0 0
-hosts /net autofs
➥rw,relatime,fd=13,pgrp=1822,timeout=300,minproto=5,maxproto=5,indirect 0 0
```

```
/dev/sr0 /media/VBOXADDITIONS_5.0.2_102096 iso9660 ro,nosuid,nodev,relatime,uid=500,
➥ gid=500,
iocharset=utf8,mode=0400,dmode=0500 0 0
/dev/sda1 /boot ext4 rw,seclabel,relatime,barrier=1,data=ordered,usrquota,grpquota 0 0
```

Although both of these files contain information about currently mounted filesystems, there are some differences that you should be aware of:

- The **/etc/mtab** file is managed by the **mount** and **umount** commands. The **mount** command has an option (**-n**) that means "do not update the **/etc/mtab** file," so it is possible that this file might not be accurate.
- The **/proc/mounts** file is managed by the kernel and is more likely to be accurate.
- The **/proc/mounts** file typically has more information (for example, look at the mount options for the **/dev/sda1** device in Example 10-13 and compare that to Example 10-14).

Mounting Filesystems Manually

To mount a filesystem, you should specify two arguments to the **mount** command: the device to mount and the mount point. For example, the following commands first demonstrate that **/dev/sda1** is mounted, then unmount the **/dev/sda1** device, and then remount it under the **/boot** partition:

```
[root@onecoursesource ~]# mount | grep /dev/sda1
/dev/sda1 on /boot type ext4 (rw,usrquota,grpquota)
[root@onecoursesource ~]# umount /dev/sda1
[root@onecoursesource ~]# mount /dev/sda1 /boot
[root@onecoursesource ~]# mount | grep /dev/sda1
/dev/sda1 on /boot type ext4 (rw)
```

If you look closely, you see a difference between how the device is mounted originally and how it was mounted the second time. The **usrquota** and **grpquota** options are missing in the output of the second **mount** command. The reason for this is that the **/dev/sda1** device was originally mounted with these options enabled as a result of an entry in the **/etc/fstab** file, a file covered later in this chapter.

To enable mount options manually, use the **-o** option:

```
[root@onecoursesource ~]# mount | grep /dev/sda1
/dev/sda1 on /boot type ext4 (rw)
[root@onecoursesource ~]# umount /dev/sda1
[root@onecoursesource ~]# mount -o usrquota,grpquota /dev/sda1 /boot
[root@onecoursesource ~]# mount | grep /dev/sda1
/dev/sda1 on /boot type ext4 (rw,usrquota,grpquota)
```

Security Highlight

Another useful mount option is the **ro** option, which allows you to mount a filesystem as read-only. If the filesystem is currently mounted as read-write, you can change it to read-only by executing the **mount -o remount,ro /dev/*device_name*** command. Mounting a filesystem as read-only can be useful for troubleshooting a problem or attempting to identify a hacker's backdoor without allowing problematic code to be executed.

As previously mentioned, there are many mount options, and these options can either apply to multiple filesystem types or are specific to an individual filesystem type. Mount options are discussed in more detail later in this chapter.

Another command-line option of the **mount** command is the **-t** option, which allows you to specify the filesystem type. In most cases, the **mount** command is smart enough to choose the right filesystem type by probing the filesystem before mounting it. However, if you need to specify a filesystem type, use the following syntax:

```
mount -t ext4 /dev/sda1 /boot
```

Problems Unmounting Filesystems

A filesystem cannot be unmounted if it is currently in use. There are several reasons why a filesystem may be in use, including the following:

- A file is open from the filesystem.
- A process is running from the filesystem.
- A user shell is "in" the filesystem. In other words, either the mount point directory or a subdirectory under the mount point is the current directory for a user's shell.

This can be frustrating for the sysadmin who needs to unmount a filesystem. You do not want to see the following error message:

```
[root@onecoursesource ~]# umount /boot
umount: /boot: device is busy.
        (In some cases useful info about processes that use
         the device is found by lsof(8) or fuser(1))
```

Note that the error message includes a suggestion of using either the **lsof** or **fuser** command. The **lsof** command is a great command for listing open files (excellent for troubleshooting many different problems), but the **fuser** command is more useful in this case.

Executing the **fuser** command with the mount point of the filesystem as an argument reveals which process is currently using the filesystem:

```
[root@onecoursesource ~]# fuser /boot
/boot:                4148c
```

The value 4148 in this example indicates the PID of the process and the **c** indicates how the process is being used. The following comes directly from the **fuser** man page documentation:

```
c      current directory.
e      executable being run.
f      open file. f is omitted in default display mode.
F      open file for writing. F is omitted in default display mode.
r      root directory.
m      mmap'ed file or shared library.
```

So, **c** means that the process with the PID of 4148 is using the **/boot** directory (or a subdirectory of the **/boot** directory) as the current directory. If you use the **-v** option (for "verbose"), you can see more detail:

```
[root@onecoursesource ~]# fuser -v /boot
                     USER        PID ACCESS COMMAND
/boot:               bob        4148 ..c.. bash
```

So, now you can hunt down the user bob and ask him to get out of the **/boot** directory. Or, you can use another useful option to the **fuser** command to kill the process that is causing you headaches:

```
[root@onecoursesource ~]# fuser -k /boot
/boot:                4148c
[root@onecoursesource ~]# fuser -v /boot
[root@onecoursesource ~]# umount /boot
```

Security Highlight

When the **fuser -k** command is executed, it sends a signal to all processes on the filesystem that are preventing you from unmounting the filesystem. This signal is called a SIGKILL signal, and it poses a potential security issue because it forces all these processes to be stopped without providing any opportunity to gracefully shut down. This means that if a process were to perform cleanup operations (such as deleting temporary files or saving data into files or databases) normally when it exits, the process wouldn't have the opportunity to perform these tasks.

It is better to attempt a graceful shutdown of all processes first. This can be accomplished by including the **-15** option when using the **-k** option to the **fuser** command. If the processes don't stop within a short period of time after running **fuser -k -15**, then execute **fuser -k** without the **-15** option.

More details about process control are covered in Chapter 24, "Process Control."

Mounting Filesystems Automatically

Several filesystems are mounted automatically at boot. Which filesystems are mounted depends on the settings in the **/etc/fstab** file. See Example 10-15 for a sample **/etc/fstab** file.

10

Example 10-15 *The /etc/fstab File*

```
[student@onecoursesource ~]$ more /etc/fstab
# Accessible filesystems, by reference, are maintained under '/dev/disk'
# See man pages fstab(5), findfs(8), mount(8) and/or blkid(8) for more info
#
/dev/mapper/vg_livecd-lv_root /                  ext4   defaults 1
UUID=974e2406-eeec-4a49-9df7-c86d046e97f9 /boot    ext4   usrquota,grpquota,defaults
➥1 2
/dev/mapper/vg_livecd-lv_swap swap               swap   defaults        0 0
tmpfs                   /dev/shm                 tmpfs  defaults        0 0
devpts                  /dev/pts                 devpts gid=5,mode=620  0 0
sysfs                   /sys                     sysfs  defaults        0 0
proc                    /proc                    proc   defaults        0 0
```

Each line of the **/etc/fstab** file contains six fields of data, separated by whitespace, that are used to describe the location of the filesystem, the filesystem type, where to mount the filesystem (mount point), and how to mount it (mount options). The six fields are

```
device_to_mount   mount_point   fs_type   mount_options
dump_level   fsck_value
```

Table 10-7 describes these fields in more detail.

Table 10-7 Fields of the **/etc/fstab** File

Option	Description
device_to_mount	This is a descriptor of the device that contains the filesystem to be mounted. There is some variety as to how you can specify this name, including using a device filename (such as **/dev/sda1**), a label, or a UUID (universally unique identifier). The pros and cons of each of these are discussed later in this chapter in the "Device Descriptors" section.
mount_point	The directory where the filesystem is to be placed within the directory tree structure.
fs_type	The filesystem type. An entry of btrfs, ext4, xfs, or vfat is common for filesystems on devices. Using nfs or cifs (Windows file sharing) is common for network filesystems. Having tmpfs, proc, or devpts is typical for pseudo filesystems. The entry swap is for devices used as memory (such as hard drive caching or operating system swap space).
mount_options	The options to use when mounting the filesystem. See the "Mount Options" section later in this chapter.
dump_level	This value is used by the **dump** command to determine which filesystems to back up. A value of 1 means "back this up," and a value of 0 means "do not back this up." The **dump** command is rarely used on modern Linux distributions, so most administrators habitually put a value of 0 in this field.
fsck_value	When the system is booted, the **fsck** command performs checks on local Linux filesystems. Which filesystems it checks and in which order depend on this field. A value of 0 means "do not check"; this should be the value on all non-Linux filesystems, including remotely mounted filesystems. A value of 1 or higher means "run the **fsck** command on this filesystem." Most administrators use a value of 1 for the **/** filesystem and a value of 2 for all others. The filesystems are checked in order starting at the value of 1. If all the partitions are located on a single hard drive, there is no advantage to using any other value, as only one partition can be checked at a time. However, if you have multiple hard drives, you may want to use the same value for similar-sized partitions on different drives to speed the process of running the **fsck** command. This is because the **fsck** command can be run in parallel on different hard drives. So, if **/dev/sda1** and **/dev/sdb6** are about the same size, use the same **fsck** value on them.

Device Descriptors

If you add a new filesystem, you should carefully consider what device descriptor you use to mount that filesystem. For example, suppose you added a new hard drive to your system, created a partition with a device name of **/dev/sdb1**, and placed an ext4 filesystem on the partition. You could then add a line like the following to the **/etc/fstab** file:

```
/dev/sdb1  /data  ext4  defaults 0 1
```

Most likely this will work just fine from this point on, but there is a potential problem: Device names can change. If you add or remove hard disks to or from your system, the firmware program (BIOS, for example) might think that new hard disk is the "first" disk, resulting in the device names of existing disks being changed. Even deleting partitions on a device might cause the existing partitions to be renumbered.

So, instead of using device names for regular partitions, you could use labels. A *label* is a name that you place on a partition. If the device name changes, the label will still "stick" to that partition, making this a better method of mounting. To create a label, use the **e2label** command:

```
[root@onecoursesource ~]# e2label /dev/sdb1 data
```

Use the following syntax in the **/etc/fstab** file:

```
LABEL="data"  /data  ext4  defaults 0 1
```

Note that you can display labels using either the **e2label** command or the **blkid** command:

```
[root@onecoursesource ~]# e2label /dev/sda2
data
[root@onecoursesource ~]# blkid | grep sda2
/dev/sda2: UUID="974e2406-eeec-4a49-9df7-c86d046e97f9" TYPE="ext4" LABEL="data"
```

Although using labels to mount devices is better than using device names, it still is not ideal. If you take this disk from the current system and add it to another system, it is possible that there could be a label conflict. If the new system also has a partition with the label of "data," this causes problems.

The most stable solution is to use UUID numbers. The universally unique identifier is a number assigned to the device when it is created. Because of how large this number is (128 bits) and how it is generated, it is virtually impossible that two devices will have the same number. The **blkid** command displays a device's UUID:

```
[root@onecoursesource ~]# blkid | grep sda2
/dev/sda2: UUID="974e2406-eeec-4a49-9df7-c86d046e97f9" TYPE="ext4" LABEL="data"
```

To use the UUID in the **/etc/fstab** file, use the following syntax:

```
UUID=974e2406-eeec-4a49-9df7-c86d046e97f9  /data  ext4  defaults 0 1
```


Finally, it is important to note that not all devices require the use of UUIDs or labels. Consider the following line from the **/etc/fstab** file:

```
/dev/mapper/vg_livecd-lv_swap swap                  swap    defaults        0 0
```

The **/dev/mapper/vg_livecd-lv_swap** device is a logical volume (logical volumes are discussed in detail later in Chapter 11, "Manage Local Storage: Advanced Features"). Logical volume device names do not change unless you, the administrator, change the names. Other devices, such as network drives and software RAID devices, also do not require UUIDs or labels.

Mount Options

How a filesystem behaves is partly based on the mount options you provide. Dozens of different mount options are available. The most important options to know are those related to the keyword defaults. When you specify defaults as a mount option in the **/etc/fstab** file, you are really specifying the options **rw**, **suid**, **dev**, **exec**, **auto**, **nouser**, **async**, and **relatime**. Table 10-8 describes these options in more detail.

Table 10-8 Default Options

Option	Description
rw	Mounts the filesystem as read-write. To mount the filesystem as read-only, use the option **ro**.
suid	Enables the SUID permission set on files in the filesystem (see Chapter 9, "File Permissions," for details regarding the SUID permission). Use the **nosuid** option to disable the SUID permission set. Disabling the SUID permission set on filesystems is normally done to prevent a user from creating an SUID program, which could result in a security risk. (Note: The **/** and **/usr** filesystems should never be mounted with the **nosuid** option.)
dev	Permits device files to be used on the filesystem. Normally device files are only placed under the **/dev** directory, so for security purposes, using the **nodev** option on all filesystems (besides the **/** filesystem) would result in a more secure system.
exec	Enables executable files in the filesystem. Use the **noexec** option to disable executable files. Disallowing executable files might be a good idea on servers to prevent users from introducing new programs to the server.
auto	This option is used when the administrator uses the **-a** option to the **mount** command. The **-a** option means "mount all filesystems that have the **auto** option in the **/etc/fstab** file." Keep in mind that when the system boots, the **mount -a** command is used to mount filesystems, so using the **noauto** option would also mean the filesystem is not mounted automatically during the boot process.
nouser	Does not permit a regular user to mount the filesystem. This is typically the best option for security reasons, but there are some cases where you might want a user to mount a removable device. In those cases, use the **user** option. If you employ the **user** option, then once the filesystem is mounted, only that user can unmount the filesystem. Also be aware of the option **user**, which also allows any user to mount the filesystem. However, this option also allows any user to unmount the filesystem.
async	The process of performing a sync is to ensure all data has been written to the hard drive. Normally when files are created or modified, the contents of the file are written directly to the hard drive, but the metadata (information about the file) is stored temporarily in memory. This reduces excessive hard drive writes and prevents thrashing, a situation that occurs when the hard drive is overtaxed. At regular intervals this metadata is written to the hard drive, a process called syncing. The **async** option is what causes metadata to be stored temporarily in memory. In some cases this can cause issues because this metadata could be lost if the system is improperly powered off. If this metadata is critical, consider using the **sync** option, but realize this could slow down your system considerably. Note: If you are using the **async** option, you can always write the metadata to the hard drive by executing the **sync** command.
relatime	Each file has three timestamps: the last time the contents of the file were modified, the last time the metadata was changed, and the last time the file was accessed. The file access time is normally not critical, but it can cause a lot of system writes, especially if you execute a command that recursively executes on a directory structure (such as **grep -r**). The **relatime** option enables updating the access timestamp. If this causes a performance issue, consider changing the option to **norelatime**.

As previously mentioned, these are not the only options; there are in fact many more. To discover these additional options, explore the man page for the **mount** command. First look at the section titled "Filesystem Independent Mount Options," as this covers options that work for most filesystems. Then search for the filesystem you are using. Example 10-16 shows a portion of the **mount** man page related to ext4 filesystems.

Example 10-16 *Mount Options for ext4 Filesystems*

```
Mount options for ext4
       The ext4 filesystem is an advanced  level  of  the  ext3  filesystem
       which  incorporates  scalability  and reliability enhancements for sup-
       porting large filesystem.

       The  options  journal_dev,  noload,  data,  commit,  orlov,   oldalloc,
       [no]user_xattr [no]acl, bsddf, minixdf, debug, errors, data_err, grpid,
       bsdgroups, nogrpid sysvgroups,  resgid,  resuid,  sb,  quota,  noquota,
       grpquota,  usrquota  and  [no]bh are backwardly compatible with ext3 or
       ext2.

       journal_checksum
              Enable checksumming of  the  journal  transactions.  This  will
              allow  the recovery code in e2fsck and the kernel to detect cor-
              ruption in the kernel. It is a compatible change  and  will  be
              ignored by older kernels.

       journal_async_commit
              Commit block can be written to disk without waiting for descrip-
              tor blocks. If enabled older kernels cannot  mount  the  device.
```

10

Mounting Removable Media

When removable media, such as a CD-ROM or DVD, is automatically mounted, it is typically made available under the **/media** directory. There is no need to configure this process on a modern Linux distribution that is using a GUI, such as Gnome or KDE, as these software programs recognize new removable media and automatically mount.

However, on a system that does not have a running GUI, this automatic mount process does not take place. You can configure the system so a regular user can mount a removable device by using the following **/etc/fstab** entry:

```
/dev/cdrom /media udf,iso9660 noauto,owner 0 0
```

Swap Space

Swap space is used by the operating system when available RAM runs low. Data in RAM not currently being used is "swapped" to the dedicated space on the hard drive reserved for this use to make room for other processes to use RAM.

Typically you create a swap partition as part of the installation process. At some point after installation, you may decide to add additional swap space. This can be in the form of another swap partition or a swap file.

To see your currently active swap devices, execute the **swapon** command with the **-s** option:

```
[root@onecoursesource ~]# swapon -s
Filename                Type         Size       Used      Priority
/dev/dm-1               partition    1048568
```

From the output of the **swapon -s** command, you can see the device name (**/dev/dm-1**) that holds the swap filesystem, the size (in bytes) of the swap filesystem, and how much of this space has been used. The priority indicates which swap filesystem should be used first.

Creating Swap Devices

A swap device can be either a storage device (a partition, logical volume, RAID, and so on) or a file. Typically storage devices are a bit quicker than swap files because the kernel doesn't have to go through a filesystem to access swap space on a storage device. However, you are not always able to add a new device to the system, so you may find swap files are more often used for secondary swap devices.

Assuming that you have already created a new partition with a tag type of 82 (**/dev/sdb1** in this example), you can format it as a swap device by executing the following command:

```
[root@onecoursesource ~]# mkswap /dev/sdb1
Setting up swapspace version 1, size = 203772 KiB
no label, UUID=039c21dc-c223-43c8-8176-da2f4d508402
```

You can add this to existing swap space with the **swapon** command:

```
[root@onecoursesource ~]# swapon -s
Filename                  Type         Size         Used         Priority
/dev/dm-1                 partition    1048568      37636        -1
root@onecoursesource ~]# swapon /dev/sdb1
[root@onecoursesource ~]# swapon -s
Filename                  Type         Size         Used         Priority
/dev/dm-1                 partition    1048568      37636        -1
/dev/sdb1                 partition    203768       0            -2
```

Remember that the **swapon** command is only a temporary solution. Add an entry like the following to **/etc/fstab** to make this a permanent swap device:

```
UUID=039c21dc-c223-43c8-8176-da2f4d508402 swap    defaults    0 0
```

To create a swap file, you first need to create a large file. This is most easily accomplished by using the **dd** command. Example 10-17 shows how to create a 200MB file named **/var/extra_swap** and then enable it as swap space.

Example 10-17 *Creating a File and Enabling Swap Space*

```
[root@onecoursesource ~]# dd if=/dev/zero of=/var/extra_swap bs=1M count=200
200+0 records in
200+0 records out
209715200 bytes (210 MB) copied, 4.04572 s, 51.8 MB/s
[root@onecoursesource ~]# mkswap /var/extra_swap
mkswap: /var/extra_swap: warning: don't erase bootbits sectors
        on whole disk. Use -f to force.
Setting up swapspace version 1, size = 204796 KiB
no label, UUID=44469984-0a99-45af-94b7-f7e97218d67a
[root@onecoursesource ~]# swapon /var/extra_swap
[root@onecoursesource ~]# swapon -s
```

```
Filename            Type        Size      Used     Priority
/dev/dm-1           partition   1048568   37664    -1
/dev/sdb1           partition   203768    0        -2
/var/extra_swap     file        204792    0        -3
```

If you decide that you want to manually remove a device from the current swap space, use the **swapoff** command:

```
[root@onecoursesource ~]# swapon -s
Filename          Type        Size      Used     Priority
/dev/dm-1         partition   1048568   27640    -1
/var/extra_swap   file        204792    0        -2
[root@onecoursesource ~]# swapoff /var/extra_swap
[root@onecoursesource ~]# swapon -s
Filename          Type        Size      Used     Priority
/dev/dm-1         partition   1048568   27640    -1
```

Summary

In this chapter, you learned how to create partitions and filesystems and to perform essential filesystem manipulation tasks. This was done through mounting partitions both manually and automatically and using different options available during the mounting and unmounting operations.

Key Terms

Physical filesystem, virtual filesystem, mount point, mounting, label, UUID, syncing, swap space, journal, snapshot, inode

Review Questions

1. Which of the following is a filesystem used on CD-ROM discs? (Choose two.)

- **A.** ext2
- **B.** HFS
- **C.** ISO9660
- **D.** UDF

2. The _____ command is used to unmount a filesystem.

3. Which commands can be used to determine what is preventing you from unmounting a filesystem? (Choose two.)

- **A.** **mount**
- **B.** **umount**
- **C.** **fuser**
- **D.** **lsof**

10

4. Which option to the **fuser** command displays the owner of the process that is keeping the filesystem busy?

   A. -k

   B. -o

   C. -v

   D. All of the above

5. Which of the following commands displays the UUID of a device?

   A. **e2label**

   B. **mount**

   C. **sync**

   D. **blkid**

6. The _____ command removes a swap device from current use.

7. Which filesystem supports files up to 2TB in size?

   A. ext2

   B. ext3

   C. ext4

   D. None of the above

8. Which of the following commands can be used to create a partition?

   A. **mkfs**

   B. **fsck**

   C. **dumpe2fs**

   D. **fdisk**

9. Fill in the blank to make an ext4 filesystem: _____

10. The _____ option to the **tune2fs** command allows you to change the percentage of the filesystem reserved for the superuser.

Manage Local Storage: Advanced Features

The focus of this chapter is managing advanced local storage device features. The first part of this chapter covers encrypting filesystems so you can secure mobile devices.

Next, the feature of autofs is explored. This feature allows you to automatically make devices appear in the directory structure when a user moves into a specific directory. This feature is useful for both local and remote storage devices. Remote storage devices are covered in Chapter 12, "Manage Network Storage."

Lastly, you learn the basics of logical volume management, a replacement for traditional partitions.

After reading this chapter and completing the exercises, you will be able to do the following:

Create and mount encrypted filesystems

Manage autofs

Manage logical volumes

Set up disk quotas

Manage hard and soft links

Encrypted Filesystems

You may have used software such as the GnuPG to encrypt files. This technology, called *file level encryption*, is designed to encrypt specific files, normally to ensure they are securely transported. The purpose of encrypting filesystems is similar, but is normally performed for a different reason.

Consider a situation in which you need to transfer thousands of files to another individual on a USB thumb drive. Encrypting each file individually would be a tedious process (as would the decryption process). Encrypting the entire filesystem provides just as much of a security advantage (in fact, more advantages) as encrypting individual files.

How is encrypting the entire filesystem better than encrypting individual files? Consider that when you encrypt a single file, some of the file data (ownership, permissions, timestamps, and so on) is still visible to a potential threat. If you encrypt the entire filesystem, these details wouldn't be available unless the filesystem was decrypted.

Additionally, if your laptop contains sensitive data, encrypting the filesystems could prevent unauthorized access in the event that your laptop is lost or stolen.

An important technology you want to be aware of when it comes to Linux filesystem encryption is the specification LUKS (Linux Unified Key Setup). When we say that LUKS is a specification, we mean that it describes how filesystems are to be encrypted on Linux. It does not provide any software, and it is not an official standard (although specifications are commonly referred to as "unofficial standards").

Because it is a specification, LUKS does not force you to use any one specific software tool to encrypt a filesystem. Different tools are available, but for the purposes of this book, we will demonstrate a kernel-based implementation called DMCrypt.

DMCrypt is a kernel module that allows the kernel to understand encrypted filesystems. In addition to the DMCrypt module, you should be aware of two commands you can use to create and mount an encrypted filesystem: the **cryptsetup** and **cryptmount** commands. Note that you would only use one of the two commands (most likely the **cryptsetup** command) to configure an encrypted filesystem.

The following steps demonstrate how to create a new encrypted filesystem using the **cryptsetup** command. To begin, you may need to load some kernel modules (see Chapter 28, "System Booting," for details regarding the **modprobe** command):

```
[root@onecoursesource ~]# modprobe dm-crypt
[root@onecoursesource ~]# modprobe aes
[root@onecoursesource ~]# modprobe sha256
```

Next, create a LUKS-formatted password on a new partition. Note that if you are using an existing partition, you first need to back up all data and unmount the partition. The following command overrides data on the **/dev/sda3** partition:

```
[root@onecoursesource ~]# cryptsetup --verbose --verify-passphrase
➥luksFormat /dev/sda3
WARNING!
========
This will overwrite data on /dev/sda3 irrevocably.
Are you sure? (Type uppercase yes): YES
Enter passphrase:
Verify passphrase:
Command successful.
```

Notice from the previous output of the **cryptsetup** command that you are prompted to provide a passphrase (a string of characters such as a sentence or simple phrase). This passphrase will be needed to decrypt the filesystem whenever you need to mount the filesystem.

11

Next, you need to run a command to create a new encrypted device file. The following creates a file called **/dev/mapper/data**, which is used later to mount the encrypted filesystem. The passphrase you type must match the one you created by the previous **cryptsetup** command.

```
[root@onecoursesource ~]# cryptsetup luksOpen /dev/sda3 data
Enter passphrase for /dev/sda3:
```

Now that the filesystem is open (you can think of this as "unlocked" or "decrypted"), create a filesystem on the new device, as shown in Example 11-1.

Example 11-1 *Creating a Filesystem*

```
[root@onecoursesource ~]# mkfs -t ext4 /dev/mapper/data
mke2fs 1.42.9 (28-Dec-2013)
Filesystem label=
OS type: Linux
Block size=4096 (log=2)
Fragment size=4096 (log=2)
Stride=0 blocks, Stripe width=0 blocks
34480 inodes, 137728 blocks
6886 blocks (5.00%) reserved for the super user
```

```
First data block=0
Maximum filesystem blocks=142606336
5 block groups
32768 blocks per group, 32768 fragments per group
6896 inodes per group
Superblock backups stored on blocks:
    32768, 98304
Allocating group tables: done
Writing inode tables: done
Creating journal (4096 blocks): done
Writing superblocks and filesystem accounting information: done
```

Notice in the previous command that the device **/dev/mapper/data** was used as the device to create the filesystem on. It is very important that you *not* create the filesystem on the partition (**/dev/sda3** in this example).

Create the mount point directory and entries in the **/etc/crypttab** and **/etc/fstab** files. The **/etc/crypttab** file matches the new **/dev/mapper/data** device with the **/dev/sda3** partition. This association is used by the system during the boot process to mount **/dev/mapper/data** under the **/data** directory.

```
[root@onecoursesource ~]# mkdir /data
[root@onecoursesource ~]# echo "data /dev/sda3 none" >> /etc/crypttab
[root@onecoursesource ~]# echo "/dev/mapper/data /data ext4 defaults 1 2" >> /etc/fstab
```

Each time you boot the system, you are prompted for the passphrase to mount the **/dev/mapper/data** device. See Figure 11-1 for an example.

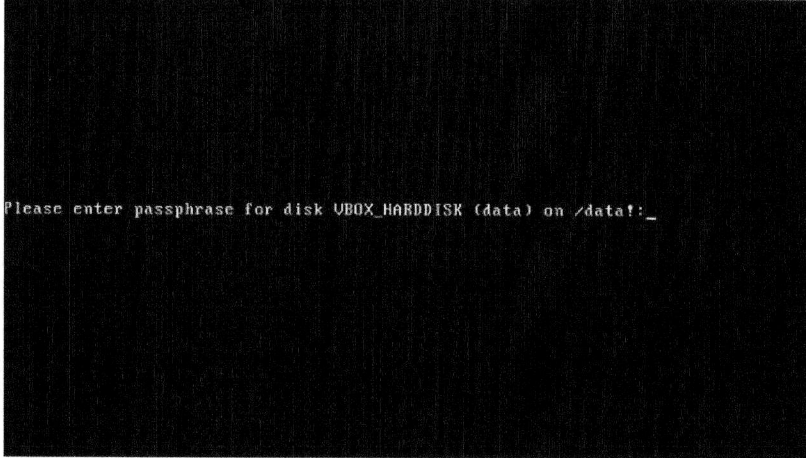

Figure 11-1 *Prompting for Password During Boot*

It is possible to automate this process by changing **none** in the **/etc/crypttab** file to a setting that provides the password, but that defeats the reason why you encrypted the filesystem in the first place.

Managing autofs

The purpose of autofs is to have filesystems automatically mounted when a user (or any process) accesses the mount point. After the mount point has not been used for a period of time, the filesystem is automatically unmounted.

The starting point of autofs is the **/etc/auto.master** file, which allows you to specify what to mount when a mount point is accessed. Typically your distribution will already have an **/etc/auto.master** file, but its exact contents may vary slightly from one distribution to another. Example 11-2 shows the **/etc/auto.master** file on a CentOS 7.x system.

Example 11-2 *The /etc/auto.master File on a CentOS 7.x System*

```
[root@onecoursesource Desktop]# more /etc/auto.master
#
# Sample auto.master file
# This is a 'master' automounter map and it has the following format:
# mount-point [map-type[,format]:]map [options]
# For details of the format look at auto.master(5).
#
/misc    /etc/auto.misc
#
# NOTE: mounts done from a hosts map will be mounted with the
#     "nosuid" and "nodev" options unless the "suid" and "dev"
#     options are explicitly given.
#
/net    -hosts
#
# Include /etc/auto.master.d/*.autofs
# The included files must conform to the format of this file.
#
+dir:/etc/auto.master.d
#
# Include central master map if it can be found using
# nsswitch sources.
#
# Note that if there are entries for /net or /misc (as
# above) in the included master map any keys that are the
# same will not be seen as the first read key seen takes
# precedence.
#
+auto.master
```

Note that most of the default file is composed of comments and that only four settings currently exist in this file. Three of these settings are fairly basic and are described in Table 11-1.

Table 11-1 Default **/etc/auto.master** Settings

Setting	Description
/net -hosts	This setting provides a useful feature to automatically mount NFS (Network File System) devices that have been shared from remote systems. When this setting is enabled, you can just navigate directly to **/net/*machine_name*** to automatically mount all NFS devices that have been shared by that remote machine. For example, if you navigate to **/net/server1**, then autofs would automatically mount all NFS shares from the machine with the hostname of server1. Or, if you go to **/net/192.168.1.1**, then autofs would automatically mount all NFS shares from the machine with an IP address of 192.168.1.1. Note: NFS shares will be covered in detail in Chapter 12.

11

Setting	Description
+dir:/etc/auto.master.d	This setting allows you to create files in the **/etc/auto.master.d** directory with additional autofs settings. Most administrators will likely modify the **/etc/auto.master** file directly, but the advantage of the **/etc/auto.master.d** directory is that software vendors that want to add autofs mounts can do so by placing a file in this directory rather than trying to edit the **/etc/auto.master** file during the installation process.
+auto.master	As you can see from the comments in the **/etc/auto.master** file, this setting is used to "Include central master map if it can be found using nsswitch sources." If you look at the **/etc/nsswitch.conf** file, there will be an entry that looks like this: **automount: files**. If you had autofs settings from another source, like NIS (Network Information Server), then you could incorporate them on the local system by changing the entry in the **/etc/nsswitch.conf** file to look something like this: **automount: files nis**.

In addition to the settings from Table 11-1, there is another entry in the typical **/etc/auto.master** file:

```
/misc    /etc/auto.misc
```

This entry is the beginning of what is called an *indirect autofs map*. An indirect map requires settings in two files: the **/etc/auto.master** file and the file specified as the second value of the line (**/etc/auto.misc** in this example). To the automount daemon, this means "if a user or process changes into a subdirectory under the **/misc** directory, then look at the entries in **/etc/auto.misc** for the rest of the information."

If there is an entry that refers to the **/etc/auto.misc** file in your default **/etc/auto.master** file, then there should also be a default **/etc/auto.misc** file. Example 11-3 demonstrates the default **/etc/auto.misc** file on a CentOS 7.x system.

Example 11-3 *The /etc/auto.misc File on a CentOS 7.x System*

```
[root@onecoursesource Desktop]# more /etc/auto.misc
#
# This is an automounter map and it has the following format
# key [ -mount-options-separated-by-comma ] location
# Details may be found in the autofs(5) manpage

cd         -fstype=iso9660,ro,nosuid,nodev        :/dev/cdrom

# the following entries are samples to pique your imagination
#linux         -ro,soft,intr         ftp.example.org:/pub/linux
#boot          -fstype=ext2          :/dev/hda1
#floppy        -fstype=auto          :/dev/fd0
#floppy        -fstype=ext2          :/dev/fd0
#e2floppy      -fstype=ext2          :/dev/fd0
#jaz           -fstype=ext2          :/dev/sdc1
#removable     -fstype=ext2          :/dev/hdd
```

Most of these lines are commented out, but one line does provide a setting that is currently enabled:

```
cd         -fstype=iso9660,ro,nosuid,nodev     :/dev/cdrom
```

The first field (**cd** in this example) contains the rest of the path to generate the mount point. The second field contains the mount options, and the third field is the device to mount. In other words, based on the entry in Example 11-3, if a user or process were to enter the **/misc/cd** directory, then the local **/dev/cdrom** device would be mounted with the **-fstype=iso9660,ro,nosuid,nodev** mount options.

On modern Linux distributions that have a GUI running, the GUI automatically mounts CD-ROMs. However, this would not happen on a server that was not running a GUI, so this setting might make it easier for regular users to access the CD-ROM (normally they would not be allowed to mount the CD-ROM).

Suppose you wanted to create an automount that mounts the NFS share of **server1:/usr/share/doc** under the **/nfs/doc** directory and creates an automount that mounts the NFS share of **plan9:/aliens** under the **/nfs/aliens** directory. First add the following entry in the **/etc/auto.master** file:

```
/nfs            /etc/auto.custom
```

Then add the following entries in the **/etc/auto.custom** file:

```
Doc        -fstype=nfs    server1:/usr/share/doc
Aliens     -fstype=nfs    plan9:/aliens
```

Next, create the **/nfs** directory (note that on modern systems, this step might not be necessary, but it does no harm either):

```
mkdir /nfs
```

Do not create any subdirectories; **/nfs/doc** and **/nfs/aliens** will be created by the automount daemon as required (and then deleted when no longer required).

Finally, either start or restart the autofs service. Assuming you are working on a SysVinit system, execute the following:

```
/etc/init.d/autofs start
```

Note that you can also create a direct map, which is less complex and recommended for simple mounts. For direct maps, you add an entry like the following in the **/etc/auto.master** file:

```
/-     /etc/auto.direct
```

Then you place the complete mount point, mount options, and device to mount in the **/etc/auto.direct** file:

```
/remote/aliens    -fstype=nfs    plan9:/aliens
```

Remember to restart the autofs services whenever you make changes to any of these map files.

Logical Volume Manager

The partitioning technology that has been used on x86 platforms for decades has limitations. For example, the entire partition must reside on a single disk, making it difficult to take advantage of disk space when a new hard drive is added to the system. It is also not easy to resize traditional partitions.

Logical Volume Manager (LVM) is a technology that can be used in place of traditional partitions. Using LVM you can incorporate new storage space into an existing storage device, essentially extending the capacity of a device that already contains a filesystem. LVM also allows you to create "snapshots," enabling you to create backups of live filesystems.

Logical Volume Manager Concepts

NOTE This section introduces some terms that are critical to understand: Logical Volume Manager (LVM), volume group, physical volume, physical extent, and so on. When reading documentation on LVM, you will almost always see these terms abbreviated (volume group = VG, physical volume = PV, and so on). As a result, this chapter follows the same convention of using abbreviations after introducing a term. This is designed to help you become comfortable with this convention.

You have been tasked with installing a new database server on an existing system. You inform your manager that you need 100GB of additional storage space, to which he replies, "No problem, I will have that sent to your office." The next day a package arrives, containing three new 40GB hard drives. You realize a problem immediately, as the database software requires a single 100GB storage container. When you inform your boss about this problem, you are told that you must make do with what you have been provided. Now what?

You could put the three hard disks into a software RAID 0 device, but you realize that this will pose problems if more space is required for the database server in the future. You also know that getting a solid backup of the database while it is being used is important. Fortunately, you know of a technology that allows you to add more space on the fly and provides a technique to make backups on live filesystems: LVM (Logical Volume Manager).

Typically, two mental barriers seem to stop administrators from embracing LVM:

- Understanding why LVM is so much better than regular partitions
- Understanding the concept of how LVM works

So, before diving into the commands that you need to know to implement LVM, we explore the advantages and concepts of this technology.

NOTE There are two primary implementations of LVM: LVM1 and LVM2. Most of the topics in this chapter apply to both. When there are differences, they are covered. To avoid confusion, the term LVM refers to both LVM1 and LVM2.

The following list describes some of the advantages of LVM:

- LVM can be used to take multiple storage devices and merge them together into a device that the kernel perceives as a single storage device. This means you can take three hard drives of 40GB and merge them into a single storage device that is 120GB. In fact, the devices don't all have to be the same size or the same type, so you can combine a 30GB hard drive, a 20GB USB drive (just don't remove it!), and a 25GB iSCSI device into a single storage device. You can even use part of a hard disk by creating a partition and adding that to the LVM.
- With LVM, you can add space to existing filesystems by adding a new physical storage device and adding this device to the LVM. Examples of this are provided later in this chapter.
- Even if you don't need really large storage containers and are not worried about increasing the size of your filesystems, LVM can still be useful if you have multiple hard disks in your system. By using the LVM feature of striping, you can have data written to multiple hard disks concurrently, which can increase your I/O (input/output) speed substantially.
- Backing up a live filesystem is often problematic because of how backup tools work. These tools often back up filesystem metadata first and then back up the file contents. On live filesystems, this can cause problems if the files' contents change between backing up the metadata and backing up the file contents. LVM has a feature called a *snapshot* that allows you to back up a frozen image of the filesystem while the real filesystem remains active. This is explained in greater detail later in this chapter.

It sounds like LVM is perfect for everything. Granted, in most cases you probably should use LVM instead of traditional partitions, but LVM has a couple of disadvantages that you should consider:

- LVM doesn't provide redundancy like RAID does (then again, neither do traditional partitions). However, you can solve this problem by creating software RAID 1 devices and including them as the storage devices used within your LVM. LVM2 also has a feature that incorporates software RAID (but for level 4, 5, or 6, not for level 1).
- Some older firmware and bootloaders don't know how to access LVM devices. As a result, you often see the **/boot** filesystem placed on a regular partition. However, this has started to change recently as more modern firmware and bootloaders can access LVM devices.

Advantages of LVM on a System with a Single Drive

You may be wondering why you should use LVM on a system that has just a single hard disk. To answer that question, let us tell you about a situation that we have had to deal with many times in our careers as system administrators.

We are often tasked with installing a new system, and we always try to create partitions that make sense given the situation. For example, if we are installing a mail server, we would make sure to create a separate **/var** filesystem. If we are installing a machine that has multiple users, we would make sure the **/home** filesystem is on a separate partition. Therefore, it wouldn't be uncommon to end up with a partition layout that looks like the layout described in Table 11-2.

Table 11-2 Sample Partition Layout

Partition	Mount Point	Size
/dev/sda1	**/boot**	200MB
/dev/sda2	**/var**	1.5GB
/dev/sda5	**/**	5GB (Note: **/dev/sda3** is not used and **/dev/sda4** is the extended partition.)
/dev/sda6	**/tmp**	500MB
/dev/sda7	**/home**	2.5GB

Typically, the filesystem layout described in Table 11-2 works just fine for some time. However, that doesn't always last because the filesystem space needs change over time. For example, on one occasion it was discovered that the **/tmp** filesystem was filling up on a regular basis, but the **/home** filesystem wasn't even 10% full. It would be great to take some of the space from the **/home** filesystem (located in the **/dev/sda7** partition) and give it to the **/tmp** filesystem (located in the **/dev/sda6** partition), but that is not an easy task. The general steps would be as follows:

Step 1. Back up the data in **/home** (**/tmp** is temporary data, so backing up that filesystem should not be necessary).

Step 2. Unmount both **/home** and **/tmp** (which likely requires switching to single user mode).

Step 3. Destroy the **/dev/sda7** and **/dev/sda6** partitions.

Step 4. Create new, resized **/dev/sda7** and **/dev/sda6** partitions.

Step 5. Create filesystems on the new partitions.

Step 6. Restore the data.

Step 7. Mount the **/home** and **/tmp** filesystems.

If you think that is a lot of work, consider taking space from the **/home** (**/dev/sda7**) filesystem and giving it to the **/var** (**/dev/sda2**) filesystem. This would require having to change all partitions except the **/dev/sda1** partition, which would take a lot of time and effort.

If these were LVM storage devices instead of regular partitions, the process would be much easier, requiring much less data backup and downtime. You can easily reduce the space of an LVM storage device and give that space to another LVM storage device, or you can just add a new storage device to the system and provide that space to the filesystem that needs more space.

LVM Essentials

Hopefully by now you are convinced of the benefits of LVM and are at least willing to abandon regular partitions in favor of LVM. The next hurdle is to understand the concepts of LVM.

NOTE If you want to practice LVM commands, consider using virtual machines. If you are using a virtual machine, you can easily create three new virtual hard drives to practice the LVM commands, which are described in this chapter.

Returning to the original scenario: You have three 40GB hard disks and you need to make the kernel treat a total of 100GB of this space as a single storage device. The first step to this process, after installing these devices, is to convert them to physical volumes (PVs). This is accomplished by executing the **pvcreate** command. For example, if you have three drives with device names of **/dev/sdb**, **/dev/sdc**, and **/dev/sdd**, you can convert them to PVs by executing the following command:

```
[root@onecoursesource Desktop]# pvcreate /dev/sdb /dev/sdc /dev/sdd
  Physical volume "/dev/sdb" successfully created
  Physical volume "/dev/sdc" successfully created
  Physical volume "/dev/sdd" successfully created
```

To think of this conceptually, look at what has been created so far in Figure 11-2.

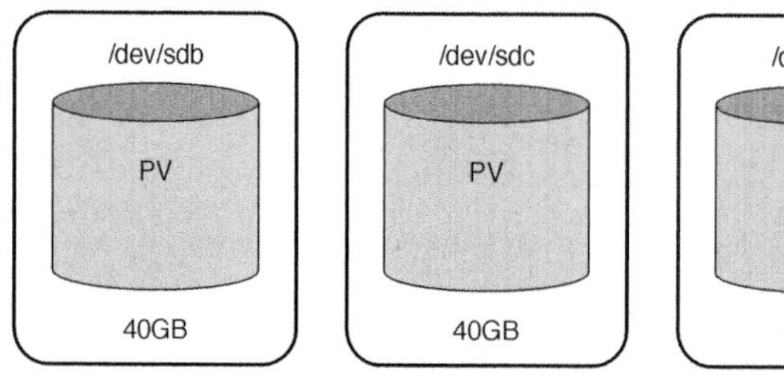

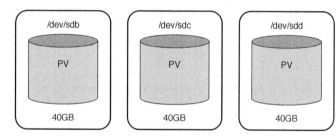

Figure 11-2 *Physical Volumes*

Now that you have formatted the PVs, you need to place them inside a new volume group (VG). You can create this VG and place the PVs inside it by executing the following command:

```
[root@onecoursesource ~]# vgcreate VG0 /dev/sdb /dev/sdc /dev/sdd
  Volume group "VG0" successfully created
```

The VG is a container used to group PVs together. The space available within the VG can be used to create logical volumes (LVs). Logical volumes work just like partitions; you can create filesystems on LVs and mount them just like regular partitions.

Before exploring how to create an LV, look at Figure 11-3 to see a visual representation of a VG.

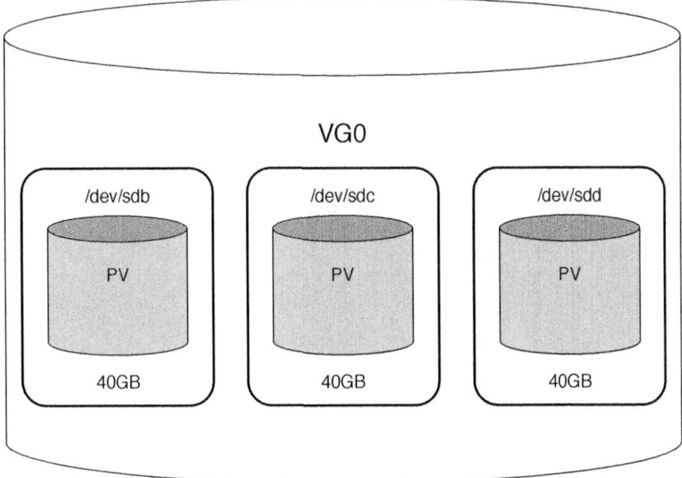

Figure 11-3 *The VG0 Volume Group*

Extents

When the VG was created, the space made available by the PVs was broken into small chunks called *physical extents*. By default, the extent size is 4MB, but this is something you can specify when you create the VG by using the **-s** option:

```
[root@onecoursesource ~]# vgcreate -s 16MB VG0 /dev/sdb /dev/sdc /dev/sdd
```

Note that the extent size is not something that can be adjusted at a later time. For LVM1, this is an important feature because you build the LVs using these extents and there is a limit of how many extents you can use for each LV. For example, if the VG has extents that are 4MB, you could build a 20MB LV by using five extents from the VG.

If your system is using LVM1, it is critical to know that each LV can have at most 65,534 extents. If you do the math, this means if your VG has 4MB extents, the largest an LV can be is 256GiB (see http://wintelguy.com/gb2gib.html for a review of the difference between GB and GiB). In most cases that should be plenty, but in the event that it isn't, create the VG with a larger extent size.

The 65,534 extent limitation was removed in LVM2, which is most likely the version of LVM that you are using if you are using a modern distribution. However, using small extents on large LVs can slow down the LVM tools (although it should have no impact on input/output performance).

The largest extent size is 16GiB, so you might wonder why you wouldn't just use the largest extent size. The problem with this approach is that each LV must use a whole multiple of the extent size. In other words, if your extent size is 16GiB, then your LVs can be 16GiB, 32GiB, 48GiB, and so on. This isn't a flexible approach.

To visualize the concept of physical extents, look at the black boxes in Figure 11-4 (but imagine a lot more of them, because each PV in our scenario is 40GB and each extent is only 4MB).

11

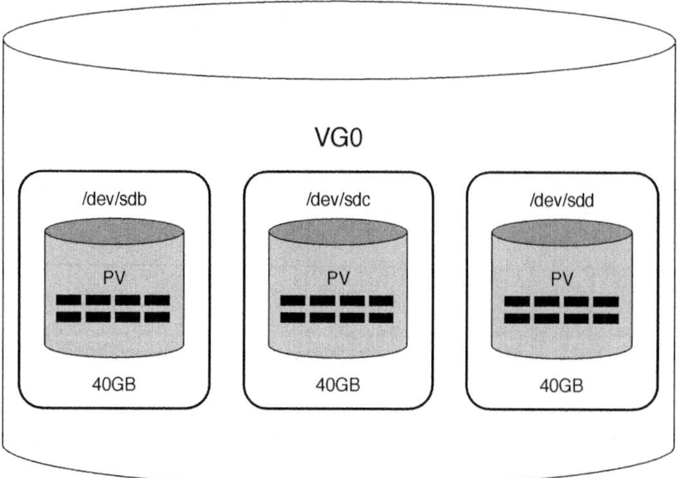

Figure 11-4 *Physical Extents*

If you want to see the size of the extents, as well as other useful VG information, execute the **vgdisplay** command, as shown in Example 11-4.

Example 11-4 *The **vgdisplay** Command*

```
[root@onecoursesource ~]# vgdisplay VG0
  --- Volume group ---
  VG Name               VG0
  System ID
  Format                lvm2
  Metadata Areas        3
  Metadata Sequence No  1
  VG Access             read/write
  VG Status             resizable
  MAX LV                0
  Cur LV                0
  Open LV               0
  Max PV                0
  Cur PV                3
  Act PV                3
  VG Size               1.49 GiB
  PE Size               4.00 MiB
  Total PE              381
  Alloc PE / Size       0 / 0
  Free  PE / Size       381 / 1.49 GiB
  VG UUID               AbRpPe-vaV3-1SKI-eFMB-IN48-Fdkt-U54OW7
```

NOTE Although the original scenario was to use three 40GB hard disks, this example uses three 500MB virtual hard disks. If you are practicing these commands on a virtual machine, we suggest using small virtual hard disks rather than wasting space creating huge virtual hard disks.

Notice that the format is set to **lvm2**, so on this system we don't have a limitation of 65,534 extents per LV. The **VG Size** value indicates how much space is available in the VG, and the **Total PE** value indicates the total number of physical extents available to assign to LVs.

If you use the **-v** option to the **vgdisplay** command, you also see information about any PVs and LVs associated with the VG. At this point we haven't created any LVs, so executing the **vgdisplay -v** command provides the additional information shown in Example 11-5.

Example 11-5 *The vgdisplay -v Command*

```
--- Physical volumes ---
PV Name               /dev/sdb
PV UUID               K6ikZy-yRxe-mwVf-ChQP-0swd-OvNA-L56QNT
PV Status             allocatable
Total PE / Free PE    127 / 127

PV Name               /dev/sdc
PV UUID               leCbvm-FzNb-479B-5OAv-CTje-YWEe-gJhcyK
PV Status             allocatable
Total PE / Free PE    127 / 127

PV Name               /dev/sdd
PV UUID               7KUVBt-Un5l-0K3e-aeOy-deqP-iUW4-24fXwI
PV Status             allocatable
Total PE / Free PE    127 / 127
```

You can also see detailed information about a PV by executing the **pvdisplay** command, as shown in Example 11-6.

Example 11-6 *The pvdisplay Command*

```
[root@onecoursesource ~]# pvdisplay /dev/sdb
 --- Physical volume ---
 PV Name               /dev/sdb
 VG Name               VG0
 PV Size               512.00 MiB / not usable 4.00 MiB
 Allocatable           yes
 PE Size               4.00 MiB
 Total PE              127
 Free PE               127
 Allocated PE          0
 PV UUID               K6ikZy-yRxe-mwVf-ChQP-0swd-OvNA-L56QNT
```

NOTE When referring to extents on a PV, we call them *physical extents*. When an LV is using these physical extents, they are called *logical extents*. They aren't two different things, but rather the same thing from two different perspectives. They are typically just called extents, but you should be aware that some LVM documentation uses either the term PE or the term LE.

Logical Volumes

To create an LV using space from a VG, execute the **lvcreate** command. You can enable several options when you create an LV. A simple example would be to create an LV specifying how many extents you want to use:

```
[root@onecoursesource ~]# lvcreate -l 6 -n lv0 VG0
  Logical volume "lv0" created.
```

11

The **-n** option is used to specify a name for the LV. The **-l** option is used to specify how many extents to use to create the LV. To specify the size of the new LV, use the **-L** option instead of the **-l** option (for example, **lvcreate -L 120M -n lv0 VG0**).

To understand what happens when you executed the **lvcreate** command, look at Figure 11-5.

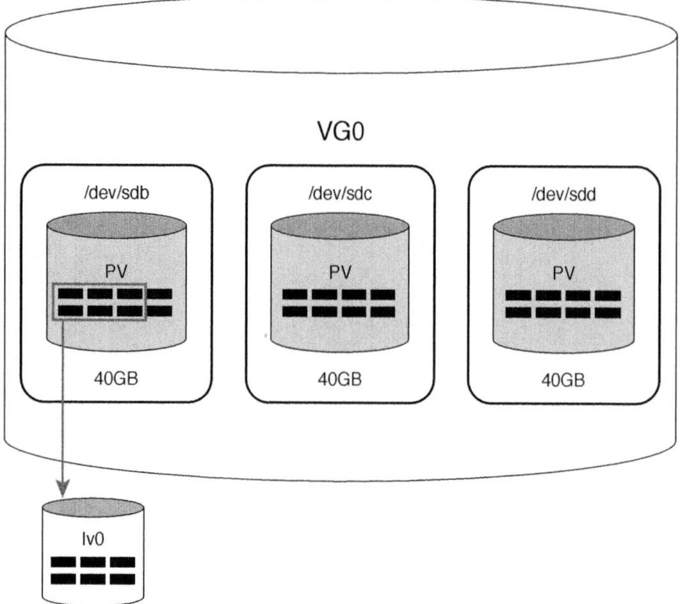

Figure 11-5 *Logical Volume*

The new LV was built using six PEs from the first PV in the VG. You could have chosen to use two PEs from each PV by using the **-i** option to the **lvcreate** command. The **-i** option is used to indicate how many PVs (referred to as *stripes*) to use when creating the LV. Here's an example:

```
[root@onecoursesource ~]# lvcreate -i 3 -l 6 -n lv1 VG0
 Using default stripesize 64.00 KiB.
 Logical volume "lv1" created.
```

Device Naming

Now that there are two new devices, lv0 and lv1, you can see the device names that have been created in the **/dev** directory structure. In fact, you now have three methods to refer to each device: the LVM1 method, the LVM2 method, and the "real" device name.

In LVM1, a directory is created under the **/dev** directory that matches the name of the VG, and within that directory files are created that match the name of the LVs. So, if you have a VG named VG0 and two LVs named lv0 and lv1, then you should see the following files:

```
[root@onecoursesource ~]# ls /dev/VG0
lv0  lv1
```

However, these are not the real device names, but rather symbolic links to the real device names. You can see this by looking at the output of the following command:

```
[root@onecoursesource ~]# ls -l /dev/VG0
total 0
lrwxrwxrwx. 1 root root 7 Oct 27 09:14 lv0 -> ../dm-3
lrwxrwxrwx. 1 root root 7 Oct 27 09:24 lv1 -> ../dm-4
```

The real device names are **/dev/dm-3** and **/dev/dm-4**. Why create the symbolic link instead of using the device names of **/dev/dm-3** and **/dev/dm-4**? Because it is easier for you to remember names that you create.

LMV2 introduced a new naming convention (although the LMV1 naming convention of **/dev/VG/LV** still exists). The newer naming technique is **/dev/mapper/VG-LV**. So, if you have a VG named VG0 and two LVs named lv0 and lv1, then you should see the following files:

```
[root@onecoursesource ~]# ls -l /dev/mapper/VG0*
lrwxrwxrwx. 1 root root 7 Oct 27 09:14 /dev/mapper/VG0-lv0 -> ../dm-3
lrwxrwxrwx. 1 root root 7 Oct 27 09:24 /dev/mapper/VG0-lv1 -> ../dm-4
```

Most Linux distributions use LVM2, so both naming conventions should be available. It doesn't matter which one you use because they both point to the same **dm-*** files.

Using Logical Volumes and Additional LVM Commands

Now comes the easy part: Think of **/dev/VG0/lv0** (or **/dev/mapper/VG0-lv0**) as if it were a regular partition. What would you do with a partition to make it available to the operating system?

1. Create a filesystem.
2. Make a mount point.
3. Mount the filesystem under the mount point.
4. Verify the mount.
5. Make an entry in **/etc/fstab** to mount the filesystem at bootup.

Start by creating a filesystem, as shown in Example 11-7.

Example 11-7 *Creating the Filesystem*

```
[root@onecoursesource ~]# mkfs -t ext4 /dev/mapper/VG0-lv0
mke2fs 1.41.12 (17-May-2010)
Filesystem label=
OS type: Linux
Block size=1024 (log=0)
Fragment size=1024 (log=0)
Stride=0 blocks, Stripe width=0 blocks
6144 inodes, 24576 blocks
1228 blocks (5.00%) reserved for the super user
First data block=1
Maximum filesystem blocks=25165824
3 block groups
8192 blocks per group, 8192 fragments per group
2048 inodes per group
Superblock backups stored on blocks:
        8193
Writing inode tables: done
Creating journal (1024 blocks): done
Writing superblocks and filesystem accounting information: done
This filesystem will be automatically checked every 20 mounts or
180 days, whichever comes first. Use tune2fs -c or -i to override.
```

11

Now create a mount point, mount the filesystem, and verify the mount, like so:

```
[root@onecoursesource ~]# mkdir /storage-lv0
[root@onecoursesource ~]# mount /dev/mapper/VG0-lv0 /storage-lv0
[root@onecoursesource ~]# mount | grep lv0
/dev/mapper/VG0-lv0 on /storage-lv0 type ext4 (rw)
```

Finally, add an entry like the following to the **/etc/fstab** file:

```
/dev/mapper/VG0-lv0  /storage  ext4  defaults 0 2
```

Displaying LVM Information

Several commands display LVM information, including a couple we already introduced. For example, recall that the **vgdisplay** command provides information about a VG. Now that two new LVs have been created, notice the difference in the output from when the **vgdisplay** command was previously executed by looking at Example 11-8.

Example 11-8 *The **vgdisplay** Command After LV Creation*

```
[root@onecoursesource ~]# vgdisplay -v VG0
    Using volume group(s) on command line.
  --- Volume group ---
  VG Name               VG0
  System ID
  Format                lvm2
  Metadata Areas        3
  Metadata Sequence No  5
  VG Access             read/write
  VG Status             resizable
  MAX LV                0
  Cur LV                2
  Open LV               1
  Max PV                0
  Cur PV                3
  Act PV                3
  VG Size               1.49 GiB
  PE Size               4.00 MiB
  Total PE              381
  Alloc PE / Size       12 / 48.00 MiB
  Free  PE / Size       369 / 1.44 GiB
  VG UUID               AbRpPe-vaV3-1SKI-eFMB-IN48-Fdkt-U54OW7

  --- Logical volume ---
  LV Path                /dev/VG0/lv0
  LV Name                lv0
  VG Name                VG0
  LV UUID                m3cZlG-yydW-iNlh-I0Ky-HL3C-vWI8-AUKmRN
  LV Write Access        read/write
  LV Creation host, time onecoursesource.localdomain, 2017-10-27 09:14:21 -0700
  LV Status              available
  # open                 1
  LV Size                24.00 MiB
  Current LE             6
  Segments               1
```

```
Allocation              inherit
Read ahead sectors      auto
- currently set to      256
Block device            253:3

--- Logical volume ---
LV Path                 /dev/VG0/lv1
LV Name                 lv1
VG Name                 VG0
LV UUID                 GBhvzW-osp5-hf0D-uY1n-7KuA-Ulix-U3vaJ7
LV Write Access         read/write
LV Creation host, time onecoursesource.localdomain, 2017-10-27 09:24:42 -0700
LV Status               available
# open                  0
LV Size                 24.00 MiB
Current LE              6
Segments                1
Allocation              inherit
Read ahead sectors      auto
- currently set to      768
Block device            253:4

--- Physical volumes ---
PV Name                /dev/sdb
PV UUID                K6ikZy-yRxe-mwVf-ChQP-0swd-OvNA-L56QNT
PV Status              allocatable
Total PE / Free PE     127 / 119

PV Name                /dev/sdc
PV UUID                1eCbvm-FzNb-479B-5OAv-CTje-YWEe-gJhcyK
PV Status              allocatable
Total PE / Free PE     127 / 125

PV Name                /dev/sdd
PV UUID                7KUVBt-Un5l-0K3e-aeOy-deqP-iUW4-24fXwI
PV Status              allocatable
Total PE / Free PE     127 / 125
```

Note that some of the changes include information regarding the new LVs and changes to the information provided for the PVs. This information can also be viewed by using the **pvdisplay** and **lvdisplay** commands, as shown in Example 11-9.

Example 11-9 *The **pvdisplay** and **lvdisplay** Commands*

```
[root@onecoursesource ~]# pvdisplay /dev/sdb
  --- Physical volume ---
  PV Name               /dev/sdb
  VG Name               VG0
  PV Size               512.00 MiB / not usable 4.00 MiB
  Allocatable           yes
  PE Size               4.00 MiB
  Total PE              127
  Free PE               119
```

11

```
  Allocated PE          8
  PV UUID               K6ikZy-yRxe-mwVf-ChQP-0swd-OvNA-L56QNT

[root@onecoursesource ~]# lvdisplay /dev/mapper/VG0-lv0
  --- Logical volume ---
  LV Path                /dev/VG0/lv0
  LV Name                lv0
  VG Name                VG0
  LV UUID                m3cZlG-yydW-iNlh-I0Ky-HL3C-vWI8-AUKmRN
  LV Write Access        read/write
  LV Creation host, time onecoursesource.localdomain, 2017-10-27 09:14:21 -0700
  LV Status              available
  # open                 1
  LV Size                24.00 MiB
  Current LE             6
  Segments               1
  Allocation             inherit
  Read ahead sectors     auto
  - currently set to     256
  Block device           253:3
```

Additional LVM Commands

There are dozens of additional LVM commands (LVM is a huge topic). It is useful to know that almost all LVM-related commands are subcommands of the **lvm** command.

The LVM commands demonstrated in this chapter are normally executed by symbolic links that refer to the **/sbin/lvm** command:

```
[root@onecoursesource ~]# which pvcreate
/sbin/pvcreate
[root@onecoursesource ~]# ls -l /sbin/pvcreate
lrwxrwxrwx. 1 root root 3 Oct 22 10:55 /sbin/pvcreate -> lvm
```

This can be critical to know in rescue environments, where the **lvm** command exists but the link commands to the **lvm** command do not exist. (Note: A rescue environment is one in which you boot the system from a recovery CD and attempt to fix system problems.)

When executing the **lvm** command with no arguments, you are provided an **lvm>** prompt where you can also execute these subcommands, as demonstrated in Example 11-10.

Example 11-10 *The lvm Command*

```
[root@onecoursesource ~]# lvm
lvm> help
  Available lvm commands:
  Use 'lvm help <command>' for more information

  dumpconfig      Dump active configuration
  formats         List available metadata formats
  help            Display help for commands
  lvchange        Change the attributes of logical volume(s)
  lvconvert       Change logical volume layout
  lvcreate        Create a logical volume
  lvdisplay       Display information about a logical volume
```

```
  lvextend        Add space to a logical volume
  lvmchange       With the device mapper, this is obsolete and does nothing.
  lvmdiskscan     List devices that may be used as physical volumes
  lvmsadc         Collect activity data
  lvmsar          Create activity report
  lvreduce        Reduce the size of a logical volume
  lvremove        Remove logical volume(s) from the system
  lvrename        Rename a logical volume
  lvresize        Resize a logical volume
  lvs             Display information about logical volumes
  lvscan          List all logical volumes in all volume groups
  pvchange        Change attributes of physical volume(s)
  pvresize        Resize physical volume(s)
  pvck            Check the consistency of physical volume(s)
  pvcreate        Initialize physical volume(s) for use by LVM
  pvdata          Display the on-disk metadata for physical volume(s)
  pvdisplay       Display various attributes of physical volume(s)
  pvmove          Move extents from one physical volume to another
  pvremove        Remove LVM label(s) from physical volume(s)
  pvs             Display information about physical volumes
  pvscan          List all physical volumes
  segtypes        List available segment types
  vgcfgbackup     Backup volume group configuration(s)
  vgcfgrestore    Restore volume group configuration
  vgchange        Change volume group attributes
  vgck            Check the consistency of volume group(s)
  vgconvert       Change volume group metadata format
  vgcreate        Create a volume group
  vgdisplay       Display volume group information
  vgexport        Unregister volume group(s) from the system
  vgextend        Add physical volumes to a volume group
  vgimport        Register exported volume group with system
  vgmerge         Merge volume groups
  vgmknodes       Create the special files for volume group devices in /dev
  vgreduce        Remove physical volume(s) from a volume group
  vgremove        Remove volume group(s)
  vgrename        Rename a volume group
  vgs             Display information about volume groups
  vgscan          Search for all volume groups
  vgsplit         Move physical volumes into a new or existing volume group
  version         Display software and driver version information
lvm> quit
```

11

Resizing Logical Volumes

Resizing an LV is a two-step process. If you are making the LV smaller, you first need to shrink the size of the filesystem and then shrink the LV with the **lvreduce** command. Some filesystems don't permit you to shrink the filesystem size, but making an LV smaller is rare anyway.

Most likely you are going to increase the size of the LV. In this case, you first increase the LV and then "grow" the filesystem. Note that these steps are the opposite order of the steps you take to decrease the size of an LV.

Not only do most filesystems permit growth, but many of them allow this to take place without you having to unmount the filesystem.

Before beginning this process, view the current size of the filesystem; in this example, it is about 23MB:

```
[root@onecoursesource ~]# df -h /dev/mapper/VG0-lv0
Filesystem            Size  Used Avail Use% Mounted on
/dev/mapper/VG0-lv0    23M  204K   21M   1% /storage-lv0
```

Also look at the size of the LV as displayed in Example 11-11, which is slightly larger because the filesystem requires some space for metadata, making the available size smaller than the container that holds the filesystem.

Example 11-11 *Logical Volume Display Size*

```
[root@onecoursesource ~]# lvdisplay /dev/mapper/VG0-lv0
 --- Logical volume ---
 LV Path                /dev/VG0/lv0
 LV Name                lv0
 VG Name                VG0
 LV UUID                m3cZlG-yydW-iNlh-I0Ky-HL3C-vWI8-AUKmRN
 LV Write Access        read/write
 LV Creation host, time onecoursesource.localdomain, 2017-10-27 09:14:21 -0700
 LV Status              available
 # open                 1
 LV Size                24.00 MiB
 Current LE             6
 Segments               1
 Allocation             inherit
 Read ahead sectors     auto
 - currently set to     256
 Block device           253:3
```

Notice that this filesystem is currently mounted and contains files. This is to demonstrate that you can perform the process of increasing the size of the LV and filesystem even though the filesystem is currently being used:

```
[root@onecoursesource ~]# mount | grep lv0
/dev/mapper/VG0-lv0 on /storage-lv0 type ext4 (rw)
[root@onecoursesource ~]# ls /storage-lv0
group  hosts  lost+found  words
```

Increase the size of the LV by using the **lvextend** command. In this case, the size is increased by 40MB:

```
[root@onecoursesource ~]# lvextend -L +40M /dev/mapper/VG0-lv0
  Size of logical volume VG0/lv0 changed from 24.00 MiB (6 extents) to 64.00 MiB (16 extents).
  Logical volume lv0 successfully resized
```

Verify that the LV is now larger:

```
[root@onecoursesource ~]# lvdisplay /dev/mapper/VG0-lv0 | grep Size
  LV Size                64.00 MiB
```

Note that the filesystem size is unchanged:

```
[root@onecoursesource ~]# df -h /dev/mapper/VG0-lv0
Filesystem           Size  Used Avail Use% Mounted on
/dev/mapper/VG0-lv0   23M  5.0M   17M  24% /storage-lv0
```

Now resize the filesystem with the **resize2fs** command (use the **xfs_growfs** command if you are resizing an xfs filesystem) and verify that this command was successful, as shown in Example 11-12.

Example 11-12 *Resizing the Filesystem*

```
[root@onecoursesource ~]# resize2fs /dev/mapper/VG0-lv0
resize2fs 1.41.12 (17-May-2010)
Filesystem at /dev/mapper/VG0-lv0 is mounted on /storage-lv0; on-line resizing required
old desc_blocks = 1, new_desc_blocks = 1
Performing an on-line resize of /dev/mapper/VG0-lv0 to 65536 (1k) blocks.
The filesystem on /dev/mapper/VG0-lv0 is now 65536 blocks long.

[root@onecoursesource ~]# df -h /dev/mapper/VG0-lv0
Filesystem           Size  Used Avail Use% Mounted on
/dev/mapper/VG0-lv0   61M  5.3M   53M  10% /storage-lv0
[root@onecoursesource ~]# df -h /dev/mapper/VG0-lv00
Filesystem            Size  Used Avail Use% Mounted on
/dev/mapper/VG0-lv0    62M  6.3M   53M  11% /storage-lv0
[root@onecoursesource ~]# ls /storage-lv0
group  hosts  lost+found  words
```

Although you can tell the **resize2fs** command what size to grow to, the command is smart enough to grow to the size of its container. Only if you are making the filesystem smaller do you need to specify a size value for the **resize2fs** command.

To shrink the size of an LV, there are five important steps, and they must be executed in order; otherwise, the procedure will fail and potentially cause filesystem damage:

1. Unmount the mount point or logical volume with the **umount** command.
2. Force **fsck** to check the filesystem.
3. Use **resize2fs** to reduce the filesystem.
4. Use **lvreduce** to reduce the size of the logical volume.
5. Mount the filesystem with the **mount** command.

See Example 11-13 for a demonstration of this process.

Example 11-13 *Reducing the Size of a Logical Volume*

```
[root@onecoursesource ~]# umount /storage-lv0/
[root@onecoursesource ~]# fsck -f /dev/mapper/VG0-lv0
fsck from util-linux-ng 2.17.2
e2fsck 1.41.12 (17-May-2010)
Pass 1: Checking inodes, blocks, and sizes
Pass 2: Checking directory structure
Pass 3: Checking directory connectivity
Pass 4: Checking reference counts
Pass 5: Checking group summary information
/dev/mapper/VG0-lv0: 14/16384 files (0.0% non-contiguous), 8429/65536 blocks
[root@onecoursesource ~]# resize2fs /dev/mapper/VG0-lv0 24M
```

```
resize2fs 1.41.12 (17-May-2010)
Resizing the filesystem on /dev/mapper/VG0-lv0 to 24576 (1k) blocks.
The filesystem on /dev/mapper/VG0-lv0 is now 24576 blocks long.

[root@onecoursesource ~]# lvreduce -L -40M /dev/mapper/VG0-lv0
  WARNING: Reducing active logical volume to 24.00 MiB
  THIS MAY DESTROY YOUR DATA (filesystem etc.)
Do you really want to reduce lv0? [y/n]: y
  Reducing logical volume lv0 to 24.00 MiB
  Logical volume lv0 successfully resized
[root@onecoursesource ~]# mount /dev/mapper/VG0-lv0 /storage-lv0
[root@onecoursesource ~]# df -h /dev/mapper/VG0-lv0
Filesystem            Size  Used Avail Use% Mounted on
/dev/mapper/VG0-lv0    24M  6.0M   17M  27% /storage-lv0
```

NOTE You can grow ext3, ext4, and xfs filesystems while they are mounted. To make these filesystems smaller, you need to unmount them first.

LVM Snapshots

Many backup utilities take the following approach to backing up a filesystem:

1. Record the metadata for the files being backed up.
2. Record the metadata for the directories being backed up.
3. Back up the directories (which really is the list of files that belong in each directory).
4. Back up the file's contents.

You can see this with a utility like the **dump** command. Note the bold lines in the output of Example 11-14.

Example 11-14 *The **dump** Command*

```
[root@onecoursesource ~]# dump -f /tmp/backup /storage-lv0
 DUMP: Date of this level 0 dump: Tue Oct 27 22:17:18 2017
 DUMP: Dumping /dev/mapper/VG0-lv0 (/storage-lv0) to /tmp/backup
 DUMP: Label: none
 DUMP: Writing 10 Kilobyte records
 DUMP: mapping (Pass I) [regular files]
 DUMP: mapping (Pass II) [directories]
 DUMP: estimated 4880 blocks.
 DUMP: Volume 1 started with block 1 at: Tue Oct 27 22:17:18 2017
 DUMP: dumping (Pass III) [directories]
 DUMP: dumping (Pass IV) [regular files]
 DUMP: Closing /tmp/backup
 DUMP: Volume 1 completed at: Tue Oct 27 22:17:18 2017
 DUMP: Volume 1 4890 blocks (4.78MB)
 DUMP: 4890 blocks (4.78MB) on 1 volume(s)
 DUMP: finished in less than a second
 DUMP: Date of this level 0 dump: Tue Oct 27 22:17:18 2017
 DUMP: Date this dump completed:  Tue Oct 27 22:17:18 2017
 DUMP: Average transfer rate: 0 kB/s
 DUMP: DUMP IS DONE
```

The problem with this technique is when live (mounted) filesystems are backed up. It is possible that between backing up the metadata and the file data that changes take place in the filesystem. For example, after the metadata is backed up for the **/storage-lv0/hosts** file, if the file was deleted before its contents were backed up, this would cause problems with the backup.

It is best to unmount the filesystem before backing it up, but this isn't always possible on production machines. So instead you can make use of an LVM snapshot. A snapshot provides a "frozen image" of the filesystem within an LV. By backing up the frozen image, you ensure a good (error free) backup.

To create a snapshot, use the **lvcreate** command with the **-s** option:

```
[root@onecoursesource ~]# lvcreate -L 20M -s -n snap0 /dev/mapper/VG0-lv0
  Logical volume "snap0" created.
```

Now there is a new device named **/dev/mapper/VG0-snap0**. The **-s** option specifies that you want a snapshot LV. The **-n** option specifies the name of the new LV. The last argument is the name of the LV that the new LV is a snapshot of.

Create a mount point for this new device and mount it as read-only so no changes take place in the "frozen" filesystem:

```
[root@onecoursesource ~]# mkdir /backup
[root@onecoursesource ~]# mount -o ro /dev/mapper/VG0-snap0 /backup
```

You can now back up the **/backup** filesystem with the backup utility of your choice. You can see that it currently contains the same data as the original LV:

```
[root@onecoursesource ~]# ls /backup
group  hosts  lost+found  words
[root@onecoursesource ~]# ls /storage-lv0
group  hosts  lost+found  words
```

So, how is backing up the **/backup** filesystem any different than backing up the **/storage-lv0** filesystem? Whereas the **/storage-lv0** filesystem is live and can be modified, the **/backup** filesystem cannot be changed, as demonstrated by the following commands:

11

```
[root@onecoursesource ~]# rm /storage-lv0/hosts
rm: remove regular file '/storage-lv0/hosts'? y
[root@onecoursesource ~]# ls /storage-lv0
group  lost+found  words
[root@onecoursesource ~]# rm /backup/words
rm: remove regular file '/backup/words'? y
rm: cannot remove '/backup/words': Read-only file system
[root@onecoursesource ~]# ls /backup
group  hosts  lost+found  words
```

After completing the backup, you should destroy the LVM snapshot by first unmounting the snapshot VM and then executing the **lvremove** command:

```
[root@onecoursesource ~]# lvremove /dev/mapper/VG0-snap0
```

Knowing how to create and use an LVM snapshot is an important skill. Knowing how it works is not critical, but it can help you understand why backing up a snapshot LV is better than backing up a live filesystem.

To begin with, assume you just created the **/dev/mapper/VG0-snap0** snapshot and have mounted it under the **/backup** directory. A way to conceptualize this process is to look at the graphic in Figure 11-6.

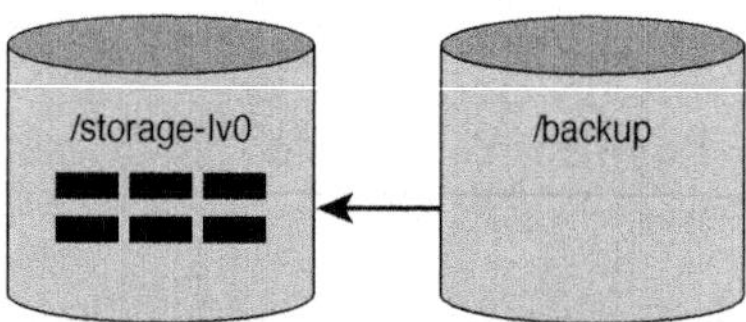

Figure 11-6 *Initial LVM Snapshot*

The boxes in the LV represented by the **/storage-lv0** cylinder are files. As you can see, all the files are initially stored in the LV mounted under the **/storage-lv0** mount point. If someone lists the files under that **/backup** mount point, the kernel knows to look at files from the **/storage-lv0** directory.

When a file is removed from the **/storage-lv0** directory, it is not immediately deleted from that LV. First, it is copied over to the snapshot LV and then removed from the original LV. Figure 11-7 demonstrates what happens during the removal of the file from the **/storage-lv0** directory, and Figure 11-8 demonstrates how the LVs look after the removal.

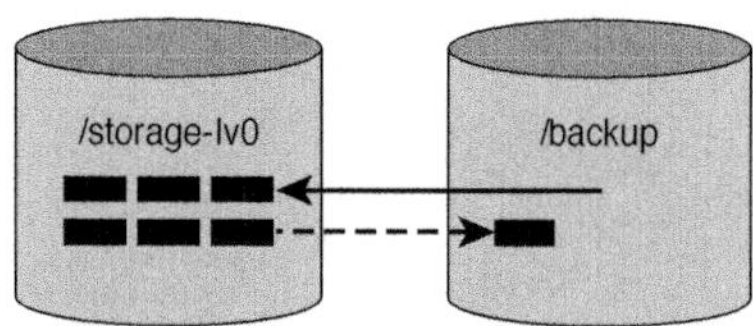

Figure 11-7 *LVs During File Removal*

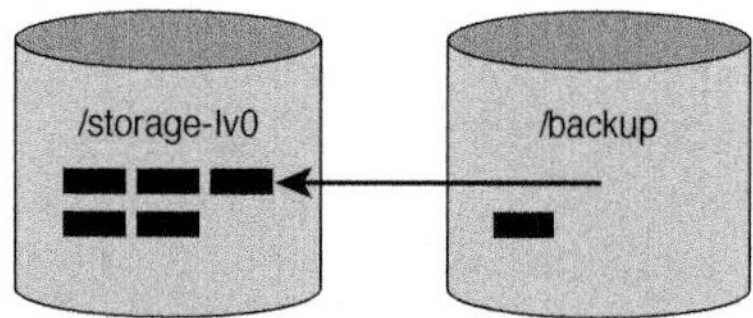

Figure 11-8 *LVs After File Removal*

Now you might be wondering how the file is copied over to the snapshot when it was mounted as read-only. The read-only mount process means you can't make changes to the filesystem via the mount point. However, this file is being copied over "under the hood," not by a simple filesystem **cp** command. Although you can't make any changes to files under the **/backup** mount point, the kernel certainly can make changes in the **/dev/mapper/VG0-snap0** device. It is the kernel that ends up copying this file.

Disk Quotas

Regular users can have a negative impact on a filesystem by creating many large files. A user can completely fill an entire filesystem with large files, making the filesystem unusable for others.

Disk quotas are designed to eliminate this problem. As an administrator, you can limit how much space a user can use in each filesystem. The limitation can be applied to individual users or all members of a group.

For example, you can enable disk quotas for the user ted that limits him to 300MB of space by creating a *hard limit*. You can also create a *soft limit*, which would result in a warning if the user exceeds this limit (but doesn't prevent additional file creation until the hard limit is reached).

If you create disk quotas for a group, the quota applies individually for each member of the group. For example, if the nick, sarah, and julia users were members of the payroll group and there was a 100MB hard limit in the **/home** filesystem, then each user could use up to 100MB in that filesystem.

It is also important to limit how many files a user can create. Each file requires an inode, the part of the file that stores the file's metadata, such as file ownership, permissions, and timestamps. Each filesystem has a limited number of inodes, and although this limit is typically very generous, a determined user could create a large number of empty files that could result in using up all the possible inodes. So, even if there is more space available, without any additional inodes, no one else can create files in that filesystem.

Lastly, note that this discussion has been using the term *filesystem*. This is because disk quotas are applied on an entire filesystem, not on a directory.

Setting Up a Disk Quota for a Filesystem

To enable user quotas, you must mount the filesystem with the **usrquota** mount option. This can be accomplished by adding **usrquota** to the mount option field of the **/etc/fstab** file:

```
/dev/sdb1       /               ext4    usrquota            1   1
```

Then, remount the filesystem with the following command (the following commands must be executed by the root user):

```
[root@localhost ~]$ mount -o remount /
```

After mounting the filesystem with the **usrquota** option enabled, you need to create the initial quota databases by executing the following **quotacheck** command:

```
[root@localhost ~]$ quotacheck -cugm /dev/sdb1
```

This will result in new files in the mount point directory of the filesystem:

```
[root@localhost ~]$ ls /aquota*
/aquota.group  /aquota.user
```

Important options for the **quotacheck** command are shown in Table 11-3.

Table 11-3 Options for the **quotacheck** Command

Option	Description
-c	Create database file(s).
-g	Only create the **aquota.group** file, which means only group quotas will be enabled unless the **-u** option is also used.
-m	Do not attempt to unmount the filesystem while creating the quota file(s).
-u	Only create the **aquota.user** file, which means only user quotas will be enabled unless the **-g** option is also used.

11

Editing, Checking, and Generating User Quota Reports

After setting up disk quotas as described in the previous section, follow these steps to enable and display quotas for users:

1. Turn on disk quotas by executing the **quotaon** command.
2. Create or edit a user quota by using the **edquota** command.
3. Display quota information by using the **quota** or **repquota** command.

quotaon

The **quotaon** command is used to turn quotas on for a filesystem. Normally when the system is booted, this will happen automatically. However, you may turn off quotas by executing the

quotaoff command followed by the name of the filesystem (the following commands must be executed by the root user):

```
[root@localhost ~]$ quotaoff /dev/sdb1
[root@localhost ~]$ quotaon /dev/sdb1
```

edquota

To create or edit a user's quotas, execute the **edquota** command followed by the username (the following command must be executed by the root user):

```
[root@localhost ~]$ edquota sarah
```

The **edquota** command will enter an editor (vi is typically the default) and display all the user's quotas. The output will appear to be something like the following:

```
Disk quotas for user sarah (uid 507):
  Filesystem  blocks   soft   hard   inodes   soft   hard
  /dev/sdb1   550060      0      0    29905      0      0
```

Table 11-4 describes the fields of the quota.

Table 11-4 Fields of Quota

Key	Description
Filesystem	The partition that contains the filesystem with quotas enabled.
blocks	How many blocks the user currently uses in the filesystem.
soft	A value that represents a soft quota for blocks; if the user creates a file that results in exceeding this block limit, a warning is issued.
hard	A value that represents a hard quota for blocks; if the user creates a file that results in exceeding this block limit, an error is issued and no additional files can be created in the filesystem.
inodes	How many files the user currently has in the filesystem.
soft	A value that represents a soft quota for files; if the user creates a file that results in exceeding this file limit, a warning is issued.
hard	A value that represents a hard quota for files; if the user creates a file that results in exceeding this file limit, an error is issued and no additional files can be created in the filesystem.

NOTE The grace period can be set by executing the **edquota –t** command. See the "quota" section for more details regarding the grace period.

quota

The **quota** command can be executed by a user to display the quotas for the account:

```
[sarah@localhost ~]$ quota
Disk quotas for user sarah (uid 507):
     Filesystem  blocks   quota   limit   grace   files   quota   limit   grace
      /dev/sda1   20480   30000   60000               1       0       0
```

Note the output when a user has exceeded a soft quota; in the following example, the user sarah is above the soft limit for block size:

```
[sarah@localhost ~]$ quota
Disk quotas for user sarah (uid 507):
     Filesystem  blocks   quota   limit   grace   files   quota   limit   grace
      /dev/sda1   40960*  30000   60000   7days       2       0       0
```

Once the user has exceeded a soft quota, a grace period is provided. The user must reduce the space used in the filesystem to be below the soft quota within the grace period or else the current usage converts to a hard quota limit.

NOTE The grace period can be set by the root user by executing the **edquota –t** command.

Here are some important options for the **quota** command:

Option	Description
-g	Display group quotas instead of specific user quotas.
-s	Display information in human-readable sizes rather than block sizes.
-l	Display quota information only for local filesystems (rather than network-based filesystem quotas).

repquota

The **repquota** command is used by the root user to display quotas for an entire filesystem (the following command must be executed by the root user):

```
[root@localhost ~]$ repquota /
*** Report for user quotas on device /dev/sda1
Block grace time: 7days; Inode grace time: 7days
                        Block limits                File limits
User            used    soft     hard  grace    used  soft  hard  grace
----------------------------------------------------------------------
root      -- 4559956       0        0         207396     0     0
daemon    --      64       0        0              4     0     0
man       --    1832       0        0            145     0     0
www-data  --       4       0        0              1     0     0
libuuid   --      40       0        0              6     0     0
syslog    --    3848       0        0             23     0     0
messagebus --      8       0        0              2     0     0
landscape --       8       0        0              2     0     0
pollinate --       4       0        0              1     0     0
vagrant   --  550060       0        0          29906     0     0
colord    --       8       0        0              2     0     0
statd     --      12       0        0              3     0     0
puppet    --      44       0        0             11     0     0
ubuntu    --      36       0        0              8     0     0
sarah     +-   40960   30000    60000  6days       2     0     0
```

Important options for the **repquota** command include:

Option	Description
-a	Display quotas for all filesystems with quota mount options specified in the **/etc/fstab** file.
-g	Display group quotas instead of specific user quotas.
-s	Display information in human-readable sizes rather than block sizes.

Hard and Soft Links

There are two different types of file links on Linux:

- **Hard links**: When you create a hard link to a file, there is no way to distinguish the "original" file from the "linked" file. They are just two filenames that point to the same inode, and hence the same data. If you have 10 hard-linked files and you delete any nine of these files, the data is still maintained in the remaining file.

  Figure 11-9 demonstrates hard links.

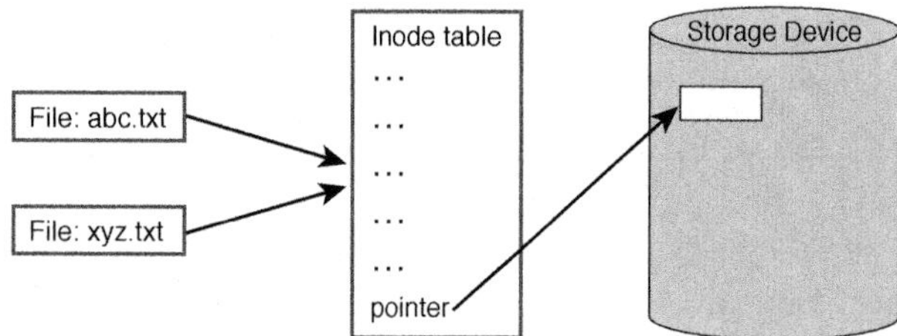

Figure 11-9 *Hard Links*

  In Figure 11-9, the **abc.txt** and **xyz.txt** files are hard-linked together. This means that they share the same inode tables. The ellipsis (...) in the inode table represents metadata—information about the file such as the user owner and permissions. Included with this metadata are pointers that refer to blocks within the storage device where the file data is stored.

- **Soft links**: When you create a soft link, the original file contains the data while the link file "points to" the original file. Any changes made to the original will also appear to be in the linked file because using the linked file always results in following the link to the target file. Deleting the original file results in a broken link, making the link file worthless and resulting in complete data loss.

  Figure 11-10 demonstrates soft links.

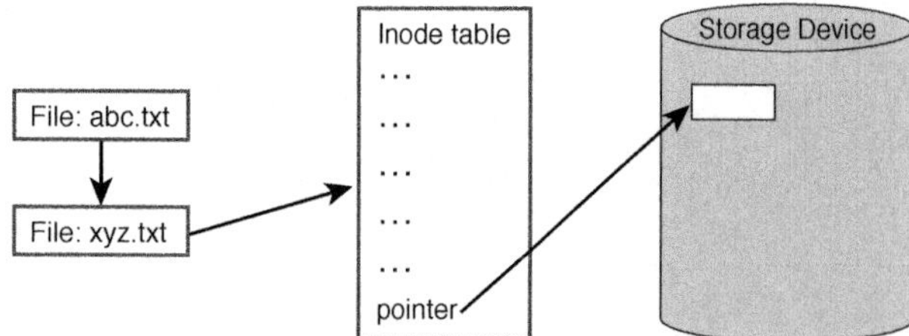

Figure 11-10 *Soft Links*

  In Figure 11-10, the **abc.txt** file is soft-linked to the **xyz.txt** file. The **abc.txt** file points to the filename **xyz.txt**, not the same inode table (although not shown in this figure, the **abc.txt** file has its own inode table). By following the link, the data for the **xyz.txt** file is accessible via the **abc.txt** file.

Why Use Links?

One common use of links for system administration tasks is when an administrator decides to move the location of a key file to a different directory location (or give the file a different name). This can cause some confusion for users who are used to the original file location and name.

For example, suppose a key configuration file is named **/etc/setup-db.conf** and the administrator wants to move this file into the **/etc/db** directory. After the file has been moved, a symbolic link can be created to help other users (and perhaps programs) to find the correct data (be sure to run the following command as the root user):

```
[root@onecoursesource ~]$ ln -s /etc/db/setup-db.conf /etc/setup-db.conf
```

The **/etc** directory has several examples of this use of links:

```
[root@onecoursesource ~]$ ls -l /etc | grep "^l"
lrwxrwxrwx   1 root root          12 Jan 26  2017 drupal -> /etc/drupal6
lrwxrwxrwx   1 root root          56 Dec 17  2017 favicon.png -> /usr/share/icons/
➥hicolor/16x16/apps/fedora-logo-icon.png
lrwxrwxrwx   1 root root          22 Jan 23  2017 grub2.cfg -> ../boot/grub2/grub.cfg
lrwxrwxrwx   1 root root          22 Dec 17  2017 grub.conf -> ../boot/grub/grub.conf
lrwxrwxrwx   1 root root          11 Jan 23  2017 init.d -> rc.d/init.d
lrwxrwxrwx   1 root root          41 Feb 18  2017 localtime -> ../usr/share/zoneinfo/
➥America/Los_Angeles
lrwxrwxrwx   1 root root          12 Dec 17  2017 mtab -> /proc/mounts
lrwxrwxrwx   1 root root          10 Jan 23  2017 rc0.d -> rc.d/rc0.d
lrwxrwxrwx   1 root root          10 Jan 23  2017 rc1.d -> rc.d/rc1.d
lrwxrwxrwx   1 root root          10 Jan 23  2017 rc2.d -> rc.d/rc2.d
lrwxrwxrwx   1 root root          10 Jan 23  2017 rc3.d -> rc.d/rc3.d
lrwxrwxrwx   1 root root          10 Jan 23  2017 rc4.d -> rc.d/rc4.d
lrwxrwxrwx   1 root root          10 Jan 23  2017 rc5.d -> rc.d/rc5.d
lrwxrwxrwx   1 root root          10 Jan 23  2017 rc6.d -> rc.d/rc6.d
lrwxrwxrwx   1 root root          14 Sep 10 12:58 redhat-release -> fedora-release
lrwxrwxrwx   1 root root          14 Sep 10 12:58 system-release -> fedora-release
```


Creating Links

To create a link, execute the **ln** command in the following manner: **ln [-s]** *target_file link_file*. For example, to create a hard link from the **/etc/hosts** file to a file in the current directory called **myhosts**, execute the following command:

```
[root@onecoursesource ~]$ ln /etc/hosts myhosts
```

Hard-link files share the same inode. You can only make a hard link to a file (not a directory) that resides on the same filesystem as the original file. Creating hard links to files on other filesystems or to directories will result in errors:

```
[root@onecoursesource ~]$ ln /boot/initrd.img-3.16.0-30-generic initrd
ln: failed to create hard link 'initrd' => '/boot/initrd.img-3.16.0-30-generic': Invalid
➥cross-device link
[root@onecoursesource ~]$ ln /etc myetc
ln: '/etc': hard link not allowed for directory
```

Soft links (also called *symbolic links*) are files that point to other files (or directories) via the filesystem. You can create a soft link to any file or directory:

```
[root@onecoursesource ~]$ ln -s /boot/initrd.img-3.16.0-30-generic initrd
```

Displaying Linked Files

The **ls** command can be used to display both soft and hard links. Soft links are very easy to see, as the target file is displayed when the **ls -l** command is executed:

```
[root@onecoursesource ~]$ ls -l /etc/vtrgb
lrwxrwxrwx 1 root root 23 Jul 11  2015 /etc/vtrgb -> /etc/alternatives/vtrgb
```

Hard links are more difficult because a hard-link file shares an inode with another filename. For example, the value **2** after the permissions in the following output indicates this is a hard-link file:

```
[root@onecoursesource ~]$ ls -l myhosts
-rw-r--r-- 2 root root 186 Jul 11  2015 myhosts
```

To view the inode number of a file, use the **-i** option to the **ls** command:

```
[root@onecoursesource ~]$ ls -i myhosts
263402 myhosts
```

Then use the **find** command to search for files with the same inode:

```
[root@onecoursesource ~]$  find / -inum 263402 -ls 2> /dev/null
263402     4 -rw-r--r--   2 root     root        186 Jul 11  2015 /root/myhosts
263402     4 -rw-r--r--   2 root     root        186 Jul 11  2015 /etc/hosts
```

Summary

In this chapter, you learned about encrypting filesystems and the value of encrypting an entire filesystem over individual files for security. Additional topics covered in this chapter included autofs, the management of logical volumes, disk quotas, and links.

Key Terms

LUKS, autofs, LVM, snapshot, PV, PE, LE, LV, VG

Review Questions

1. The _____ command is used to create volume groups.
2. Which option to the **vgcreate** command specifies the extent size for the physical volumes?
   - **A.** -e
   - **B.** -t
   - **C.** -s
   - **D.** -p
3. On an LVM1 system, what is the maximum number of extents that can be assigned to a logical volume?
   - **A.** 100,000
   - **B.** 97,400
   - **C.** 65,534
   - **D.** None of the above
4. The _____ command displays information about a physical volume.

5. Which option to the **vgdisplay** command provides detailed information about a volume group, including information about which physical volumes are in the volume group?

   A. -t

   B. -d

   C. -V

   D. None of the above

6. The _____ option to the **lvcreate** command is used to specify the name of the logical volume.

   A. -i

   B. -l

   C. -s

   D. -n

7. Which command allows you to add a new physical volume to an existing volume group?

   A. **pvadd**

   B. **pvextend**

   C. **vgadd**

   D. **vgextend**

8. The _____ command is used to change the size of an ext4 filesystem.

Manage Network Storage

There are many ways to provide users with the ability to transfer files from one system to another. For example, on Linux you can make use of a SAMBA server. The advantage of using a SAMBA server is that the protocol used to perform the transfer is not just a "Linux thing." This makes it easier to transfer files between different operating systems, such as between Linux and Microsoft Windows.

In this chapter, you learn about the SAMBA server, including key configuration settings. After completing this chapter, you should be able to share a directory or a printer using the SAMBA server. You should also understand how to secure these shares with SAMBA user accounts.

Once a SAMBA share has been made, you should know how to access it. You will learn a variety of methods, including how to mount a SAMBA share to make it appear to be part of the local filesystem.

Another method for sharing files that is more common within Linux and Unix is Network File System (NFS). This method allows an administrator to share a directory structure with other systems that have the NFS client software installed.

You learn how to set up an NFS server and connect to it from an NFS client. You also learn how to secure **portmap**, the service that grants access to NFS servers.

Lastly, you learn how to use iSCSI to provide network storage devices to client systems.

After reading this chapter and completing the exercises, you will be able to do the following:

Create and access Samba shares

Create and access NFS shares

Share storage locations via iSCSI

Use an iSCSI resource on a client system

Samba

One of the ways to share files between different systems is by using a protocol called SMB (Server Message Block). This protocol was invented in the mid-1980s by IBM for the purpose of being able to share directories between hosts on a local area network (LAN). The term used to describe sharing files and directories across a network is DFS (Distributed File System). In addition to SMB, NFS (Network File System) is a popular DFS for Linux (NFS is covered later in this chapter).

You may often hear the acronym CIFS (Common Internet File System) used in conjunction with SMB. CIFS is an SMB-based protocol made popular on Microsoft Windows systems. Typically, the two abbreviations are used interchangeably (or collectively, as in SMB/CIFS), but there are subtle differences between the protocols. In this book, the term *SMB* will be used from this point on.

You can also share printers using SMB as well as share files between different operating system types. In fact, one common SMB task is to share printers between Linux and Microsoft Windows systems.

The Linux-based software that allows SMB sharing is called SAMBA. Typically, there are three separate SAMBA packages you should consider installing:

- **SAMBA**: This package contains the SAMBA server software.
- **SAMBA-client**: This package contains the SAMBA client programs, which allow you to connect to SAMBA servers or Microsoft Windows DFS.
- **SAMBA-common**: This package contains software used by both the SAMBA server and client utilities.

For the purposes of testing SAMBA, we suggest installing all three of these packages. Another useful package is SAMBA-swat, which provides a web-based interface SAMBA administration tool.

SAMBA Configuration

The configuration file for SAMBA is **/etc/SAMBA/smb.conf** (on some older systems, it may be **/etc/smb/smb.conf**). It is a bit different from most other configuration files that you find in Linux. Here are some key points to note:

- The file is well documented. You will not need to consult the standard SAMBA documentation because the configuration file has detailed descriptions.
- The file is broken into sections defined using the following format:
  - **[name]**: This is often referred to as "the section" and denotes the shared item or service.
  - **[options and attributes]**: Each line is a separate configuration option for the shared item or service named above it.
- Two comment characters are used for this configuration file: the **#** and **;** characters. The **#** character is used for regular comments; whereas the **;** character is used for converting to comment lines any actual configuration settings that you do not want to use but that you should maintain in case you ever need these settings at a later time. This way, the proper naming convention and appropriate attributes are preserved within the configuration file.

To give you an idea of what a typical **smb.conf** file looks like, look at the output of Example 12-1, which demonstrates a typical default **smb.conf** file with all comment and blank lines removed.

Example 12-1 *Default smb.conf File*

```
[root@onecoursesource ~]# grep -v "#" /etc/SAMBA/smb.conf | grep -v ";" | grep -v "^$"
➥[global]
        workgroup = MYGROUP
        server string = SAMBA Server Version %v
        security = user
        passdb backend = tdbsam
        load printers = yes
        cups options = raw
[homes]
        comment = Home Directories
        browseable = no
        writable = yes
[printers]
        comment = All Printers
        path = /var/spool/SAMBA
        browseable = no
        guest ok = no
        writable = no
        printable = yes
```

What exactly did the command line in Example 12-1 do? Recall that the **grep** command is a filtering tool and that the **-v** option is an "inverted" **grep**. When the **-v** option is used, the **grep** command displays all lines except the ones matching the pattern. So, the first **grep** pattern matched any line with a **#** comment character and filtered out those lines. The second **grep** pattern matched any line with a **;** comment character and filtered out those lines. The last **grep** pattern matched blank lines and filtered out those lines. So, the output is composed of all the real configuration settings in the file (no comments and no blank lines). Repeat after us: "**grep** is my friend!" Learning to master commands like **grep** to allow the system to filter information you desire will make it much easier to administer your Linux system.

Note that there are three sections: **[global]**, **[homes]**, and **[printers]**. Additional sections are added as directories and individual printers are shared.

The [global] Section

The Samba server's primary settings are placed in the **[global]** section. Recall the default values shown in Example 12-1:

```
[global]
        workgroup = MYGROUP
        server string = SAMBA Server Version %v
        security = user
        passdb backend = tdbsam
        load printers = yes
        cups options = raw
```

You will find that the default options are enough to start the SAMBA server, but you will likely want to change at least a few of these options to fit your system needs. Table 12-1 describes these default options.

Table 12-1 Typical **[global]** Options

Option	Description
workgroup	This is the NetBIOS (Network Basic Input/Output System) workgroup or NetBIOS domain name. This is a technique for grouping together a set of machines. This may be important if you want to communicate with Microsoft Windows systems via SMB.
server string	A description of the server; this is useful when a remote system is attempting to connect to the server to determine what services the server provides. The value **%v** is replaced with SAMBA's version number. The value **%h** can be used to symbolize the server's hostname.
security	This determines what sort of user authentication method is used. A value of **user** means SAMBA user accounts will be used. If you have a DC (domain controller) on a Microsoft Windows system, you would specify the domain. To authenticate via Active Directory, specify **ads**.
passdb backend	This specifies how the SAMBA account data is stored. Typically, this is not something you would change unless you were an expert.
load printers	This option, if set to **yes**, tells SAMBA to share all CUPS printers by default. (The Common UNIX Printing System is a common printing protocol in Linux and Unix.) Although this can be handy, you don't always want to share all CUPS printers on the SAMBA server. Individual printer shares can be handled in separate sections. Note: For SAMBA to be able to load all CUPS printers automatically, the **[printers]** section needs to be properly configured (this is described in a later section).
cups options	Options regarding CUPS; this is rarely modified and should only be done by an expert.

The [homes] Section

In a later section of this chapter, you learn how to create SAMBA user accounts. These SAMBA users are associated with Linux user accounts (typically sharing the same name, but this is not a requirement), and of course these Linux user accounts have home directories.

To make it easier for these users to share their home directories via the SAMBA server, the **[homes]** section is designed to automatically share these directories. Keep in mind that normal Linux permissions apply, so these shares normally only make the home directory available for the user who owns the home directory.

The default **[homes]** share typically looks like this:

```
[homes]
        comment = Home Directories
        browseable = no
        writable = yes
```

The values in this section are defined in the following list:

- **comment**: The description of the share.
- **browseable**: If this is set to **yes**, the share would be visible via a client utility that's displaying information about available shares on the SAMBA server. If it's set to **no**, the share is available, but the user who is using the client utility must know about the share.

Security Highlight

Using the feature **browseable = no** provides some additional security, but keep in mind that it just obfuscates the share. It doesn't make it completely protected, and a determined hacker may be able to guess the share name and access the share as a result.

- **writable**: If this is set to **yes**, the home directories are shares with read-write access. Remember that regular permissions still apply. If it's set to **no**, the home directories are shares with read-only access. Keep in mind that underlying filesystem permissions still apply. As a result, access could be granted via this SAMBA setting, but denied by the filesystem.

WHAT COULD GO WRONG? If you connect to a system via SAMBA and can't access a file or directory, try to log directly in to the system via local login or Secure Shell (see Chapter 22, "Connecting to Remote Systems," to learn about Secure Shell) and then try to access the file directly. If you can't, then what went wrong was the local file permissions. If you can, then what went wrong was how the SAMBA share was created.

The [printers] Section

Recall the **load printers** setting in the **[global]** section. When that setting is **yes**, SAMBA looks for the **[printers]** section to automatically share all the CUPS printers. A typical **[printers]** section would look like this:

```
[printers]
        comment = All Printers
        path = /var/spool/SAMBA
        browseable = no
        guest ok = no
        writable = no
        printable = yes
```

In most cases, you are unlikely to make changes to this section. However, you should realize what the default settings in this section mean:

- **comment**: The description of the share.
- **path**: The location of the CUPS spool directory (this is where the items sent to the printer are stored prior to printing).
- **browseable**: If this is set to **yes**, the share would be visible via a client utility that's displaying information about available shares on the SAMBA server. If it's set to **no**, the share is available, but the user who is using the client utility must know about the share.
- **guest ok**: This permits access to the CUPS printers to the guest account. More details regarding that account are given later in this chapter.
- **writeable**: Should be set to **no** because this is not a directory share.
- **printable**: Should be set to **yes** because this is a printer share.

Custom Shares

You can create custom shares of directories or printers. For directory shares, the syntax is much like the **[homes]** section. You start by creating a section name and then set the parameters. In the following example, the **/usr/share/doc** directory is shared as read-only. This is useful when you want to save space and have just one system that contains documentation:

```
[doc]
    comment = System documentation
    path = /usr/share/doc
    guest ok = yes
    browseable = yes
    writeable = no
```

For this share, the resource is shared as read-only because there is no need to make changes to the resource. Users who have a SAMBA account are the only users who are able to view the documentation.

If you want to add more security to the share, you can limit which SAMBA users can access it (and how) by using the following options:

- **valid users**: A list of SAMBA users who can access this share. Example: **valid users = bob, ted**. Think of this like "whitelisting" users by explicitly noting the usernames.
- **invalid users**: A list of SAMBA users who cannot access this share. All other SAMBA users are allowed access. Think of this like "blacklisting" users by explicitly noting the usernames.
- **read list**: A list of SAMBA users who can access the share, but as read-only.
- **write list**: A list of SAMBA users who have read-write access to the share.

To share a specific printer, first make sure that the **loadprinters** setting in the **[global]** section is set to **no**. Then create a section like the following:

```
[hp-101]
       path = /var/spool/SAMBA/
       browseable = yes
       printable = yes
       printer name = hp-101
```

SAMBA Server

After you have made changes to the **/etc/SAMBA/smb.conf** file and before starting the SAMBA server, you should execute the **testparm** command. This command verifies the syntax of the configuration file, as shown in Example 12-2.

Example 12-2 *The **testparm** Command*

```
[root@onecoursesource ~]# testparm
Load smb config files from /etc/SAMBA/smb.conf
Processing section "[homes]"
Processing section "[printers]"
Processing section "[doc]"
Loaded services file OK.
Server role: ROLE_STANDALONE
Press enter to see a dump of your service definitions

[global]
        workgroup = MYGROUP
        server string = SAMBA Server Version %v
        passdb backend = tdbsam
        cups options = raw

[homes]
        comment = Home Directories
        read only = No
        browseable = No

[printers]
        comment = All Printers
        path = /var/spool/SAMBA
        printable = Yes
        browseable = No

[doc]
        comment = System documentation
        path = /usr/share/doc
        guest ok = Yes
```

WHAT COULD GO WRONG? If there are any errors that the **testparm** command can discover, you will see messages in the output like the following (in this case, the error occurred because the value of **lp_bool** had to be a Boolean; in other words, a value of 0 or 1):

```
[root@onecoursesource ~]# testparm
Load smb config files from /etc/SAMBA/smb.conf
Processing section "[homes]"
Processing section "[printers]"
Processing section "[doc]"
ERROR: Badly formed boolean in configuration file: "nope".

lp_bool(nope): value is not boolean!
```

Once you have a valid configuration file, start the SAMBA server (the service is called "smb," not "SAMBA"). You see two services start: **smbd** and **nmbd**. The **smbd** service handles the shares, and the **nmbd** process handles NetBIOS operations:

```
[root@onecoursesource ~]# ps -fe | egrep "smbd|nmbd"
root     20787     1  0 12:18 ?        00:00:00 smbd -D
root     20790     1  0 12:18 ?        00:00:00 nmbd -D
root     20792 20787  0 12:18 ?        00:00:00 smbd -D
```

Security Highlight

Often, seeing multiple processes of the same name may indicate a problem. For example, a hacker may have placed a rogue program on the system that has spawned multiple processes.

In this case, don't be concerned about multiple **smbd** processes. Each client request results in the spawning of a new **smbd** process to handle that client's request.

Both **nmbd** and **smbd** have separate log files under the **/var/log/SAMBA** directory:

```
[root@onecoursesource ~]# ls /var/log/SAMBA
nmbd.log  smbd.log
```

NOTE If you are used to administering Active Directory on Microsoft Windows systems, you may be familiar with a command-line utility called **net**. The SAMBA software also provides this utility to manage SAMBA and CIFS-based servers.

For example, the following command lists all the users in the test domain:

```
net rpc user -S 10.0.2.20 -U test/user%pw -n myname -W test
```

SAMBA Accounts

Before users can access the SAMBA server, you need to create a SAMBA user account. This account also needs to be associated with a system account. For this example, the system already has a "student" user account:

```
[root@onecoursesource ~]# grep student /etc/passwd
student:x:500:500::/home/student:/bin/bash
```

To create a new SAMBA account for a Linux user account, use the **smbpasswd** command (note that after the "password" prompts, a password is entered, but not displayed on the screen):

```
[root@onecoursesource ~]# smbpasswd -a student
New SMB password:
Retype new SMB password:
Added user student.
```

The **-a** option is used to add a new account. If you wanted to change the password of an existing SAMBA account, omit the **-a** option.

Mapping Local Accounts

Using the same name for the system account and the SAMBA account is normal and causes less confusion for the user. However, if you want to have a different name for each, you can use a username map. Start by including a setting in the **[global]** section:

```
username map = /etc/SAMBA/usermap.txt
```

In the **/etc/SAMBA/usermap.txt** file, create entries like the following:

```
bobsmith = student
nickjones = teacher
```

The first value is the Linux account name, and the second value is the SAMBA account name. Do not forget that you need to create the SAMBA accounts for this to work, and because you made a change in the **[global]** section, you need to restart SAMBA.

Keep in mind that if you are using a Microsoft Windows Active Directory or domain server to authenticate SAMBA users, the left side of the **=** character should be the Microsoft Windows account name.

Recall the **guest ok** setting previously discussed:

```
[doc]
    comment = System documentation
    path = /usr/share/doc
    guest ok = yes
    browseable = yes
    writeable = no
```

One way to identify which SAMBA user that this guest account is linked to is to use the following entry in a shared section, such as the **[doc]** section:

```
    guest account = test
```

Then create the "test" SAMBA account using the **smbpasswd** command.

Accessing SAMBA Servers

To discover SAMBA servers in your workgroup, execute the **nmblookup** command:

```
[root@onecoursesource ~]# nmblookup MYGROUP
querying MYGROUP on 10.0.2.255
10.0.2.15 MYGROUP<00>
```

After you have discovered a SAMBA server, you can see what shares are available on the SAMBA server by executing the **smbclient** command, as shown in Example 12-3.

Example 12-3 *Displaying SAMBA Server Shares*

```
[root@onecoursesource ~]# smbclient -U student -L 10.0.2.15
Password:
Domain=[ONECOURSESOURCE] OS=[Unix] Server=[SAMBA 3.0.33-3.40.el5_10]

        Sharename       Type      Comment
        ---------       ----      -------
        doc             Disk      System documentation
        IPC$            IPC       IPC Service (SAMBA Server Version 3.0.33-3.40.el5_10)
        student         Disk      Home Directories
Domain=[ONECOURSESOURCE] OS=[Unix] Server=[SAMBA 3.0.33-3.40.el5_10]

        Server               Comment
        ---------            -------

        Workgroup            Master
        ---------            -------
        MYGROUP              ONECOURSESOURCE
```

In Example 12-3, the **-U** option allows you to specify the SAMBA account you will use to access the server. Note that you are prompted for a password for this SAMBA account. The **-L** option is used to state that you want to list the files and services available on the server. The server is identified by providing the IP address (10.0.2.15 in this example).

To access a specific share, execute the following **smbclient** command:

```
[root@onecoursesource ~]# smbclient -U student //10.0.2.15/doc
Password:
Domain=[ONECOURSESOURCE] OS=[Unix] Server=[SAMBA 3.0.33-3.40.el5_10]
smb: \>
```

Once you have connected, you can execute commands similar to FTP commands. See Example 12-4 for a brief demonstration.

Example 12-4 *Using the **smbclient** Command*

```
smb: \> help
?               altname         archive         blocksize    cancel
case_sensitive cd              chmod           chown        close
del             dir             du              exit         get
getfacl         hardlink        help            history      lcd
link            lock            lowercase       ls           mask
md              mget            mkdir           more         mput
newer           open            posix           posix_open   posix_mkdir
posix_rmdir     posix_unlink    print           prompt       put
pwd             q               queue           quit         rd
recurse         reget           rename          reput        rm
rmdir           showacls        setmode         stat         symlink
tar             tarmode         translate       unlock       volume
vuid            wdel            logon           listconnect showconnect
!
smb: \> cd zip-2.31
smb: \zip-2.31\> ls
  .                       D        0  Fri Oct  9 18:22:37 2018
  ..                      D        0  Sat Jan  2 21:29:14 2018
  CHANGES                      60168  Tue Mar  8 20:58:06 2018
  TODO                          3149  Sun Feb 20 21:52:44 2018
  WHERE                        19032  Tue Apr 18 18:00:08 2018
  README                        8059  Sat Feb 26 19:22:50 2018
  LICENSE                       2692  Sun Apr  9 15:29:41 2018
  WHATSNEW                      2000  Tue Mar  8 20:58:28 2018
  algorith.txt                  3395  Sat Dec 14 05:25:34 2018
  BUGS                           356  Sat Dec 14 05:25:30 2018
  MANUAL                       40079  Sun Feb 27 23:29:58 2018

                46868 blocks of size 131072. 13751 blocks available
smb: \zip-2.31\> get README
getting file \zip-2.31\README of size 8059 as README (231.5 kb/s) (average 231.5 kb/s)
smb: \zip-2.31\> quit
```

Most of the commands demonstrated in Example 12-4 are similar to Linux commands that you already know. One that is different—the **get** command—downloads a file from the remote system to the local system.

You can see the status of the SAMBA server, including which machines are connected to it and what resource is being accessed, by executing the **smbstatus** command. As you can see from the following output, the SAMBA server was connected to by someone on the local system (hence the same IP address of 10.0.2.15):

```
[root@onecoursesource zip-2.31]# smbstatus
SAMBA version 3.0.33-3.40.el5_10
PID     Username      Group         Machine
-------------------------------------------------------------------
21662   student       student       onecoursesource    (10.0.2.15)
Service      pid     machine       Connected at
-------------------------------------------------------
doc          21662   onecoursesource     Sun Jan  3 17:45:24 2016
No locked files
```

Mounting SAMBA Shares

Instead of requiring users to connect manually to the SAMBA or Microsoft Windows share, you can have these shares appear within the local filesystem by mounting each one. For example:

```
[root@onecoursesource ~]# mkdir /doc
[root@onecoursesource ~]# mount -t cifs -o user=student //10.0.2.15/doc /doc
Password:
```

The mount process should be straightforward because it is similar to mounts you have performed in the past (for more information on mounting, review Chapter 10, "Manage Local Storage: Essentials"). The **-t** option is used to specify the filesystem type. The **-o** option is used to provide options—in this case, the name of the SAMBA user account. The **//10.0.2.15/doc** argument is the device to mount, and the **/doc** argument is the mount point.

WHAT COULD GO WRONG? Notice that the path to the share is preceded with two slash (/) characters, not one like a directory path. Using just one / character will cause this command to fail.

In most cases, you want to mount the SAMBA share automatically during the boot process. The following line added to the **/etc/fstab** file can accomplish this task:

```
//10.0.2.15/doc    /doc    cifs    user=student,password=sosecret    0    0
```

Of course, it is a horrible idea to include the SAMBA password directly in the **/etc/fstab** file, which is what the setting **password=sosecret** does. All users on the local system can see the contents of the **/etc/fstab** file, so instead you should use a credentials file:

```
//10.0.2.15/doc    /doc    cifs    credentials=/etc/SAMBA/student 0    0
```

In the **/etc/SAMBA/student** file, you place entries like the following:

```
user=student
password=sosecret
```

Security Highlight

Make sure the permissions for the file that holds the SAMBA username and password are correctly secured. The permissions should only allow the root user to view the contents of this file, so consider securing it with a command like the following: **chmod 600 /etc/SAMBA/student**.

Network File System

Network File System (NFS) is a Distributed File System (DFS) protocol that has been in use for more than 40 years. NFS was originally created by Sun Microsystems in 1984 to provide an easy way for administrators to share files and directories from one UNIX system to another.

Since its inception, NFS has been ported to several different operating systems, including Linux and Microsoft Windows. Although it may not be as popular as SAMBA, there are many organization that still use NFS to share files.

Configuring an NFS Server

On most Linux distributions, the NFS software is installed by default; you can simply start NFS via the **nfs**, **nfsserver,** or **nfs-kernel-service** startup script (the script name depends on the distribution; you will learn more about scripting in Chapter 15, "Scripting"). In some cases, you may need to install the **nfs-utils** or **nfs-kernel-server** package, but typically the NFS software is installed by default. See Chapter 26, "Red Hat-Based Software Management," and Chapter 27, "Debian-Based Software Management," if you are unsure how to install this software.

There is a little trick to NFS, though. It requires another service called RPC (Remote Procedure Call). RPC acts as a go-between for interactions between the NFS client and NFS server. The RPC service is provided by a utility called **portmap**; if the **portmap** server is not running when you try to start the NFS server, you get an error message similar to the following:

```
Cannot register service: RPC: Unable to receive; errno = Connection refused
rpc.rquotad: unable to register (RQUOTAPROG, RQUOTAVERS, udp).
```

The /etc/exports File

The primary configuration for the NFS server is the **/etc/exports** file. This is the file that you use to specify what directories you want to share with the NFS clients. The syntax of this file is

```
Directory     hostname(options)
```

The value of **Directory** should be replaced with the name of the directory you want to share (for example, **/usr/share/doc**). The value **hostname** should be a client hostname that can be resolved into an IP address. The **options** value is used to specify how the resource should be shared.

For example, the following entry in the **/etc/exports** file would share the **/usr/share/doc** directory with the NFS client jupiter (with the options of read-write) and the NFS client mars (with the option of read-only):

```
/usr/share/doc jupiter(rw) mars(ro)
```

Note that there is a space between the **jupiter** and **mars** name/options, but no space between the hostname and its corresponding option. A common mistake of novice administrators is to provide an entry like the following:

```
/usr/share/doc jupiter (rw)
```

The previous line would share the **/usr/share/doc** directory with the jupiter host with the default options, and all other hosts would have access to this share as read-write.

When you're specifying a hostname in the **/etc/exports** file, the following methods are permitted:

- **hostname**: A hostname that can be resolved into an IP address.
- **netgroup**: An NIS netgroup using the designation of @groupname.
- **domain**: A domain name using wildcards. For example, *.onecoursesource.com would include any machine in the onecoursesource.com domain.
- **Network**: A network defined by IP addresses using either VLSM (Variable Length Subnet Mask) or CIDR (Classless Inter-Domain Routing). Examples: 192.168.1.0/255.255.255.0 and 192.168.1.0/24.

There are many different NFS sharing options, including these:

- **rw**: Share as read-write. Keep in mind that normal Linux permissions still apply. (Note that this is a default option.)
- **ro**: Share as read-only.
- **sync**: File data changes are made to disk immediately, which has an impact on performance, but is less likely to result in data loss. On some distributions this is the default.
- **async**: The opposite of **sync**; file data changes are made initially to memory. This speeds up performance but is more likely to result in data loss. On some distributions this is the default.
- **root_squash**: Map the root user and group account from the NFS client to the anonymous accounts, typically either the nobody account or the nfsnobody account. See the next section, "User ID Mapping," for more details. (Note that this is a default option.)
- **no_root_squash**: Map the root user and group account from the NFS client to the local root and group accounts. See the next section, "User ID Mapping," for more details.

User ID Mapping

To make the process of sharing resources from the NFS server to the NFS client as transparent as possible, make sure that the same UIDs (user IDs) and GIDs (group IDs) are used on both systems. To understand this concept, first look at Figure 12-1.

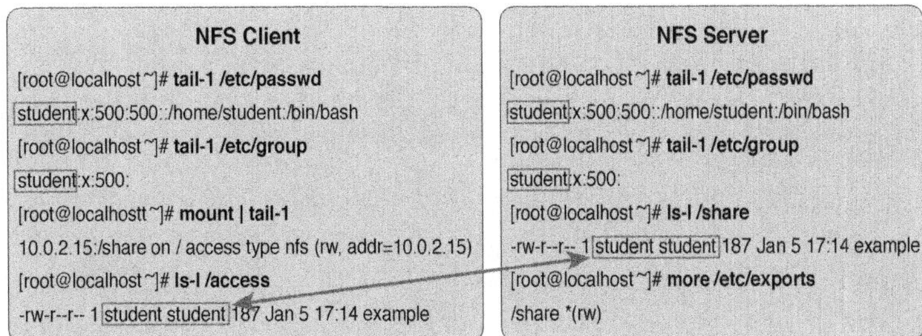

Figure 12-1 *NFS ID Mapping—Same User and Group Name*

In Figure 12-1, the NFS server and NFS client both have the same student user and group account. Both systems are using the UID of 500 and the GID of 500 for these accounts. The NFS server has the **/share** directory shared with the NFS client, which has it mounted under the **/access** directory. Now when the student user tries to access the **/access/example** file, that user will have **rw-** permissions on that file.

Now consider the situation described in Figure 12-2.

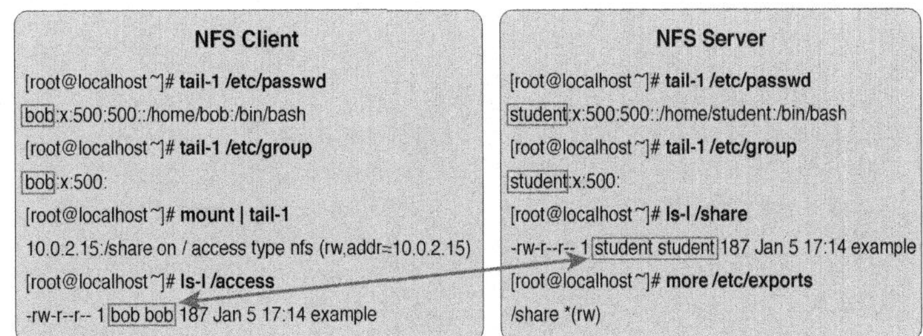

Figure 12-2 *NFS ID Mapping—Different User and Group Name*

The NFS client in the example in Figure 12-2 has a user and group named bob assigned to the UID and GID of 500. This means when the bob user on the NFS client accesses the **/access/example** file, which is really the **/share/example** file on the NFS server, bob is provided with ownership access to the file. In other words, the user bob on the NFS client has read and write permissions to the file owned by the student user on the NFS server!

This is one of the reasons why you do not see NFS used outside a LAN. There are other reasons (such as security issues), but this UID and GID mapping is an important aspect of NFS to understand.

Security Highlight

One way to avoid mismatched accounts is to use a central authentication system, such as an NIS or LDAP server. Using a central authentication system is also better for security than using local accounts on multiple systems (imagine the headache of deleting or locking the same account on dozens of systems, not to mention that you could forget one or more).

NIS and LDAP configuration are covered in Chapter 19, "Network Configuration."

Recall that one of the share options for the **/etc/exports** file is **root_squash**. This is because you likely do not want the root account on the NFS client to have root privileges on the files on the NFS server. The **root_squash** share option results in a rare case where a regular user has more rights to something on the filesystem than the root user does. Here's an example:

```
[root@onecoursesource ~]# mount | tail -1
192.168.1.22:/share on /access type nfs (rw,addr=192.168.1.22)
 [root@onecoursesource ~]# ls -l /access/example
-rw-r--r--. 1 student student 187 Jan  5 17:14 /access/example
[root@onecoursesource ~]# echo "no way" > /access/example
bash: /access/example: Permission denied
```

NFS Server Processes

So far you have learned that to have a system be an NFS server, you need to perform the following steps:

1. Create at least one share entry in the **/etc/exports** file.
2. Start the **portmap** service.
3. Start the NFS service.

The NFS service actually consists of several different processes working together, as demonstrated from the output shown in Example 12-5.

Example 12-5 *NFS Server Processes*

```
[root@onecoursesource ~]# ps -fe | grep 'rpc\.'
rpcuser   2074     1  0 Jan03 ?        00:00:00 rpc.statd
root     26445     1  0 17:15 ?        00:00:00 rpc.rquotad
root     26460     1  0 17:15 ?        00:00:00 rpc.mountd
root     26515     1  0 17:15 ?        00:00:00 rpc.idmapd
[root@onecoursesource ~]# ps -fe | grep nfs
root     26449    15  0 17:15 ?        00:00:00 [nfsd4]
root     26450     1  0 17:15 ?        00:00:00 [nfsd]
root     26451     1  0 17:15 ?        00:00:00 [nfsd]
root     26452     1  0 17:15 ?        00:00:00 [nfsd]
root     26453     1  0 17:15 ?        00:00:00 [nfsd]
root     26454     1  0 17:15 ?        00:00:00 [nfsd]
root     26455     1  0 17:15 ?        00:00:00 [nfsd]
root     26456     1  0 17:15 ?        00:00:00 [nfsd]
root     26457     1  0 17:15 ?        00:00:00 [nfsd]
```

Depending on what RPC-based services you have running on your system, you may see some additional lines of output if you run the commands shown in Example 12-5. The list provided in Example 12-5 is just displaying the processes related to NFS. The process are as follows:

- **rpc.statd**: This process handles the recovery process if the NFS server is rebooted when NFS clients are actively using the NFS server's resources.
- **rpc.rquotad**: This process works in conjunction with the filesystem's quota system.
- **rpc.mountd**: This process handles the initial NFS client mount requests. (Note that this is listed as just **mountd** on the LPIC-2 exam objectives, so expect it to be referred to either way when taking the exam.)
- **rpc.idmapd**: This process exists only on systems that run NFSv4. It can be used to modify the way user and group names are mapped between systems.
- **nfsd**: Also referred to as **rpc.nfsd**, this process handles the bulk of the client/server relationship. If your system uses both NFSv3 and NFSv4, you will also see an **nfsd4** or **rpc.nfsd4** process.

Understanding portmap

Think of the **portmap** utility as one of those old-fashioned telephone operators. You may have seen these in older movies, where someone picks up the phone and says, "Operator, connect me to Boston 4567." The operator knows which connection to make to connect the parties. If you cannot envision that example, consider that **portmap** provides a map of the ports in use by the various services and programs on the computer, much like a legend on a map identifies each element.

That is **portmap**'s primary job. When an RPC-based service starts, it tells **portmap** how it can be reached by providing **portmap** with a network port number. When a client system tries to connect to a server, it asks the **portmap** utility which port the service is using.

If you are logged in to the NFS server, you can see this information by executing the **rpcinfo** command, as shown in Example 12-6.

Example 12-6 *The rpcinfo Command*

```
[root@onecoursesource ~]# rpcinfo -p
   program vers proto   port
    100000    2   tcp    111  portmapper
    100000    2   udp    111  portmapper
    100021    1   udp  56479  nlockmgr
    100021    3   udp  56479  nlockmgr
    100021    4   udp  56479  nlockmgr
    100021    1   tcp  36854  nlockmgr
    100021    3   tcp  36854  nlockmgr
    100021    4   tcp  36854  nlockmgr
    100011    1   udp    758  rquotad
    100011    2   udp    758  rquotad
    100011    1   tcp    761  rquotad
    100011    2   tcp    761  rquotad
    100003    2   udp   2049  nfs
    100003    3   udp   2049  nfs
    100003    4   udp   2049  nfs
    100003    2   tcp   2049  nfs
    100003    3   tcp   2049  nfs
    100003    4   tcp   2049  nfs
    100005    1   udp    772  mountd
    100005    1   tcp    775  mountd
```

12

```
100005    2   udp    772  mountd
100005    2   tcp    775  mountd
100005    3   udp    772  mountd
100005    3   tcp    775  mountd
```

Security Highlight

You can also see this information from a remote system by including the IP address of the server (for example, **rpcinfo -p 192.1**68.1.22). This is one of the reasons why some administrators prefer to use Samba over NFS (having many visible network ports open poses a potential security risk).

You can also block access to the NFS server for specific NFS clients by blocking access to the **portmap** service. The **portmap** service uses a library called TCP Wrappers, also known as **libwrap**.

TCP Wrappers uses two files to provide you with the means to allow or block access to services: the **/etc/hosts.allow** and **/etc/hosts.deny** files. Each of these files contains rules designed to match a connection attempt. For example, the following rule matches an attempt to connect to the **portmap** service from the machine 192.168.1.100:

```
portmap: 192.168.1.100
```

The rules are applied in the following manner:

1. If the rule matches in the **/etc/hosts.allow** file, the connection is *granted.*
2. If the rule matches in the **/etc/hosts.deny** file, the connection is *not allowed.*
3. If no rule matches from either file, the connection is *granted.*

So, no rules in either file means all connections from all systems are granted. Suppose you wanted to deny access to all machines in the 192.168.1.0/24 network, except allow one machine in that network (192.168.1.100) and allow all other machines outside that network access to the **portmap** utility. You could use the following rules:

```
root@onecoursesource ~]# more /etc/hosts.allow
portmap: 192.168.1.100
root@onecoursesource ~]# more /etc/hosts.deny
portmap: 192.168.1.0/24
```

In most cases, you want to grant access to a few machines and deny all others. For example, the following rulesets would allow all machines in the 192.168.1.0/24 network access to the **portmap** utility and deny all others:

```
root@onecoursesource ~]# more /etc/hosts.allow
portmap: 192.168.1.0/24
root@onecoursesource ~]# more /etc/hosts.deny
portmap: ALL
```

NOTE There is more to TCP Wrappers than what is discussed in this chapter. For a more complete coverage of TCP Wrappers, see Chapter 23, "Develop a Network Security Policy."

NFS Server Commands

The **exportfs** command can be used on the NFS server to display what is currently shared:

```
[root@onecoursesource ~]# exportfs
/share          <world>
```

The **exportfs** command can also be used to temporarily share a resource, assuming the NFS services have already been started:

```
[root@onecoursesource ~]# exportfs -o ro 192.168.1.100:/usr/share/doc
[root@onecoursesource ~]# exportfs
/usr/share/doc  192.168.1.100
/share          <world>
```

The **-o** option is used to specify the share options. The argument includes the name of the systems to share with, as well as the directory to share, separated by a colon (:) character.

If you make changes to the **/etc/exports** file, any newly added share will be enabled after a reboot. If you want to enable these changes immediately, execute the following command: **exportfs –a**.

The **nfsstat** command can display useful NFS information. For example, the following command displays what is currently mounted by NFS clients:

```
[root@onecoursesource ~]# nfsstat -m
/access from 10.0.2.15:/share
 Flags: rw,vers=3,rsize=131072,wsize=131072,hard,proto=tcp,timeo=600,
➥retrans=2,sec=sys,addr=10.0.2.15
```

The **showmount** command displays similar information:

```
[root@onecoursesource ~]# showmount -a
All mount points on onecoursesource.localdomain:
10.0.2.15:/share
```

Configuring an NFS Client

Mounting an NFS share is not much different from mounting a partition or logical volume. First create a regular directory:

```
[root@onecoursesource ~]# mkdir /access
```

Next, use the **mount** command to mount the NFS share:

```
[root@onecoursesource ~]# mount 192.168.1.22:/share /access
```

You can verify the mount was successful either by executing the **mount** command or by viewing the **/proc/mounts** file. The advantage of viewing the **/proc/mounts** file is that it provides more detail:

```
[root@onecoursesource ~]# mount | tail -1
192.168.1.22:/share on /access type nfs (rw,addr=192.168.1.22)
[root@onecoursesource ~]# tail -1 /proc/mounts
192.168.1.22:/share /access nfs rw,relatime,vers=3,rsize=131072,wsize=131072,namlen=255,
➥hard,proto=tcp, timeo=600,retrans=2,sec=sys,mountaddr=192.168.1.22,mountvers=3,
➥mountport=772,mountproto=udp,local_lock=none,addr=192.168.1.22 0 0
```

If the NFS client was rebooted, this mount would not be reestablished after the system boots. To make this a persistent mount across reboots, add an entry like the following in the **/etc/fstab** file:

```
[root@onecoursesource ~]# tail -1 /etc/fstab
192.168.1.22:/share     /access  nfs     defaults      0     0
```

After adding this entry to the **/etc/fstab** file, unmount the NFS share (if necessary) and test the new entry by only providing the mount point when executing the **mount** command:

```
[root@onecoursesource ~]# umount /access
[root@onecoursesource ~]# mount /access
```

```
[root@onecoursesource ~]# mount | tail -1
192.168.1.22:/share on /access type nfs (rw,addr=192.168.1.22)
```

Recall that the fourth field of the **/etc/fstab** file contains the mount options. Several mount options are available for NFS, including some default mount options. Table 12-2 describes these options, with the default option in **bold**.

Table 12-2 NFS Mount Options

Options	Description
soft | **hard**	The NFS client attempts to mount the NFS server for a specific period of time (see the **timeo=** option). If the server does not respond and the **hard** option is used, the NFS client continues to try to mount indefinitely. If the **soft** option is used, the NFS client stops attempting to mount the server. This is important during the boot process. You do not want your system to hang, repeatedly attempting to mount an NFS server resource that is unreachable (perhaps the server is down or there is a network issue).
fg | bg	Perform foreground (**fg**) mount or background (**bg**) mount during the boot process. If you decide to use the **hard** option, consider placing the mount in the **bg** mode so the system continues to boot and does not potentially hang when an NFS server is unavailable.
timeo=	Sets the timeout value using 1/10 second. For example, **timeo=300** means a 30-second timeout value.
retrans=	Specifies how many times to retry to mount an NFS share. By default, three UDP attempts are made and two TCP attempts are made.
retry=	How many attempts to try before timing out. The default depends on your distribution and version of NFS.
rsize=	The maximum byte size of each READ request. Administrators typically set this to a value of 8192 (the default can be 1024, 4096, or 8192, depending on your distribution). The maximum depends on your version of NFS. Benchmarking (testing different configurations to determine which is best) is recommended to determine the best rate.
wsize=	The maximum byte size of each WRITE request. Administrators typically set this to a value of 8192 (the default can be 1024, 4096, or 8192, depending on your distribution). The maximum depends on your version of NFS. Benchmarking is recommended to determine the best rate.
rw | ro	Attempts to mount the NFS share as read-write (**rw**) or read-only (**ro**). If the resource is shared as read-only, the mount is read-only regardless of this option.

iSCSI

iSCSI (Internet Small Computer System Interface) is a network storage solution based on the communication protocol provided by SCSI. Recall that SCSI is a protocol designed to provide an interface between the kernel and a SCSI device.

Conversational Learning™—Advantages of iSCSI

Gary: Hey, Julia. Can I pick your brain?

Julia: Anytime.

Gary: I am trying to understand what advantages iSCSI provides.

Julia: Well, first thing you really need to think about is what advantages remote storage provides over local storage. Keep in mind that unlike a local hard disk, iSCSI provides access to a remote storage device.

Gary: OK, that I understand. For example, local disk space can be very limited, whereas remote storage can make use of large datacenter devices, right?

Julia: That is one advantage. There are others, but you are on the right track. For example, consider how reliable network connectivity is. That's very important if you are using remote storage.

Gary: So, if I decide to go with remote storage, what choices do I have?

Julia: You can use a file-sharing service like Samba or NFS. These are commonly referred to as NAS, or Network-Attached Storage. Although these services have some advantages, they are really designed to share a portion of a filesystem. iSCSI provides the client system with a device that works like a local hard disk, but is obviously remotely located.

Gary: OK, so are there alternatives to iSCSI that I should also consider?

Julia: Yes, you could also go with Fibre Channel, which is commonly referred to as FC.

Gary: So, what are the advantages and disadvantages of FC?

Julia: It isn't always a cut-and-dry answer, but typically FC is going to have very strong performance and reliability, but with a higher cost than NAS and iSCSI solutions. Also, FC provides a good solution in a local area network, but NAS and iSCSI are better solutions for wide area networks.

Gary: OK, this gives me a good starting point. It sounds like I really should get more details for each solution before making a decision.

Julia: Yes, this is something you don't want to just jump into. Map out your network storage requirements and determine which solution fits best before taking any action.

Gary: More homework! I suppose I should be getting used to that.

Julia: Just do what you can to avoid getting an "F"!

To understand iSCSI, you first need to know about some key terms:

- **Target**: This term describes the storage device, which resides on a server. The server can either be on a LAN or a WAN. Think of the target as the storage device being shared. Also, keep in mind that a target is considered a device, not a filesystem. When the client system accesses this device, it can be treated as if it was a hard disk.
- **Initiator**: This is the client that connects to the target. In some cases, the initiator is referred to as the iSCSI client.
- **WWID**: World Wide Identifier; this is an identifier guaranteed to be unique throughout the world. This unique number is important for iSCSI devices connected to the Internet to ensure that no other iSCSI device has that same identification number. It is similar in concept to the MAC address on your network card (which is a unique identifier that no other network card has). On the iSCSI server, there would be an association made via a symbolic link file and the actual device filename. The term WWN (Word Wide Name) is sometimes used interchangeably with WWID.
- **LUN**: Logical Unit Number; this is a value used by the target to identify a iSCSI device. The concept originates with SCSI, where on each system a SCSI device can be identified by a LUN that looks like this: **/dev/dsk/c0t0d0s0**. The **c0t0d0s0** indicates the controller card, target, disk, and slice (partition) of the SCSI device that you want to access. For iSCSI, it is important to understand that WWID is a name unique on the Internet, whereas LUN is only unique on the local system.

Target Configuration

To configure your system as an iSCSI server, you first need to install the **scsi-target-utils** package and its dependencies. This package is not normally installed by default on most distributions. (See Chapter 26, "Red Hat-Based Software Management," and Chapter 27, "Debian-Based Software Management," for information on how to manage software packages.) Keep in mind that the **scsi-target-utils** package also has some dependency packages that also need to be installed. See Chapters 26 and 27 if you are unsure how to install this software.

After installing the software package, edit the **/etc/tgt/targets.conf** file to create the target. The entry should look something like the following:

```
<target iqn.2018-10.localdomain.onecoursesource:test1>
        backing-store /dev/VolGroup/iscsi
        initiator-address 10.0.2.15
</target>
```

Here, **iqn.2018-10.localdomain.onecoursesource:test1** is a method of creating a unique name for this target, similar to the WWID mentioned previously. The format of this should be **iqn.year-month.domain_in_opposite_order:name_for_target**. For example, if you wanted to create a target called **firefly** on the machine **test.sample.com** and it is October, 2018, then the name you create is **iqn.2018-10.com.sample.test:firefly**.

The **backing-store** value should be a device that has no data or filesystem stored on it, such as a newly created partition or logical volume. Remember, you are creating a device target, not sharing an existing filesystem.

The **initiator-address** describes which systems are permitted to access this target.

Next, start the **tgtd** daemon. On a SysVinit system, execute the following:

```
[root@onecoursesource ~]# /etc/init.d/tgtd start
Starting SCSI target daemon:                           [  OK  ]
```

Finally, execute the **tgt-admin --show** command to verify that the target has been enabled, as shown in Example 12-7.

Example 12-7 *The tgt-admin --show Command*

```
[root@onecoursesource ~]# tgt-admin --show
Target 1: iqn.2018-10.localdomain.onecoursesource:test1
    System information:
        Driver: iscsi
        State: ready
    I_T nexus information:
    LUN information:
        LUN: 0
            Type: controller
            SCSI ID: IET     00010000
            SCSI SN: beaf10
            Size: 0 MB, Block size: 1
            Online: Yes
            Removable media: No
            Prevent removal: No
            Readonly: No
            Backing store type: null
            Backing store path: None
```

```
            Backing store flags:
        LUN: 1
            Type: disk
            SCSI ID: IET     00010001
            SCSI SN: beaf11
            Size: 264 MB, Block size: 512
            Online: Yes
            Removable media: No
            Prevent removal: No
            Readonly: No
            Backing store type: rdwr
            Backing store path: /dev/VolGroup/iscsi
            Backing store flags:
    Account information:
    ACL information:
        10.0.2.20
```

Initiator Configuration

To configure your system as an iSCSI initiator, you first need to install the **iscsi-initiator-utils** package and its dependencies. This package is not normally installed by default on most distributions.

After you have installed the package, you can use the **iscsiadm** command to see the name of the targets provided by a iSCSI server. To perform this task, use the following **iscsiadm** command:

```
[root@onecoursesource ~]# iscsiadm -m discovery -t sendtargets -p 10.0.2.15
Starting iscsid:                                           [  OK  ]
10.0.2.20:3260,1 iqn.2018-10.localdomain.onecoursesource:test1
```

Note that the first time you execute this command, it automatically starts the **iscsid** daemon.

What you are looking for in the output of the **iscsiadm** command is which machine(s) can act as an initiator (10.0.2.20, in this case) and the IQN (iSCSI qualified name). The list of initiators should include the machine you are executing commands on (the client) for you to be able to attach to the iSCSI target.

Now that the target has been discovered, an easy way to connect to it is to start the **iscsi** service:

```
[root@onecoursesource ~]# /etc/init.d/iscsi restart
```

The **iscsi** script starts the **iscsid** daemon, which manages iSCSI targets on the initiator side. Although you probably will not change the configuration script for the **iscsid** daemon, you should be aware that it is located in the **/etc/iscsi/iscsid.conf** file.

The **iscsi** script is also a great way to determine the device name that the target has been assigned on the local system, as the highlighted output in Example 12-8 demonstrates.

Example 12-8 *Determining Local Device Name for iSCSI Target*

```
[root@onecoursesource ~]# /etc/init.d/iscsi status
iSCSI Transport Class version 2.0-870
version 6.2.0-873.13.el6
Target: iqn.2018-10.localdomain.onecoursesource:test1 (non-flash)
        Current Portal: 10.0.2.15:3260,1
        Persistent Portal: 10.0.2.15:3260,1
                **********
                Interface:
```

```
**********
Iface Name: default
Iface Transport: tcp
Iface Initiatorname: iqn.1994-05.com.redhat:392559bc66c9
Iface IPaddress: 10.0.2.15
Iface HWaddress: <empty>
Iface Netdev: <empty>
SID: 1
iSCSI Connection State: LOGGED IN
iSCSI Session State: LOGGED_IN
Internal iscsid Session State: NO CHANGE
 *********
 Timeouts:
 *********
 Recovery Timeout: 120
 Target Reset Timeout: 30
 LUN Reset Timeout: 30
 Abort Timeout: 15
 *****
 CHAP:
 *****
 username: <empty>
 password: ********
 username_in: <empty>
 password_in: ********
 ************************
 Negotiated iSCSI params:
 ************************
 HeaderDigest: None
 DataDigest: None
 MaxRecvDataSegmentLength: 262144
 MaxXmitDataSegmentLength: 8192
 FirstBurstLength: 65536
 MaxBurstLength: 262144
 ImmediateData: Yes
 InitialR2T: Yes
 MaxOutstandingR2T: 1
 ************************
 Attached SCSI devices:
 ************************
 Host Number: 3    State: running
 scsi3 Channel 00 Id 0 Lun: 0
 scsi3 Channel 00 Id 0 Lun: 1
         Attached scsi disk sdb      State: running
```

Recall that the **udev** system creates and manages device files. In this case, the **udev** daemon works in conjunction with the **scsi_id** command to map the target with the **sdb** device (the **/dev/sdb** file), hence the output in Example 12-8: **Attached scsi disk sdb**. Although you can execute the **scsi_id** command yourself, it is normally used by the **udev** daemon to create the device file.

The nice thing about the target is that it appears as a regular device to the local filesystem. You can make a partition on it, create a filesystem, and mount the filesystem, as shown in Example 12-9.

Example 12-9 *Using the iSCSI Target on the Local System*

```
[root@onecoursesource ~]# fdisk /dev/sdb
Device contains neither a valid DOS partition table, nor Sun, SGI or OSF disklabel
Building a new DOS disklabel with disk identifier 0xafa8a379.
Changes will remain in memory only, until you decide to write them.
After that, of course, the previous content won't be recoverable.

Warning: invalid flag 0x0000 of partition table 4 will be corrected by w(rite)

WARNING: DOS-compatible mode is deprecated. It's strongly recommended to
       switch off the mode (command 'c') and change display units to
       sectors (command 'u').

Command (m for help): n
Command action
   e   extended
   p   primary partition (1-4)
p
Partition number (1-4): 1
First cylinder (1-1024, default 1):
Using default value 1
Last cylinder, +cylinders or +size{K,M,G} (1-1024, default 1024):
Using default value 1024

Command (m for help): w
The partition table has been altered!

Calling ioctl() to re-read partition table.
Syncing disks.
[root@onecoursesource ~]# mkfs -t ext4 /dev/sdb1
mke2fs 1.41.12 (17-May-2010)
Filesystem label=
OS type: Linux
Block size=1024 (log=0)
Fragment size=1024 (log=0)
Stride=0 blocks, Stripe width=0 blocks
64512 inodes, 258020 blocks
12901 blocks (5.00%) reserved for the super user
First data block=1
Maximum filesystem blocks=67371008
32 block groups
8192 blocks per group, 8192 fragments per group
2016 inodes per group
Superblock backups stored on blocks:
        8193, 24577, 40961, 57345, 73729, 204801, 221185
Writing inode tables: done
Creating journal (4096 blocks): done
Writing superblocks and filesystem accounting information: done
This filesystem will be automatically checked every 22 mounts or
180 days, whichever comes first. Use tune2fs -c or -i to override.
[root@onecoursesource ~]# mkdir /test
[root@onecoursesource ~]# mount /dev/sdb1 /test
```

12

Here are a few important notes to consider:

- Make sure you enable the **iscsi** script to start automatically at boot (that is, use the **chkconfig** command if you are working on a SysVinit system).
- Make sure you enable the filesystem mount in the **/etc/fstab** file. You should probably include the **_netdev** mount option, as this ensures networking is up before trying to mount the resource.
- There is more to iSCSI than discussed in this book. If you are thinking about implementing iSCSI in your environment, you may want to consider other features, such as ways to secure the target. For example, there is a way to enable an authentication technique called CHAP (Challenge-Handshake Authentication Protocol), which would need to be configured on the target and on the initiator (by modifying the **/etc/iscsi/iscsid.conf** file).
- You do not need two systems to test iSCSI. The system that acts as the target can also be the initiator. This is not normally done outside of testing, but it does provide you with an easy way to test these commands.
- You may find some subtle differences in how iSCSI works on different distributions. The iSCSI examples provided in this book were performed on a CentOS 7.x system.

Summary

In this chapter, you learned how to administer remote storage devices. First, you were introduced to SAMBA, a tool that allows you to share directories between Linux and other operating systems. You also learned how to share directory structures between Linux systems using NFS. Lastly, you learned how to create a shared storage device using iSCSI.

Key Terms

SMB, DFS, NFS, CIFS, NetBIOS, Active Directory, RPC, user ID mapping, TCP Wrappers, iSCSI, target, initiator, WWID, LUN

Review Questions

1. The _____ software package provides SAMBA client utilities.
2. Which of the following characters can be used for commenting a line in the **/etc/SAMBA/smb.conf** file? (Choose two.)

   A. #

   B. *

   C. ;

   D. /
3. Which of the following is used to specify a description of the SAMBA server when placed in the **[global]** section of the **smb.conf** file?

   A. **comment =**

   B. **server =**

   C. **description =**

   D. **server string =**

4. The _____ section of the **smb.conf** file is used to share a SAMBA user's home directories by default.

5. Which of the following is used to share a directory as read-only when placed in a directory share within the **smb.conf** file?

   A. **read-only = yes**

   B. **unwritable = yes**

   C. **writable = no**

   D. **changeable = no**

6. The _____ setting in a SAMBA share section of the **smb.conf** file permits guest user account access.

   A. **guest = yes**

   B. **unsecure = yes**

   C. **guest ok = yes**

   D. **guest access = yes**

7. Fill in the missing setting for the following SAMBA printer share:

```
[hp-101]
        _____ = /var/spool/SAMBA/
        browseable = yes
        printable = yes
        printer name = hp-101
```

8. Starting the SAMBA server results in two server processes starting: _____ and _____.

9. Fill in the blank for the following command to create a new SAMBA user account named student:

```
smbpasswd _____student
```

   A. **-c**

   B. **-a**

   C. **-n**

   D. **-s**

10. The _____ setting can be used to match Windows account names to local user accounts when placed in the **[global]** section of the **smb.conf** file.

11. The _____service provides the functionality of RPC.

12. Which of the following are valid NFS software package names? (Choose two.)

    A. nfs

    B. nfs-server

    C. nfs-utils

    D. nfs-kernel-server

12

13. Fill in the blank in the following entry in the **/etc/exports** file to share the **/share** directory with the test machine with read-only access:

```
/share   test(_____)
```

A. **read-only**

B. **readonly**

C. **norw**

D. **ro**

14. The _____ share option results in better performance but has the potential for data loss.

15. Based on the following share from the **/etc/exports** file, which systems have the capability to access the share as read-write?

```
/share   test (rw)
```

A. Only the test machine.

B. Only machines in the local network.

C. No machines because the entry is invalid.

D. All machines.

16. Which of the following are valid ways to specify NFS clients in the **/etc/exports** file? (Choose two.)

A. domain

B. URL

C. ADS name

D. IP network

17. The _____ process handles the NFS client mount requests.

18. You can see RPC port information on the system by executing the _____ command.

19. You can secure the **portmap** service by modifying which of the following files? (Choose two.)

A. **/etc/hosts**

B. **/etc/hosts.allow**

C. **/etc/hosts.access**

D. **/etc/hosts.deny**

20. The _____ mount option attempts to mount the share once and then stops trying.

21. Which file would you edit to define your iSCSI targets?

A. **/etc/targets.conf**

B. **/etc/tgt/targets.conf**

C. **/etc/tgt/tgt.conf**

D. **/etc/tgt.conf**

22. The _____ command is used by the **udev** daemon to map an iSCSI target to a local device file.

Develop a Storage Security Policy

Securing storage devices poses a challenge because often the individuals who compromise these devices already have valid access to these systems. This chapter focuses on how to secure data using the skills you learned in Chapters 9–12.

The security of storage devices is not just about keeping people from seeing sensitive data. It also includes ensuring that critical data is not lost. You also learn how to create backups of files and directories as well as develop a backup policy to ensure you can recover lost data.

After reading this chapter and completing the exercises, you will be able to do the following:

Develop a security plan for securing storage devices

Create a backup strategy

Utilize backup utilities

Developing the Plan

While developing a security plan for storage devices, you should consider the following:

- Sensitive data needs to be secure from prying eyes, including users who have valid access to the system.
- Consider where all data should be stored. For example, a critical database with private company data should not be stored in an external-facing web server (or any external-facing server for that matter).
- All critical data needs to be backed up on a regular basis in the event that a storage device fails or a disaster (such as fire or flood) destroys the storage devices.
- A data recovery system should be put in place to allow for the quick recovery of lost data.

The essentials you need to know to protect data have already been covered in previous chapters (Chapters 9–12), and more information will be provided in later chapters. The following is a summary of these essentials and how you should consider them when developing a security plan:

- Protect files from users who already have access to the system using a combination of file permissions, file attributes, and SELinux (covered in Chapter 9, "File Permissions"). Your security policy should clearly define these security settings on every system-critical file and all files that contain sensitive data.
- Create scripts (covered in Chapter 15, "Scripting") to run automatically (covered in Chapter 14, "crontab and at") to probe key files to determine whether the file permissions and attributes are correctly set. (Note that you can find scripts like this via Internet searches; Kali Linux does not include tools that provide these functions.)
- For any mobile devices such as laptops, make sure you enable filesystem encryption (covered in Chapter 11, "Manage Local Storage: Advanced Features").
- For any network storage device, make sure you use features such as a firewall (covered in Chapter 31, "Firewalls") to best limit access to the storage devices.

Backing Up Data

Almost all seasoned system administrators, as well as many end users, have horror stories that revolve around lost data. Millions of dollars have been lost and heads have rolled because either no backup strategy was put in place or the backup strategy was insufficient or not properly followed.

Securing data is a serious business, and you do not want to be the one, hat in hand, explaining why critical company data has been lost forever. You must create a solid backup strategy and make sure it is implemented correctly.

Creating a Backup Strategy

As an administrator, it is your responsibility to develop a solid backup strategy. To create this strategy, you need to answer the following questions:

- **What needs to be backed up?** This is a critical question because it has an impact on the answers to the rest of the questions. While answering this question, you should consider breaking down your filesystem into smaller logical components to create a more efficient backup strategy.
- **How often?** Several factors come into play when answering this question. If you have broken down your filesystem into smaller logical components, you should answer this question for each component, as the answer varies depending on what type of data is backed up.
- **Full or incremental?** A full backup is when everything is backed up, regardless of whether any changes have been made since the last backup. An incremental backup is when a backup is performed only on the files that have changed since a previous backup. Some backup utilities allow for complex backup strategies based on several different levels of incremental backups. Incremental backups are faster, but a full backup allows for easier reinstatement of data in the event of a loss or accident.
- **Where will the backup be stored?** Will you use tape devices, optical devices (CD-ROMs/DVDs), external storage devices (USB drives), or network-accessible storage locations? Each storage location has inherent advantages and disadvantages.
- **What backup tool will be used?** The decision that you make regarding the backup tool has a significant impact on the process of backing up and restoring data. Most Linux distributions come with several tools installed by default, such as the **dd** and **tar** commands. In many cases, additional tools are freely available; you just need to install each tool from the distribution repository. In addition to the tools that come with the distribution, you may want to consider exploring third-party tools, which typically offer more robust solutions.

What Needs to Be Backed Up?

One of the reasons why administrators tend to use multiple partitions (or logical volumes) when installing the operating system is that this lends to developing good backup strategies. Certain directories change more often than others. By making these separate filesystems, you can make use of filesystem features to perform the backup.

For example, it is normally a good idea to back up data not actively being modified. However, this can pose challenges when backing up users' home directories. By making **/home** a separate partition, you can then unmount the partition and perform a backup directly from the partition. Even better, you can make the **/home** filesystem on a logical volume and use Logical Volume Manager (LVM) snapshots to create a "frozen" view of the filesystem in the **/home** directory. This allows users to continue to work on the filesystem while you back up the data.

This does not mean that you will always make separate filesystems for each directory structure that you want to back up. In fact, in some cases (for example, the **/etc** directory), this is not even possible (**/etc** must be in the same filesystem as the **/** filesystem). However, whenever possible, it is generally a good idea to create separate filesystems for directory structures that you are incorporating into your backup strategy.

NOTE You will see that we tend to use the terms *directory* and *filesystem* interchangeably in this chapter. As you know, not all directories represent entire filesystems—just those that are mount points. However, because we strongly suggest that the directories in Table 13-1 be mount points for filesystems, we decided to use the terms *directory, directory structure*, and *filesystem* interchangeably when discussing these sorts of directories.

So, what directories/filesystems should you consider including in your backup strategy? Table 13-1 highlights those that are commonly part of a backup strategy.

Table 13-1 Directories/Filesystems to Consider Including in Your Backup Strategy

Directory/Filesystem	Reasons for Consideration
/home	If your system has any regular users, this directory structure is certain to be a part of your backup strategy. On servers with no regular users, however, this directory is normally ignored in the backup strategy.
/usr	The **/usr** directory rarely changes because this is the location of most of the system's commands, documentation, and programs. This directory structure normally only changes when new software is added to the system or when existing software is updated. Some administrators argue not to ever back up **/usr** because if something goes wrong, you can always just reinstall the software. The flaw in this reasoning is that few administrators keep a list of all the software installed on all the systems they administer. So, you should include this directory in your backup strategy.
/bin	If you back up the **/usr** directory, consider including the **/bin** directory because some of the operating system software is installed in this directory structure.
/sbin	If you back up the **/usr** directory, consider including the **/sbin** directory because some of the operating system software is installed in this directory structure.
/opt	If you have a lot of third-party software installed on your system, you might consider backing up this directory. This isn't typically the case in most Linux distributions.
/var	The primary data stored in the **/var** directory structure includes log files, the incoming email queue, and the print queue. The print queue should not need backing up, but log files and the email queue might be important, depending on the function of the system. Typically this filesystem is backed up on servers but often ignored on desktop systems.
/boot	The kernel is located in this directory structure. If you install a new kernel, consider backing up this directory structure. Typically it is not backed up on a regular basis.
/lib and **/lib64**	If you back up the **/usr** directory, consider including the **/lib** and **/lib64** directories because the operating system libraries are installed in these directory structures. As software is added to the system, new libraries are sometimes added as well.
/etc	This directory structure is often overlooked in the backup strategy, but it is also often the directory that changes most frequently. Regular system administration tasks, such as administering software configuration files and managing user/group accounts, result in changes in the **/etc** directory structure. On an active system, this directory should be backed up on a regular basis. (Note that the **/etc** directory *must* be a part of the **/** filesystem; it cannot be a separate filesystem.)

Which directories/filesystems should you never back up? The following directories either are not stored on the hard drive or contain temporary information that never needs to be backed up:

- **/dev**
- **/media**
- **/mnt**
- **/net**
- **/proc**
- **/srv**
- **/sys**
- **/var/tmp**

How Often?

There is no exact rule that tells you how often to perform backups. To determine how often to perform backups, determine which directories/filesystems you are going to back up and then get an idea of how often data changes on each.

Based on your observations, you should be able to determine how often to perform backups. It will likely be a different schedule for different directories, and you also need to consider how often to perform full versus incremental backups.

Full or Incremental?

Not all software tools provide the flexibility to perform incremental backups. But if you are using one that does provide this feature, consider including it in your backup strategy.

If the backup tool does provide incremental backups, there are probably several different levels available. Here are some examples:

- A Level 0 backup would be a full backup.
- A Level 1 backup would back up all files that have changed since the last lower-level backup (Level 0).
- A Level 2 backup would back up all files that have changed since the last lower-level backup (Level 0 or 1).

Typically these incremental backups would include the values 1–9. So a Level 9 backup would back up all files that have changed since the last lower-level backup (which could be Level 0, Level 1, Level 2, and so on).

To better understand incremental backups, first look at Figure 13-1.

13

	Sun	Mon	Tue	Wed	Thu	Fri	Sat
Week 1	0	2	3	4	5	6	7
	Sun	Mon	Tue	Wed	Thu	Fri	Sat
Week 2	1	2	3	4	5	6	7
	Sun	Mon	Tue	Wed	Thu	Fri	Sat
Week 3	1	2	3	4	5	6	7
	Sun	Mon	Tue	Wed	Thu	Fri	Sat
Week 4	1	2	3	4	5	6	7

Figure 13-1 *Backup Strategy #1*

The strategy in Figure 13-1 demonstrates a four-week backup period. Every four weeks, this cycle repeats. On the first day of the period, a full (Level 0) backup is performed. The next day, Monday, a Level 2 backup is performed. This backs up everything that has changed since the last lower-level backup (Level 0). This is essentially one day's worth of changes.

On Tuesday, a Level 3 back up is performed. This backs up everything that has changed since the last lower-level backup (the Level 2 performed on Monday). Each day during the week, a backup is performed that backs up the last 24 hours of changes to the directory/filesystem.

The following Sunday, a Level 1 backup is performed. This backs up all changes since the last lower-level backup (the Level 0 performed at the beginning of the cycle). Essentially, this backs up a week's worth of changes.

The advantage of this backup plan is that the backups each night take comparatively little time. Sunday's backups take longer each week, but the rest of the week is a relatively small backup. Because most businesses close earlier on Sunday, this presents little impact to the need for business access to these systems.

The disadvantage of this backup plan is in the recovery. If the filesystem must be restored because the data was lost on Friday of the third week, then the following restores must be performed, in this order:

- The Level 0 backup
- The Level 1 backup performed on Sunday of Week 3
- The Level 2 backup performed on Monday of Week 3
- The Level 3 backup performed on Tuesday of Week 3
- The Level 4 backup performed on Wednesday of Week 3
- The Level 5 backup performed on Thursday of Week 3

Now compare the backup strategy from Figure 13-1 with the backup strategy shown in Figure 13-2.

	Sun	Mon	Tue	Wed	Thu	Fri	Sat
Week 1	0	5	5	5	5	5	5
	Sun	Mon	Tue	Wed	Thu	Fri	Sat
Week 2	1	5	5	5	5	5	5
	Sun	Mon	Tue	Wed	Thu	Fri	Sat
Week 3	1	5	5	5	5	5	5
	Sun	Mon	Tue	Wed	Thu	Fri	Sat
Week 4	1	5	5	5	5	5	5

Figure 13-2 *Backup Strategy #2*

With the backup strategy on Figure 13-2, you also perform a full backup on the first day of the cycle. The backups performed Monday through Saturday back up all files that have changed since Sunday. The backup performed on the following Sunday includes all files that have changed since the first backup of the cycle.

The disadvantage of this method is that each backup takes more time as the week progresses. The advantage is the recovery process is easier and quicker. If the filesystem must be restored because the data was lost on Friday of the third week, then the following restores must be performed, in order:

- The Level 0 backup
- The Level 1 backup performed on Sunday of Week 3
- The Level 5 backup performed on Thursday of Week 3

There are many other backup strategies, including the famous Tower of Hanoi, which is based on a mathematical puzzle game. The important thing to remember is that you should research the different methods and find the one that is right for your situation.

Where Will the Backup Be Stored?

You have many options for media on which you can store backup data. Table 13-2 describes the most popular media and provides some of the advantages and disadvantages you should consider.

Table 13-2 Backup Storage Locations

Location	Advantage	Disadvantage
Tape	Low cost Medium shelf life	Slow Requires special hardware Requires a lot of maintenance
Disk	Fast Easily available	Not portable
Remote	Normally easily available Easy to have data secured offsite	Depends on network access Could be expensive Could be slow
Optical media	Decent speed Low cost Hardware easy to obtain and affordable	Low storage capacity Most often "write once" can't be reused

NOTE Consider following the 3-2-1 Rule: Store three copies of all important backup data. Use at least two types of media for the backups. Make sure at least one backup is offsite.

What Backup Tool Will Be Used?

You can use many different tools to back up data, including those that are already a part of most Linux distributions, as well as third-party tools. In this chapter, we cover the following tools:

- **dd**
- **tar**
- **rsync**
- Amanda
- Bacula

In addition to the backup tools, you should be aware of a few other tools used for creating and restoring files:

- **dump/restore**: Not used as often as in the past, these tools were designed to back up and restore entire filesystems. These tools support both full and incremental backups, which makes them some of the few standard backup tools that have this feature.

13

- **cpio**: Similar to the **tar** command, the **cpio** command can be used to merge files from multiple locations into a single archive.
- **gzip/gunzip**: Although the **gzip** command does not provide an essential feature that you want in a backup tool (namely, it does not merge files together), it does compress files. As a result, it could be used to compress a backup file.
- **bzip2/bunzip2**: Although the **bgzip2** command does not provide an essential feature that you want in a backup tool (namely, it does not merge files together), it does compress files. As a result, it could be used to compress a backup file.
- **zip/unzip**: An advantage of this tool is that it merges files together and compresses those files; plus, it uses a standard compression technique employed on multiple operating systems, including many non-Linux operating systems.

Standard Backup Utilities

These utilities are considered standard because you can expect them to be on just about every distribution of Linux. The advantage of this is that you use the tools to perform a backup on just about every system, but even more importantly, you can view and restore the backups on just about every system. It is frustrating and time consuming to deal with an esoteric backup file for which you lack the software to even determine the contents of the backup.

The dd Command

The **dd** command is useful to back up entire devices, whether entire hard disks, individual partitions, or logical volumes. For example, to back up an entire hard disk to a second hard disk, execute a command like the following:

```
[root@onecoursesource~]# dd if=/dev/sda of=/dev/sdb
```

The **if** option is used to specify the input device. The **of** option is used to specify the output device. Make sure when you execute this command that the **/dev/sdb** hard disk is at least as large as the **/dev/sda** hard disk.

What if you do not have a spare hard disk, but you have enough room on a device (such as an external USB hard disk)? In this case, place the output into an image file:

```
[root@onecoursesource ~]# dd if=/dev/sda of=/mnt/hda.img
```

You can also use the **dd** command to back up the contents of a CD-ROM or DVD into an ISO image:

```
[root@onecoursesource ~]# dd if=/dev/cdrom of=cdrom.iso
```

The ISO image file can be used to create more CD-ROMs, or it can be shared via the network to make the contents of the CD-ROM easily available (rather than passing the disc around the office).

It is also helpful to know that both image and ISO files can be treated as regular filesystems in the sense both types can be mounted and explored:

```
[root@onecoursesource ~]# mkdir /test
[root@onecoursesource ~]# mount -o loop /mnt/had.img /test
```

One of the advantages of the **dd** command is that it can back up anything on the hard disk, not just files and directories. For example, at the beginning of each disk is an area called the MBR (Master Boot Record). For the boot disk, the MBR contains the bootloader (GRUB) and a copy of the partition table. It can be useful to have a backup of this data:

```
[root@onecoursesource ~]# dd if=/dev/sda of=/root/mbr.img bs=512 count=1
```

The **bs** option indicates the block size, and the **count** indicates how many blocks to back up. The values of 512 and 1 make sense because the MBR size is 512 bytes.

We suggest storing the MBR image on an external device. If the system fails to boot because of a corrupted MBR, you can boot off a recovery CD-ROM and restore the MBR with a single command:

```
[root@onecoursesource ~]# dd if=mbr.img of=/dev/sda
```

The tar Command

The tape archive (**tar**) command was originally designed to back up filesystems to tape devices. Although many people now use the **tar** command to back up to non-tape devices, you should be aware of how to use tape devices as well.

Tape device names in Linux follow the **/dev/st*** and **/dev/nst*** convention. The first tape device is assigned the device name of **/dev/st0**, and the second tape device is accessible via the **/dev/st1** device name.

The name **/dev/nst0** also refers to the first tape device, but it sends a "no rewind" signal to the tape device. This is important for when you need to write multiple volumes to the tape. The default behavior of the tape drive is to automatically rewind when the backup is complete. If you wrote another backup to the same tape, you would overwrite the first backup unless you used the **/dev/nst0** device name when performing the first backup.

If you are working with tape devices, you should be aware of the **mt** command. This command is designed to allow you to directly manipulate the tape devices, including moving from one volume to another and deleting the contents of a tape. Here are some common examples:

```
[root@onecoursesource ~]# mt -f /dev/nst0 fsf 1     #skip forward one file (AKA, volume)
[root@onecoursesource ~]# mt -f /dev/st0 rewind     #rewinds the tape
[root@onecoursesource ~]# mt -f /dev/st0 status     #prints information about tape device
[root@onecoursesource ~]# mt -f /dev/st0 erase      #erases tape in tape drive
```

NOTE For the following examples, we assume that you do not have a tape drive in your system. The examples provided for the **tar** command place the tar ball (the result of the **tar** command) in a regular file; however, if you have a tape drive, you can just replace the filename with your tape device file.

To create a backup (or tar ball) with the **tar** utility, use the **-c** (create) option in conjunction with the **-f** (filename) option:

```
[root@onecoursesource ~]# tar -cf /tmp/xinet.tar /etc/xinetd.d
tar: Removing leading `/' from member names
```

The leading **/** characters are removed from the filenames, so instead of absolute pathnames being backed up, the pathnames are relative. This makes it easier to specify where the files are restored. Having the leading **/** would result in files always being stored in the exact same location.

To see the contents of a tar ball, use the **-t** (table of contents) option in conjunction with the **-f** option, as shown in Example 13-1.

Example 13-1 *Contents of a Tar Ball Using **tar -tf***

```
[root@onecoursesource ~]# tar -tf /tmp/xinet.tar
etc/xinetd.d/
etc/xinetd.d/rsync
```

```
etc/xinetd.d/discard-stream
etc/xinetd.d/discard-dgram
etc/xinetd.d/time-dgram
etc/xinetd.d/echo-dgram
etc/xinetd.d/daytime-stream
etc/xinetd.d/chargen-stream
etc/xinetd.d/daytime-dgram
etc/xinetd.d/chargen-dgram
etc/xinetd.d/time-stream
etc/xinetd.d/telnet
etc/xinetd.d/echo-stream
etc/xinetd.d/tcpmux-server
```

You often want to see detailed information when listing the contents of the tar ball. Include the **-v** (verbose) option to see additional information, as shown in Example 13-2.

Example 13-2 *The –v Option to See Details of the Tar Ball*

```
[root@onecoursesource ~]# tar -tvf /tmp/xinet.tar
drwxr-xr-x root/root         0 2018-11-02 11:52 etc/xinetd.d/
-rw-r--r-- root/root       332 2017-03-28 03:54 etc/xinetd.d/rsync
-rw------- root/root      1159 2016-10-07 10:35 etc/xinetd.d/discard-stream
-rw------- root/root      1157 2016-10-07 10:35 etc/xinetd.d/discard-dgram
-rw------- root/root      1149 2016-10-07 10:35 etc/xinetd.d/time-dgram
-rw------- root/root      1148 2016-10-07 10:35 etc/xinetd.d/echo-dgram
-rw------- root/root      1159 2016-10-07 10:35 etc/xinetd.d/daytime-stream
-rw------- root/root      1159 2016-10-07 10:35 etc/xinetd.d/chargen-stream
-rw------- root/root      1157 2016-10-07 10:35 etc/xinetd.d/daytime-dgram
-rw------- root/root      1157 2016-10-07 10:35 etc/xinetd.d/chargen-dgram
-rw------- root/root      1150 2016-10-07 10:35 etc/xinetd.d/time-stream
-rw------- root/root       302 2018-11-02 11:52 etc/xinetd.d/telnet
-rw------- root/root      1150 2016-10-07 10:35 etc/xinetd.d/echo-stream
-rw------- root/root      1212 2016-10-07 10:35 etc/xinetd.d/tcpmux-server
```

To extract all the contents of the tar ball into the current directory, use the **-x** (extract) option in conjunction with the **-f** option, as shown in Example 13-3.

Example 13-3 *Using **tar –xf** for Extracting Contents from the Tar Ball*

```
[root@onecoursesource ~]# cd /tmp
[root@onecoursesource tmp]# tar -xf xinet.tar
[root@onecoursesource tmp]# ls
backup          pulse-iqQ3aLCZD30z  virtual-root.MLN2pc  virtual-root.zAkrYZ
etc             pulse-lZAnjZ6xlqVu  virtual-root.o6Mepr  xinet.tar
keyring-9D6mpL  source              virtual-root.vtPUaj  zip-3.0-1.el6.src.rpm
orbit-gdm       virtual-root.7AHBKz virtual-root.y6Q4gw
orbit-root      virtual-root.EaUiye virtual-root.Yelrtc
[root@onecoursesource tmp]# ls etc
xinetd.d
[root@onecoursesource tmp]# ls etc/xinetd.d
chargen-dgram   daytime-stream  echo-dgram   tcpmux-server  time-stream
chargen-stream  discard-dgram   echo-stream  telnet
daytime-dgram   discard-stream  rsync        time-dgram
```

Suppose your tar ball contains thousands of files and you only need a few files. You can list the file-names at the end of the **tar** command to perform this partial restore:

```
[root@onecoursesource tmp]# tar -xf xinet.tar etc/xinetd.d/rsync
[root@onecoursesource tmp]# ls etc/xinetd.d
rsync
```

The **tar** command has many options; consult Table 13-3 to learn about some of the more useful ones (including those already covered).

Table 13-3 Useful **tar** Options

Option	Description
-A	Append to an existing tar ball.
-c	Create a tar ball.
-C	Set the current directory.
-d	Display the difference between an existing tar ball and what is currently on the filesystem.
--delete	Delete files from the tar ball (not possible on tapes).
-j	Compress tar ball with the **bzip2** command.
-t	List the table of contents of the tar ball.
-x	Extract the contents of the tar ball.
-z	Compress the tar ball with the **gzip** command.
-W	Attempt to verify after writing.

The rsync Command

The **rsync** command provides a different set of backup features than those provided by the **tar** and **dd** commands. It is designed to back up files to a remote system. It can communicate via Secure Shell (SSH), making the backup process secure. Additionally, it only backs up files that have changed since the last backup.

For example, the command shown in Example 13-4 performs a recursive backup of the **/etc/xinetd.d** directory to the **/backup** directory of the **server1** machine.

Example 13-4 *The **rsync** Command*

```
[root@onecoursesource ~]# rsync -av -e ssh /etc/xinetd.d server1:/backup
root@server1's password:
sending incremental file list
xinetd.d/
xinetd.d/chargen-dgram
xinetd.d/chargen-stream
xinetd.d/daytime-dgram
xinetd.d/daytime-stream
xinetd.d/discard-dgram
xinetd.d/discard-stream
xinetd.d/echo-dgram
xinetd.d/echo-stream
xinetd.d/rsync
xinetd.d/tcpmux-server
xinetd.d/telnet
```

```
xinetd.d/time-dgram
xinetd.d/time-stream

sent 14235 bytes  received 263 bytes  1159.84 bytes/sec
total size is 13391  speedup is 0.92
```

The options used from the previous command are **-v** (verbose), **-a** (archive), **-e ssh** (execute via SSH). The first argument is what to copy, and the second argument is where to copy it.

Suppose a change takes place to one of the files in the **/etc/xinetd.d** directory:

```
[root@onecoursesource ~]# chkconfig telnet off      #changes /etc/xinetd.d/telnet
```

Note that when the **rsync** command is executed again, only the modified file is transferred:

```
[root@onecoursesource ~]# rsync -av -e ssh /etc/xinetd.d server1:/backup
root@server1's password:
sending incremental file list
xinetd.d/
xinetd.d/telnet

sent 631 bytes  received 41 bytes  192.00 bytes/sec
total size is 13392  speedup is 19.93
```

Third-party Backup Utilities

Many third-party backup utilities are available for Linux. The following is a brief summary of two of the more popular utilities.

Amanda

The Advanced Maryland Automatic Network Disk Archiver (aka Amanda) is an open source software tool popular on both Unix and Linux distributions. Although there is a freely available community version, an enterprise version is available that provides support (for a fee, of course).

Amanda provides a scheduler, making it easier for system administrators to automate the backup process. It also supports writing to either tape device or hard disk.

Bacula

Bacula is an open source product that supports clients from different platforms, including Linux, Microsoft Windows, macOS, and Unix. One of the compelling features of Bacula is the capability to automate backup, freeing the system administrator from this routine task.

Configuration of Bacula on the server side can be accomplished via a web interface, GUI-based tools, or command-line tools.

One disadvantage of Bacula is that the format of the backup data is not compatible with other backup formats, such as the **tar** command's format. This makes it difficult to deal with the backup data unless you have the Bacula tools installed on the system.

Summary

In this chapter, you explored how to create a storage device security plan. Many of the topics from Chapters 9–12 included security features for storage devices. These features are the heart of a solid security plan. This chapter reviewed these key features as well as introduced how to create data backups and restore data from these backups.

Key Terms

Tower of Hanoi, tape device, tar ball, Amanda, Bacula

Review Questions

1. For tools that use numbers to specify full and incremental backups, the number _____ specifies a full backup.

2. Which of the following directories do not need to be backed up?

   A. **/etc**

   B. **/var**

   C. **/dev**

   D. **/sys**

3. Which of the following directories do not need to be backed up?

   A. **/usr**

   B. **/tmp**

   C. **/proc**

   D. **/boot**

4. The _____ command is used to remotely back up data; by default, it only backs up data that has changed since the last time the command was used.

5. Which of the following backup storage locations is likely to be the fastest?

   A. CD-ROM

   B. Tape

   C. Hard disk

   D. Remote network location

6. Which option to the **dd** command specifies the device that you are backing up?

   A. **count=**

   B. **bs=**

   C. **of=**

   D. **if=**

7. The "no rewind" device name for the first tape device on the system is **/dev/**_____.

8. Which option to the **tar** command is used to extract data from a tar ball?

   A. **-a**

   B. **-x**

   C. **-e**

   D. **-X**

9. The _____ option to the **rsync** command is used to enable data transfer via SSH.

13

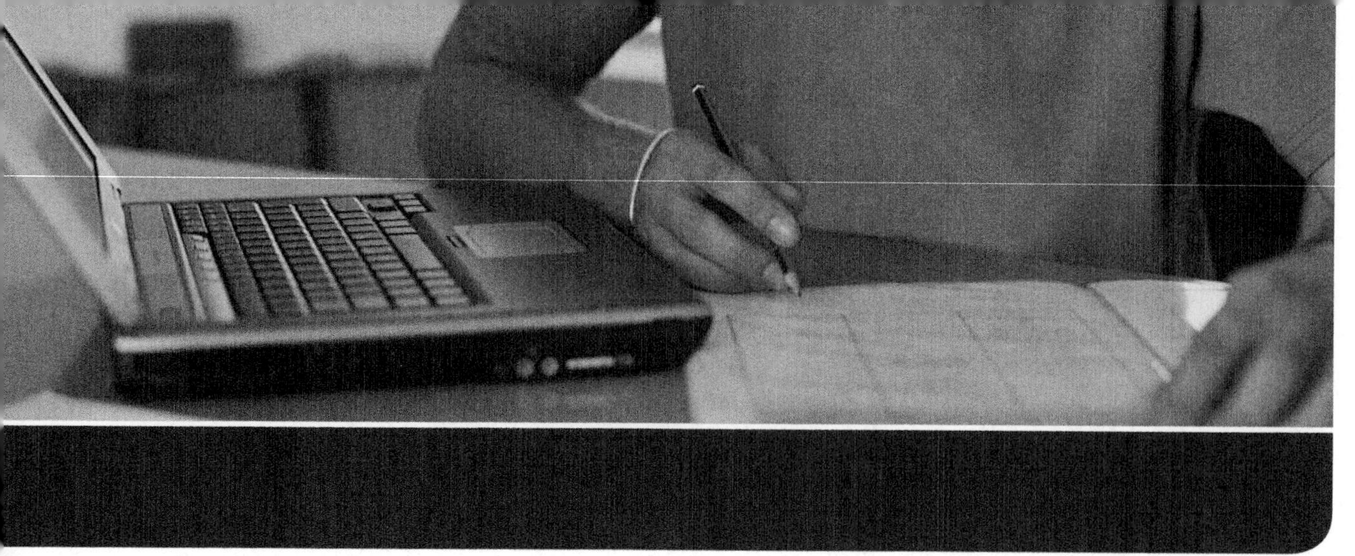

The goal of automation is to make the process of managing the system easier and more foolproof. With that in mind, you should also realize that automation is often used to make the system more secure. For example, you can automate the process of scanning your system for weaknesses.

Part IV

Automation

In Part IV, "Automation," you will explore the following chapters:

- Chapter 14, "crontab and at," covers two sets of tools that allow you to automatically execute processes at future times. The **crontab** system allows users to execute programs at regular intervals, such as once a month or twice a week. The **at** system provides users with a way to execute a program at one specific time in the future.
- Chapter 15, "Scripting," covers the basics of placing BASH commands into a file in order to create a more complex set of commands. Scripting is also useful for storing instructions that may be needed at a later time.
- Chapter 16, "Common Automation Tasks," covers the sort of tasks that both regular users and system administrators routinely automate. The focus of this chapter is on security, but additional automation tasks are demonstrated, particularly those related to topics covered in previous chapters.
- Chapter 17, "Develop an Automation Security Policy," provides you with the means to create a security policy using the knowledge you acquire in Chapters 14, 15, and 16.

crontab and at

Nobody wants to sit at a computer for 24 hours a day, monitoring the system health and ensuring routine tasks are completed. This is where the automation tools of **crontab** and **at** come into play.

By default, any user can create a **crontab** entry that will result in a daemon executing a program on a routine basis. Regular users make use of this feature to perform routine operations that they would normally have to remember to perform manually. System administrators use this feature to ensure the health and security of the operating system.

However, if you want to execute a program just once in the future, the **at** system is a better solution. With this feature, you can schedule the execution of a command or a set of commands at one specific time in the future.

This chapter covers both of these automation tools, including how a system administrator can secure them from misuse.

After reading this chapter and completing the exercises, you will be able to do the following:

Set up user crontab tables

Administer system crontab tables

Configure a command to execute once in the future with the at **command**

Secure the crontab **and** at **commands by limiting which users can schedule tasks using these commands**

Using crontab

The **crontab** command allows a user to view or modify their **crontab** file. The **crontab** file allows a user to schedule a command to be executed on a regular basis, such as once an hour or twice a month.

Important options for the **crontab** command are included in Table 14-1.

Table 14-1 Important **crontab** Command Options

Option	Description
-e	Edit the **crontab** file.
-l	List the entries in the **crontab** file.
-r	Remove all entries in the **crontab** file.
-u	Specify a user account.

Each line of the **crontab** table is broken into fields, separated by one or more space characters. Table 14-2 describes these fields.

Table 14-2 Fields of the **crontab** Table

Field	Description
First field: Minute	The minute that the command should execute. Values can be between 0 and 59. You can use a single value or a list of values, such as **0,15,30,45**. Range values (**1-15**) can also be used. An asterisk (*) character means "all possible values."
Second field: Hour	The hour that the command should execute. Values can be between 0 and 23. You can use a single value or a list of values, such as **0,6,12,18**. Range values (**8-16**) can also be used. An asterisk (*) character means "all possible values."
Third field: Day of the Month	The day of the month that the command should execute. Values can be between 1 and 31. You can use a single value or a list of values, such as **1,15**. Range values (**1-10**) can also be used. An asterisk (*) character means "not specified," unless the fifth field is also an * character, in which case it means "all possible values."
Fourth field: Month	The month that the command should execute. Values can be between 1 and 12. You can use a single value or a list of values, such as **6,12**. Range values (**1-3**) can also be used. An asterisk (*) character means "all possible values."
Fifth field: Day of the Week	The day of the week that the command should execute. Values can be between 0 and 7 (0=Sunday, 1=Monday...6=Saturday, 7=Sunday). You can use a single value or a list of values, such as **1,3,5**. Range values (**1-5**) can also be used. An asterisk (*) character means "not specified," unless the third field is also an * character, in which case it means "all possible values."
Sixth field: command**name**	The name of the command to execute.

For example, the following **crontab** entry will execute the **/home/bob/rpt.pl** script during every weekday (Monday–Friday) every month starting at 08:30 in the morning and every half hour until 16:30 (4:30 p.m.) in the afternoon:

```
0,30 8-16 * 1-12 1-5 /home/bob/rpt.pl
```

To create a **crontab** entry, execute the **crontab** command with the **-e** option:

```
student@onecoursesource:~# crontab -e
```

The **crontab** command will place you into an editor to allow for creation or editing of **crontab** entries. By default, it will use the vi editor. You can modify this by changing the **EDITOR** variable, which was covered in the "Environment Variables" section of Chapter 2, "Working on the Command Line."

WHAT COULD GO WRONG? Note that if you make any syntax mistakes while adding or modifying **crontab** entries, the **crontab** command will notify you of this when you exit the editor. For example, in the following output, there was an error in the minute field of line number 1:

```
"/tmp/crontab.6or0Y9":1: bad minute
errors in crontab file, can't install.
Do you want to retry the same edit?
```

You can answer **Y** or **N** at the prompt. An answer of **Y** will place you back in the editor where you will need to fix your error and then exit the editor again. An answer of **N** will discard all changes you made to the **crontab** table.

Be aware, however, that if what you enter is a logical mistake, such as typing 4 for the hour instead of 16, the system will not alert you because the command syntax is valid.

When finished editing your **crontab** entries, just exit the editor as you normally would. For example, if you are using the vi editor, enter **:wq** while in the command mode.

Security Highlight

Each user has their own collection of **crontab** entries. These entries are stored in files that only the root user has access to. These files are typically located in the **/var/spool/**cron directory.

To display the current user's **crontab** table, execute the **crontab** command with the **-l** option:

```
student@onecoursesource:~# crontab -l
0,30 8-16 * 1-12 1-5 /home/bob/rpt.pl
```

As an administrator, you can view or edit **crontab** tables of other users by using the **-u** option:

```
root@onecoursesource:~# crontab -l -u student
0,30 8-16 * 1-12 1-5 /home/bob/rpt.pl
```

To remove the entire **crontab** table, execute the **crontab** command with the **-r** option:

```
student@onecoursesource:~# crontab -r
```

Configure User Access to the cron Service

As the administrator, you can use configuration files to determine if a user can use the **crontab** commands. The **/etc/cron.deny** and **/etc/cron.allow** files are used to control access to the **crontab** command.

The format of each of these files is one user name per line. Here's an example:

```
[root@localhost ~]$ cat /etc/cron.deny
alias
backup
bin
daemon
ftp
games
gnats
guest
irc
lp
mail
man
nobody
operator
proxy
sync
sys
www-data
```

Table 14-3 describes how the **/etc/cron.deny** and **/etc/cron.allow** files work, and Figure 14-1 provides some additional information.

Table 14-3 Details Regarding How the **/etc/cron.deny** and **/etc/cron.allow** Files Work

Situation	Description
Only the **/etc/cron.deny** file exists	All users listed in this file are denied access to the **crontab** command while all other users can execute the **crontab** command successfully. Use this file when you want to deny access to a few users but allow access to most users.
Only the **/etc/cron.allow** file exists	All users listed in this file are allowed access to the **crontab** command while all other users cannot execute the **crontab** command successfully. Use this file when you want to allow access to a few users but deny access to most users.
Neither file exists	On most Linux distributions, this means that only the root user can use the **crontab** command. However, on some platforms, this results in all users being allowed to use the **crontab** command, so be careful and fully understand the Linux distribution you administer.
Both files exist	Only the **/etc/cron.allow** file is consulted and the **/etc/cron.deny** file is completely ignored.

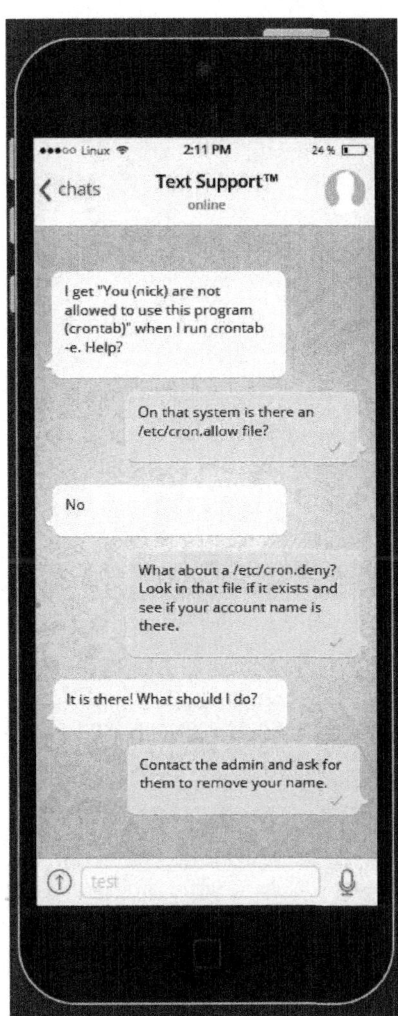

Figure 14-1 *Text Support™—Why Can't I Use* ***crontab?***

Security Highlight

On systems where regular users normally work, it is better to use the **/etc/cron.deny** file and place all system accounts in that file. Then, if more regular users are added to the system, they have access to the **crontab** command without any additional work.

On systems where regular users are not supposed to work (like servers), it is better to use the **/etc/cron.allow** file and only include the select few accounts that should have access to the **crontab** command.

/etc/crontab

The **/etc/crontab** file acts as the system **crontab**. The system administrator edits this file to enable executing system-critical processes at specific intervals.

Security Highlight

The **/etc/crontab** file is critical not only to perform system maintenance, but also to automate security scans. Only the root user has access to modify this file, but regular users can view the contents by default on most distributions. Consider removing the read permission of the "others" permission set to avoid prying eyes from seeing what scans you are performing.

Here is a sample **/etc/crontab** file:

```
[root@localhost ~]$ more /etc/crontab
SHELL=/bin/sh
PATH=/usr/local/sbin:/usr/local/bin:/sbin:/bin:/usr/sbin:/usr/bin

# m h dom mon dow user  command
17 *    * * *   root    cd / && run-parts /etc/cron.hourly
```

Each configuration line describes a process to execute, when to execute it, and what user name to use when executing the process. Each line is broken into fields, separated by one or more space characters. Table 14-4 describes these fields.

Table 14-4 Fields of the **/etc/crontab** File

Field	Description
First field: Minute	The minute that the command should execute. Values can be between 0 and 59. You can use a single value or a list of values, such as **0,15,30,45**. Range values (**1-15**) can also be used. An asterisk (*) character means "all possible values."
Second field: Hour	The hour that the command should execute. Values can be between 0 and 23. You can use a single value or a list of values, such as **0,6,12,18**. Range values (**8-16**) can also be used. An asterisk (*) character means "all possible values."
Third field: Day of the Month	The day of the month that the command should execute. Values can be between 1 and 31. You can use a single value or a list of values, such as **1,15**. Range values (**1-10**) can also be used. An asterisk (*) character means "not specified," unless the fifth field is also an * character, in which case it means "all possible values."
Fourth field: Month	The month that the command should execute. Values can be between 1 and 12. You can use a single value or a list of values, such as **6,12**. Range values (**1-3**) can also be used. An asterisk (*) character means "all possible values."

Field	Description
Fifth field: Day of the Week	The day of the week that the command should execute. Values can be between 0 and 7 (0=Sunday, 1=Monday…6=Saturday, 7=Sunday). You can use a single value or a list of values, such as **1,3,5**. Range values (**1-5**) can also be used. An asterisk (*) character means "not specified," unless the third field is also an * character, in which case it means "all possible values."
Sixth field: Username	The name of the user that the command should run as.
Seventh field: command**name**	The name of the command to execute.

Most default **/etc/crontab** files are designed to execute a script called **run-parts**. This script accepts a directory name as an argument. The script will execute all the programs (likely scripts themselves) in the specified directory.

For example, in the following **/etc/crontab** entry, the current directory is first changed to the **/** directory by the **cd** command, and then all the programs in the **/etc/cron.hourly** directory are executed:

```
[root@localhost ~]$ tail -n 1 /etc/crontab
17 *    * * *   root    cd / && run-parts /etc/cron.hourly
```

Most distributions will have **/etc/crontab** entries for **run-parts** for the following directories:

- **/etc/cron.hourly**: Contains programs that will be executed once per hour
- **/etc/cron.daily**: Contains programs that will be executed once per day
- **/etc/cron.weekly**: Contains programs that will be executed once per week
- **/etc/cron.monthly**: Contains programs that will be executed once per month

This means that if you want to execute something once per day, you do not have to create an entry in the **/etc/crontab** file. You could place a program in the **/etc/cron.daily** directory instead. This is how many developers handle tasks that need to be automated. As a result, after you install some software, you may find a new program in one or more of these directories.

Security Highlight

Keep in mind that any program placed in any of the **/etc/cron.{hourly,daily,weekly,monthy}** directories will be executed as the root user. Because of this elevated privilege, you should be careful with any program you place in these directories. After installing software, be sure to check these directories to check for new entries. You can also automate this task, as you will learn in Chapter 15, "Scripting."

In addition to the entries in the **/etc/crontab** file, system **crontab** entries can be found in the **/etc/cron.d** directory. This makes it easier for software developers to add custom entries (as opposed to editing the **/etc/crontab** file directly). So, look at all the files in the **/etc/cron.d** directory as well as the entries in the **/etc/crontab** file when determining all the system cron jobs that will be executed.

Security Highlight

Become familiar with all the files and directories mentioned in this section. Be aware of what is supposed to be in these locations, because hackers will often add entries in the system **crontab** file or the **/etc/cron.{hourly,daily,weekly,monthy}** directories to create backdoors into the system. This technique is used after the hacker gains root access to the system and is designed to make it easy to regain access even after their breach is discovered.

For example, if a hacker gains access to the system as the root user, then they could create a small script in the **/etc/cron.daily** directory that resets the root password (to something that they know). Even if they are discovered, they just need to wait until the next day because the root password will soon be set to something they know.

If you find an entry you do not recognize, go view the contents of the file that will be executed to determine whether the file is legitimate or if there is a potential security issue if the file is allowed to execute.

/etc/anacrontab

The component of the **crontab** system that executes commands as scheduled is the **crond** daemon. This is a process that runs in the background, waking up every minute and executing commands as necessary.

One issue with the system **crontab** (the **/etc/crontab** file and the files in the **/etc/cron.d** directory) is what happens when the system is turned off and a command is supposed to be executed. Important system commands can be skipped in situations like this. Consider the following scenario: There are several **crontab** entries on a user's Linux laptop that are designed to run at night. This user routinely will shut down the laptop every day before leaving work. The next morning, the user turns on the laptop. Unfortunately, none of the aforementioned **crontab** entries will be executed because when the commands were supposed to be executed, the **crond** daemon was not running because the laptop was not turned on.

The **/etc/anacrontab** file is used by the **anacron** command to determine how to execute commands that were missed by the **crond** daemon while a system was shut down. A typical **/etc/anacrontab** file looks like the following:

```
[root@localhost ~]$ cat /etc/anacrontab
SHELL=/bin/sh
PATH=/sbin:/bin:/usr/sbin:/usr/bin
MAILTO=root
# the maximal random delay added to the base delay of the jobs
RANDOM_DELAY=45
# the jobs will be started during the following hours only
START_HOURS_RANGE=3-22

#period in days  delay in minutes  job-identifier   command
1         5     cron.daily      nice run-parts /etc/cron.daily
7        25     cron.weekly     nice run-parts /etc/cron.weekly
@monthly 45cron.monthly    nice run-parts /etc/cron.monthly
```

The lines at the bottom of this file describe what commands to run and when to run them. Each line is broken into fields, separated by one or more space characters. Table 14-5 describes these fields.

Table 14-5 Fields of the **/etc/anacrontab** File

Field	Description
First field: period	The **anacron** command looks in the log files to determine the last time the command listed in the third field was executed. The first field means "if it has been more than this number of days since the last time that command was executed, then execute the command after the boot process has completed."
Second field: wait time	Wait this period of time (in minutes) after the system has completed booting before executing the command in the fourth field.
Third field: command name	The name of the command that was skipped.
Fourth field: command to execute	The command that should be executed.

For example, the following line means "execute the **nice run-parts /etc/cron.daily** command 5 minutes after the system boots if it has been one day or more since the last time the **cron.daily** command was executed":

```
1      5      cron.daily       nice run-parts /etc/cron.daily
```

NOTE On some modern Linux distributions, the **anacron** utility has been made obsolete because the modern **crond** daemon handles this function. However, if your system still uses the **anacron** utility, you should be aware of how it works because you should maintain this file to match the operations that the system **crontab** tables perform.

Using at

The **at** command is used to schedule one or more commands to be executed at one specific time in the future. The syntax for the command is **at** *time*, where *time* indicates when you want to execute a command. For example, the following will allow you to schedule a command to run at 5:00 p.m. tomorrow:

```
at 5pm tomorrow
at>
```

When provided the **at>** prompt, enter a command to execute at the specified time. To execute multiple commands, press the **Enter** key for another **at>** prompt.

When complete, hold down the Ctrl key and press the letter **d**. This results in an <EOT> message and creates the **at** job. Here's an example:

```
[root@localhost ~]$ at 5pm tomorrow
at>/home/bob/rpt.pl
at>echo "report complete" | mail bob
at><EOT>
job 1 at Thu Feb 23 17:00:00 2017
```

atq

The **atq** command lists the current user's **at** jobs:

```
[root@localhost ~]$ atq
1       Thu Feb 23 17:00:00 2018 a bob
```

The output includes a job number (1 in the previous example), the date the command will execute, and the user name (bob).

atrm

To remove an **at** job before it is executed, run the **atrm** command followed by the job number to remove. For example:

```
[root@localhost ~]$ atq
1       Thu Feb 23 17:00:00 2018 a bob
[root@localhost ~]$ atrm 1
~/shared$ atq
```

Configure User Access to at Services

As the administrator, you can use configuration files to determine if a user can use the **at** command. The **/etc/at.deny** and **/etc/at.allow** files are used to control access to the **at** command. Note that this is the same method as controlling access to the **crontab** command, but the filenames are different.

The format of each of these files is one user name per line. For example:

```
[root@localhost ~]$ cat /etc/at.deny
alias
backup
bin
daemon
ftp
games
gnats
guest
irc
lp
mail
man
nobody
operator
proxy
sync
sys
www-data
```

Table 14-6 describes how the **/etc/at.deny** and **/etc/at.allow** files work.

Table 14-6 Details Regarding How the **/etc/at.deny** and **/etc/at.allow** Files Work

Situation	Description
Only the **/etc/at.deny** file exists	All users listed in this file are denied access to the **at** command while all other users can execute the **at** command successfully. Use this file when you want to deny access to a few users but allow access to most users.
Only the **/etc/at.allow** file exists	All users listed in this file are allowed access to the **at** command while all other users cannot execute the **at** command successfully. Use this file when you want to allow access to a few users but deny access to most users.
Neither file exists	On most Linux distributions, this means that only the root user can use the **at** command. However, on some platforms, this results in all users being allowed to use the **at** command.

Situation	Description
Both files exist	Only the **/etc/at.allow** file is consulted, and the **/etc/at.deny** file is completely ignored.

Conversational Learning™—crontab vs. at

Gary: Hi, Julia. Can you explain in which situations I would use the **crontab** command versus when I would use the **at** command?

Julia: Sure, suppose you want to run a command sometime in the future. For example, you want to see who is logged in to the system at 2 p.m. next Saturday. In that case, you could use the **at** command to execute the **who** command at that specific time.

Gary: OK, so when would I use the **crontab** command?

Julia: Suppose you need to execute a command on a regular basis. For example, every two weeks you need to automate the executing of the payroll batch program. In that case, you would use the **crontab** command.

Gary: OK, makes sense. Thank you.

Julia: No problem!

Summary

The Linux operating system offers several ways to schedule tasks such as running programs in the future. Two tools, **crontab** and **at**, were covered in this chapter. Learning to automate repetitive tasks aids in efficiency, both for you as a system administrator and for system consistency. The "Security Highlight" sidebars in this chapter help to identify areas to check, as automation may pose a security risk.

Key Terms

at, daemon, crontab

Review Questions

1. The _____ option to the **crontab** command will remove all entries in the current user's **crontab**.

2. Which field of a **crontab** file is used to specify the day of the week?

   A. 2

   B. 3

   C. 4

   D. 5

3. Which files are used to control who can use the **crontab** command? (Choose two.)

   A. /etc/cron.deny

   B. /etc/cron.permit

   C. /etc/cron.block

   D. /etc/cron.allow

4. The **/etc/**_____ file is used by the system administrator to execute system-critical processes at specific intervals.

5. The _____ command will display the current user's **at** jobs.

14

Scripting

Imagine you find yourself typing the same set of commands daily (or maybe even multiple times per day). After doing this over and over, day after day, you will likely begin to ask yourself, "Is there another way?"

Some folks turn to the history list to make this easier. Recall from Chapter 2, "Working on the Command Line," that you can re-execute previous commands either by pressing the up-arrow key until you see the correct command or by typing *!cmd*, replacing *cmd* with the command you want to execute. Sometimes this solution works, but history lists can change, and pressing the up-arrow key 75 times to get to a specific command presents a level of frustration in itself.

This is where scripting makes more sense. Scripting is essentially creating small programs based on the Linux commands that you want to routinely (or occasionally) execute. Scripting also provides some programming features, such as flow control and the passing of parameters to the script. In this chapter, you will learn how to create and read BASH shell scripts.

After reading this chapter and completing the exercises, you will be able to do the following:

Describe key features of different scripting languages, including Perl, Python, and BASH scripting

Create and read BASH scripts

Linux Programming

Most Linux programming languages can be placed into two general categories: scripting languages (sometimes called "interpreted" languages) and compiled languages. There is no strict definition that separates these categories, but the following are the essential differences between the two:

- Compiled languages cannot be executed directly from source code. The source code must be converted into compiled code first.
- Scripts traditionally are not compiled.
- Scripting languages are typically easier to learn.
- Scripts often take less coding to perform a task.

As an example of how these categories are not strictly defined, consider this: Perl is a popular scripting language that is executed directly from source code, but before executing it is compiled into memory, and the compiled form of the code is executed.

Because the scope of this book is focused on Linux, this chapter will concentrate on BASH scripting. However, you should be aware that other scripting languages are often used on Linux distributions. The following sections provide a brief overview of BASH, Perl, and Python scripting—the three most commonly used scripting languages on Linux.

BASH Shell Scripting

In previous chapters, you learned the basics of working in Linux and the BASH shell. The commands you learned can also be used in shell scripting programs. For example, suppose you routinely execute the following commands:

```
cd /home
ls -l /home > /root/homedirs
du -s /home/* >> /root/homedirs
date >> /root/homedirs
```

Instead of executing each of these commands manually, day after day, you can place all of the commands into a file, make the file executable, and then run the file as a program:

```
[root@onecoursesource ~]$ more /root/checkhome.sh
#!/bin/bash

cd /home
ls -l /home > /root/homedirs
du -s /home/* >> /root/homedirs
date >> /root/homedirs
[root@onecoursesource~]$ chmod a+x /root/checkhome.sh
[root@onecoursesource~]$ /root/checkhome.sh
```

Because you can use Linux commands natively in BASH shell scripts, this scripting language can be extremely powerful. Another advantage of using this language is that you can be confident that just about every Linux (and Unix) distribution will have the BASH shell, making it easy to port a script from one system to another.

In addition to being able to use Linux commands in BASH shell scripts, you should be aware that this language has other programming features, such as the following:

- Variables
- Loop controls (**if**, **while**, and so on)
- Exit status values
- The ability to source code from other files

With all of its advantages, there are some disadvantages to BASH shell scripting:

- It lacks some advanced programming features, such as object-oriented programming.
- It is often much slower than executing other languages because each command is normally executed as a separate process.

Even with these disadvantages, BASH shell scripting is very popular in Linux. In fact, a search for BASH scripts (files that end in **.sh**) on a typical Linux distribution normally will result in hundreds of results:

```
[root@onecoursesource ~]$ find / -name "*.sh" | wc -l
578
```

Hint: The previous command provides you with the means to find existing BASH shell scripts. This is useful because learning BASH shell scripting includes reading existing scripts.

Perl Scripting

In the mid-1980s, a developer named Larry Wall began work on a new scripting language that would eventually be named Perl. At the time he was working on Unix-based systems that had tools such as the C programming language, the Bourne Shell scripting language (precursor to BASH), and sed and awk (more about these tools later). However, none of these tools worked as he wanted, so he created his own language.

Of course, Larry did not want to lose the features he did like about these tools, so he combined the features that he liked into his new language. This resulted in a language that looks a bit like C, a bit like shell scripting, and a bit like a hodgepodge collection of Unix utilities.

There are several aspects of Perl that Linux users like, including the following:

- You can very quickly write Perl code because much of what you need for basic scripting is already built in to the core language.
- Perl code is very flexible; you are not limited by the structure as much as some other languages.
- Perl's syntax is fairly simple, derived primarily from the C language.
- It normally does not take very long to learn Perl.
- Perl has very powerful features, such as robust regular expressions.

Although Perl can be used for many different applications, it is often used for the following:

- **Data parsing**: Perl has powerful regular expression features, which makes it ideal for data munging (pulling chunks from data and generating reports).
- **Web development**: Perl is often a component of LAMP-based (LAMP = Linux, Apache HTTP Server, MySQL, and Perl or PHP) technology because of its web development features, including Common Gateway Interface (CGI).
- **Code testing**: Because Perl is easy and quick to code, developers will often use it to create tools to test their applications.
- **GUI programs**: Additional Perl modules (libraries), such as WxPerl and Tk, provide Perl programmers with the option of easily creating a GUI interface for users to interact with the Perl code.
- **Administrative tools**: System administrators will often create Perl scripts to help them automate administrative tasks.

NOTE Perl scripting is a very large topic and beyond the scope of this book. However, as your experience in Linux grows, Perl is a language that you should consider learning because it has powerful features that allow you to automate tasks on Linux.

Python Scripting

The beginnings of Python are best described by Guido van Rossum, its creator, who wrote the following as a forward for a book on Python published in 1996:

> "Over six years ago, in December 1989, I was looking for a 'hobby' programming project that would keep me occupied during the week around Christmas. My office … would be closed, but I had a home computer, and not much else on my hands. I decided to write an interpreter for the new scripting language I had been thinking about lately: a descendant of ABC that would appeal to Unix/C hackers. I chose Python as a working title for the project, being in a slightly irreverent mood (and a big fan of Monty Python's Flying Circus)."

Little did he know that Python would one day become one of the world's most popular scripting languages. Since that fateful Christmas break in the late 1980s, Python has developed into a robust programming language that is the core of many Linux tools and open source projects.

One of the driving philosophies of Python is well-structured code. Python enforces this with rules such as a very rigid indentation scheme. You can see how seriously Python developers take the concept of well-structured code by reading some of the rules defined by the document "Zen of Python":

- Beautiful is better than ugly.
- Explicit is better than implicit.
- Simple is better than complex.
- Complex is better than complicated.
- Flat is better than nested.
- Sparse is better than dense.
- Readability counts.

In addition to Python being a well-structured language, the following components make Python a popular language:

- It has object-oriented features.
- It has a large standard library.
- It is extendable or embedded.
- The data structures provided by Python are more diverse than those of many languages.

Although Python can be used for many different applications, it is often used for the following:

- **Network-based applications**: By using Twisted, a Python-based network framework, you can develop network-based applications.
- **Web development**: The Apache Web Server provides the option of using Python scripts for dynamic websites.
- **Scientific applications**: Several libraries are available for Python that make it a good choice to create scientific applications.
- **System tools**: Python is often used by Linux developers to create system tools for the operating system.

NOTE Python scripting is a very large topic and beyond the scope of this book. However, as your experience in Linux grows, Python is a language that you should consider learning because it has powerful features that allow you to automate tasks on Linux.

Conversational Learning™—Which Language Is Best?

Gary: Hi, Julia! I'm about to create a script, but I'm not sure which language is the best. I'm thinking of either Perl, Python, or BASH. Which one is the best language?

Julia: I believe trying to list the pros and cons of each scripting language is a mistake. To begin with, this is often a matter of opinion.

Gary: What do you mean?

Julia: For example, Perl is a very flexible language, whereas Python is more structured. If I want to write a quick script and I am not worried about maintaining the code long term, then flexibility might be a pro and structure a con. However, if I was working with multiple developers on a larger product, then structure might be a pro and flexibility a con.

Gary: Well, then, how do I decide which language to use?

Julia: Rather than trying to compare and contrast the pros and cons of each scripting language, try to focus on what people usually like about each language and what each language is typically used for. It is better to decide what aspect of a language is a feature versus a liability.

Gary: OK, I suppose this makes sense because if there was one "best language," then everyone would just use that one language.

Julia: There you go—you got the idea.

Basics of BASH Scripting

To an extent, you already know many of the basics of BASH scripting because you have already learned many features of the BASH shell in this book. For example, you learned about shell variables in Chapter 2. Shell variables are used in BASH scripting to store values.

To start a BASH script, enter the following as the first line of the script file in a text editor, such as the vi or vim editor:

```
#!/bin/bash
```

This special sequence is called the *shebang*, and it tells the system to execute this code as a BASH script.

Comments in a BASH script start with a **#** character and extend to the end of the line. For example:

```
echo "Tux for President"   #prints "Tux for President" to the screen
```

As shown in the previous example, the **echo** command can be used to display information to the user who is running a program. The arguments to the **echo** command can contain any text data and can also include the value of a variable:

```
echo "The answer is $result"
```

After creating your BASH script and saving it, you make it executable:

```
[student@onecoursesource ~]$ more hello.sh
#!/bin/bash
#hello.sh

echo "Tux for President"
[student@onecoursesource ~]$ chmod a+x hello.sh
```

Security Highlight

Scripts should never have the SUID permission set. This permission could allow someone to hijack the script and run commands as the owner of the script.

Now your code can be run as a program by using the following syntax:

```
[student@onecoursesource ~]$./hello.sh
Tux for President
```

Note the need to place **./** before the name of the command. This is because the command may not be in one of the directories specified by the **$PATH** variable:

```
[student@onecoursesource ~]$ echo $PATH
/usr/local/sbin:/usr/local/bin:/usr/sbin:/usr/bin:/sbin:/bin:/usr/games:/usr/local/games
```

To avoid the need to include **./** whenever you want to run your script, you can modify the **$PATH** variable to include the directory in which your script is stored. For example, typically regular users create a "**bin**" directory in their home directory and place scripts in this location:

```
[student@onecoursesource ~]$ mkdir bin
[student@onecoursesource ~]$ cp hello.sh bin
[student@onecoursesource ~]$ PATH="$PATH:/home/student/bin"
[student@onecoursesource ~]$ hello.sh
hello world!
```

In addition to the built-in variables that were discussed in Chapter 2, there are variables available in BASH scripts that represent the arguments passed into the script. For example, consider the following execution of a script called **test.sh**:

```
[student@onecoursesource ~]$ test.sh Bob Sue Ted
```

The values **Bob**, **Sue**, and **Ted** are assigned to variables within the script. The first argument (**Bob**) is assigned to the **$1** variable, the second argument is assigned to the **$2** variable, and so on. Additionally, all arguments collectively are assigned to the **$@** variable.

For additional details regarding these positional parameter variables or anything related to BASH scripting, consult the man page for BASH:

```
[student@onecoursesource ~]$ man bash
```

Conditional Expressions

Several conditional statements are available for the BASH shell, including the **if** statement:

```
if [ cond ]
then
    statements
elif [ cond ]
then
    statement
else
    statements
fi
```

Note the following:

- An "else, if" statement is spelled **elif** and is not required if you don't want to perform additional conditional checks.
- After the **if** and **elif**, you need a **then** statement. However, after an **else**, do not include a **then** statement.
- End the **if** statement with the word "if" spelled backwards: **fi**.

See Example 15-1 for an example of an **if** statement.

Example 15-1 *Sample if Statement*

```
#!/bin/bash
#if.sh

color=$1

if [ "$color" = "blue" ]
```

15

```
then
   echo "it is blue"
elif [ "$color" = "red" ]
then
   echo "it is red"
else
   echo "no idea what this color is"
fi
```

NOTE BASH allows you to use either **==** or **=** for numeric equality.

In Example 15-1, the following conditional statement was used:

["$color" = "blue"]

This syntax performs an implicit call of a BASH command named **test** that can be used to perform several comparison tests. This can include integer (numeric) comparisons, string comparisons, and file testing operations. For example, use the following syntax to test whether the string value that is stored in the **$name1** variable does not equal the string stored in the **$name2** variable:

```
[ "$name1" != "$name2" ]
```

WHAT COULD GO WRONG? Common mistakes when creating an **if** statement include forgetting to put a **then** after the **if** and **elif** statements. Also, people often mistakenly put a **then** after an else statement, but this is incorrect.

IMPORTANT NOTE The spacing around the square brackets is very important. There should be a space before and after each square bracket. Without these spaces, an error message will occur.

Get in the habit of putting double quotes around your variables in BASH scripts. This is important in the event the variable has not been assigned a value. For example, suppose the script in Example 15-1 was executed with no arguments. The result would be that the **color** variable is unassigned and the resulting conditional statement would be **if ["" = "blue"]**.

The result would be false, but without the quotes around **$color**, the result would be an error message and the script would exit immediately. This is because the resulting conditional statement would be missing one of its key components after the value of **$color** has been returned: **if [= "blue"]**.

In addition to determining whether two strings are equal or not equal, you may also find the **-n** option useful. This option will determine whether a string is not empty, which is useful when testing user input. For example, the code in Example 15-2 will read data from user input (the keyboard), assign the input to the **$name** variable, and test to make sure the user typed something for the name.

Example 15-2 *Testing User Input*

```
[student@onecoursesource ~]$ more name.sh
#!/bin/bash
#name.sh

echo "Enter your name"
read name
```

```
if [ -n "$name" ]
then
   echo "Thank you!"
else
   echo "hey, you didn't give a name!"
fi
[student@onecoursesource ~]$./name.sh
Enter your name
Bo
Thank you!
[student@onecoursesource ~]$./name.sh
Enter your name

hey, you didn't give a name!
```

Integer Comparisons

If you want to perform integer (numeric) comparison operations, use the following:

- **-eq**: True if values are equal to each other.
- **-ne**: True if values are not equal to each other.
- **-gt**: True if first value is greater than second value.
- **-lt**: True if first value is less than second value.
- **-ge**: True if first value is greater than or equal to second value.
- **-le**: True if first value is less than or equal to second value.

File Test Comparisons

You can also perform test operations on files and directories to determine information about the file's status. These operations include the following:

- **-d**: True if the "file" is a directory.
- **-f**: True if the "file" is a regular file.
- **-r**: True if the file exists and it is readable by the user running the script.
- **-w**: True if the file exists and it is writable by the user running the script.
- **-x**: True if the file exists and it is executable by the user running the script.
- **-L**: True if the first value is less than or equal to the second value.

Flow Control Statements

In addition to **if** statements, the BASH scripting language has several other flow control statements:

- **The while loop**: Executes a block of code repeatedly as long as the conditional statement is true.
- **The until loop**: Executes a block of code repeatedly as long as the conditional statement is false. Essentially the opposite of a **while** loop.
- **The case statement**: Similar to an **if** statement but provides an easier branching method for multiple situations. The **case** statement ends with **esac** ("case" spelled backwards).
- **The for loop**: Executes a block of code for each item in a list of values.

The while Loop

The following code segment will prompt the user for a five-digit number. If the user complies, the program will continue as the condition of the **while** loop will be false. However, if the user provides incorrect data, the condition of the **while** loop will be true and the user will be prompted for the correct data again:

```
echo "Enter a five-digit ZIP code: "
read ZIP

while echo $ZIP | egrep -v "^[0-9]{5}$" > /dev/null 2>&1
do
   echo "You must enter a valid ZIP code - five digits only!"
   echo "Enter a five-digit ZIP code: "
   read ZIP
done

echo "Thank you"
```

The **egrep** command from the previous example is a bit tricky. To begin with, the regular expression pattern is matching a value that is exactly five digits. The **-v** option is used to return a value if the pattern is not found. So, if **$ZIP** contains a valid five-digit number, then **egrep** returns a false result because it is trying to find lines that don't contain a five-digit number. The **egrep** command returns a true result if the **$ZIP** contains something besides a five-digit number.

Why the **> /dev/null 2>&1**? Because you do not want to display anything from the **egrep** command, just make use of its true/false return value. All operating system (OS) commands return a true or false value (technically each returns 0 for "true" and a positive number for false) when executed, and that is what is needed here. Any **STDOUT** (regular command output) or **STDERR** (command error messages) from the command is unnecessary and only serves to confuse matters if it is displayed to the user.

The for Loop

A **for** loop enables you to perform an operation on a set of items. For example, the following command, when run as the root user, will create five user accounts:

```
for person in bob ted sue nick fred
do
    useradd $person
done
```

Loop Control

Like most languages, BASH scripting provides a way to prematurely exit a loop or to stop the current iteration of a loop and start a new iteration of a loop. Use the **break** command to immediately exit a **while**, **until**, or **for** loop. Use the **continue** command to stop the current iteration of a **while**, **until**, or **for** loop and start the next iteration of the loop.

The case Statement

A **case** statement is designed for when you want to perform multiple conditional checks. Although you could use an **if** statement with multiple **elif** statements, the syntax of **if/elif/else** is often more cumbersome than a **case** statement.

Here is the syntax for a **case** statement (note that **cmd** represents any BASH command or programming statement):

```
case var in
cond1)   cmd
         cmd;;
cond2)   cmd
         cmd;;
esac
```

For the previous syntax example, **var** represents a variable's value that you want to conditionally check. For example, consider the following code:

```
name="bob"

case $name in
ted)   echo "it is ted";;
bob) echo "it is bob";;
*)      echo "I have no idea who you are"
esac
```

The "condition" is a pattern that uses the same matching rules as file wildcards. An asterisk (*) matches zero or more of any character, a ? matches a single character, and you can use square brackets to match a single character of a specific range. You can also use a pipe (|) character to represent "or." For example, consider Example 15-3, which is used to check a user's answer to a question.

Example 15-3 *Example of a* ***case*** *Statement*

```
answer=yes

case $answer in
y|ye[sp]) echo "you said yes";;
n|no|nope) echo "you said no";;
*)   echo "bad response";;
esac
```

User Interaction

The example in Example 15-3 is a bit of a puzzle because it is intended to check user input. However, the variable is hard-coded. It would make more sense to use actual user input, which can be gathered by the **read** statement:

```
read answer
```

The **read** statement will prompt the user to provide information and read that data (technically from **STDIN**, which is where the program reads data from and is set to the user's keyboard by default) into a variable that is specified as the argument to the **read** statement. See Example 15-4 for an example.

Example 15-4 *Example of a* ***read*** *Statement*

```
read answer

case $answer in
y|ye[sp]) echo "you said yes";;
n|no|nope) echo "you said no";;
*)   echo "bad response";;
esac
```

15

To assign values to different variables, use the following syntax:

```
read var1 var2 var3
```

Use the **-p** option to issue a prompt to the user:

```
read -p "Enter your name" name
```

Using Command Substitution

Command substitution is the process of executing a subcommand within a larger command. It is typically used to gather data and store this data into a variable. For example, the following command stores the output of the **date** command into the **$today** variable:

```
today=$(date)
```

Command substitution can be performed by using one of two methods:

- Method 1: **$(cmd)**
- Method 2: **`cmd`**

Note that Method 2 uses backquote characters (also called "backtick" characters), not single-quote characters. Both methods yield the same results; however, Method 1 is generally considered more "readable" because it is difficult to see the difference between single-quote and backquote characters.

Additional Information

Want to learn more about creating BASH scripts? The following are good resources for additional information:

- **man bash**: The man page for the BASH shell has a great deal of information about writing BASH scripts.
- **http://tldp.org**: A website that is (sadly) mostly out of date. However, there is one gem of a document called the "Advanced Bash-Scripting Guide." Click the "Guides" link under the "Documents" section and scroll down until you see this guide. The author of this guide normally updates it on a regular basis. Since the guides are listed by publication date, this guide is almost always at the top of the list.

Summary

A key feature of automation is the ability to batch commands into a single executable file. Scripting languages, such as Python, Perl, and BASH scripting, provide this powerful feature. In this chapter, you learned the basics of creating scripts, with a primary focus on BASH scripting.

Key Terms

Perl, Python, conditional expression, variable

Review Questions

1. The _____ permission must be added to a script before it can be run like a program.
2. Which command is used to display messages?

   A. print

   B. display

   C. show

   D. -echo

3. A **while** statement is required to have a **then** statement directly following which of these? (Choose two.)

   A. if

   B. fi

   C. else

   D. -elif

4. The _____ operator is used to determine if one integer is less than or equal to another integer.
5. The _____ command gathers user input and stores the value that the user types into a variable.

Common Automation Tasks

After exploring **crontab** and scripting in Chapter 14, "crontab and at," and Chapter 15, "Scripting," you now have the tools to automate! Most likely you are now thinking "OK, but what will I automate?" This chapter explores some common automation use cases and provides demonstration scripts and **crontab** entries.

After reading this chapter and completing the exercises, you will be able to do the following:

Plan common automation tasks

Exploring Scripts that Already Exist on Your System

To start, there is some good news: you have many examples of Linux automation already available on your system that you can use to model your own solutions. You just need to know where to look.

The /etc/cron.* Directories

Recall in Chapter 14 that several directories contain scripts that are run on a regular schedule:

- **/etc/cron.hourly**: Contains programs that will be executed once per hour
- **/etc/cron.daily**: Contains programs that will be executed once per day
- **/etc/cron.weekly**: Contains programs that will be executed once per week
- **/etc/cron.monthly**: Contains programs that will be executed once per month

This means that on your system you already have examples of automation. What exactly you have in these directories will depend on what software you have installed. For example, consider the following output from a Fedora system:

```
[root@onecoursesource cron.daily]# ls -l
total 20
-rwxr-xr-x 1 root root 180 Aug  1  2012 logrotate
-rwxr-xr-x 1 root root 618 Nov 13  2014 man-db.cron
-rwxr-x--- 1 root root 192 Aug  3  2013 mlocate
```

These three scripts perform specific tasks that are designed to promote the health and security of the distribution. What do these do? To determine that, you just need to read the scripts.

logrotate

Review the **logrotate** script (note that the **nl** command displays a file with a number at the beginning of each line):

```
[root@onecoursesource cron.daily]#nl -ba logrotate
     1  #!/bin/sh
     2
     3  /usr/sbin/logrotate /etc/logrotate.conf
```

```
4   EXITVALUE=$?
5   if [ $EXITVALUE != 0 ]; then
6       /usr/bin/logger -t logrotate "ALERT exited abnormally
7   fi
8   exit 0
```

From Line 1, you can tell this is a BASH script (**/bin/sh** is a symbolic link to **/bin/bash**).

Line 3 is executing the **/usr/sbin/logrotate** program. To determine what sort of program this is, use the **file** command:

```
[root@onecoursesource cron.daily]#file /usr/sbin/logrotate
/usr/sbin/logrotate: ELF 64-bit LSB executable, x86-64, version 1 (SYSV),
dynamically linked (uses shared libs), for GNU/Linux 2.6.32,
BuildID[sha1]=21ac008a2855900ed1819a1fb6c551c54a84a49f, stripped
```

Since the output of the **file** command does not indicate that this is a text file, you should not look at it directly. However, given that it is located in the **/usr/sbin** directory, it likely has a man page. After executing **man logrotate**, you can see that this command's function "… rotates, compresses, and mails system logs," and if you look at the **SYNOPSIS** section of the man page, you will discover that the argument to the **logrotate** command is its configuration file:

```
logrotate [-dv] [-f|--force] [-s|--state file] config_file ..
```

Note that we will discuss the **logrotate** command in more depth in Chapter 25, "System Logging," when we discuss system logs. The purpose of this discussion is to gather ideas of what sort of automation processes can be created to better service the system. The first paragraph of the **DESCRIPTION** of the man page provides an excellent reason for this command to be executed daily:

> "logrotate is designed to ease administration of systems that generate large numbers of log files. It allows automatic rotation, compression, removal, and mailing of log files. Each log file may be handled daily, weekly, monthly, or when it grows too large."

But what about the rest of the script? Line 4 introduces something new that you have not learned about BASH scripting yet: when a command or program finishes execution, it will return an exit status value to the calling program. This is a numeric value that is 0 if the command executed successfully and a positive value if the command failed. This exit status value is stored in the **$?** variable.

Line 4 stores this value in a new variable called **EXITVALUE**, and line 5 contains code that you should already understand from topics that were discussed in Chapter 15. The **if** statement determines if the **EXITVALUE** is not 0, and if it is not 0, then the **logger** command will execute. What does the **logger** command do?

Again, consult the man page: "logger makes entries in the system log." So, if the **logrotate** command fails, then the **logger** utility will create an entry about this failure.

Line 8 just exits the script with a "success" return value of 0.

man-db.cron

This script is a bit larger, so not every line will be examined, and the **grep** command is used to filter out comment lines and blank lines:

```
[root@onecoursesource cron.daily]#grep -v "^#" man-db.cron | grep -v "^$" | nl
     1  if [ -e /etc/sysconfig/man-db ]; then
     2      . /etc/sysconfig/man-db
     3  fi
```

```
 4  if [ "$CRON" = "no" ]; then
 5     exit 0
 6  fi
 7  renice +19 -p $$ >/dev/null 2>&1
 8  ionice -c3 -p $$ >/dev/null 2>&1
 9  LOCKFILE=/var/lock/man-db.lock
10  [[ -f $LOCKFILE ]] && exit 0
11  trap "{ rm -f $LOCKFILE ; exit 0; }" EXIT
12  touch $LOCKFILE
13  mandb $OPTS
14  exit 0
```

Lines 1–3 make use of a feature called *sourcing*. If the **/etc/sysconfig/man-db** file exists, it is executed as if the code from that file was embedded within this script. This is typically used to import variables from an external file.

Lines 4–12 perform some setup tasks that are necessary for the command on Line 13 to run correctly. Most of these lines are straightforward (Line 9 creates a variable, Line 12 creates a file, and so on). Some commands, like the **renice** command, will be covered in later chapters.

Line 13 is the heart of this script. According to the man page, the **mandb** command (described as **%mandb%** in the man page) performs the following:

> "%mandb% is used to initialiseor manually update index database caches that are usually maintained by %man%. The caches contain information relevant to the current state of the manual page system and the information stored within them is used by the man-db utilities to enhance their speed and functionality."

Why is this useful? As you add and update software to the system, new man pages are introduced. By executing this command automatically on a daily basis, the functionality of the man page is optimized.

mlocate

In Chapter 2, "Working on the Command Line," you were introduced to the **find** command, which is used to search the live filesystem for files based on filename, ownership, permissions, and other file metadata. In addition to the **find** command is a command called **locate** that also looks for files:

```
[root@onecoursesource cron.daily]#locate motd
/etc/motd
/extract/etc/motd
/usr/lib64/security/pam_motd.so
/usr/libexec/usermin/caldera/motd
/usr/libexec/usermin/caldera/motd/images
/usr/libexec/usermin/caldera/motd/images/icon.gif
/usr/libexec/webmin/pam/pam_motd.so.pl
/usr/share/doc/pam/html/sag-pam_motd.html
/usr/share/doc/pam/txts/README.pam_motd
/usr/share/man/man8/pam_motd.8.gz
```

There are several differences between the **find** and **locate** commands, but the biggest difference is that the **locate** command doesn't search the live filesystem, but rather searches from a database that is generated automatically daily. This makes the **locate** command faster than the **find** command because searching the live filesystem is more time consuming.

How is the database that the **locate** command uses generated daily? As you can probably guess by now, it is the **mlocate** script:

```
[root@onecoursesource cron.daily]#nl -ba mlocate
     1  #!/bin/sh
     2  nodevs=$(< /proc/filesystems awk '$1 == "nodev" && $2 != "rootfs"
➥{ print $2 }')
     3  renice +19 -p $$ >/dev/null 2>&1
     4  ionice -c2 -n7 -p $$ >/dev/null 2>&1
     5  /usr/bin/updatedb -f "$nodevs"
```

Try to read this one on your own. Here are some hints:

- You learned about the **$()** feature in Chapter 15.
- The code inside **$()** is a bit tricky. However, you can just run Line 2 in a standard BASH shell and then look at the value of the **nodevs** variable.
- The man pages will help you with the **renice**, **ionice**, and **updatedb** commands. It is the **updatedb** command that actually creates the database that is used by the **locate** command.

Before continuing to the next section in this chapter, consider looking for and reading more scripts in the **/etc/cron.daily**, **/etc/cron.hourly**, **/etc/cron.weekly**, and **/etc/cron.monthly** directories. The more you explore, the better you will understand automation.

Repositories

A *repository*, in coding terms, is a location where people share programs. You should consider exploring several BASH shell repositories, including the following:

- **Daniel E. Singer's Scripts**: ftp://ftp.cs.duke.edu/pub/des/scripts/INDEX.html
- **John Chambers' directory of useful tools**: http://trillian.mit.edu/~jc/sh/
- **Cameron Simpson's Scripts**: https://cskk.ezoshosting.com/cs/css/
- **Carlos J. G. Duarte's Scripts**: http://cgd.sdf-eu.org/a_scripts.html

Not only will exploring these repositories provide you with access to useful scripts (and not just BASH scripts), but we have found that this practice also serves to ignite your imagination to help you create your own automation scripts.

Conversational Learning™—Can I Use This Script?

Gary: Hi, Julia! I found some cool scripts online… can I use them however I want?

Julia: That depends. Typically if the author is sharing the script, then the intention is to make it available for anyone to use. But sometimes there are strings attached.

Gary: What do you mean?

Julia: Some authors will place a license on the script that limits its use. For example, you may be able to use it in noncommercial situations but not include it with other commercial software.

Gary: Are there other restrictions besides that?

Julia: There might be. Some code you can't legally modify. In some cases, if you do modify the code and give the modified version to someone else, you need to credit the original author. There are other possible restrictions—again based on the license applied to the code.

Gary: OK, how do I figure out what I can do?

Julia: Sometimes the license is embedded in the code itself, or at least a reference to a site that describes the license. In some cases, you might just need to contact the owner. If you are going to use the code at work, you might also want to check with your manager, who can consult the company legal team.

Gary: OK. Thanks, Julia!

Creating Your Own Automation Scripts

The process of creating your own automation scripts may seem daunting at first, but after you take the time to explore existing examples, it will come easier to you. The following are just a few suggestions when creating your scripts:

- Pay attention to tasks that you routinely perform. If you find yourself executing the same or a similar set of commands over and over, then automating these commands with a script makes sense.
- Is there a command that takes a lot of time on the system? How about one that uses a lot of system resources (memory, CPU, network bandwidth, and so on)? Maybe that command should be executed via a **cron** or **at** job in the middle of the night when nobody is on the system.
- Do you find that other users in your organization struggle with complex command-line utilities? You can create an interactive script that prompts the user to answer questions and then executes the correct command with all those complicated options for the user who runs your script.
- Need to run a critical security audit on a regular basis? Make that audit into a script and add it to the system **crontab** file.
- Are people forgetting to attend your important weekly meeting? Make a script that automatically generates a reminder email 10 minutes before the meeting.
- Want to know who is logged into the system on Friday at 8 p.m.? Make a **cron** job that runs the **who** command and mails a message to you.
- Forget to routinely update software on the system? Make that a **cron** job, and you do not need to worry about it anymore.
- Do you regularly back up your files, or do you find yourself days in the future when you realize you should have made a backup and now it is too late because the system has crashed or someone has overwritten your file? Put together a better backup policy.

Sounds like a large list of tasks, but in the big picture, this is small potatoes. The possibilities of how you can automate your system are practically endless.

WHAT COULD GO WRONG? OK, not everything should be automated. For example, if a hacker has compromised your system, do not rely on automated scripts to protect you. Some tasks still need human intervention (thankfully).

Summary

Knowing how to create automated processes is just half the battle. Knowing what you should automate is the other half. In this chapter, we explored some ideas and concepts that are designed to assist you in determining what tasks you should automate on your system.

Key Terms

Exit status, sourcing, repository

Review Questions

1. The _____script rotates, compresses, and mails system logs.
2. Which directories contain scripts that execute on a regular basis? (Choose two.)
   - **A.** **/etc/cron.d**
   - **B.** **/etc/crond.minutely**
   - **C.** **/etc/cron.daily**
   - **D.** **/etc/cron.hourly**
3. Which variable is used to store the exit status of a command?
   - **A.** **$!**
   - **B.** **$$**
   - **C.** **$^**
   - **D.** **$?**
4. The _____command displays files, including line numbers.
5. In coding terms, a _____ is a location where people share programs.

Develop an Automation Security Policy

Now that you have learned how to automate processes (Chapter 14, "crontab and at") and create BASH scripts (Chapter 15, "Scripting," and Chapter 16, "Common Automation Tasks"), it is time to learn how to create a security policy for these features. This chapter focuses on what you should consider when creating an automation security policy.

After reading this chapter and completing the exercises, you will be able to do the following:

Create a security policy for the use of crontab **and** at

Create a security policy for BASH scripts

Securing crontab and at

Some of the security features for **crontab** and **at** were covered in Chapter 14. Recall that you can determine who has access to the **crontab** command by modifying the contents of either the **/etc/cron.allow** or **/etc/cron.deny** file. The **/etc/at.allow** and **/etc/at.deny** files are used to determine who can use the **at** command.

Your security policy should clearly indicate who can use these commands. The decision should be made for each system in your environment. The following describes some of the considerations that have an impact on your decision:

- On system-critical servers, consider removing access to the **crontab** and **at** commands for all users. These commands can impact system performance (if users have system-intensive **crontab** and **at** jobs) and potentially provide the means for a hacker to exploit the system.
- On workstations, considering only providing access to users who routinely use the workstations and deny all others.
- Monitor **crontab** and **at** jobs on a regular basis. Explore the commands that are executed (these are stored in text files in the **/var/spool/cron** and **/var/spool/at** directories) for suspicious jobs or jobs that use large amounts of system resources.
- Create written rules for the use of **crontab** and **at** that all users must follow. Include consequences for misuse.

It is also important to make sure specific files and directories that are related to the **crontab** and **at** jobs are properly secured. Consider the following permission suggestions (typical default permissions shown in parentheses):

- **/var/spool/cron (drwx------)**: This default permission set is as secure as you can make this directory.
- **/var/spool/at (drwx------)**: This default permission set is as secure as you can make this directory.

- **/etc/crontab (-rw-r--r--)**: On most systems, regular users have no need to access this file, so consider changing the permissions to **-rw------**.
- **/etc/cron.d (drwxr-xr-x)**: On most systems, regular users have no need to access this file, so consider changing the permissions to **drwx-----**.
- **/etc/cron.daily (drwxr-xr-x)**: On most systems, regular users have no need to access this file, so consider changing the permissions to **drwx-----**.
- **/etc/cron.hourly (drwxr-xr-x)**: On most systems, regular users have no need to access this file, so consider changing the permissions to **drwx-----**.
- **/etc/cron.monthly (drwxr-xr-x)**: On most systems, regular users have no need to access this file, so consider changing the permissions to **drwx-----**.
- **/etc/cron.weekly (drwxr-xr-x)**: On most systems, regular users have no need to access this file, so consider changing the permissions to **drwx-----**.
- **/etc/cron.deny (-rw-r--r--)**: On most systems, regular users have no need to access this file, so consider changing the permissions to **-rw------**.
- **/etc/cron.allow (-rw-r--r--)**: On most systems, regular users have no need to access this file, so consider changing the permissions to **-rw------**.
- **/etc/at.deny (-rw-r--r--)**: On most systems, regular users have no need to access this file, so consider changing the permissions to **-rw------**.
- **/etc/at.allow (-rw-r--r--)**: On most systems, regular users have no need to access this file, so consider changing the permissions to **-rw------**.
- **/usr/bin/crontab (-rwsr-xr-x)**: To ensure no user besides the root user can execute the **crontab** command, remove the SUID permission and the permissions for group and other: **-rwx------**.
- **/usr/bin/at (-rwsr-xr-x)**: To ensure no user besides the root user can execute the **at** command, remove the SUID permission and the permissions for group and other: **-rwx------**.
- **/etc/anacrontab (-rw-r--r--)**: On most systems, regular users have no need to access this file, so consider changing the permissions to **-rw------**.

Two additional concerns that you should take into consideration when creating a security policy for **crontab** and **at**:

- Remember that each system has its own **crontab** and **at** systems. The policy you create has to take into consideration different rules for different systems.
- If you remove a user's ability to use the **crontab** and **at** commands, then any of that user's existing **crontab** and **at** jobs would still execute. Disabling access only limits the user's ability to create more **crontab** and **at** jobs. Your security policy should also have a procedure in place to identify and remove existing jobs when a user is blocked access.

Securing BASH Scripts

BASH scripts allow you to create tools. Often folks who write shell scripts do not consider security; however, hackers will make use of existing scripts to compromise the system, so having a security policy for BASH scripts is important. This section outlines some security features you should consider when creating a security policy for BASH scripts.

Access to Scripts

Some scripts are meant to be tools for everyone, but some are for specific users (database administrators, system administrators, and so on). Carefully consider where you place scripts, and make sure only the authorized users have access to the scripts and the ability to execute them.

Also consider on which systems you place scripts. Placing BASH scripts on a publicly accessible system poses a greater threat than on an internal server.

Do not allow anyone the ability to modify a script, except for the owner of the script. For example, a good permission set for a script would be **-rwxr-x---** whereas a bad permission set would be **-rwxrwx---**. The second permission set would allow any group member the ability to modify the contents of the script.

Never place SUID or SGID permission on a BASH script. A hacker who knows BASH can take advantage by running extra commands from the script, which could provide access to files that the hacker would normally not be able to access.

Script Contents

In order to execute a script, the read permission has to be enabled for a user. This means that, unlike with most system binary commands, a user can see everything in a BASH script. As a result, you should have a script security policy that requires all scripts to be free of any sensitive data (user names, passwords, and so on).

It is also safer to use the absolute path when executing commands in a script. For example, consider the following:

```
#!/bin/bash
cd /data
ls -l jan_folder
rm jan_folder/file1
```

A safer script would be this:

```
/usr/bin/cd /data
/usr/bin/ls -l jan_folder
/usr/bin/rm jan_folder/file1
```

If you do not use the absolute path, then the user's **PATH** variable is used to determine the location of the command. This could lead to a situation where the wrong command is executed. For example, hackers like to place rouge **rm**, **ls**, and **cd** commands in directories like **/tmp** (these commands will exploit or damage the system).

Dealing with Data

One area of concern when writing shell scripts is user data. This data can be gathered by command-line arguments, via user-created environment variables, or through interaction with the user (for example, the **read** command). When dealing with user data, consider the following:

- Avoid running critical commands that are based on user data. For example, do not accept a value from the user and then try to execute the **passwd** command using that value.
- Do not trust that environment variables are set correctly.
- Perform validity checks on all user-related data. For example, if you are expecting a user to provide a ZIP code of five digits, verify they provide exactly five digits.

Shell Settings

Consider the following shell settings:

- **set -u**: This setting causes your shell script to exit prematurely if an unset variable is used.
- **set -f**: This setting causes the expansion of wildcards to be avoided. Wildcard expansion can be an issue with data that comes from users.
- **set -e**: This setting causes a script to exit automatically if any command in the script fails.

Shell Style

Although it is not just a security-based topic, you should also consider reviewing Google's Shell Style Guide (https://google.github.io/styleguide/shell.xml). It has many best practices that can result in better shell scripts. This could also lead to more secure code, as best practices often mean you are following a good set of rules and are less likely to create a security hole in your code.

Lastly, if you ever execute another user's script, read the script first to make sure it executes the correct commands. This is especially true for any script you find on the Internet.

Summary

In this chapter, you explored several topics related to creating a security policy for automation tools (**crontab** and **at**) and BASH scripts.

Review Questions

1. The permissions for the **/var/spool/cron** directory should be **d**_____.
2. Which command will result in only allowing the root user the ability to run the **crontab** command?
   - A. **rm /etc/crontab**
   - B. **rm -r /var/spool**
   - C. **chmod 0700 /usr/bin/crontab**
   - D. **rm /usr/bin/crontab**
3. BASH scripts should never have the _____ and SGID permissions set.
4. Which of the following will cause a BASH script to exit when a command in the script fails?
   - A. **set -u**
   - B. **set -f**
   - C. **set -e**
   - D. **set -v**
5. Which of the following will cause a BASH script to exit when an unset variable is used?
   - A. **set -u**
   - B. **set -f**
   - C. **set -e**
   - D. **set -v**

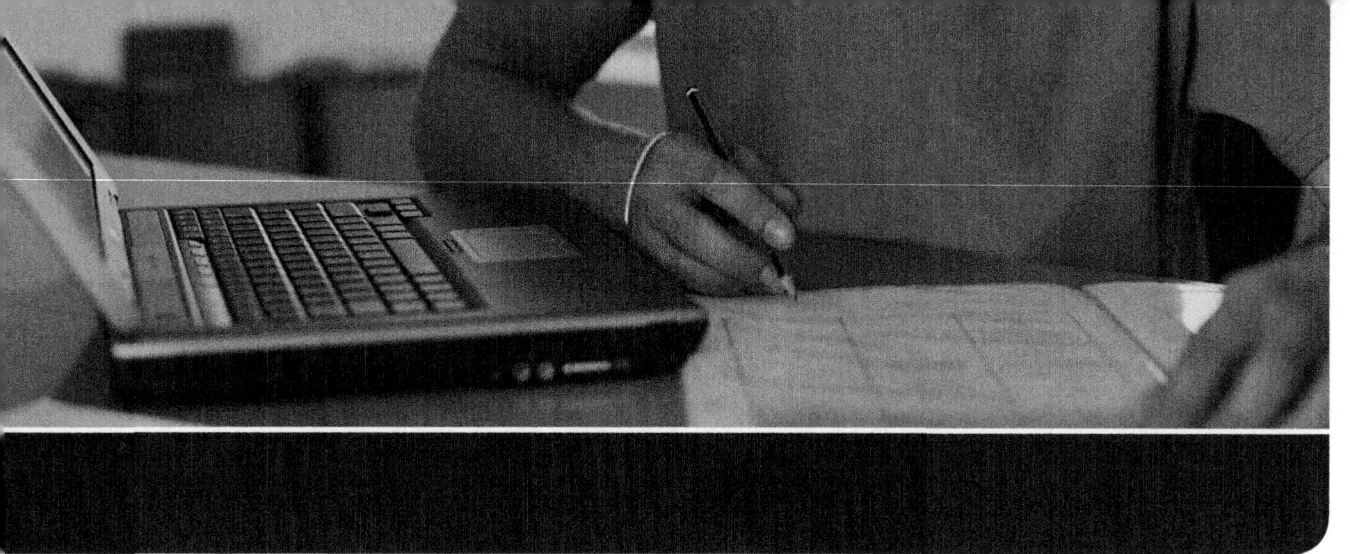

Networking is a key component of modern-day operating systems. Networking provides the means to connect to other systems, either to access network-based services or gain access to useful information. From a security perspective, networking also poses one of the greatest risks to a secure environment. Hackers often use the network to gain unauthorized access to remote systems, often using well-known vulnerabilities. As a result, you really need to understand how networking works and how to implement features to protect your system from network-based attacks.

Part V

Networking

In Part V, "Networking," you will explore the following chapters:

- Chapter 18, "Networking Basics," covers the essentials you should know before configuring and securing your network connections.
- Chapter 19, "Network Configuration," covers the process of configuring your system to connect to the network.
- Chapter 20, "Network Service Configuration: Essential Services," covers the process of configuring several network-based tools, including DNS, DHCP, and email servers.
- Chapter 21, "Network Service Configuration: Web Services," covers the process of configuring several network-based tools, including the Apache Web Server and Squid.
- Chapter 22, "Connecting to Remote Systems," discusses how to connect to remote systems via the network.
- Chapter 23, "Develop a Network Security Policy," provides you with the means to create a security policy using the knowledge you acquire in Chapters 18, 19, 20, 21, and 22.

Networking Basics

In order to correctly configure your network, be able to troubleshoot network issues, and properly secure network connections, you need to understand some basic principles of networking first. The goal of this chapter is to cover these principles.

We start by discussing some essential network terms, including hosts, IP addresses, and protocols. Also included in this chapter is a discussion on subnetting and network ports.

It is important to keep in mind that this chapter focuses on the essentials of networking. Networking is a very large topic, and entire books are devoted to the principles and features of modern networking environments. We encourage you to learn more about networking than what is provided in this chapter, but in terms of the goal of learning Linux and configuring a Linux network, the content in this chapter provides you with the foundation you need.

After reading this chapter and completing the exercises, you will be able to do the following:

Explain essential network terminology

Define network addresses, including subnetting

Describe common network ports

Identify the primary differences between IPv4 and IPv6

Describe common network protocols

Network Terminology

A network is created when two or more computers communicate through some sort of connection. This connection could be created via several different technologies, including Ethernet, fiber optic, and wireless.

Each computer on the network is called a *host*, and it can include a large number of different systems, such as desktop and laptop computers, printers, routers, switches, and even cell phones. Although the focus in this chapter is on computers that have a Linux operating system, you should consider any system that communicates on the network as a host.

There are two general classes of networks:

- **LAN (local area network)**: This network describes all the hosts that communicate directly with one another on the same network.
- **WAN (wide area network)**: This network describes a collection of LANs that are able to communicate through a series of routers or switches. Routers and switches have the ability to transfer network communications from one network to another.

Figure 18-1 provides an example that illustrates a LAN versus a WAN.

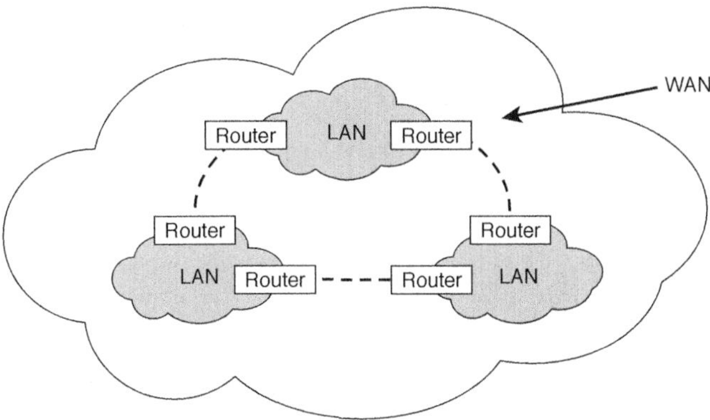

Figure 18-1 *LAN and WAN*

Data is sent across networks using a *network packet*. A network packet is a well-defined message that includes the data as well as metadata (called the *packet header*). The packet header provides information about how the network packet is to reach its destination. You can think of a network packet like a letter you would send in the mail. The letter in the envelope is the data, and the address information written on the envelope is the packet header. In reality, the packet header will contain much more information than appears on the envelope of a letter that you mail, but the analogy is apropos.

Included in the packet header are two pieces of information that help determine the destination of the packet: the *IP (Internet Protocol) address* of the destination host and the *port* of the destination host. An IP address is a unique numeric-based value that is like the street name on a traditional envelope. For example, suppose you sent a letter as shown in Figure 18-2.

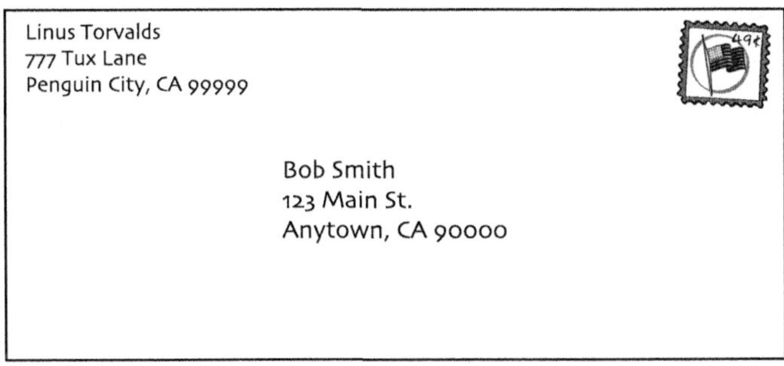

Figure 18-2 *Traditional Mailing Address*

You can consider the IP address to be "123 Main St.", which means you can think of that one house as analogous to a host. The port is a numeric value that is associated to a *service*, which is a program that is running on the host that is listening for incoming messages on a specific port number. For example, you could have a web server installed on a host that will listen to incoming network packets destined for port 80. Going back to our traditional mail message analogy, you can consider a port number to be like the person's name identifying to whom the envelope is addressed (Bob Smith in the previous example).

Recall that a WAN is a collection of LANs that can communicate with each other through routers or switches. The way that a router or switch determines which LAN to send a message to is via a *subnet* value. The subnet value, when combined with the IP address, creates a unique network address. How this happens is covered later in this chapter. You can think of the subnet value for a traditional mail message like the city, state, and ZIP code of a letter, which allows mail carriers to route the envelope to the correct geographic location. In a sense, you could also consider each city to be analogous to a LAN and the entire country (or world even) to be analogous to a WAN.

Within the network packet resides the data. The data must be formatted in a way that the receiving system understands. This is partly handled by protocols. A *protocol* is a well-defined standard for network communications between two hosts. For example, web servers often use HTTP (Hypertext Transfer Protocol) as the means of communication between the client host and the server. A *server* is a host on a network that offers a service; it serves something to the receiver, which is known as a *client*. That is why when you use a web browser, you typically type a web address like this: http://www.OneCourseSource.com.

A server may understand multiple protocols. For example, web servers also understand FTP (File Transfer Protocol) and HTTPS (HTTP Secure).

Protocols are used at a higher level of networking to define networking operations. For example, recall that each host on a network has a unique IP address (Internet Protocol address). This protocol is used to determine where to send information across a network. Other common network protocols include TCP (Transmission Control Protocol), UDP (User Datagram Protocol), and ICMP (Internet Control Message Protocol). Critical details regarding these protocols are provided later in this chapter.

NOTE There are literally hundreds of standard protocols, and in most cases you do not have to worry about the details of the protocols. However, if you want to learn more about a protocol than what is provided in this book, then visit one of the many sites that describe RFCs (requests for comments), such as https://www.rfc-editor.org.

IPv4 Versus IPv6

The two different versions of IP are IPv4 and IPv6. IPv4 has been a standard on the Internet for a very long time and is slowly being replaced by IPv6. There are many differences between these two versions, but a complete discussion is beyond the scope of this book. Instead, we will consider one of the major differences and then provide a chart that illustrates some of the other differences.

To understand this major difference, first consider this: there are 4,294,967,296 total possible unique IPv4 addresses. That may seem like a lot, and perhaps even more than we could possibly need, but the way in which these IP addresses are categorized and distributed resulted in a shortage of available IP addresses that was first recognized in the 1990s. Every device that is connected to the Internet needs a unique identifier so that communication with the device works properly We will go more into this in a later section on how IPv4 addresses work, but for now realize that there was a time when we had a valid concern that we would run out of IPv4 addresses.

IPv4 uses a technique called *dotted decimal notation* (also known as *dot delimited*), a 32-bit number divided into four octets that results in about 4.3 billion possible IP addresses. IPv6 uses a different technique called hexadecimal notation, a 128-bit number. This technique results in 340,282,366,920,938,463,463,374,607,431,768,211,456 IPv6 addresses (if this number is too big to comprehend, think "340 trillion, trillion, trillion" or "many trillion addresses available for each person alive today"). In other words, we have plenty of IP addresses for all the hosts on the Internet now and the foreseeable future.

IPv6 has other advantages over IPv4, as described in Table 18-1.

Table 18-1 Some Differences Between IPv4 and IPv6

Difference	Description
Address scheme	IPv4: dotted decimal notation, a 32-bit number divided into four octets. IPv6: hexadecimal notation, a 128-bit number

Difference	Description
Number of available hosts	IPv4: Approximately 4.3 billion with no extra subnetting. *Subnetting* is the process of dividing a larger network into a smaller one and results in the loss of assignable IP addresses. IPv6: A lot more than IPv4—approximately 340,000,000,000,000,000,000, 000,000,000,000,000,000. No need to subnet with the available number of addresses.
Routing	IPv6 has a more efficient routing technique. Routing is how network packets are moved from one network to another.
Autoconfiguration	IPv6 can be configured to auto-assign an IP address, much like DHCP (Dynamic Host Configuration Protocol) in IPv4, but without needing a DHCP server. DHCP is a service that provides a host with an IP address and subnet.
Packet header	Each network package has a header that contains information about the packet. The header in IPv6 is much more flexible.
Security	IPv4 relies on other protocols to provide security for the network packets, whereas IPv6 has built-in security features.

Security Highlight

IPv6 is generally considered more secure, but keep in mind that if you use IPv6 on systems connected to the Internet, at some point the network packets are likely to be converted into IPv4 packets (usually soon after leaving your network). As a result, the security features offered by IPv6 are typically only useful within your own organization.

Note that Table 18-1 is not a complete description of the differences between IPv6 and IPv4, but it should provide you with the general idea that IPv6 is a better overall protocol. This might lead you to wonder why it is "slowly" replacing IPv4—and, by the way, we do mean *slowly*. IPv6 was introduced in January of 1996, and by its 20th birthday it was only enabled on about 10% of the world's computers. More recent estimates have this number approaching 25%.

There are many reasons why the Internet has not switched completely to IPv6, but here are two of the most common reasons:

- Switching an entire network from IPv4 to IPv6 is not a trivial task. The protocols are vastly different in many ways, so a lot of care and work must take place to make this switch happen smoothly and transparently. And even if your organization did switch to IPv6, at some point to connect to the rest of the Internet, network communication must be converted into IPv4 because most of the Internet is still using IPv4.
- Recall the concern about running out of IPv4 addresses? That concern was just about eliminated by the invention of an IPv4 feature called NAT (Network Address Translation). With NAT, a single host (in this case, a router) can have one IPv4 address that can communicate directly on the network. The LAN that the router is connected to uses a set of IP addresses (called private IP addresses) that cannot be used directly on the Internet. The router translates all incoming and outgoing network packets between the Internet and the internal private network, allowing the hosts in the internal private network indirect access to the Internet though the NAT router. Almost all hosts today, including your cell phone and devices within your home (like many flat screen televisions, and even refrigerators), have internal private IP addresses. With the wide spread adoption of NAT, the concern about running out of IPv4 address is eliminated because only a small number of routers with live IP addresses are required to allow hundreds of hosts indirect access to the Internet.

Because IPv4 is still the dominant protocol used on the Internet, this book will focus on IPv4 rather than IPv6. However, you should know the differences between the two, as described in this chapter, and you should consider learning more about IPv6 for the future.

IPv4 Addresses

An IPv4 address consists of four numbers separated by a dot character (for example, 192.168.100.25). Each number represents an octet, a number that can be represented by a binary value, like so:

11000000.10101000.01100100.00011001

192 can be represented by the binary number 11000000 because each binary value represents a numeric value, as shown in Figure 18-3.

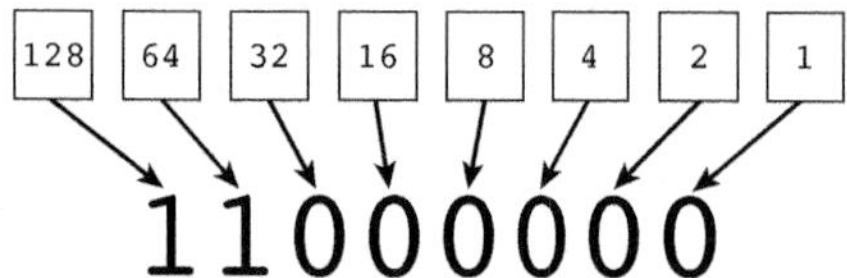

Figure 18-3 *Binary Representation of Numeric Values*

IPv4 addresses are divided into classes, and there are five classes total. These classes are defined by the first octet (the first number of the IP address). For example, the IP address of 192.168.100.25 uses the 192 value to define in which of the five primary classes the IP resides. Table 18-2 describes these standard IPv4 address classes.

Table 18-2 IPv4 Classes

Class	Description
A	Ranges 1.x.x.x to 126.x.x.x. Allows for 127 networks, each with up to 16 million hosts. The first octet defines the network address, and the remaining octets define the host addresses.
B	Ranges 128.x.x.x to 191.x.x.x. Allows for approximately 16,000 networks, each with up to 65,000 hosts.
C	Ranges 192.x.x.x to 223.x.x.x. Allows for approximately 2 million networks, each with up to 254 million hosts.
D	Ranges 224.x.x.x to 239.x.x.x. Only used for multicast groups.
E	Ranges 240.x.x.x to 254.x.x.x. Only used for research and development.

So, a Class A network of 55.x.x.x can have up to 16 million host IP addresses that run from 55.0.0.1 (55.0.0.0 is reserved for the network itself) to 55.254.254.254 (technically the highest value is 255, but those IP addresses are reserved for broadcasting messages to the entire network).

Organizations that have been assigned large networks (Class A or B, although even Class C networks apply here) do not want to have millions or even thousands of hosts on a single network. Subnetting provides a method of dividing a large network into smaller sections. This is accomplished by making smaller networks (subnetworks) by using IP addresses that are normally used by hosts to define the network and broadcast IP addresses.

There are two common network situations in which you should know how subnets work:

- When a system already has an IP address and a subnet address, you want to know how to determine the subnetwork that is created.

- When you have a larger IP network and want to know how to divide it into smaller networks. This is important if you have several smaller physical networks in your organization because each physical network must be on a separate subnetwork.

In both of these situations, you can use one of the many IP address calculators freely available on the Internet to aid you in the process. The purpose of showing you how to perform these tasks by hand is to aid you in understanding how subnetting works.

Determining a Network Address from an IP Address and Subnet

Suppose you were using a full Class C network of 192.168.100.0. This means that the first three octets (**192.168.100.**0) are used for the network address, the last possible IP address is the broadcast address (192.168.100.**255**), and all other IP addresses (192.168.100.1 to 192.168.1.254) can be assigned to hosts on the network.

Perhaps having 254 hosts in a single physical network does not work for your situation and you want to divide this class C network into smaller networks. Before doing this, consider how the network is defined in the first place by looking at Table 18-3.

Table 18-3 Class C Network Definition

Category	IP Address	Binary Format of IP Address
Address	192.168.100.25	11000000.10101000.01100100.00011001
Netmask	255.255.255.0 or 24	11111111.11111111.11111111.00000000
Network	192.168.100.0	11000000.10101000.01100100.00000000
Broadcast	192.168.100.255	11000000.10101000.01100100.00011111
First IP	192.168.100.1	11000000.10101000.01100100.00010001
Last IP	192.168.100.254	11000000.10101000.01100100.00011110
Maximum hosts in network	254	

In Table 18-3, the IP address is displayed in both dotted decimal notation (192.168.100.25) and binary format. The subnet mask is displayed in three formats:

- **Variable-Length Subnet Mask (VLSM) format**: Essentially the same format as dotted decimal notation.
- **Classless Inter-Domain Routing (CIDR) format**: This is the same value as VLSM, but described in a different way. This value is the number of "1" values in the binary format (add them up and you will get 24 "1" values for the netmask in Table 18-3).
- **Binary format**: As shown in Table 18-3.

To determine which part of the IP address represents the network, just look at all the bits in the binary format that are a value of "1" for both the IP address and the subnet mask. To make this easier to see, this has been highlighted in Table 18-3.

The first possible address in this network defines the network itself (192.168.100.0 in Table 18-3) and the last possible address in this network defines the broadcast address (192.168.100.255 in Table 18-3).

The example in Table 18-3 is straightforward because it is one of the standard classes. Look at the example in Table 18-4 and see how a different, nonstandard subnet (255.255.255.240) would affect the various IP addresses.

Table 18-4 Nonstandard Subnet Mask Example

Category	IP Address	Binary Format of IP Address
Address	192.168.100.25	11000000.10101000.01100100.00011001
Netmask	255.255.255.240 or 28	11111111.11111111.11111111.11110000
Network	192.168.100.0	11000000.10101000.01100100.00000000
Broadcast	192.168.100.31	11000000.10101000.01100100.00001111
First IP	192.168.100.17	11000000.10101000.01100100.00010001
Last IP	192.168.100.30	11000000.10101000.01100100.00011110
Maximum hosts in network	14	

NOTE It may take some time to understand the process of subnetting. We highly encourage you to practice by using one of the many subnet calculators freely available on the Internet, such as the one found at the following address: https://www.adminsub.net/ipv4-subnet-calculator.

Private IP Addresses

As previously mentioned, private IP addresses are used with routers that utilize NAT. One network per Internet class (A, B, and C) has been set aside for private IP addresses. Any host with an IP address in one of these ranges must connect to the Internet via a router that utilizes NAT.

Most organizations use private IP addresses for most hosts, using public IP for systems like firewalls, web servers, and other hosts that need to be directly available on the Internet. As a result, you should be familiar with the ranges of IP addresses that are for private use only:

- 10.0.0.0-10.255.255.255
- 172.16.0.0-172.31.255.255
- 192.168.0.0-192.168.255.255

Common Protocol Suites

You should be familiar with the following protocol suites:

- **IP (Internet Protocol)**: This protocol is responsible for delivering network packets between hosts. Its functions include routing, or sending packets from one physical network to another. Often network packets are forwarded through several routers before reaching the correct destination.
- **TCP (Transmission Control Protocol)**: This protocol compliments IP (Internet Protocol), which is why you will commonly hear the term TCP/IP. TCP is designed to ensure that the network packages arrive in a reliable and ordered manner. With TCP, data packages are *connection based*, which means error checking is performed to determine if packages are lost in transmission. If a packet is lost, a replacement packet is created and sent. TCP is generally slower than UDP (see the definition of UDP) because error-checking each package requires more "work." Also, the loss of a package requires a request to resend the packages, which can have an impact on subsequent packages. However, it is more reliable than UDP because all packages are verified. One example of the use of TCP is the downloading of a software program.
- **UDP (User Datagram Protocol)**: Like TCP, this protocol complements IP (Internet Protocol). It performs a similar function to TCP; however, data packages are connectionless,

which means no error checking is performed to determine if packages are lost in transmission. As a result, it is faster than TCP because connectionless data transfer requires less "work." It is also less reliable than TCP because of the lack of error checking. One example of the use of UDP is live streaming of video, in which the loss of an occasional packet does not have any major impact on the overall data flow.

- **ICMP (Internet Control Message Protocol)**: This protocol is used primarily to send error messages and for determining the status of network devices. It is unlike TCP or UDP in that it is designed to send simple messages, not transfer data between devices or establish connections between devices. One example of the use of ICMP is the **ping** command (see Chapter 19, "Network Configuration"), which is used to verify that a host can be contacted via the network.

Network Ports

The **/etc/services** file is the traditional location where services are mapped to ports. It is considered traditional in the sense that historically services would look at this file to determine which port the service should use. However, most modern services have a setting in the configuration file that is used to determine the actual port that the service will use.

The **/etc/services** file is still useful to administrators in that it contains ports that have been assigned to services by the Internet Assigned Numbers Authority (IANA).

Each line in this file describes one service-to-port mapping. The format of the line is as follows:

```
service_name      port/protocol     [alias]
```

For example:

```
[root@localhost ~]# grep smtp /etc/services
smtp             25/tcp           mail
smtp             25/udp           mail
rsmtp            2390/tcp                 # RSMTP
rsmtp            2390/udp                 # RSMTP
```

Table 18-5 lists the usage for common ports and services. Note that the descriptions are intentionally short, and much more detail is necessary to fully understand each protocol. However, understanding generally the protocol's function is the primary goal here. For many of these protocols, you will be introduced to the software services that use the protocols in Chapter 19.

Table 18-5 Common Network Ports

Port	Service
20 and 21	FTP (File Transfer Protocol). Used for transferring files between hosts.
22	SSH (Secure Shell). Used for connecting to remote systems and executing commands.
23	telnet. Used for connecting to remote systems and executing commands.
25	SMTP (Simple Mail Transfer Protocol). Used to send email.
53	DNS (Domain Name Service). Used to translate hostnames to IP addresses.
80	HTTP (Hypertext Transfer Protocol). Used to communicate with web servers.
110	POP3 (Post Office Protocol). Used to retrieve email.

Port	Service
123	NTP (Network Time Protocol). Used to synchronize system clocks.
139	NETBIOS (Network Basic Input/Output System). Used for LAN communications.
143	IMAP (Internet Message Access Protocol). Used to retrieve email.
161 & 162	SNMP (Simple Network Management Protocol). Used to gather information about network devices.
389	LDAP (Lightweight Directory Access Protocol). Used to provide network-based information, such as network account information.
443	HTTPS (Hypertext Transfer Protocol, Secured). Used to communicate with web servers via encrypted messages.
465	SMTPS (Simple Mail Transfer Protocol, Secured). Used to send encrypted email messages.
514	Syslog (system log). Used to send system log messages to remote systems.
636	LDAPS (Lightweight Directory Access Protocol, Secured). Used to provide network-based information via encryption, such as network account information.
993	IMAPS (Internet Message Access Protocol, Secured). Used to retrieve email via encrypted connections.
995	POP3S (Post Office Protocol, Secured). Used to retrieve email via encrypted connections.

Conversational Learning™—Making Sense of Protocols

Gary: Hey, Julia.

Julia: Gary, you seem down. What's going on?

Gary: I'm just trying to get my head around all of these protocols. I've just begun to understand what a protocol is, and now I found out there are so many that do a lot of different things.

Julia: I understand. Even experienced administrators can find the large number of protocols overwhelming. Maybe I can provide you with some advice?

Gary: Anything would help!

Julia: First, understand that you don't have to know everything about every protocol. Each system or host will only have a handful of services, perhaps even just one that it provides to the network. For example, a server that provides network accounts via LDAP isn't likely to also be a web server and a mail server.

Gary: OK, so I should focus on the services that are provided by the hosts that I am going to maintain, right?

Julia: That is a great place to start. Also realize that understanding the details of the protocol isn't normally so important. Knowing how to configure the service to use the protocol and how to implement key security features is what is really important.

Gary: Ah, that makes me feel a bit better! I tried to read through one of those RFCs and my head started spinning.

Julia: Trust me, you aren't the only one who has experienced that!

Summary

In this chapter, you explored several key networking concepts. The goal of this chapter was not to make you a networking expert, but to introduce you to these concepts to make the process of configuring, maintaining, troubleshooting, and securing a network easier.

Key Terms

LAN, WAN, network packet, packet header, IP address, host, network, Ethernet, fiber optic, subnet, protocol, dotted decimal notation, hexadecimal notation, routing, DHCP, FTP, SSH, telnet, VLSM, CIDR, NAT, private IP addresses, IP, TCP, UDP, ICMP, SMTP, DNS, HTTP, POP3, NTP, NetBIOS, IMAP, SNMP, LDAP, HTTPS, SMTPS, syslog, LDAPS, IMAPS

Review Questions

1. A _____ is a well-defined standard for network communications between two hosts.
2. Which is true about TCP?
   - **A.** It is connectionless.
   - **B.** It is generally faster than UDP.
   - **C.** It ensures data arrives in a reliable manner.
   - **D.** It does not perform error checking.
3. Which protocol is designed for determining the status of network devices?
   - **A.** FTP
   - **B.** POP3
   - **C.** telnet
   - **D.** ICMP
4. The **/etc/**_____ file contains traditional service-to-port mappings.
5. The _____ protocol is used to translate hostnames to IP addresses.

Network Configuration

Now that you have learned some of the essential networking principles in Chapter 18, "Networking Basics," you will explore how to configure network devices in this chapter. We primarily focus on Ethernet devices—the most common network device you will find on Linux systems.

You learn how to assign an IP address and subnet mask to a network interface. You also discover how to configure routes as well as define the DNS servers your system will use.

This chapter also explores wireless network device configuration in the event you need to configure networking on a laptop.

After reading this chapter and completing the exercises, you will be able to do the following:

- **Configure network devices, both on the fly and persistently**
- **Define network routes**
- **Perform network troubleshooting tasks**
- **Configure wireless network devices**

Ethernet Network Interfaces

One of the most common network devices is the Ethernet port. If your desktop or laptop does not communicate on the network wirelessly, then you probably connect a blue network cable, like the one shown in Figure 19-1, into your computer.

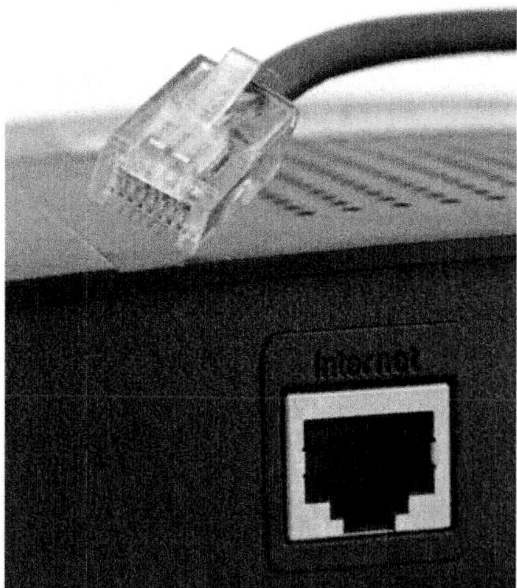

Figure 19-1 *Ethernet Connection*

In this section, you learn how to configure Ethernet port devices.

Displaying Ethernet Port Configurations

One of the commonly used commands to display network information is the **ifconfig** command. When executed with no arguments, it lists active network devices, as shown in Example 19-1.

Example 19-1 *Using **ifconfig** to Display Network Information*

```
[root@onecoursesource ~]# ifconfig
eth0: flags=4163<UP,BROADCAST,RUNNING,MULTICAST>  mtu 1500
        inet 192.168.1.16  netmask 255.255.255.0  broadcast 192.168.1.255
        inet6 fe80::a00:27ff:fe52:2878  prefixlen 64  scopeid 0x20<link>
        ether 08:00:27:52:28:78  txqueuelen 1000  (Ethernet)
        RX packets 20141  bytes 19608517 (18.7 MiB)
        RX errors 0  dropped 0  overruns 0  frame 0
        TX packets 2973  bytes 222633 (217.4 KiB)
        TX errors 0  dropped 0 overruns 0  carrier 0  collisions 0

lo: flags=73<UP,LOOPBACK,RUNNING>  mtu 65536
        inet 127.0.0.1  netmask 255.0.0.0
        inet6 ::1  prefixlen 128  scopeid 0x10<host>
        loop  txqueuelen 0  (Local Loopback)
        RX packets 3320  bytes 288264 (281.5 KiB)
        RX errors 0  dropped 0  overruns 0  frame 0
        TX packets 3320  bytes 288264 (281.5 KiB)
        TX errors 0  dropped 0 overruns 0  carrier 0  collisions 0
```

The output shows network information for two devices: the primary Ethernet network card (**eth0**) and the local loopback address (**lo**). If the system had additional Ethernet network cards, they would be displayed as **eth1**, **eth2**, and so on. The purpose of the loopback address is to allow software to communicate with the local system using protocols and services that would normally require the communication to occur on a network. In most cases, there is not much for you to administer or troubleshoot in regard to the loopback address.

WHAT COULD GO WRONG? If you are working on a virtual machine, you may see something like **enp0s3** instead of **eth0**. This is because the virtual machine manager does not always treat the virtual machine as if it was a true network card (it depends on what sort of network interface you configure within the virtual machine). Consider **enp0s3** to be the same as **eth0**; the commands in this chapter should work just fine on this device.

You should understand the lines of output for the **eth0** section. Table 19-1 describes the key portions of this output in detail.

Table 19-1 Output of the **ifconfig** Command

Output Component	Description
flags=4163<UP,BROADCAST,RUNNING,MULTICAST>	Parameters that are set for the interface. Additional details regarding flags are provided after this table.
mtu 1500	Maximum transmission unit; a value can be used by an operating system to compute the cost of a network route. Traditionally, this is set to 1500, which is considered an optimal value.

Output Component	Description
inet 192.168.1.16	The interface's IPv4 address.
netmask 255.255.255.0	The interface's IPv4 netmask.
broadcast 192.168.1.255	The interface's IPv4 broadcast address.
inet6 fe80::a00:27ff:fe52:2878 prefixlen 64	The interface's IPv6 address and "prefixlen" (a value that plays a role similar to what the netmask does for IPv4 addresses).
ether 08:00:27:52:28:78	The machine's MAC (Media Access Control) address. MAC addresses are typically hardwired into the network card.
txqueuelen 1000 (Ethernet)	The speed at which this device can transmit (1000Mbps in this example).
RX packets	Statistics regarding how many network packets have been received correctly.
RX errors	Statistics regarding how many network packets had some error occur in the receiving process.
TX packets	Statistics regarding how many network packets have been sent correctly.
TX errors	Statistics regarding how many network packets had some error occur in the transmission process.

Many different flags can be assigned an interface. Some of the more important flags include the following:

- **UP**: Indicates the interface is active. When the interface is down, the **flags** line is not displayed at all.
- **BROADCAST**: Indicates that the broadcast address has been set for the device.
- **MULTICAST**: Indicates whether the multicast address is enabled on this device.
- **PROMISC**: Indicates whether the device is in promiscuous mode. Normally a device only listens to network packets sent to its own IP address. In promiscuous mode, the device listens for all network traffic. This can be helpful for analyzing network traffic.

Security Highlight

Enabling promiscuous mode allows you to *sniff* the network. This means you can observe network traffic either to determine issues or to discover a potential security breech.

Changing Ethernet Port Settings

The **ifconfig** command can also be used to change network settings temporarily; these changes are not persistent across reboots. For example, the following command sets the IPv4 address, netmask, and broadcast addresses:

```
[root@onecoursesource ~]# ifconfig eth0 192.168.1.16 netmask 255.255.255.0 broadcast
➥ 192.168.2.255
```

To enable promiscuous mode, execute the following command:

```
[root@onecoursesource ~]#ifconfig eth0 promisc
```

The previous command changes the **flags** section of the **ifconfig** command output. This can be verified by executing the **ifconfig** command without any arguments:

```
[root@onecoursesource ~]# ifconfig | grep eth0
eth0: flags=4163<UP,BROADCAST,RUNNING,PROMISC,MULTICAST>  mtu 1500
```

To disable promiscuous mode, execute the following command:

```
[root@onecoursesource ~]#ifconfig eth0 -promisc
```

An upcoming section describes the Address Resolution Protocol (ARP). In a nutshell, ARP is for keeping track of IP-to-MAC-address resolution. Normally this feature is turned on automatically for Ethernet devices. You can temporarily turn off this protocol by executing the following command:

```
[root@onecoursesource ~]#ifconfig eth0 -arp
```

The previous command changes the **flags** section of the **ifconfig** command output. This can be verified by executing the **ifconfig** command without any arguments:

```
[root@onecoursesource ~]# ifconfig | grep eth0
eth0: flags=4163<UP,BROADCAST,RUNNING,NOARP,MULTICAST>  mtu 1500
```

To enable ARP, execute the following command:

```
[root@onecoursesource ~]#ifconfig eth0 arp
```

Note that you can also activate (bring up) a network interface with the **ifup** command (**ifup eth0**) and deactivate (bring down) a network interface with the **ifdown** command **(ifdown eth0**).

Network Configuration Tools

Some modern systems include additional automated tools that configure your network settings. For example, your Linux distribution may have a tool called Network Manager installed. This tool is designed to configure the network without any interaction on your part.

These tools can be helpful in some cases, such as when end users have Linux laptops. However, on servers, these tools can make it difficult to define the network settings that you want to use.

To determine if the Network Manager is running on your system, use the following command:

```
[root@onecoursesource ~]# nmcli device status
Error: NetworkManager is not running.
```

As you can see from the output of the previous command, Network Manager is not running on this system. If it was running, you could stop it by executing the following command:

```
[root@onecoursesource ~]# systemctl stop NetworkManager
```

This is only a temporary solution. After a system reboot, the Network Manager will be running again. To disable the Network Manager from starting at boot, execute the following command:

```
[root@onecoursesource ~]# systemctl disable NetworkManager
```

See Figure 19-2 for information about how Network Manager can affect a system.

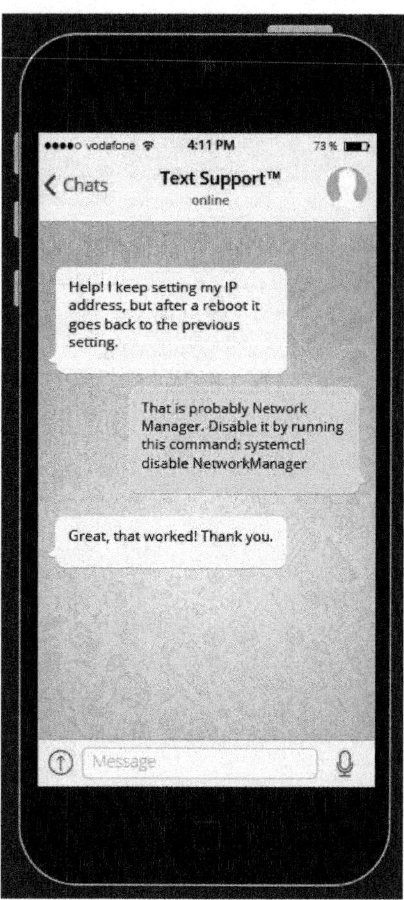

Figure 19-2 *Text Support™—Problem Setting Network Configuration*

The arp Command

Most users and administrators use hostnames to communicate with remote systems. This hostname must be translated into an IP address because the Internet Protocol (IP) uses IP addresses rather than hostnames. This function is provided by a resolver, such as a DNS server. More details regarding DNS servers are provided in Chapter 20, "Network Service Configuration: Essential Services."

The IP is part of a seven-layer networking model called the ISO-OSI (International Organization of Standardization–Open System Interconnection) network model. At Layer 2 of this model, devices communicate using the network card's MAC address. In most cases, for two hosts to communicate, not only do they need to know each other's IP addresses, but they also need to know each other's MAC addresses.

Initially the local system does not know the MAC addresses of any other host. When a remote IP address is first used, a broadcast request is sent on the network that matches that IP address. The machine with the matching IP address responds to the original request, reporting to the original host what its MAC address is. The original system then stores this MAC address and corresponding IP address in a memory address called the ARP table.

The **arp** command is used to view the ARP table or make changes to it. When executed with no arguments, the **arp** command displays the ARP table:

```
[root@onecoursesource ~]# arp
Address                  HWtype  HWaddress           Flags Mask      Iface
192.168.1.11             ether   30:3a:64:44:a5:02   C                eth0
```

WHAT COULD GO WRONG? In the event that a remote system has its network card replaced, it may be necessary to delete an entry from the ARP table. This can be accomplished by using the **-d** option to the **arp** command:

```
[root@onecoursesource ~]# arp -i eth0 -d 192.169.1.11
```

Once the address has been removed from the ARP table, there should be no need to add the new address manually. The next time the local system uses this IP address, it sends a broadcast request on the appropriate network to determine the new MAC address.

The route Command

When a network packet is destined for a host on the local network, it is broadcast on that network and picked up by the appropriate host. When the network packet is destined for a host not on the local network, the packet needs to be passed through a gateway (also called a router). The gateway has a live IP address on both the local network and at least one other network.

The gateway is connected either to the Internet (either directly or through additional gateways) or to an internal, private network. The local system keeps track of the gateways it can directly communicate with by storing information in the routing table.

The **route** command either displays or modifies the routing table. To display the routing table, execute the **route** command without any arguments:

```
[root@onecoursesource ~]# route
Kernel IP routing table
Destination     Gateway         Genmask         Flags Metric Ref    Use Iface
default         192.168.1.1     0.0.0.0         UG    100    0        0 eth0
192.168.1.0     0.0.0.0         255.255.255.0   U     100    0        0 eth0
```

The line from the output of the previous command that begins with 192.168.1.0 specifies how to handle network traffic destined for the 192.168.1.0/255.255.255.0 network. The gateway for this line is 0.0.0.0, which means "broadcast these network packets on the local network."

The default line from the output of the previous command means "unless specified by another rule, use this line." The gateway on this line indicates where to send the network traffic. In this example, if the network packet is not destined for the 192.168.1.0/255.255.255.0 network, it should be sent to the 192.168.1.1 gateway. The flag setting of **UG** means Up + Gateway (an active gateway).

Suppose there was a gateway with the IP address of 192.168.1.100 connected to an internal network of 192.168.2.0/255.255.255.0. You could add this gateway by running the following command:

```
[root@onecoursesource ~]# route add -net 192.168.2.0 netmask 255.255.255.0 gw
➥ 192.168.1.100
[root@onecoursesource ~]# route
Kernel IP routing table
Destination     Gateway         Genmask         Flags Metric Ref    Use Iface
default         192.168.1.1     0.0.0.0         UG    100    0        0 eth0
192.168.1.0     0.0.0.0         255.255.255.0   U     100    0        0 eth0
192.168.2.0     192.168.1.100   255.255.255.0   U     0      0        0 eth0
```

To delete this gateway, execute the following command:

```
[root@onecoursesource ~]# route del -net 192.168.2.0 netmask 255.255.255.0 gw
➥ 192.168.1.100
[root@onecoursesource ~]# route
Kernel IP routing table
```

```
Destination     Gateway         Genmask         Flags Metric Ref    Use Iface
default         192.168.1.1     0.0.0.0         UG    100    0        0 eth0
192.168.1.0     0.0.0.0         255.255.255.0   U     100    0        0 eth0
192.168.2.0     0.0.0.0         255.255.255.0   U     0      0        0 eth0
```

You can also delete and add the default gateway using the following syntax:

```
[root@onecoursesource ~]# route del default
[root@onecoursesource ~]# route add default gw 192.168.1.1
```

The ip Command

Now that you have learned all about the **ifconfig**, **arp**, and **route** commands, we have some bad news (sort of) for you. If you look at the man page of any of these commands while working on a modern distribution of Linux, you will likely see the following statement:

```
NOTE
       This  program  is obsolete!
```

Now, you might be wondering why you spent the time learning about these programs if they are obsolete. That is a good question, and we have several good answers:

- Although the **ip** command is designed to replace the **ifconfig**, **arp**, and **route** commands (and some other network tools), on most distributions these tools still exist (and likely will for a long time). The reason for this is that many shell scripts have been written over the years that use these programs. Upgrading all these programs to use the new **ip** command takes time and, in the opinion of a good number of script maintainers, is not worth the trouble. If you come across one of those scripts, you should know what these commands do, even if you use the **ip** command yourself normally.
- Although the **ifconfig**, **arp**, and **route** commands are no longer under development, they still work just fine. You should know that the **ip** command provides more features and is an active project. However, many administrators already know how to use the **ifconfig**, **arp**, and **route** commands and use these on a regular basis. As a result, you should be aware of these tools as well.
- If you inherit an older or legacy system, the **ip** command might not exist. So, knowing the older commands is useful.

The **ip** command can do essentially everything that the **ifconfig**, **arp**, and **route** commands can do, plus a lot more. Table 19-2 demonstrates how to execute the **ip** command to perform any of the **ifconfig**, **arp**, and **route** commands demonstrated in this chapter. Try both the **ip** command and the corresponding "older" command to see how they can be slightly different in the way they display information.

Table 19-2 The **ip** Command

ifconfig/arp/route Command	ip Command
ifconfig	ip addr show #more information ip link show #less information Note: The **show** command is the default on most versions of the **ip** command, so **ip link** should do the same thing as **ip link show**.

ifconfig/arp/route Command	ip Command
ifconfig eth0 192.168.1.16 netmask 255.255.255.0 broadcast 192.168.2.255	ip addr add 192.168.1.16 /24 broadcast 192.168.2.255 dev eth0
ifconfig eth0 promisc	ip link set eth0 promisc on
ifconfig eth0 -promisc	ip link set eth0 promisc off
ifconfig eth0 -arp	ip link set eth0 arp off
ifconfig eth0 arp	ip link set eth0 arp on
arp	ip neigh show #neigh = neighbor
arp -i eth0 -d 192.169.1.11	ip neigh del 192.168.1.11 dev eth0
route	ip route show
route add -net 192.168.2.0 netmask 255.255.255.0 gw 192.168.1.100	ip route add 192.168.2.0/24 via 192.168.1.100
route del -net 192.168.2.0 netmask 255.255.255.0 gw 192.168.1.100	ip route del 192.168.2.0/24 via 192.168.1.100
route del default	ip route del default
route add default gw 192.168.1.1	ip route add default via 192.168.1.1

The hostname Command

The **hostname** command can display or change the system hostname:

```
[root@onecoursesource ~]# hostname
onecoursesource
[root@onecoursesource ~]# hostname myhost
[root@myhost ~]# hostname
myhost
```

WHAT COULD GO WRONG? Note that this change is temporary and, after a system reboot, will return to the original value. Later in this chapter you will see how to make this a persistent change.

The host Command

The **host** command is normally used to perform simple hostname-to-IP-address translation operations (also called *DNS queries*):

```
[root@onecoursesource ~]# host google.com
google.com has address 172.217.4.142
google.com has IPv6 address 2607:f8b0:4007:800::200e
google.com mail is handled by 30 alt2.aspmx.l.google.com.
google.com mail is handled by 50 alt4.aspmx.l.google.com.
google.com mail is handled by 20 alt1.aspmx.l.google.com.
google.com mail is handled by 10 aspmx.l.google.com.
google.com mail is handled by 40 alt3.aspmx.l.google.com.
```

Table 19-3 describes common options for the **host** command.

Table 19-3 Options for the ***host*** Command

Option	Description
-t	Specify a type of query that you want to display; for example, **host -t ns google.com** will display Google's name servers.
-4	Only perform IPv4 queries.
-6	Only perform IPv6 queries.
-v	Verbose; display additional information.

The dig Command

The **dig** command is useful for performing DNS queries on specific DNS servers. Think of it as a more powerful version of the **host** command. The format of the command is demonstrated here:

```
[root@onecoursesource ~]# dig google.com

; <<>> DiG 9.9.4-RedHat-9.9.4-38.el7_3 <<>> google.com
;; global options: +cmd
;; Got answer:
;; ->>HEADER<<- opcode: QUERY, status: NOERROR, id: 56840
;; flags: qr rd ra; QUERY: 1, ANSWER: 1, AUTHORITY: 0, ADDITIONAL: 1

;; OPT PSEUDOSECTION:
; EDNS: version: 0, flags:; udp: 512
;; QUESTION SECTION:
;google.com.            IN    A

;; ANSWER SECTION:
google.com.        268    IN    A    216.58.217.206

;; Query time: 36 msec
;; SERVER: 192.168.1.1#53(192.168.1.1)
;; WHEN: Sun Mar 05 17:01:08 PST 2018
;; MSG SIZE  rcvd: 55
```

Note that the output of this command will become clear when DNS servers are covered in Chapter 20.

To query a specific DNS server, rather than the default DNS servers for your host, use the following syntax: **dig @server host_to_lookup**.

Table 19-4 describes common options for the **dig** command.

Table 19-4 Options for the ***dig*** Command

Option	Description
-f *file*	Use the content of *file* to perform multiple lookups; the file should contain one hostname per line.
-4	Only perform IPv4 queries.
-6	Only perform IPv6 queries.
-x address	Perform a reverse lookup (return the hostname when provided an IP address).

The netstat Command

The **netstat** command is useful for displaying a variety of network information. It is a key utility when troubleshooting network issues. Table 19-5 describes common options for the **netstat** command.

Table 19-5 Options for the **netstat** Command

Option	Description
-t or --tcp	Display TCP information.
-u or --udp	Display UDP information.
-r or --route	Display the routing table.
-v or --verbose	Verbose; display additional information.
-i or --interfaces	Display information based on a specific interface.
-a or --all	Apply to all.
-s or --statistics	Display statistics for the output.

For example, the following command will display all active TCP connections:

```
[root@onecoursesource ~]# netstat -ta
Active Internet connections (servers and established)
Proto Recv-Q Send-Q Local Address          Foreign Address         State
tcp        0      0 192.168.122.1:domain   0.0.0.0:*               LISTEN
tcp        0      0 0.0.0.0:ssh            0.0.0.0:*               LISTEN
tcp        0      0 localhost:ipp          0.0.0.0:*               LISTEN
tcp        0      0 localhost:smtp         0.0.0.0:*               LISTEN
tcp6       0      0 [::]:ssh               [::]:*                  LISTEN
tcp6       0      0 localhost:ipp          [::]:*                  LISTEN
tcp6       0      0 localhost:smtp         [::]:*
```

Persistent Network Configurations

In many cases, the content presented in this book works equally well on most any Linux distribution. However, there are some situations when that is not the case. For example, in order to set or modify network configuration, you will need to edit a series of files. Some of these files will be "universal," working on most Linux distributions, but in some cases these files will be different on different distributions.

Typically there are two major varieties: Red Hat (which includes Red Hat Enterprise Linux, Fedora, CentOS, and others) and Debian (Debian, Mint OS, Ubuntu, and others). In this section, each file discussed will be marked as "universal," "Red Hat," or "Debian."

The /etc/hostname File (Universal)

The **/etc/hostname** file is where the local system's hostname is stored:

```
[root@onesourcesource ~]#more /etc/hostname
server.sample999.com
```

The /etc/hosts File (Universal)

The **/etc/hosts** file is where hostname-to-IP-address translation is defined:

```
[root@onesourcesource ~]#more /etc/hosts
192.168.1.24 server.sample999.com
```

```
127.0.0.1    localhost onesourcesource
::1          localhost onesourcesource
```

Each line describes one translation. The first field is the IP address, the second field is the hostname, and the optional third field shows the alias addresses.

In most cases, this file is only used for the local host itself or for hosts on the local network. Normally hostname-to-IP-address translation is handled by a DNS server.

The /etc/resolv.conf File (Universal)

The **/etc/resolv.conf** file contains a list of the DNS servers for the system. A typical file looks like the following:

```
[root@onesourcesource ~]# cat /etc/resolv.conf
search sample999.com
nameserver 192.168.1
```

If your system is a DHCP client, then this file is normally dynamically populated using data from the DHCP server. For servers that use static IP address settings, this file is typically manually defined. See more details about static versus dynamic IP settings later in this chapter.

Table 19-6 describes common settings for the **/etc/resolv.conf** file.

Table 19-6 Common Settings for the **/etc/resolv.conf** File

Setting	Description
nameserver	The IP address of the DNS server; there can be up to three **nameserver** lines in the file.
domain	Used to specify the local domain, which allows for use of short names for DNS queries.
search	A list of optional domains on which to perform DNS queries when using short names.

The /etc/nsswitch.conf File (Universal)

The Name Service Switch (NSS) configuration file, **/etc/nsswitch.conf**, is used by applications to determine the sources from which to obtain name-service information, as well as in what order. For example, for networking, this file contains the location of the name server resolver, the utility that provides hostname-to-IP-address translation:

```
[root@onesourcesource ~]#grep hosts /etc/nsswitch.conf
#hosts:     db files nisplus nis dns
hosts:      files dns
```

The value of **files dns** means "look at the local **/etc/hosts** file first, then look at the DNS server if the required translation isn't in the local file."

Table 19-7 describes common hostname-to-IP-address translation utilities.

Table 19-7 Common Hostname-to-IP-Address Translation Utilities

Utility	Description
files	The local **/etc/hosts** file
dns	A DNS server

Utility	Description
NIS	A Network Information Service server

The /etc/sysctl.conf File (Universal)

The **/etc/sysctl.conf** file is used to define parameters for the kernel. The kernel is the component of the operating system that controls many of its functions, such as system boot and communicating with hardware devices.

There are hundreds of possible kernel settings, some of which can affect networking. For example, if you decide that you want to completely turn off IPv6 networking for the system, you should include the following two settings in the **/etc/sysctl.conf** file:

```
net.ipv6.conf.all.disable_ipv6=1
net.ipv6.conf.default.disable_ipv6=1
```

A complete discussion of all possible network configuration settings for the **/etc/sysctl.conf** file is beyond the scope of this book. Consult the kernel documentation for additional details.

See Figure 19-3 for details on how to disable responses to **ping** requests.

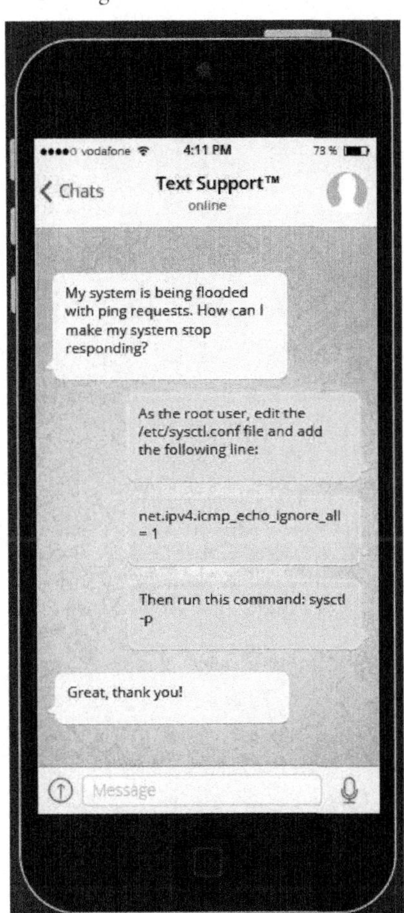

Figure 19-3 *Text Support™—Disable* ***ping*** *Responses*

The /etc/sysconfig/network File (Red Hat)

By default, this Red Hat–based configuration file contains two settings: the system hostname and a setting that determines if networking should be started automatically during the boot process:

```
[root@onesourcesource ~]#more /etc/sysconfig/network
HOSTNAME=onecoursesource
NETWORKING=yes
```

NOTE If you want to permanently change the hostname on Red Hat–based systems, you should change this file. You could also change the **/etc/hostname** file, but that file should be autogenerated by the system during the boot process from the **HOSTNAME** setting in the **/etc/sysconfig/network** file.

There are other possible settings that you can place in this file. For example, the following entry would define a default router (also called a default gateway):

```
GATEWAY=192.168.100.1
```

However, in most cases this setting is placed in a different file (the **/etc/sysconfig/network-scripts/ifcfg-eth0** file), so it is rare to see the **GATEWAY** setting in the **/etc/sysconfig/network** file.

The /etc/sysconfig/network-scripts/ifcfg-*interface-name* Files (Red Hat)

For each network interface (**eth0**, **eth1**, and so on), there is a separate configuration file on Red Hat–based systems. For example, to configure the primary interface for a static IP address, use the following:

```
[root@onesourcesource ~]#more /etc/sysconfig/network-scripts/ifcfg-eth0
DEVICE=eth0
BOOTPROTO=static
ONBOOT=yes
IPADDR=192.168.100.50
NETMASK=255.255.255.0
GATEWAY=192.168.100.1
```

A static IP address is one that is the same each time the system is booted and the network interface is brought up. Another option is to have the IP address (and other corresponding network values, such as the subnet mask) provided by a DHCP (Dynamic Host Configuration Protocol) server. In a DHCP client configuration, the **ifcfg-eth0** file would look like the following:

```
[root@onesourcesource ~]#more /etc/sysconfig/network-scripts/ifcfg-eth0
DEVICE=eth0
BOOTPROTO=dhcp
ONBOOT=yes
```

The possible settings in this configuration file include those shown in Table 19-8.

Table 19-8 Settings for the Configuration File

Setting	Description
DEVICE	The name of the device (for example, **eth0** for the primary Ethernet device).

Setting	Description
BOOTPROTO	Typically set to **static** or **dhcp**, this setting specifies how the networking settings are established. The value **static** means "use the settings indicated in this file," and the value **dhcp** means "contact the DHCP server and get the network settings from that server."
ONBOOT	When **ONBOOT** is set to **yes**, the network device will be activated during the boot process. When it's set to **no**, the network device will not be activated during the boot process.
IPADDR	The IP address to assign to this device.
NETMASK	The subnet mask for this device.
GATEWAY	The default router for the system.

The /etc/network/interfaces File (Debian)

On Debian systems, a single file is used to specify the IP address settings for all interfaces. In the following example, the local loopback address (**lo**) and two network interfaces (**eth0** and **eth1**) are defined:

```
[root@onesourcesource ~]#more /etc/network/interfaces
auto lo
iface lo inet loopback

auto eth0
iface eth0 inet static
    address 192.0.2.7
    netmask 255.255.255.0
    gateway 192.0.2.254

auto eth1
allow-hotplug eth1
iface eth1 inet dhcp
```

In the previous example, the **eth0** device was set with a static IP address, and the **eth1** device was configured via DHCP. Here are some important settings of the **/etc/network/interfaces** file:

- **auto**: This means to activate the device during the boot process if the device exists and is attached to the network. In some cases, like on laptops, the device might not currently be attached.
- **allow-hotplug**: This means to activate the device automatically if detected while the operating system is running.

Network Troubleshooting Commands

In situations when there are network configuration errors, it is helpful to know some network troubleshooting commands. This section focuses on some of these commands.

The ping Command

The **ping** command is used to verify that a remote host can respond to a network connection:

```
[root@onesourcesource ~]#ping -c 4 google.com
PING google.com (172.217.5.206) 56(84) bytes of data.
```

```
64 bytes from lax28s10-in-f14.1e100.net (172.217.5.206): icmp_seq=1 ttl=55 time=49.0 ms
64 bytes from lax28s10-in-f206.1e100.net (172.217.5.206): icmp_seq=2 ttl=55 time=30.2 ms
64 bytes from lax28s10-in-f14.1e100.net (172.217.5.206): icmp_seq=3 ttl=55 time=30.0 ms
64 bytes from lax28s10-in-f206.1e100.net (172.217.5.206): icmp_seq=4 ttl=55 time=29.5 ms

--- google.com ping statistics ---
4 packets transmitted, 4 received, 0% packet loss, time 3008ms
rtt min/avg/max/mdev = 29.595/34.726/49.027/8.261 ms
```

By default, the **ping** command will continuously send "pings" to the remote system until the user cancels the command (Ctrl+C). The **-c** option specifies a count of how many **ping** requests to send.

Conversational Learning™—Using the ping Command

Gary: Hey, Julia. I have a question about pinging a system.

Julia: What's your question?

Gary: I used **ping** to determine if a system is up and it didn't respond. But when I went to the system, it was up and running.

Julia: OK, well first of all, keep in mind that **ping** isn't meant to determine if a host is running. It is designed to determine if the host is reachable via the network.

Gary: How could it be up but not reachable?

Julia: It might have an issue with its network configuration. Or the network cable could simply be unplugged. Or there could be a firewall blocking access. Some administrators block **ping** requests via the firewall.

Gary: Are there any other reasons why it might not respond?

Julia: Yes, there is also a kernel setting that says "don't respond to **ping** requests." Plus, the problem might not be with the machine you are trying to ping at all. The host you are running the **ping** command on may have network issues.

Gary: Hmmm... so, really what **ping** does is determine if the remote host is reachable from the local system only. It could be responding to other hosts or it could respond to other network connections, just not **ping**?

Julia: Exactly. If **ping** responds back successfully, that means it is reachable, but a failure to respond doesn't necessarily mean there is a problem. Further exploring is required.

Gary: OK. Thanks again, Julia.

NOTE The **ping6** command is similar to the **ping** command, except it is used to ping IPv6 addresses, whereas the **ping** command is used to ping IPv4 addresses.

The traceroute Command

The **traceroute** command is used to display the router hops from one system to another (in other words, from one router to another):

```
[root@onesourcesource ~]#traceroute google.com
traceroute to google.com (172.217.4.142), 30 hops max, 60 byte packets
 1  * * *
 2  * * *
 3  * * *
 4  * * *
```

```
5  * * *
6  * paltbprj02-ae1-308.rd.pt.cox.net (68.105.31.37)  49.338 ms  53.183 ms
7  108.170.242.83 (108.170.242.83)  53.041 ms 108.170.242.82 (108.170.242.82)  57.529 ms
➥ 108.170.242.227 (108.170.242.227)  60.106 ms
8  209.85.246.38 (209.85.246.38)  56.051 ms 209.85.246.20 (209.85.246.20)  59.853 ms
➥ 209.85.249.63 (209.85.249.63)  64.812 ms
9  64.233.174.204 (64.233.174.204)  59.018 ms 64.233.174.206 (64.233.174.206)  59.307 ms
➥ 64.233.174.204 (64.233.174.204)  57.352 ms
10  64.233.174.191 (64.233.174.191)  67.186 ms  66.823 ms 209.85.247.0 (209.85.247.0)
➥ 65.519 ms
11  108.170.247.193 (108.170.247.193)  65.097 ms 108.170.247.225 (108.170.247.225)
➥ 65.039 ms 108.170.247.193 (108.170.247.193)  38.324 ms
12  72.14.238.213 (72.14.238.213)  41.229 ms  40.340 ms  41.887 ms
13  lax17s14-in-f142.1e100.net (172.217.4.142)  43.281 ms  40.650 ms  43.394 ms
```

NOTE The value of * means that the data for that hop could not be retrieved.

Table 19-9 describes common options for the **traceroute** command.

Table 19-9 Common Options for the **traceroute** Command

Option	Description
-n	Only display IP addresses; don't resolve to hostnames.
-6	Perform an IPv6 **traceroute** (IPv4 is used by default).
-g or --gateway	Specify the router (gateway) to perform the **traceroute** through.
-i or --interface	Specify the interface (network device) to perform the **traceroute** through.

The **traceroute6** command is the same as the **traceroute** command when the **-6** option is used.

The netcat Command

The **netcat** command (just **nc** or **ncat** on many distributions) is a utility that can be used for debugging network issues. For example, you can have the **nc** command act as a server that is listening on a specific port:

```
[root@onesourcesource ~]#nc -l 9000
```

You can also use the **nc** command to connect to a server on a specific port:

```
[root@onesourcesource ~]#nc localhost 9000
```

Now whatever messages you send on the client side show up on the server side, and vice versa. This utility allows you to test interactions with existing servers as well as allows you to create your own simple network server.

Table 19-10 describes common options for the **nc** command.

Table 19-10 Options for the **nc** Command

Option	Description
-4	Allow only IPv4 communication.
-6	Allow only IPv6 communication.
-l or **--listen**	Open a port to listen on.

Option	Description
-k or **--keep-open**	Don't close the server port when client disconnects; keep the server alive for additional connections.
-m or **--max-conns**	Establish the maximum number of connections allowed to the server.

Access to Wireless Networks

NOTE Practicing the following commands can be difficult for a few reasons. To begin with, you need a system that has wireless devices, which likely means either a laptop or a system with a supported external wireless device (like a USB wireless network dongle). Using a virtual machine will not be possible because wireless devices from the host operating system appear as Ethernet devices within the virtual machine.

Wireless networks can be trickier to configure than Ethernet devices. This is normally due to the fact that hardware vendors have struggled to develop true standards for wireless devices, whereas Ethernet devices have been standardized for many years now. There are certainly some wireless standards, but it is not uncommon for vendors to include nonstandard features in their wireless devices.

The iwconfig Command

To display the parameters of your wireless network interface, execute the **iwconfig** command, as shown in Example 19-2.

Example 19-2 *The iwconfig Command*

```
[root@onecoursesource~]# iwconfig
lo        no wireless extensions.
eth0      no wireless extensions.
wlan0     IEEE 802.11bgn  ESSID:"test1"
          Mode:Managed  Frequency:2.412 GHz  Access Point: Not-Associated
          Tx-Power=20 dBm
          Retry min limit:7   RTS thr:off   Fragment thr=2352 B
          Power Management:off
          Link Quality:0  Signal level:0  Noise level:0
          Rx invalid nwid:0  Rx invalid crypt:0  Rx invalid frag:0
          Tx excessive retries:0  Invalid misc:0   Missed beacon:0
```

Because the **lo** and **eth0** devices are not wireless devices, no data is provided for them. Based on the output of the previous command, the **wlan0** device supports wireless types b, g, and n, which is important when determining which wireless routers to connect to. The **ESSID** parameter indicates that this device is already attached to a wireless router named **test1**.

You could specify several different values for the **Mode** setting. This setting is well described in the man page for the **iwconfig** command:

> "Set the operating mode of the device, which depends on the network topology. The mode can be Ad-Hoc (network composed of only one cell and without Access Point), Managed (node connects to a network composed of many Access Points, with roaming), Master (the node is the synchronisation master or acts as an Access Point), Repeater (the node forwards packets between other wireless nodes), Secondary (the node acts as a backup master/repeater), Monitor (the node is not associated with any cell and passively monitor all packets on the frequency) or Auto."

You can change wireless network settings with the **iwconfig** command. For example, to change the mode to **Ad-Hoc**, execute the following command:

```
[root@onecoursesource~]# iwconfig wlan0 mode Ad-Hoc
```

The iwlist Command

If you are trying to attach a wireless device to a wireless access point (wireless router), you could execute the **iwlist** command to see a list of available wireless routers, as shown in Example 19-3.

Example 19-3 *The iwlist Command*

```
[root@onecoursesource ~]# iwlist scan
lo        Interface doesn't support scanning.

eth0      Interface doesn't support scanning.

wlan0     Scan completed :
          Cell 01 - Address: 08:00:27:FF:E7:E1
                    ESSID:"test1"
                    Mode:Master
                    Channel:1
                    Frequency:2.412 GHz (Channel 1)
                    Quality=42/100  Signal level:-84 dBm  Noise level=-127 dBm
                    Encryption key:on
                    IE: WPA Version 1
                        Group Cipher : TKIP
                        Pairwise Ciphers (1) : TKIP
                        Authentication Suites (1) : PSK
                    IE: IEEE 802.11i/WPA2 Version 1
                        Group Cipher : TKIP
                        Pairwise Ciphers (2) : CCMP TKIP
                        Authentication Suites (1) : PSK
                    IE: Unknown: 2D1A2C0217FFFF0000000000000000000000000000000000000000
                    Bit Rates:1 Mb/s; 2 Mb/s; 5.5 Mb/s; 11 Mb/s; 6 Mb/s
                              9 Mb/s; 12 Mb/s; 18 Mb/s; 24 Mb/s; 36 Mb/s
                              48 Mb/s; 54 Mb/s
                    Extra:tsf=0000003d7dfe8049
                    Extra: Last beacon: 1840ms ago
          Cell 02 - Address: 08:00:27:93:6F:3D
                    ESSID:"test2"
                    Mode:Master
                    Channel:6
                    Frequency:2.437 GHz (Channel 6)
                    Quality=58/100  Signal level:-73 dBm  Noise level=-127 dBm
                    Encryption key:on
                    IE: WPA Version 1
                        Group Cipher : TKIP
                        Pairwise Ciphers (2) : CCMP TKIP
                        Authentication Suites (1) : PSK
                    IE: IEEE 802.11i/WPA2 Version 1
                        Group Cipher : TKIP
                        Pairwise Ciphers (2) : CCMP TKIP
                        Authentication Suites (1) : PSK
```

```
              Bit Rates:1 Mb/s; 2 Mb/s; 5.5 Mb/s; 11 Mb/s; 18 Mb/s
                        24 Mb/s; 36 Mb/s; 54 Mb/s; 6 Mb/s; 9 Mb/s
                        12 Mb/s; 48 Mb/s
              Extra:tsf=0000007a7d5a1b80
              Extra: Last beacon: 1616ms ago
    Cell 03 - Address: 08:00:27:93:6F:DD
              ESSID:"test3"
              Mode:Master
              Channel:6
              Frequency:2.437 GHz (Channel 6)
              Quality=84/100  Signal level:-49 dBm  Noise level=-127 dBm
              Encryption key:on
              IE: WPA Version 1
                  Group Cipher : TKIP
                  Pairwise Ciphers (2) : CCMP TKIP
                  Authentication Suites (1) : PSK
              IE: IEEE 802.11i/WPA2 Version 1
                  Group Cipher : TKIP
                  Pairwise Ciphers (2) : CCMP TKIP
                  Authentication Suites (1) : PSK
              Bit Rates:1 Mb/s; 2 Mb/s; 5.5 Mb/s; 11 Mb/s; 18 Mb/s
                        24 Mb/s; 36 Mb/s; 54 Mb/s; 6 Mb/s; 9 Mb/s
                        12 Mb/s; 48 Mb/s
              Extra:tsf=000001b2460c1608
              Extra: Last beacon: 1672ms ago
```

The **iwlist** command probes your system's network devices; if it finds one that's a wireless device, it attempts to scan the networks available to the device. The output of this command can depend on the remote routers because different types of wireless routers provide different features.

Each cell section of the output describes a wireless router. Here are some of the important values:

- **ESSID**: Extended Service Set Identification; this is essentially a name given to the wireless router to distinguish it between other wireless routers nearby. Some vendors refer to this as simply SSID. This is the name that administrators assign to the wireless access point.
- **IE: WPA Version 1**: WPA (Wi-Fi Protected Access) is an encryption specification used to secure the wireless router from unauthorized users. WEP (Wireless Encryption Protocol) is an older encryption specification; WPA was designed to replace WEP.

Summary

In this chapter, you explored several key networking concepts. The goal of this chapter was not to make you a networking expert, but to introduce you to these concepts to make the process of configuring, maintaining, troubleshooting and securing a network easier.

Key Terms

ARP table, ARP, ESSID, eth0, gateway, lo, MAC, promiscuous mode, route, router, WAP, WEP

Review Questions

1. Based on the output of the **ifconfig** command shown next, _____ is the IPv4 address for the **eth0** device.

```
eth0: flags=4163<UP,BROADCAST,RUNNING,MULTICAST>  mtu 1500
        inet 192.168.1.16  netmask 255.255.255.0  broadcast 192.168.1.255
        inet6 fe80::a00:27ff:fe52:2878  prefixlen 64  scopeid 0x20<link>
        ether 08:00:27:52:28:78  txqueuelen 1000  (Ethernet)
        RX packets 20141  bytes 19608517 (18.7 MiB)
        RX errors 0  dropped 0  overruns 0  frame 0
        TX packets 2973  bytes 222633 (217.4 KiB)
        TX errors 0  dropped 0 overruns 0  carrier 0  collisions 0
```

2. Which device name represents the local loopback device?

   A. **eth0**

   B. **eth1**

   C. **lo**

   D. **loop**

3. The _____ command displays information about the table that contains IP-address-to-MAC-address translation.

4. Which command can display the default gateway? (Choose two.)

   A. **arp**

   B. **ifconfig**

   C. **ip**

   D. **route**

5. Fill in the blank in the following command to add a gateway for the 192.168.2.0/255.255.255.0 network:

```
route add _____ 192.168.2.0 netmask 255.255.255.0 gw 192.168.1.100
```

6. The _____ command is the replacement command for the **ifconfig**, **arp**, and **route** commands.

7. Which option to the **iwlist** command provides a list of available routers?

   A. **display**

   B. **search**

   C. **find**

   D. **scan**

Network Service Configuration: Essential Services

As an administrator, you should know how to correctly set up and secure key network servers. In this chapter, you explore some of these servers, including DNS, DHCP, and mail servers.

You will start by learning key components of the Doman Name Service (DNS) and how to configure a BIND DNS server. Then you learn how to set up a Dynamic Host Configuration Protocol (DHCP) server and discover how this server can interact with a DNS server.

This chapter concludes with an in-depth discussion on email services, including setting up and configuring Postfix, procmail, and Dovecot.

After reading this chapter and completing the exercises, you will be able to do the following:

Configure and secure a BIND DNS server

Set up a DHCP server

Explain key email features

Configure a Postfix server

Configure email delivery software, including procmail and Dovecot

DNS Servers

DNS (Domain Name Service) is a protocol designed to provide name-to-IP-address resolution. It is part of the standard TCP/IP protocol suite and one of several protocols that can provide this functionality; others include the Network Information Service (NIS) and LDAP.

What distinguishes DNS from other similar protocols is that its sole focus is name resolution; NIS and LDAP provide other resolution operations, such as network user and group accounts. DNS is also the de facto standard name resolution solution for the majority of systems connected to the Internet.

DNS client configuration is simple—just specify the DNS server in the local system's **/etc/resolv.conf** file:

```
[root@onesourcesource ~]#cat /etc/resolv.conf
nameserver 192.168.1.1
```

DNS server configuration can be much more complex. In order to properly configure a DNS server, you should understand some of the concepts behind DNS.

Essential Terms

The following are some important terms associated with DNS:

- **Host**: Typically a host is a computer (desktop, laptop, tablet, or mobile phone) that is attached to a network. Another way of looking at the term is that a host is a device that can communicate on a network.
- **Domain name**: Hosts on the Internet address each other by using IP address numbers. These numbers are difficult for humans to remember, so a unique name is often assigned to a host. When this name is registered on an authorized DNS server, the name is considered a "domain name."
- **Top-level domain**: Domain names are structurally organized in a tree-like fashion, much like files are organized in a virtual filesystem structure. The very top level of the DNS structure is simply referred to as "dot" and symbolized by the "." character. The domains directly beneath "." are the top-level domains. The original top-level domains were .com, .org, .net, .int, .edu, .gov, and .mil. Many others have been added in recent years.
- **FQDN:** An FQDN, or fully qualified domain name, is the domain name of a host starting from the top of the DNS structure. For example, the name "www.onecoursesource.com." would be an FQDN. Notice the dot (.) character at the very end of the FQDN. It is the domain above the top level. This character is often omitted when regular users provide a domain name, as the dot is assumed to be the last character of an FQDN in most cases. However, you should get used to including the dot character if you are going to administer DNS servers because it will be required in some of the DNS server configuration files.
- **Subdomain**: A subdomain is any domain that is a component of a larger domain. For example, suppose you wanted to have three domains in your organization to functionally organize the hosts. You might call these domains "sales," "eng," and "support." If your company's domain is "onecoursesource.com.", these three subdomains would be called "sales.onecoursesource.com.", "eng.onecoursesource.com.", and "support.onecoursesource.com.", respectively.
- **Name server**: A name server is a system that responds to DNS client requests. Name servers provide the translation from IP address to domain names (and, sometimes, provide the opposite: domain-name-to-IP-address translation). Note that a name server either has a copy of this information stored locally (called a *zone file*) or stores information obtained by other name servers temporarily in memory or passes on the query to another server (or servers) that has the information.
- **Authoritative name server**: An authoritative name server is one that returns results based on information stored locally on the system (the original master records).
- **Zone file**: The name of the file that is used to store IP-address-to-domain-name translation information (aka, the DNS records). This file also contains information that is used to define the domain itself.
- **Record**: Within the zone file, a record is an entry that defines a single chunk of information for the zone, such as the data that would translate an IP address to domain name.
- **Caching name server**: A caching name server is one that returns results based on information obtained from another name server, such as an authoritative name server. The primary advantage of a caching name server is that it can speed up the IP-address-to-domain-name resolution because it will cache results and be able to respond to future requests using the information in this cache.
- **TTL**: The data stored in a caching name server is typically not stored permanently. The name server that provides the data also provides the caching name server with a TTL, or a *time to live*. The caching name server will store the information in memory until this TTL period ends. Typically this period of time is 24 hours, but this can vary depending on how often the records in the authoritative name server are updated.

- **DNS forwarder**: A DNS server designed to take DNS queries from an internal network and send them to an external DNS server.
- **Forward lookup**: The process of translating an IP address into a domain name. Most DNS servers provide this functionality.
- **Reverse lookup**: The process of translating a domain name into an IP address. While many DNS servers provide this functionality, it is less common than a forward lookup.
- **BIND**: Berkeley Internet Name Domain; the DNS software that is most widely used on the Internet. Originally the software was developed at the University of California Berkeley. The current release of BIND is referred to as BIND 9.

How Name Resolution Works

The following example is purposefully simplistic to provide you with the idea of how name resolution works. Many factors can alter the exact nature of how this process works, including specifics about how each DNS server described in the example has been configured.

For this example, consider a situation in which you are using your web browser to surf to the www.onecoursesource.com domain. In order to determine the IP address of this domain name, your system first needs to determine which DNS servers it can query. The **/etc/resolv.conf** file is consulted for this information:

```
[root@onesourcesource ~]#cat /etc/resolv.conf
nameserver 192.168.1.1
```

In most cases, it is best to have at least two name server settings. If the first name server is unavailable, the second one can answer queries. However, you will find that some smaller companies only provide one name server for their systems. Additionally, if you are using a virtual machine (VM), then typically the VM manager serves as the only name server for the VM. So, do not be surprised if you end up with only one name server setting in the **/etc/resolv.conf** file.

The query is sent to the name server with the IP address of 192.168.1.1, which is the DNS server within the organization. You can determine this because the IP address is a “private” IP (not routable on the Internet). Although this DNS server may have cached the results of a previous query for www.onecoursesource.com, we will assume that the local DNS server does not have this information. In this case, the DNS server needs to pass off the request to another DNS server.

Although it is possible to configure a DNS server to pass off requests to other specific DNS servers, in most cases the query is passed off the DNS servers at the top of the DNS domain structure. These are called the “root servers,” and there are 13 of them; Example 20-1 displays these servers as they are described in the BIND zone files.

Example 20-1 *The Root Servers*

```
;; ANSWER SECTION:
.                       518400  IN      NS      a.root-servers.net.
.                       518400  IN      NS      b.root-servers.net.
.                       518400  IN      NS      c.root-servers.net.
.                       518400  IN      NS      d.root-servers.net.
.                       518400  IN      NS      e.root-servers.net.
.                       518400  IN      NS      f.root-servers.net.
.                       518400  IN      NS      g.root-servers.net.
.                       518400  IN      NS      h.root-servers.net.
.                       518400  IN      NS      i.root-servers.net.
.                       518400  IN      NS      j.root-servers.net.
.                       518400  IN      NS      k.root-servers.net.
```

```
.                        518400   IN      NS       l.root-servers.net.
.                        518400   IN      NS       m.root-servers.net.
;; ADDITIONAL SECTION:
a.root-servers.net.      3600000  IN      A        198.41.0.4
a.root-servers.net.      3600000  IN      AAAA     2001:503:ba3e::2:30
b.root-servers.net.      3600000  IN      A        192.228.79.201
c.root-servers.net.      3600000  IN      A        192.33.4.12
d.root-servers.net.      3600000  IN      A        199.7.91.13
d.root-servers.net.      3600000  IN      AAAA     2001:500:2d::d
e.root-servers.net.      3600000  IN      A        192.203.230.10
f.root-servers.net.      3600000  IN      A        192.5.5.241
f.root-servers.net.      3600000  IN      AAAA     2001:500:2f::f
g.root-servers.net.      3600000  IN      A        192.112.36.4
h.root-servers.net.      3600000  IN      A        128.63.2.53
h.root-servers.net.      3600000  IN      AAAA     2001:500:1::803f:235
i.root-servers.net.      3600000  IN      A        192.36.148.17
i.root-servers.net.      3600000  IN      AAAA     2001:7fe::53
j.root-servers.net.      3600000  IN      A        192.58.128.30
j.root-servers.net.      3600000  IN      AAAA     2001:503:c27::2:30
k.root-servers.net.      3600000  IN      A        193.0.14.129
k.root-servers.net.      3600000  IN      AAAA     2001:7fd::1
l.root-servers.net.      3600000  IN      A        199.7.83.42
l.root-servers.net.      3600000  IN      AAAA     2001:500:3::42
m.root-servers.net.      3600000  IN      A        202.12.27.33
m.root-servers.net.      3600000  IN      AAAA     2001:dc3::35
```

See Figure 20-1 for a demonstration of the queries described so far.

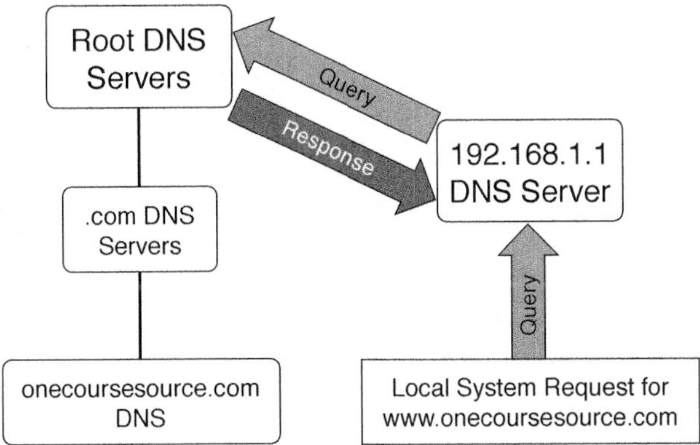

Figure 20-1 *Querying the Root DNS Servers*

These root servers are aware of the DNS servers for the top-level domains (.com, .edu, and so on). Although they do not know about the www.onecoursesource.com domain, they are able to direct the query to the DNS servers responsible for the ".com" domain, as shown in Figure 20-2.

The ".com" DNS servers are also unaware of the www.onecoursesource.com domain, but they do know which DNS servers are responsible for the onecoursesource.com domain. The query is passed on to the DNS server that is responsible for the onecoursesource.com domain, which returns the IP address for the www.onecoursesource.com domain (see Figure 20-3).

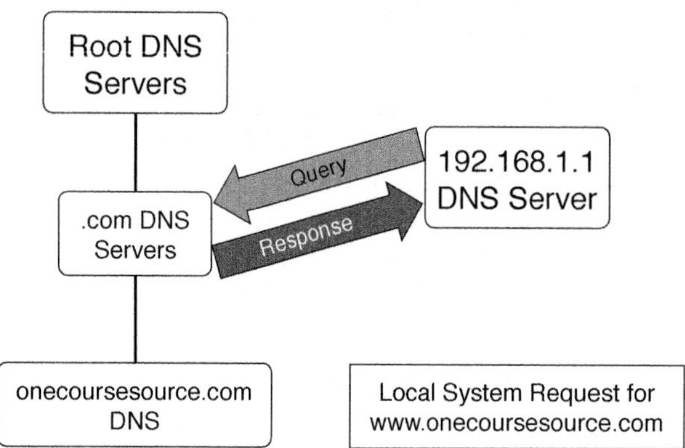

Figure 20-2 *Querying the ".com" DNS Servers*

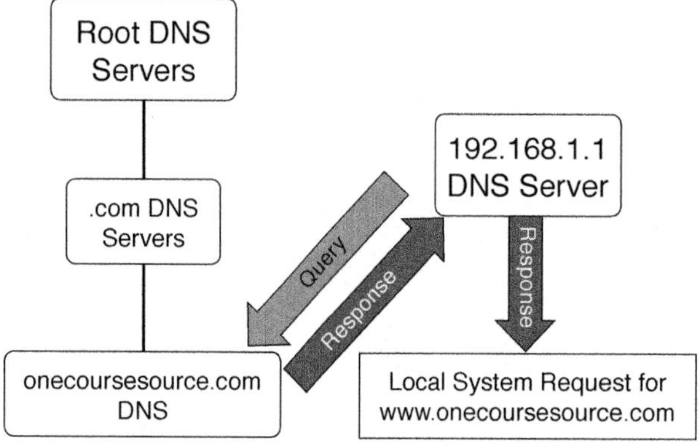

Figure 20-3 *Querying the "onecoursesrouce.com" DNS Servers*

Basic BIND Configuration

Configuring BIND involves many components. Which of these components you will configure depends on several factors, such as the type of BIND server (caching, forwarder, or authoritative) and what features you want the BIND server to have (security features, for example).

The focus of this chapter is the basic configuration files.

The /etc/named.conf File

The primary configuration file for the BIND server is the **/etc/named.conf** file. This file is read by the BIND server (called named) when it is started. See Example 20-2 for a sample **/etc/named.conf** file.

Example 20-2 *Sample /etc/named.conf File*

```
//
// named.conf
//
// Provided by Red Hat bind package to configure the ISC BIND named(8) DNS
// server as a caching only nameserver (as a localhost DNS resolver only).
//
// See /usr/share/doc/bind*/sample/ for example named configuration files.
//

options {
```

```
        listen-on port 53 { 127.0.0.1; };
        listen-on-v6 port 53 { ::1; };
        directory       "/var/named";
        dump-file       "/var/named/data/cache_dump.db";
        statistics-file "/var/named/data/named_stats.txt";
        memstatistics-file "/var/named/data/named_mem_stats.txt";
        allow-query     { localhost; };

        /*
         - If you are building an AUTHORITATIVE DNS server, do NOT enable recursion.
         - If you are building a RECURSIVE (caching) DNS server, you need to enable
           recursion.
         - If your recursive DNS server has a public IP address, you MUST enable
           access control to limit queries to your legitimate users. Failing to do so
           will cause your server to become part of large scale DNS amplification
           attacks. Implementing BCP38 within your network would greatly
           reduce such attack surface
        */
        recursion yes;

        dnssec-enable yes;
        dnssec-validation yes;
        dnssec-lookaside auto;

        /* Path to ISC DLV key */
        bindkeys-file "/etc/named.iscdlv.key";

        managed-keys-directory "/var/named/dynamic";

        pid-file "/run/named/named.pid";
        session-keyfile "/run/named/session.key";
};

logging {
        channel default_debug {
                file "data/named.run";
                severity dynamic;
        };
};

zone "." IN {
        type hint;
        file "named.ca";
};

include "/etc/named.rfc1912.zones";
include "/etc/named.root.key";
```

You should not be intimidated by all these settings! Most of them are really straightforward once you understand how the DNS server works.

It is important to understand that the configuration file provided in Example 20-2 is for a caching name server (recall that this term was defined earlier in this chapter). When you install the BIND package, the default configuration file provided is for a caching name server. This is actually very handy because it makes it really easy to configure a caching name server; just install the BIND server package and start the BIND server.

Here are some syntax notes:

- There are three ways to make comments in the **/etc/named.conf** file. A single-line comment starts with **//** (called "C++ style") or **#** (Unix style). A multiline comment starts with a line that contains **/*** and ends on a line that contains ***/** (called "C style").
- Values in the **/etc/named.conf** file are separated by the semicolon (;) character. This is extremely important; many administrators have lost a lot of hair (from pulling it out) because of the headaches created by a missing semicolon.

Review Table 20-1 to learn about the different settings in the **options** section of the file displayed in Example 20-1. The **options** section is used to provide general settings for the DNS server.

Table 20-1 Settings in the **default /etc/named.conf** File

Setting	Meaning
listen-on	This contains the port number and interfaces that the BIND server will "listen to." For example, the value in Example 20-2 is **port 53 { 127.0.0.1; };**, which means "listen to incoming requests on port 53 for the interface that has the IP address of 127.0.0.1." This means that the server only listens for requests from the local machine. Suppose the primary network card has an IP address of 192.168.1.1. To have the BIND server listen to requests on that interface (or, in other words, on the network for that interface), adjust the **listen-on** value to the following: **listen-on port 53 { 127.0.0.1; 192.168.1.1; };** You can also specify multiple **listen-on** statements, which is useful if you want to listen to a different port number for another interface. Commenting out this directive will cause the service to listen on all interfaces for port 53.
listen-on-v6	The same concept as the **listen-on** setting, but **listen-on** is for IPv4 addresses whereas this setting is for IPv6 addresses.
directory	The "working directory" for the server. This is the location where additional information, including zone files, can be found. In most cases, this should be the /var/named directory. However, this will be set to a different directory if you run your DNS server in a "chroot jail," which is a topic covered later in this chapter.
allow-query	Whereas **listen-on** specifies the port and interface to listen to incoming requests, the **allow-query** setting indicates the systems to which the BIND server will respond. More details on this setting can be found later in this chapter.
recursion	If this setting is **yes**, the DNS server will attempt to find the answer by performing all necessary DNS queries. If this setting is **no**, the DNS server will respond with referral data (basically which DNS server to query next).
dnssec-enable	When set to **yes**, this setting enables DNSSEC (Domain Name System Security Extensions). The primary purpose of DNSSEC is to provide a means of authenticating DNS data. DNSSEC is covered in detail later in this chapter.

Setting	Meaning
dnssec-validation	When set to **yes**, this setting makes use of "trusted" or "managed" keys.
dnssec-lookaside	When set to **auto**, this setting makes use of an alternative repository of trusted keys as defined in the **bindkeys-file** setting (typically the repository hosted by dlv.isc.org).
bindkeys-file	This is the file used when the **dnssec-lookaside** setting is set to **auto**.
managed-keys-directory	This setting indicates which directory is used to store a list of DNSSEC trusted keys.
pid-file	The process ID of the DNS server is stored in this file.
session-keyfile	This setting contains the name of a file where a TSIG session key is stored. TSIG (transaction signature) is used to allow authenticated updates to the DNS database. The nsupdate command makes use of the TSIG key to allow for these authenticated DNS database updates. TSIG is covered later in this chapter.

The allow-query Setting

In some cases, you will want to limit which systems can query your DNS server. One way of doing this is to use the allow-query setting in the /etc/named.conf file. The allow-query setting accepts an argument in the form of { address_match_list; address_match_list; …};, where address_match_list can be one of the following:

- An IPv4 or IPv6 address.
- A network in the format 192.168.100/24 or 2001:cdba:9abc:5678::/64.
- An ACL, which is a nickname assigned to multiple IP addresses or networks.
- A predefined address. Four options are available: **none** matches no IP addresses, **any** matches all IP addresses, **localhost** matches the IP address of the DNS server itself, and **localnets** matches all the IP addresses of the network that the DNS server is on.

You can also use a **!** character to negate one of the aforementioned values. For example, **!192.168.100.1** means *not* 192.168.100.1. This is useful when you want to exclude an IP address from a network. For example, the following would allow transfers from every machine in the 192.168.100/24 network except the machine with the IP address of 192.168.100.1:

```
allow-query      { localhost; !192.168.100.1; 192.168.100/24};
```

The **acl** address match mentioned previously can be very useful if you find yourself using the same address sets for different settings in the **/etc/resolv.conf** file. For example, consider the following:

```
acl "permit"     { localhost; !192.168.100.1; 192.168.100/24};
        allow-query      { "permit"};
```

Not only can the **permit** ACL be used with the **allow-query** setting, but it can be used with other settings that support **address_match_list** arguments. The **address_match_list** format is used with several other DNS configuration settings, such as **listen-on** and **listen-on-v6**.

Security Highlight

Generally speaking, you want to disallow DNS queries for internal hosts from external systems. In other words, only systems within your organization can perform DNS queries for hosts that should not be accessed by systems outside of your network.

Additional /etc/named.conf Settings

You should be aware of three additional settings in the /etc/named.conf file:

- **logging**: This setting allows you to specify several logging features, such as where log entries are stored (defined in the **file** setting) and the severity level of log messages that are recorded (the **severity** setting). The **channel** setting can be used to define a set of rules. This allows you to have different rules (such as different log files) for different log messages (such as different severity levels). Note that the severity levels are much like the syslog severity levels.

Security Highlight

Logging is a key element to determine if inappropriate DNS queries are performed, so be sure to set **logging** to a value that provides you with the necessary information to discover a breach. See Chapter 25, "System Logging," for more details about system logs.

- **zone**: This is where you specify the type of zone files and the location of the zone file. This is covered in more detail later in this chapter.
- **include**: This allows you to place additional DNS settings in a separate file. Typically the **include** setting appears at the end of the **/etc/named.conf** file, but wherever it is placed is where the rules from the other file are inserted. The advantages of using an **include** file is that you can enable or disable a large set of rules by either uncommenting or commenting a single **include** setting from the **/etc/named.conf** file.

Note that if you explore the **name.conf** man page, you will quickly realize that we have just scratched the surface of potential settings. For now, keep in mind that we are focusing on the basics, and you should not be overwhelmed by all the other settings. However, if you are going to be a DNS administrator for your organization, you should explore additional settings because they can be extremely useful.

Zone Files

Previously in this chapter you learned about the basic configuration of BIND by modifying the / etc/named.conf file. One of the settings in that file, the **directory** setting, was used to indicate the location of additional configuration files, like so:

```
[root@onesourcesource ~]#grep "directory" /etc/named.conf
        directory       "/var/named";
```

On a standard BIND setup, the zone files are stored in the **/var/named** directory. These zone files are used to define the hostname-to-IP-address translation as well as additional information about DNS domains.

In this section, you learn how to configure these zone files for an authoritative DNS server for one or more domains. You learn the syntax of these zone files as well as how to create and administer resource records within the zone files.

Zone File Basics

By default, you should see two zone files in the /var/named directory:

- **/var/named/named.ca**: This file contains a list of the root servers. In most cases you should never modify this file directly. If more root servers are added (a rare event), a future update of the BIND software should update the **/var/named/named.ca** file.
- **/var/named/named.localhost**: This file defines the local host. It also is rarely modified because it is only used to define a single host. Example 20-3 shows a typical **/var/named/named.localhost** file.

Example 20-3 *Sample /var/named/named.localhost File*

```
[root@onesourcesource ~]#more /var/named/named.localhost
$TTL 1D
@       IN SOA  ns.onecoursesource.com. root.onecoursesource.com. (
                                        0       ; serial
                                        1D      ; refresh
                                        1H      ; retry
                                        1W      ; expire
                                        3H )    ; minimum
        NS      ns.onecoursesource.com
        A       127.0.0.1
        AAAA    ::1
```

Each of the settings you see in Example 20-3 is covered in greater detail later in this chapter.

Zone File Entries in the /etc/named.conf File

To use zone files, you need to make entries in the /etc/named.conf file first. If the changes to the zone are created on the local machine, you would make an entry like the following:

```
zone "onecoursesource.com" {
type master;
file "named.onecoursesource.com";
};
```

This defines a forward zone file that could be used to translate domain names into IP addresses. The type of master identifies this as the machine on which changes to the zone file are made. The file setting specifies the location of the file that contains the zone information, relative to the directory setting (**/var/named**) previously described.

Typically, you set up another DNS server that contains a copy of the zone file obtained from the master via a process classed as a *zone transfer*. To set up this secondary DNS server (a DNS *slave* server), place the following entry in the **/etc/named.conf** file on the other secondary machine:

```
zone "onecoursesource.com" {
type slave;
file "named.onecoursesource.com";
masters { 38.89.136.109; }
};
```

One advantage of having both master and slave servers is that you can spread the query load between different machines. Another advantage is that if one server becomes unavailable, another server is available to respond to queries.

The terms *master name server*, *slave name server*, and *authoritative name server* may be a bit confusing:

- A master name server is the system where you make changes directly to the zone files.
- A slave name server is a system that holds a copy of the master name server zone files.
- An authoritative name server is a name server that has the authority to respond to DNS queries. This includes both the master name server and the slave name servers.

Although not required, you may want to define reverse lookup zones. With a reverse lookup zone, the query provides an IP address, and the DNS server returns the domain name. To create a reverse lookup zone, you first need an entry like the following in the **/etc/named.conf** file:

```
zone    "136.89.38.in-addr.arpa" {
type   master;
file   "db.38.89.136";
};
```

Security Highlight

Although you are not required to provide reverse lookups, you should be aware that not creating reverse lookups may break some network services. Some of these services verify hostnames and IP addresses by performing a forward lookup and then a reverse lookup to ensure that the values are the same "both ways." So, without a reverse lookup zone file, these network services would return a failure when performing this security check.

Note the format of the zone definition: **136.89.38.in-addr.arpa**. This is the network address (octets) in reverse, with **in-addr.arpa** added to the end. As with forward lookup zone files, you should define one master DNS server and optionally additional slave DNS servers.

The **/etc/named.conf** zone entries previously described are the minimum settings that you need to have. Table 20-2 describes additional settings that you should consider when setting up zone file entries.

Table 20-2 Zone Settings in the /etc/named.conf File

Setting	Description
allow-query	Just like the **allow-query** entry in the **options** section, but **allow-query** in a zone setting only applies to this specific zone.
allow-transfer	This setting is important if you plan to have slave DNS servers. You can limit which DNS servers can transfer the entire zone file by making this entry in the zone setting on the master DNS's **/etc/named.conf** file.
allow-update	Useful if you decide to implement a DNS feature called Dynamic DNS; this feature allows DHCP servers to update records in the master DNS's zone file. The **allow-update** setting allows you to specify which IP addresses can update their domain name.

Zone File Syntax

The syntax of the zone file (the files that you place in the /var/named directory) must be correct; otherwise, the DNS server will not load the zone file properly. In most cases it is probably best to copy an existing zone file and modify it to suit your needs. A simple Internet search results in many sample zone files.

Here are a few things to consider when creating a zone file:

- Comment lines begin with a semicolon (;) character and continue to the end of the line.
- Each line defines a record, and in most cases the end of the line is the end of the record. In some cases, the record can be spread across multiple lines (see the SOA example later in this chapter for an example).
- Each record consists of fields of data separated by either spaces or tabs (whitespace). The fields are defined as **name**, **ttl**, **record class**, **record type**, and **record data**. Each of these fields is described in greater detail in Table 20-3.
- The **@** character has a special meaning within the zone file. It means "the current origin," which refers to the current domain. So, in a forward zone file for the onecoursesource.com

domain, the **@** character means onecoursesource.com. (Note the trailing dot character, which is required in zone files.) You can change the meaning of the **@** character by using the **$ORIGIN** setting (for example, **$ORIGIN example.com.**).

- Each zone file should start with a **$TTL** setting, which is used to set the default time to live (TTL). The TTL is how long caching DNS servers should store information from this DNS server. This default TTL can be overridden by individual records; see the **ttl** field in Table 20-3 for further details.
- When times are given in the zone file, the default time value is seconds. For example, an entry of **$TTL 86400** sets the default time to live to 86,400 seconds (which equates to one day). You can specify time values in minutes (**30m**, for example) hours (**3h**), days (**2d**), or weeks (**1w**). This option is not case sensitive (later examples use capital letters, which is what we normally use), and you can even combine values (**2h30m**, for example).

Table 20-3 Zone File Record Fields

Field	Description
name	The domain name associated with this record.
ttl	The time to live for this record. This is how long the record is considered valid when stored on a caching name server (or a client program like a web browser). After this period of time the client should discard the record from the local cache. Note that this field can be omitted. If it is omitted for a record, the default zone file value is used. This default is defined by the **$TTL** directive (for example, **$TTL 1D**).
record class	This is a predefined value and is most commonly set to IN (which stands for Internet). Although there are a few recognized classes, you will almost always use the IN record class.
record type	This is the type of record. Many types are available and are defined later in this chapter.
record data	The record data varies depending on the record type. It could be a single value or a collection of values, depending on the record type. Examples of this data are described later in this chapter.

NOTE It is important that you include the trailing dot character (the period at the end of onecoursesource.com.) whenever using an FQDN in the zone file. Relative domain names do not require a trailing dot character because they are prepended to the value of **$ORIGIN**.

Zone Record Types

Although dozens of possible zone record types are available, you do not need to be aware of each one. In this section, you learn about the zone record types most commonly used in zone files.

The SOA Record Type

The SOA (Start of Authority) record type is used to define the authoritative information about the zone (think of it as the operating instructions for the zone). A typical SOA record type looks like the following:

```
@       IN SOA  ns.onecoursesource.com. root.onecoursesource.com. (
                                        0       ; serial
                                        1D      ; refresh
```

```
                                    1H       ; retry
                                    1W       ; expire
                                    3H )     ; minimum
```

The parentheses allow you to spread the data across multiple lines and provide comments for each data value. Although this for easier reading, it isn't required. You may sometimes see the record in a single-line format:

```
@       IN SOA  ns.onecoursesource.com. root.onecoursesource.com. 0 1D 1H 1W  3H
```

In the **name** field, the name for the entire domain should be provided. Recall that the shortcut value **@** represents the current domain name, which is determined by the **zone** entry in the **/etc/named.conf** file.

Typically, the **ttl** field is set to the default value by the field being omitted. The IN class is almost always used, and the record type is set to SOA.

The record data field includes seven values, as described in Table 20-4.

Table 20-4 SOA Record Data

Data	Description
Name server	This is the domain name of the master name server. Example: ns.onecoursesource.com.
Email address	The email address of the DNS administrator for this domain. Instead of using an @ to separate the user name from the domain name, a "." character is used instead. For example, root.onecoursesource.com. is the equivalent of root@onecoursesource.com.
Serial number	This number is important if you have slave servers because this value is used to determine whether a zone transfer should be initiated. On a regular basis, the slave servers query the master server to determine whether the serial number has been updated. For example, suppose the current serial number is 100 and the zone file on the master is modified. The administrator who performs the modification should increase the serial number by a value of at least 1 (101, for example). Then the slave servers know changes have been made and request these changes from the master server through a process called a *zone transfer*. The serial number is limited to a total of 10 digits. However, this allows you to use a format that always results in an increasing number while also documenting the last time the zone file was modified: YEARmonthDAYrev. YEAR is a four-digit year value, month is a two-digit month value, DAY is a two-digit day of the month value, and rev is which version of the file on that particular day. For example, the first zone file change on January 31, 2017, would be a serial number of 2017013100. This allows for up to 100 zone file updates per day until December 31, 9999. If you are wondering what happens if you need to update the zone file more than 100 times per day, you should really think about how you administer zone files. It is rare to update your zone file more than a handful of times per day. And if you are wondering what happens in the year 10,000, we suggest that will most likely be someone else's problem!

Data	Description
Refresh	How often does the slave server query the master server to determine whether the serial value has changed? The refresh value provides the slave server with this information. Typically, a value such as **1D** is used to tell the slave server to check every 24 hours; however, in a domain where the zone file changes frequently, you may choose a value like **1H** or **6H** to have the slave query the master every one or six hours, respectively.
Retry	Suppose the refresh is set to **1D**, and the slave attempts to query the master for an update. If the master does not respond, the retry value is checked. The retry value is how long the DNS slave server waits before attempting to query the DNS master server again. For example, a value of **1H** could have the slave wait one hour and then attempt to query the master server again.
Expiry	If the master server continues to be unreachable, the expiry value is used to determine when the slave servers should no longer respond to DNS client requests. The idea here is that since the DNS master hasn't responded in so long, the DNS entries may no longer be valid. Typically this is set to one or two weeks.
Minimum	This one is tricky; consider the following situation: Your company has a caching server and you try to resolve the domain name test.onecoursesource.com. This is a new machine, and its DNS record has not been updated on the master DNS server, so your caching server receives a "no such host" response. Because it is a caching server, it stores this in its cache. But for how long should it be stored? Recall that the default time to live is normally set at one day, much too long for a negative DNS response to be cached. Once that new domain name has been added to the master DNS server, you don't want your caching server to be serving up "no such host" responses for the next 24 hours. The minimum setting is used to provide a length of time to cache negative DNS responses. If your domain is updated frequently, you want this to be a low value (perhaps **1h** or less). If your domain rarely changes, you want this to be a high value (but likely not higher than **1d**).

The Address Record Type

An address record is used to define a domain-name-to-IP-address translation. A typical example would look like the following:

```
www            IN      A      38.89.136.109
```

The first field is the domain name (for example, www). In this case, the domain is given relative to the default domain defined by **$ORIGIN**, but it can also be provided as a fully qualified name:

```
www.onecoursesource.com.          INA38.89.136.109
```

The value of A indicates that this line represents an address record type, and the value of 38.89.136.109 is the IP address associated with the www.onecoursesource.com. domain.

Note that address records are only placed in forward lookup zone files.

The Canonical Name Type

In some cases, you may have a host in your domain that provides more than one role and, as a result, should be accessible with more than one domain name. For example, the web server for onecoursesource.com may also act as the FTP server, so it would make sense to have this single system be accessible either via www.onecoursesource.com or ftp.onecoursesource.com.

However, you should only have one address record per IP address. So, to allow for more than one domain name to be translated to a single IP address, use canonical records. A canonical record (also called a *cname*) is like a nickname and typically looks like the second record shown in the following snippet:

```
www.onecoursesource.com.          IN      A      38.89.136.109
ftp                                                   IN      CNAME      www
```

With an entry like this, the domain name ftp.onecoursesource.com would be translated to the domain name www.onecoursesource.com, which is further translated into the IP address of 38.89.136.109.

The Name Server Record Type

As mentioned previously, each domain can have one or more name servers; these can be defined by NS records. The primary (or master) name server is specified in the SOA record, but also needs to have an NS record. Additional (secondary or slave) name servers also need to be defined with NS records. You can define name servers by creating records like the following:

```
@      INNSns.sample.com.
@      IN      NSns2.sample.com.
```

All of your name servers should have an NS entry, even the master server. Additionally, the NS entry data specifies a domain name, not an IP address, so it is important to also have an address record for each name server.

Note that the @ character in the NS example could have been removed completely. If the first field of data is omitted, it is assumed to be the value of **$ORIGIN**.

The Mail eXchange Record Type

Suppose an email is sent to info@onecoursesource.com. The MTA (mail transfer agent) from the sending domain needs to be able to determine which machine handles inbound email for the one-coursesource.com domain. The MTA accomplishes this by querying the domain name servers for the Mail eXchange (MX) records.

The MX records for a domain typically look like the following:

```
@INMX10mail1.onecoursesource.com
@INMX20mail2.onecoursesource.com
```

Most of the MX record should be straightforward now that you understand record types. The values of 10 and 20 are different from what you have seen so far. These numbers provide a priority value, where the lower the number, the higher its priority.

The priority value is often confused by administrators. If one mail server has a priority of 10 and another has a priority of 20, the MTA from the sending domain initially attempts to send mail to the server with the priority of 10. If the server does not respond, the mail server with the priority of 20 is then contacted. It is likely that the second mail server will never be used because most mail servers are available 24/7.

It is more common to have the same priority value for each mail server to allow for load balancing. In this case, the mail servers are roughly equally utilized ("roughly" because caching DNS servers can unbalance the load a bit).

It is not uncommon to have just one MX record because many small-to-midsize companies do not need multiple mail servers to handle incoming email.

The Pointer Record Type

The address record type described previously is used in forward lookup zone files to translate domain names into IP addresses. The Pointer (PTR) record type is used in reverse lookup zone files to translate IP addresses into domain names. Here's an example of a typical Pointer record:

```
109.136.89.38.in-addr.arpa. IN PTR www.onecoursesource.com.
```


It is critical to understand that the IP address for a Pointer record type is given in reverse of the actual IP address, followed by **in-addr.arpa**. For example, the value **109.136.89.38.in-addr.arpa.** is for the IP address of 38.89.136.109.

In most cases, you will not need to specify this fully qualified IP address name because **$ORIGIN** should be set to the current reverse lookup network domain (for example, **.136.89.38.in-addr.arpa.**) If that is the case, you could just provide the host IP portion of the IP address:

```
109 IN PTR www.onecoursesource.com.
```

Putting It All Together

Creating a DNS server from scratch is often a daunting task for the novice DNS administrator. When you create your first DNS server, use the KISS principle (Keep It Simple, Silly). If you try to implement a lot of fancy DNS settings, it will be hard to determine what went wrong.

It is also important to look at the log files when things do not work correctly. We are often blind to our own errors (especially simple typos), making log files very useful in determining what went wrong.

Sometimes it helps to see the big picture after focusing on specifics. With that in mind, let's look at a simple DNS configuration. In this example, we create the necessary files for the sample.com domain. As this is just a test domain, we use private IP addresses.

First, see Example 20-4 for the **/etc/named.conf** file. Note that the comments have been removed from this file for brevity.

Example 20-4 *New /etc/named.conf File*

```
options {
        listen-on port 53 { 127.0.0.1; };
        listen-on-v6 port 53 { ::1; };
        directory       "/var/named";
        dump-file       "/var/named/data/cache_dump.db";
        statistics-file "/var/named/data/named_stats.txt";
        memstatistics-file "/var/named/data/named_mem_stats.txt";
        allow-query     { localhost; };
        recursion yes;
        dnssec-enable yes;
        dnssec-validation yes;
        dnssec-lookaside auto;
        bindkeys-file "/etc/named.iscdlv.key";
        pid-file "/run/named/named.pid";
        session-keyfile "/run/named/session.key";
};

logging {
        channel default_debug {
                file "data/named.run";
                severity dynamic;
```

```
        };
};

zone "." IN {
        type hint;
        file "named.ca";
};

include "/etc/named.rfc1912.zones";
include "/etc/named.root.key";

zone "sample.com" {
type master;
file "named.sample.com";
};

zone    "1.168.192.in-addr.arpa" {
        type   master;
        file   "db.192.168.1";
};
```

Based on the entries in Example 20-4, you should be able to tell that both a forward and reverse lookup zone were defined. Additionally, you should be able to determine that this system serves as the master name server for the sample.com domain, which means all changes to the zone files should be made on this machine.

If this was a slave server, you would not create zone files because these are automatically created during the first zone transfer from the master server. However, because this is the master server, you need to create a forward zone file, as shown in Example 20-5.

Example 20-5 *The /var/named/named.sample.com File*

```
$TTL 1D
@       IN SOA  ns.sample.com. root.sample.com. (
                                        0       ; serial
                                        1D      ; refresh
                                        1H      ; retry
                                        1W      ; expire
                                        3H )    ; minimum
; Nameservers:
@    INNSns1.sample.com.
@    INNSns2.sample.com.
; Address records:
wwwINA    192.168.1.100
ns1          INA    192.168.1.1
ns2          INA    192.168.1.2
mail1        INA    192.168.1.200
mail2        IN    A    192.168.1.201
test         INA    192.168.1.45

; Aliases:
ftpINCNAMEwww
```

```
; MX records
@         IN    MX    10    mail1.onecoursesource.com.
@         INMX20mail2.onecoursesource.com.
```

WHAT COULD GO WRONG? A lot could go wrong when editing the zone file. After you have made these changes, restart your BIND server and perform some simple tests (which can be done with the **dig** command, as shown later in this discussion).

You should create a reverse zone file, which is simpler because you only need an SOA record, NS records, and Pointer records (see Example 20-6).

Example 20-6 *The /var/named/db.192.168.1 File*

```
$TTL 1D
@       IN SOA  ns.sample.com. root.sample.com. (
                                       0        ; serial
                                       1D       ; refresh
                                       1H       ; retry
                                       1W       ; expire
                                       3H )     ; minimum
; Nameservers:
@     IN    NSns1.sample.com.
@     IN    NSns2.sample.com.
;
; Address records:
100          IN    PTR       www
1            IN    PTR       ns1
2            IN    PTR       ns1
200          IN    PTR       mail1
201          IN    PTR       mail2
45INPTR     text
```

You might be thinking, what about ftp.sample.com? Why is that not in the reverse lookup zone file? The IP address can only return one hostname, so you need to pick which one you want to have returned: either www.sample.com or ftp.sample.com.

Slave BIND Servers

The example provided in this section describes how to set up a master DNS server. Setting up a slave server requires several additional steps, including the following:

- Setting up the **/etc/named.conf** file on the slave server.
- Adding the slave server as an NS record on the master server's zone file. This should also require creating an A record and PTR record for the slave server, assuming it is a new machine for the network.
- Modifying the **/etc/named.conf** file on the master server to allow the slave server to perform a zone transfer (using the **allow-transfer** statement).

Keep in mind that these are general steps. Knowing the specifics of setting up a slave server is beyond the scope of this book.

Testing the DNS Server

After you have set up all your DNS configuration files, you can restart the named server. However, it might be a good idea to first verify that the syntax of the configuration files is correct. This can be accomplished by using the **named-checkconf** and **named-checkzone** commands.

The **named-checkconf** command is used to verify the syntax of the **/etc/named.conf** file. If there are no problems with the file, no output is produced. However, if there is a syntax error, you receive an error message like the following:

```
[root@onesourcesource ~]# named-checkconf
/etc/named.conf:12: missing ';' before 'listen-on-v6'
```

The error message from the previous example includes the filename, the line number (12), and the syntax error.

Perhaps the best part of the **named-checkconf** command is that it is aware of which settings are valid and which are not, as you can see from the output of the following command:

```
[root@onesourcesource ~]# named-checkconf
/etc/named.conf:12: unknown option 'listen-onv6'
```

The **named-checkzone** command checks the syntax of a specific zone file. In addition to specifying the zone file as an argument, you specify the name of the zone:

```
[root@onesourcesource ~]# named-checkzone sample.com
➥/var/named/named.sample.com
zone sample.com/IN: loaded serial 0
OK

[root@onesourcesource ~]# named-checkzone 1.168.192.in-addr.arpa
➥/var/named/db.192.168.1
zone 1.168.192.in-addr.arpa/IN: loaded serial 0
OK
```

The error messages are not perfect, but they do help you find problems. For example, consider the output of the following commands:

```
[root@onesourcesource ~]# named-checkzone sample.com
➥/var/named/named.sample.com
zone sample.com/IN: NS 'ns1.sample.com.sample.com' has no address
➥records (A or AAAA)
zone sample.com/IN: not loaded due to errors.
[root@onesourcesource ~]# grep ns1 /var/named/named.sample.com
@       IN      NS      ns1.sample.com
ns1                     IN      A       192.168.1.1
```

The problem with the file is a missing dot character at the end of ns1.sample.com. (It should be "ns1.sample.com." instead.)

The dig Command

After you restart the named server, you can perform a test lookup by executing the **dig** command, as shown in Example 20-7.

Example 20-7 *Testing with the* ***dig*** *Command*

```
[root@onesourcesource ~]#dig www.sample.com @localhost
; <<>> DiG 9.9.4-RedHat-9.9.4-18.el7_1.5 <<>> www.sample.com @localhost
```

```
;; global options: +cmd
;; Got answer:
;; ->>HEADER<<- opcode: QUERY, status: NOERROR, id: 28530
;; flags: qr aa rd ra; QUERY: 1, ANSWER: 1, AUTHORITY: 2, ADDITIONAL: 3

;; OPT PSEUDOSECTION:
; EDNS: version: 0, flags:; udp: 4096
;; QUESTION SECTION:
;www.sample.com.                       IN      A

;; ANSWER SECTION:
www.sample.com.        86400   IN      A       192.168.1.100

;; AUTHORITY SECTION:
sample.com.            86400   IN      NS      ns1.sample.com.
sample.com.            86400   IN      NS      ns2.sample.com.

;; ADDITIONAL SECTION:
ns1.sample.com.        86400   IN      A       192.168.1.1
ns2.sample.com.        86400   IN      A       192.168.1.2

;; Query time: 0 msec
;; SERVER: ::1#53(::1)
;; WHEN: Mon Nov 30 07:38:52 PST 2018
;; MSG SIZE  rcvd: 127
```


The **dig** command produces a lot of output, and it is difficult to read if you are not familiar with DNS zone file syntax. However, now that you are familiar with this syntax, you can see that the responses are in the same format as the zone file records. For example, consider the output below **ANSWER SECTION**:

```
www.sample.com.        86400   IN      A       192.168.1.100
```

This output includes the fully qualified hostname (including the trailing "." character), the TTL (86400 seconds, which is one day) for this record, the class for the record (IN), the record time (A for address), and the IP address. Keep in mind, this is the information that the DNS server is providing, not exactly what you have in your zone file. For example, you might not have included the TTL value, but that was included by the server when it responded to the **dig** request.

Securing BIND

BIND servers are often directly accessible to the Internet. Any time you have a system that can be directly accessed via the Internet, security becomes a big concern. Concerns include someone compromising the data on the server (sometimes called "poisoning" the data) and hackers seizing control of the exposed server process, allowing the hijacked server to have unauthorized access to other system files.

This section covers some of the more common methods for securing the BIND server.

Sending BIND to Jail

Before we dive into putting the named server in a "jail," there are two things you should understand: what a jail is and why you would lock up the BIND server.

Traditionally, the **named** process ran as the root user, but this is rare on modern Linux distributions where the **named** process normally runs as the "named" user. This type of user is also known as a service account:

```
[root@onecoursesource ~]# ps -fe | grep named
root       9608  9563  0 17:35 pts/3     00:00:00 grep --color=auto named
named     19926     1  0 Nov30 ?         00:00:07 /usr/sbin/named -u named
```

Running as a non-root user is much better than running as the root user because the capability of the **named** process to make critical changes to the operating system is limited. However, there are still some security concerns when the **named** process runs as a non-root user.

To begin with, think about the fact that the **named** process is going to be interacting with network-based connections when it handles incoming DNS queries. Any time a process is network accessible, there is the potential that this process may be vulnerable to a hijack attack. In this type of attack, a user on a remote system takes control of the local process. Once this user has control, they can access the local system, including viewing or modifying files.

The danger is limited when a hijacked process runs as a non-root user. However, consider critical system files like the **/etc/passwd** file:

```
[root@onecoursesource ~]# ls -l /etc/passwd
-rw-r--r--. 1 root root 2786 Sep  7 07:46 /etc/passwd
```

Every user on the system, including the named user account, can view the contents of the **/etc/passwd** file because everyone has read permission on this file. Now ask yourself this question: Do you want some unknown hacker to be able to compromise your named server and view the contents of your **/etc/passwd** file (or any system file for that matter)?

The purpose of a chroot jail is to limit access to system files. The named process is placed into a jail, where it can only see files that pertain to BIND. This is accomplished by placing BIND configuration files into a specific subdirectory and starting the **named** process so that it appears that the root of the filesystem is the aforementioned subdirectory (chroot stands for *change root*, as in "change the root of the filesystem for this process").

Security Highlight

Although it is not covered in this chapter, you should be aware of another method to protect system files from processes: SELinux. With SELinux, you can limit which files and directories a process can access, regardless of the user running the process.

Creating the chroot Directory and Files

To start the process of creating a chroot jail, you first need to create directories where all the files are placed:

```
[root@onecoursesource ~]# mkdir -p /chroot/named
[root@onecoursesource ~]# mkdir -p /chroot/named/dev
[root@onecoursesource ~]# mkdir -p /chroot/named/etc
[root@onecoursesource ~]# mkdir -p /chroot/named/var/named
[root@onecoursesource ~]# mkdir -p /chroot/named/var/run
```

You may be wondering what all these directories are used for. The following list describes the purpose of each of these directories:

- **/chroot/named/dev**: The location of the device files needed by the **named** process.
- **/chroot/named/etc**: The location of the **named.conf** file. Depending on your current configuration, you may also need to create additional files and subdirectories under the **/chroot/named/etc** directory, such as the **/chroot/named/etc/named** directory. Look at the current contents of the **/etc** directory on your system to see what else might need to be created.
- **/chroot/named/var/named**: The location where the zone files are placed.
- **/chroot/named/var/run**: The location where the **named** process stores data, such as the PID of the process.

In the next step, you copy the files from your current configuration into the new locations:

```
[root@onecoursesource ~]# cp -p /etc/named.conf /chroot/named/etc
[root@onecoursesource ~]# cp -a /var/named/* /chroot/named/var/named
[root@onecoursesource ~]# cp /etc/localtime /chroot/named/etc
```

The preceding commands assume a fairly standard DNS configuration. You may need to copy additional files, depending on customization to the DNS server.

Next, make sure all the new files are owned by the named user and group accounts (although if you use the **-p** and **-a** options with all the aforementioned **cp** commands, the following **chown** command won't be necessary):

```
[root@onecoursesource ~]# chown -R named:named /chroot/named
```

Finally, you need to create a couple of device files:

```
[root@onecoursesource ~]# mknod /chroot/named/dev/null c 1 3
[root@onecoursesource ~]# mknod /chroot/named/dev/random c 1 8
[root@onecoursesource ~]# chmod 666 /chroot/named/dev/*
```

Configuring named to Start in the Jail

After creating and copying all the appropriate files and directories, you need to configure the **named** process to start in a chrooted jail. How you do this may depend on your distribution. The following example should work on most Red Hat–based systems:

```
[root@onecoursesource ~]# more /etc/sysconfig/named
# BIND named process options
-t /chroot/named
```

The **–t** option to the **named** command places the **named** service in a chrooted jail. After making this change to the **/etc/sysconfig/named** file, restart your **named** service.

NOTE If you want to practice creating a chroot jail, use an older distribution, such as CentOS 5.x. Modern distributions provide a package named **bind-chroot** that automatically configures a chroot jail for BIND.

If that package is available, it is considered the recommended (and much easier) way to create a chrooted jail for BIND. However, if this package is not available, then you should know how to create a chroot jail manually. Additionally, the techniques used by the **bind-chroot** package are similar to the manual method, so by understanding the manual method, you will have a better understanding of the **bind-chroot** package.

Split BIND Configuration

To understand a split DNS server configuration, you first should understand why you would want to configure this sort of setup in the first place. Consider the situation in which you have three "public facing" servers:

- www.onecoursesource.com
- ftp.onecoursesource.com
- secure.onecoursesource.com

In this situation, you want any machine on the Internet to be able to query your DNS server for domain-name-to-IP-address resolution for these three machines. But, suppose you had other hosts within your company not intended for external access. This could include systems with domain names such as sales.onecoursesource.com, test.onecoursesource.com, and eng.onecoursesource.com.

These systems may be behind a firewall that prevents access from outside your private network. Or, they may have private IP addresses and can only access the Internet via NAT (Network Address Translation). In other words, while you want users within your organization to be able to perform DNS queries for these internal domain names (as well as the external facing systems), there is no reason for these internal systems to be accessible outside your private network. The solution: a split DNS.

You can actually use a couple of different techniques to create this split DNS environment:

- **Use DNS views**: With the **view** statement (placed in the **/etc/named.conf** file), you can have your DNS server respond to DNS queries based on where the query originates. For example, you can have one view for the internal network that uses a zone file containing all the DNS records and another view for the external network that uses a zone file that contains only a few of the DNS records (the external facing systems). Views are an easy way to create a split DNS.
- **Use two DNS servers**: This method is more secure because you create two DNS master servers: a private one with a complete zone file and a public one with a partial zone file. It is more secure because if the **named** process of the external DNS server is compromised (hijacked), those private domain names and IP addresses are not exposed. With views, that data would be available because the **named** process could view any zone file because it is readable for the **named** process.

The configuration of a split DNS using two servers is not complicated. The concept will likely be more challenging, so an example is provided with more detail. To begin with, Figure 20-4 shows an internal network (the grey box) and an external network (the white box). The systems mentioned earlier are also shown in the network they belong in (www = www.onecoursesource.com, for example).

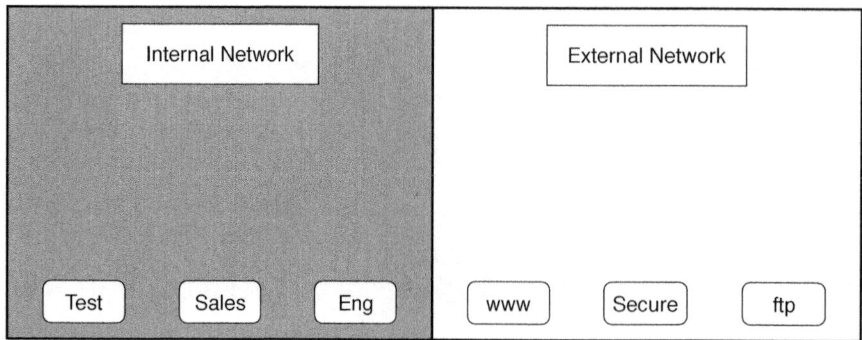

Figure 20-4 *Internal and External Networks*

Next, we introduce two DNS servers: in-ns.onecoursesource.com and ex-ns.onecoursesource.com. The in-ns name server zone file contains both the private and public domain names, and the ex-ns name server zone file contains only the public domain names. Of course, the private network needs to communicate with the outside world, so the router (which could also act as a firewall or NAT system) is also added to the diagram. See Figure 20-5 for a visual example.

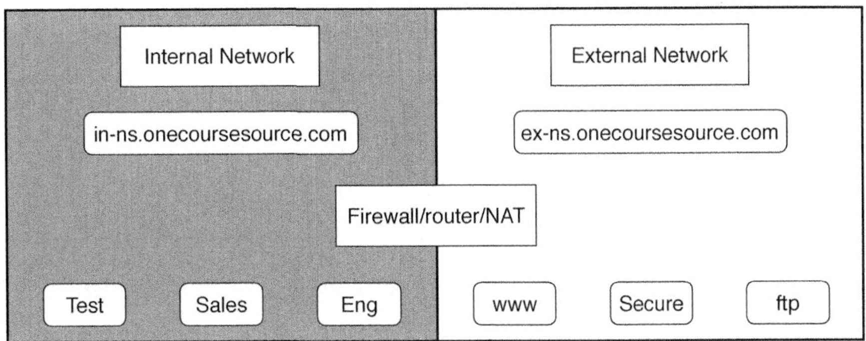

Figure 20-5 *Internal and External Name Servers*

You could also take one additional step. It is common in a scenario like this to have the internal DNS server use the external DNS server as the forwarder. Recall that the forwarder is placed in the **/etc/named.conf** file and is used in cases where the DNS server doesn't have the answer to the query in its zone files.

For example, suppose someone in the internal lookup performs a query for www.sample.com. This domain name is not in the zone files for the in-ns.onecoursesource.com DNS server. It needs to be forwarded to either the top-level (root) servers or to another DNS server.

Why forward this to the external server? Keep in mind you are trying to hide the internal IP address and domain names from the external network. Even a forward query from the internal DNS server can provide a potential security leak, as external DNS servers will be made aware of your internal DNS server. By funneling the request through your external DNS server, you make your internal DNS server a bit more secure.

Security Highlight

We did not provide a full example of configuring a split DNS because once you understand the concept, it is easy to set up. Just use the information that you learned from the previous sections in this chapter to create your internal DNS server. Copy these files to your external DNS server and remove the private address and pointer records from the zone files. After both DNS servers are working, add a **forwarder** statement in the **options** statement of the **/etc/named.conf** file on your internal server, and have it point to the external server.

Have your internal systems point to the internal DNS server (by using the **nameserver** setting in the **/etc/resolv.conf** file) and share the external DNS server with the world.

Transaction Signatures

Previously in this chapter, the concepts of DNS master and slave servers were discussed. Recall that both types of DNS servers can respond to DNS queries, but the master server is the system where you make direct changes to the zone files. The slave servers copy this information into their zone files through a process called a *zone transfer*.

Limiting what machines can initiate a zone transfer was also covered briefly. The **allow-transfer** setting can be applied either to a specific zone (by placing **allow-transfer** in the zone setting of the

/etc/named.conf file) or to the entire master server (by placing **allow-transfer** in the options setting of the **/etc/named.conf** file). By limiting which systems can perform a zone transfer, you are creating a more secure environment. If any system could perform a zone transfer, it would be easy for a potential hacker to gather a list of all the domain names and IP addresses within your domain. This would make it easier for the hacker to find machines to probe.

Another potential security risk can exist in the DNS system. It may be possible for a fake DNS server to provide incorrect data when a query is performed. This is known as *DNS cache poisoning* or *DNS spoofing*. The concern here is that the domain-name-to-IP-address translation of a sensitive system (like a bank's website) could point to a rogue server designed to capture user names and passwords.

Security Highlight

One example of DNS cache poisoning is the Great Firewall of China (also called the Golden Shield Project). This project was designed and implemented by the Ministry of Public Security of the government of China. One of the goals of this project is to prevent Chinese citizens from accessing websites deemed "inappropriate." This is accomplished by DNS cache poisoning; DNS servers within China do not provide the correct IP addresses for domain names associated with what the Chinese government deems as inappropriate websites.

The Great Firewall cache poisoning is not always limited to people in China. In 2010, these invalid DNS responses "escaped" from China and were found on many DNS caching servers in the United States.

There is a way to limit the likelihood of DNS cache poisoning: use transaction signatures (TSIG). With TSIG, private and public digital signatures are used to ensure that DNS data is coming from the correct source. This technology can be used to verify zone transfers as well as DNS queries. The most common way to implement TSIG for DNS is to use Domain Name System Security Extensions (DNSSEC).

The dnssec-keygen Command

To use DNSSEC, you first need to create a private key and a public key. This is accomplished by first switching to the directory that contains the zone files (**/var/named**, for example) and then executing the **dnssec-keygen** command. Here's an example:

```
[root@onecoursesource ~]# cd /var/named
[root@onecoursesource named]# dnssec-keygen -a RSASHA1 -b 768
➥-n ZONE sample.com
Generating key pair.....++++++++ ........++++++++
Ksample.com.+005+05451
```

Note that the **dnssec-keygen** command may appear to hang (freeze), especially on a system that has been recently booted, is not very active, or is virtualized. This is because the command makes use of data from the **/dev/random** file, a file that contains random data derived from system activity, such as mouse movement, disk movement, or keyboard strokes.

You can speed up the process by performing these sorts of operations, but that may require significant mouse movements or banging on the keyboard. A quick way to populate the **/dev/random** file is by using the following **rngd** command:

```
rngd -r /dev/urandom -o /dev/random -b
```

After you execute the **dnssec-keygen** command, there are two new files in the current directory:

```
[root@onecoursesource named]# ls K*
Ksample.com.+005+05451.key  Ksample.com.+005+05451.private
```

The **Ksample.com.+005+05451.key** file contains the public key. This file should be provided to other DNS servers, such as the DNS slave servers. There isn't a method within DNS that allows you to transfer this file to other systems, so you should use another technology, such as Secure Shell.

The **Ksample.com.+005+05451.private** file contains the private key. It is used to generate a digitally signed zone file.

The dnssec-signzone Command

The zone file used when DNSSEC is implemented is not the standard zone file. Instead, a digitally signed zone file is used. This digitally signed zone file is created using the private key generated by the **dnssec-keygen** command, and the digital signature can only be verified by the public key generated by the **dnssec-keygen** command.

To create this encrypted zone file, create a plain-text zone file first and then use the **dnssec-signzone** command to generate the encrypted file (note that on your distribution, you may need to use the **-S** option for smart signing):

```
[root@onecoursesource named]# dnssec-signzone -o sample.com
➥named.sample.com Ksample.com.+005+15117
```

The result is a new file named **named.sample.com.signed**, which you should now use as the zone file for the domain.

Security Highlight

There is more to this process than described in this book. For example, you should make sure you have some additional settings in the **/etc/named.conf** file (such as the **dnssec-enable** setting). The focus of this section is the concepts behind the **dnssec-keygen** and **dnssec-signzone** commands.

DHCP Server

DHCP (Dynamic Host Configuration Protocol) gives you the ability to dynamically assign network-related information to client systems. This information can include providing a system with an IP address, subnet mask, and DNS server information.

DHCP is especially important in any network where hosts are mobile (for example, laptops, tablets, and cell phones). These devices are often moved from one network to another, and the owners of these devices want an easy way to connect their devices to the network. Part of that process is assigning IP network information to the devices.

The default installation of most distributions does not include the DHCP server package. (However, the DHCP client package is almost always installed by default.) The package name can vary between distributions. Common DHCP server package names include **dhcp**, **dhcp-server**, **isc-dhcp-server**, **dhcp3-server**, and **dhcp4-server**.

Note that in most cases, we suggest using virtual machines to practice setting up configurations. However, that poses a bit of a problem with DHCP because typically your Virtual Machine Manager acts as a DHCP server. There are ways around this, but in this case it may be easier to actually use two different physical machines connected to a physical network (not wireless) to practice setting up a DHCP server and client.

WHAT COULD GO WRONG? Do not connect your DHCP server to a network that needs to be used by other systems. Otherwise, your DHCP server might provide incorrect information to those systems. Creating a "rogue" DHCP server can prevent an entire network from functioning correctly.

DHCP Configuration Basics

After installing the correct DHCP server package, you can configure the server by editing the **/etc/dhcpd.conf** file (on some distributions the configuration file may be the **/etc/dhcp/dhcpd.conf** file). Typically, this file is entirely empty or contains only comments, as shown in the following output:

```
[root@onecoursesource ~]# more /etc/dhcpd.conf
#
# DHCP Server Configuration file.
#   see /usr/share/doc/dhcp*/dhcpd.conf.sample
#
```

The sample file that is mentioned within the **/etc/dhcpd.conf** file is useful in putting together an initial **/etc/dhcpd.conf** file. See Example 20-8 for the contents of the sample file.

Example 20-8 *Sample dhcpd.conf File*

```
[root@onecoursesource ~]# more /usr/share/doc/dhcp*/dhcpd.conf.sample
ddns-update-style interim;
ignore client-updates;

subnet 192.168.0.0 netmask 255.255.255.0 {

# --- default gateway
        option routers                  192.168.0.1;
        option subnet-mask              255.255.255.0;

        option nis-domain               "domain.org";
        option domain-name              "domain.org";
        option domain-name-servers      192.168.1.1;

        option time-offset              -18000; # Eastern Standard Time
#       option ntp-servers              192.168.1.1;
#       option netbios-name-servers     192.168.1.1;
# --- Selects point-to-point node (default is hybrid). Don't change this unless
# -- you understand Netbios very well
#       option netbios-node-type 2;

        range dynamic-bootp 192.168.0.128 192.168.0.254;
        default-lease-time 21600;
        max-lease-time 43200;

        # we want the nameserver to appear at a fixed address
        host ns {
                next-server marvin.redhat.com;
                hardware ethernet 12:34:56:78:AB:CD;
                fixed-address 207.175.42.254;
        }
}
```

The file displayed in Example 20-8 has three primary directives, including the **subnet** directive. Within the **subnet** directive are additional option directives, some of which could also be provided as primary directives (sometimes you see these outside the subnet directive, as each can be global network directives).

Some of the directives in the default file shown in Example 20-8 are beyond the scope of this book. The rest of this section focuses on the critical directives.

The ddns-update-style and ignore client-updates Directives

The concept of Dynamic DNS (DDNS) was briefly introduced earlier in this chapter. In the /etc/named.conf file (the configuration file for the DNS server), the allow-update setting is described as follows: "Useful if you decide to implement a DNS feature called Dynamic DNS; this feature allows DHCP servers to update records in the master DNS's zone file."

How this feature is implemented is defined in the **/etc/dhcpd.conf** file by the **ddns-update-style** directive. Four possible values can be set for the **ddns-update-style** directive:

- **none**: Does not attempt to update DNS servers.
- **ad-hoc**: Based on a script language, this is an older method that was retired in DHCP 4.3.0.
- **interim**: Written in C and considered a better solution than **ad-hoc**. Called "interim" because it served as a temporary solution to the shortcomings of **ad-hoc**. It was released as the new Dynamic DNS standards were being written.
- **standard**: The newest technique was released in DHCP 4.3.0. It was designed to incorporate the new standards for DDNS.

DHCP clients can also perform DDNS updates. The **ignore client-updates** directive tells the DHCP server to suggest to the client that it perform the update itself. The **deny client-updates** directive tells the DHCP server to inform the client that it is not permitted to perform its own update.

The subnet Directive

The subnet directive is used to define a network for which the DHCP server provides IP information. There are many possible subdirectives for this directive. The best way of understanding the subnet directive is to see an example that shows the typical minimum subdirectives:

```
subnet 192.168.0.0 netmask 255.255.255.0 {
        option routers                  192.168.0.1;
        option subnet-mask              255.255.255.0;
        option domain-name              "domain.org";
        option domain-name-servers      192.168.1.1;
        range 192.168.0.128 192.168.0.254;
        default-lease-time 21600;
        max-lease-time 43200;
}
```

Each of these directives is described in Table 20-5.

Table 20-5 Components of the **subnet** Directive

Component	Description
subnet 192.168.0.0 netmask 255.255.255.0 { }	The subnet directive starts with a network IP address, the **netmask** keyword, and then the subnet address. The last part of this directive is a collection of subdirectives listed within curly brace characters.

Component	Description
option routers	Defines the router for the DHCP client.
option subnet-mask	Defines the subnet mask for the DHCP client.
domain-name	Defines the domain name for the DHCP client.
domain-name-servers	Defines the DNS servers for the DHCP client.
range	This is the range of IP address that can be handed out to the DHCP clients. Be careful to not include the static IP address assigned to the DHCP server.
default-lease-time	DHCP information is given out to DHCP clients for a period of time. This is called a *DHCP lease*. The default-lease-time tells the client that it is provided a lease of the IP address for a specific period of time; this value is in seconds by default. After this period of time, the client can request a renewal of the lease. If a renewal is not requested, the IP address is released and available for another DHCP client. The client can ask for a longer initial lease time, in which case the default least time is not used. Note: This directive could be placed outside the subnet directive as a directive for the entire DHCP server.
max-lease-time	The maximum period of time a DHCP client can keep the lease. After this period of time, the client must request a new lease and, potentially, receive a new IP address. Note: This directive could also be placed outside the subnet directive as a directive for the entire DHCP server.

Configuring Static Hosts

Suppose you have a user who brings the same laptop to the same network each day. It makes sense to ensure that this laptop gets the same IP address each day. To accomplish this, you define a static host (also known as a reservation) within the subnet directive of the **/etc/dhcpd.conf** file:

```
host julia {
        hardware ethernet 12:34:56:78:AB:CD;
        fixed-address 192.168.0.101;
        option host-name "julia";
}
```

The host directive has a value of the hostname for the system (**"julia"** in the previous example). This hostname could be defined on the client or assigned with the **option host-name** directive. The key to this working is the **hardware ethernet** directive. You must determine the Ethernet (or MAC) address of the client to create this static assignment.

There are a couple of ways to determine this. One is to execute the **ifconfig** command on the client system. The other is to look at the **dhcpd.leases** file on the server (typically located under the **/var** directory structure; the exact location varies). It contains details about DHCP leases that have already been given out. A typical entry in this file looks like the following (which could vary slightly depending on your version of DHCP):

```
lease 192.168.0.101{
    starts 6 2018/12/27 00:40:00;
```

```
    ends 6 2018/12/27 12:40:00;
    hardware ethernet 12:34:56:78:AB:CD;
    uid 01:00:50:04:53:D5:57;
    client-hostname "julia";
}
```


Using the **dhcpd.leases** file to determine the Ethernet address requires the remote machine to first secure a DHCP lease from the server. Another technique is to view the information provided by the **arp** command:

```
[root@onecoursesource ~]# arp
Address          HWtype  HWaddress           Flags Mask    Iface
192.168.1.1      ether   C0:3F:0E:A1:84:A6   C             eth0
192.168.1.101    ether   12:34:56:78:AB:CD   C             eth0
```

DHCP Log Files

In addition to the **dhcpd.leases** file previously mentioned, you should be aware that the DHCP server may store log information either in the **/var/log/messages** file (Red Hat–based systems) or the **/var/log/daemon.log** file (Debian-based systems). Example 20-9 demonstrates a potential DHCP server message. We purposely made a mistake in the configuration file, and when the DHCP server was started, it provided a useful message (see the bold line).

Example 20-9 */var/log/messages Entry*

```
Jan  6 20:26:16 localhost dhcpd: Internet Systems Consortium DHCP Server V3.0.5-RedHat
Jan  6 20:26:16 localhost dhcpd: Copyright 2004-2006 Internet Systems Consortium.
Jan  6 20:26:16 localhost dhcpd: All rights reserved.
Jan  6 20:26:16 localhost dhcpd: For info, please visit http://www.isc.org/sw/dhcp/
Jan  6 20:26:16 localhost dhcpd: Address range 192.168.1.128 to 192.168.1.254 not on net
➥192.168.0.0/255.255.255.0!
Jan  6 20:26:16 localhost dhcpd:
Jan  6 20:26:16 localhost dhcpd: If you did not get this software from ftp.isc.org, please
Jan  6 20:26:16 localhost dhcpd: get the latest from ftp.isc.org and install that before
Jan  6 20:26:16 localhost dhcpd: requesting help.
Jan  6 20:26:16 localhost dhcpd:
Jan  6 20:26:16 localhost dhcpd: If you did get this software from ftp.isc.org and have not
Jan  6 20:26:16 localhost dhcpd: yet read the README, please read it before requesting help.
Jan  6 20:26:16 localhost dhcpd: If you intend to request help from the
➥dhcp-server@isc.org
Jan  6 20:26:16 localhost dhcpd: mailing list, please read the section on the README about
Jan  6 20:26:16 localhost dhcpd: submitting bug reports and requests for help.
Jan  6 20:26:16 localhost dhcpd:
Jan  6 20:26:16 localhost dhcpd: Please do not under any circumstances send requests for
Jan  6 20:26:16 localhost dhcpd: help directly to the authors of this software - please
Jan  6 20:26:16 localhost dhcpd: send them to the appropriate mailing list as described in
Jan  6 20:26:16 localhost dhcpd: the README file.
Jan  6 20:26:16 localhost dhcpd:
Jan  6 20:26:16 localhost dhcpd: exiting.
```

Email Servers

In this section, you learn techniques to manage email servers—specifically Postfix. Postfix has become the most widely used email server on Linux, with many distributions providing it as the default email server. You will learn features such as configuring email addresses, implementing email quotas, and managing virtual email domains.

Early in the career of one of the authors of this book, he asked a senior administrator to explain SMTP (Simple Mail Transfer Protocol) and sendmail (which at the time was the predominant email server). This senior administrator said, "Just go read RFC 821 and once you understand all of that, I will explain sendmail to you." If you take a look at RFC 821 (actually, you should look at 2821, which defines the more modern ESMTP, Extended SMTP), you will realize that the joke was on the author. This document definitely defines SMTP, but it is not for the faint of heart, nor is it an enjoyable read for a novice administrator.

Fortunately, you do not need to read RFC 821 or 2821 to understand the essentials of SMTP. However, you should realize that basic knowledge of the SMTP protocol is key to understanding how email servers function.

SMTP Basics

As a protocol, SMTP defines how email is transmitted and stored. It is part of the application layer of the TCP/IP protocol, and it provides the set of rules that all email-based programs agree to follow. Simply put: Without SMTP, there would be no email.

To understand SMTP, it is helpful to understand some of the major components to email: the mail user agent (MUA), the mail submission agent (MSA), the mail transfer agent (MTA), and the mail delivery agent (MDA).

- **MUA**: The mail user agent is the client program that the user uses to create email messages. A variety of MUAs are available on Linux, including command-line-based utilities (like mutt), GUI-based programs (like Thunderbird), and web-based interfaces (like SquirrelMail).
- **MSA**: A mail submission agent accepts an email message from the MUA and communicates with an MTA to begin the process of transferring the message to the intended recipient. In most cases, the software program that functions as the MSA also functions as the MTA.
- **MTA:** The mail transfer agent is responsible for accepting the email message from the MUA and sending it to the correct receiving mail server (another MTA). The communication might not be direct because the message may need to pass through a series of MTAs before reaching its final destination. Examples of MTA servers in Linux include Postfix, sendmail, and exim.
- **MDA:** The mail delivery agent takes the message from the MTA and sends it to the local mail spool (typically a file on the hard drive). Typically, MTA servers can also act as MDAs; however, there are programs specifically designed to act as MDAs, such as procmail and maildrop. The advantage of the MDA is that it can be configured to perform operations on the message before sending it to the spool. For example, the MDA can be used as a filter, perhaps to block junk mail.
- **Post Office Protocol (POP) and Internet Message Access Protocol (IMAP)**: These protocols are used by MUAs to retrieve email.

Figure 20-6 presents a visual example of the process of transporting an email message. In this figure, user1 wants to send an email to user2. Working on an MUA, user1 composes and sends the message. The message is sent to the company MSA and then to the company MTA (although these could be the same system). The highlighted box represents multiple possible MTAs between the domain for user1's MTA and the MTA for user2.

Eventually the message arrives at the MTA for user2's domain. From there it could be sent directly to the mail spool (typically a file in **/var/spool** on the mail server), but it may be first sent to the MDA for filtering—hopefully for user1's sake, it makes it past the junk filter! When user2 wants to read new emails, his MUA connects to the POP or IMAP server to download the message.

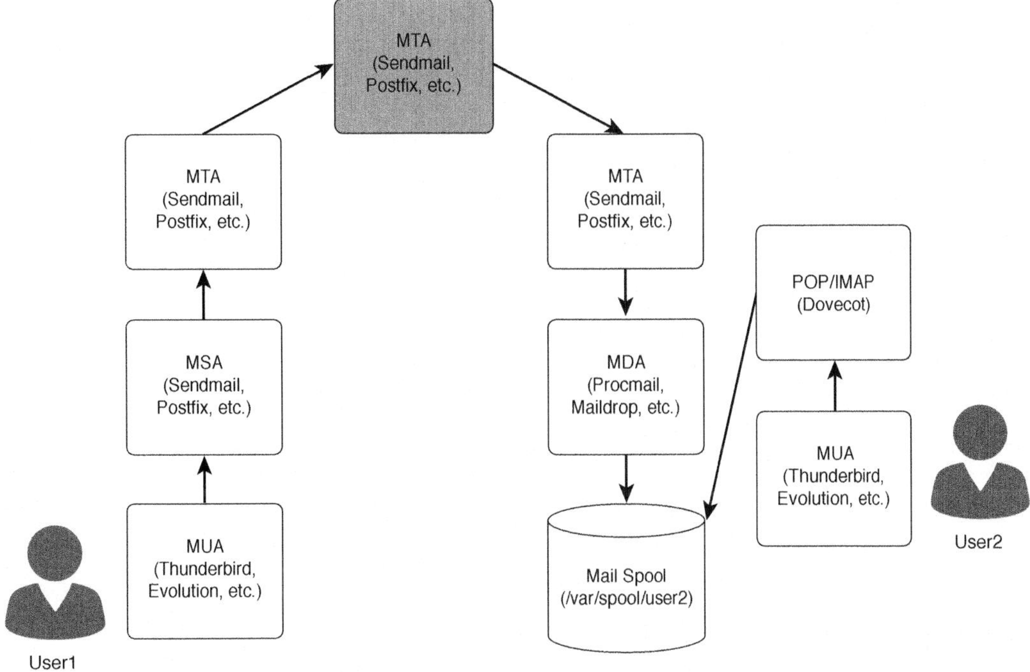

Figure 20-6 *Transporting an Email Message*

WHAT COULD GO WRONG? Keep in mind that there is another important part of the process of sending an email message. The sending MTA must be able to determine which MTA is responsible for receiving the email message. This is handled by the MX records provided by the DNS servers, a topic that was covered earlier in this chapter.

Configuring Postfix

For many years the sendmail server was the standard SMTP server in both UNIX and Linux. Many argue that the standard is now Postfix, with sendmail relegated to older systems or esoteric distributions.

NOTE Although most of the changes you make to Postfix will be within files in the **/etc** directory, you should be aware that Postfix stores information, such as incoming email messages, in the **/var/spool/postfix** directory. Email messages are initially stored in subdirectories until a filtering process (such as the **qmgr** utility) processes the messages and stores each in the user's spool (a file named after the user's name: **/var/spool/mail/*username***).

Postfix Configuration File

The primary configuration file for postfix is the **/etc/postfix/main.cf** file. The format of the settings in this file is like setting a shell variable:

```
setting = value
```

You can either modify this file by hand or use the **postconf** command to make changes. The **postconf** command has the advantage of providing some basic syntax checking, making it less likely that you will make errors. It also can be used to easily display the current configuration of Postfix.

Normally all settings are displayed by default (the first command here is just to show you how many settings there can be):

```
[root@onecoursesource ~]# postconf |wc -l
816
[root@onecoursesource ~]# postconf | head -5
2bounce_notice_recipient = postmaster
access_map_defer_code = 450
access_map_reject_code = 554
address_verify_cache_cleanup_interval = 12h
address_verify_default_transport = $default_transport
```

As you can see, the **postconf** command displays all configuration settings by default. This includes all the default settings, not just the ones specified in the configuration file. If you only want to see the custom settings defined in the configuration file, use the **-n** option to the **postconf** command, as shown in Example 20-10.

Example 20-10 *The postconf -n Command*

```
[root@onecoursesource ~]# postconf -n
alias_database = hash:/etc/aliases
alias_maps = hash:/etc/aliases
command_directory = /usr/sbin
config_directory = /etc/postfix
daemon_directory = /usr/libexec/postfix
data_directory = /var/lib/postfix
debug_peer_level = 2
debugger_command = PATH=/bin:/usr/bin:/usr/local/bin:/usr/X11R6/bin ddd
➥$daemon_directory/$process_name $process_id & sleep 5
html_directory = no
inet_interfaces = localhost
inet_protocols = all
mail_owner = postfix
mailq_path = /usr/bin/mailq.postfix
manpage_directory = /usr/share/man
mydestination = $myhostname, localhost.$mydomain, localhost
newaliases_path = /usr/bin/newaliases.postfix
queue_directory = /var/spool/postfix
readme_directory = /usr/share/doc/postfix-2.10.1/README_FILES
sample_directory = /usr/share/doc/postfix-2.10.1/samples
sendmail_path = /usr/sbin/sendmail.postfix
setgid_group = postdrop
unknown_local_recipient_reject_code = 550
```

You can also view a specific setting by providing the setting name as a parameter:

```
[root@onecoursesource ~]# postconf inet_interfaces
inet_interfaces = localhost
```

To make a changes, use the **-e** option and the following syntax:

```
[root@onecoursesource ~]# postconf -e inet_interfaces=all
[root@onecoursesource ~]# postconf inet_interfaces
inet_interfaces = all
```

Although it is not perfect, the **postconf** command does include some error checking. For example, it is aware of what legal settings are allowed in the **main.cf** file:

```
[root@onecoursesource ~]# postconf ine_interfaces
postconf: warning: ine_interfaces: unknown parameter
```


Important Postfix Settings

As you can see by running the **postconf** command, the Postfix server has hundreds of possible settings:

```
[root@onecoursesource ~]# postconf |wc -l
816
```

If you are going to administer a companywide Postfix server, you certainly want to explore a lot of these settings. However, for basic Postfix configuration, the settings described in Table 20-6 should be sufficient.

Table 20-6 Essential Postfix Settings

Setting	Description
myhost	A fully qualified hostname for the system. Normally you do not need to set this because the value is derived by Postfix by executing the **hostname** command.
disable_vrfy_command	Should be set to **yes** on publicly accessible Postfix servers to prevent techniques that are used to harvest email addresses (for example, mail.onecoursesource.com).
mydomain	The domain part of the system's hostname. If not set, the value of the **myhostname** setting is used, with the relative hostname removed (for example, onecoursesource.com).
myorigin	If the client system does not provide an outgoing hostname (this is a configuration feature of MUAs), the value of the **myorigin** setting is used. If not set, the value of the **myhostname** setting is used.
inet_interfaces	Which interfaces Postfix should listen on. By default, it is set to **localhost**, which means it only accepts inbound email that originates from the local machine. Set it to **all** or a specific network interface to accept email from outside the local machine.
mydestination	Set to the value of **myhostname** by default, this is a list of the domains or hosts for which Postfix accepts email. Keep in mind that this is a destination address, so setting **mydestination** to onecoursesource.com means Postfix is accepting inbound email for the onecoursesource.com domain.
relay_domains	If you want Postfix to function as a relay (send email to other domains), use this setting followed by a comma-separated list of where Postfix can relay to.
relayhost	In some cases, you may want to send messages to an outbound SMTP server within your organization, rather than have Postfix send them directly onto the Internet. The **relayhost** option accepts the value of this outbound SMTP server.

NOTE After you make changes to the Postfix configuration file, make sure you restart Postfix to have the settings take effect.

Aliases

You may want to configure some email aliases for your Postfix server. For example, the user account on your system may be bob, but you want to have a more descriptive email address, such as bob.smith@onecoursesource.com. You can set up an alias so email that arrives for bob.smith is sent to the bob account by creating an entry in the **/etc/aliases** file similar to the one in Example 20-11.

Example 20-11 *The /etc/aliases File*

```
[root@onecoursesource ~]# head -20 /etc/aliases
#
#  Aliases in this file will NOT be expanded in the header from
#  Mail, but WILL be visible over networks or from /bin/mail.
#
#       >>>>>>>>>>      The program "newaliases" must be run after
#       >> NOTE >>      this file is updated for any changes to
#       >>>>>>>>>>      show through to sendmail.
#

# Basic system aliases -- these MUST be present.
mailer-daemon:  postmaster
postmaster:     root

# General redirections for pseudo accounts.
bin:            root
daemon:         root
adm:            root
lp:             root
sync:           root
shutdown:       root
```

Each line in this file follows this format:

```
alias: local_acount
```

So, to send incoming email for bob.smith to the local account bob, add the following to the **/etc/aliases** file:

```
bob.smithbob
```

Note that in some cases, the **/etc/mail/aliases file** is used. This is more likely on some older distributions using sendmail.

You can also send email to multiple accounts. For example, to have the email for webmaster go to the bob, sue, and nick local accounts, add the following line to the **/etc/aliases** file:

```
webmaster: bob, sue, nick
```

After changing the **/etc/aliases** file, you must run the **newaliases** command. This converts the text-based file into a binary file (the **/etc/aliases.db** file) used by Postfix:

```
[root@onecoursesource ~]# newaliases
[root@onecoursesource ~]# ls /etc/aliases*
/etc/aliases  /etc/aliases.db
```


Postfix Virtual Domains

The **/etc/aliases file** is useful to redirect email to local user accounts. The **/etc/postfix/virtual** file is designed to perform a similar task, but instead of redirecting email just to local accounts, it can be configured to also redirect email to virtual and remote destinations. This can be useful in situations where you have multiple domains or when you want to hide the destination location.

The format of the **/etc/postfix/virtual** file is as follows:

```
inbound_addressrelay.to_address
```

For example, suppose the Postfix server handles inbound email for two domains: example.com and sample.com. The following **/etc/postfix/virtual** file settings may be used:

```
bob@example.combobsmith
bob@sample.combobjones
```

You could also use the following line to forward inbound email for one account to a different account:

```
bob@example.combob@sample.com
```

After making changes to the **/etc/postfix/virtual** file, you must take a few steps for this to work. The first step is to modify **the /etc/postfix/main.cf** file to include the following line:

```
virtual_alias_maps = hash:/etc/postfix/virtual
```

Next, you must convert the text-based **/etc/postfix/virtual** file into a binary file (hence the hash in the previous line) by executing the following command:

```
postmap /etc/postfix/virtual
```

Finally, you need to either restart the Postfix service or reload its configuration files.

Managing Local Email Delivery

This section focuses on the procmail tool. The procmail program is designed to perform filtering of email messages. This can be useful to perform actions like blocking SPAM, redirecting mail to other user accounts, and making copies of the email message and sending them to other accounts.

Although a technique presented previously allows you to redirect mail to other user accounts using aliases, the technique is limited to redirection based on the inbound user's name. With procmail, you can create complex rules that use regular expressions to match data from any part of the email message. As a result, the procmail program provides a much more robust method of filtering inbound email.

Some systems (such as Postfix) do not use procmail but rather have the MTA store the incoming email messages directly in the mail spool. This might lead you to wonder why you should use procmail.

The advantage that procmail has over MTAs is the capability to use rules to perform actions on messages before they are sent to the mail spool. These rules can be anything from simple (redirecting messages from one account to another) to complex (regular expressions pattern matching of the contents of the message).

procmail Basics

It is important to note that procmail is not a typical service started at bootup. Instead, it is a program called by the MTA when needed. The procmail package is installed by default on most distributions and is often enabled for Postfix and sendmail.

One way to determine whether procmail is automatically used by the MTA is to create a simple rule in a user's procmail configuration file, the **$HOME/.procmailrc** file:

```
:0c:
$HOME/mail.backup
```

The previous rule should make a backup of all inbound messages to the **mail.backup** directory in that user's home directory (more details about how this rule works in the next section). As that user (the student user in the following example), create the following backup directory:

```
[student@localhost ~]# mkdir $HOME/mail.backup
```

Now as the root user, send a message to that user account:

```
[root@onecoursesource ~]# mail student
Subject: test
test
EOT
```

The result should be something like the following:

```
[root@onecoursesource ~]# ls /home/student/mail.backup
msg.e1mmB  msg.f1mmB
```

You may wonder how you can read these messages if they are in a different directory. Most mail clients have a means to specify a different directory for the mail spool. For example, using the command-line mail program, you would do the following:

```
[student@localhost ~]$ mail -f mail.backup/msg.e1mmB
Heirloom Mail version 12.5 7/5/10. Type ? for help.
"mail.backup/msg.e1mmB": 1 message 1 unread
>U  1 root                  Sat Jan 16 14:47  19/622   "test"
&
```

So, what if it doesn't work? That just means your MTA is not configured to automatically use procmail. You could configure it to automatically use MTA, but a better solution could be to have users who want to use procmail add the following file to their home directories. (Note: Check the location of procmail on your system, as it may differ from the path specified here.)

```
[student@localhost ~]$ more .forward
| /bin/procmail
```

Why is this better than reconfiguring the MTA? There are a couple of things to take into consideration:

- While you can make a global procmail configuration (the **/etc/procmailrc** file), this is typically only done if you are using procmail as a SPAM filter. Because specific SPAM filter programs are more robust than procmail, procmail is not commonly used for this feature (except on an individual user basis). If there is no valid procmail configuration file, only individual configuration files are used.
- Not all users want to use procmail. Most novice users find the process of creating the rules to be challenging. If the MTA is configured to use procmail and only a handful of users are creating rules, the procmail is called repeatedly for no valid reason.

Security Highlight

As a system administrator, you can place procmail rules in the **/etc/procmailrc** file. However, you should avoid placing any rules that execute external commands. The commands are run as the root user, and that could be used to cause security issues on your system.

So, unless the majority of users are using procmail rules or you are using a global configuration file, it makes sense for users to call procmail via their own **.forward** file. You also provide the users with an easy way to temporarily disable procmail by commenting out that one line from their own **.forward** file.

procmail Rules

The syntax of a **procmail** rule is as follows:

```
:0 [flags] [:[lockfile]]
* [conditions]
Action
```

The **:0** tells procmail that this is the start of a new rule. The **[flags]** are used to modify how the rule matching works. Table 20-7 describes these flags.

Table 20-7 procmail Flags

Flag	Description
H	Match only the header section of the message. This is the default.
B	Match within the body of the message.
D	Case-sensitive matching. (Case-insensitive is the default.)
c	Perform match on the carbon copy (cc).
w	Wait for the action to complete. The action fails; then procmail continues to parse the matching rules.
W	Works like **w** but suppresses the "Program failure" messages.

Some additional filters can be viewed by executing the **procmail -h** command, as shown in Example 20-12.

Example 20-12 *The procmail-h Command*

```
[student@localhost ~]$ procmail -h 2>&1 | tail -12
Recipe flag quick reference:
        H  egrep header (default)       B  egrep body
        D  distinguish case
        A  also execute this recipe if the common condition matched
        a  same as 'A', but only if the previous recipe was successful
        E  else execute this recipe, if the preceding condition didn't match
        e  on error execute this recipe, if the previous recipe failed
        h  deliver header (default)     b  deliver body (default)
        f  filter                       i  ignore write errors
        c  carbon copy or clone message
        w  wait for a program           r  raw mode, mail as is
        W  same as 'w', but suppress 'Program failure' messages
```

The **[:[lockfile]]** is a filename (or a **:** character) that tells the procmail utility which file to use to inform other processes that it is working with a file. This prevents duplicate actions from taking place on the same message. In most cases, it is just easy to specify **:** for the lockfile, allowing the procmail utility to pick its own filename.

The **[conditions]** line is used to perform the pattern matching itself. The **[condition]** line must start with an * character to be valid.

The procmail utility uses the **egrep** command to perform pattern matching. You should be aware of the **egrep** command from previous experience; Table 20-8 serves as a reminder of some of the more important pattern matching characters that the **egrep** utility supports.

Table 20-8 The egrep Pattern-Matching Characters

<table>
<tr><th>Character</th><th>Description</th></tr>
<tr><td>*</td><td>Match zero or more of the previous character.</td></tr>
<tr><td>+</td><td>Match one or more of the previous character.</td></tr>
<tr><td>{x,y}</td><td>Match the previous character x to y times.</td></tr>
<tr><td>.</td><td>Match any single character (except the newline character).</td></tr>
<tr><td>[range]</td><td>Match a single character listed within the square brackets.</td></tr>
<tr><td>^</td><td>Match the beginning of a line.</td></tr>
<tr><td>$</td><td>Match the end of a line.</td></tr>
<tr><td>|</td><td>Alternation (or operation): this|that.</td></tr>
<tr><td>\n</td><td>Match a newline character.</td></tr>
</table>

To see additional regular expression characters that the **egrep** command supports, view the man page for the **egrep** command.

The last part of the rule is the action. This can be different sorts of actions, including those described in Table 20-9.

Table 20-9 procmail Actions

<table>
<tr><th>Action</th><th>Description</th></tr>
<tr><td>Filename</td><td>This can be either a filename or a directory name. If it is a directory name, it tells the procmail utility which directory to store the message in.

The file or directory name can be an absolute path or relative to the $MAILDIR variable. Other variables, such as $HOME, can also be used.

There are two formats that messages can be stored in: mbox and Maildir. The default is mbox, but you can have the procmail utility store the message in Maildir format by providing a / character to the end of the path.</td></tr>
<tr><td>Another program</td><td>You can have the message sent to another program by using the following syntax:

<code>|program_name</code></td></tr>
<tr><td>Email address</td><td>To send the message on to another email address, use the following syntax:

<code>~email_address</code></td></tr>
</table>

Action	Description

Nested block	You can place a rule within a rule. For example, what if you want to perform a complex match that includes matching something specifically within the header and then something else within the body of the message. This would require two separate rule sets. You can place the second set as part of the action by using the following syntax:
	`:0 [flags] [:[lockfile]]`
	`* [conditions]`
	`{`
	`    :0 [flags] [:[lockfile]]`
	`    * [conditions]`
	`    action`
	`}`

20

procmail Examples

To understand procmail rules, it helps to see some examples. The following example sorts all mail messages sent to bob and places those in the **bobfile** directory:

```
:0:
* ^TObob
bobfile
```

The next rule is more complex. The rule in Example 20-13 matches any message from support that contains "reboot" in the subject line. If the match occurs, a copy of the message is sent to bo@onecoursesource.com and the message is stored in the **$MAILDIR/support-reboot** directory.

Example 20-13 *Complex procmail Rule*

```
:0:
* ^From.*support.*
* ^Subject:.*reboot.*
{
   :0 c
   ! bo@onecoursesource.com

   :0
   support-reboot
}
```

NOTE Putting together good rules requires knowing regular expressions really well. It also requires a lot of testing and a decent amount of patience!

mbox and Maildir Formats

Two different formats are used to store mail messages: mbox and Maildir. The mbox format has been the standard format used by MTAs for quite some time. In this format, all the mail for the user is stored in a single file, typically located in the **/var/spool/mail** directory. Each user has a file named after their user name. Thus, the user bob would have a single mail file named **/var/spool/mail/bob**.

When a new massage is sent to the MTA to the user bob, the MTA locks the **/var/spool/mail** file and appends the message to the end. The file is unlocked when the process is complete.

The nice thing about the single file format is that a user can search all of their messages using a utility like the **grep** command. I have done this myself to find a particular message that seemed to have mysteriously disappeared when I downloaded it to my email client.

The problem with this single file format is that the locking process sometimes causes issues. There is also the potential for the file to become corrupted, resulting in the loss of all the email messages.

By default, Postfix writes to mbox format, although it can be configured to write to Maildir format. With the Maildir format, a directory is created for each user who receives email. This directory contains three subdirectories: **new**, **cur**, and **temp**.

The Maildir format is considered faster, and if you know the **grep** command well you can still search for messages in the directory structure.

You should know that the procmail utility understands both formats, as does the Dovecot program (an MDA), which is discussed in the next section.

Remote Email Delivery

Recall the way that an email message travels from the originating system to the destination by reviewing Figure 20-6 earlier in this chapter. Servers like Postfix act as MTAs (mail transmission agents), and the primary focus of these servers is to transmit an email message from one domain to another. MTAs are referred to as push servers because the sending MTA actively “pushes” the message from the origin to the destination.

Once the message has arrived and gone through the filter process (recall the **procmail** program), the message is placed on the mail spool. It sits in the mail spool until the user’s MUA (mail user agent) requests the message be sent. This request is sent to the server’s MDA (mail delivery agent) either using the POP or IMAP protocol. Because the request originates from the client, the MDA is referred to as a *pull server*.

IMAP and POP Essentials

To administer an MDA server, you want to have a basic understanding of the POP and IMAP protocols. The knowledge level is similar to what you should know about SMTP when administering an MTA server: You do not necessarily need to be an expert, but you should understand the essentials.

In some ways, understanding IMAP and POP is more important than understanding SMTP because you have the option to have the MDA server use one or the other (or both). Both are designed to allow an MUA to request access to email messages, but there are differences that could make one protocol better in certain situations than the other protocol.

Table 20-10 provides a summary of the major differences between the two protocols.

Table 20-10 IMAP versus POP

Feature	POP	IMAP
Ease of implementation	POP is generally considered a simpler protocol, resulting in an easier implementation.	IMAP is more complex, and this results in a more difficult implementation.

Feature	POP	IMAP
Message handling	By default, most POP servers delete the mail message after it has been downloaded by the MUA. The advantage of this is less disk space usage on the mail server. However, this also means potential loss of the message if deleted on the MUA.	By default, most IMAP servers leave a copy of the message on the server. The MUA receives a copy of the message to be stored locally.
Folders (mailboxes)	POP has no concept of folders.	IMAP supports the feature of folders or mailboxes and allows the client to perform operations such as creating, renaming, or deleting mailboxes.
Connection	Only one client can be currently connected to the mailbox.	Allows multiple simultaneous connections.
Retrieval	All of the message is retrieved.	Individual parts of the message can be retrieved separately.

The Dovecot Server

Dovecot supports both the IMAP and POP protocols. Dovecot also supports both types of mailboxes: mbox and Maildir.

More than likely, you should have the Dovecot server installed on your distribution because this package is the standard MDA for most distributions. The Dovecot server is configured by modifying the primary configuration file, the **/etc/dovecot/dovecot.conf** file.

One of the nice features of Dovecot is the capability to see a clean configuration by executing the **dovecot -n** command, as shown in Example 20-14. Instead of reading through the configuration file, you can see the current settings by executing this command. This is useful because much of the **/etc/dovecot/dovecot.conf** file consists of commands. Also, the configuration files in the **/etc/dovecot/conf.d** directory are also included, making it difficult to see the full picture that the **dovecot -n** command provides.

Example 20-14 *The dovecot -n Command*

```
[root@onecoursesource ~]# dovecot -n
# 2.2.10: /etc/dovecot/dovecot.conf
# OS: Linux 3.10.0-229.14.1.el7.x86_64 x86_64 CentOS Linux release 7.1.1503 (Core)
mbox_write_locks = fcntl
namespace inbox {
  inbox = yes
  location =
  mailbox Drafts {
    special_use = \Drafts
  }
  mailbox Junk {
    special_use = \Junk
  }
  mailbox Sent {
    special_use = \Sent
  }
  mailbox "Sent Messages" {
    special_use = \Sent
```

```
    }
    mailbox Trash {
      special_use = \Trash
    }
    prefix =
  }
  passdb {
    driver = pam
  }
  ssl = required
  ssl_cert = </etc/pki/dovecot/certs/dovecot.pem
  ssl_key = </etc/pki/dovecot/private/dovecot.pem
  userdb {
    driver = passwd
  }
```

Most of the default Dovecot configuration file consists of comments that explain the more important settings. The format for these settings is the standard *setting=value*; however, there is a twist because the value can actually be multiple values and there can be subsettings that override default settings for specific values when a value is followed by a set of curly braces (**{}**). If you look at Example 20-14 again, you can see this by looking at the namespace setting.

There are many possible settings for the Dovecot server. Table 20-11 describes some of the most important settings.

Table 20-11 Dovecot Settings

Setting	Description
protocols	Describes which protocols to support. Example: **protocols = imap pop3**.
listen	Defines which local network interface to listen to for inbound requests. A value of * means all IPv4 interfaces. A value of :: means all IPv6 interfaces. To specify both, separate them by a comma (**listen = *, ::**). Example: **listen = 192.168.1.100**.
base_dir	The location of where Dovecot stores its data. This is not typically changed.
!include	Include the configuration files in the specified directory. Example: **!include conf.d/*.conf**. See more details about this setting later in this section.
mail_location	If you store the mailboxes in a standard place, Dovecot is likely to find them. However, if you choose a custom location, you may need to use this setting. Here are some examples: **mail_location = maildir:~/Maildir** **mail_location = mbox:~/mail:INBOX=/var/mail/%u** **mail_location = mbox:/var/mail/%d** The **%char** values are as follows: ■ **%u**: Username ■ **%n**: User part of user@domain ■ **%d**: Domain part of user@domain ■ **%h**: User's home directory

It is important to understand how the **!include** setting works. First, do not be thrown off by that **!** character, which makes it seem like the setting should mean "do not include." The **!** character is supposed to be there, and it does mean include.

Second, having this **include** directory provides a good way of breaking the settings into categories. The following is an example of the files that you may see in the **include** directory:

```
[root@onecoursesource ~]$ ls /etc/dovecot/conf.d
10-auth.conf        20-imap.conf                 auth-dict.conf.ext
10-director.conf    20-lmtp.conf                 auth-ldap.conf.ext
10-logging.conf     20-pop3.conf                 auth-master.conf.ext
10-mail.conf        90-acl.conf                  auth-passwdfile.conf.ext
10-master.conf      90-plugin.conf               auth-sql.conf.ext
10-ssl.conf         90-quota.conf                auth-static.conf.ext
15-lda.conf         auth-checkpassword.conf.ext  auth-system.conf.ext
15-mailboxes.conf   auth-deny.conf.ext           auth-vpopmail.conf.ext
```

The concept is that if you want to make a configuration setting concerning how IMAP works, you would modify the **/etc/dovecot/conf.d/20-imap.conf** file. This can be a great system, but it can also lead to problems. For example, if you make a change to the **/etc/dovecot/dovecot.conf** file that affects IMAP, it would take precedence over a setting in the **20-imap.conf** file if it appears after the **!include** setting in the **/etc/dovecot/dovecot.conf** file. But, if it appears before the **!include** setting, the value provided by the **20-imap.conf** file would be applied.

Also, the numbers in front of the files in the **/etc/dovecot/conf.d** directory provide an order. This can cause confusion and misconfigurations if you are not careful.

If you want to have a single configuration file, but changes have already been made to the settings in the configuration files in the **/etc/dovecot/conf.d** directory, the easy way to handle this is to execute the following commands:

```
[root@onecoursesource ~]$ cp /etc/dovecot/dovecot.conf
➥/etc/dovecot/dovecot.conf.backup
[root@onecoursesource ~]$ doveconf -n > /etc/dovecot/dovecot.conf
```

The result of the previous commands is to make a backup of the original configuration file and then override the **dovecot.conf** file with the current configuration settings.

Note that you can use the **telnet** command for basic testing of a POP server, as shown in Example 20-15.

Example 20-15 *Testing with **telnet***

```
[root@onecoursesource ~]# telnet localhost 110
Trying 127.0.0.1...
Connected to localhost.localdomain (127.0.0.1).
Escape character is '^]'.
+OK Dovecot ready.
user student
+OK
pass student
+OK Logged in.
retr 1
+OK 537 octets
Return-Path: <root@localhost.example.com>
X-Original-To: student@localhost
Delivered-To: student@localhost.example.com
```

```
Received: from example.com (localhost.localdomain [127.0.0.1])
        by ldap.example.com (Postfix) with SMTP id 6575F11802F
        for <student@localhost>; Sun, 31 Jan 2019 15:36:34 -0800 (PST)
Subject: Sending a message without a MUA
Message-Id: <20160131233644.6575F11802F@ldap.example.com>
Date: Sun, 31 Jan 2019 15:36:34 -0800 (PST)
From: root@localhost.example.com
To: undisclosed-recipients:;

Body of message
```

Summary

In this chapter you explored how to configure several important network services. You learned how to correctly set up and secure BIND DNS servers and how to configure DHCP servers. You also learned how to configure a variety of email servers, including Postfix, procmail, and Dovecot.

Key Terms

push server, pull server, mail spool, mbox, Maildir, SMTP, ESMTP, MUA, MSA, MDA, POP, IMAP, DHCP, static hosts, Domain Name Service (DNS), fully qualified domain name (FQDN), subdomain, name server, authoritative name server, record, caching, name server, forward lookup, reverse lookup, DNS forwarder, Berkeley Internet Name Domain (BIND), root servers, DNS master, DNS slave, zone transfer, forward DNS lookup, reverse DNS lookup, time to live (TTL)

Review Questions

1. Which of the following would you find in a zone file?

   A. The **directory** setting

   B. The A record

   C. The **dump-file** setting

   D. The **recursion** setting

2. Which type of name server returns results based on original records stored locally on the system?

   A. Caching name server

   B. Forwarder name server

   C. Authoritative name server

   D. Local name server

3. A _____ file is used to store IP-address-to-domain-name translation information (also called "records").

4. Fill in the blank to create a master DNS server entry in the **/etc/named.conf** file:

```
zone "onecoursesource.com" {
type master;
_____ "named.onecoursesource.com";
};
```

5. Which of the following zone files should you see in the **/var/named** directory by default? (Choose two.)

   A. **/var/named/named.ca**

   B. **/var/named/sample.com**

   C. **/var/named/named.localhost**

   D. **/var/named/localhost.ca**

6. Which of the following settings allows for a zone transfer when placed in the appropriate place within the **/etc/named.conf** file?

   A. **allow-query**

   B. **allow-zone**

   C. **allow-zone-transfer**

   D. **allow-transfer**

7. Which of the following directives tells the DHCP server to suggest to the client that it perform the update itself?

   A. **allow client-updates**

   B. **permit client-updates**

   C. **ignore client-updates**

   D. **avoid client-updates**

8. The _____ directive is used to define a network that the DHCP server provides IP information for.

9. Which of the following is an example of an MDA?

   A. mailget

   B. mailserv

   C. Dovecot

   D. procmail

10. Which part of the following procmail rule is used to specify the lockfile name?

```
:0:
* ^TObob
bobfile
```

   A. The first **:** character

   B. The second **:** character

   C. **bobfile**

   D. None of the above

Network Service Configuration: Web Services

One of the most common server types is a web server. By most estimates, there are over 100 million web servers directly attached to the Internet, but there are certainly many more used internally within corporate and government organizations.

Because most of these web servers are accessible directly through the Internet, security is paramount. In this chapter, you not only learn how to configure a popular Linux web server (the Apache Hypertext Transfer Protocol Server), but you learn how to enable important security features.

This chapter also introduces you to proxy servers. Proxy servers are used for several reasons, including to speed up access to data and to provide an extra layer of security to servers (including web servers). You learn the basics of proxy servers and how to configure two of the more popular proxy servers.

After reading this chapter and completing the exercises, you will be able to do the following:

Configure an Apache Web Server

Enable security features on Apache Web Servers

Configure a proxy server

Apache Web Server

Typically, when people say they installed Apache on their system, they are referring to the web server provided by the Apache Software Foundation. This organization actually provides many open source projects, but because it is most famously known for the Apache Hypertext Transfer Protocol Server, the term "Apache" in software terms has become synonymous with this web server (we typically refer to it as the Apache Web Server). It is also commonly referred to as "httpd," as that is normally the name of the web server process.

Hypertext Transfer Protocol (HTTP, or simply *hypertext*) is a protocol that has been a standard for web pages since the 1990s. This protocol allows for a client program (web browser) to request data from a server program (the httpd process, for example). Often this data is formatted by a markup language called Hypertext Markup Language (HTML), which is in turn converted into a human-readable web page.

Before you start to configure the Apache Web Server, you first need to search for the location of the primary configuration file. Depending on your distribution, this file should be located in one of the following directories:

- **/etc/apache**
- **/etc/apache2**
- **/etc/httpd**
- **/etc/httpd/conf**

For example, on an Ubuntu system, the configuration file is located under the **/etc/apache2** directory, while on a CentOS system it is located under the **/etc/httpd/conf** directory. Even the main configuration filename can vary from one distribution to another. For example, it is named **httpd.conf** on CentOS and **apache2.conf** on Ubuntu. As frustrating as this may be, the good news is that regardless of where the configuration file is located, the syntax within the file should be the same.

Basic Apache Web Server Configuration

The default Apache Web Server configuration file consists of comments and directives, which are parameters, and can therefore be assigned values. An example of a portion of an Apache configuration file follows:

```
# ServerRoot: The top of the directory tree under which the server's
# configuration, error, and log files are kept.
#
# Do not add a slash at the end of the directory path. If you point
# ServerRoot at a non-local disk, be sure to specify a local disk on the
# Mutex directive, if file-based mutexes are used. If you wish to share the
# same ServerRoot for multiple httpd daemons, you will need to change at
# least PidFile.
#
ServerRoot "/etc/httpd"
```

Typically, each directive (at least the default directives) is well commented (***#comment***), making it easier to determine the purpose of each directive. There are hundreds of possible directives, some of which are described in more detail later in this chapter. The basic directives that you should be aware of are described in Table 21-1. (Descriptions in comment format are taken directly from the configuration file.)

Table 21-1 Basic Apache Directives

Directive	Description

ServerRoot	`# ServerRoot: The top of the directory tree under which the server's`
	`# configuration, error, and log files are kept.`
	Example: **ServerRoot "/etc/httpd"**

Listen	`# Listen: Allows you to bind Apache to specific IP addresses and/or`
	`# ports, instead of the default. See also the <VirtualHost>`
	`# directive.`
	Example: **Listen 12.34.56.78:80**
	Example: **Listen 80**
	Further discussion on this directive occurs later in this chapter.

DocumentRoot	`# DocumentRoot: The directory out of which you will serve your`
	`# documents. By default, all requests are taken from this directory, but`
	`# symbolic links and aliases may be used to point to other locations.`
	Example: **DocumentRoot "/var/www/html"**

Directive	Description

LogLevel	`# LogLevel: Control the number of messages logged to the error_log.`
	`# Possible values include: debug, info, notice, warn, error, crit,`
	`# alert, emerg.`
	Example: **LogLevel warn**
	This can be a critical setting when your web server is not performing correctly. Consider changing the LogLevel to debug and restart your web server. A lot of useful log messages now appear in the log files.

In some cases, directives require multiple values. The syntax for multiple-line directives is a bit different than single-line directives:

```
<Directory />
    AllowOverride All
    Require all granted
</Directory>
```

The **<Directory />** line starts the directive, and it continues until **</Directory>**. In the preceding example, **AllowOverride** and **Require** are also directives (you can consider these subdirectives).

Starting the Apache Web Server

After you install the Apache Web Server software package, you should be able to start the server using the default configuration file. Although it will not serve up useful content, it is good to know that the server is functioning correctly without the need for any changes to the configuration files.

The Apache Web Server process is named **httpd**. You can start this process using either the usual startup scripts or by using the **apache2ctl** (or **apachectl**) program.

After starting the server, you can verify it is responding to requests by opening a web browser on the same machine as the server and typing **localhost** in the URL. The result should be something like what's shown in Figure 21-1.

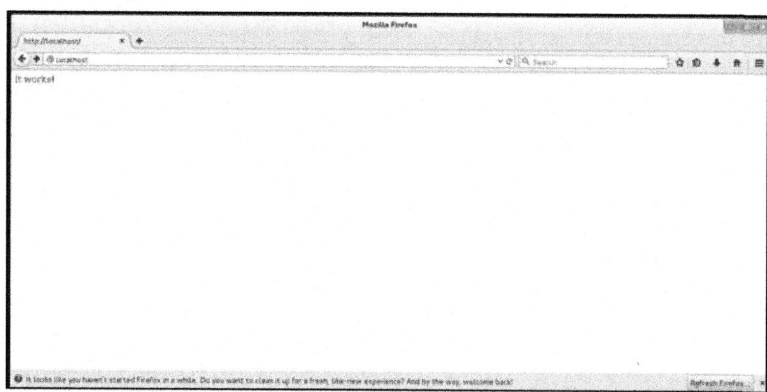

Figure 21-1 *Default Apache Web Page*

By default, the location where web pages reside is the **/var/www/html** directory (you can confirm or change the exact location by looking for the **DocumentRoot** setting in the primary configuration file). After a fresh installation of the Apache software, this directory should be empty. If you want to further test your server's functionality, create a small text file (or HTML if you are familiar with that language) in the **/var/www/html** directory:

```
[root@localhost ~]# echo "testing, 1, 2, 3, testing" > /var/www/html/test
```

Apache Web Server Log Files

Two log files are useful when testing and troubleshooting the Apache Web Server: the **access_log** and the **error_log**. The **access_log** contains information about attempts to access content from the web server. The **error_log** contains messages regarding when problems arise on the web server.

The following demonstrates the last two entries in the **access_log**:

```
[root@localhost ~]# tail -2 /var/log/httpd/access_log
::1 - - [09/Dec/2018:05:02:22 -0800] "GET /tes HTTP/1.1" 404 201 "-"
"Mozilla/5.0 (X11; Linux x86_64; rv:38.0) Gecko/20100101 Firefox/38.0"
::1 - - [09/Dec/2018:05:02:28 -0800] "GET /test HTTP/1.1" 200 26 "-"
"Mozilla/5.0 (X11; Linux x86_64; rv:38.0) Gecko/20100101 Firefox/38.0"
```

Note that in each line, the **"GET"** portion of the line indicates what file was requested. The access_log does not indicate whether the file was actually sent, just that there was a request.

Security Highlight

Many random access attempts could be the result of someone trying to hack into your system or find information about your system. Monitor the access log regularly, especially for "404" errors (which indicate that someone tried to get a web page that does not exist), "403" (or Forbidden) errors, and "401" errors (where access has been denied for security reasons). These are often all examples of probe attacks.

Enable Scripting

You can add features to the Apache Web Server by enabling modules. Many modules come with the default installation of Apache, and others are available on the Internet.

At the very least, you should know how to enable the modules that permit Perl and PHP scripting. These modules allow web developers to create more dynamic web pages by using scripting.

Security Highlight

This is a brief introduction of enabling scripting on web servers. In the real world, you should be careful about implementing scripting because it can allow a hacker to gain unauthorized access to your system. Although you need to know these basics, consider this a topic that you really should explore in more detail before implementing on a live web server.

To enable PHP scripting, take the following steps:

Step 1. Make sure PHP is installed on your system. For example, the following command verifies PHP is installed on a CentOS system (see Chapter 26, "Red Hat–Based Software Management" and Chapter 27, "Debian-Based Software Management," for instructions on how to install software, if necessary):

```
[root@localhost ~]# yum list installed | grep php
php.x86_64                    7.2.3-36.el7_1           @updates
php-cli.x86_64                7.2.3.el7_1              @updates
php-common.x86_64             7.2.3.el7_1              @updates
```

Step 2. Verify that the **libphp7.so** file is in the Apache Web Server module directory. This file should have been installed with the PHP software package. On a CentOS system, the Apache Web Server modules are in the **/etc/httpd/modules** directory:

```
[root@localhost ~]# ls /etc/httpd/modules/*php*
/etc/httpd/modules/libphp7.so
```

Step 3. Configure the Apache Web Server to enable PHP. This can be accomplished by modifying the primary configuration file or by creating a file in the module's **include** directory. For example, on a CentOS system, the following line appears in the primary configuration file:

```
[root@localhost ~]# grep Include /etc/httpd/conf/httpd.conf
Include conf.modules.d/*.conf
    #   Indexes Includes FollowSymLinks SymLinksifOwnerMatch ExecCGI
➥MultiViews
    # (You will also need to add "Includes" to the "Options" directive.)
IncludeOptional conf.d/*.conf
```

And in the **/etc/httpd/conf.modules.d** directory, the following file exists:

```
[root@localhost ~]# cat /etc/httpd/conf.modules.d/10-php.conf
#
# PHP is an HTML-embedded scripting language which attempts to make it
# easy for developers to write dynamically generated webpages.
#
<IfModule prefork.c>
  LoadModule php5_module modules/libphp5.so
</IfModule>
```

Step 4. Restart the Apache Web Server.

Keep in mind that the previous steps should provide basic PHP functionality. There may be additional configuration settings that you want to explore for a real-world Apache Web Server.

How can you tell whether it worked? First, create the following file (name it **hello.php**) in the **DocumentRoot** directory (**/var/www/html** for example):

```
<html>
<head>
<title>PHP Test</title>
</head>
<body>
<?php echo '<p>Hello World</p>'; ?>
</body>
</html>
```

Then test the script by pointing your web browser to the **localhost/hello.php** URL. The result should look like Figure 21-2.

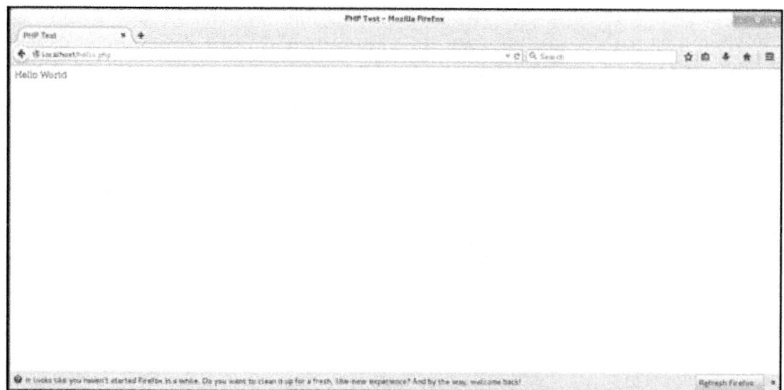

Figure 21-2 *PHP Test Page*

WHAT COULD GO WRONG? The **IfModule prefork.c** directive is used to specify when to load the module. The critical element is the **LoadModule** line, so do not remove this value.

To enable Perl scripting, take the following steps:

Step 1. Make sure the Perl Apache modules are installed on your system. For example, the following command verifies PHP is installed on a CentOS system:

```
[root@localhost ~]# yum list installed | grep mod_perl
mod_perl.x86_64                              2.0.8-10.20140624svn1602105.el7 @epel
```

Step 2. Verify that the **mod_perl.so** file is in the Apache Web Server module directory. This file should have been installed with the mod_perl software package. On a CentOS system the Apache Web Server modules are in the **/etc/httpd/modules** directory:

```
[root@localhost ~]# ls /etc/httpd/modules/*perl*
/etc/httpd/modules/mod_perl.so
```

Step 3. Configure the Apache Web Server to enable Perl. This can be accomplished by modifying the primary configuration file or by creating a file in the module's **include** directory, as shown:

```
[root@localhost ~]# cat /etc/httpd/conf.modules.d/02-perl.conf
#
# Mod_perl incorporates a Perl interpreter into the Apache web server,
# so that the Apache web server can directly execute Perl code.
# Mod_perl links the Perl runtime library into the Apache web server
# and provides an object-oriented Perl interface for Apache's C
# language API. The end result is a quicker CGI script turnaround
# process, since no external Perl interpreter has to be started.
#
LoadModule perl_module modules/mod_perl.so
```

Step 4. Add the following to the primary Apache Web Server configuration file:

```
<Directory /var/www/html/perl>
AllowOverride All
SetHandler perl-script
PerlHandler ModPerl::Registry
PerlOptions +ParseHeaders
Options ExecCGI
Order allow,deny
Allow from all
</Directory>
```

This allows you to place Perl scripts in the **/var/www/html/perl** directory.

Step 5. Restart the Apache Web Server.

How can you tell whether it worked? First, create the following file (name it **hello.pl**) in the **/var/www/html/perl** directory:

```
print "Content-type: text/plain\r\n\r\n";
print "hello\n";
```

Then test the script by pointing your web browser to the **localhost/perl/hello.pl** URL. The result should look like Figure 21-3.

WHAT COULD GO WRONG? On older systems, the required package name may be different (for example, **apache-mod_perl** or **libapache2-mod-perl2**).

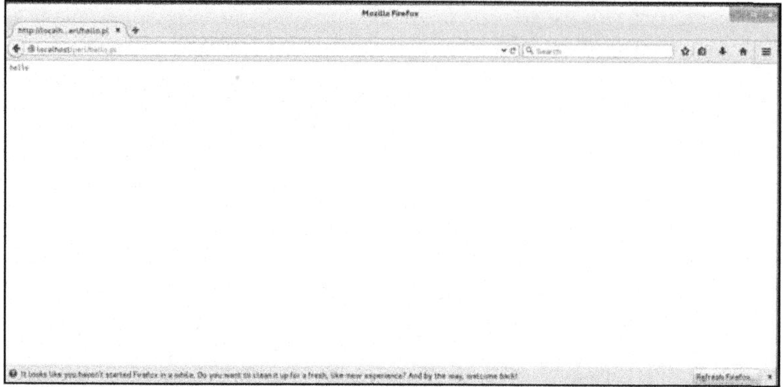

Figure 21-3 *Perl Test Page*

Security Highlight

For security purposes, you may want to use a redirect statement to store Perl scripts in another location. This can be accomplished with an **Alias** directive, as shown here:

```
Alias /perl/ /var/httpd/perl/
```

Now when files under the **/perl** directory on your web server are accessed, the Apache Web Server looks in the **/var/httpd/perl** directory.

Apache Web Server Security

Your company web server is going to be placed on a machine visible to the Internet and all those "bad actors" who would love to take advantage of weak spots. There are many generic ways to secure your web server, including the following:

- Limit the number of user accounts on the system.
- Install only the minimum software required for the system to function correctly.
- Limit which processes are running on the system.
- Secure critical directories and files with permissions (or, perhaps, SELinux, which was covered in Chapter 9, "File Permissions").
- Implement a firewall (discussed in Chapter 31, "Firewalls").

In addition to securing the system, there are settings within the Apache Web Server that help make it more secure.

Essential Settings

In the primary configuration file for the Apache Web Server, you can limit client access by the following settings:

```
StartServers 10
MinSpareServers 5
MaxSpareServers 15
MaxClients 150
MaxRequestsPerChild 5000
```

See Table 21-2 for details regarding these settings.

Table 21-2 Client Restriction Settings for the Apache Web Server

Setting	Description
StartServers	When the Apache Web Server starts, it initially starts a single process owned by the root user. This process never handles client requests. Instead, other processes are started that are owned by the Apache user (or some other non-root account) that handles client requests. This protects the system as processes run because the Apache user has limited access to system files. The **StartServers** setting specifies how many processes that run as the Apache user should be started. See Example 21-1 to see how the **StartServers** setting value of **10** results in multiple **httpd** processes running. The value that you choose for this depends on the web server load. Starting dozens of these processes on a slow web server results in wasted system resources. Not starting enough can have a performance impact when many clients connect to the server.
MinSpareServers	As client requests are made, the **httpd** processes are assigned to handle them. Once an **httpd** process has been assigned to a client, it can't be used for any other clients until it is finished with the client, so new servers need to be started. The **MinSpareServers** directive makes sure that a specific number of **httpd** processes are always available.
MaxSpareServers	If the demand on the Apache Web Server decreases, there could be a bunch of **httpd** processes "sitting around," waiting for client requests. The **MaxSpareServers** directive is used to tell Apache to "kill off" extra servers when not in use.
MaxClients	In a sense, this could be called "MaxServers." Recall that each server handles a client. If the **MaxClients** directive is set to **150**, then a maximum of 150 servers will be started. As a result, the maximum number of clients is also 150.
MaxRequestsPerChild	In a denial of service (DoS) attack, multiple client machines could flood an Apache Web Service with requests. If there are enough of these client machines (as in the number of **MaxClients**), this attack could effectively disable a web server. Setting **MaxRequestPerChild** to a value such as **5000** can limit the effectiveness of a DoS attack.

Example 21-1 *Starting **httpd** Processes*

```
[root@localhost perl]# ps -fe | grep httpd
root      24007     1  2 17:02 ?        00:00:00 /usr/sbin/httpd -DFOREGROUND
apache    24009 24007  0 17:02 ?        00:00:00 /usr/sbin/httpd -DFOREGROUND
apache    24010 24007  0 17:02 ?        00:00:00 /usr/sbin/httpd -DFOREGROUND
apache    24011 24007  0 17:02 ?        00:00:00 /usr/sbin/httpd -DFOREGROUND
apache    24012 24007  0 17:02 ?        00:00:00 /usr/sbin/httpd -DFOREGROUND
apache    24013 24007  0 17:02 ?        00:00:00 /usr/sbin/httpd -DFOREGROUND
apache    24014 24007  0 17:02 ?        00:00:00 /usr/sbin/httpd -DFOREGROUND
apache    24015 24007  0 17:02 ?        00:00:00 /usr/sbin/httpd -DFOREGROUND
apache    24016 24007  0 17:02 ?        00:00:00 /usr/sbin/httpd -DFOREGROUND
```

```
apache    24017 24007  0 17:02 ?        00:00:00 /usr/sbin/httpd -DFOREGROUND
apache    24018 24007  0 17:02 ?        00:00:00 /usr/sbin/httpd -DFOREGROUND
```

User Authentication

On a public web server, you may decide to limit access to specific directories. This can be accomplished by setting an authentication method that requires the client user to know a user name and password. (Note that these are not regular user names, but a user name specifically for the Apache Web Server.)

To use this feature, you need to make sure that the mod_auth module is loaded. This can be loaded from the primary configuration file or in the module's **include** directory.

To secure portions of the website, you need to create a password file. Execute the **htpasswd** command, as shown here:

```
[root@localhost ~]# htpasswd -c /etc/httpd/conf/password bob
New password:
Re-type new password:
Adding password for user bob
```

The **-c** option creates a password file. The argument after the **-c** option is the location of the password file. It should be in a secure location; a good place is under the **/etc/httpd/conf** directory (or wherever the configuration files for the Apache Web Server are stored on your system). The last argument (**bob**) is the user name associated with the password.

You have two places where you can choose to configure security for a specific directory. In the primary configuration file you can add an entry like the following:

```
<Directory /var/www/html/secure>
AuthName "Secure folder"
AuthType Basic
AuthUserFile /etc/httpd/conf/password
Require valid-user
</Directory>
```

Or you can create a file named **.htaccess** within the **/var/www/html/secure** directory. This file would have the following directives:

```
AuthName "Secure folder"
AuthType Basic
AuthUserFile /etc/httpd/conf/password
Require valid-user
```

Virtual Hosts

In some cases, you may want to host more than one website on a single physical machine. If your organization has more than one website that you must administer, having all the servers on a single system can eliminate a lot of administrative work. Additionally, web-hosting companies often have multiple clients share a single physical machine.

To place more than one website on a single machine, you need to use virtual hosting. There are two methods that you can use:

- **IP-based virtual hosts**: With this technique, each web domain has a separate IP address. This means you need to know how to configure multiple IP addresses for a single network interface (a process called IP aliasing) or install multiple network interfaces. The focus of this chapter is how to configure this functionality via the Apache Web Server; however, configuring multiple IP addresses is easy.

- **Name-based virtual hosts**: This technique is the more common of the two. All web domains share a single IP address. When the web server receives a client request, the request itself is used to determine which website to serve up.

Configuring IP-Based Virtual Hosts

For this configuration, the assumption is that your system already has unique IP addresses for the www.example.com and the www.sample.com domains. In the primary Apache Web Server file, you would add the lines shown in Example 21-2.

Example 21-2 *Sample IP-Based Virtual Hosts*

```
<VirtualHost www.example.com>
ServerAdmin webmaster@mail.example.com
DocumentRoot /var/www/example/html
ServerName www.example.com
ErrorLog /var/log/example/error_log
</VirtualHost>

<VirtualHost www.sample.com>
ServerAdmin webmaster@mail.sample.com
DocumentRoot /var/www/sample/html
ServerName www.sample.com
ErrorLog /var/log/sample/error_log
</VirtualHost>
```

Configuring Name-Based Virtual Hosts

For this example, the assumption is that both the www.example.com and www.sample.com domains resolve to the 192.168.1.100 IP address. In the primary Apache Web Server file, you would add the lines shown in Example 21-3.

Example 21-3 *Sample Named-Based Virtual Hosts*

```
NameVirtualHost 192.168.1.100

<VirtualHost 192.168.1.100>
ServerName www.example.com
DocumentRoot /var/www/example/html
</VirtualHost>

<VirtualHost 192.168.1.100>
ServerName www.sample.com
DocumentRoot /var/www/sample/html
</VirtualHost>
```

NOTE Just a reminder that as with many of the topics covered in this book, you are not expected to become an expert at this topic, but rather understand its concepts and some of the configuration options. There are many more details regarding virtual hosts that we could dive into; however, the focus of this book is to provide you with the essentials.

For example, when configuring IP-based virtual hosts, you could choose to set up multiple daemons instead of having one daemon respond to multiple IP addresses.

The point is that that if you really want to be an Apache Web Server administrator, there is a lot more to learn than what we are providing in this book!

Conversational Learning™—IP-Based Versus Name-Based Virtual Hosts

Gary: Hey, Julia. I'm setting up some web servers and I am not sure which technique I should use.

Julia: What do you mean by "which technique"?

Gary: Well, I need to set up three web servers on one system, and I can either use the IP-based method or the name-based method.

Julia: Ah, yes, OK. Well, typically if you are going to be a web server provider and want to host several different websites on a single machine, you would use the IP-based technique.

Gary: Why is that?

Julia: Well, keep in mind that with the IP-based method, you likely only have one network card and you will assign multiple IP addresses to that one network card. This is ideal for a web-hosting organization because they don't want to have to install a bunch of network cards, and each website should have a separate IP address.

Gary: OK, so that would be the best solution then?

Julia: That may depend. Are you planning on these being internal servers or servers available on the Internet?

Gary: Internal only.

Julia: Then you may find that the name-based technique is easier. You only need one IP address on that network card, and you just need to update the name server to have it serve up the same IP address for each domain name or URL.

Gary: OK, that does seem best for this situation. Thanks, Julia.

HTTPS

It's payday! Time for you to log in to your bank's online website and pay those bills. You type in the URL of your bank and notice that the letters "https://" magically appear before the website's name. Previously in this chapter, you were introduced to HTTP (Hypertext Transfer Protocol), but now there is an "s" added to that abbreviation.

HTTPS is a newer, more secure protocol. Most people call this HTTP Secure or HTTP SSL (SSL stands for Secure Sockets Layer, a security-based protocol). HTTPS offers two primary advantages: the identity of the website is authenticated, and the data exchanged between the client (the web browser) and the server (the web server) is more secure because it is encrypted.

NOTE If you look at documentation regarding HTTPS, you will discover that a newer cryptographic protocol called TLS (Transport Layer Security) is also now commonly used. TLS was designed to replace SSL, but the community often refers to TLS as SSL.

While administering the Apache Web Server, you should realize that HTTPS uses port 443, whereas HTTP uses port 80 for network communication.

SSL Essentials

The technique used by SSL is called *asymmetric cryptography* (it is also referred to as *PKC*, or *public key cryptography*). With asymmetric cryptography, two keys are used: a public key and a private key. These keys are used to encrypt and decrypt data.

The public key is used to encrypt the data sent to the Apache Web Server. This key is provided to all systems upon request. For example, when a web browser first connects to an Apache Web Server that is using SSL, the web browser asks for the public key of the server. This public key is freely given to the web browser.

Any additional data sent from the web browser to the server, such as account names and passwords, is encrypted using this public key. This data can only be decrypted by the server using the private key. This is where the term *asymmetric cryptography* comes into play. With *symmetric cryptography* the same key is used to encrypt and decrypt data. Two separate keys are needed when asymmetric cryptography is used: one to encrypt data and the other to decrypt. This means that only the web server can decrypt the data sent by the web browser.

You might be wondering how the web browser really knows that it reached the correct web server and not some "rogue" web server. When the web server sends its public key, it includes a digital signature (also called a *message digest*). This digital signature can be sent to a CA (Certificate Authority) server, a trusted third-party system used to verify the digital signature.

From the user's perspective, all this takes place behind the scenes and is completely transparent—at least until something goes wrong and warning messages are displayed by the web browser. Because digital certificates typically have an expiration date, the most common problem is when the CA does not have an updated digital certificate—or when the user changes the date on their computer!

See Figure 21-4 for a visual example of this process.

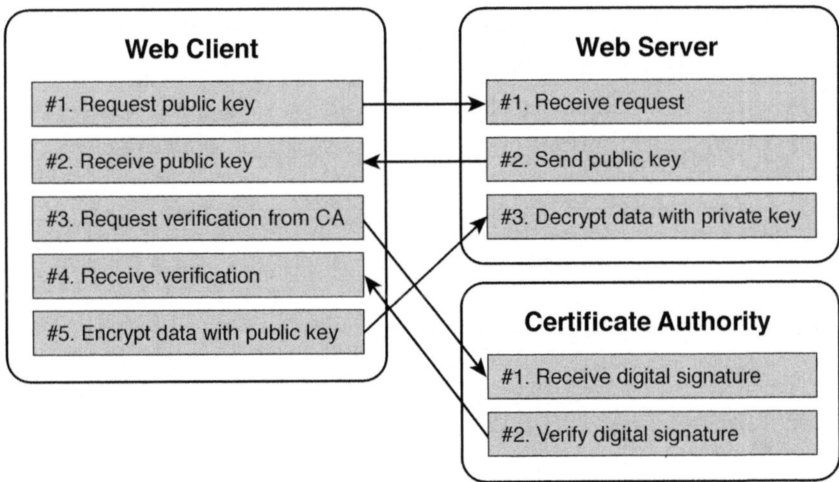

Figure 21-4 *SSL Process*

SSL Issues

SSL is not a perfect solution. Here are a few security concerns regarding SSL use:

- Having a large number of Certificate Authority (CA) machines increases the chance that one could be compromised. Most web browsers have a large list of CAs that can be used.
- Trust is also an issue. The purpose of digital signatures is that your web browser will not blindly trust the website it is communicating with. And yet your web browser does blindly trust the CA, at least to some extent. There is a hierarchy of CAs, the topmost being the root CA. The concept

is that a sub-CA is trusted because its parent CA says so, but at the top of the structure the root CA has no means to say "trust me because some other CA says so." It basically says "trust me because I am the root CA."

- Man-in-the-middle attacks are also possible. This would be when you connect through a router (typically an untrusted wireless router) that can exploit the connection and read the data as it is passed through.
- If you have virtual hosts, SSL is also a bit of a challenge. Each virtual host should have its own digital signature. However, when the client (web browser) first contacts the server (Apache Web Server), the client does not include the name of the website when requesting the public key. As a result, the server has no idea which digital signature to send to the client. There are workarounds for this issue, the details of which are beyond the scope of this book. You should be aware of the issues that virtual hosts pose when using SSL.
- As with any asymmetric cryptography technique, the security of the private key is critical. If this key is made available to the wrong element, the encrypted data can be compromised.

Self-Signing

It is important to note that not all websites use a third-party CA to verify the identity of the website (although hopefully your bank website does!). There is a cost involved for an organization to have a third-party CA perform verifications. As a result, it is not uncommon for smaller organizations to use a process that involves what is called a *self-signed certificate*.

Essentially a self-signed certificate is one that requires no third-party CA for verification. With a self-signed certificate, the web server presents its public key and the digital signature, which essentially says "trust me, I am the right website."

SSL and Apache

You can implement SSL in several different ways. The technique in this section is to use a module named mod_ssl. Another method is to use an Apache Web Server named Apache-SSL (http://www.apache-ssl.org/). This is the combination of the core Apache Web Server plus software from the OpenSSL project. Some commercial products also provide customized SSL-based Apache Web Servers.

Implementing mod_ssl is simple. You just need to add a line like the following in your Apache configuration file:

```
LoadModule ssl_module /path/to/modules/mod_ssl.so
```

In fact, it might be even easier than that. If you install the mod_ssl software package, the configuration process might happen automatically. For example, on a typical CentOS system, the following file appears after the mod_ssl software package is installed:

```
[root@localhost ~]# ls /etc/httpd/conf.modules.d
00-base.conf  00-lua.conf  00-proxy.conf  00-systemd.conf  02-perl.conf
00-dav.conf   00-mpm.conf  00-ssl.conf    01-cgi.conf      10-php.conf
[root@localhost ~]# more /etc/httpd/conf.modules.d/00-ssl.conf
LoadModule ssl_module modules/mod_ssl.so
```

Recall from earlier in this chapter that files in the **/etc/htppd/conf.modules.d** directory were included in the configuration process of the Apache Web Server on this CentOS system.

If the Apache Web Server is restarted now, it accepts both regular HTTP and HTTPS requests. Most likely you only want to accept HTTPS requests; however, right now that presents a bit of a problem because if you attempt to connect to the web server via HTTPS at this point, you should get a warning message like the one shown in Figure 21-5.

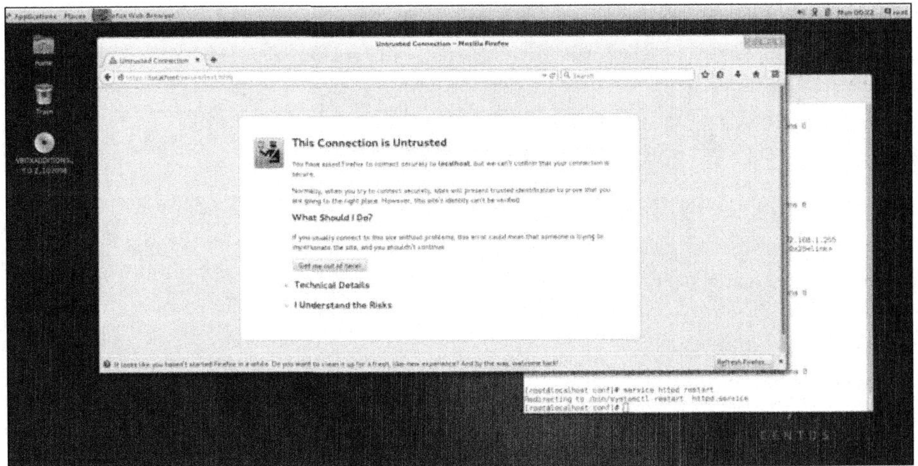

Figure 21-5 *Web Browser Warning Message*

This warning is because you have not set up a digital signature and had it signed by a CA. That process is described in the next section.

SSL Server Certificate

To create the SSL certificate, you must have the openssl software package installed. Recall that you have two choices: either you can have a CA digitally sign your certificate or you can self-sign it. If you are going to use a CA, you start by executing the **openssl** command to generate an RSA key file. The syntax looks like the following:

```
[root@localhost ~]# openssl genrsa -des3 -out server.key 1024
Generating RSA private key, 1024 bit long modulus
..++++++
.........................................................................................
..............++++++
e is 65537 (0x10001)
Enter pass phrase for server.key:
Verifying - Enter pass phrase for server.key:
```

The argument **genrsa** tells the **openssl** command to create an RSA key file. Another option is to generate a DSA key file; however, RSA for this situation is typically preferred. DSA is faster in signing, but slower in verification (which is going to happen a lot more often than signing when used with web servers).

NOTE What does RSA stand for? The acronym is composed of the first initial of the last names of the creators of the technology: Ron Rivest, Adi Shamir, and Leonard Adleman. What does DSA stand for? Digital Signature Algorithm.

The **-des3** option specifies the algorithm used for the encryption (Triple DES), the **server.key** argument indicates the filename to store the key in, and the **1024** argument specifies the size in bits of the key. The passphrase is necessary if you use the data within the key file.

The next step is to execute the command found in Example 21-4 to generate a CSR (Certificate Signing Request).

Example 21-4 *Generating a CSR*

```
[root@localhost ~]# openssl req -new -key server.key -out server.csr
Enter pass phrase for server.key:
You are about to be asked to enter information that will be incorporated
into your certificate request.
What you are about to enter is what is called a Distinguished Name or a DN.
There are quite a few fields but you can leave some blank
For some fields there will be a default value,
If you enter '.', the field will be left blank.
-----
Country Name (2 letter code) [XX]:US
State or Province Name (full name) []:CA
Locality Name (eg, city) [Default City]:San Diego
Organization Name (eg, company) [Default Company Ltd]:OCS
Organizational Unit Name (eg, section) []:
Common Name (eg, your name or your server's hostname) []:OCS
Email Address []:bo@onecoursesource.com

Please enter the following 'extra' attributes
to be sent with your certificate request
A challenge password []:linuxrocks
An optional company name []:
```

The **req** argument is used to specify that you want to make a CSR, the **-new** option is to create a new CSR, the **-key** option is used to specify the existing key that you previously created, and the **-out** option is used to create the file that you send to the CA.

To self-sign the key, you first need to install the **openssl-perl** package. Then you execute the command shown in Example 21-5. (Note: The exact location of the **CA.pl** file may differ on your system.)

Example 21-5 *Setting Up the CA*

```
[root@localhost ~]# mkdir /tmp/test
[root@localhost ~]# cd /tmp/test
[root@localhost test]#  /etc/pki/tls/misc/CA.pl -newca
CA certificate filename (or enter to create)

Making CA certificate ...
Generating a 2048 bit RSA private key
....................................+++
...+++
writing new private key to '/etc/pki/CA/private/cakey.pem'
Enter PEM pass phrase:
Verifying - Enter PEM pass phrase:
-----
You are about to be asked to enter information that will be incorporated
into your certificate request.
What you are about to enter is what is called a Distinguished Name or a DN.
There are quite a few fields but you can leave some blank
For some fields there will be a default value,
If you enter '.', the field will be left blank.
-----
```

```
Country Name (2 letter code) [XX]:US
State or Province Name (full name) []:CA
Locality Name (eg, city) [Default City]:San Diego
Organization Name (eg, company) [Default Company Ltd]:OCS
Organizational Unit Name (eg, section) []:
Common Name (eg, your name or your server's hostname) []:OCS
Email Address []:bo@onecoursesource.com

Please enter the following 'extra' attributes
to be sent with your certificate request
A challenge password []:linuxrocks
An optional company name []:
Using configuration from /etc/pki/tls/openssl.cnf
Enter pass phrase for /etc/pki/CA/private/cakey.pem:
Check that the request matches the signature
Signature ok
Certificate Details:
        Serial Number: 12294451229265977217 (0xaa9eaa4114c35f81)
        Validity
            Not Before: Dec 14 09:43:55 2017 GMT
            Not After : Dec 13 09:43:55 2020 GMT
        Subject:
            countryName               = US
            stateOrProvinceName       = CA
            organizationName          = OCS
            commonName                = OCS
            emailAddress              = bo@onecoursesource.com
        X509v3 extensions:
            X509v3 Subject Key Identifier:
                3F:DD:38:62:16:2A:65:12:09:B8:63:55:E5:9B:AB:2B:24:0A:C1:E0
            X509v3 Authority Key Identifier:
                keyid:3F:DD:38:62:16:2A:65:12:09:B8:63:55:E5:9B:AB:2B:24:0A:C1:E0

            X509v3 Basic Constraints:
                CA:TRUE
Certificate is to be certified until Dec 13 09:43:55 2020 GMT (1095 days)

Write out database with 1 new entries
Data Base Updated
```

Note that the **/etc/pki/tls/misc/CA.pl** script creates a file named **/etc/pki/CA/private/cakey.pem**. This sets up the next process so that it works correctly. The next step would be to create a signing request, as shown in Example 21-6.

Example 21-6 *Creating a Signing Request*

```
[root@localhost test]# /etc/pki/tls/misc/CA.pl -newreq
Generating a 2048 bit RSA private key
....................................................+++
.................................................................................
.....+++
writing new private key to 'newkey.pem'
Enter PEM pass phrase:
```

```
Verifying - Enter PEM pass phrase:
-----
You are about to be asked to enter information that will be incorporated
into your certificate request.
What you are about to enter is what is called a Distinguished Name or a DN.
There are quite a few fields but you can leave some blank
For some fields there will be a default value,
If you enter '.', the field will be left blank.
-----
Country Name (2 letter code) [XX]:US
State or Province Name (full name) []:CA
Locality Name (eg, city) [Default City]:San Diego
Organization Name (eg, company) [Default Company Ltd]:OCS
Organizational Unit Name (eg, section) []:
Common Name (eg, your name or your server's hostname) []:OCS
Email Address []:bo@onecoursesource.com

Please enter the following 'extra' attributes
to be sent with your certificate request
A challenge password []:linuxrocks
An optional company name []:
Request is in newreq.pem, private key is in newkey.pem
```

The last step in this process is to sign the certificate by executing the **CA.pl** script with the **-signreq** option, as shown in Example 21-7.

Example 21-7 *Signing the Request*

```
[root@localhost test]# /etc/pki/tls/misc/CA.pl -signreq
Using configuration from /etc/pki/tls/openssl.cnf
Enter pass phrase for /etc/pki/CA/private/cakey.pem:
Check that the request matches the signature
Signature ok
Certificate Details:
        Serial Number: 12294451229265977218 (0xaa9eaa4114c35f82)
        Validity
            Not Before: Dec 15 03:00:07 2017 GMT
            Not After : Dec 14 03:00:07 2020 GMT
        Subject:
            countryName               = US
            stateOrProvinceName       = CA
            localityName              = San Diego
            organizationName          = OCS
            commonName                = OCS
            emailAddress              = bo@onecoursesource.com
        X509v3 extensions:
            X509v3 Basic Constraints:
                CA:FALSE
            Netscape Comment:
                OpenSSL Generated Certificate
            X509v3 Subject Key Identifier:
                C5:04:9F:4C:07:BE:1D:EE:0E:36:44:C7:DF:7B:68:3C:5C:B3:4D:B2
            X509v3 Authority Key Identifier:
                keyid:3F:DD:38:62:16:2A:65:12:09:B8:63:55:E5:9B:AB:2B:24:0A:C1:E0
```

```
Certificate is to be certified until Dec 14 03:00:07 2018 GMT (365 days)
Sign the certificate? [y/n]:y


1 out of 1 certificate requests certified, commit? [y/n]y
Write out database with 1 new entries
Data Base Updated
Signed certificate is in newcert.pem
```


You should now have three files in the current directory:

```
[root@localhost test]# ls
newcert.pem  newkey.pem  newreq.pem
```

You need **newcert.pem** (the signed certificate) and **newkey.pem** (the private key file), but you don't need the **newreq.pem** file any more, as this was just to make the request for signing.

Security Highlight

These filenames are generic; it is a good practice to change the names and place the files into a different location. The two locations where certificates are typically stored are the **/etc/ssl** directory and the **/etc/pki** directory:

```
[root@localhost test]# mv newcert.pem /etc/ssl/example.com-cert.pem
[root@localhost test]# mv newkey.pem /etc/ssl/example.com-private.pem
[root@localhost test]# rm newreq.pem
rm: remove regular file 'newreq.pem'? y.
```

Apache SSL Directives

To use the certificate file and the private key file, you need to use the **SSLCertificateFile** and the **SSLCertificateKeyFile** directives within the Apache Web Server configuration file:

```
SSLCertificateFile /etc/ssl/example.com-cert.pem
SSLCertificateKeyFile /etc/ssl/example.com-private.pem
```

In addition to these SSL-based Apache directives, you should be aware of the ones shown in Table 21-3.

Table 21-3 Critical Apache SSL Directives

Directive	Description
SSLEngine	This directive allows you to turn off (or on) SSL by setting the directive to **off** (or **on**). It is useful because you can use it within virtual host directives to enable SSL for specific virtual hosts.
SSLCertificateChainFile	Recall that there is a hierarchy of CAs, with the top being the root CA. In most cases, web browsers can discover the chain of CAs that lead to the root CA, but if this poses a problem, you can insert all this information within the certificate (it is listed at the bottom of the file, one line per CA, with the root CA being the last one). Creating this more complex file is beyond the scope of this book; however, if this file does exist, you should know that the **SSLCertificateChainFile** directive is how you refer to the file. Use this instead of the **SSLCertificateFile** directive.

Directive	Description
SSLCACertificateFile	Until now the authentication described has been one directional: The client authenticates the server. However, you can set up a file on the server that can be used to authenticate the client. A single file that contains a concatenation of all the Certificates of CA serves this purpose. If you have such a file, use the **SSLCACertificateFile** to specify its location.
SSLCACertificatePath	Like the **SSLCACertificateFile** directive, the **SSLCACertificatePath** directive is used to authenticate client systems. Rather than place all the Certificates of CA into a single file, you can place them in separate files in a directory. The **SSLCACertificatePath** directive is used to specify the location of this directory.
SSLProtocol	Recall that SSL can refer to either Secure Sockets Layer or Transport Layer Security. You can specify which protocol to use and which version of that protocol by using the **SSLProtocol** directive. This is useful when you need to use an older protocol for backward compatibility or for when you want to use a specific protocol. Arguments to the **SSLProtocol** directive include **SSLv2**, **SSLv3**, **TLSv1**, **TLSv1.1**, **TLSv1.2**, and **ALL**.
SSLCipherSuite	The **SSLCipherSuite** directive is used to specify the cipher for creating the public/private key combination (for example, RSA). Several other cipher types are available, but you don't need to memorize the types for the exam.
ServerTokens	For security reasons, you may want to limit how much information the client receives about the server. The **ServerTokens** directive allows you to specify what information is returned in the response header field. For example, the statement **ServerTokens Prod** only returns the type of web server (Apache), whereas the statement **ServerTokens OS** returns the web server type (Apache), the web server version (for example, 2.4.1), and the operating system type (Linux). This directive also controls information provided by the **ServerSignature** directive (from Apache 2.0.44 and higher).
ServerSignature	This directive relates to documents created by the Apache Web Server. It is used to create footers with useful information for debugging purposes. It can be set to either **On** or **Off**. The **ServerTokens** directive is also used by this directive to add server and operations system information to these documents.
TraceEnable	An SSL trace is used for debugging purposes. By default, it is typically turned off. Use the **TraceEnable** directive with the **On** option to enable the SSL trace feature.

Proxy Servers

A *proxy server* is a system that serves to facilitate the communications between a client and a server. There are several different types of proxy servers as well as different advantages, depending on the design of the proxy server. The different types of proxy servers include tunneling proxy servers, forward proxy servers, and reverse proxy servers.

Tunneling Proxy

This type of proxy is designed to act as a gateway between two networks. An example would be when an IPv4-based network needs to communicate with an IPv6-based network. See Figure 21-6 for a visual example of a tunneling proxy.

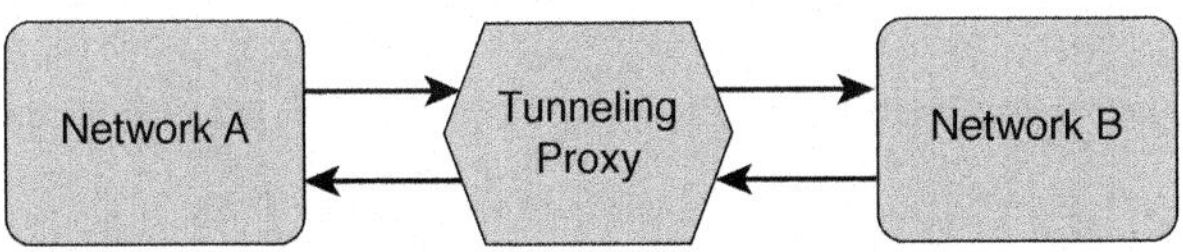

Figure 21-6 *Tunneling Proxy*

Forward Proxy

This type of proxy is designed to work on the client side of the communication. For example, a web browser can point to a proxy server instead of communicating directly with the web server. Typically, when someone calls a system the proxy server, they are referring to a system functioning as a forward proxy. See Figure 21-7 for a visual example of a forward proxy.

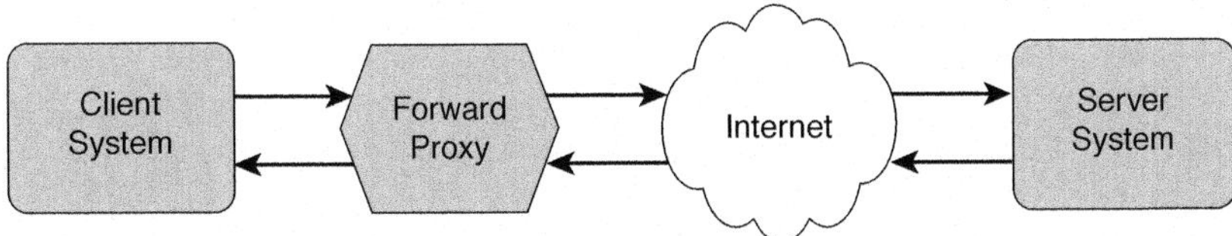

Figure 21-7 *Forward Proxy*

A forward proxy server can provide several key functions:

- It can act as a filter by blocking access to external resources.
- It can act as a buffer between the client and the server, as the server "sees" the request coming from the proxy, not the original client. This can hide the original client data, such as its IP address or location. Some users prefer this because it allows for anonymous browsing. This is also useful to get around restrictions (for example, a website that only allows access from a geographic region). In this case, a proxy server located in the correct geographic region could permit the required access.
- Proxy servers can cache static data (for example, websites that have static web pages). When multiple proxy clients attempt to retrieve the same data, the proxy server can serve to speed up the process by returning the data directly, rather than querying the web server repeatedly.
- The proxy server can be used to log client activity.

Reverse Proxy

A reverse proxy server is one that is configured on the server side. For example, instead of having web clients directly connect to your company web server, you have them connect to the proxy server initially. The proxy server then communicates with the web server for the required data. See Figure 21-8 for a visual example of a reverse proxy.

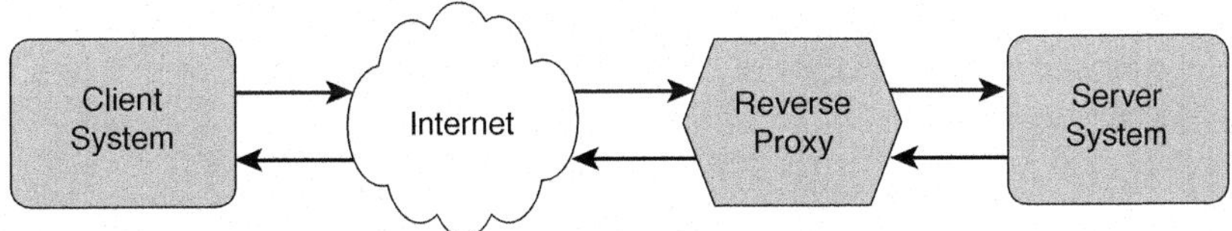

Figure 21-8 *Reverse Proxy*

There are several advantages to using a reverse proxy server:

- Load balancing can be provided by the proxy server because it can send queries to multiple web servers.
- The proxy server can limit the load from the server by caching static data.
- For SSL-based web servers, the proxy server can perform the SSL-based operations instead of the web server. If the proxy server is equipped with SSL accelerated hardware, this can be a tremendous advantage.
- The proxy server can effectively hide the web server from the client, making the web server more secure. Without direct access to the web server, it is more difficult to exploit the web server.
- The proxy server can optimize communication by compressing the data, increasing the speed of data transport.

Many software projects provide proxy servers. Here are two of the most common proxy servers:

- **Squid**: This software is used both as a forward and a reverse proxy server. It originated from the Harvest Object Cache Project, developed at the University of Colorado, Boulder. It was forked from this original project and named Squid (*forked* in this situation refers to a project that starts with the source code from another software project). A commercial version (NetCache), now no longer under development, was also forked from the project. This chapter focuses on how to configure Squid as a proxy server.
- **Nginx (pronounced "engine x")**: Nginx can function as a reverse proxy server for several protocols, including HTTP and HTTPS. Typically it is used to provide load balancing and caching functions for web servers. It can also be set up as a web server by itself.

Squid Basics

Although is it fairly common to have the Apache Web Server installed by default on a typical Linux distribution, it is not common to have Squid installed by default. So, your first task is to use your software management system (**yum** or **apt-get**, see Chapter 26 and Chapter 27 for details) to install Squid.

The installation should include a basic Squid configuration file (**squid.conf**), typically located in the **/etc/squid** directory. Table 21-4 describes several settings you should be familiar with.

Table 21-4 Squid Configuration Settings

Squid Setting	Description
cache_dir	When Squid is acting as a forward proxy server, it should be configured to cache static data. To set this up, use a setting like the following: **cache_dir ufs /var/spool/squid 100 16 256** Here are the arguments to this setting: ■ The value **ufs** indicates the type of storage. ■ The value **/var/spool/squid** is the location of the cache directory. ■ The value **100** is the maximum size of the cache files (combined) in megabytes. The values **16** and **256** refer to how many first-level and second-level subdirectories will be created under the cache directory.

Squid Setting	Description
http_port	This is the port number that the Squid server listens to for incoming HTTP requests. Normally this is set to a value of **3128**, but it is also common to set this to a value of **8080**. Example: **http_port 3128**
auth_param	This option allows you to perform authentication of the client using a variety of authentication methods. For example, you could authenticate using LDAP or Samba servers. In most cases you limit access to the Squid server by specifying which client systems are allowed access.
acl	This option provides you with the ability to group source and destination networks, addresses, ports, and other security settings together and assign a name to the group. This is useful when you want to allow or deny access to the Squid server. The **acl** option is described in more detail in the next section. Note: The term ACL stands for "access control list."
http_access	This option is used to specify which **acl** name is allowed to use the Squid server as an HTTP forward proxy server. The **http_access** option is described in more detail in the next section.

Squid Access Rules

In most cases you want to limit access to your company Squid server to specific systems. This is accomplished by first creating groups of machines with **acl** statements and then using the **http_access** statement to allow (or deny) access.

The default Squid configuration file normally has both **acl** and **http_access** statements. These not only help you by providing a baseline of what systems should be allowed to access the Squid server, but they also help by demonstrating the syntax of the **acl** and **http_access** statements. See Example 21-8 for an example of the default **squid.conf** file.

Example 21-8 *Default **squid.conf** File*

```
[root@localhost ~]# grep -v '^#' /etc/squid/squid.conf | grep -v '^$'
acl localnet src 10.0.0.0/8     # RFC1918 possible internal network
acl localnet src 172.16.0.0/12  # RFC1918 possible internal network
acl localnet src 192.168.0.0/16 # RFC1918 possible internal network
acl localnet src fc00::/7       # RFC 4193 local private network range
acl localnet src fe80::/10      # RFC 4291 link-local (directly plugged) machines
acl SSL_ports port 443
acl Safe_ports port 80          # http
acl Safe_ports port 21          # ftp
acl Safe_ports port 443         # https
acl Safe_ports port 70          # gopher
acl Safe_ports port 210         # wais
acl Safe_ports port 1025-65535  # unregistered ports
acl Safe_ports port 280         # http-mgmt
acl Safe_ports port 488         # gss-http
acl Safe_ports port 591         # filemaker
acl Safe_ports port 777         # multiling http
acl CONNECT method CONNECT
http_access deny !Safe_ports
```

```
http_access deny CONNECT !SSL_ports
http_access allow localhost manager
http_access deny manager
http_access allow localnet
http_access allow localhost
http_access deny all
http_port 3128
coredump_dir /var/spool/squid
refresh_pattern ^ftp:           1440    20%     10080
refresh_pattern ^gopher:        1440    0%      1440
refresh_pattern -i (/cgi-bin/|\?) 0     0%      0
refresh_pattern .               0       20%     4320
```

The basic syntax for an acl statement is

```
acl name type data
```

The ***name*** is something that you make up. For example, in the following entries, **localnet** is not some special, predefined name, but rather just a name given based on what it describes (local networks):

```
acl localnet src 10.0.0.0/8     # RFC1918 possible internal network
acl localnet src 172.16.0.0/12  # RFC1918 possible internal network
acl localnet src 192.168.0.0/16 # RFC1918 possible internal network
acl localnet src fc00::/7       # RFC 4193 local private network range
acl localnet src fe80::/10      # RFC 4291 link-local (directly plugged) machines
```

There are many ***type*** values, and they are used to indicate to Squid what sort of data this acl is designed to define. Here are the ones you are most likely to use:

- **src**: Used to indicate that the data describes a source IP/network combination. A source would be the system that requested the connection.
- **dst**: Used to indicate that the data describes a destination IP/network combination. A destination would be the system that the outbound network packet is to be sent to.
- **time**: This can be used to describe a time; useful if you want to allow access to the proxy server for specific times or days.
- **Safe_ports**: The ports on which HTTP connections are permitted.
- **SSL_ports**: The ports on which SSL connections are permitted.

Note that in Example 21-8 there are multiple **acl localnet src** lines. These could have been written in a single, less readable line:

```
acl localnet src 10.0.0.0/8 172.16.0.0/12 192.168.0.0/16 fc00::/7 fe80::/10
```

Later in the configuration file when the value **localnet** is provided, it refers to all the IP addresses that match the values in the line that defines the **localnet acl**.

Built-In ACLs

The following access control lists are already defined in the Squid configuration file:

- **all**: Refers to all systems.
- **manager**: A special ACL for the management of Squid's cache.

- **localhost**: Refers to the source IP address for the local machine (the server itself). Use this if you need to refer to the local machine with the **src** setting.
- **to_localhost**: Refers to the destination IP address for the local machine (the server itself). Use this if you need to refer to the local machine with the **dst** setting.

Understanding the Squid Rules

Note the following lines from the output of Example 21-8:

```
http_access deny !Safe_ports
http_access deny CONNECT !SSL_ports
http_access allow localhost manager
http_access deny manager
http_access allow localnet
http_access allow localhost
http_access deny all
```

Here, **http_access** uses the data from the configuration file to determine which ports are available and which systems can connect to the Squid proxy server. The following list describes each **http_access** line from the output of Example 21-8:

- **http_access deny !Safe_ports**: Deny access to all ports that don't match the **Safe_ports** ACL. All other ports are permitted by default.
- **http_access deny CONNECT !SSL_ports**: Deny the ability to connect to the Squid proxy server via SSL for all ports that don't match the **SSL_ports** ACL. All other ports are permitted by default.
- **http_access allow localhost manager**: Allow the machine that matches the **localhost** ACL the ability to access the cache manager.
- **http_access deny manager**: Deny all other machines the ability to access the cache manager. Order is important here. If this line appeared before the **http_access allow localhost manager** line, then this allow line would be meaningless.
- **http_access allow localnet**: Allow the machine that matches the **localnet** ACL the ability to use the Squid proxy server as a client.
- **http_access allow localhost**: Allow the machine that matches the **localhost** ACL the ability to use the Squid proxy server as a client.
- **http_access deny all**: Deny all other machines the ability to access the Squid proxy server as a client. Again, the order is important here, as this line should be after all **http_access** lines.

Nginx Configuration

If you are configuring a reverse proxy server, you could also choose to use Nginx (pronounced "engine x"), a server that can act as both a proxy server or a standalone web server.

> **NOTE** When you're considering which web server to use for your company website, the choice often comes down to picking either the Apache Web Server or Nginx. A comparison of the two is beyond the scope of this book, but in the real world you should devote some time and effort into understanding the advantages and disadvantages of each software product.

Nginx provides several features when it is used as a reverse proxy server, including the following:

- **Load balancing**: Nginx can be used to balance the load between multiple back-end web servers. However, you should realize that as of 2013, this is a feature available on Nginx Plus, a commercial version of Nginx that requires the purchase of a support contract.

- **Web acceleration**: This is provided by a combination of features, including compression of both inbound and outbound data and caching static web server content. This feature is available on both the Nginx open source product and Nginx Plus.
- **Support for multiple protocols**: In addition to supporting reverse proxy operations for HTTP, Nginx supports TCP, IMAP, POP3, and SMTP reverse proxy services. The level of support varies between the open source and Plus products.
- **Authentication**: In addition to SSL, Nginx supports additional authentication techniques as well as provides bandwidth-management features.

Although is it common to have the Apache Web Server installed by default on a typical Linux distribution, it is not common to have Nginx installed by default. So, your first task is to use your software management system (**yum** or **apt-get**) to install Nginx.

After installation, there should be a new configuration file for Nginx: the **/etc/nginx/nginx.conf** file. The default configuration file is designed to have Nginx act as a web server. It should look similar to the output displayed in Example 21-9.

Example 21-9 *Default nginx.conf File*

```
[root@localhost nginx]# more nginx.conf.backup
# For more information on configuration, see:
#   * Official English Documentation: http://nginx.org/en/docs/
#   * Official Russian Documentation: http://nginx.org/ru/docs/

user nginx;
worker_processes auto;
error_log /var/log/nginx/error.log;
pid /run/nginx.pid;

events {
    worker_connections 1024;
}

http {
    log_format  main  '$remote_addr - $remote_user [$time_local] "$request" '
                      '$status $body_bytes_sent "$http_referer" '
                      '"$http_user_agent" "$http_x_forwarded_for"';

    access_log  /var/log/nginx/access.log  main;

    sendfile            on;
    tcp_nopush          on;
    tcp_nodelay         on;
    keepalive_timeout   65;
    types_hash_max_size 2048;

    include             /etc/nginx/mime.types;
    default_type        application/octet-stream;

    # Load modular configuration files from the /etc/nginx/conf.d directory.
    # See http://nginx.org/en/docs/ngx_core_module.html#include
    # for more information.
    include /etc/nginx/conf.d/*.conf;
```

```
    server {
        listen       80 default_server;
        listen       [::]:80 default_server;
        server_name  _;
        root         /usr/share/nginx/html;

        # Load configuration files for the default server block.
        include /etc/nginx/default.d/*.conf;

        location / {
        }

        error_page 404 /404.html;
            location = /40x.html {
        }

        error_page 500 502 503 504 /50x.html;
            location = /50x.html {
        }
    }
}
```

Unless you want to perform major customizations, the default configuration file is good for a basic web server, although a few tweaks to the server section are necessary:

- Have a single listen setting with the argument of **80**.
- Specify the domain for the website after the **server_name** setting.
- Change the directory specified by the root setting to the location of the root of your website.
- Create the error pages indicated by the error page settings.

Note that you likely already have the Apache Web Server running on the system. To start the Nginx server, you first must stop the Apache Web Server.

Finally, if you want to configure Nginx as a basic reverse proxy server, replace the entire **server** section of the configuration file with the following:

```
server {
        listen 80;
        location / {
             proxy_pass http://10.1.1.252;
        }
}
```

Note that as you probably realize, there are many other configuration settings for Nginx. However, the goal of this section is to introduce you to the features of Nginx, not to make you an expert on the software.

Client Configuration

After configuring a proxy server, you may want to test it by setting up a client system to use the proxy server. The exact method that you use depends on which browser you are using. For this demonstration, Firefox ESR 38.3.0 is used, as shown in Figure 21-9.

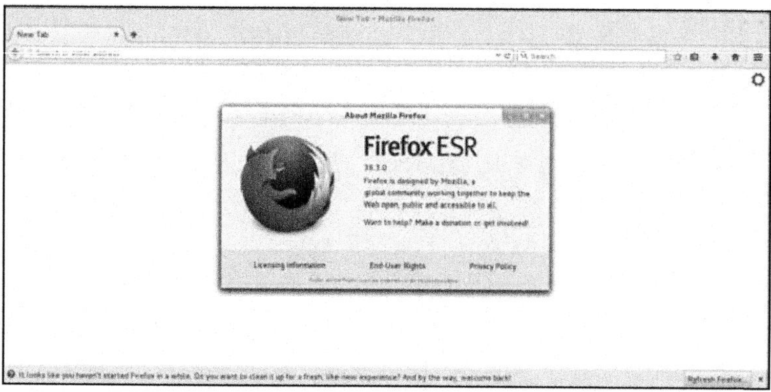

Figure 21-9 *Firefox ESR 38.3.0*

Step 1. Access the menu options for the browser. For this version of Firefox, the icon that looks like three horizontal bars opens the menu option, as shown in Figure 21-10.

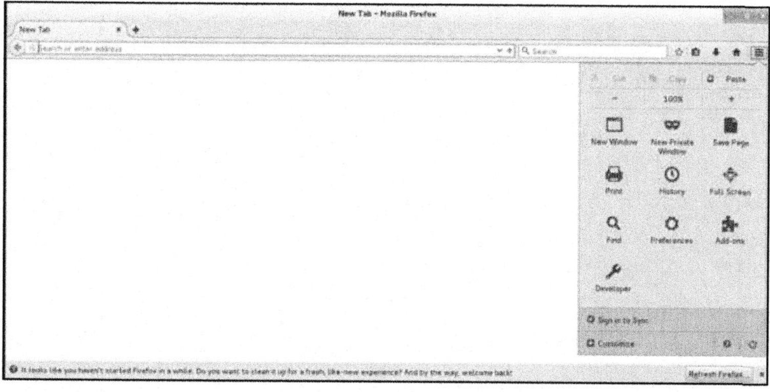

Figure 21-10 *Firefox Menu Options*

Step 2. Click the **Preferences** button. On some browsers this button is labeled **Options**. The result is similar to that shown in Figure 21-11.

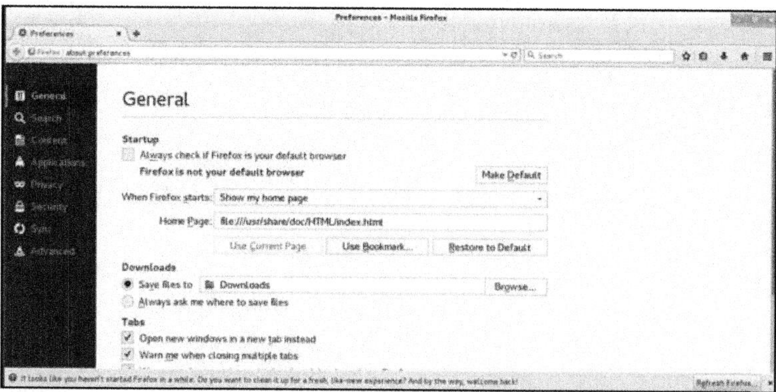

Figure 21-11 *Firefox Preferences*

Step 3. Typically proxy settings are under the Advanced section. In this example, click **Advanced** in the left-hand menu and then click **Network** on the menu that appears (see Figure 21-12).

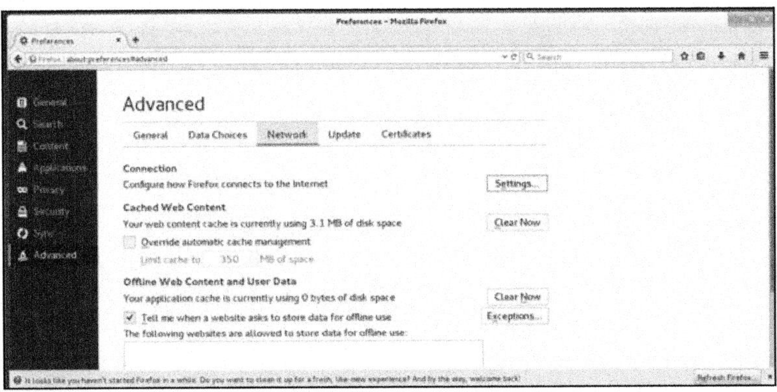

Figure 21-12 *Firefox Advanced Network Settings*

Step 4. Click the **Settings** button next to **Configure how Firefox connects to the Internet**. The dialog box shown in Figure 21-13 appears.

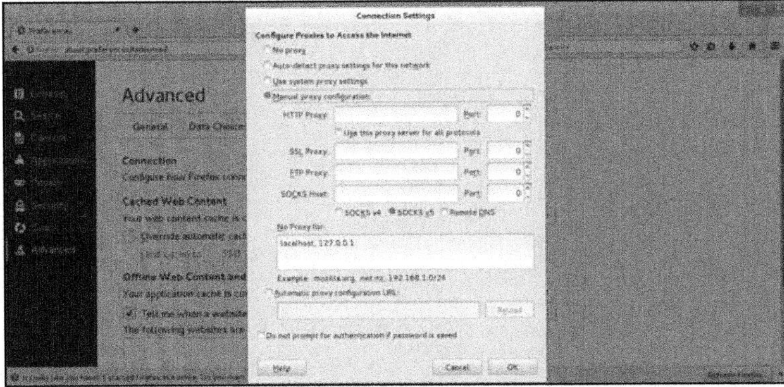

Figure 21-13 *Firefox Connection Settings Dialog Box*

Step 5. Click the **Manual proxy configuration** radio button and fill in the IP address of your Squid server in the box next to **HTTP Proxy**. If you set the Squid server on the local machine, you can use the local machine's IP address or 127.0.0.1.

Step 6. Click **OK** to finish. In some cases, you may need to restart Firefox for this new proxy setting to work properly.

Summary

In this chapter, you learned how to set up and secure an Apache Web Server. You also learned how to implement two different proxy servers: Squid and Nginx.

Key Terms

virtual host, Apache, HTTP, HTML, PHP, Perl, HTTPS, SSL, TLS, asymmetric cryptography, PKC, CA, man-in-the-middle attack, self-signing, proxy server

Review Questions

1. The directive used to specify the directory that contains the web files that will be served by the Apache Web Server is the _____ directive.

2. Which of the following Apache Web Server directives is used to specify what level of log messages will be logged to the error_log file?

   A. **Log**

   B. **ErrorLog**

   C. **LogLevel**

   D. **InfoLevel**

3. Fill in the blank:

```
<Directory />
    AllowOverride All
    Require all granted
<______>
```

   A. **END**

   B. **Directory/**

   C. **Directory**

   D. **/ Directory**

4. Fill in the blank to create a name-based virtual host:

```
_____ 192.168.1.100

<VirtualHost 192.168.1.100>
     ServerName www.example.com
     DocumentRoot /var/www/example/html
</VirtualHost>

<VirtualHost 192.168.1.100>
     ServerName www.sample.com
     DocumentRoot /var/www/sample/html
</VirtualHost>
```

   A. **VirtualHost**

   B. **NameVirtualHost**

   C. **NameVHost**

   D. **NameVH**

5. The _____ protocol is used when a web browser communicates with an Apache Web Server using SSL.

6. Which of the following are SSL security issues? (Choose all that apply.)

   A. Man-in-the-middle attacks

   B. Virtual hosts

   C. The security of the public key

   D. The security of the private key

7. Fill in the blank for the following command to generate an RSA key file:

```
_____genrsa -des3 -out server.key 1024
```

8. A _____ proxy server acts as a gateway between two networks.

9. The configuration file for Squid is **/etc/squid/_____**.

10. The _____ setting within the Squid configuration file is used to specify the location of the cache directory.

    A. **dir**

    B. **c_dir**

    C. **caching_dir**

    D. **cache_dir**

Connecting to Remote Systems

Several different types of network servers can be found on most networks, and you will need to be able to create connections to these servers and maintain them. Lightweight Directory Access Protocol (LDAP) servers provide database-like access to key network information, such as network users and groups. File Transfer Protocol (FTP) servers are used to transfer files between systems. When you need to connect to any remote Linux system in order to run commands on that system, Secure Shell (SSH) is the most common method.

This chapter discusses the essential setup and configuration of these servers as well as how to connect and communicate with each from the client side.

After reading this chapter and completing the exercises, you will be able to do the following:

Configure an LDAP server

Define values in an LDAP server

Connect a client system to an LDAP server

Configure and connect to an FTP server

Establish secure connections via SSH

LDAP

LDAP (Lightweight Directory Access Protocol) is a distributed directory service. Directory services are often compared to databases in the sense that directory services store information in an organized manner, much like a database program. However, a database is simply a collection of information. Databases do not really provide any sort of service to client systems; databases provide information that can be accessed using various tools.

There are several differences between a directory service and a database. Databases are normally designed to be equally efficient at writing data as reading data. Directory services are designed to provide an efficient method of reading data. Directory services are also specifically designed to provide sets of records organized in a hierarchical structure (much like the Internet's domain structure). As a result, directory services provide company data that mirrors the company structure.

Several different types of LDAP-based software programs are available. For example, Microsoft's Active Directory is an LDAP-based directory service. For Linux, OpenLDAP is the most commonly used open source directory service (there are also several commercial LDAP-based Linux programs).

Before you can connect to an LDAP server, you first have to have one available. As a result, we will first discuss the fundamentals of LDAP, then its installation and configuration, and lastly how to connect to an LDAP server.

The OpenLDAP software is not installed by default on most Linux distributions. The first step in configuring an OpenLDAP server is to install the **openldap-server** package (see Chapter 26, "Red Hat-Based Software Management," and Chapter 27, "Debian-Based Software Management," for information on how to install software packages).

After you have installed the software, a configuration file for the OpenLDAP server should have been saved to the system. Typically, this is located in the **/etc/openldap** directory, and the file-name is **slapd.conf**. The name of the OpenLDAP server is **slapd**.

Key LDAP Terms

One aspect of LDAP that makes it challenging for new LDAP administrators is learning the many LDAP terms. These terms, listed in Table 22-1, are important to understanding the concept of LDAP and properly administering it.

Table 22-1 Key LDAP Terms

Term	Description
Object	An object (also called an *entry* or *record*) is a single item within the LDAP directory. The object is used to describe things like computers, a user account, or any other data structure allowed by the schema. The definition of an object is called an object class. This is defined in a file called the schema.
Attribute	An attribute is a component of an object. For example, if the object type is a user account, the UID (user ID) of that account would be an attribute. The attributes collectively make up the object. These attributes are not random bits of data, but rather data types defined by the schema.
Schema	The schema is used to define the attributes and objects. For example, the schema may define a user account object as something that has a UID attribute, a user name attribute, and a home directory attribute—but hopefully not just these three attributes! The schema also defines the attributes and specifies what the attributes can store. For example, you do not want the value of ABC stored in the UID attribute. So, the schema could be used to define the UID attribute as "an integer value from 0 to 65,000." More details regarding schemas are provided in a later section in this chapter.
LDIF	The LDAP Data Interchange Format is used to create LDAP objects. Using the attributes of an object type, along with specific values for these attributes, you can place the LDIF format in a file and use it to create an object.

Term	Description
DN	Each object must have a unique name within the LDAP server directory. This name is developed by creating containers used to create an organized structure in the directory. For example, you could create a top-level container named "com" and a secondary-level container under the com container called "example." Each container is also called a domain component, or DC for short. Within the example container you could create a user account object named "bob." The DN (distinguished name) is the full name of this object, which includes the domains in which it resides. It would be written as follows within LDAP: cn=bob,dc=example,dc=com It might help to think of CN as a file and DC as a directory. In this sense, you have what is like a full pathname to a file, except in the opposite order that you are used to.
CN	The CN (or common name) is the relative name of an object. This name does not include the container within which the object is stored. For example, bob in the following DN is a CN: cn=bob,dc=example,dc=com
SSSD	The System Security Services Daemon's function is to provide authentication of user accounts using different services that provide user account data. For example, you can use SSSD to authenticate a user using data from an LDAP server.

Before you configure your LDAP server, you really should consider what sort of structure you are going to use. Choose wisely; it is not easy to change this structure at a later date!

You can organize your LDAP directory structure in several different ways. Figure 22-1 demonstrates one technique, which is used to mirror the company's domain name structure (a non-white circle denotes a DC and a white circle denotes a CN).

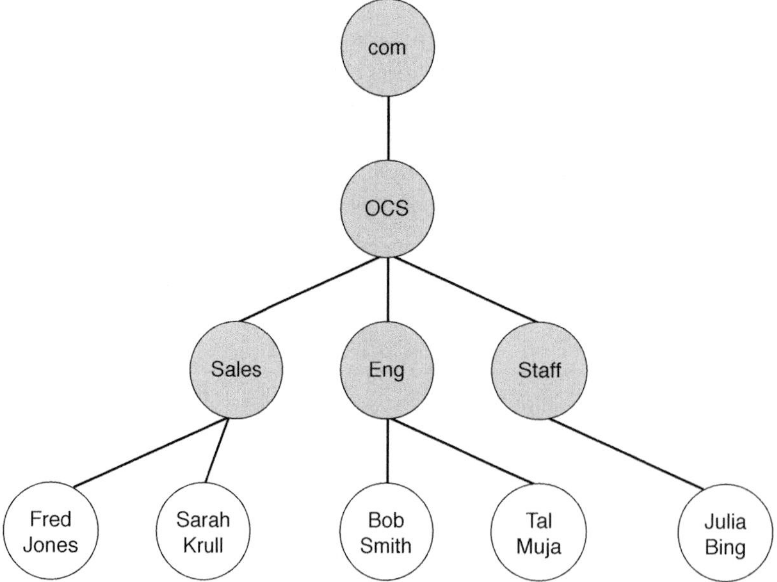

Figure 22-1 *Domain Name–based LDAP Structure*

Figure 22-2 demonstrates another technique in which the LDAP directory structure is designed to mirror the company's geographic locations (a non-white circle denotes a DC and a white circle denotes a CN).

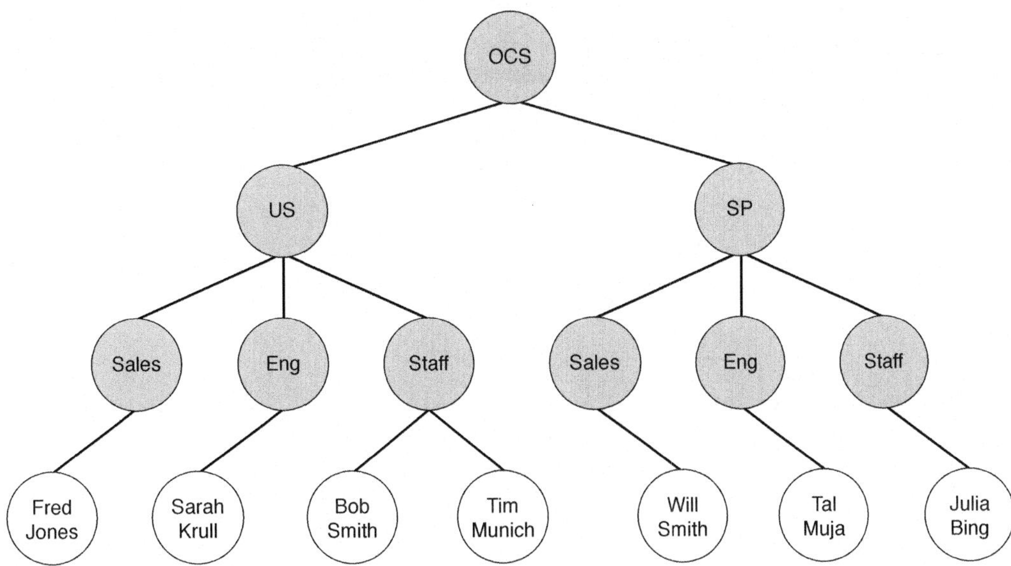

Figure 22-2 *Geographic-based LDAP Structure*

The slapd.conf File

The **slapd.conf** file has several components. In many cases you will not make changes to certain sections and you do not need to know all of the sections for basic LDAP configuration. The first component that you should know about includes some lines that import the LDAP schema:

```
include         /etc/openldap/schema/core.schema
include         /etc/openldap/schema/cosine.schema
include         /etc/openldap/schema/inetorgperson.schema
include         /etc/openldap/schema/nis.schema
```

These schemas could be placed directly in the **slapd.conf** file, but they are large and would make it difficult to manage the primary OpenLDAP configuration file. Also, by using these **include** statements, you can add more schemas to LDAP by downloading (or creating) a schema file and using the **include** statement in the **slapd.conf** file to import the schema.

Customizing Your LDAP Domain

You may likely never make any schema changes, but you should know how to include new schemas in the event your company requires new object types. However, the following highlighted settings are definitely ones you should consider changing:

```
database        bdb
suffix          "dc=my-domain,dc=com"
rootdn          "cn=Manager,dc=my-domain,dc=com"
# Cleartext passwords, especially for the rootdn, should
# be avoided. See slappasswd(8) and slapd.conf(5) for details.
# Use of strong authentication encouraged.
# rootpw                secret
# rootpw                {crypt}ijFYNcSNctBYg
```

Table 22-2 describes the bolded lines from this example.

Table 22-2 LDAP Configuration Settings

Setting	Description
suffix "dc=my-domain,dc=com"	This is designed to start the top levels of the LDAP structure. Consider the directory structure described in Figure 22-1. To start that directory structure, you would modify the suffix line as follows: **suffix "dc=OCS,dc=com"** The suffix line for the directory structure described in Figure 22-2 would be this: **suffix "dc=OCS"**
rootdn "cn=Manager,dc=my-domain,dc=com"	This is the root account for the LDAP server. Note that this is not a regular Linux account, but an LDAP-only account. This root LDAP account is important because it will be used to add new objects to the LDAP directory. Consider the directory structure described in Figure 22-1. To set the **rootdn** for this structure, use the following line: **rootdn "cn=root,dc=OCS,dc=com"** Note: We prefer an LDAP administrator account actually named "root."

rootpw	This is the password for the **rootdn** LDAP account. At this point, you see that there are two commented-out lines. One demonstrates a plain-text password and the other demonstrates an encrypted password.
	
	A plain-text password is easier to manage but does pose risks. If the **slapd.conf** file is displayed on a monitor that is not secure, someone could see the **rootdn** password. Although the permissions of the file should keep it secure, a change in permissions could leave the file open for viewing.
	
	To create an encrypted password, use the **slappasswd** command:
	
	`[root@onecoursesource ~]# slappasswd`
	`    New password:`
	`    Re-enter new password:`
	`{SSHA}lpEFwp3XkQPEEZ8qJCDxCT+EPvfleMBf`

Configuring Logging

A **slapd.conf** configuration setting you should be aware of that is not in the default configuration file is the **loglevel** setting. The **loglevel** setting allows you to specify the sort of logging information you want to have sent to the system logger.

This setting is a bit more complicated than how most Linux services define what is logged. Log messages are placed in categories; the following describes these categories as defined within the **slapd.conf** man page:

```
1      (0x1 trace) trace function calls
2      (0x2 packets) debug packet handling
4      (0x4 args) heavy trace debugging (function args)
8      (0x8 conns) connection management
16     (0x10 BER) print out packets sent and received
```

```
32      (0x20 filter) search filter processing
64      (0x40 config) configuration file processing
128     (0x80 ACL) access control list processing
256     (0x100 stats) stats log connections/operations/results
512     (0x200 stats2) stats log entries sent
1024    (0x400 shell) print communication with shell backends
2048    (0x800 parse) entry parsing
4096    (0x1000 cache) caching (unused)
8192    (0x2000 index) data indexing (unused)
16384   (0x4000 sync) LDAPSync replication
32768   (0x8000 none) only messages that get logged whatever log level is set
```


Each category can be described in one of three different ways: decimal, hexadecimal, or name. For example, the entry parsing can be referred to as the integer value **2048**, the hexadecimal value **0x800**, or the name **parse**:

```
loglevel 2048
loglevel 0x800
loglevel parse
```

More than one category can be defined. Each of the following lines would have the LDAP server log entry parsing and LDAPSync replication messages:

```
loglevel 204816384
loglevel 0x800 0x4000
loglevel parse sync
```

Configuring the Database Directory

This is a setting that will probably not need any changes, but you should be aware of it because if it is not set up correctly, the LDAP server will not start correctly. The directory setting in the **/etc/openldap/slapd.conf** file is used to specify where the LDAP database files are stored:

```
# The database directory MUST exist prior to running slapd AND
# should only be accessible by the slapd and slap tools.
# Mode 700 recommended.
directory       /var/lib/ldap
```

Here are a few considerations you should be aware of:

- If this directory does not exist, **slapd** will not start.
- If the OpenLDAP package was installed correctly, this directory should already exist. However, it is a good idea to double-check after installation.
- It is common to keep the **directory** setting assigned to the **/var/lib/ldap** directory.
- If you read the comment in the **slapd.conf** file, above the **directory** setting, you see that it says "# Mode 700 recommended." This is important because you do not want users to access this data directly and mode (or permission) 700 only gives access to the **slapd** service (and the root user, of course).

Starting the LDAP Server

After you have saved the changes to the **slapd.conf** file, you should run the **slaptest** command to verify there are no problems with the file:

```
[root@onecoursesource ~]# slaptest -u -v
config file testing succeeded
```

Normally if there are any problems, the **slaptest** command provides some clue as to what the problem is (unfortunately, sometimes you only get the "bad configuration file!" error, leaving you to look through the configuration file by hand). The following error occurred because the **rootdn** setting was not configured correctly:

```
[root@onecoursesource ~]# slaptest -u -v
/etc/openldap/slapd.conf: line 93: <rootpw> can only be set when rootdn is
➥under suffix
slaptest: bad configuration file!
```

If the test is successful, start the OpenLDAP server using the correct technique for your distribution. Note that although the process name is **slapd**, the name of the startup script will likely be **ldap**. The following example is from a system with traditional SysV-init scripts (see Chapter 28, "System Booting," for more details about starting services):

```
[root@onecoursesource ~]# /etc/init.d/ldap start
Starting slapd:                                           [  OK  ]
```

The **ldapsearch** command is designed to search for directory information from the client system. Although details for this command are discussed later in this chapter, it is useful to use this command to verify that the OpenLDAP server is responding to queries. To perform this verification, first install the openldap-clients package and then run the command demonstrated in Example 22-1. If the DN result matches what you placed in the configuration file, the server is working correctly.

Example 22-1 *Testing the OpenLDAP Server*

```
[root@onecoursesource ~]# ldapsearch -x -b '' -s base '(objectclass=*)' namingContexts
# extended LDIF
#
# LDAPv3
# base <> with scope baseObject
# filter: (objectclass=*)
# requesting: namingContexts
#

#
dn:
namingContexts: dc=OCS,dc=com

# search result
search: 2
result: 0 Success

# numResponses: 2
# numEntries: 1
```

The following options are used in the **ldapsearch** command demonstrated in Example 22-1:

- **-x**: Indicates to use simple authentication instead of SASL (Simple Authentication and Security Layer). In this case, no additional authentication is necessary.
- **-b**: The search base. The value of a null string (two single quotes, as shown in Example 22-1) starts the search at the top level of the LDAP domain structure.
- **-S**: Determines the return order of the values. See the man page for **ldap_sort** for additional details.

OpenLDAP Objects

To create an object in OpenLDAP, you first need to create an LDIF (LDAP Data Interchange Format) file. The format of this file is as follows:

```
dn: dc=OCS,dc=com
dc: OCS
description: A training company
objectClass: dcObject
objectClass: organization
o: OCS, Inc.
```

In some ways you may find parts of the LDIF file understandable based on what you have learned about objects. For example, you should realize now that the first line in the previous example (dn: dc=OCS,dc=com) specifies a container that already exists. To understand the rest, you need to understand a bit about schemas.

22

Security Highlight

The LDIF file can be stored in any directory because it is just used to create the object. However, you should either remove the file after you have created the object or make sure this file is located in a secure directory (only root should have access) as it may contain sensitive account date stored in it.

OpenLDAP Schemas

Recall that the schema is used to organize how data is stored in the OpenLDAP directory. More specifically, it is used to define the object types and which attributes make up the components of the objects.

For casual LDAP configuration you do not need to know specifics about the format of the schemas. However, if you really want to administer an OpenLDAP server, you should learn about how schemas are formatted. The core schema (located in the **/etc/openldap/schema/core.schema** file) contains the entry shown in Example 22-2.

Example 22-2 *Formatting Schemas*

```
objectclass ( 2.5.6.4 NAME 'organization'
        DESC 'RFC2256: an organization'
        SUP top STRUCTURAL
        MUST o
        MAY ( userPassword $ searchGuide $ seeAlso $ businessCategory $
                x121Address $ registeredAddress $ destinationIndicator $
                preferredDeliveryMethod $ telexNumber $ teletexTerminalIdentifier $
                telephoneNumber $ internationaliSDNNumber $
                facsimileTelephoneNumber $ street $ postOfficeBox $ postalCode $
postalAddress $ physicalDeliveryOfficeName $ st $ l $ description ) )
```

You do not need to worry about all these settings. The following are the most important:

- Each object type definition is referred to as an **objectclass**. Each **objectclass** has a unique object ID (2.5.6.4 in the previous example). This object ID is supposed to be globally unique. These unique IDs are maintained by the Internet Assigned Numbers Authority (IANA).
- Know how to determine the name of the object (**NAME 'organization'**).

- Read the **DESC** to determine the object's use.
- Understand that **MUST** specifies what attributes are required and **MAY** describes what attributes are allowed but not required.

Recall the LDIF file shown previously and notice the lines highlighted in bold:

```
dn: dc=OCS,dc=com
dc: OCS
description: A training company
objectClass: dcObject
objectClass: organization
o: OCS, Inc.
```

These two lines create an organization object with the required **o** attribute. What is the **o** attribute type? The following is according to the schema:

```
attributetype ( 2.5.4.10 NAME ( 'o' 'organizationName' )
        DESC 'RFC2256: organization this object belongs to'
        SUP name )
```

You may encounter the term *schema white page*, which refers to a schema specifically designed to provide information about users. The term comes from the "white pages" used by telephone companies to publish the phone numbers of people in a geographic area.

OpenLDAP Database Changes

To add the content of an LDIF file into the LDAP directory, execute the **ldapadd** command, as shown in Example 22-3.

Example 22-3 *The **ldapadd** Command*

```
[root@onecoursesource ~]# more ldif.txt
dn: dc=OCS,dc=com
dc: OCS
description: A training company
objectClass: dcObject
objectClass: organization
o: OCS, Inc.
[root@onecoursesource ~]# ldapadd -x -D "cn=root,dc=OCS,dc=com" -W -f ldif.txt
Enter LDAP Password:
adding new entry "dc=OCS,dc=com"
```

The options used in the **ldapadd** command demonstrated in Example 22-3 are as follows:

- **-x**: Indicates to use simple authentication instead of SASL (Simple Authentication and Security Layer). In this case, because changes are being made to the data, you must supply the password for the rootdn account.
- **-D**: The DN of the OpenLDAP account authorized to administer the server (in other words, the DN of the rootdn).
- **-W**: Has the **ldapadd** command query for the rootdn password.
- **-f**: Used to specify the name of the file that contains the LDIF information.

You can verify these changes by running the **slapcat** command, as shown in Example 22-4.

Example 22-4 *The **slapcat** Command*

```
[root@onecoursesource ~]# slapcat
dn: dc=OCS,dc=com
dc: OCS
description: A training company
objectClass: dcObject
objectClass: organization
o: OCS, Inc.
structuralObjectClass: organization
entryUUID: 2159172e-4ab6-1035-90c7-df99939a0cfb
creatorsName: cn=root,dc=OCS,dc=com
createTimestamp: 20160109004614Z
entryCSN: 20160109004614Z#000000#00#000000
modifiersName: cn=root,dc=OCS,dc=com
modifyTimestamp: 20160109004614Z
```


NOTE A benefit of the **slapcat** command is that the output format is LDIF. This means you can use this information to create your own LDIF files, which you can then modify to generate new content.

You should also be aware of the additional commands designed to make modifications to the OpenLDAP database:

- **ldapmodify**: Using an LDIF file, this command changes an existing object.
- **ldapdelete**: Used to delete an existing object. No LDIF file is required for this command; the object is specified on the command line.
- **slapindex**: An index is used to make it easier to find data. Remember that LDAP, as a directory service, is optimized for reading data. Having data indexed makes reading data quicker. The **slapindex** command creates this index for the objects in the database.

The ability to execute these commands successfully depends on a security feature called *access control*. Within the **slapd.conf** file you can create rules that define who can modify what within the LDAP database. When your organization becomes large and this database becomes difficult to manage, it is useful to be able to offload some work to other people.

The downside to this is that the syntax of access control is complex. The **slapd.access** man page describes the details; however, a complete discussion of these details is beyond the scope of this book. To give you an idea of the complexity of configuring access control, look at Example 22-5, which shows the syntax of the **oclAccess** directive, as provided by the OpenLDAP documentation.

Example 22-5 *An Access Control Example*

```
        olcAccess: <access directive>
<access directive> ::= to <what>
                [by <who> [<access>] [<control>] ]+
<what> ::= * |
                [dn[.<basic-style>]=<regex> | dn.<scope-style>=<DN>]
                [filter=<ldapfilter>] [attrs=<attrlist>]
<basic-style> ::= regex | exact
<scope-style> ::= base | one | subtree | children
<attrlist> ::= <attr> [val[.<basic-style>]=<regex>] | <attr> , <attrlist>
<attr> ::= <attrname> | entry | children
```

```
<who> ::= * | [anonymous | users | self
                        | dn[.<basic-style>]=<regex> | dn.<scope-style>=<DN>]
                [dnattr=<attrname>]
                [group[/<objectclass>[/<attrname>][.<basic-style>]]=<regex>]
                [peername[.<basic-style>]=<regex>]
                [sockname[.<basic-style>]=<regex>]
                [domain[.<basic-style>]=<regex>]
                [sockurl[.<basic-style>]=<regex>]
                [set=<setspec>]
                [aci=<attrname>]
<access> ::= [self]{<level>|<priv>}
<level> ::= none | disclose | auth | compare | search | read | write | manage
<priv> ::= {=|+|-}{m|w|r|s|c|x|d|0}+
<control> ::= [stop | continue | break]
```

Using the ldapdelete Command

After populating your database, you might decide that you want to delete an entry in the database. This does not require creating an LDIF file. Instead, you specify on the command line what you want to delete:

```
[root@onecoursesource ~]# ldapdelete "uid=named,ou=People,dc=OCS,dc=com"
➥-x -D "cn=root,dc=OCS,dc=com" -W
Enter LDAP Password:
```

This is one of those cases in which no news is good news. If the object was not deleted, you would see an error message:

```
[root@onecoursesource ~]# ldapdelete "uid=named,ou=People,dc=OCS,dc=com"
➥-x -D "cn=root,dc=OCS,dc=com" -W
Enter LDAP Password:
ldap_delete: No such object (32)
        matched DN: ou=People,dc=OCS,dc=com
```

You can make sure the entry is deleted by using the **slapcat** command:

```
[root@onecoursesource ~]# slapcat | grep named
```

Again, no news is good news. If the named object was in the database, something would be displayed by the **grep** command.

You can also use the **ldapsearch** tool, described in the next section.

The following breaks down the different components of the **ldapdelete** command:

- **"uid=named,ou=People,dc=OCS,dc=com"** is what you want to delete.
- **-x** means "use simple authentication." Because a change is being made to the database, a password is required.
- **-D "cn=root,dc=OCS,dc=com"** specifies the LDAP account that can make changes (the rootdn).
- **-W** specifies to prompt the user for the password. You could also include the password on the command line with the **-w** option, but that poses potential security problems (someone nearby looking over your shoulder, the line is recorded in your history, and so on).

Using the ldapsearch Command

After you have a database populated with information, you will find the **slapcat** command to be difficult to use:

```
[root@onecoursesource ~]# slapcat | wc -l
1077
```

The previous command produces more than 1000 lines of output, and that is just a handful of entries. Expect to have tens (or hundreds) of thousands of output lines when running the **slapcat** command on a live database.

The **ldapsearch** tool provides a much better way to view details from the OpenLDAP database (however, unlike the **slapcat** command, this command requires the LDAP server to be running). Many search options are available; Example 22-6 demonstrates viewing all objects that are account object types and returning the **uid** attribute of those objects.

Example 22-6 *Searching for Account Objects*

```
[root@onecoursesource ~]# ldapsearch -x -b 'ou=People,dc=OCS,dc=com'
➥'(objectclass=account)' uid
# extended LDIF
#
# LDAPv3
# base <ou=People,dc=OCS,dc=com> with scope subtree
# filter: (objectclass=account)
# requesting: uid
#

# root, People, OCS.com
dn: uid=root,ou=People,dc=OCS,dc=com
uid: root

# bin, People, OCS.com
dn: uid=bin,ou=People,dc=OCS,dc=com
uid: bin

# daemon, People, OCS.com
dn: uid=daemon,ou=People,dc=OCS,dc=com
uid: daemon
```

Here are some important notes regarding the output of Example 22-6:

- Recall that using **-x** means "use simple authentication." In this case, no password is required.
- The **-b** option is used to specify the base to search from. You could have just used **'dc=OCS,dc=com'** and the results would have been the same. However, the search could have taken longer if there were additional DCs or OUs (Organization Units). Plus, on a real OpenLDAP server, additional results from other DCs or OUs may have appeared. It is best to use the "deepest" possible base when performing searches.
- The **'(objectclass=account)'** is the filter—essentially what records to search inside. The **uid** is what attribute to return.
- Many additional results were returned. However, to avoid a large amount of output, only the first three results are displayed.

You can also search by CN. Remember that the CN (or common name) is the name of an object without specifying the domain (DM) to which it belongs. See Example 22-7 to see a demonstration of searching by CN.

Example 22-7 *Searching by CN*

```
[root@onecoursesource ~]# ldapsearch -x -b 'ou=People,dc=OCS,dc=com' '(cn=bin)' uid
# extended LDIF
#
# LDAPv3
# base <ou=People,dc=OCS,dc=com> with scope subtree
# filter: (cn=bin)
# requesting: uid
#

# bin, People, OCS.com
dn: uid=bin,ou=People,dc=OCS,dc=com
uid: bin

# search result
search: 2
result: 0 Success

# numResponses: 2
# numEntries: 1
```

The output of the **ldapsearch** command is likely more information than you really need. You can use one or more **-L** options to limit how much additional information is displayed or change how it is displayed:

- **-L**: Display output in an older version (LDAP, version 1).
- **-LL**: Display only the results and the version of LDAP.
- **-LLL**: Display only the results.

See Example 22-8 for a demonstration of using the **-LL** option.

Example 22-8 *The -LL Option*

```
[root@onecoursesource ~]# ldapsearch -LL -x -b 'ou=People,dc=OCS,dc=com'
➥'(cn=bin)' uid
version: 1

dn: uid=bin,ou=People,dc=OCS,dc=com
uid: bin

[root@onecoursesource ~]# ldapsearch -LLL -x -b 'ou=People,dc=OCS,dc=com'
➥'(cn=bin)' uid
dn: uid=bin,ou=People,dc=OCS,dc=com
uid: bin
```

You can use Boolean operators when specifying the filter:

- | is the logical OR operator
- & is the logical AND operator.
- ! is the logical NOT operator.

However, you may find the syntax of these complex filters to be a bit strange:

```
[root@onecoursesource ~]# ldapsearch -LLL -x -b 'ou=People,dc=OCS,dc=com'
➥'(|(cn=bin)(cn=root))' uid
dn: uid=root,ou=People,dc=OCS,dc=com
uid: root

dn: uid=bin,ou=People,dc=OCS,dc=com
uid: bin
```

There is also flexibility in the filter expression:

- **=**: Must match exactly.
- **=*string*string***: Asterisk acts as a wildcard.
- **>=**: Equal to or greater than.
- **<=**: Equal to or less than.
- **~=**: Approximate match.

Here's an example:

```
[root@onecoursesource ~]# ldapsearch -LLL -x -b 'ou=People,dc=OCS,dc=com'
➥'(cn=*bo*)' uid
dn: uid=nobody,ou=People,dc=OCS,dc=com
uid: nobody

dn: uid=vboxadd,ou=People,dc=OCS,dc=com
uid: vboxadd
```

Using the ldappasswd Command

As you can see from the following command, user accounts in the OpenLDAP database have passwords stored in the **userPassword** attribute:

```
[root@onecoursesource ~]# ldapsearch -LLL -x -b 'ou=People,dc=OCS,dc=com'
➥'(cn=bin)' uid userPassword
dn: uid=bin,ou=People,dc=OCS,dc=com
uid: bin
userPassword:: e2NyeXB0fSo=
```

You can change the password for an OpenLDAP user by executing the **ldappasswd** command:

```
[root@onecoursesource ~]# ldappasswd -x -D "cn=root,dc=OCS,dc=com" -s
➥newpassword -W uid=bin,ou=People,dc=OCS,dc=com
Enter LDAP Password:
Result: Success (0)
```

The **-x**, **-D**, and **-W** options have the same meanings as with the **ldapdelete** and **ldapadd** commands. The **-s** option allows you to specify the new password for the OpenLDAP user. The output of the command should be "Success," and you can verify the change by running the **ldapsearch** command again:

```
[root@onecoursesource ~]# ldapsearch -LLL -x -b 'ou=People,dc=OCS,dc=com'
➥'(cn=bin)' uid userPassworddn: uid=bin,ou=People,dc=OCS,dc=com
uid: bin
userPassword:: e1NTSEF9NGNUcW81U29taW1QS3krdFdOUHowS2hLdXp2UzZ5Ris=
```

If you want to avoid specifying the new password on the command line when you execute the **ldappasswd** command, use the **-S** option instead of the **-s** option:

```
[root@onecoursesource ~]# ldappasswd -x -D "cn=root,dc=OCS,dc=com" -S -W
➥uid=bin,ou=People,dc=OCS,dc=com
New password:
Re-enter new password:
Enter LDAP Password:
Result: Success (0)
```

The first two password prompts are for the new password for the OpenLDAP user. The third prompt is for the rootdn password.

Connecting to an LDAP Server

LDAP servers can be used in a variety of ways because the purpose of an LDAP server is to provide information to client systems, and the LDAP server has the flexibility to store a wide variety of information. With that said, there are two specific operations that LDAP servers are commonly used for: as a replacement for DNS internally within an organization and as a means to provide login information for client systems.

Different distributions have different tools to help you manage an LDAP client. For example, if you are working on an Ubuntu system, the general steps and tools you would use to configure access to LDAP user and group accounts are as follows:

1. Make sure the ldap-auth-client package is installed.
2. Make sure the nscd package is installed. This includes software that helps the system manage user, group, and host lookups.
3. Execute the **auth-client-config** command to tell the system to authenticate via an LDAP server.
4. Modify settings in the **/etc/ldap/ldap.conf** file.

Some Red Hat–based distributions make use of a utility named authconfig to configure access to an LDAP server.

Additional considerations when setting up LDAP on the client side include the following:

- Setting up automounting to mount network home directories
- Modifying PAM (Pluggable Authentication Modules) features to provide more functionality and security on LDAP clients
- Modifying the lookup order of accounts (local accounts first, network accounts second, and so on)

Because the techniques and tools vary from one distribution to another, specific examples are not provided in this book. This is one of the areas where you really need a "deep dive" into the documentation for the distribution on which you are working.

FTP Servers

An FTP (File Transfer Protocol) server is used to provide an easy and standard way to transfer files across the network. Several different FTP servers are available for Linux:

- **vsftpd**: The Very Secure FTP daemon is a popular Linux-based FTP server (it exists on many UNIX-based flavors as well). This server is the default for most of the major Linux distributions. Keep in mind that the standard FTP protocol itself is not secure because data is sent via the network in unencrypted format. The **vsftpd** process is considered very secure because of how the process interacts with the filesystem. The **vsftpd** software also provides additional features, including bandwidth throttling, limitations based on source IP, and per-user configuration. There is a reason why it is the default for so many distributions!

- **Pure-FTPd**: This software is designed to be a simpler (yet secure) FTP server. Although it may not have the robust features that **vsftpd** has, it provides the key components needed for most organizations that implement an FTP server.
- **ProFTPd**: This software is designed to be more user friendly in the sense that it opens configuration options to end users. It is known for being highly configurable.

Although there are differences between how these servers are configured, they are all designed to perform the same function. As a result, only the **vsftpd** server will be covered in detail in this book.

Configuring vsftpd

You should be able to use either the **yum** or **apt-get** commands on just about any distribution to install the **vsftpd** software package (see Chapters 26 and 27 for details on installing software). In fact, it may already be installed on your system. The **/etc/vsftpd/vsftpd.conf** file is used to configure this server.

As with any server discussed in this book, many configuration settings are available for **vsftpd**, but you only need to know some of them to perform essential administration tasks.

Anonymous FTP

The feature called *anonymous FTP* allows people to connect to the FTP server even if they do not have a local user account. Typically, this is set up to allow the anonymous user only to download content, not upload, as that can pose legal issues and other problems.

Security Highlight

It is a bad idea to allow the anonymous account to upload content. In the event that this is discovered, people could use your FTP server for illegal activity, such as sharing copyrighted content (movies, music, books, and so on). That puts your organization at risk.

Additionally, allowing anonymous accounts to upload content can result in the **/var** partition becoming full quickly. This can have an impact on system services that require the capability to write data to the **/var** partition, such as mail, log files, and print spooling.

Several settings in the **/etc/vsftpd/vsftpd.conf** file are related to anonymous FTP. See Table 22-3 for the details regarding these settings.

Table 22-3 Anonymous FTP Settings

Setting	Description
anonymous_enable=	If set to **YES**, this allows a user to connect via the anonymous account. The value **NO** does not allow anonymous access. Important: If this setting does not exist or is commented out, the default value of **YES** is used.
anon_upload_enable=	If set to **YES**, this allows the anonymous user to upload content. The value **NO** does not allow anonymous users to upload content. Important: If this setting does not exist or is commented out, the default value of **NO** is used.

Setting	Description
anon_mkdir_write_enable=	If set to **YES**, this allows the anonymous user to create directories. The value **NO** does not allow anonymous users to create directories. Important: If this setting does not exist or is commented out, the default value of **NO** is used.
local_enable=	It is common to disable regular user FTP access for FTP servers that allow anonymous access. To not allow regular users to log in to the FTP server, set **local_enable** to **NO** or comment out the **local_enable** option because the default is **NO**.
dirmessage_enable=	If set to **YES**, the contents of the message file are displayed when the user enters the directory. This is useful to warn anonymous users of the proper use for this FTP server.

To test whether your **vsftpd** server has the correct anonymous settings, either start or restart the server and then attempt to connect using either the **anonymous** account or the **ftp** account (they are the same account from FTP's perspective). Example 22-9 demonstrates an FTP server that permits anonymous access.

Example 22-9 *Anonymous Access Permitted*

```
[root@onecoursesource ~]# ftp localhost
Connected to localhost.localdomain.
220 (vsFTPd 2.0.5)
530 Please login with USER and PASS.
530 Please login with USER and PASS.
KERBEROS_V4 rejected as an authentication type
Name (localhost:root): anonymous
331 Please specify the password.
Password:
230 Login successful.
Remote system type is UNIX.
Using binary mode to transfer files.
ftp>
```

Note that the password can be anything. In the "olden days," it was supposed to be your email address, but that is no longer necessary. (How did it know whether it was your email address anyway?)

Example 22-10 demonstrates an FTP server that does not permit anonymous access.

Example 22-10 *Anonymous Access Not Permitted*

```
[root@onecoursesource ~]# ftp localhost
Connected to localhost.localdomain.
220 (vsFTPd 2.0.5)
530 Please login with USER and PASS.
530 Please login with USER and PASS.
KERBEROS_V4 rejected as an authentication type
Name (localhost:root): anonymous
331 Please specify the password.
Password:
530 Login incorrect.
Login failed.
ftp>
```

Limiting User Accounts

You may choose to limit which regular users can access the FTP server. This can be accomplished either by using a feature provided by PAM (see Chapter 7, "Managing User Accounts," for details about PAM) or by using a feature embedded in the **vsftpd** server.

The PAM feature allows you to add a user account name to the **/etc/vsftpd.ftpusers** file to prevent the user from logging in via FTP. This feature exists because of the **pam_listfile.so** line in the **/etc/pam.d/vsftpd** file, as shown in Example 22-11.

Example 22-11 *pam_listfile.so*

```
[root@onecoursesource ~]# more /etc/pam.d/vsftpd
#%PAM-1.0
session    optional     pam_keyinit.so    force revoke
auth       required     pam_listfile.so item=user sense=deny file=/etc/vsftpd/ftpusers
➥onerr=succeed
auth       required     pam_shells.so
auth       include      system-auth
account    include      system-auth
session    include      system-auth
session    required     pam_loginuid.so
```

The **/etc/vsftpd.ftpusers** file should include one user name per line:

```
[root@onecoursesource ~]# more /etc/vsftpd.ftpusers
root
student
```

Security Highlight

This PAM technique is useful because normally you want to limit access to a few users. However, what if you only want to allow access for a few users? If you have 100 users and only five should be able to log in via FTP, it would be a pain to have to add 95 user names to the **/etc/vsftpd.ftpusers** file. Also, you would have to remember to add any new user to this file unless they are supposed to be allowed to use FTP as well.

Another solution is to use the **userlist_enable**, **userlist_file**, and **userlist_deny** directives:

- When set to **YES**, the **userlist_enable** directive allows you to use the file defined by the **userlist_file** directive to either allow or block user access to the FTP server. The **userlist_enable** directive is set to **NO** by default.
- The **userlist_file** directive allows you to specify a filename where the list of user accounts is stored. If this is not set, the default **/etc/vsftpd/user_list** is used.
- The **userlist_deny** directive allows you to specify whether the users in the file are allowed or denied access. If set to **YES**, this essentially does the same thing as the PAM **/etc/vsftpd.ftpusers** file, denying access to the FTP server for these users. If it is set to **NO**, only users in the file can access the FTP server. The default for this directive is **YES**.

The most common use of these directives is shown in the following output. This allows you to place the names of users authorized to access the FTP server in the **/etc/vsftpd/user_list** file (all other users would be denied):

```
userlist_enable=YES
# userlist_file  - commented out because most administrators use the default file
userlist_deny=NO
```

Additional Settings

You can set numerous directives in the **/etc/vsftpd/vsftpd.conf** file. Table 22-4 provides a brief summary of some of the more important ones.

Table 22-4 vsftpd.conf Directives

Setting	Description
banner_file=	The banner is a message displayed before the login attempt takes place. By default, the **vsftpd** server displays its version information: **220 (vsFTPd 2.0.5)** This can cause security issues because knowing the version of a server can provide a hacker with information to exploit the server. Instead of displaying the **vsftpd** server version, consider creating a file with a warning about confidentiality or proper use and set the **banner_file=** directive to point to this warning file.
ftpd_banner=	Only need to display a small, pre-login message? Instead of using a file, just use **ftpd_banner=***Your message here*. Replace *Your message here* with your actual message, of course.
chroot_local_users=	When set to **YES**, this directive places local user accounts in a chrooted jail, limiting access to the system to their own home directory only.
write_enable=	When set to **NO**, this directive does not permit regular users to upload files.
max_clients=	Limits how many FTP clients can connect to the server at one time. This is useful to prevent DDoS attacks.
max_per_ip=	Limits how many FTP clients can connect from a single IP address. This is important when the **max_clients** directive is used to prevent one user from using all the possible connections.
anon_max_rate=	The rate, in bytes per second, that can be transferred by anonymous users. This limits the anonymous users from flooding the FTP server with data transfer operations.
local_max_rate=	The rate, in bytes per second, that can be transferred by regular users. This limits the local users from flooding the FTP server with data transfer operations.

Connecting to an FTP server

As previously demonstrated, you connect to an FTP server by executing the **ftp** command followed by the hostname or IP address of the FTP server. Once you have successfully logged in, there are a series of commands you can execute to transfer files or perform other tasks on the remote system. To see a summary of these commands, use the **help** command at the **ftp>** prompt, as shown in Example 22-12.

Example 22-12 *Using **ftp> help** to See a Summary of Commands*

```
ftp> help
Commands may be abbreviated.  Commands are:

!         dir         mdelete    qc         site
$         disconnect  mdir       sendport   size
account   exit        mget       put        status
```

```
append    form      mkdir     pwd       struct
ascii     get       mls       quit      system
bell      glob      mode      quote     sunique
binary    hash      modtime   recv      tenex
bye       help      mput      reget     tick
case      idle      newer     rstatus   trace
cd        image     nmap      rhelp     type
cdup      ipany     nlist     rename    user
chmod     ipv4      ntrans    reset     umask
close     ipv6      open      restart   verbose
cr        lcd       prompt    rmdir     ?
delete    ls        passive   runique
debug     macdef    proxy     send
```


To see a brief description of one of these commands, execute a command like the following:

```
ftp> help ls
ls              list contents of remote directory
```

It is important to note that when a command performs an operation on the "remote" system, it is performing the operation on the FTP server. For example, the **cd** command changes directories on the remote server:

```
ftp> help cd
cd              change remote working directory
ftp> cd /tmp
250 Directory successfully changed.
```

When a command performs an operation on the "local" system, it is performing on the system on which you originally ran the **ftp** command to connect to the server:

```
ftp> help lcd
lcd             change local working directory
ftp>lcd /etc
Local directory now /etc
```

Many of the commands are very similar to the Linux commands you have already learned:

```
ftp> help ls
ls              list contents of remote directory
ftp> ls
200 PORT command successful. Consider using PASV.
150 Here comes the directory listing.
-rw-------    1 1000     1000            0 Jan 21 15:44 config-err-qCpjfZ
226 Directory send OK.
```

Security Highlight

Note the warning "Consider using PASV." This is an important security feature that is discussed in the next section, titled "Active versus Passive Mode."

To copy a file from the current local directory to the current remote directory, use the **put** command: **put file123**. Multiple files can be copied using the **mput** command and wildcards: **mput *.txt**.

To copy files from the current remote system to the current local directory, use the **get** command: **get file123**. Multiple files can be copied using the **mget** command and wildcards: **mget *.txt**.

> **WHAT COULD GO WRONG?** Unlike regular Linux commands, you do not ever use the pathname when copying files. The commands always work only on the current local and remote directories.

Active versus Passive Mode

To understand the difference between active and passive mode, you first need to understand a common feature used in firewalls. Administrators often want to permit internal machines to establish connections to external machines, but prevent the reverse, except in a few rare cases.

For example, your company web server may be behind the company firewall, so the firewall might be configured to allow inbound connections for ports 80 and 443. Other communications that initiate on any other port from outside the firewall are blocked.

Normally any communication initiated from within the firewall, regardless of the port, is permitted. So, if you were on a host within the firewall and attempted to connect to an SSH server outside the firewall, that connection should be permitted by the firewall.

This works well for almost all servers, with FTP being an exception. By default, FTP connections use a feature called "active." In an active FTP connection, the FTP client uses a random unprivileged port (a port number greater than 1023) to initiate the connection to port 21 (called the command port) on the FTP server. The FTP server initially responds to the port the client provided, handling the login process for the user.

See Figure 22-3 for a diagram of how the active FTP connection is established.

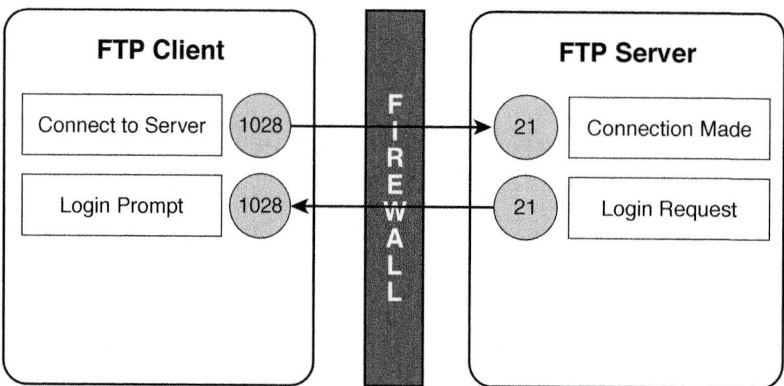

Figure 22-3 *Establishing an Active FTP Connection*

Once this initial connection is established, some additional actions take place. The user is prompted for a user name and a password to log in to the FTP server. Once the user is successfully logged in, any data transfer (uploading or downloading of files, for example) takes place on different ports. On the server, port 20 is used. On the client, the port number is one higher than the connection port. So, for the example in Figure 22-4, this is port 1029.

All commands issued from the client (and responses from the server) continue to be sent via the original ports. But data transfer uses the new ports and is initiated by the server. This is a problem because firewalls on the client side are typically designed to block these sorts of connections. You might think you could just allow the inbound connection for that port, but remember that this port is a moving target. The client randomly picks the client-side ports when the connection is first established.

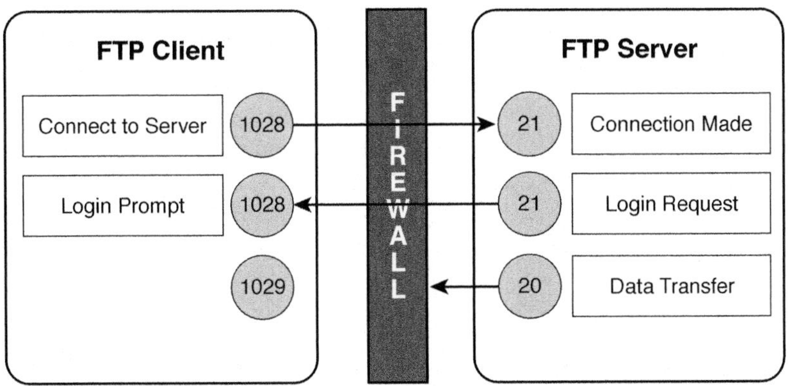

Figure 22-4 *FTP Data Transfer*

The result of this is that the FTP server appears to freeze when the client attempts to download or upload a file. Everything else to that point appears to work just fine.

When passive mode is used, the FTP server is told to not initiate the data transfer communication and to wait for the client to establish the connection. This satisfies the firewall rules (if they are configured correctly) because the data being set by the FTP server is deemed a response to the FTP client's connection request (firewall rules normally allow for responses from connections that are established on the client side).

The way you establish passive mode is to log in to the FTP server and then issue the **passive** command, as demonstrated in Example 22-13.

Example 22-13 *Enabling Passive Mode*

```
[root@onecoursesource ~]# ftp localhost
Connected to localhost.localdomain.
220 (vsFTPd 2.0.5)
530 Please login with USER and PASS.
530 Please login with USER and PASS.
KERBEROS_V4 rejected as an authentication type
Name (localhost:root): anonymous
331 Please specify the password.
Password:
230 Login successful.
Remote system type is UNIX.
Using binary mode to transfer files.
ftp> passive
Passive mode on.
ftp>
```

Secure Shell

Secure Shell is designed to replace unsecure remote communication operations, such as the **telnet**, **ftp**, **rlogin**, **rsh**, **rcp**, and **rexec** commands/protocols. The primary issue with previous communication methods is that these methods send data across the network in plain text, rather than encrypted format. In some cases, such as **telnet** and **ftp**, this can include sending user account data (name and password) across the network in plain text.

The Secure Shell (SSH) protocol provides a better level of security by encrypting the data sent across the network. SSH has become such a standard in Linux that almost all distributions include both the client and server software by default. In the event that you do not have this software installed on your system, you should install the openssh, openssh-server, openssh-clients, and openssh-askpass software packages (see Chapters 26 and 27 for more details regarding installing software).

Configuring the Secure Shell Server

The **/etc/ssh** directory is the location where the Secure Shell configuration files are stored. The configuration file for the SSH server is the **/etc/ssh/sshd_config** file. Don't confuse this with the **/etc/ssh/ssh_config** file, which is used to configure client utilities, such as the **ssh**, **scp**, and **sftp** commands.

Basic Configuration Settings

The two different SSH protocols are numbered 1 and 2. These are not versions, but rather two separate protocols developed to provide secure data connections. There was a time when both protocols were commonly used, but now almost all SSH clients use only protocol 2. To set the protocol that your SSH server accepts, use the **Protocol** keyword:

```
Protocol 2
```

If you have some older SSH clients that require protocol 1, you can configure your SSH server to accept both protocol connections by using the following keyword setting in the **/etc/ssh/sshd_config** file:

```
Protocol 1,2
```

Security Highlight

Protocol 1 is no longer supported and should be avoided if possible. Protocol 2 has better security features and is actively receiving improvements. In general, you should always stay away from software that is no longer supported or actively maintained because security holes are not fixed when discovered by hackers.

In some cases, you may have multiple network cards (or virtual interfaces) and you want to limit the SSH server to listen to only some of the network cards. To do this, use the **ListenAddress** keyword and specify the IP address assigned to the network cards that SSH should accept connections on. Here is an example:

```
ListenAddress 192.168.1.100:192.168.1.101
```

The standard port number that the SSH server listens to is port 22. You can modify the SSH server to listen to another port by using the **Port** keyword:

```
Port 2096
```

Security Highlight

Using a nonstandard port makes it a bit more difficult for a hacker to discover a service. However, there are tools that allow hackers to probe a system for ports that are "open" (that is, ports to which services are responding). Therefore, changing the port will not completely hide the SSH service. However, many hackers also just use scripts with hardcoded values (like port numbers), so you might be able to avoid a casual hacking attempt by using a different port number.

You might need to change what sort of log messages you want the SSH server to record. This can be set by using the **LogLevel** keyword. Here are the levels available:

- **QUIET**
- **FATAL**
- **ERROR**
- **INFO**
- **VERBOSE**
- **DEBUG**
- **DEBUG1** (same as **DEBUG**)
- **DEBUG2**
- **DEBUG3**

Like system logging (see Chapter 25, "System Logging," for details about system logs), these levels build on each other. For example, the **INFO** level includes all the logs generated at the **ERROR** and **FATAL** levels (technically **QUIET** as well, but there are no messages at this level). Be careful when changing to **DEBUG**, **DEBUG2**, or **DEBUG3**, as this may cause security issues on real SSH servers.

Security Highlight

The **sshd_config** man page states, "Logging with a **DEBUG** level violates the privacy of users and is not recommended." If you set the **LogLevel** keyword to **DEBUG** on a test machine and then restart the SSH server, connect to the SSH server, and look at the **/var/log/secure** file (Red Hat–based systems) or **/var/log/auth.log** file (Debian), you should see why (data such as user names and passwords are captured).

Settings That Affect User Access

To disallow the root user from logging in via SSH, change the **PermitRootLogin** value to **no**:

```
PermitRootLogin no
```

Security Highlight

You might want to consider not allowing the root user to log in directly via SSH, especially if the system is connected to the Internet. Allowing root login via SSH provides potential hackers with the ability to use a brute-force attack by trying multiple passwords to gain access.

A better choice is to permit regular user login, allowing the user to switch to the root account using the **su** or **sudo** command. Although the brute-force attack can still be attempted with the regular user, the hacker would have to know the account exists and then, after gaining access, attempt to hack into the root account.

What if you have a regular user who has no reason to log in via SSH? In this case, you have two choices: **AllowUsers** or **DenyUsers**. Both of these keywords allow you to specify a list of user names:

```
AllowUsers bob sue ted
```

If you use the **AllowUsers** keyword, only those users are allowed to connect to the SSH server. If you use the **DenyUsers** keyword, all users can connect to the SSH server except for those users listed. Note that if you use both keywords, **DenyUsers** takes precedence.

You can use wildcard characters to match patterns:

```
DenyUsers guest*#denies any user with a name that begins with "guest"
DenyUsers ????app#denies any user with a name that contains 4 characters
and ends with "app"
```

Security Highlight

You can also use the **AllowGroups** and **DenyGroups** keywords.

Several different authentication methods are available for the SSH server. Here are the critical ones you should know about:

- **PasswordAuthentication**: When set to **yes** (the default), this setting allows users to log in by providing their user name and password. If set to **no**, users can log in using an Authentication key only. Authentication keys will be covered in detail later in this chapter.
- **PubkeyAuthentication**: When this is set to **yes**, a user can store a public key on the server. The public key is generated by the **ssh-keygen** command on the user's client system. This process is covered in greater detail in a later section of this chapter.

Table 22-5 describes additional useful SSH server settings that affect user login.

Table 22-5 SSH Server Settings

Setting	Description
Banner	Specifies a file of which the contents are displayed prior to the user authentication process.
PrintMotd	If this is set to **yes** (the default), the contents of the **/etc/motd** file are displayed when a user logs in to the system via SSH.
X11Forwarding	If set to **yes** (the default is **no**), this provides an easy way to allow graphical programs to be executed on the SSH server and displayed on the SSH client. This requires the SSH client command (the **ssh** command) be executed with the **-X** or **-Y** option.
MaxAuthTries	Set to a numeric value that indicates how many attempts a user has to enter the correct password. The default is **6**.
PermitEmptyPasswords	If this is set to **no** (the default), users cannot log in via SSH if the password field for the user account is empty.

Secure Shell Client Commands

You need to be aware of several different SSH client commands, including the following:

- **ssh**: Allows you to log in to an SSH server and work on the server via the command line
- **scp**: Allows you to transfer files to and from an SSH server via the command line
- **sftp**: Allows you to connect to an SSH server and execute FTP-like commands

You should be aware of the function of each of these commands as well as some of the key settings in the **/etc/ssh/ssh_config** file.

The ssh_config File

A few components of the **ssh_config** file are different from the **sshd_config** file. To begin with, there is the systemwide **/etc/ssh/ssh_config** file, which applies to all users. Additionally, each user can create a file in their home directory (**~/.ssh/config**) that can be used to override the settings in the **/etc/ssh/ssh_config** file.

In addition to the files, command-line options can override the values specified in the configuration files. Here is the order in which all this information is parsed:

1. Command-line options
2. The user's **~/.ssh/config** file
3. The **/etc/ssh/ssh_config** file

Important

The first parameter found is the one used. For example, if **ConnectTimeout** is set in the user's **~/.ssh/config** file and a different value is set in the **/etc/ssh/ssh_config** file, the user's configuration file is used to set this value.

Another important difference between the **ssh_config** file and the **sshd_config** file is that most of the settings in the **ssh_config** file are subsettings of the **Host** setting. The **Host** setting allows you to specify different rules for different SSH servers you are connecting to. For example, the following would apply the **ConnectTimeout** value of **0** when connecting to server1.onecoursesource.com and a value of **600** when connecting to test.example.com:

```
Host server1.onecoursesource.com
ConnectTimeout 0
Host test.example.com
ConnectTimeout 600
```

Many of the settings in the **ssh_config** file are related to settings in the SSH server configuration file. Recall, for example, the following **/etc/ssh/sshd_config** file setting:

```
X11Forwarding yes
```

On the client side, this feature is typically enabled by using the **-X** or **-Y** option when executing the **ssh**-based commands. However, if you want this feature to be the default, the following settings could be used in either the **/etc/ssh/ssd_config** or the **~/.ssh/config** file:

```
ForwardX11 and ForwardX11Trusted
```

The ssh Command

The first time you attempt to connect to a machine via the **ssh** command, you are prompted to verify the RSA key fingerprint:

```
[student@onecoursesource ~]$ ssh 192.168.1.22
The authenticity of host '192.168.1.22 (192.168.1.22)' can't be established.
RSA key fingerprint is 7a:9f:9b:0b:7b:06:3a:f0:97:d1:c7:e9:94:a8:84:03.
Are you sure you want to continue connecting (yes/no)? yes
Warning: Permanently added '192.168.1.22' (RSA) to the list of known hosts.
student@192.168.1.22's password:
[student@testmachine ~]$
```

Consider the RSA key fingerprint to be like an actual fingerprint. Many modern laptops and phones have fingerprint scanners to verify your identity as a means of logging on to or unlocking the device. To use this feature, you first need to register it. This is what is happening when you answer **yes** to the **ssh** prompt "Are you sure you want to continue connecting (yes/no)?"

When you register your fingerprint on your laptop or phone, the device just assumes you are who you claim to be (the owner of the account or device). Essentially, this is what happens when you accept the RSA key fingerprint. You are accepting that the computer you are connecting to is the correct computer.

Future attempts to connect to this computer invoke a process in which the current fingerprint on the SSH server matches the one that you accepted when you first connected. This fingerprint is stored in the **~/.ssh/known_hosts** file (each user has a separate set of accepted fingerprints):

```
[student@onecoursesource ~]$ cat .ssh/known_hosts
192.168.1.22 ssh-rsa AAAAB3NzaC1yc2EAAAABIwAAAQEAz98zgUakM93uWfXw/iF5QhCsPrSnNKHVBD/
o9qwSTh8sP6MKtna8vMw1U2PltXN3/BMm7hrT0sWe1hjkAqFjrx7Hp6uzjslikfPSRerybsE+CAR+KywbiiInvp
4ezm/IHPjhwjasskSzcWHwdQ+1YaYNkoaoGrRz87/xbiXUxWVb7VVn6RZKxiVIh2+XgCr4dWct0ciJf3eM9eel-
2SL81G5M1jUMB8g9jzUpWITvuj2e86LJw8RwpqRZ9oUaCwZFkp8FaBpLvA1xBTaGIjB6J9qBAoERfTv5TChqG-
MoK1zyz/KF9LC/22dwZ2hnU21fdS34COJ6RuxNA4P/hSGFxrw==
```

As a user, you do not really need to know specifics about the fingerprint; this process is handled by the SSH client utility and the SSH server. However, this is a situation regarding the fingerprint that you should be aware of. It is related to the following message:

```
@@@@@@@@@@@@@@@@@@@@@@@@@@@@@@@@@@@@
@ WARNING: REMOTE HOST IDENTIFICATION HAS CHANGED! @
@@@@@@@@@@@@@@@@@@@@@@@@@@@@@@@@@@@@
IT IS POSSIBLE THAT SOMEONE IS DOING SOMETHING NASTY!
Someone could be eavesdropping on you right now (man-in-the-middle attack)!
It is also possible that the RSA host key has just been changed.
The fingerprint for the RSA key sent by the remote host is
7a:9f:9b:0b:7b:06:3a:f0:97:d1:c7:e9:94:a8:84:03
Please contact your system administrator.
```

This error message could appear for several reasons:

- The SSH server software was reinstalled; this could result in a new RSA key fingerprint.
- The SSH server itself was reinstalled or replaced with a new system.
- The man-in-the-middle from the warning could be the cause.

Security Highlight

A "man-in-the-middle" is a hacking technique in which a rouge computer will insert itself in between the client and server. The goal is to gather information for a hacker so they can further compromise systems.

The administrator of the SSH server should know whether one of the first two situations has occurred. If that is the case, the solution is to delete the entry for this SSH server from the **~/.ssh/known_hosts** file. If the first two situations have not occurred, it is time to do some exploring to determine what is really going on.

To log in as a different user from the user you are logged in as on the client machine, use one of the following syntax methods:

```
ssh -l username ssh_server
ssh username@ssh_server
```

To execute a command on the remote system, but immediately return to your client system, use the following syntax:

```
ssh ssh_server command
```

The scp and sftp Commands

The **scp** command uses many of the same options and features provided by the **ssh** command. To copy a file from your current system to a remote system, use the following syntax:

```
[student@onecoursesource ~]$ scp /etc/hosts 192.168.1.22:/tmp
student@192.168.1.22's password:
hosts                                            100%  187     0.2KB/s   00:00
```


Here are a few useful **scp** options:

- **-r**: Copies entire directory structures
- **-v**: Verbose mode; displays details helpful in debugging transfer issues
- **-q**: Quiet mode
- **-p**: Preserves timestamps and permissions

The **sftp** command connects to an SSH server and provides an FTP-like client interface. See Example 22-14 for a demonstration.

Example 22-14 *Connecting via sftp*

```
[student@onecoursesource ~]$ sftp 192.168.1.22
Connecting to 192.168.1.22...
student@192.168.1.22's password:
sftp>cd /tmp
sftp>ls
gconfd-root          hosts                keyring-GhtP1j       mapping-root
nis.6788.ldif        nis.6818.ldif        nis.6836.ldif        orbit-root
ssh-ysXgwO2672       uplist               virtual-root.9QNCsb
sftp>get hosts
Fetching /tmp/hosts to hosts
/tmp/hosts                                  100%  187     0.2KB/s   00:00
sftp>ls h*
hosts
sftp>quit
```

Advanced SSH Features

A question often asked by novice administrators is, how can SSH encrypt the data transfer to ensure it is secure? The technique used involves public and private keys. When the SSH client connects to the SSH server, the server provides the client with its public key.

As a session is being established, a symmetric session key is generated by the client and server, which is then used to encrypt all the data exchanged between the hosts. The client then encrypts all data with the public key before sending it to the server. The data can only be decrypted by the private key, which is stored only on the server.

These keys are created when the SSH server is installed, and they are stored in the **/etc/ssh** directory.

If a user routinely logs in to a specific SSH server, that user may want to set up passwordless log-ins. To do this, you would follow these steps:

Step 1. On the SSH client machine, execute the **ssh-keygen** command, as shown in Example 22-15. When prompted for a passphrase, press the Enter key to leave this blank (or, you could use the **-N** option with the **ssh-keygen** command, which results in no passphrase prompt).

Example 22-15 *The ssh-keygen Command*

```
[student@onecoursesource ~]$ ssh-keygen -t rsa
Generating public/private rsa key pair.
Enter file in which to save the key (/home/student/.ssh/id_rsa):
Enter passphrase (empty for no passphrase):
Enter same passphrase again:
Your identification has been saved in /home/student/.ssh/id_rsa.
Your public key has been saved in /home/student/.ssh/id_rsa.pub.
The key fingerprint is:
b4:77:29:40:b8:aa:d1:1c:3a:cb:e6:b8:5d:9b:07:fb student@localhost.localdomain
The key's randomart image is:
+--[ RSA 2048]----+
|       ..        |
|      ..         |
|       .o        |
|    . .. o   .   |
|   + o  S o o    |
|  + =     . o    |
| . =.o           |
| o=..o.          |
|o+o ooE          |
+-----------------+
```

Step 2. There is now a public key in the **~/.ssh/id_rsa.pub** file. This needs to be copied to the remote server, into the **~/.ssh/authorized_keys** file of your account on the remote machine (you may need to create this directory and set the permissions to **770**). This can be done with the following commands:

```
student@localhost ~]$ cat .ssh/id_rsa.pub | ssh 192.168.1.22 'cat >> .ssh/
authorized_keys'
student@192.168.1.22's password:
```

Step 3. Set the permissions of the **authorized_keys** file to **640**:

```
[student@onecoursesource ~]$ ssh 192.168.1.22 'chmod 640 /home/student/.ssh/
➥ authorized_keys'
student@192.168.1.22's password:
```

Security Highlight

On some distributions, you can use the **ssh-copy-id** command to complete both Step 2 and Step 3. However, you should also know how to use the manual method described in these steps.

You now should be able to log in to the SSH server without any password:

```
[student@onecoursesource ~]$ ssh 192.168.1.22 date
Mon Jan 11 16:59:32 PST 2019
```

Some security experts point out that having no passphrase for your key poses a security risk. However, if you do have a passphrase, each time you try to connect to the SSH server from the client, instead of being asked for your password, you are asked for the passphrase (and having to type a password/passphrase is what you were trying to avoid in the first place):

```
[student@onecoursesource ~]$ ssh 192.168.1.22 date
Enter passphrase for key '/home/student/.ssh/id_rsa':
Mon Jan 11 17:17:00 PST 2019
```


A method that you can use to have a passphrase for the RSA key and avoid having to type it for each connection is to use a utility called **ssh-agent**. The following steps demonstrate how this works:

Step 1. Start a new BASH shell with the **ssh-agent** utility:

```
ssh-agent /bin/bash
```

Step 2. Execute the following command:

```
ssh - add ~/.ssh/id_rsa
```

From this point on, when you use the **ssh-agent** shell to remotely connect to the SSH server, the connection takes place without the passphrase.

Summary

The focus of this chapter was to configure, secure, and connect to key servers. You learned about the LDAP server and how it provides directory-based information for features like networked user accounts. You also learned how to share files using an FTP server. Lastly, you learned how to connect to a remote Linux system via SSH. With SSH, you were able to log into a remote system and execute commands.

Key Terms

LDAP, OpenLDAP, Active Directory, object, attribute, schema, LDIF, DN, CN, SSSD, white pages, anonymous FTP, active FTP mode, passive FTP mode

Review Questions

1. An _____ is a component of an object.
2. The format of the file used to create LDAP objects is called _____.

   A. schema

   B. LDAP

   C. LDIF

   D. DN
3. Which command is used to create a rootdn password?

   A. rootpw

   B. slappasswd

   C. ldappasswd

   D. rootpasswd

4. The permissions of the OpenLDAP database directory should be set to _____. (Provide an octal value.)

5. The _____ command can be used to test the OpenLDAP configuration file before starting the server.

6. Fill in the blank to provide the rootdn password on the command line:

```
ldapadd -x -D "cn=root,dc=OCS,dc=com" _____ rootdnpw -f newpasswd.ldif
```

   A. -p

   B. -r

   C. -a

   D. -w

7. Which option means "use simple authentication" when using one of the **ldap**-based commands (such as **ldapsearch**)?

   A. -S

   B. -x

   C. -p

   D. -a

8. The _____directive in the **vsftpd.conf** file is used to allow anonymous FTP connections.

9. Which of the following **vsftpd.conf** directives are related to creating a list that allows specific users to access the FTP server? (Choose all that apply.)

   A. **userlist_enable**

   B. **userlist_file**

   C. **userlist_allow**

   D. **userlist_deny**

10. The _____ setting in the **/etc/ssh/sshd_config** file is used to specify which interfaces to accept SSH connections on.

11. The _____ setting of the **/etc/ssh/sshd_config** file is used to specify which users can connect to the SSH server.

Develop a Network Security Policy

For each network service, a variety of methods can be used to secure the service. For example, part of securing the BIND DNS service includes placing BIND in a chroot jail, implementing a split BIND configuration, and using Transaction Signature (all of which were covered in Chapter 20, "Network Service Configuration: Essential Services"), but many additional security settings can be used to make a more secure BIND server.

Your security policy should include specific steps to properly secure each network-based service. This can be a daunting task because there are so many different services, including many that are not covered in this book.

The previous three chapters covered several network-based services. The essential security features of each service were covered, so these will not be covered again in this chapter. Realize, however, that these security features are important when you're creating a security policy. Also important are the additional security features that these network-based services provide (something you will need to explore more if you end up implementing these services in a live environment).

Additionally, some network-based security features will be covered in more detail later in this book. For example, a firewall (covered in detail in Chapter 31, "Firewalls") can be used to block incoming connections to a system. Although firewalls will be a major part of any network security policy, they are not discussed in this chapter. Instead, this chapter focuses on the three key components of a network security policy: kernel parameters, TCP Wrappers, and the Network Time Protocol.

After reading this chapter and completing the exercises, you will be able to do the following:

Modify kernel parameters to provide better network security

Implement TCP Wrappers

Configure the system time manually

Configure the system to use a Network Time Protocol server

Kernel Parameters

Chapter 28, "System Booting," introduces you to a topic that is related to kernel parameters. You can use kernel parameters to modify the behavior of the kernel by adjusting key features. They can be used to change how the kernel manages devices, optimize memory usage, and enhance the security of the system.

Because a complete discussion of kernel parameters is provided in Chapter 28, this chapter focuses on the essentials of kernel parameters as well as some of the more important kernel parameters for network security.

The /etc/sysctl.conf File

Kernel parameters can be modified by making changes in the **/etc/sysctl.conf** file; see Example 23-1 for an example of this file.

Example 23-1 *The /etc/sysctl.conf File*

```
[root@onecoursesource ~]#head /etc/sysctl.conf
# Kernel sysctl configuration file for Red Hat Linux
#
# For binary values, 0 is disabled, 1 is enabled. See sysctl(8) and
# sysctl.conf(5) for more details.

# Controls IP packet forwarding
net.ipv4-ip_forward = 0

# Controls source route verification
net.ipv4.conf.default.rp_filter = 1
```


To modify a kernel parameter, you set the value of the parameter (**net.ipv4-ip_forward**, for example) to a new value in this file. For example, the **net.ipv4-ip_forward** kernel parameter determines if this system will act as a router. A router will forward network packets between networks. If you set **net.ipv4-ip_forward** to a value of 1 (0=false or no, 1=true or yes), then this machine can act as a router. A full router would also need two network connections (one for each network), but the point of this discussion is to point out how to change a kernel parameter, not how to set up a router.

Note that any changes you make to the **/etc/sysctl.conf** file will not have an immediate effect because the contents of this file are only read during system boot. Either reboot the system or run the **systemctl --system** command to have changes take place immediately.

It is important to note that there are thousands of kernel parameters, and many of them are designed to make the system more secure. This chapter only covers some of the more common security-based kernel parameters.

Ignoring ping Requests

The **ping** command is often used to determine if a remote host is accessible through the network. It does this by sending an Internet Control Message Protocol (ICMP) echo request packet to the remote host, expecting a response packet if the remote system is reachable. This poses two security challenges:

- A hacker can use **ping** to probe for active systems, trying to find systems that they can break into. Although this is not the only way to probe for active systems (see Chapter 30, "Footprinting," for other methods), it is a very common one. As a result, it is best to ignore **ping** requests for mission-critical systems.
- Responding to **ping** requests can leave a system vulnerable to denial of service (DoS) attacks. A DoS attack is when a large number of network packets are sent to a system, making it difficult for the system to handle all the data and rendering the system nonresponsive. This can also be accomplished via a distributed denial of service (DDoS) attack when packets are sent from multiple systems to overwhelm a host. Because of this vulnerability, it is best to ignore **ping** requests for mission-critical systems.

To ignore **ping** requests, use the following setting in the **/etc/sysctl.conf** file:

```
net.ipv4.icmp_echo_ignore_all = 1
```

WHAT COULD GO WRONG? If you set all of your systems to ignore **ping** requests, that means you cannot use the **ping** command to determine if a machine is responding via the network. Keep this in mind while trying to troubleshoot network issues.

Ignoring Broadcast Requests

Broadcast requests can be used for DoS and DDoS attacks, using a technique similar to that of **ping** requests. To ignore broadcast requests, use the following setting in the **/etc/sysctl.conf** file:

```
net.ipv4.icmp_echo_ignore_broadcasts = 1
```

Enabling TCP SYN Protection

A SYN flood attack is another DoS attack where SYN requests are used to make a system unresponsive. To ignore SYS requests, use the following setting in the **/etc/sysctl.conf** file:

```
net.ipv4.tcp_syncookies = 1
```

Disabling IP Source Routing

IP source routing is a feature that enables the sender of a packet to specify the network route that should be taken. This feature bypasses routing tables and makes your system vulnerable because hackers can employ man-in-the-middle attacks (interjecting a system between client-to-server communications) or they can use this feature to map your network or bypass your firewalls.

Each network interface has a separate IP source routing kernel parameter. So, to disable this feature from a specific network device, use a setting like the following:

```
net.ipv4.conf.eth0.accept_source_route = 0
```

TCP Wrappers

TCP wrappers are used when server programs that have been compiled with the **libwrap** library call that library when a system tries to access the service. For example, the Secure Shell server (**sshd**) calls the **libwrap** library when someone tries to connect to the Secure Shell service. The **libwrap** library uses configuration files to determine whether the SSH connection should be allowed, based on what machine is initiating the connection. The files used are the **/etc/hosts.allow** and **/etc/hosts.deny** files.

Before exploring the configuration files, you first need to be able to determine which services use the **libwrap** library. An easy way to do that is to use the **ldd** command:

```
[root@onecoursesource ~]# ldd /usr/sbin/sshd | grep libwrap
libwrap.so.0 => /lib64/libwrap.so.0 (0x00007efeb9df7000)
```

If the **ldd** command returns **libwrap.so.0**, then the program uses TCP wrappers. One way to find these "libwrapped" services is by executing a command like the one shown in Example 23-2.

Example 23-2 *Displaying "libwrapped" Programs*

```
[root@onecoursesource ~]# for i in /usr/sbin/*
>do
>ldd $i | grep libwrap && echo $i
>done
libwrap.so.0 => /lib64/libwrap.so.0 (0x00007facd0b05000)
/usr/sbin/exportfs
libwrap.so.0 => /lib64/libwrap.so.0 (0x00007fd295593000)
/usr/sbin/rpcinfo
libwrap.so.0 => /lib64/libwrap.so.0 (0x00007fd87537c000)
/usr/sbin/rpc.mountd
libwrap.so.0 => /lib64/libwrap.so.0 (0x00007f5251e30000)
/usr/sbin/rpc.rquotad
```

```
libwrap.so.0 => /lib64/libwrap.so.0 (0x00007f96e8b39000)
/usr/sbin/sshd
libwrap.so.0 => /lib64/libwrap.so.0 (0x00007f5a93020000)
/usr/sbin/xinetd
```

NOTE There may be services located in the **/usr/bin** and **/sbin** directories that use the **libwrap** library, so you should also search those directories.

To understand how the **/etc/hosts.allow** and **/etc/hosts.deny** files work, you first need to understand the order in which these two files are evaluated. When the **libwrap** library is asked by a service (**sshd**, for example) to authorize a connection, it first looks in the **/etc/hosts.allow** file to determine whether there is any rule that matches. The rules will be described in more detail, but essentially a rule includes a service (**sshd**) and a machine specification (IP address, hostname, and so on). If a rule matches in the **/etc/hosts.allow** file, the library utility tells the service to permit this access.

If no rule in the **/etc/hosts.allow** file matches, then the **libwrap** library looks at the rules in the **/etc/hosts.deny** file. If a rule matches in that file, then the **libwrap** library tells the service not to permit this access.

If no rules in either file match, then the **libwrap** library tells the service to permit this access. That means the default policy is to permit access, and you would need a rule in the **/etc/hosts.deny** to block access. See Figure 23-1 for a visual representation of this process.

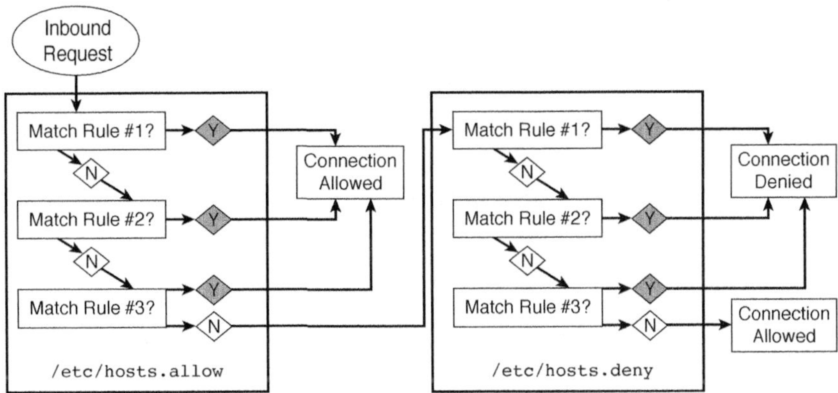

Figure 23-1 *TCP Wrappers*

The syntax of the rules in the **/etc/hosts.allow** and **/etc/hosts.deny** files is

```
service_list: client_list [options]
```

The service is the name of the binary executable service program (for example, **sshd** or **xinetd**). The client list is what system(s) this rule should apply to. Consider the following simple example:

```
[root@onecoursesource ~]# more /etc/hosts.allow
[root@onecoursesource ~]# more /etc/hosts.deny
sshd: test.onecoursesource.com
```

In the previous example, all clients are permitted to access the local system to connect to any service, except that clients from the test.onecoursesource.com system cannot connect via the **sshd** service.

The service list can consist of multiple services:

```
[root@onecoursesource ~]# more /etc/hosts.allow
[root@onecoursesource ~]# more /etc/hosts.deny
xinetd,sshd: test.onecoursesource.com
```

The previous example would deny access to users from the test.onecoursesource.com system who attempt to connect to the **sshd** or **xinetd** service on the local machine.

The keyword **ALL** could also be used to specify all services:

```
[root@onecoursesource ~]# more /etc/hosts.allow
[root@onecoursesource ~]# more /etc/hosts.deny
ALL: test.onecoursesource.com
```

The **client_list** is also flexible. The following list details the different values you can provide:

- **IP address**: Example: 192.168.0.100.
- **Network**: Example: 192.168.0.0/255.255.255.0 or 192.168.0.
- **Entire domain**: Example: **.example.com**.
- **ALL**: Matches every possible client.
- **LOCAL**: Matches clients without a dot in their hostname. Example: test1.
- **UNKNOWN**: Matches clients that can't be resolved via the hostname resolver (DNS, local hosts file, and so on).
- **KNOWN**: Matches clients that can be resolved via the hostname resolver (DNS, local hosts file, and so on).

Consider the following example:

```
[root@onecoursesource ~]# more /etc/hosts.allow
ALL: test.onecoursesource.com
[root@onecoursesource ~]# more /etc/hosts.deny
ALL: .onecoursesource.com
```

This would deny access to all systems within the onecoursesource.com domain *except* the test.onecoursesource.com machine.

Network Time Protocol

Maintaining an accurate system clock is critical for network security because many network services have time-based security features. For example, a network service may allow a login to be considered valid for a specific period of time. Or a network service might use PAM (Pluggable Authentication Modules, discussed in Chapter 7, "Managing User Accounts," and Chapter 8, "Develop an Account Security Policy") to allow access to services on specific dates or times.

The system clock can be set manually or configured from a Network Time Protocol (NTP) server. In this section, we first cover how to set the system clock manually. Although using an NTP server is more ideal, you should at least understand how to set a system clock manually in the event a reliable NTP server is not available.

Setting the System Clock Manually

You can use the **date** command to display the system clock:

```
[root@onecoursesource ~]#date
Tue Feb 28 22:15:33 PST 2019
```

The output of the **date** command is commonly used to generate unique filenames because the command has a very flexible output format. Here's an example:

```
[root@onecoursesource ~]#date "+%F"
2019-02-28
[root@onecoursesource ~]#touch data-$(date "+%F")
[root@onecoursesource ~]#ls data*
data-2019-02-28
```

Table 23-1 details some of the more commonly used date formats.

Table 23-1 Date Formats

Format	Description
%a	Abbreviated weekday name (Sun)
%A	Full weekday name (Sunday)
%b	Abbreviated month (Jan)
%B	Full month (January)
%d	Day of the month
%D	Same as **%m/%d/%y**
%F	Same as **%Y-%m-%d**
%m	Month
%n	A newline character
%y	Two-digit year (19)
%Y	Four-digit year (2019)

As the root user, you can use the **date** command to set the system clock using the following syntax:

```
[root@onecoursesource ~]#date Tue Feb 28 22:15:33 PST 2019
```

On some systems, the **timedatectl** command is used to display or set the system clock, as shown in Example 23-3.

Example 23-3 *The* ***timedatectl*** *Command*

```
[root@onecoursesource ~]#timedatectl
      Local time: Tue 2019-02-28 22:07:39 PST
  Universal time: Wed 2019-03-01 06:07:39 UTC
        RTC time: Sun 2018-06-12 17:50:56
        Timezone: America/Los_Angeles (PST, -0800)
     NTP enabled: yes
NTP synchronized: no
 RTC in local TZ: no
      DST active: no
 Last DST change: DST ended at
                  Sun 2018-11-06 01:59:59 PDT
                  Sun 2018-11-06 01:00:00 PST
 Next DST change: DST begins (the clock jumps one hour forward) at
                  Sun 2019-03-12 01:59:59 PST
                  Sun 2019-03-12 03:00:00 PDT
```

As the root user, you can use this command to set the system clock. Table 23-2 demonstrates the more commonly used methods of changing the system clock.

Table 23-2 Changing the System Clock

Method	Description
set-time [*time*]	Sets the system clock to the specified *time*
set-timezone [*zone*]	Sets the system time zone to the specified zone
set-ntp [*0*|*1*]	Enables (1) or disables (0) the Network Time Protocol

Setting the System Time Zone Manually

The **tzselect** utility is a menu-driven, CLI-based tool that allows a user to select a time zone. An example is provided in Example 23-4.

Example 23-4 *Executing the **tzselect** Command*

```
[root@onecoursesource~]#tzselect
Please identify a location so that time zone rules can be set correctly.
Please select a continent, ocean, "coord", or "TZ".
 1) Africa
 2) Americas
 3) Antarctica
 4) Arctic Ocean
 5) Asia
 6) Atlantic Ocean
 7) Australia
 8) Europe
 9) Indian Ocean
10) Pacific Ocean
11) coord - I want to use geographical coordinates.
12) TZ - I want to specify the time zone using the Posix TZ format.
#? 2
Please select a country whose clocks agree with yours.
 1) Anguilla               28) Haiti
 2) Antigua & Barbuda           29) Honduras
 3) Argentina               30) Jamaica
 4) Aruba                31) Martinique
 5) Bahamas                32) Mexico
 6) Barbados                33) Montserrat
 7) Belize                34) Nicaragua
 8) Bolivia                35) Panama
 9) Brazil                36) Paraguay
10) Canada                37) Peru
11) Caribbean Netherlands     38) Puerto Rico
12) Cayman Islands          39) St Barthelemy
13) Chile               40) St Kitts & Nevis
14) Colombia                41) St Lucia
15) Costa Rica               42) St Maarten (Dutch part)
16) Cuba               43) St Martin (French part)
17) Curacao               44) St Pierre & Miquelon
18) Dominica                45) St Vincent
```

```
19) Dominican Republic          46) Suriname
20) Ecuador                     47) Trinidad & Tobago
21) El Salvador                 48) Turks & Caicos Is
22) French Guiana               49) United States
23) Greenland                   50) Uruguay
24) Grenada                     51) Venezuela
25) Guadeloupe                  52) Virgin Islands (UK)
26) Guatemala                   53) Virgin Islands (US)
27) Guyana
#? 49
Please select one of the following time zone regions.
 1) Eastern Time
 2) Eastern Time - Michigan - most locations
 3) Eastern Time - Kentucky - Louisville area
 4) Eastern Time - Kentucky - Wayne County
 5) Eastern Time - Indiana - most locations
 6) Eastern Time - Indiana - Daviess, Dubois, Knox & Martin Counties
 7) Eastern Time - Indiana - Pulaski County
 8) Eastern Time - Indiana - Crawford County
 9) Eastern Time - Indiana - Pike County
10) Eastern Time - Indiana - Switzerland County
11) Central Time
12) Central Time - Indiana - Perry County
13) Central Time - Indiana - Starke County
14) Central Time - Michigan - Dickinson, Gogebic, Iron & Menominee Counties
15) Central Time - North Dakota - Oliver County
16) Central Time - North Dakota - Morton County (except Mandan area)
17) Central Time - North Dakota - Mercer County
18) Mountain Time
19) Mountain Time - south Idaho & east Oregon
20) Mountain Standard Time - Arizona (except Navajo)
21) Pacific Time
22) Pacific Standard Time - Annette Island, Alaska
23) Alaska Time
24) Alaska Time - Alaska panhandle
25) Alaska Time - southeast Alaska panhandle
26) Alaska Time - Alaska panhandle neck
27) Alaska Time - west Alaska
28) Aleutian Islands
29) Hawaii
#? 23

The following information has been given:

     United States
     Alaska Time

Therefore TZ='America/Anchorage' will be used.
Local time is now:        Tue Feb 28 21:03:15 AKST 2019.
Universal Time is now:    Wed Mar  1 06:03:15 UTC 2019.
Is the above information OK?
1) Yes
```

```
2) No
#? 1

You can make this change permanent for yourself by appending the line
     TZ='America/Anchorage'; export TZ
to the file '.profile' in your home directory; then log out and log in again.

Here is that TZ value again, this time on standard output so that you
can use the /usr/bin/tzselect command in shell scripts:
America/Anchorage
```

The output of the **tzselect** command is displayed on the screen, and it includes the value (for example, America/Anchorage) used on Debian-based systems to set the time zone for the system.

The location of the system time zone on Debian-based systems is located in the following file:

```
[root@onecoursesource ~]#more /etc/timezone
America/Anchorage
```

This file can be modified manually by using the output of the **tzselect** command.

On Red Hat–based distributions, the system time zone is set by the **/etc/localtime** file. This file is a symbolic link to a binary time zone file:

```
[root@onecoursesource ~]#ls -l /etc/localtime
lrwxrwxrwx 1 root root 41 Feb 18  2019 /etc/localtime ->
../usr/share/zoneinfo/America/Los_Angeles
[root@onecoursesource ~]#file /usr/share/zoneinfo/America/Los_Angeles
/usr/share/zoneinfo/America/Los_Angeles: timezone data, version 2,
4 gmt time flags, 4 std time flags, no leap seconds, 185 transition times,
4 abbreviation chars
```

To change the time zone on a system that uses the **/etc/localtime** file, create a new symbolic link:

```
[root@onecoursesource ~]# rm /etc/localtime
[root@onecoursesource ~]# ln -s /usr/share/zoneinfo/America/Goose_Bay/etc/localtime
[root@onecoursesource~]#ls -l /etc/localtime
lrwxrwxrwx 1 root root 36 Feb 28  2019 /etc/localtime ->
../usr/share/zoneinfo/America/Goose_Bay
```

Note that the **tzselect** output is still useful when setting a time zone on a Red Hat–based distribution because the output (for example, America/Anchorage) can be added to **/usr/share/zoneinfo** to create a full path to the time zone file: **/usr/share/zoneinfo/America/Anchorage**.

Setting the System Date Using NTP

The Network Time Protocol daemon (**ntpd**) is a process that ensures the system clock is in sync with the time provided by remote NTP servers. Most of the configuration for this process is handled via the **/etc/ntp.conf** file. Table 23-3 shows the important settings of the **/etc/ntp.conf** file.

Table 23-3 Settings for the **/etc/ntp/conf** File

Option	Description
driftfile	File that contains a value that represents the typical delta (change) over time from the NTP-reported time and the system clock. This value is used to regularly update the system clock without having to access an NTP server.

Option	Description
restrict	Used to indicate restrictions for the daemon, including what machines can access this NTP server when it is used as a service.
server	Used to list an NTP server for this machine when it is used as an NTP client.

See Example 23-5 for an example of a typical **/etc/ntp.conf** file.

Example 23-5 *Typical **/etc/ntp.conf** File*

```
# For more information about this file, see the man pages
# ntp.conf(5), ntp_acc(5), ntp_auth(5), ntp_clock(5), ntp_misc(5), ntp_mon(5).

driftfile /var/lib/ntp/drift

# Permit time synchronization with our time source, but do not
# permit the source to query or modify the service on this system.
restrict default kod nomodify notrap nopeer noquery

# Permit all access over the loopback interface.  This could
# be tightened as well, but to do so would effect some of
# the administrative functions.
restrict 127.0.0.1
restrict ::1

# Hosts on local network are less restricted.
#restrict 192.168.1.0 mask 255.255.255.0 nomodify notrap

# Use public servers from the pool.ntp.org project.
# Please consider joining the pool (http://www.pool.ntp.org/join.html).
server 0.fedora.pool.ntp.org iburst
server 1.fedora.pool.ntp.org iburst
server 2.fedora.pool.ntp.org iburst
server 3.fedora.pool.ntp.org iburst

# Enable public key cryptography.
#crypto

includefile /etc/ntp/crypto/pw

# Key file containing the keys and key identifiers used when operating
# with symmetric key cryptography.
keys /etc/ntp/keys
```

The **pool.ntp.org** address is a link to a cluster of NTP servers that are geographically spread throughout the world. These servers can be freely used within the **/etc/ntp.conf** file. For example, the following servers are provided by the Fedora project (note that these are often mirrors, pointing to other systems, so the resulting hostnames for these servers will be different once you have connected to them):

0.fedora.pool.ntp.org

1.fedora.pool.ntp.org

2.fedora.pool.ntp.org

3.fedora.pool.ntp.org

The **ntpq** command allows you to perform queries on NTP servers. For example, the **ntpq** command shown in Example 23-6 displays a summary of the status of NTP servers.

Example 23-6 *ntpq Command*

```
[root@onecoursesource ~]# ntpq -p
     remote           refid      st t when poll reach   delay   offset  jitter
==============================================================================
*propjet.latt.ne 68.110.9.223     2 u  120 1024  377   98.580    7.067   4.413
-services.quadra 208.75.88.4      3 u  272 1024  377   72.504  -10.689   1.612
+mirror          216.93.242.12    3 u  287 1024  377   20.406   -2.555   0.822
+108.61.194.85.v 200.23.51.102    2 u  741 1024  377   69.403   -3.670   1.610
```

Table 23-4 lists some important options to the **ntpq** command.

Table 23-4 Options for the **ntpq** Command

Option	Description
-d	Enable debugging mode
-n	List host IP addresses rather than names
-p	Print a list of all peers

NOTE: Using Kali Linux Some excellent tools are provided in Kali Linux that let you probe the network security of a system. However, given that we have not yet fully covered all the network security topics introduced in this book, further discussion of these tools is deferred until later chapters.

Summary

In this chapter, you studied several key elements of putting together a network security policy, including kernel parameters and how to implement TCP wrappers. You also learned how to configure the system clock, both manually and via NTP.

Key Terms

NTP, router, libwrap, DoS attack, DDoS attack, SYN flood attack, IP source routing, man in-the-middle attack

Review Questions

1. The primary configuration file for kernel parameters is the **/etc/**_____ file.

2. Which of the following parameters can be used to prevent a DoS attack? (Choose two.)

   A. **net.ipv4.icmp_echo_ignore_all**

   B. **net.ipv4.dos.trap**

   C. **net.ipv4.conf.eth0.accept_source_route**

   D. **net.ipv4.tcp_syncookies**

3. The _____ library is used to implement TCP wrappers.

4. Which of the following files are used with TCP wrappers? (Choose two.)

   A. **/etc/hosts.reject**

   B. **/etc/hosts.accept**

   C. **/etc/hosts.allow**

   D. **/etc/hosts.deny**

5. The _____ command allows you to perform queries on NTP servers.

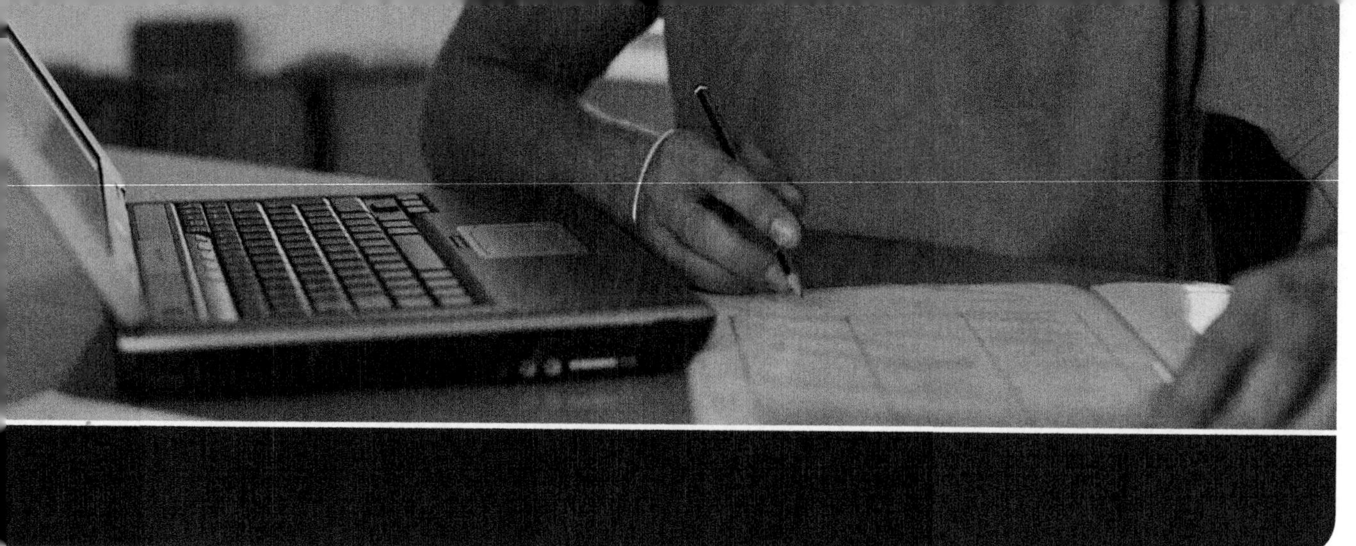

A program that runs on a Linux distribution is called a process. Knowing how to view processes and control (stop, pause, and restart) them is important for overall system health, as well as for security reasons. For example, while viewing processes, you may discover one that is taking a very large amount of system resources (CPU or RAM), which can have an impact on system performance.

Often, data is collected regarding how a process is functioning. This data is useful because it can help you troubleshoot software problems or discover hacking attempts.

Part VI

Process and Log Administration

In Part VI, "Process and Log Administration," you will explore the following chapters:

- Chapter 24, "Process Control," covers how to start, view, and control processes (programs).
- Chapter 25, "System Logging," covers how to view system logs as well as how to configure the system to create custom log entries.

Process Control

On any operating system, it is important to have the ability to determine what programs are running and to alter the states of these programs. In Linux, this can be accomplished by a collection of commands that allow you to display running programs, pause and restart programs, stop programs, and change program CPU priority. During this chapter you explore these topics as well as how to display essential CPU and memory information.

After reading this chapter and completing the exercises, you will be able to do the following:

Describe what processes and jobs are

Start and stop processes and jobs

List processes and jobs that are currently running

Change process priority

Display CPU and RAM information

Viewing Processes

Process is just a fancy way of saying "a program that is running on the system." It could be a command that you executed from a BASH shell, a web browser, or some program started by the operating system.

Both regular users and system administrators should know how to start and stop processes. Typically you start a process by executing a command or clicking an icon or menu option within the GUI, but there are other techniques you can use to start a process. Some of these additional techniques can provide the process with access to more system resources.

Before discussing detailed methods of starting and stopping processes, we'll first focus on how to view process information.

The ps Command

The **ps** command is used to list processes that are running on the system. With no arguments, the command will list any child process of the current shell as well as the BASH shell itself, as shown here:

```
[student@onecoursesource ~]$ps
  PID TTY          TIME CMD
18360 pts/0    00:00:00 bash
18691 pts/0    00:00:00 ps
```

Each line describes one process. By default, the **ps** command displays the following information:

- **PID**: Process ID number; each process has a unique ID that can be used to control the process.
- **TTY**: This is the terminal window that started the process. A terminal window is essentially a place where a user is able to issue commands from the command line. Originally this was a physical terminal (a machine that provided keyboard input to an operating system). In fact,

TTY stands for *Teletype*, a terminal that was used to connect to some of the original Unix systems. Terminals that start with "pts" are GUI-based virtual terminals, windows in which shell programs run, or remote connections (such as an SSH connection). You may also see "tty," which indicates a non-GUI-based virtual terminal. A "?" indicates a process that was not started from a terminal, but rather from another process (perhaps during system boot).

- **TIME**: CPU time; how much time the process has used to execute code on the CPU. Although this number can grow over time, it is typically a very small number (a handful of seconds or maybe a few minutes, but rarely more), unless something is wrong with the process.
- **CMD**: The command.

To list all processes running on the system, add the **-e** option, as shown next. This is useful because the process you want to view might have been started from a different shell (or by a different user), but the result of this command is dozens, perhaps even hundreds of lines of output.

```
[student@onecoursesource ~]$ps -e | wc -l
194
```

Recall that **wc -l** will display the number of lines of data; in the previous example, that would be the number of lines that the **ps** command produced. Each process is displayed on a separate line, so this system has 193 processes running (one line is the header information— PID, TTY, TIME, and so on). As a result, you likely will want to use a **grep** command to filter the output by command name:

```
[student@onecoursesource ~]$ps -e | grep xeyes
 4896 pts/2    00:00:00 xeyes
```

Another useful option to the **ps** command is the **-f** option, which displays "full information" about a process:

```
[student@onecoursesource ~]$ps -f
UID          PID  PPID  C STIME TTY          TIME CMD
student     3872  3693  0 16:41 pts/5    00:00:00 bash
student     4934  3872  0 21:05 pts/5    00:00:00 ps -f
```

The following new columns of data are included when you use the **-f** option:

- **UID**: User ID; the name of the user who started the process. This user "owns" the process, which is important because to control a process, you either need to be the root user or own the process.
- **PPID**: Parent process ID; this is the PID of the process that started the process described on this line. For example, in the previous output, the **ps -f** command was launched by the **bash** command, so the PPID of the **ps -fe** command matches the PID of the **bash** command. This can be useful to find a specific process in the event that more than one execution of a command or program is currently running.
- **C**: State; a value of 1 means it is currently executing code on the CPU (or has code in the CPU queue), and a value of 0 means it is currently "sleeping" (waiting for something to happen so it can perform an action).
- **STIME**: Start time; when the command was started. If a command has been running for more than 24 hours, this will be displayed as a date rather than as a time.

There are many more useful options to the **ps** command. This is one of those situations where you really want to explore the documentation and find additional options that will be useful for your daily work.

The pgrep Command

Often you will use a combination of the **ps** and **grep** commands to display specific processes:

```
[student@onecoursesource ~]$ps -e | grep sleep
25194 pts/0    00:00:00 sleep
```

The **pgrep** command can also provide a similar function:

```
[student@onecoursesource ~]$pgrep sleep
25194
```

Important options to the **pgrep** command are shown in Table 24-1.

Table 24-1 Options for **pgrep** Command

Option	Description
-G *name*	Match processes by group name.
-l	Display process name and PID.
-n	Display most recently started processes first.
-u *name*	Match processes by user *name*.

The top Command

The **top** command displays process information that is updated on a regular basis (by default, every two seconds). The first half of the output of the **top** command contains overall information, whereas the second half displays a select list of processes (by default, the processes with the most CPU utilization).

See Figure 24-1 for a typical output of the **top** command.

```
top - 16:09:10 up 2 days,  3:07,  2 users,  load average: 0.00, 0.07, 0.12
Tasks: 119 total,   2 running, 117 sleeping,   0 stopped,   0 zombie
%Cpu(s):  1.3 us,  1.0 sy,  0.0 ni, 97.0 id,  0.3 wa,  0.0 hi,  0.3 si,  0.0 st
KiB Mem:   4048292 total,  3832140 used,   216152 free,   356468 buffers
KiB Swap:        0 total,        0 used,        0 free.  1610568 cached Mem

  PID USER      PR  NI    VIRT    RES    SHR S %CPU %MEM     TIME+ COMMAND
26159 root      20   0 2461400 1.243g  24040 S  2.7 32.2  44:59.94 java
  965 root       0 -20       0      0      0 S  0.3  0.0   0:35.58 loop0
27545 nobody    20   0   87524   3616    892 S  0.3  0.1   0:05.32 nginx
28770 root      20   0   12824    940    776 S  0.3  0.0   0:14.39 ping
    1 root      20   0   33604   2952   1476 S  0.0  0.1   0:00.98 init
    2 root      20   0       0      0      0 S  0.0  0.0   0:00.00 kthreadd
    3 root      20   0       0      0      0 S  0.0  0.0   0:05.72 ksoftirqd/0
    5 root       0 -20       0      0      0 S  0.0  0.0   0:00.00 kworker/0:0H
    7 root      20   0       0      0      0 S  0.0  0.0   1:12.43 rcu_sched
    8 root      20   0       0      0      0 R  0.0  0.0   1:39.49 rcuos/0
    9 root      20   0       0      0      0 S  0.0  0.0   0:00.00 rcu_bh
   10 root      20   0       0      0      0 S  0.0  0.0   0:00.00 rcuob/0
   11 root      rt   0       0      0      0 S  0.0  0.0   0:00.00 migration/0
```

Figure 24-1 *The* ***top*** *Command*

The **top** command provides both general system statistics as well as process information. Table 24-2 describes the output displayed in Figure 24-1.

Table 24-2 Output of the **top** Command

Output	Description
First line	Output derived from the **uptime** command; see "The uptime Command" section in this chapter for further details.
Second line	A summary of processes running on the system.

Output	Description
Third line	CPU statistics since the last time top data was refreshed.
Fourth line	Physical memory statistics. (Note: Type **E** while in the **top** command to change the value from kilobytes to another value.)
Fifth line	Virtual memory statistics.
Remaining lines	A list of processes and associated information.

See Figure 24-2 for information about how **top** can be used to help solve system problems.

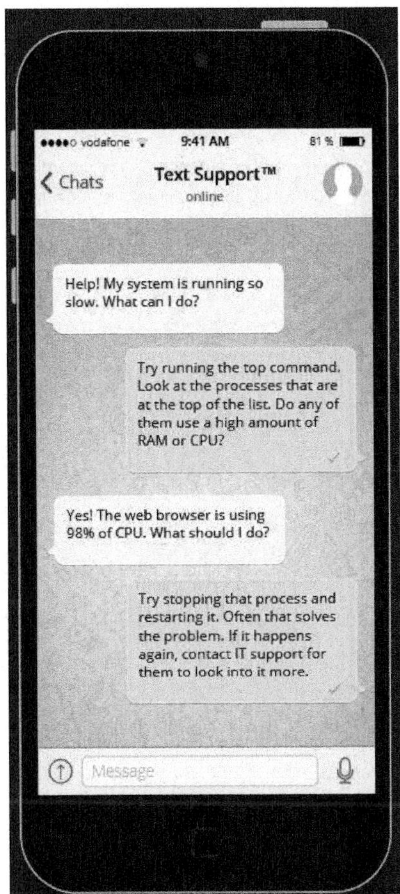

Figure 24-2 *Text Support™—Solving Issues on Systems that Lag*

While the **top** command is running, you can type interactive commands to perform actions such as change display values, reorder the process list, and kill (stop) processes. These interactive commands are single characters. The more important interactive commands are provided in Table 24-3.

Table 24-3 Commands Within the Execution of the **top** Command

Command	Description
h	Help; display a summary of interactive commands.
E	Change the default value from kilobytes to another value; the available values are "cycled" through until the display is back to kilobytes.

Command	Description
Z	Toggle color highlighting on; use lowercase **z** to toggle color and non-color.
B	Toggle bold on and off.
<>	Move the sort column to the left (<) or the right (>).
s	Set the update value to a different value other than the default of 2 seconds.
k	Kill a process by providing a PID.
q	Quit the **top** command.

The **top** command also supports several command-line options. Important options are displayed in Table 24-4.

Table 24-4 Important Options to the **top** Command

Option	Description
-d	Set the time between data refreshes. For example, **top -d 5** would mean that the data is refreshed every 5 seconds, rather than the default of every 2 seconds.
-n *number*	Maximum number of data refreshes until the **top** command exits.
-u *username*	Display only processes owned by *username*.

The uptime Command

Although the **uptime** command doesn't display individual process data, it does provide stats regarding overall process activity. The **uptime** command displays how long the system has been up for and its load average, as shown here:

```
[student@onecoursesource ~]$ uptime
 15:06:13 up 2 days,  9:09,  3 users,  load average: 0.01, 0.02, 0.05
```

The load average indicates the CPU usage over the last 1, 5, and 15 minutes (0.01, 0.02 and 0.05, for example). Load average is related to the number of CPUs, as described next:

- A load average of 1.0 on a single CPU system means 100% utilization.
- A load average of 2.0 on a single CPU system means 200% utilization (meaning that processes were often waiting for the CPU because it was busy).
- A load average of 1.0 on a system with two CPUs means 50% utilization.
- A load average of 2.0 on a system with two CPUs means 100% utilization.

The information provided by the **uptime** command can be useful in determining if the CPU is overloaded. Consistent utilization of the CPU over 100% indicates a problem and can cause servers to lag in response time.

Security Highlight

A high load average may indicate a hacking attempt. Even worse, it could be the result of a successful hack in which the hacker has placed intelligence-gathering scripts on the system.

The free Command

The **free** command displays memory statistics. Although this command does not display how much memory each individual process uses, it does provide a good overview of how much memory is available and how much is currently used. Here's an example:

```
[student@onecoursesource ~]$ free
             total       used       free     shared    buffers     cached
Mem:       4048292    3891592     156700        460     370640    1617812
-/+ buffers/cache:    1903140    2145152
Swap:       400000          0          0
```

Values are displayed in bytes by default. The important areas to focus on are how much is the total memory and how much is the amount of free memory. The columns **shared**, **buffers**, and **cache** are more important for developers.

Swap refers to "swap space," a topic that's discussed in Chapter 10, "Manage Local Storage: Essentials," and Chapter 11, "Manage Local Storage: Advanced Features." Recall that swap space is hard drive storage that is temporarily used to store data from memory in the event that system RAM becomes full.

Important options to the **free** command include those shown in Table 24-5.

Table 24-5 Options for the **free** Command

Option	Description
-k	Display memory usage in kilobytes.
-m	Display memory usage in megabytes.
-g	Display memory usage in gigabytes.
-s *n*	Update display every *n* seconds.
-t	Display a line that shows the total of each column.

Running Processes

Typically, processes are started as foreground jobs. When a process is in the foreground, the BASH shell from which the process was launched is not available. A process that is run in the background leaves the BASH shell available for the user to execute additional commands.

The terms *job* and *process* are essentially interchangeable. Any program running on the system is a process. A job is a process that is executed from the command line. Each BASH shell keeps track of jobs that were launched from that BASH shell.

Conversational Learning™—Processes Versus Jobs

Gary: Hi, Julia. Can you explain something to me? I'm not really understanding the difference between a process and a job.

Julia: Hi, Gary. No problem. Let's start by describing a process. A process is any command, program, or application that is running on the system. This includes anything that was started during the boot process, by other users, or programs started by other processes.

Gary: OK, I understand that.

Julia: A job is also a process. Consider jobs to be a subset of all the processes running on the system. Not all processes are jobs. For example, any process started at boot is not considered a job.

Gary: So, which processes are considered to be jobs?

Julia: Any process that is started by a user in a shell. In other words, any command or program that you start by typing the command or program name in a shell.

Gary: Why are these processes called jobs?

Julia: Because there are some commands and features you can use on jobs that you can't use on other processes. For example, the **jobs** command displays all the processes that were started in the current shell.

Gary: OK, but I could also see those "job processes" by using the **ps** command, right?

Julia: Yes, but the point is that often you just want to focus on the processes started by your current shell, so the **jobs** command often makes more sense in these cases. Also, jobs have job numbers that are unique for each shell. You can see these job numbers by using the **jobs** command, and you can use them with commands like the **kill** command.

Gary: OK, this all makes more sense now. Thank you!

Running a process in the background allows you to continue to work in the BASH shell and execute additional commands. To execute a process in the background, add an ampersand (**&**) character to the end of the command:

```
[student@onecoursesource ~]$xeyes &
```

Each BASH shell keeps track of the processes that are running from that BASH shell. These processes are referred to as *jobs*. To list the currently running jobs, execute the **jobs** command from the BASH shell:

```
[student@onecoursesource ~]$jobs
[1]-  Running                  xeyes&
[2]+  Running                  sleep 777 &
```

Each job is assigned a job number to control the job. Refer to this job number by the following syntax: *%job_number*.

Pausing and Restarting Processes

To pause a program that is running in the foreground, hold down the **Ctrl** key and press **z**. You can then see whether that job is stopped (paused) by running the **jobs** command.

A paused process is restarted in the background by using the **bg** command, like so:

```
[student@onecoursesource ~]$jobs
[1]+  Stopped                  sleep 999
[student@onecoursesource ~]$bg %1
[1]+ sleep 999 &
[student@onecoursesource ~]$jobs
[1]+  Running                  sleep 999 &
```

A paused process is restarted in the foreground by using the **fg** command, as shown here:

```
[student@onecoursesource ~]$jobs
[1]+  Stopped                  sleep 999
[student@onecoursesource ~]$fg %1
sleep 999
```

Killing Processes

As morbid as it sounds, the phrase "kill a process" is used to describe when you completely stop a process, not just pause it. Several methods are available to kill a process, including the following:

- The **kill** command
- The **pkill** command
- The **killall** command
- The **xkill** command
- Clicking the close box of a GUI-based program

The kill Command

The **kill** command can be used to change the state of a process, including to stop (kill) a process. To stop a process, first determine its process ID or job number and then provide that number as an argument to the **kill** command. Both the process ID and job number methods are demonstrated in Example 24-1.

Example 24-1 *Stopping Jobs with the **kill** Command*

```
[student@onecoursesource ~]$jobs
[1]-  Running                  sleep 999 &
[2]+  Running                  sleep 777 &
[student@onecoursesource ~]$kill %2
[student@onecoursesource ~]$jobs
[1]-  Running                  sleep 999 &
[2]+  Terminated               sleep 777
[student@onecoursesource ~]$ps -fe | grep sleep
student  17846 12540  0 14:30 pts/2    00:00:00 sleep 999
student  17853 12540  0 14:31 pts/2    00:00:00 grep --color=auto sleep
[student@onecoursesource ~]$kill 17846
[student@onecoursesource ~]$ps -fe | grep sleep
student  17856 12540  0 14:31 pts/2    00:00:00 grep --color=auto sleep
[1]+  Terminated               sleep 999
```

The **kill** command sends a signal to the process to inform the process what action to take. This signal can be specified as either a numeric argument or a keyword argument. Example 24-2 demonstrates how you can list all the possible signals that the **kill** command can send to a process.

Example 24-2 *Listing Kill Signals*

```
[student@onecoursesource ~]$ kill -l | head -5
 1) SIGHUP 2) SIGINT3) SIGQUIT4) SIGILL 5) SIGTRAP
 6) SIGABRT7) SIGBUS8) SIGFPE 9) SIGKILL10) SIGUSR1
11) SIGSEGV12) SIGUSR213) SIGPIPE14) SIGALRM15) SIGTERM
16) SIGSTKFLT17) SIGCHLD18) SIGCONT19) SIGSTOP20) SIGTSTP
21) SIGTTIN22) SIGTTOU23) SIGURG24) SIGXCPU25) SIGXFSZ
```

The output in Example 24-2 was truncated with the **head** command because the later kill signals are more esoteric and not as important as the earlier signals shown in the output. Some of the more important kill signals are described in Table 24-6.

Table 24-6 Important Kill Signals

Signal	Description
-1 or **SIGHUP**	Sends an HUP signal. See "The nohup Command" section later in this chapter for more details. Example: **kill -1** ***PID***.
-2 or **SIGINT**	Keyboard interrupt; same as pressing Ctrl+C to stop a process that is running in the foreground. Note that some processes ignore signal 2, so this might not stop these processes. Example: **kill -2** ***PID***.
-9 or **SIGKILL**	Force kill; does not provide the process any choice, forcing the process out of memory. A potential negative side effect is that the process does not have the chance to perform operations like saving data or deleting temporary files. Example: **kill -9*PID***.
-15 or **SIGTERM**	Standard kill; this signal is sent by default. Note that some processes ignore signal 15, so it might not stop those processes. Example: **kill -15** ***PID***.

Security Highlight

Because of potential negative side effects, avoid using signal 9 when stopping processes, at least initially. Allow processes to shut down gracefully by issuing a regular **kill** command, wait about 30 seconds, and then attempt the **kill -9** command.

The **-9** option may be necessary if the developer of the program you are trying to stop decided to ignore regular kill signals, or if a hacker has taken control or executed potentially harmful processes on the system.

The pkill Command

When sending signals to a process using the **kill** command, you indicate which process by providing a PID (process ID). With the **pkill** command, you can provide a process name, a username, or another method to indicate which process (or processes) to send a signal. For example, the following will send a kill signal to all processes owned by the user sarah:

```
[student@onecoursesource ~]$pkill -u sarah
```

Important options include those shown in Table 24-7.

Table 24-7 Options for the **pkill** Command

Option	Description
-G *name*	Match processes by group *name*.
-u *name*	Match processes by user *name*.

The killall Command

The **killall** command is used to stop all the processes of a specific name. Here's an example:

```
[student@onecoursesource ~]$killall firefox
```

Important options include those shown in Table 24-8.

Table 24-8 Options for the **killall** Command

Option	Description
-I	Case-insensitive match.
-i	Interactive; prompt before sending the signal to the process.
-r *pattern*	Match processes by regular expression *pattern*.
-s *signal*	Send *signal* to process instead of the default signal.
-v	Verbose; report if process was successfully sent the signal.

The xkill Command

You can kill a process by running the **xkill** command and then just clicking the process that you want to stop. Refer to Figure 24-3 to see the first step in using the **xkill** command.

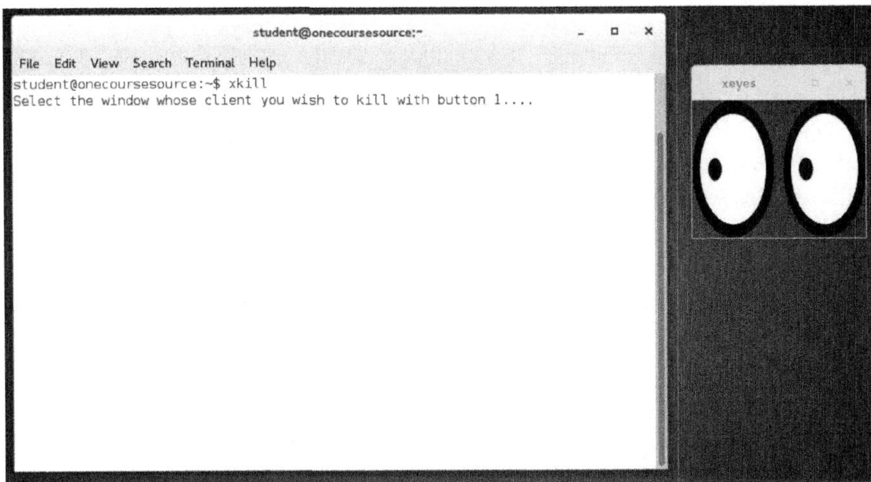

Figure 24-3 *Starting the **xkill** Command*

The first step of running the **xkill** command is to make sure you can see the window of the program you want to stop. In this case, the **xkill** command will be used to stop the **xeyes** program (the pair of "eyes" to the right of the terminal window). Note the message that is displayed after running the **xkill** command and then see the result of clicking the **xeyes** program in Figure 24-4.

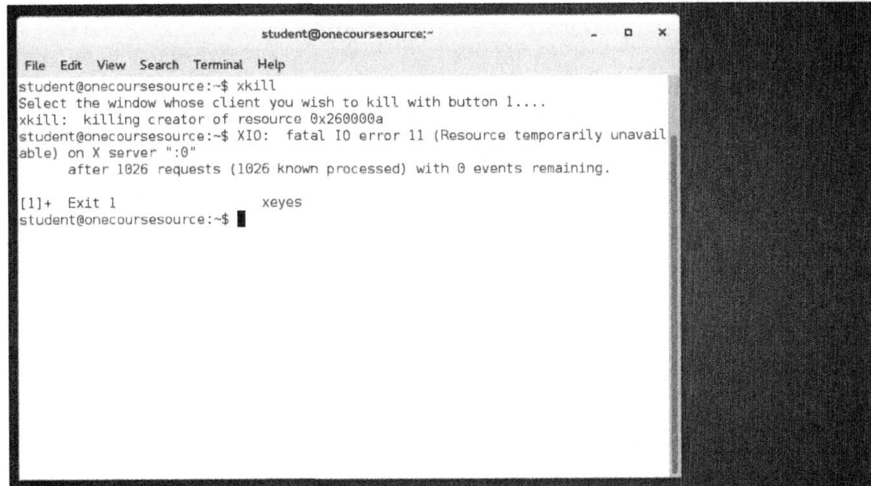

Figure 24-4 *Stopping the xeyes Program*

The nohup Command

Each process has a parent process that started it. For example, if you execute a command in a BASH shell, then that command's parent process is the BASH shell process.

When a parent process is stopped, an HUP signal is sent to all the child processes. This HUP signal is designed to stop the child processes. By default, a child process will stop when sent an HUP signal.

To avoid this, execute the child process with the **nohup** command:

```
[student@onecoursesource ~]$nohup some_command
```

This technique is typically used when you remotely log in to a system and want to have some command continue to run even if you are disconnected. When you are disconnected, all the programs you have running are sent HUP signals. Using the **nohup** command allows this specific process to continue running.

Process Priority

"Nice" values are used to indicate to the CPU which process has the higher priority for access to the CPU. The values range from **-20** (highest priority) to **19** (lowest priority). The default priority of any job created by a user is **0**. You can set the priority value of a new process by running the process with the **nice** command. To change the priority value of an existing process, use the **renice** command.

The nice Command

To specify a different "nice" value than the default, execute the job via the **nice** command:

```
[student@onecoursesource ~]$  nice -n 5 firefox
```

Note that regular users cannot assign a negative nice value. These values can only be used by the root user.

To view the nice value of a process, use the **-o** option with the **ps** command and include the value of "nice":

```
[student@onecoursesource ~] ps -o nice,pid,cmd
 NI   PID CMD
  0 23865 -bash
  5 27967 firefox
  0 27969 ps -o nice,pid,cmd
```

The renice Command

Use the **renice** command to change the nice value of an existing job, as shown in Example 24-3.

Example 24-3 *Using **renice** to Change the Nice Value of an Existing Job*

```
[student@onecoursesource ~] ps -o nice,pid,cmd
 NI   PID CMD
  0 23865 -bash
 5 28235 sleep 999
  0 28261 ps -o nice,pid,cmd
[student@onecoursesource ~] renice -n 10 -p 28235
28235 (process ID) old priority 5, new priority 10
[student@onecoursesource ~] ps -o nice,pid,cmd
 NI   PID CMD
```

```
 0 23865 -bash
10 28235 sleep 999
 0 28261 ps -o nice,pid,cmd
```

NOTE Regular (non-root) users can only change the priority of an existing process to a lower priority. Only the root user can alter a process priority to a high priority.

Important options for the **renice** command include those shown in Table 24-9.

Table 24-9 Options for the **renice** Command

Option	Description
-g *group*	Change the priority of all files owned by *group*.
-u *user*	Change the priority of all files owned by *user*.

Summary

In this chapter, you explored how to control processes, including how to start, pause, resume, and stop processes. You also learned several techniques to display process information as well as change process CPU priority.

Key Terms

Process, PID, TTY, terminal, kill, job, background process, foreground process, HUP

Review Questions

1. The _____ command is used to display all processes running on the system.
2. Which command is used to display process information on a regular basis (every 2 seconds by default)?
   - A. **free**
   - B. **uptime**
   - C. **top**
   - D. **jobs**
3. The highest CPU priority for a process is specified by the nice value of _____.
4. Which command can stop a process from executing? (Choose all that apply.)
   - A. **stop**
   - B. **skill**
   - C. **pkill**
   - D. **xkill**
5. The _____ command can be used to prevent a process from terminating if its parent process stops running.

System Logging

System logs are critical for several reasons: These logs provide administrators with useful information to aid in troubleshooting problems. They are also useful in identifying potential hacking attempts. Additionally, logs can be used to provide general information about services, such as which web pages have been provided by a web server.

One area that may complicate matters is the different logging methods available for Linux. Some distributions make use of an older technique called **syslog** (or newer versions of **syslog** called **rsyslog** or **syslog-ng**), whereas other distributions use a newer technique called **journald**. Both of these techniques are covered in this chapter.

After reading this chapter and completing the exercises, you will be able to do the following:

View system logs

Configure syslog to create custom log entries

Rotate older log files

View journald logs

Customize journald

Syslog

The **syslog** service has existed since 1980. Although advanced at the time it was created, its limitations have grown over time as more complex logging techniques were required.

In the late 1990s, the **syslog-ng** service was created to extend the features of the traditional **syslog** service. Remote logging (including TCP support) was included.

In the mid-2000s, the **rsyslog** service was created, also as an extension of the traditional **syslog** service. The **rsyslog** service includes the ability to extend the **syslog** capabilities by including modules.

In all three cases, the configuration of the services (the format of **syslog.conf** file) is consistent, with the exception of slightly different naming conventions (**rsyslog.conf**, for example) and additional features available in the log files.

The syslogd Daemon

The **syslogd** daemon is responsible for the logging of application and system events. It determines which events to log and where to place log entries by configuration settings that are located in the **/etc/syslog.conf** file.

Important options to the **syslogd** command are displayed in Table 25-1.

Table 25-1 Important ***syslogd*** Options

Option	Description
-d	Enable debugging mode.

Option	Description
-f	Specify the configuration file (**/etc/syslog.conf** is the default).
-m *x*	Create a timestamp in the log files every *x* minutes. Set this to **0** to omit timestamps.
-r	Enables the **syslogd** daemon to accept logs from remote systems.
-S	Verbose mode.
-x	Disable DNS lookups for IP addresses.

Security Highlight

Log entries typically include a timestamp, so using the **-m** option to introduce additional timestamps is unnecessary and could result in more disk space usage.

Most modern distributions use **rsyslogd** instead of **syslogd**. However, from a configuration standpoint, there is very little difference: A few options are different, and the primary configuration file is **/etc/rsyslog.conf** instead of **/etc/syslog.conf**.

Keep in mind that the **syslog.conf** (or **rsyslog.conf**) file is used to specify what log entries to create. This file is discussed in more detail later in this chapter. You should also be aware that there is a file in which you can specify the **syslogd** or **rsyslogd** options. This file varies depending on your distribution. Here are two locations where you might find this file on distributions that use **rsyslogd**:

- On Ubuntu, go to **/etc/default/rsyslog**.
- On Fedora, go to **/etc/sysconfig/rsyslog**.

Regardless of where the file resides, its contents should look something like the following:

```
root@onecoursesource:~# more /etc/default/rsyslog
# Options for rsyslogd
# -x disables DNS lookups for remote messages
# See rsyslogd(8) for more details
RSYSLOGD_OPTIONS=""
```

You specify the options described in Table 25-1 by using the **RSYSLOGD_OPTIONS** variable. For example, to configure the current system as a syslog server, use the following:

```
RSYSLOGD_OPTIONS="-r"
```

NOTE If you are working on an older system that still uses **syslogd**, the only real difference in terms of this log file is its name (**syslog**, not **rsyslog**). Also, **rsyslogd** supports a few more options that were not mentioned in this chapter.

The /var/log Directory

The **/var/log** directory is the standard location for log files to be placed by the **syslogd** and **rsyslogd** daemons. The exact files created by these daemons can vary from one distribution to another. The following describes some of the more commonly created files:

- **/var/log/auth.log**: Log entries related to authentication operations (typically users logging into the system).
- **/var/log/syslog**: A variety of log entries are stored in this file.

- **/var/log/cron.log**: Log entries related to the **crond** daemon (**crontab** and **at** operations).
- **/var/log/kern.log**: Log entries from the kernel.
- **/var/log/mail.log**: Log entries from the email server (although Postfix normally stores its log entries in a separate location).

Not all log files in the **/var/log** directory are created by the **syslogd** daemon. Many modern services create and manage log files separate from **syslogd**. Consider the entries from the **syslogd** daemon as fundamentally part of the operating system, while separate processes (such as web servers, print servers, and file servers) create log files for each process. Exactly what additional files you will find in the **/var/log** directory depends largely on what services your system is providing.

Security Highlight

The non-**syslogd** log files are just as important as those managed by **syslogd**. When you develop a security policy for handling log files, take these additional log files into consideration.

The /etc/syslog.conf File

The **/etc/syslog.conf** file is the configuration file for the **syslogd** daemon that tells the daemon where to send the log entries it receives. The following demonstrates a typical **syslog.conf** file with comments and blank lines removed:

```
[root@localhost ~]# grep -v "^$" /etc/syslog.conf | grep -v "^#"
*.info;mail.none;authpriv.none;cron.none        /var/log/messages
authpriv.*                                       /var/log/secure
mail.*                   -/var/log/maillog
cron.*                                           /var/log/cron
*.emerg                                         *
uucp,news.crit                                   /var/log/spooler
local7.*                   /var/log/boot.log
```

Each line represents one logging rule that is broken into two primary parts: the selector (for example, **uucp,news.crit**) and the action (for example, **/var/log/spooler**). The selector is also broken into two parts: the facility (for example, **uucp,news**) and the priority (for example, **crit**).

The following list shows the available facilities, along with a brief description:

- **auth (or security)**: Log messages related to system authentication (like when a user logs in).
- **authpriv**: Log messages related to non-system authentication (like when a service such as Samba authenticates a user).
- **cron**: Log message sent from the **crond** daemon.
- **daemon**: Log messages sent from a variety of daemons.
- **kern**: Log messages sent from the kernel.
- **lpr**: Log messages sent from older, outdated printer servers.
- **mail**: Log messages sent from mail servers (typically sendmail).
- **mark**: Log message designed to place a timestamp in log files.
- **news**: Log messages for the news server (an outdated Unix server).
- **syslog**: Log messages generated by **syslogd**.
- **user**: User-level log messages.
- **uucp**: Log messages generated by uucp (an outdated Unix server).

- **local0 through local7**: Custom log messages that can be generated by nonstandard services or shell scripts. See the discussion of the **logger** command later in this chapter for more details.
- *: Represents all the facilities.

The following list shows the available priority levels in order from least serious to most serious:

- **debug**: Messages related to debugging issues with a service.
- **info**: General information about a service.
- **notice**: A bit more serious than info messages, but not quite serious enough to warrant a warning.
- **warning (or warn)**: Indicates some minor error.
- **err (or error)**: Indicates a more serious error.
- **crit**: A very serious error.
- **alert**: Indicates that a situation must be resolved because the system or service is close to crashing.
- **emerg (or panic)**: The system or service is crashing or has crashed completely.
- *: Represents all the levels.

It is actually the choice of the software developer as to what priority level is used to send a message. For example, the folks who developed the **crond** daemon may have considered a mistake in a **crontab** file to be a warning-level priority, or they may have chosen to make it an error-level priority. Generally speaking, **debug**, **info**, and **notice** priority levels are FYI-type messages, whereas **warning** and **error** mean "this is something you should look into," and **crit**, **alert**, and **emerg** mean "do not ignore this; there is a serious problem here."

Once the severity has been established, the **syslogd** daemon needs to determine what action to take regarding the log entry. The following list shows the available actions:

- **Regular file**: A file in the **/var/log** directory to place the log entry.
- **Named pipes**: This topic is beyond the scope of this book, but essentially it's a technique to send the log entry to another process.
- **Console or terminal devices**: Recall that terminal devices are used to display information in a login session. By sending the message to a specific terminal window, you cause it to be displayed for the user who currently has that terminal window open.
- **Remote hosts**: Messages are sent to a remote log server.
- **User(s)**: Writes to the specified user's terminal windows (use * for all users).

Security Highlight

You will see two formats for specifying a file to write log entries to:

/var/log/maillog

-/var/log/maillog

If you do not have a hyphen (the "-" character) before the filename, every log entry will result in the **syslogd** daemon writing to the hard drive. This will have a performance impact on systems such as mail servers, where each new mail message received or sent would result in a log entry.

If you place a hyphen before the filename, the **syslogd** daemon will "batch" writes, meaning every log entry does not result in a hard drive write, but rather the **syslogd** daemon will collect a group of these messages and write them all at one time.

So, why is this a security issue? If your syslogd daemon generates so many hard drive writes that it drastically impacts the performance of the system, then critical operations might fail, resulting in data loss or the inability to access critical data.

Conversational Learning™—Remote Log Servers

Gary: Julia… got a question for you.

Julia: What's that?

Gary: I have been asked to send a log message from one of our servers to a remote log server. Why is that important?

Julia: Ah, this is common on system-critical servers, especially if they have a presence on the Internet. Pretend for a moment that you are a hacker and you have gained unauthorized access to the server in question. Once you have access, you probably want to hide your tracks. Guess what you will probably do?

Gary: Oh, I see! I'd delete the log files! Then nobody could tell how I accessed the system. Shoot, they might not even know that I have accessed the system at all!

Julia: Right, but what if those log files were also copied over to another server?

Gary: Ah, then it would be much harder to hide my tracks. I'd have to hack into yet another system, probably one that has different accounts and services, making it much more difficult.

Julia: And now you know why you want a copy of the log files sent to another server.

Gary: Thanks, Julia!

Julia: Always happy to help out, Gary.

The /etc/rsyslog.conf File

Most modern systems make use of the **rsyslogd** daemon instead of the **syslogd** daemon. The newer **rsyslod** daemon has more functionality, but most of the features of the older **syslogd** daemon still work.

For example, although there are features in the **/etc/rsyslog.conf** file that do not exist in the **/etc/syslog.conf** file, the contents described earlier in this chapter are still valid for the newer configuration file.

You should be aware of a few features that are new to the **/etc/rsyslog.conf** file. One feature is the ability to use modules. Modules provide more functionality; for example, the following module will allow the **rsyslogd** daemon to accept log messages from remote systems via the TCP protocol:

```
# provides TCP syslog reception
#$ModLoad imtcp
#$InputTCPServerRun 514
```

Also, a new section in the **/etc/rsyslog.conf** file called **GLOBAL DIRECTIVES** allows you to provide settings for all log file entries. For example, the following will set the user owner, group owner, and permissions of any new log file that is created by the **rsyslogd** daemon:

```
# Set the default permissions for all log files.
#
$FileOwner syslog
$FileGroup adm
$FileCreateMode 0640
```

The last major change is that most log rules are not stored in the **/etc/rsyslog.conf** file, but rather in files in the **/etc/rsyslog.d** directory. These files can be included in the main configuration file as follows:

```
# Include all config files in /etc/rsyslog.d/
#
$IncludeConfig /etc/rsyslog.d/*.conf
```

By using an "include" directory, you can quickly add or remove large sets of log rules by adding or removing a file from the directory.

Creating Your Own /etc/syslog.conf Entry

The ability to read existing **/etc/syslog.conf** entries is important, but being able to create your own entries is also useful. Creating an entry consists of modifying the **/etc/syslog.conf** file first, then restarting the **syslogd** server. After the **syslogd** server has restarted, you should test your new entry by using the **logger** command.

Adding an Entry

First, determine what sort of entry you want to capture. For example, typically all **crond** daemon log messages are sent to the **/var/log/cron** file because of the following entry in the **/etc/syslog.conf** file:

```
cron.*                                              /var/log/cron
```

What if you also want **cron** messages at **crit** priority and higher sent to the root user's terminal window? You could add the following entry to the **/etc/syslog.conf** file:

```
cron.crit                                           root
```

When you specify a priority, all messages at that priority level and above (more serious) are sent to the destination. To capture only messages at a specific priority level, use the following syntax:

```
cron.=crit                                          root
```

25

Another way of sending messages is from a script that you create. You can issue **logger** commands (see the next section) within your script to create log entries, but you do not want to use the standard facilities, such as **cron** and **mail**, as these are associated with specific services already. Instead, use one of the custom facilities (**local0**, **local1**, and so on). The highest of these values is **local7**. Here's an example:

```
local7.* /var/log/custom
```

After making these changes and saving the **/etc/syslog.conf** file, restart the **syslogd** service (see Chapter 28, "System Booting," for details about restarting services). Then use the **logger** command to test your new entry.

WHAT COULD GO WRONG? Errors in the **/etc/syslog.conf** file could have an impact on existing log rules. Make sure you always use the **logger** command to test new rules.

Using the logger Command

The **logger** utility can be used to send a log entry to the **syslogd** daemon:

```
[root@localhost ~]# logger -p local7.warn "warning"
```

Important options to the **logger** command are provided in Table 25-2.

Table 25-2 Important **logger** Command Options

Option	Description
-i	Log the PID of the logger process.
-s	Output the message to STDERR as well as send it to the **syslogd** daemon.

Option	Description
-f *file*	Use the contents of ***file*** as the message to send to the **syslogd** daemon.
-p	Specify the facility and priority.
-t	Mark the log entry with a tag for searching purposes.

The logrotate Command

The **logrotate** command is a utility designed to ensure that the partition that holds the log files has enough room to handle the log files. Log file sizes increase over time as more entries are added. The **logrotate** command routinely makes backup copies of older log files and eventually removes older copies, limiting the filesystem space that the logs use.

This command is configured by the **/etc/logrotate.conf** file and files in the **/etc/logrotate.d** directory. Typically the **logrotate** command is configured to run automatically as a **cron** job:

```
[root@localhost ~]# cat /etc/cron.daily/logrotate
#!/bin/sh

/usr/sbin/logrotate /etc/logrotate.conf
EXITVALUE=$?
if [ $EXITVALUE != 0 ]; then
    /usr/bin/logger -t logrotate "ALERT exited abnormally with [$EXITVALUE]"
fi
exit 0
```

The /etc/logrotate.conf File

The **/etc/logrotate.conf** file is the primary configuration file for the **logrotate** command. A typical **/etc/logrotate.conf** file looks like Example 25-1.

Example 25-1 *Typical /etc/logrotate.conf File*

```
[root@localhost ~]#cat /etc/logrotate.conf
# see "man logrotate" for details
# rotate log files weekly
weekly

# keep 4 weeks worth of backlogs
rotate 4

# create new (empty) log files after rotating old ones
create

# uncomment this if you want your log files compressed
#compress

# RPM packages drop log rotation information into this directory
include /etc/logrotate.d

# no packages own wtmp -- we'll rotate them here
/var/log/wtmp {
    monthly
```

```
    minsize 1M
    create 0664 root utmp
    rotate 1
}
```

The top part of the **/etc/logrotate.conf** file is used to enable global settings that apply to all files that are rotated by the **logrotate** utility. These global settings can be overridden for individual files by a section defined like the following:

```
/var/log/wtmp {
    monthly
    minsize 1M
    create 0664 root utmp
    rotate 1
}
```

Typically these sections are found in files located in the **/etc/logrotate.d** directory, but they can be placed directly in the **/etc/logrotate.conf** file, as in the previous example of **/var/log/wtmp**.

Important settings in the **/etc/logrotate.conf** file include those shown in Table 25-3.

Table 25-3 Settings in the **/etc/logrotate.conf** File

Settings	Description
daily | weekly | monthly	How often to rotate files.
rotate *x*	Keep ***x*** number of old (backup) files.
create	Create a new log file when backing up the old log file.
compress	Compress the backup log file, using the **gzip** command by default; the **compress** command can be changed by the **compresscmd** setting.
compresscmd	Specify the compression utility to use when compressing backup log files.
datetext	Backup log files are normally named by the convention **logfile.*x*** where ***x*** represents a number (0, 1, 2, and so on); using **datetext** will change the extension to a date value (YYYYMMDD).
mail *address*	Mails the backup log file to ***address***.
minsize *X*	Only rotate the log file if the size is at least the value specified by ***X***.
nocompress	Do not compress the backup copy of the log file.
olddir *dir*	Place the backup log files in the ***dir*** directory.

Files in the **/etc/logrotate.d** directory are used to override the default settings in the **/etc/logrotate.conf** file for the **logrotate** utility. The settings for these files are the same as the settings for the **/etc/logrotate.conf** file.

By using this "include" directory, you can easily insert or remove log rotate rules by adding or deleting files in the **/etc/logrotate.d** directory.

The journalctl Command

On modern Linux systems, the logging process is handled by the **systemd-journald** service. To query **systemd** log entries, use the **journalctl** command, as shown in Example 25-2.

Example 25-2 *Using the **journalctl** Command*

```
[root@localhost ~]#journalctl | head
-- Logs begin at Tue 2019-01-24 13:43:18 PST, end at Sat 2019-03-04 16:00:32 PST. --
Jan 24 13:43:18 localhost.localdomain systemd-journal[88]: Runtime journal is using 8.0M
(max allowed 194.4M, trying to leave 291.7M free of 1.8G available → current
➥limit 194.4M).
Jan 24 13:43:18 localhost.localdomain systemd-journal[88]: Runtime journal is using 8.0M
(max allowed 194.4M, trying to leave 291.7M free of 1.8G available → current
➥limit 194.4M).
Jan 24 13:43:18 localhost.localdomain kernel: Initializing cgroup subsys cpuset
Jan 24 13:43:18 localhost.localdomain kernel: Initializing cgroup subsys cpu
Jan 24 13:43:18 localhost.localdomain kernel: Initializing cgroup subsys cpuacct
Jan 24 13:43:18 localhost.localdomain kernel: Linux version 3.10.0-327.18.2.el7.x86_64
(builder@kbuilder.dev.centos.org) (gcc version 4.8.3 20140911 (Red Hat 4.8.3-9) (GCC) ) #1
SMP Thu May 12 11:03:55 UTC 2016
Jan 24 13:43:18 localhost.localdomain kernel: Command line: BOOT_IMAGE=/vmlinuz-3.10.0-
327.18.2.el7.x86_64 root=/dev/mapper/centos-root ro rd.lvm.lv=centos/root rd.lvm.
lv=centos/swap crashkernel=auto rhgb quiet LANG=en_US.UTF-8
Jan 24 13:43:18 localhost.localdomain kernel: e820: BIOS-provided physical RAM map:
Jan 24 13:43:18 localhost.localdomain kernel: BIOS-e820: [mem 0x0000000000000000-
0x000000000009fbff] usable
```

Important options to the **journalctl** command include those shown in Table 25-4.

Table 25-4 Options to the **journalctl** Command

Option	Description
--all or -a	Show all fields in full format.
-r	Reverse the log order so newest entries are displayed first.
-k	Show only kernel messages.
--priority=*value*	Only show messages that match the priority ***value*** (**emerg**, **alert**, **crit**, **err**, **warning**, **notice**, **info**, or **debug**).

The /etc/systemd/journald.conf file

The **/etc/systemd/journald.conf** file is used to configure the **systemd-journald** service. Typically this file contains all commented-out values by default. Important settings for the **/etc/systemd/journald.conf** file include those shown in Table 25-5.

Table 25-5 Settings for the **/etc/systemd/journald.conf** File

Setting	Description
Storage=*value*	Where to store the journal date; ***value*** can be **"volatile"**, **"persistent"**, **"auto"**, or **"none"**. If this is set to **"persistent"**, then the **systemd-journald** service stores journal entries in files located in the **/var/log/journal** directory.
Compress=*[1|0]*	If this is set to **1** (true), journal entries are compressed before writing to file.

Summary

In this chapter, you explored how to view and create log file entries using one of the **syslogd** services. You also learned how to prevent log files from growing to the size that quickly fills the **/var** partition.

Key Terms

Log, facility, priority

Review Questions

1. The **/etc/**_____ file is the primary configuration file for the **rsyslogd** daemon.
2. Which syslog facility is used to log messages related to non-system authentication?
   - **A.** **auth**
   - **B.** **authpriv**
   - **C.** **authnosys**
   - **D.** **authsys**
3. Log entries that are generated by the kernel are typically stored in the **/var/log/**_____ file.
4. The _____ syslog priority indicates that the system or a service has crashed.
   - **A.** **info**
   - **B.** **warning**
   - **C.** **crit**
   - **D.** **emerg**
5. The _____ command can be used to send a log entry to the **syslogd** daemon.

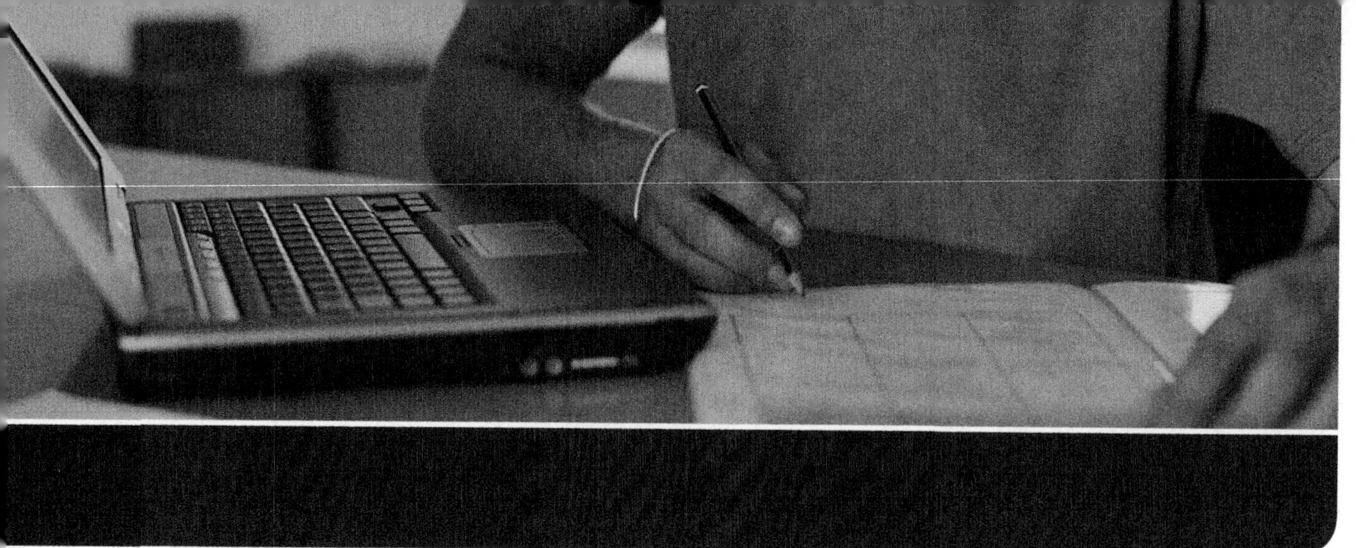

As the requirements of a Linux system grow, there will be a need to install additional software. This is one area in which different Linux distributions diverge. Some distributions make use of a series of commands and utilities, originally created by Red Hat, to manage software. Other distributions opt to use similar tools available from Debian, another popular Linux distribution. Because you will likely work on multiple distributions, knowing both methods is important.

After installing software, you need to know how to start server processes automatically during the boot process. This part of the book includes a chapter that describes how the boot process works and how you can modify the boot process to include additional server processes.

Part VII

Software Management

In Part VII, "Software Management," you will explore the following chapters:

- Chapter 26, "Red Hat–Based Software Management," covers how to administer software on Red Hat–based systems such as Fedora and CentOS.
- Chapter 27, "Debian–Based Software Management," covers the process of configuring your system to connect to the network.
- Chapter 28, "System Booting," covers the process of configuring several network-based tools.
- Chapter 29, "Develop a Software Management Security Policy," provides you with the means to create a security policy using the knowledge you acquire in Chapters 26, 27, and 28.

Red Hat–Based Software Management

Most distributions offer a variety of tools to help you manage software. For Red Hat–based distributions, there are three commonly used tools. The **rpm** command allows you to view various information regarding installed packages. The command also allows you to install and remove packages.

The **yum** and **dnf** commands also provide the ability to view, install, and remove packages. However, these tools provide a higher level of functionality, as the commands are able to connect to software repositories and handle issues related to software dependencies.

These software management tools, along with additional theory about software packages, will be covered in this chapter.

After reading this chapter and completing the exercises, you will be able to do the following:

View package information with the rpm **and** yum **commands**

Install software packages using the rpm **and** yum **commands**

Use the rpm **and** yum **commands to delete software packages**

Perform advanced package management operations, including creating software repositories

Red Hat Packages

A software package is a file that contains a software program and additional required components. For example, consider a web server software program. The program serves up web pages to web clients, but it needs additional data, such as configuration file data, in order to perform its job.

In a sense, a software package is like the tar files discussed in Chapter 2, "Working on the Command Line." It contains a collection of files that make up the complete software program. However, it also contains additional information, such as metadata (information about the software; who created it, when it was released, and so on) and dependencies. *Dependency* is the term for when one software program relies on another program.

The Red Hat package naming convention (for example, **ntpdate-4.7.6p5-22.fc27.x86_64.rpm**) is described in Figure 26-1.

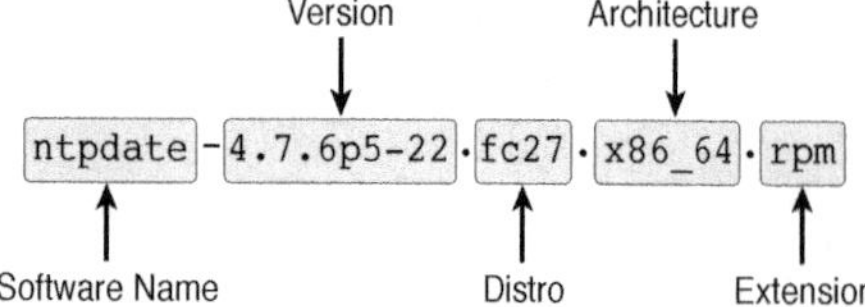

Figure 26-1 *Components of a Red Hat Package Name*

The package name provides basic information about the package itself. The package may be named after the primary command provided by the package, or it may be named after the entire software project.

Package versions can be a bit confusing, as there are no rules regarding versions. Typically the first number of the version ("4" for **ntpdate-4.7.6p5-22.fc27.x86_64.rpm**) is a major release version, and the second number ("7" for **ntpdate-4.7.6p5-22.fc27.x86_64.rpm**) is a minor release version. Beyond that, it is really up to the software vendor. Some vendors use up to six numbers in their version, and some use alpha characters (for example, "6p5").

The developers who maintain the Linux distributions often add a "distro" number to the package name. For example, the "fc27" in Figure 26-1 means "Fedora, release 27." This indicates that some changes may have been made to the software specifically for that distribution before it was repackaged.

The architecture is normally either for a 32-bit platform ("x86") or a 64-bit platform ("x86_64"), but distributions that support non-Intel platforms will have different values for the architecture. You may also see "noarch," which means the software in the package is not dependent on any specific architecture.

How to Obtain Packages

If you are using a command like **yum** or **dnf**, these tools can download software packages automatically for you. However, if you are using the **rpm** command to install software packages, you need to find and download packages manually (or use an option to the **rpm** command to tell it where to get the packages).

There are several sources for packages, including the following:

- **The distribution site**: Each distribution has its own servers.
- **www.rpmfind.net**: A website that has RPM packages.
- **rpm.pbone.net**: A website that has RPM packages.
- **Independent project sites**: Any software vendor that creates software designed to run on Red Hat–based distributions will likely have a website where the software can be downloaded directly.
- **GitHub.com**: Many software vendors also share code via this website.

Security Highlight

Be very careful when you download software. Because software must be installed by the root user, it provides an easy way for hackers to compromise your system. These hackers will repackage valid software with some additional tools designed to compromise your system.

The /var/lib/rpm Directory

Although you rarely need to perform any task directly on the **/var/lib/rpm** directory, you should be aware that this is the location where all package metadata is stored. Package metadata is information about packages, such as the date a package was built and the vendor who built the package. Whenever you install new software (or remove software), changes are made to the database in the **/var/lib/rpm** directory:

```
[root@onecoursesource ~]#ls /var/lib/rpm
Basenames     __db.002  Group       Obsoletename  Requirename  Triggername
Conflictname  __db.003  Installtid  Packages      Sha1header
__db.001      Dirnames  Name        Providename   Sigmd5
```

Although you should realize that this directory exists and that its purpose is to store information about packages, you shouldn't modify any of these files directly. Occasionally you may need to rebuild the databases in these files, but this should be accomplished by executing the **rpm --rebuilddb** command.

Using the rpm Command

RPM originally was an acronym for Red Hat Package Manager. As more distributions started using the RPM system to manage software packages, RPM was repackaged to mean RPM Package Manager (a recursive acronym—technically a "backronym," since the acronym already existed and a definition was provided). Many distributions use RPM, including RHEL (Red Hat Enterprise Linux), Fedora, CentOS, and SUSE.

The **yum** and **dnf** commands are "front-end" applications that eventually run **rpm** commands. Although you may find the **yum** or **dnf** command to be easier to use, you will encounter situations in which it is better to use the **rpm** command. Read the Conversational Learning™ box for reasons why the **rpm** command can be useful to execute directly.

Conversational Learning™—Why Use the rpm Command?

Gary: Hi, Julia. I'm wondering if you can explain something about the **rpm** command for me?

Julia: I'll do my best.

Gary: OK, it seems like **yum** and **dnf** are easier to use and provide more functionality, like the ability to download and automatically install dependency packages. So, why should I ever use the **rpm** command?

Julia: There are several reasons. For example, suppose you have a package file that has no dependencies. You can easily install that with the **rpm** command.

Gary: OK, are there other situations?

Julia: Yes, you will find that the **rpm** command is very good at performing database queries. While many of these queries can be performed by the **yum** and **dnf** commands, the **rpm** command has more features.

Gary: Ah, good point. Any other examples?

Julia: Suppose someone sends you an **rpm** file and you want to see information about it. The **rpm** command works well for that scenario.

Gary: Good point. I don't want to install that package without taking a look at it first!

Julia: Exactly. Also, you can manually extract files from a package without installing them by using an **rpm**-based command called **rpm2cpio**.

Gary: OK, OK, you have me convinced! I should study the **rpm** command and its features in more detail. Thanks, Julia.

Listing rpm Information

To display all installed packages, execute the **rpm -qa** command. The **-q** option stands for "query" and the **-a** option stands for "all" (note that the **head** command was used to limit the output because there are usually hundreds of packages on a typical system), as shown in Example 26-1.

Example 26-1 *The rpm -qa Command*

```
[root@onecoursesource ~]# rpm -qa | head
pciutils-libs-3.3.0-1.fc20.x86_64
iptables-services-1.4.19.1-1.fc20.x86_64
bouncycastle-pg-1.46-10.fc20.noarch
```

```
perl-HTTP-Negotiate-6.01-7.fc20.noarch
php-pdo-5.5.26-1.fc20.x86_64
vim-filesystem-7.4.475-2.fc20.x86_64
sisu-inject-0.0.0-0.4.M4.fc20.noarch
perl-DBD-Pg-2.19.3-6.fc20.x86_64
php-bcmath-5.5.26-1.fc20.x86_64
zlib-1.2.8-3.fc20.x86_64
```

To view basic package information, execute the following command: **rpm -qi *pkgname***. Replace ***pkgname*** with the name of the package you want to display. See Example 26-2 for an example.

Example 26-2 *Viewing Package Information*

```
[root@onecoursesource ~]# rpm -qi zlib
Name        : zlib
Version     : 1.2.11
Release     : 3.fc28
Architecture: x86_64
Install Date: Tue 6 Feb 2019 09:09:01 AM PST
Group       : System Environment/Libraries
Size        : 188163
License     : zlib and Boost
Signature   : RSA/SHA256, Tue 28 Aug 2017 02:04:04 AM PDT, Key ID 2eb161fa246110c1
Source RPM  : zlib-1.2.8-3.fc20.src.rpm
Build Date  : Sat 26 Aug 2017 06:42:20 AM PDT
Build Host  : buildvm-05.phx2.fedoraproject.org
Relocations : (not relocatable)
Packager    : Fedora Project
Vendor      : Fedora Project
URL         : http://www.zlib.net/
Summary     : The compression and decompression library
Description :
Zlib is a general-purpose, patent-free, lossless data compression
library which is used by many different programs.
```

26

Note that important information from the output of the **rpm -qi** command includes the version, release, and install date. The description can also be helpful to determine what the software package is designed to do.

To list files installed with the package, execute the following command: **rpm -ql *pkgname***. This is a useful command to run right after installing a software package so you are aware of which new files have been added to the system. Here's an example:

```
[root@onecoursesource ~]# rpm -ql zlib
/usr/lib64/libz.so.1
/usr/lib64/libz.so.1.2.8
/usr/share/doc/zlib
/usr/share/doc/zlib/ChangeLog
/usr/share/doc/zlib/FAQ
/usr/share/doc/zlib/README
```

If the package provides some sort of service, then the service will likely have configuration files. To list the configuration files of a package, execute the following command: **rpm -qc *pkgname***. For example:

```
[root@onecoursesource ~]# rpm -qc vsftpd
/etc/logrotate.d/vsftpd
/etc/pam.d/vsftpd
/etc/vsftpd/ftpusers
/etc/vsftpd/user_list
/etc/vsftpd/vsftpd.conf
```

Note that the **zlib** package was not used in the previous example because it has no configuration files:

```
[root@onecoursesource ~]# rpm -qc zlib
[root@onecoursesource ~]#
```

It can also be useful to view the documentation files provided by the package. This allows you to view details about how to use the software that came with the package. To list documentation files, execute the following command: **rpm -qd *pkgname***. For example:

```
[root@onecoursesource ~]# rpm -qd zlib
/usr/share/doc/zlib/ChangeLog
/usr/share/doc/zlib/FAQ
/usr/share/doc/zlib/README
```

What if you found a file that is already on the system and you want to know if anything else was installed as part of the package? This can be really useful when the file has been altered because you can retrieve the original file directly from the package. To view what package a file originated from, use the **rpm -qf *filename*** command:

```
[root@onecoursesource ~]# rpm -qf /usr/lib64/libz.so.1
zlib-1.2.8-3.fc20.x86_64
```

If one file from a package has been modified or removed, then other files from that same package may also have been modified or removed. To get a list of the state of all files of a package, use the **rpm -V *pkgname*** command:

```
[root@onecoursesource ~]# rpm -V clamd
.....UG..    /var/clamav
missing      /var/run/clamav
```

The output of the **rpm -V** command can be a bit difficult to get used to. If a file that was installed with the package is no longer on the system, then the output will mark the file as "missing." If a file has been modified, then the command provides a list of characters (and "dots," or periods) that indicate what changes have been made. These characters are defined in the man page for the **rpm** command, as shown in Example 26-3.

Example 26-3 *Man Page Description of the Output of the **rpm -V** Command*

```
[root@onecoursesource ~]#man rpm
...
       S file Size differs
       M Mode differs (includes permissions and file type)
       5 digest (formerly MD5 sum) differs
       D Device major/minor number mismatch
       L readLink(2) path mismatch
       U User ownership differs
       G Group ownership differs
       T mTime differs
P caPabilities differ
...
```

Security Highlight

Finding changes to a package's files does not automatically indicate a problem. For example, if a configuration file's size has changed, that likely means that an administrator edited the file to customize how the software runs.

Consider carefully which files should and should not change. For instance, files in the **/bin** and **/usr/bin** directories are typically binary (not text) files and should not change in size. Files in the /etc directory are typically configuration files, and you would expect these files to change in size.

Viewing Package Dependencies

Packages often need features from other packages. These features are called *dependencies*. To list the dependencies of a package, execute the following command: **rpm -qR** ***pkgname***. See Example 26-4 for an example.

Example 26-4 *The* ***rpm -qR*** *Command*

```
[root@onecoursesource ~]#rpm -qR vsftpd
/bin/bash
/bin/sh
/bin/sh
/bin/sh
config(vsftpd) = 3.0.2-6.fc20
libc.so.6()(64bit)
libc.so.6(GLIBC_2.14)(64bit)
libc.so.6(GLIBC_2.15)(64bit)
libc.so.6(GLIBC_2.2.5)(64bit)
libc.so.6(GLIBC_2.3)(64bit)
libc.so.6(GLIBC_2.3.4)(64bit)
libc.so.6(GLIBC_2.4)(64bit)
libc.so.6(GLIBC_2.7)(64bit)
libcap.so.2()(64bit)
libcrypto.so.10()(64bit)
libcrypto.so.10(libcrypto.so.10)(64bit)
libdl.so.2()(64bit)
libnsl.so.1()(64bit)
libpam.so.0()(64bit)
libpam.so.0(LIBPAM_1.0)(64bit)
libssl.so.10()(64bit)
libssl.so.10(libssl.so.10)(64bit)
libwrap.so.0()(64bit)
logrotate
rpmlib(CompressedFileNames) <= 3.0.4-1
rpmlib(FileDigests) <= 4.6.0-1
rpmlib(PayloadFilesHavePrefix) <= 4.0-1
rtld(GNU_HASH)
rpmlib(PayloadIsXz) <= 5.2-1
```

Note that the dependencies are not just package names but also features that are provided by a package. For example, in the output of Example 26-4, "logrotate" indicates a dependency on the **logrotate** package, but "/bin/bash" indicates a dependence on the **/bin/bash** command. Most of the other lines indicate libraries (small programs that are shared by other programs to provide functions).

To list what package provides a dependency, execute the following command: **rpm -q --whatprovides *capability***. Example 26-5 provides some examples.

Example 26-5 *The **rpm -q --whatprovides** Command*

```
[root@onecoursesource ~]#rpm -q --whatprovides /bin/bash
bash-4.2.53-2.fc28.x86_64
[root@onecoursesource ~]#rpm -q --whatprovides "libc.so.6()(64bit)"
glibc-2.18-19.fc28.x86_64
[root@onecoursesource ~]#rpm -q --whatprovides /sbin/ldconfig
glibc-2.18-19.fc28.x86_64
[root@onecoursesource ~]#rpm -q --whatprovides "libwrap.so.0()(64bit)"
tcp_wrappers-libs-7.6-76.fc28.x86_64
```

You also may be wondering "if this one package needs this dependency, what other packages also need this dependency?" To list what else requires a dependency, execute the following command: **rpm -q --whatrequires *capability***. For example, see the output of Example 26-6.

Example 26-6 *Output of **rpm -q --whatrequires***

```
[root@onecoursesource ~]# rpm -q --whatrequires "libwrap.so.0()(64bit)"
net-snmp-agent-libs-5.7.2-18.fc28.x86_64
net-snmp-5.7.2-18.fc28.x86_64
quota-4.01-11.fc28.x86_64
sendmail-8.14.8-2.fc28.x86_64
audit-2.4.1-1.fc28.x86_64
vsftpd-3.0.2-6.fc28.x86_64
pulseaudio-libs-5.0-25.fc28.x86_64
openssh-server-6.4p1-8.fc28.x86_64
systemd-208-31.fc28.x86_64
proftpd-1.3.4e-3.fc28.x86_64
```

The preceding output can be very useful. For example, we can tell that if we remove the package that provided the **"libwrap.so.0()(64bit)"** library, then the packages listed by the aforementioned **rpm -q --whatrequires** command will no longer work correctly.

Once you determine what package provides a specific dependency, you may also want to view what other dependencies that package provides. To list these other dependencies, execute the following command: **rpm -q--provides *pkgname***. For example:

```
[root@onecoursesource ~]# rpm -q --provides tcp_wrappers-libs-7.6-76.fc28.x86_64
libwrap.so.0()(64bit)
tcp_wrappers-libs = 7.6-76.fc28
tcp_wrappers-libs(x86-64) = 7.6-76.fc28
```

Package Listing Tricks

The **rpm** command is well known for having powerful features to list software package information. For example, suppose you suspect a new package is causing problems on the system, but you do not recall which packages have been installed lately (or you suspect a hacker has installed some new packages). Consider running the **rpm -qa --last** command, which will display installed packages in order from the installation date:

```
[root@onecoursesource ~]# rpm -qa --last | head -n 5
perl-Pod-Checker-1.60-292.fc28.noarch        Fri 10 Feb 2019 11:09:09 AM PST
```

```
perl-Pod-Parser-1.61-3.fc28.noarch          Fri 10 Feb 2019 11:09:08 AM PST
perl-Readonly-1.03-24.fc28.noarch           Fri 10 Feb 2019 10:10:25 AM PST
perl-Readonly-XS-1.05-16.fc28.x86_64        Fri 10 Feb 2019 10:10:24 AM PST
libX11-devel-1.6.1-1.fc28.x86_64            Thu 26 Jan 2019 10:26:50 AM PST
```

Recall that the **rpm -qi** command provides information about an installed package. To see the sort of information on a package that has not been installed yet, execute the command **rpm -qip** ***pkgname.rpm***. Note that the **-p** option means "this is a package file, not an installed package." See Example 26-7 for an example.

Example 26-7 *The **rpm -qip** Command*

```
[root@onecoursesource ~]#rpm -qip fedora/packages/tcl-8.5.14-1.fc28.x86_64.rpm
Name        : tcl
Epoch       : 1
Version     : 8.5.14
Release     : 1.fc28
Architecture: x86_64
Install Date: (not installed)
Group       : Development/Languages
Size        : 4592249
License     : TCL
Signature   : RSA/SHA256, Thu 15 Aug 2017 10:36:45 AM PDT, Key ID 2eb161fa246110c1
Source RPM  : tcl-8.5.14-1.fc28.src.rpm
Build Date  : Thu 15 Aug 2017 02:04:19 AM PDT
Build Host  : buildvm-13.phx2.fedoraproject.org
Relocations : (not relocatable)
Packager    : Fedora Project
Vendor      : Fedora Project
URL         : http://tcl.sourceforge.net/
Summary     : Tool Command Language, pronounced tickle
Description :
The Tcl (Tool Command Language) provides a powerful platform for
creating integration applications that tie together diverse
applications, protocols, devices, and frameworks. When paired with the
Tk toolkit, Tcl provides a fastest and powerful way to create
cross-platform GUI applications.  Tcl can also be used for a variety
of web-related tasks and for creating powerful command languages for
applications.
```

Which packages take up the most hard drive space? To list packages by size, execute the following command: **rpm -qa --queryformat '%{name} %{size}\n' | sort -n -k 2 -r**. For example:

```
[root@onecoursesource ~]# rpm -qa --queryformat '%{name} %{size}\n' |
➥ sort -n -k 2 -r | head -n 5
kernel 151587581
kernel 147584558
kernel 146572885
firefox 126169406
moodle 122344384
```

Note that in the preceding command line, the **head** command is used to reduce the amount of output to the top five largest files. The **sort** command performs a reverse numeric (higher numbers displayed first) sort on the second field of each line (the size of the package in bytes). Although the size is in bytes, this can easily be converted into megabytes or gigabytes using one of many online calculators (for example, http://whatsabyte.com/P1/byteconverter.htm).

In some cases you may want to list all packages that came from a specific vendor. This can be accomplished by executing the following command: **rpm -qa --qf '%{name} %{vendor}\n' | grep *vendor-name***. Replace ***vendor-name*** with the name of the vendor, like so:

```
[root@onecoursesource ~]# rpm -qa --qf '%{name} %{vendor}\n' | grep  "Virtualmin, Inc."
virtualmin-base Virtualmin, Inc.
```

NOTE The previous command might not work on your system if you do not have any software from "Virtualmin, Inc." So, how did we pick this particular vendor? We first ran the **rpm -qa --qf '%{name} %{vendor}\n'** command, which yielded hundreds of lines of output. Most of these lines displayed a vendor name of "Fedora Project," because the distribution we were working on is Fedora. Next, we ran the **rpm -qa --qf '%{name} %{vendor}\n' | grep -v "Fedora Project"** command to display all the packages that were not provided by the "Fedora Project" (recall that the **-v** option to the **grep** command means "match all lines that don't contain this pattern"). Then we just picked one of the results at random for the demonstration. The point of this description is to demonstrate that knowing powerful command-line tools like **grep** can make your life a lot easier!

Security Highlight

To add or remove software requires you to be logged in as the root user. However, any user can view software package information. This highlights the importance of securing regular user accounts, because knowing what software is installed on a system can provide a hacker with the means to determine a hacking technique that could further compromise the system. As a result, if a hacker can gain access to the system as a regular user, valuable information is then available to the hacker.

Installing Packages with rpm

Three different options can be used to install software packages with the **rpm** command. Table 26-1 describes these three options.

Table 26-1 Installation Methods for the **rpm** Command

Scenario	rpm -i	rpm -U	rpm -F
Previous version of the package is currently installed on the system.	A second (very likely conflicting) version of package is installed.	Package is upgraded to the new version.	Package is upgraded to the new version.
Previous version of the package is not currently installed on the system.	Package is installed.	Package is installed.	No action is taken.

You only want to use the **-i** option if you are certain that a previous version of the package is not already installed. The exception to this is the **kernel** package. No two **kernel** packages have conflicting files, and having an older version of the **kernel** package is useful if the newer version of the package fails to boot the system.

In most cases, you should use the **-U** option to install or upgrade a package. However, the **-F** option is useful in certain situations. For example, suppose your administrator copies all updated packages for the distribution into a network shared directory. This share has thousands of packages—far more than you currently have installed on your system. If you execute the **rpm -U *** command in the directory where these packages are shared, you would end up not just upgrading existing packages but also installing a lot of new packages. If you execute the **rpm -F *** command, only existing packages would be upgraded, and all "new" packages would not be installed at all.

NOTE Some packages may take a long time to install. Because there is normally no output to the **rpm** command until after the package is completely installed, this can lead to you thinking the command is not "doing anything." Consider using the **-h** option, which will display "hash marks" across the screen as the package is installed:

```
[root@onecoursesource ~]# rpm -ih /var/cache/yum/x86_64/20/
➥fedora/packages/joe-3.7-13.fc28.x86_64.rpm
################################## [100%]
Updating / installing...
################################## [100%]
```

Before You Install That Package...

Consider a situation in which you obtain a software package either from the Internet or via email. How can you tell that the package was really from the correct source versus a package that has been compromised by a hacker? You should never install a software package from an untrusted source, especially on a critical system.

You should also look at the content of the package before installing it. It would be a good idea to use a virus- or worm-scanning tool as well.

Even if you get the package from what you consider a trusted source, you should consider verifying the package. You can do this in a similar way that you could verify that a letter was written by a specific person. If you know what that person's signature looks like, you could look at the signature on the letter to verify it really came from that specific person.

The organization that created the software package should provide a digital signature, which is a unique "key" that only that organization can place on the package. There is a tool you can use to verify this digital signature, but first you need to get a signature file from a trusted location (directly from the organization itself).

Next import the signature into the RPM database by using the following command: **rpm --import *****/location/key-file***

Once you have the signature in the RPM database, you can verify an RPM file signature on a RPM file before you install the package, as demonstrated below:

```
[root@onecoursesource ~]# rpm -K /var/cache/yum/x86_64/20/fedora/packages/joe-3.7-13.
➥fc28.x86_64.rpm
/var/cache/yum/x86_64/20/fedora/packages/joe-3.7-13.fc28.x86_64.rpm: rsa
➥sha1 (md5) pgp md5 OK
```

What you primarily are looking for is the "OK" at the end of the output. Do not trust any packages that do not provide this message.

To list all signatures that are currently in the RPM databases, use the following command: **rpm -qa gpg-pubkey***. For example:

```
[root@onecoursesource rpm -qa gpg-pubkey*
gpg-pubkey-11f63c51-3c7dc11d
gpg-pubkey-5ebd2744-418ffac9
gpg-pubkey-4520afa9-50ab914c
gpg-pubkey-246110c1-51954fca
gpg-pubkey-a0bdbcf9-42d1d837
```

Use **rpm -qi** for details of specific signature, as shown in Example 26-8.

Example 26-8 *Displaying Signature Details*

```
[root@onecoursesource ~]#rpm -qi gpg-pubkey-a0bdbcf9-42d1d837
Name        : gpg-pubkey
Version     : a0bdbcf9
Release     : 42d1d837
Architecture: (none)
Install Date: Thu 15 Jan 2015 09:02:46 AM PST
Group       : Public Keys
Size        : 0
License     : pubkey
Signature   : (none)
Source RPM  : (none)
Build Date  : Sun 10 Jul 2005 07:23:51 PM PDT
Build Host  : localhost
Relocations : (not relocatable)
Packager    : Virtualmin, Inc. <security@virtualmin.com>
Summary     : gpg(Virtualmin, Inc. <security@virtualmin.com>)
Description :
-----BEGIN PGP PUBLIC KEY BLOCK-----
Version: rpm-4.11.1 (NSS-3)
```

NOTE Do not be thrown off by the build date in the output of Example 26-8. Digital signatures are often used for many years. As long as digital signatures are not compromised, the organization who builds the packages typically does not change these signatures. Some digital signatures have been used for decades.

Removing Packages with rpm

To remove a package with the **rpm** command, use the **-e** option, like so: **rpm -e joe**.

NOTE This command uses the "no news is good news" policy. If the command is successful, then no output is provided. To see a verification that the package was removed, use the **-v** option.

What if you want to see what would happen if a package was removed, but not actually remove the package? Run the following command to view the removal steps without actually removing the package: **rpm -e --test -vv*pkgname***.

WHAT COULD GO WRONG? If you attempt to remove a package that contains dependencies that are required for other installed packages, you will get an error message like the following:

```
error: Failed dependencies:
        libwrap.so.0()(64bit) is needed by (installed) net-snmp-agent-libs-1:5.7.2-18.
fc28.x86_64
```

While you can force the removal of this package by including the **--nodeps** option, keep in mind that you will be breaking other packages. Instead, consider removing the packages that present dependency issues.

rpm2cpio

Imagine a situation in which a file from a package has been removed or the contents have been altered. In a situation like this, you may want to recover the original file or contents.

The **rpm2cpio** command converts RPM files into CPIO data streams (CPIO stands for *copy input/output*). These streams can then be piped into the **cpio** command, which can extrapolate the files and directories. Here's an example:

```
[root@localhost package]# ls
libgcc-4.8.5-4.el7.x86_64.rpm
[root@localhost package]# rpm2cpio libgcc-4.8.5-4.el7.x86_64.rpm | cpio-idum
353 blocks
[root@localhost package]# ls
lib64  libgcc-4.8.5-4.el7.x86_64.rpm  usr
[root@localhost package]# ls usr/share/doc/libgcc-4.8.5
COPYING  COPYING3  COPYING3.LIB  COPYING.LIB  COPYING.RUNTIME
```

This process is useful to extract specific files from an RPM file without having to reinstall the entire RPM. The resulting files are exactly the files that are installed; however, they are placed in the current directory.

Note that a complete discussion of the **cpio** command is beyond the scope of this book. The **-idum** options essentially mean "extract all files and directories in the CPIO stream into the current directory."

The yum Command

You may be wondering why there is another command that can be used to view, add, and remove software packages on Red Hat–based systems. The reason is that the **yum** command is designed to overcome some drawbacks to the **rpm** command, such as the following:

- The **rpm** command requires that you download RPM files or manually point to a network-accessible RPM file when you install a new RPM package. With the **yum** command, remote repositories are automatically used to download the package during the installation process.
- When you install an RPM package that has a dependency and that dependency package is not already installed, the **rpm** command will fail. With the **yum** command, dependencies are handled automatically as the command will download and install all dependency packages.
- The **yum** utility is a rewrite of an older package management tool called Yellowdog Updater (YUP). In fact, YUM stands for Yellowdog Updater, Modified. Yellowdog is the name of an outdated Linux distribution.

WHAT COULD GO WRONG? You may come across the term "dependency hell." This is when you try to install an RPM package with the **rpm** command, only to find that the package has dependencies. You find these dependency packages and try to install those, only to find these also have dependencies. As you can imagine, this can result in an ugly situation where you are trying to find all the dependencies required to install the initial package. The **yum** command is designed to resolve most of these dependency issues.

Repositories

A repository (also called a *repo*) is a location, typically network accessible, that contains RPM packages and a small database that describes the relationship between these packages. The **yum** command connects to the repositories to determine which packages are available. During the installation of packages, the **yum** command will also download the packages from the repo.

Repos can either be shared across the network using FTP, HTTP, or HTTPS or be local to the system in a directory (hard drive or removable media). When a repo is shared via the network, part of the setup of the repo is configuring the FTP server or web server. See Chapter 20, "Network Service Configuration: Essential Services," and Chapter 21, "Network Service Configuration: Web Services," for details on how to configure those servers.

Accessing a Repo

To access a repo, you need to know how to configure the **yum** command. This is done by a combination of the **/etc/yum.conf** file and files in the **/etc/yum.repos.d** directory.

The **/etc/yum.conf** file is the primary configuration file for **yum** commands. For example, see Example 26-9.

Example 26-9 *The /etc/yum.conf File*

```
[main]
cachedir=/var/cache/yum/$basearch/$releasever
keepcache=0
debuglevel=2
logfile=/var/log/yum.log
exactarch=1
obsoletes=1
gpgcheck=1
plugins=1
installonly_limit=5
bugtracker_url=http://bugs.centos.org/set_project.php?project_id=23&ref=
➥ http://bugs.centos.org/bug_report_page.php?category=yum
distroverpkg=centos-release
```

Key settings of the **/etc/yum.conf** file are shown in Table 26-2.

Table 26-2 Settings of the **/etc/yum.conf** File

Setting	Description
cachedir	Directory where RPMs are placed after download.
logfile	Location of the log file that contains **yum** actions.
gpgcheck	A value of **1** means "perform **gpg** check to ensure package is valid"; a value of **0** means "do not perform **gpg** check" (this can be overridden by specific settings for each repository configuration file). See the following description of the **/etc/yum.repos.d** directory for more details.
assumeyes	A value of **1** means "always assume 'yes' to yes/no prompts;" a value of **0** means "do not make any assumption, provide prompt instead."

The **/etc/yum.repos.d** directory contains files that end in **.repo**. These files are used to specify the location of **yum** repositories. Each file defines one or more repositories, as described in Figure 26-2.

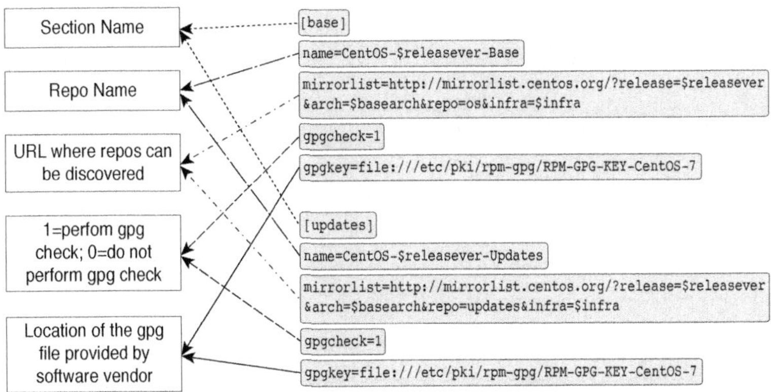

Figure 26-2 *The Format of Files in the* ***/etc/yum.repos.d*** *Directory*

Creating a Repo

Creating a repository involves the following steps:

1. Create a directory where the packages will be stored.
2. Copy all packages into this directory.
3. Run the command **createrepo** ***/directory*** (replace ***/directory*** with the directory that you created in Step 1). Note that the **createrepo** command is not typically included on the system by default. You should install the **createrepo** package to get access to this command.

Using the yum Command

The **yum** command is used to install software from repositories. It can also be used to remove software and display information regarding software. Table 26-3 highlights the primary **yum** commands and options.

Table 26-3 Primary **yum** Commands and Options

Command/Option	Description
install	Installs a package and any dependency packages from a repository (for example, **yum install zip**).
groupinstall	Installs an entire software group from a repository (for example, **yum groupinstall "Office Suite and Productivity"**).
update	Updates the specified software package.
remove	Removes the specified software package and any dependency packages from the system.
groupremove	Removes the specified software group from the system.
list	Lists information about packages, including which are installed and which are available (for example, **yum list available**).
grouplist	Lists information about software groups, including what packages are part of a group; use **yum grouplist** with no arguments to see a list of available software groups.
info	Provides information about a specific software package (for example, **yum info zip**).
groupinfo	Provides information about a specific software group.
-y	Answers "yes" automatically to any prompts (for example, **yum -y install zip**).

Displaying Package Information with yum

To display software packages with the **yum** command, use the following: **yum list *item***. Replace ***item*** with one of the following:

- **installed**: This displays all the packages already installed on the system.
- **available**: This displays packages that are available on repos, but not currently installed.
- **all**: This lists all packages, installed or not.

You can also use globs (wildcard characters) to limit the output. For example, Example 26-10 only displays packages that contain "zip" in the package name.

Example 26-10 *Packages Containing "zip"*

```
[root@onecoursesource ~]# yum list installed "*zip*"
Loaded plugins: fastestmirror, langpacks
 * base: mirror.supremebytes.com
 * epel: mirror.chpc.utah.edu
 * extras: mirrors.cat.pdx.edu
 * updates: centos.sonn.com
Installed Packages
bzip2.x86_64                       1.0.6-13.el7              @base
bzip2-libs.x86_64                  1.0.6-13.el7              @base
gzip.x86_64                        1.5-8.el7                 @base
perl-Compress-Raw-Bzip2.x86_64     2.061-3.el7               @anaconda
unzip.x86_64                       6.0-15.el7                @base
zip.x86_64                         3.0-10.el7                @anaconda
```

WHAT COULD GO WRONG? For the **yum** command to work correctly, you need to have access to the Internet. If the command fails, test your network connections.

The **yum** command also supports a **search** feature that will match a glob pattern in package names and summaries. It attempts to match the glob in the package descriptions and URLs (website links). For example, all packages that contain "joe" in the package names, summaries, and descriptions are displayed in the command in Example 26-11 (the search term is highlighted in the output).

Example 26-11 *Searching for Packages with the **yum** Command*

```
[root@onecoursesource ~]#yum search joe
Loaded plugins: fastestmirror, verify
Loading mirror speeds from cached hostfile
 * atomic: www6.atomicorp.com
 * fedora: mirrors.rit.edu
 * updates: mirrors.rit.edu
============================== N/S matched: joe ==============================
libjoedog-devel.i686 : Development files for libjoedog
libjoedog-devel.x86_64 : Development files for libjoedog
joe.x86_64 : An easy to use, modeless text editor
jupp.x86_64 : Compact and feature-rich WordStar-compatible editor
jwm.x86_64 : Joe's Window Manager
libjoedog.i686 : Repack of the common code base of fido and siege
libjoedog.x86_64 : Repack of the common code base of fido and siege
texlive-jknapltx.noarch : Miscellaneous packages by Joerg Knappen
```

You may wonder why the **jupp.x86_64** package was matched in the command from Example 26-11. If you run the **yum info jupp.x86_64** command, you will see that part of the output of that command includes what's shown in Example 26-12.

Example 26-12 *Displaying* ***yum*** *Info*

```
Description : Jupp is a compact and feature-rich WordStar-compatible editor and
            : also the MirOS fork of the JOE 3.x editor which provides easy
            : conversion for former PC users as well as powerfulness for
            : programmers, while not doing annoying things like word wrap
            : "automagically". It can double as a hex editor and comes with a
            : character map plus Unicode support. Additionally it contains an
            : extension to visibly display tabs and spaces, has a cleaned up,
            : extended and beautified options menu, more CUA style key-bindings,
            : an improved math functionality and a bracketed paste mode
            : automatically used with Xterm.
```

Software Groups

One of the benefits of the **yum** command over the **rpm** command is the ability to create software groups on the repo. By grouping packages together, it makes it easier to install a suite or collection of packages.

To display some of the software groups available on existing repositories, use the command **yum group list**, as shown in Example 26-13.

Example 26-13 *The* ***yum group list*** *Command*

```
[root@onecoursesource ~]#yum group list
Loaded plugins: fastestmirror, verify
Loading mirror speeds from cached hostfile
 * atomic: www6.atomicorp.comyu
 * fedora: mirrors.rit.edu
 * updates: mirrors.rit.edu
Installed environment groups:
   Minimal Install
Available environment groups:
   GNOME Desktop
   KDE Plasma Workspaces
   Xfce Desktop
   LXDE Desktop
   Cinnamon Desktop
   MATE Desktop
   Sugar Desktop Environment
   Development and Creative Workstation
   Web Server
   Infrastructure Server
   Basic Desktop
Installed groups:
   Development Tools
Available Groups:
   3D Printing
   Administration Tools
   Audio Production
```

```
   Authoring and Publishing
   Books and Guides
   C Development Tools and Libraries
   Cloud Infrastructure
   D Development Tools and Libraries
   Design Suite
   Editors
   Educational Software
   Electronic Lab
   Engineering and Scientific
   Fedora Eclipse
   FreeIPA Server
   Games and Entertainment
   LibreOffice
   Medical Applications
   Milkymist
   Network Servers
   Office/Productivity
   RPM Development Tools
   Robotics
   Security Lab
   Sound and Video
   System Tools
   Text-based Internet
   Window Managers
Done
```

The **yum group list** command does not display all of the software groups. Some are hidden by default and can be viewed by executing the **yum group list hidden** command. The output of this command is too large for displaying in this book. To demonstrate how using the **hidden** option will display many more software groups, look at the following output:

```
[root@onecoursesource ~]#yum group list | wc -l
51
[root@onecoursesource ~]#yum group list hidden | wc -l
142
```

Note that **wc -l** will display the number of lines from the output of the previous command. Each line represents a software group (besides a few lines that do not contain group names), so 142 lines versus 51 lines means there are about 90 additional software groups that are not displayed if you do not use the **hidden** option.

You can display information about a software group by using the **yum group info** command, as shown in Example 26-14.

Example 26-14 *The yum group info Command*

```
[root@onecoursesource ~]#yum group info "LibreOffice"
Loaded plugins: fastestmirror, verify
Loading mirror speeds from cached hostfile
 * atomic: www6.atomicorp.com
 * fedora: mirrors.rit.edu
 * updates: mirrors.rit.edu
```

```
Group: LibreOffice
 Group-Id: libreoffice
 Description: LibreOffice Productivity Suite
 Mandatory Packages:
   +libreoffice-calc
   +libreoffice-draw
   +libreoffice-emailmerge
   +libreoffice-graphicfilter
   +libreoffice-impress
   +libreoffice-math
   +libreoffice-writer
 Optional Packages:
   libreoffice-base
   libreoffice-pyuno
```

In the next section, you learn how to install packages using the package group.

Installing Software with yum

When you install a package with the **yum** command, you can either specify the package name, a glob, or a filename within the package. For example, Example 26-15 demonstrates installing the **joe** package by name.

Example 26-15 *Installing a Package with* ***yum***

```
[root@onecoursesource ~]#yum install joe
Loaded plugins: fastestmirror, verify
Loading mirror speeds from cached hostfile
 * atomic: www6.atomicorp.com
 * fedora: mirrors.rit.edu
 * updates: mirrors.rit.edu
Resolving Dependencies
--> Running transaction check
---> Package joe.x86_64 0:3.7-13.fc28 will be installed
--> Finished Dependency Resolution

Dependencies Resolved

==================================================================
 Package    Arch         Version                Repository     Size
==================================================================
Installing:
 joe        x86_64       3.7-13.fc28            fedora         382 k

Transaction Summary
==================================================================
Install   1 Package

Total size: 382 k
Installed size: 1.2 M
Is this ok [y/d/N]: y
Downloading packages:
Running transaction check
Running transaction test
```

```
Transaction test succeeded
Running transaction (shutdown inhibited)
  Installing : joe-3.7-13.fc28.x86_64                                      1/1
  Verifying  : joe-3.7-13.fc28.x86_64                                      1/1

Installed:
  joe.x86_64 0:3.7-13.fc28

Complete!
```

In the next example, a glob is used to match package names: **yum install joe***.

If you know a file that belongs to the package, you can specify a filename: **yum install /bin/joe**.

By default, the **yum** command will prompt you before downloading or installing the packages. To avoid that prompt and answer "yes" automatically, use the **-y** option to the **yum** command.

If you only want to download a package and not install any packages, use the **--downloadonly** option. This places the package in a subdirectory under the **/var/ cache/yum** directory (for example, **/var/cache/yum/x86_64/28** for version 28 of the Fedora distribution). This can be useful when creating your own repo because it provides an easy way to download packages without actually installing them.

To install packages from a group, use the **yum group install *grpname*** command (for example, **yum group install "LibreOffice"**).

Removing Software with yum

Use the **yum remove** command to remove software packages. You can either specify a package name, a glob, or a filename as an argument to the **yum remove** command:

- **yum remove joe**
- **yum remove *ruby***
- **yum remove /usr/bin/ruby**

By default, you will be asked to verify that you want to remove the package. Use the **-y** option to automatically respond with "yes."

WHAT COULD GO WRONG? Be very careful when combining the **-y** option and package arguments that include wildcard characters. You can end up deleting a lot more packages than you intended.

To remove a software group, use the following syntax: **yum group remove *grpname***.

Using yum Plug-Ins

Plug-ins are used to provide **yum** with more features and functions. Some examples of commonly used **yum** plug-ins:

- **fastmirror**: Finds the fastest mirror from the mirror list; a mirror is a repo feature that allows the repository to spread the client requests across different systems.
- **snapshot**: Automatically snapshots the filesystem during updates; a snapshot of a filesystem allows the recovery of files in the event that **yum** actions create problems.
- **versionlock**: Enables a feature to "lock" a package; when a package is locked, no updates will be performed on the package.

You can display currently installed plug-ins by executing the following command: **yum info yum**. This command will produce a large amount of output, so Example 26-16 is designed to just display one installed plug-in.

Example 26-16 *Displaying **yum** Plug-Ins*

```
[root@onecoursesource ~]#yum info yum | head -n 25
Loaded plugins: fastestmirror, verify
Loading mirror speeds from cached hostfile
 * atomic: www6.atomicorp.com
 * fedora: mirrors.rit.edu
 * updates: mirrors.rit.edu
Installed Packages
Name        : yum
Arch        : noarch
Version     : 3.4.3
Release     : 152.fc20
Size        : 5.6 M
Repo        : installed
From repo   : updates
Summary     : RPM package installer/updater/manager
URL         : http://yum.baseurl.org/
License     : GPLv2+
Description : Yum is a utility that can check for and automatically
            : download and install updated RPM packages.
            : Dependencies are obtained and downloaded
            : automatically, prompting the user for permission as
            : necessary.
```

You can enable and disable plug-ins in multiple ways:

- Each plug-in can be enabled or disabled by a setting in its specific configuration file called “enabled”. These configuration files are located in the **/etc/yum/pluginconf.d** directory. For example, to enable the **fastestmirror** plug-in for all **yum** commands, set **enabled=1** in the **/etc/yum/pluginconf.d/fastestmirror.conf** file. To disable this plug-in for all **yum** commands, set **enabled=1** in the **/etc/yum/pluginconf.d/fastestmirror.conf** file.
- To disable a plug-in for a specific **yum** command, use the **--disableplugin** option. For example: **yum --disableplugin=fastestmirror**.
- To enable plug-ins, edit the **/etc/yum.conf** file and change the value of the **plugins** setting to 1 (**plugins=1**). This does not enable all plug-ins, just the ones that are specifically enabled in the aforementioned configuration files. To disable all plug-ins for all **yum** commands, edit the **/etc/yum.conf** file and change the value of the **plugins** setting to 0 (**plugins=0**).
- To disable all plug-ins for a specific **yum** command, use the **--noplugins** option.

Additional plug-ins are available that are not currently installed on your system. You can display available plug-ins by executing the following command:

```
yum provides "/usr/lib/yum-plugins/*"
```

This **yum** command produces a large amount of output; Example 26-17 uses the **head** command to limit the output.

26

Example 26-17 *Using the **head** Command to Limit Output*

```
[root@onecoursesource ~]# yum provides "/usr/lib/yum-plugins/*" | head
Loaded plugins: fastestmirror, verify
Loading mirror speeds from cached hostfile
 * atomic: www6.atomicorp.com
 * fedora: mirrors.rit.edu
 * updates: mirrors.rit.edu
PackageKit-yum-plugin-0.8.13-1.fc22.x86_64 : Tell PackageKit to
                                           : check for updates
                                           : when yum exits
Repo        : fedora
Matched from:
Filename    : /usr/lib/yum-plugins/refresh-packagekit.py
```

To install a plug-in, use the following command: **yum install *plugin_name*** (for example, **yum install PackageKit-yum-plugin**).

Additional Tools

On distributions that use RPM, you will find that there are additional tools related to software management:

- **SUSE**: This distribution has a command-line tool called **zypper** that works very much like the **yum** command. It is a front-end utility to the **rpm** command that handles software dependencies.
- **Red Hat/CentOS/Fedora**: These distributions have a GUI-based utility called **PackageKit** that can be accessed via the menu bar. It provides similar functionality to the **yum** command, but in a GUI-based format.
- **Fedora**: On more modern versions of Fedora, a newer tool that is designed to replace **yum** is available: DNF (Dandified yum). It provides better performance, better dependency resolution, and additional improvements over the **yum** command. It is also compatible with the **yum** command and uses most of the same options (a few have been removed and some have been added). As an example of a **dnf** new feature, if you type a command that does not already exist, **dnf** suggests a command to install the correct package to provide the missing command. Note that just about every **yum** feature described in this chapter can also be executed as a **dnf** command on newer Fedora versions.

WHAT COULD GO WRONG? On newer Fedora systems, the **yum** command still technically exists, but it really executes **dnf** commands. So, any feature that only works with the **yum** command (and not the **dnf** command) will fail on newer Fedora systems, even if you execute **yum** instead of **dnf**.

Summary

In this chapter, you learned several different methods of managing packages on Red Hat–based distributions. You learned about the **rpm** command, which is primarily used to view package information, but it can also be used for simple package installations. You also learned about the advanced package management tools that the **yum** command provides, including downloading software packages from repositories and handling package dependencies.

Key Terms

Package, metadata, RPM, dependency, digital signature, repository, recursive acronym, library, plug-in, mirror

Review Questions

1. The RPM databases that contain metadata about software packages are stored in the **/var/lib/**_____ directory.
2. Which command will list all packages that are currently installed?
   - A. **rpm -ql**
   - B. **rpm -qp**
   - C. **rpm -qa**
   - D. None of these is correct.
3. The _____ command will make a repository in the specified directory.
4. The _____ option to the **rpm** command will only upgrade packages that currently have older versions already installed on the system.
   - A. **-i**
   - B. **-F**
   - C. **-g**
   - D. **-U**
5. The _____ feature of the **yum** command will match a glob pattern in package names and summaries.

Debian-Based Software Management

In Chapter 26, "Red Hat–Based Software Management," you learned how to manage software packages on distributions that make use of RPM. Another popular package management system, originally created on Debian Linux, is found on distributions like Ubuntu and Mint. Instead of using commands like **rpm**, **yum**, and **dnf**, this package management system has commands named **dpkg**, **apt**, **apt-get**, and **apt-cache**.

Conceptually, the two package management systems are very similar. The differences can be found in the specific commands, options, and, in some cases, features that are provided by each system. This chapter focuses on the Debian-based package management system and highlights the primary differences between Debian and Red Hat software management.

IMPORTANT NOTE Because this is the second chapter in this book that covers software packages, the focus is more on the "how to" rather than the theories and concepts of package management. Be sure to review Chapter 26 for information related to theories and concepts.

After reading this chapter and completing the exercises, you will be able to do the following:

View, install, and remove packages using the dpkg **command**

Create software sources for APT commands

View, install, and remove packages using APT commands

Managing Packages with dpkg

In many ways, the Debian package management tools are very much like the Red Hat package management tools. For example, the equivalent to the **rpm** command is the **dpkg** command. Both commands are good for displaying information about installed packages as well as installing locally downloaded package files.

The Debian package manager is used on many Linux distributions, including Debian, Ubuntu, and Mint. Software package files are distributed with a **.deb** extension.

Listing Package Information with dpkg

To view all the packages that are currently installed, use the **dpkg** command with the **-l** option, as shown in Example 27-1.

Example 27-1 ***dpkg*** *Command with the* ***-l*** *Option*

```
root@onecoursesource:~# dpkg -l | head
Desired=Unknown/Install/Remove/Purge/Hold
| Status=Not/Inst/Conf-files/Unpacked/halF-conf/Half-inst/trig-aWait/Trig-pend
|/ Err?=(none)/Reinst-required (Status,Err: uppercase=bad)
||/ Name                                          Version
Architecture Description
```

```
+++-=========================================-
==================================================-=============-
===============================================================================
ii  account-plugin-aim                              3.8.6-0ubuntu9.2
➥                                    amd64         Messaging account plugin for AIM
ii  account-plugin-google                           0.11+14.04.20140409.1-0ubuntu2
➥                  all              GNOME Control Center account plugin for single signon
ii  account-plugin-jabber                           3.8.6-0ubuntu9.2
➥                                    amd64         Messaging account plugin for Jabber/XMPP
ii  account-plugin-salut                            3.8.6-0ubuntu9.2
➥                                    amd64         Messaging account plugin for Local XMPP
➥ (Salut)
ii  account-plugin-yahoo                            3.8.6-0ubuntu9.2
➥                                    amd64         Messaging account plugin for Yahoo!
```

The output displayed when all packages are listed can be a bit difficult to follow because of the formatting of the output. Viewing a single package is a bit easier, as demonstrated in Figure 27-1.

```
root@onecoursesource:~# dpkg -l joe
Desired=Unknown/Install/Remove/Purge/Hold
| Status=Not/Inst/Conf-files/Unpacked/halF-conf/Half-inst/trig-aWait/Trig-pend
|/ Err?=(none)/Reinst-required (Status,Err: uppercase=bad)
||/ Name           Version      Architecture Description
+++-==============-============-============-=================================
ii  joe            3.7-2.3ubunt amd64        user friendly full screen text ed
```

Figure 27-1 *Output of the* ***dkpg -l*** *Command*

The first character of the last line of output displayed in Figure 27-1 is related to **Desired=Unknown/Install/Remove/Purge/Hold**. This **i** indicates that the normal (desired) state of this package is "install." Consider this to be a suggestion of what the state of the package should be.

The second character of the last line of output displayed in Figure 27-1 is related to **Status=Not/Inst/Conf-files/Unpacked/halF-conf/Half-inst/trig-aWait/Trig-pend**. In this case, the **i** indicates the package is currently installed.

The third character of the last line of output displayed in Figure 27-1 is used to indicate any problems or errors with the package. In this case, this is a space, which means there are no errors for this package.

The rest of the output of the last line displayed in Figure 27-1 is fairly straightforward: package name, version of the installed package, the architecture the package was built for, and a description of the package.

To display detailed information about a package, use the **-s** option, as shown in Example 27-2.

Example 27-2 *Viewing Package Information*

```
root@onecoursesource:~# dpkg -s joe | head -n 20
Package: joe
Status: install ok installed
Priority: optional
Section: editors
Installed-Size: 1313
Maintainer: Ubuntu Developers <ubuntu-devel-discuss@lists.ubuntu.com>
Architecture: amd64
Version: 3.7-2.3ubuntu1
Depends: libc6 (>= 2.14), libtinfo5
Breaks: jupp (<< 3.1.18-2~)
Conffiles:
```

27

```
 /etc/joe/ftyperc 3c915f0bb617c0e4ac2bc10a7c4e649b
 /etc/joe/jicerc.ru b7db1f92397dc0a7598065442a6827c1
 /etc/joe/jmacsrc dd24e67b67c03810922d740cebc258cc
 /etc/joe/joerc 6f9cf4e8ce4649d31c2c2dae6a337852
 /etc/joe/jpicorc 0be5c286a0a9a14b733e2fa4e42d5828
 /etc/joe/jstarrc 2fbf22c556f6199e3a49cc526300c518
 /etc/joe/rjoerc 158e89ba1c65f7089b21e567cc6368ff
Description: user friendly full screen text editor
 Joe, the Joe's Own Editor, has the feel of most PC text editors: the key
```

The output of the **dpkg -s** command includes a list of the configuration files for the package. To see a list of all the files included with a package, use the **-L** option:

```
root@onecoursesource:~# dpkg -L joe | head -n 10
/.
/etc
/etc/joe
/etc/joe/jicerc.ru
/etc/joe/rjoerc
/etc/joe/jstarrc
/etc/joe/ftyperc
/etc/joe/jpicorc
/etc/joe/joerc
/etc/joe/jmacsrc
```

You can also determine which package provides a specific file by using the **-S** command:

```
root@onecoursesource:~# dpkg -S /etc/joe/joerc
joe: /etc/joe/joerc
```

Changes to files that were installed from a package can be displayed by using the **-V** option:

```
root@onecoursesource:~# dpkg -V joe
??5?????? c /etc/joe/joerc
```

The output is very similar to the output of the **rpm -V** command that was covered in Chapter 26, as you can see from the following snippet from the man page of the **dpkg** command:

```
The output format is selectable with the --verify-format option,
which by default uses the rpm format, but that might  change  in
the  future,  and  as  such programs parsing this command output
should be explicit about the format they expect.
```

To view the contents (a list of files) of a package that has not been installed, use the **-c** option, as shown in Example 27-3.

Example 27-3 *Using the -c Option*

```
root@onecoursesource:~# dpkg -c /tmp/joe_3.7-2.3ubuntu1_amd64.deb | head
drwxr-xr-x root/root         0 2014-02-17 14:12 ./
drwxr-xr-x root/root         0 2014-02-17 14:12 ./etc/
drwxr-xr-x root/root         0 2014-02-17 14:12 ./etc/joe/
-rw-r--r-- root/root     38076 2014-02-17 14:12 ./etc/joe/jicerc.ru
-rw-r--r-- root/root     32368 2014-02-17 14:12 ./etc/joe/rjoerc
-rw-r--r-- root/root     32215 2014-02-17 14:12 ./etc/joe/jstarrc
-rw-r--r-- root/root      9327 2014-02-17 14:12 ./etc/joe/ftyperc
```

```
-rw-r--r-- root/root     30127 2014-02-17 14:12 ./etc/joe/jpicorc
-rw-r--r-- root/root     37722 2014-02-17 14:12 ./etc/joe/joerc
-rw-r--r-- root/root     34523 2014-02-17 14:12 ./etc/joe/jmacsrc
```

Security Highlight

You should list the contents of a package before installing it, especially if you obtained the package from a less than reliable source. Look for suspicious files such as **/etc/passwd** and **/etc/shadow**. Hackers interject malicious files in software packages to compromise systems.

To display information about a software package that has not already been installed, use the **-I** option, as shown in Example 27-4.

Example 27-4 *Using the -I Option*

```
root@onecoursesource:~# dpkg -I /tmp/joe_3.7-2.3ubuntu1_amd64.deb | head
 new debian package, version 2.0.
 size 350818 bytes: control archive=1821 bytes.
     118 bytes,     7 lines      conffiles
    1812 bytes,    34 lines      control
    1400 bytes,    28 lines   *  postinst             #!/bin/sh
     133 bytes,     7 lines   *  postrm               #!/bin/sh
     357 bytes,    13 lines   *  preinst              #!/bin/sh
     310 bytes,     9 lines   *  prerm                #!/bin/sh
 Package: joe
 Version: 3.7-2.3ubuntu1
```

27

Installing Software with dpkg

To install a software package with the **dpkg** command, use the **-i** option, as shown in Example 27-5.

Example 27-5 ***dpkg*** *Command Using the -i Option*

```
root@onecoursesource:~# dpkg -i /tmp/joe_3.7-2.3ubuntu1_amd64.deb
Selecting previously unselected package joe.
(Reading database ... 177428 files and directories currently installed.)
Preparing to unpack .../joe_3.7-2.3ubuntu1_amd64.deb ...
Unpacking joe (3.7-2.3ubuntu1) ...
Setting up joe (3.7-2.3ubuntu1) ...
update-alternatives: using /usr/bin/joe to provide /usr/bin/editor (editor) in auto mode
Processing triggers for man-db (2.6.7.1-1ubuntu1) ...
```

You can also specify a directory as an argument to the **-i** option. If the argument is a directory, then all files that end in **.deb** within that directory will be installed as packages.

WHAT COULD GO WRONG? It is easy to confuse the **-I** option (display information about a package file) and the **-i** option (install a software package). Be careful here, because both options are used on package files, so you can easily install a package when you really intended to display information about the package.

Reconfiguring Software with dpkg

One of the features of package management is the ability to perform custom operations during the installation (and removal) process. This is accomplished by scripts that are often interactive. In some cases, it can be useful to execute these scripts again at some point after the package installation.

For example, the **keyboard-configuration** package is designed to configure the default system keyboard. If you decided to ship a system to another country that has a different keyboard layout, then it would be useful to execute the configuration script for this package again. You can do this by executing the **dpkg-reconfigure** command. Figure 27-2 provides a demonstration of the result of executing the **dpkg-reconfigure keyboard-configuration** command.

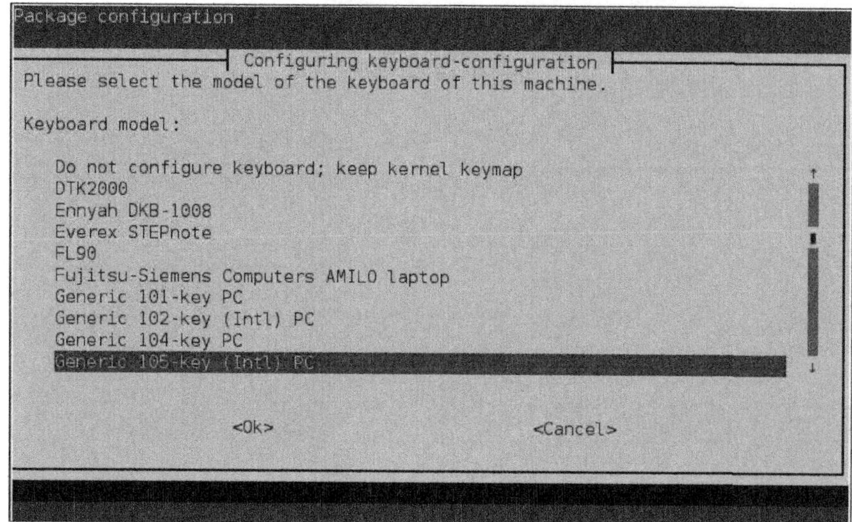

Figure 27-2 *The **dpkg-reconfigure keyboard-configuration** Command*

WHAT COULD GO WRONG? Be careful when using the **dpkg-reconfigure** command because you could "blow away" a configuration that took some time and effort to fine-tune.

Extracting Files from a Debian Package

Recall from Chapter 26 that you could extract files from an RPM package without installing the package on the system. This is useful for exploring the package files (looking for malicious code) and replacing missing or corrupted system files.

The technique to perform this task on Debian-based systems is to use the **-x** option to the **dpkg** command:

```
root@onecoursesource:~# mkdir /tmp/joe_files
root@onecoursesource:~# dpkg -x /tmp/joe_3.7-2.3ubuntu1_amd64.deb
➥/tmp/joe_files
root@onecoursesource:~# ls /tmp/joe_files
etc  usr
root@onecoursesource:~# ls /tmp/joe_files/etc
joe
root@onecoursesource:~# ls /tmp/joe_files/etc/joe
ftyperc  jicerc.ru  jmacsrc  joerc  jpicorc  jstarrc  rjoer
```

Security Highlight

Because **-x** is an option to the **dpkg** command, there is always a concern that you could accidently omit it when trying to extract package files. This would result in installing the package, which can cause serious problems if the package contains malicious software.

Removing Packages with the dpkg Command

There are two methods for removing packages on Debian-based systems:

- **dpkg -r** ***pkg_name***: This method removes the package but keeps its configuration files on the system.
- **dpkg –P** ***pkg_name***: This method removes the package, including all of the package's configuration files.

Example 27-6 demonstrates using the **dpkg -r** command.

Example 27-6 *Removing a Package with the* ***dpkg -r*** *Command*

```
root@onecoursesource:~# dpkg -r joe
(Reading database ... 177514 files and directories currently installed.)
Removing joe (3.7-2.3ubuntu1) ...
update-alternatives: using /usr/bin/jmacs to provide /usr/bin/editor (editor) in auto mode
update-alternatives: using /usr/bin/jpico to provide /usr/bin/editor (editor) in auto mode
update-alternatives: using /bin/nano to provide /usr/bin/editor (editor) in auto mode
Processing triggers for man-db (2.6.7.1-1ubuntu1) ...
root@onecoursesource:~# ls /etc/joe
editorrc  ftyperc  jicerc.ru  jmacsrc  joerc  jpicorc  jstarrc  rjoerc
```

Compare the output of the **ls** command from Example 27-6 to the output of the **ls** command in Example 27-7 when the **-P** option is used to remove a package.

27

Example 27-7 *Removing a Package with the* ***dpkg -P*** *Command*

```
root@onecoursesource:~# dpkg -P joe
(Reading database ... 177514 files and directories currently installed.)
Removing joe (3.7-2.3ubuntu1) ...
update-alternatives: using /usr/bin/jmacs to provide /usr/bin/editor (editor) in auto mode
update-alternatives: using /usr/bin/jpico to provide /usr/bin/editor (editor) in auto mode
update-alternatives: using /bin/nano to provide /usr/bin/editor (editor) in auto mode
Purging configuration files for joe (3.7-2.3ubuntu1) ...
Processing triggers for man-db (2.6.7.1-1ubuntu1) ...
root@onecoursesource:~# ls /etc/joe
ls: cannot access /etc/joe: No such file or directory
```

The lack of an **/etc/joe** directory (the location for configuration files for the **joe** package) indicates that these files have been removed from the system.

Conversational Learning™—Using the ping Command

Gary: Hi, Julia. I just learned about the **-r** and **-P** options to the **dpkg** command, and I have a question.

Julia: Fire away!

Gary: I'm trying to understand why I would want to use one option versus the other.

Julia: Ah, well, the advantage of using the **-r** option is that any customizations that have been made in the configuration files will be available in case the package is installed again in the future.

Gary: So, if I think I will install the package again and I want to use the previous configuration files, I should use the **-r** option, right? Can you give me an example?

Julia: Sure, suppose you have a fully configured web server, but you want to remove that software for now. It took a long time to configure that web server and you don't want to have to do that work again or try to retrieve the configuration from backups.

Gary: OK, then why use the **-P** option?

Julia: Consider when you know for certain that you will not be installing the package again in the future or when you want to make sure you get a "clean" installation when the package is installed again.

Gary: Ah, OK. Thanks for the information, Julia.

Managing Packages with APT

The Advanced Package Tool (APT) is a collection of commands that provide the same functionality that **yum** or **dnf** provides on Red Hat–based systems. Many tools are included in APT, but the following are the primary ones:

- **apt**: This utility can be used for most basic package management commands.
- **apt-get**: This utility provides additional features for more advanced package management operations.
- **apt-cache**: This utility provides additional features for more advanced operations and package queries.

APT Repositories

As with the **yum** and **dnf** commands, the APT commands make use of repositories from where packages can be downloaded. These repositories are called *sources* in APT and can either be placed on local drives (CD-ROMs, USB drives, and so on) or made available across the network.

To configure a system to access an APT source, you can edit either the **/etc/apt/sources.list** file or files located in the **/etc/apt/sources.list.d** directory. On some distributions, the use of the **/etc/apt/sources.list** file has been deprecated in favor of files in the **/etc/apt/sources.list.d** directory. On those systems, the **/etc/apt/sources.list** file might not exist at all or it may be an empty file.

On systems that do have a **/etc/apt/sources.list** file, it is typically a well-documented configuration file. Each line defines one source. Example 27-8 displays some typical entries (note that blank lines and commented lines were removed with the **grep** commands).

Example 27-8 */etc/apt/sources.list*

```
root@onecoursesource:~# grep -v "^$" /etc/apt/sources.list | grep -v "^#" | head
deb http://us.archive.ubuntu.com/ubuntu/ trusty main restricted
deb-src http://us.archive.ubuntu.com/ubuntu/ trusty main restricted
deb http://us.archive.ubuntu.com/ubuntu/ trusty-updates main restricted
deb-src http://us.archive.ubuntu.com/ubuntu/ trusty-updates main restricted
deb http://us.archive.ubuntu.com/ubuntu/ trusty universe
deb-src http://us.archive.ubuntu.com/ubuntu/ trusty universe
deb http://us.archive.ubuntu.com/ubuntu/ trusty-updates universe
deb-src http://us.archive.ubuntu.com/ubuntu/ trusty-updates universe
```

```
deb http://us.archive.ubuntu.com/ubuntu/ trusty multiverse
deb-src http://us.archive.ubuntu.com/ubuntu/ trusty multiverse
```

Figure 27-3 shows the typical fields of data of an APT source configuration file.

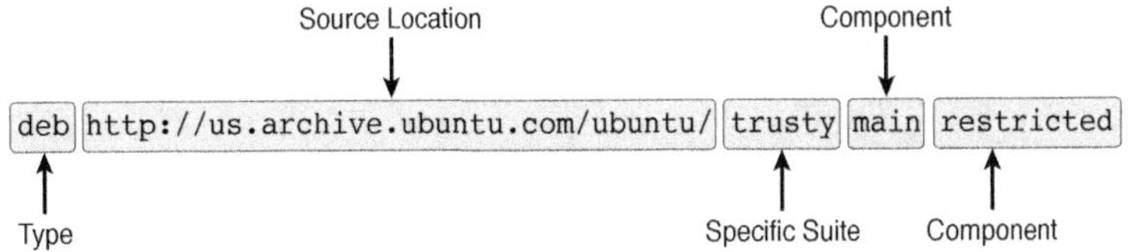

Figure 27-3 *Fields of an APT Source Configuration File*

The fields of an APT source configuration file are described in more detail in Table 27-1.

Table 27-1 Description of the Fields of an APT Configuration File

Field	Description
Type	This field indicates whether the packages in this source repository are regular packages (packages that can be installed, defined by "deb") or source packages (packages that can be downloaded to view the original source code, defined by "deb-src").
Source location	The URI (uniform resource identifier) of the source. This could be a network location (shared via a web server, for example) or a local resource (placed on local hard drive, for example).
Suite	Each source URI can have multiple repositories, located in separate directories. The value of the suite is the subdirectory under the URL where the package files are stored.
Component	Indicates what kind of packages are found on this source. There are four commonly used components: **Main**: Officially supported by the distribution and should be open source. **Restricted**: Officially supported by the distribution but is closed source software. **Universe**: Community supported and maintained, but should be open source. **Multiverse**: Not supported by the community or the distribution. Likely closed source software that may also pose copyright and patent issues.

The APT source configuration file described in Figure 27-3 and Table 27-1 uses a style called the "one-line" style. Some distributions make use of a newer style called the DEB822 style. The format for this style looks like the following:

```
Types: deb deb-src
URIs: uri
Suites: suite
Components: [component1] [component2] [...]
option1: value1
option2: value2
```

As a result, the example described using the one-line style in Figure 27-3 could be written using the DEB822 style in the following manner:

```
Types: deb
URIs: http://us.archive.ubuntu.com/ubuntu/
```

```
Suites: trusty
Components: main restricted
```

Several different options can be used with both styles. For example, you can specify the architectures of the packages for a source by using the following DEB822 style:

```
Types: deb
URIs: http://us.archive.ubuntu.com/ubuntu/
Suites: trusty
Components: main restricted
Architectures: amd64
```

There are many possible options; consult the **sources.list** man page for more details.

Creating a Source Repository

The following steps describe how to create a source repository:

1. Install the **dpkg-dev** package (if it isn't already installed). Example: **apt-get install dpkg-dev**.
2. Create a directory. Example: **mkdir /var/packages**.
3. Copy packages into the new directory. These packages can be downloaded from an existing source (this technique is described later in this chapter), or you can find the packages you need in the **/var/cache/apt/archives** directory (this is the location where packages are downloaded before being installed on the local system).
4. Run the following command in the directory that contains the packages: **dpkg-scanpackages . /dev/null | gzip -9c > Packages.gz**.

Listing Package Information with APT Commands

To list all packages, both installed and available to be installed, use the **apt list** command, as shown in Example 27-9.

Example 27-9 *The apt list Command*

```
root@onecoursesource:~# apt list | head

WARNING: apt does not have a stable CLI interface yet. Use with caution in scripts.

Listing...
0ad/trusty 0.0.15+dfsg-3 amd64
0ad-data/trusty 0.0.15-1 all
0ad-data-common/trusty 0.0.15-1 all
0ad-dbg/trusty 0.0.15+dfsg-3 amd64
0xffff/trusty 0.6~git20130406-1 amd64
2ping/trusty 2.0-1 all
2vcard/trusty 0.5-3 all
3270-common/trusty 3.3.10ga4-2build2 amd64
389-admin/trusty 1.1.35-0ubuntu1 amd64
```

Here are two key options to the **apt list** command:

- **--installed**: Used to display packages that are currently installed
- **--upgradable**: Used to display packages that are installed and have a newer version available

The **apt** command also supports listing packages using a search term. However, a more powerful way to search for packages is to use the **apt-cache** command, which provides a method to search for packages using a regular expression:

```
root@onecoursesource:~# apt-cache search "^joe"
joe - user friendly full screen text editor
joe-jupp - reimplement the joe Debian package using jupp
scheme2c - Joel Bartlett's fabled Scheme->C system
```

Consider using the **apt** command for simple package listings and the **apt-cache** command for more complex package listings.

To display information about a specific package, use the **apt show** command, as demonstrated in Example 27-10.

Example 27-10 *Listing Packaging Information with the **apt show** Command*

```
root@onecoursesource:~# apt show joe | head -n 16

WARNING: apt does not have a stable CLI interface yet. Use with caution in scripts.

Package: joe
Priority: optional
Section: universe/editors
Installed-Size: 1,345 kB
Maintainer: Ubuntu Developers <ubuntu-devel-discuss@lists.ubuntu.com>
Original-Maintainer: Josip Rodin <joy-packages@debian.org>
Version: 3.7-2.3ubuntu1
Depends: libc6 (>= 2.14), libtinfo5
Breaks: jupp (<< 3.1.18-2~)
Download-Size: 351 kB
Homepage: http://joe-editor.sourceforge.net/
Bugs: https://bugs.launchpad.net/ubuntu/+filebug
Origin: Ubuntu
APT-Sources: http://us.archive.ubuntu.com/ubuntu/ trusty/universe amd64 Packages
Description: user friendly full screen text editor
 Joe, the Joe's Own Editor, has the feel of most PC text editors.
```

NOTE The **apt-cache show** command provides a similar output. Both commands accept a glob (wildcard) as an argument to the command. So, to display all packages that begin with "vi", you can execute either the **apt show vi*** or **apt-cache show vi*** command.

The **apt-cache** command provides an option to display dependencies and reverse dependencies of a package, as shown in Example 27-11.

Example 27-11 *Listing Dependency Information with the **apt-cacheshowpkg** Command*

```
root@onecoursesource:~# apt-cache showpkg joe
Package: joe
Versions:
3.7-2.3ubuntu1 (/var/lib/apt/lists/us.archive.ubuntu.com_ubuntu_dists_trusty_universe_
➥binary-amd64_Packages)
 Description Language:
                 File: /var/lib/apt/lists/us.archive.ubuntu.com_ubuntu_dists_trusty_
➥universe_binary-amd64_Packages
```

```
                MD5: 4d6bbc0d4cf8b71ec0b3dfa1ffb8ca46
 Description Language: en
                File: /var/lib/apt/lists/us.archive.ubuntu.com_ubuntu_dists_trusty_
➥universe_i18n_Translation-en
                 MD5: 4d6bbc0d4cf8b71ec0b3dfa1ffb8ca46


Reverse Depends:
  jupp:i386,joe 3.7-2.3~
  joe:i386,joe
  jupp,joe 3.7-2.3~
  joe-jupp,joe
  joe-jupp,joe
Dependencies:
3.7-2.3ubuntu1 - libc6 (2 2.14) libtinfo5 (0 (null)) jupp (3 3.1.18-2~) jupp:i386
➥ (3 3.1.18-2~) joe:i386 (0 (null))
Provides:
3.7-2.3ubuntu1 -
Reverse Provides:
joe-jupp 3.1.26-1
```

To display the dependencies of a package, use the **apt-cache depends** command:

```
root@onecoursesource:~# apt-cache depends joe
joe
  Depends: libc6
  Depends: libtinfo5
  Breaks: jupp
  Breaks: jupp:i386
  Conflicts: joe:i386
```

To display the reverse dependencies of a package, use the **apt-cache rdepends** command:

```
root@onecoursesource:~# apt-cache rdepends joe
joe
Reverse Depends:
  jupp:i386
  joe:i386
  jupp
  joe-jupp
    joe-jupp
  joe-jupp
```

Installing Packages with APT Commands

The **apt install** command will install a package from a source, as shown in Example 27-12.

Example 27-12 *The* ***apt install*** *Command*

```
root@onecoursesource:~# apt install joe
Reading package lists... Done
Building dependency tree
Reading state information... Done
The following NEW packages will be installed:
  joe
```

```
0 upgraded, 1 newly installed, 0 to remove and 587 not upgraded.
Need to get 351 kB of archives.
After this operation, 1,345 kB of additional disk space will be used.
Get:1 http://us.archive.ubuntu.com/ubuntu/ trusty/universe joe amd64 3.7-2.3ubuntu1
➥[351 kB]
Fetched 351 kB in 2s (156 kB/s)
Selecting previously unselected package joe.
(Reading database ... 177428 files and directories currently installed.)
Preparing to unpack .../joe_3.7-2.3ubuntu1_amd64.deb ...
Unpacking joe (3.7-2.3ubuntu1) ...
Processing triggers for man-db (2.6.7.1-1ubuntu1) ...
Setting up joe (3.7-2.3ubuntu1) ...
update-alternatives: using /usr/bin/joe to provide /usr/bin/editor (editor) in auto mode
```

The **apt install** command supports the following options:

- **=pkg_version_number**: Used to indicate the specific version to install. Example: **apt-get install joe=1.2.3**.
- **/target_release**: Used to indicate which version of the distribution to use for the package version. Each distro version has a list designed for that specific distro version. Example: **apt-get install joe/trusty**.

NOTE The **apt-get install** command can be used to install software packages, and it supports the **=pkg_version_number** and **/target_release** options. However, the **apt-get install** command also supports the following options:

- **-f**: Fix broken dependencies.
- **-s**: Dry run; demonstrates what would happen if the installation was performed.
- **-y**: Assume yes (the **apt-get** command normally prompts for confirmation before installing any packages).
- **--no-upgrade**: Install if the package is new, but do not upgrade an existing package.
- **--only-update**: Upgrade if an older version of the package is already installed, but don't install if the package is new.
- **--reinstall**: Reinstall the package.

The **apt** command also provides a feature that upgrades all packages on the system: **apt full-upgrade**. This feature also removes old packages that are considered obsolete, so use this option with care.

To download, but not install, a package, use the **apt-get download** command. Notice that this command will download the package into the **/var/cache/apt/archives** directory:

```
root@onecoursesource:~# apt-get download joe
root@onecoursesource:~# ls /var/cache/apt/archives/j*
/var/cache/apt/archives/joe_3.7-2.3ubuntu1_amd64.deb
```

You may be wondering about package groups, like those that the **yum** command in Chapter 26 provides. For APT, groups work a bit different. Groups are available in the interactive **aptitude** utility, as shown in Figure 27-4.

```
 Actions  Undo  Package  Resolver  Search  Options  Views  Help
C-T: Menu  ?: Help  q: Quit  u: Update  g: Download/Install/Remove Pkgs
aptitude 0.6.8.2
--- Security Updates (389)
--- Upgradable Packages (198)
--- Installed Packages (1364)
--\ Not Installed Packages (75016)
  --- Tasks - Packages which set up your computer to perform a particular task (
  --- admin - Administrative utilities (install software, manage users, etc) (19
  --- cli-mono - Mono and the Common Language Infrastructure (322)
  --- comm - Programs for faxmodems and other communication devices (272)
  --- database - Database servers and tools (286)
  --- debug - Debugging symbols (3674)

These packages are not installed on your computer.

This group contains 75016 packages.
```

Figure 27-4 *The **aptitude** Utility*

The **aptitude** utility is normally installed by default. A similar utility, called **tasksel**, is also available, but is not normally installed by default (run **apt-get install tasksel** if you want this utility). See Figure 27-5 for a demonstration of the **tasksel** utility.

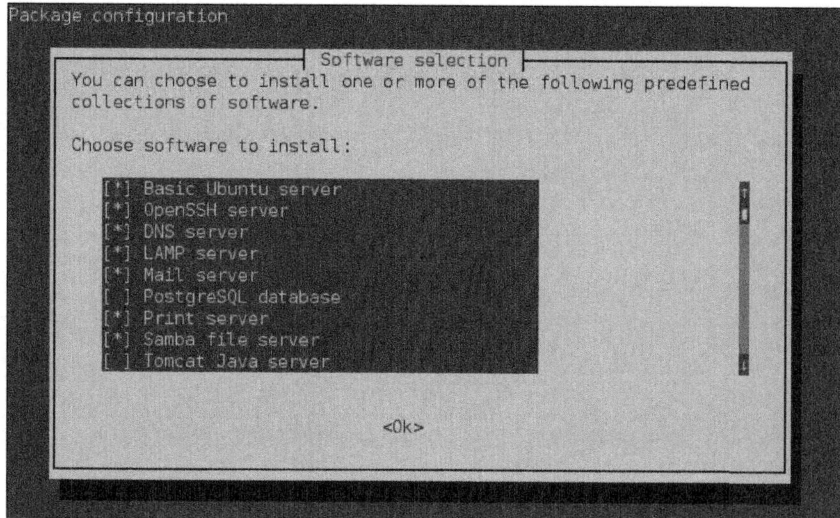

Figure 27-5 *The **tasksel** Utility*

Another option is to use the **synaptic** utility, a GUI-based package management tool. An example of this tool is displayed in Figure 27-6.

> **NOTE** The **aptitude**, **tasksel**, and **synaptic** utilities can be used to remove package and display information about packages (although the details about the packages might not be available in all the tools). Also, many distributions provide a separate GUI-based package management tool, so be sure to consult your distro's documentation.

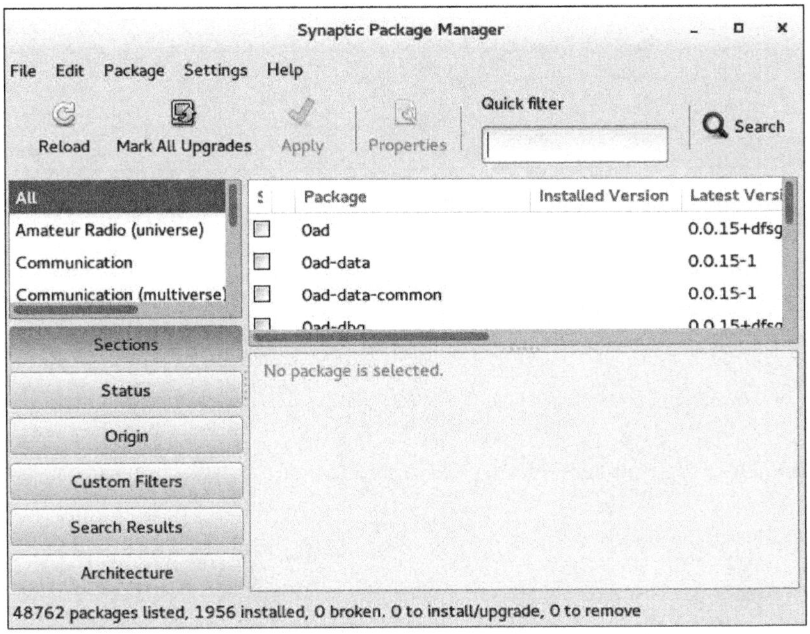

Figure 27-6 *The* ***synaptic*** *Utility*

> **WHAT COULD GO WRONG?** Becoming dependent on GUI-based package management tools can limit your ability to perform package management tasks on different systems. These tools are often not installed on production systems because the GUI itself requires a large amount of system resources (RAM, CPU, and so on). So, you really should focus your study on the command-line APT utilities.

Removing Packages with APT Commands

To remove a package, but keep its configuration files, use either the **apt remove** or **apt-get remove** command. Here's an example:

```
apt remove joe
```

To purge a package (remove all the package files, including configuration files), use the **apt-get purge** command, as demonstrated in Example 27-13.

Example 27-13 *Purging a Package with the* ***apt-getpurge*** *Command*

```
root@onecoursesource:~# apt-get purge joe
Reading package lists... Done
Building dependency tree
Reading state information... Done
The following packages will be REMOVED:
  joe*
0 upgraded, 0 newly installed, 1 to remove and 587 not upgraded.
After this operation, 1,345 kB disk space will be freed.
Do you want to continue? [Y/n] y
(Reading database ... 177514 files and directories currently installed.)
Removing joe (3.7-2.3ubuntu1) ...
```

```
update-alternatives: using /usr/bin/jmacs to provide /usr/bin/editor (editor) in auto mode
update-alternatives: using /usr/bin/jpico to provide /usr/bin/editor (editor) in auto mode
update-alternatives: using /bin/nano to provide /usr/bin/editor (editor) in auto mode
Purging configuration files for joe (3.7-2.3ubuntu1) ...
Processing triggers for man-db (2.6.7.1-1ubuntu1) ...
```

Additional APT Features

Here are a few additional features available with APT that are important to know about:

- **apt-get check**: This command is used to check for broken dependencies on all installed packages.
- **apt-get clean**: This command clears out information regarding cached source (repository) information.
- **apt-get autoclean**: This command removes old package information.

Summary

In this chapter, you learned several different methods of managing packages on Debian-based distributions. You learned about the **dkpg** command, which is primarily used to view package information, but can also be used for simple package installations and removals. You also learned about the advanced package management tools that the APT commands provide, including tools for downloading software packages from repositories and handling package dependencies.

Key Terms

Source, URI (uniform resource identifier), component, source repository

Review Questions

1. The _____ option to the **dpkg** command is used to display information about a package file.
2. Which option to the **dkpg** command will remove a package but keep its configuration files?
   - A. **-u**
   - B. **-r**
   - C. **-P**
   - D. **-c**
3. The _____ command is used to create a source repository for APT.
4. Which of the following is not a valid APT command?
   - A. **apt-cache**
   - B. **apt-get**
   - C. **apt-install**
   - D. **apt-remove**
5. The _____ option to the **apt list** command will only display packages that are currently installed on the system.

System Booting

System booting is a fairly large topic that incorporates the operations that take place during the boot process. In this chapter, you learn about the different stages of system booting, including the boot loader phase, the kernel loading phase, and the "init" phase.

After reading this chapter and completing the exercises, you will be able to do the following:

Describe the four stages of the boot process

Configure Legacy GRUB and GRUB 2

Modify key components of the kernel

Load and unload kernel modules

Modify services that are enabled at boot

Phases of the Boot Process

The boot process of a Linux operating system has four primary phases:

- BIOS/UEFI phase
- Boot loader phase
- Kernel phase
- Post-kernel phase

The BIOS/UEFI Phase

When a Linux system is first turned on, a software program is started to boot the system. This software program is not part of Linux, but rather it's a program that came with your system hardware. The two different types are BIOS (Basic Input/Output System) and UEFI (Unified Extensible Firmware Interface). While both perform similar tasks (starting the boot process), each has different features and is configured using different interfaces.

BIOS is the older of the two and is slowly being phased out. BIOS is considered *firmware*, a program embedded within the hardware. BIOS has been around for more than 30 years and has some limitations, including the devices it recognizes, limited support for large boot devices, and limits regarding partition tables.

UEFI is newer and considered a replacement for BIOS. However, because it is not firmware, but rather a software program that extends firmware, it can be used on systems that have BIOS. UEFI has several advantages over BIOS, including support for larger boot partitions, the capability to read data from different devices (RAID, LVM, and so on), and the capability to read partition tables that are GUI based.

The Bootloader Phase

The bootloader is a software program provided by the operating system that is designed to access files on the hard drive (specifically the kernel) and start the booting of the operating system. Several bootloaders are available, including LILO (which stands for Linux Loader, an older bootloader that will not be covered in this book), GRUB 2, and Legacy GRUB (Grand Unified Boot Loader).

Bootloaders can be installed on devices like hard disks (common) or USB drives (rare). If installed on a hard disk, the bootloader is normally stored in a special location called the Master Boot Record (MBR), a reserved location at the beginning of the hard disk (specifically the first 215 bytes of the boot disk). This is also where the partition table is stored.

In some cases, the bootloader might be stored in the first sector of a partition, typically when multiple bootloaders are installed on the system. It is rare to store a bootloader on a removable device, but this could be done to allow for more flexible booting (different bootloaders could be installed on different removable devices, such as a USB flash drive).

Typically the bootloader is installed during the boot process, but it is possible that the bootloader could become corrupt and require reinstallation. To install the bootloader, execute the **grub-install** command and provide the device where you want to install GRUB. For example, the following installs GRUB on the first SATA hard drive:

```
grub-install /dev/sda
```

Further details regarding configuring and using GRUB 2 and Legacy GRUB appear later in this chapter.

The Kernel Phase

The bootloader loads the kernel and passes control of the boot process to the kernel. During the kernel phase, the kernel configures itself and loads kernel modules. In general this includes the following tasks:

1. Configures the system so it can start assigning memory addresses to software.
2. Probes hardware and performs configuration operations.
3. Uncompresses the **initrd** or **initramfs** image; these files contain kernel modules that are required at boot time.
4. Initializes meta-devices such as LVM and RAID devices.
5. Mounts the root filesystem as read-only.
6. Starts the post-kernel phase, which includes starting a program that will boot the system the rest of the way.

There is not a lot an administrator will do to modify the kernel phase. You can change the behavior of the kernel by either recompiling the kernel or by passing parameters to the kernel from the bootloader. This is discussed in the GRUB sections later in this chapter.

You should be aware of the function of the **initrd** and **initramfs** images. A Linux kernel is fairly small by default, and kernel modules, which are separate software components, provide more features to the kernel. Typically the Linux kernel is configured with few kernel modules enabled by default. Additional modules are normally required during the boot process before the filesystems are mounted. These additional modules are stored within a compressed file, either **initrd** or **initramfs**.

The older of the two is **initrd**, and it is being replaced by **initramfs**. One disadvantage of **initrd** is that its image is based on a filesystem (like ext2), requiring the kernel to have filesystem support natively enabled. Another disadvantage of **initrd** is that it must be treated as a disk device, requiring I/O operations to be buffered in memory (which is redundant because the **initrd** "disk" is actually loaded into memory).

If your system uses **initrd**, you can generate a new **initrd** file by using the **mkinitrd** command. If your system uses **initramfs**, use the **dracut** command to create a new **initramfs** file. You rarely need to do this because the **initrd** or **initramfs** file created by your installer program should work just fine. Only when you add a new device that is required at initial boot would you need to create a new **initrd** or **initramfs** file. More details regarding this topic can be found later in this chapter.

The Post-Kernel Phase

Once the kernel has completed all its tasks, it starts a process that finishes booting the operating system. What process the kernel starts depends on which distribution of Linux you are using. Three bootup technologies are commonly used on modern Linux systems: SysVinit, systemd, and Upstart. Most modern systems use systemd.

GRUB

Legacy GRUB has been available for many years and was once hailed as a great replacement for older bootloader technologies, such as LILO. However, as hardware has become more sophisticated, limitations have begun to appear in Legacy GRUB's design. As a result, Legacy GRUB is no longer actively developed, but it is still available (and bug fixes are still released) for older Linux distributions.

GRUB 2 was developed to overcome the limitations of Legacy GRUB. There are actually quite a few differences between the two technologies—not only in how each functions but also in configuration. Here are a few key differences:

- GRUB 2 supports more operating systems.
- GRUB 2 can use UUIDs (universally unique identifiers) to identify disk devices; UUIDs are more reliable than the physical and logical addresses Legacy GRUB uses. For example, adding a new hard disk to the system could mess up the configuration of Legacy GRUB because the address may change for the original hard disks. This does not happen when using UUIDs. Note: Some newer versions of Legacy GRUB can make use of UUIDs, but this is a fairly recent change.
- GRUB 2 supports LVM and RAID devices, whereas Legacy GRUB cannot access these devices.
- The configuration files are different. Legacy GRUB uses a single, simple configuration file. GRUB 2 uses a more complex system in which you should not edit the actual configuration file; rather, you edit other files that are used to build the real configuration file.

Legacy GRUB Configuration

NOTE Because most mainstream distributions no longer use Legacy GRUB, practicing the topics in this chapter may be a bit more challenging. We recommend you use CentOS 5.x to gain hands-on experience with Legacy GRUB.

The primary configuration file for Legacy GRUB is the **/boot/grub/grub.conf** file, as shown in Example 28-1.

Example 28-1 *The /boot/grub/grub.conf File*

```
[root@onecoursesource grub]# more grub.conf
# grub.conf generated by anaconda
#
# Note that you do not have to rerun grub after making changes to this file
# NOTICE:  You have a /boot partition. This means that
```

```
#          all kernel and initrd paths are relative to /boot/, eg.
#          root (hd0,0)
#          kernel /vmlinuz-version ro root=/dev/VolGroup00/LogVol00
#          initrd /initrd-version.img
#boot=/dev/sda
default=0
timeout=5
splashimage=(hd0,0)/grub/splash.xpm.gz
hiddenmenu
title CentOS (2.6.18-406.el5)
        root (hd0,0)
        kernel /vmlinuz-2.6.18-406.el5 ro root=/dev/VolGroup00/LogVol00 rhgb quiet
        initrd /initrd-2.6.18-406.el5.img
title CentOS (2.6.18-398.el5)
        root (hd0,0)
        kernel /vmlinuz-2.6.18-398.el5 ro root=/dev/VolGroup00/LogVol00 rhgb quiet
        initrd /initrd-2.6.18-398.el5.img
```

The first portion of this file contains general configuration information for Legacy GRUB. Table 28-1 describes the more common of these configuration settings.

Table 28-1 Common Legacy GRUB Configuration Settings

Setting	Description
default	Indicates which title to boot if a title is not selected before the timeout value is reached. Titles are numbered in the order they appear in the file, with the first title assigned the numeric value of 0, the second title assigned the numeric value of 1, and so on.
timeout	Indicates a value in seconds to wait for the user to choose a title to boot to. If no title is chosen during this timeout period, the default title is used. During this period, a countdown timer is displayed.
splashimage	A "splashimage" is a graphic displayed when the Legacy GRUB boot menu is displayed. It must be a specific file type, limited to 14 colors, 640x480, and have an extension of **.xpm.gz** (**.xpm** is a specific graphic format and **.gz** is a gzipped file).
hiddenmenu	This setting has no value assigned to it. If this setting is present, the GRUB menu is not displayed, only the countdown timer. If a key is pressed on the keyboard, the countdown ends and the menu is displayed.

28

Each title section consists of several lines:

```
title CentOS (2.6.18-406.el5)
    root (hd0,0)
    kernel /vmlinuz-2.6.18-406.el5 ro root=/dev/VolGroup00/LogVol00 rhgb quiet
initrd /initrd-2.6.18-406.el5.img
```

Table 28-2 describes the settings for the **title** section.

Table 28-2 Legacy GRUB **title** Settings

Setting	Description
title	The value of this setting is displayed in the GRUB menu during the boot process. Typically this includes the name of the distribution and the version of the kernel, but it can be modified to provide any information.
root	This describes the device that contains the boot files (the kernel file and the initrd file). A value of **(hd0, 0)** refers to the hard disk and partition on that device. See more details on this following this table.
kernel	This is the location of the kernel to be loaded, relative to the device indicated by the **root** parameter. In addition to the kernel location, values can be added that will be passed to the kernel as it is started. For example, **ro** tells the kernel to mount the root filesystem as read-only. Additionally, **root=/dev/VolGroup00/LogVol00** tells the kernel the location of the root filesystem (in this case, an LVM device). The value **quiet** tells the kernel to not display verbose boot messages, and value **rhgb** tells the kernel to use the Red Hat graphical boot feature (which provides a nice progress bar during bootup instead of displaying boot messages). There are dozens of possible other values that you can pass to the kernel.
initrd	This is the location of the **initrd** file, relative to the device indicated by the **root** parameter.

The device specified by the **root** parameter may cause confusion. Recall that partitions in Linux are typically referred to as device files (for example, **/dev/hda1**).

Typically hard disks are either IDE (**/dev/hda**, **/dev/hdb**, and so on) or SATA (**/dev/sda**, **/dev/sdb**). The devices are represented by a letter (a = first, b = second), and partitions are numbered starting from the value 1 (**/dev/hda1**, **/dev/hda2**, and so on).

The naming convention is different in GRUB. There is no distinction between IDE and SATA drives. All drives are "hd" devices. Numbers are assigned to drives instead of letters (0 = /dev/[hs]da, 1=/dev/[hs]db). Partitions are numbered starting from the value 0, not from 1, which is standard for device files.

As a result, a device that you may refer to as **/dev/sda1** would be **(hd0, 0)** in Legacy GRUB. The **/dev/hdb2** device is **(hd1, 2)** in Legacy GRUB.

You might be wondering what you would change in this configuration file. Consider the following scenarios:

- The system is in a location that is not physically secure and you want to limit the ability of someone to make changes to GRUB during the boot process. One way of doing that is to change the timeout value to 0. The default title will be automatically and immediately used by GRUB. This may seem like a dangerous thing to do because you cannot interrupt the boot process, but keep in mind that you could boot off an external device. The point of this step is that your system is not physically secure, so making it hard to perform an alternative boot is the goal.
- You may discover a useful kernel parameter that you want to enable. In this case, you would add this parameter to the kernel line of one of the titles.
- If the system is a lab machine on which you are testing new kernel features (such as recompiling new kernels), seeing verbose kernel messages during the boot process can help you troubleshoot problems that may arise during your testing. Remove the **quiet** and **rhgb** kernel parameters from one of the titles to enable verbose kernel messages.

Security Highlight

Setting the GRUB timeout value to 0 is a good security measure on systems that are not physically secure because it lessens the chance of someone compromising the system during the boot process. Here are other steps you should take:

- Remove any external drives and ports, such as CD-ROM drives and USB ports.
- Place a password on the BIOS to prevent booting from other devices.
- Place a physical lock on the case of the system so the hard drive can't be removed and used in a different system.
- Place a password on GRUB (this method will be covered later in this chapter).

Changing Legacy GRUB During Boot

During the boot process, you can perform operations that change how the system boots. These operations include:

- Selecting an alternative title for booting
- Modifying parameters for a title
- Executing GRUB commands via the GRUB command line

The most common task is to choose an alternative title to boot from. After the GRUB menu appears, use the arrow keys to select a title and then press the Enter key when you are ready to boot the system. See Figure 28-1 for an example of the screen that permits you to choose a title.

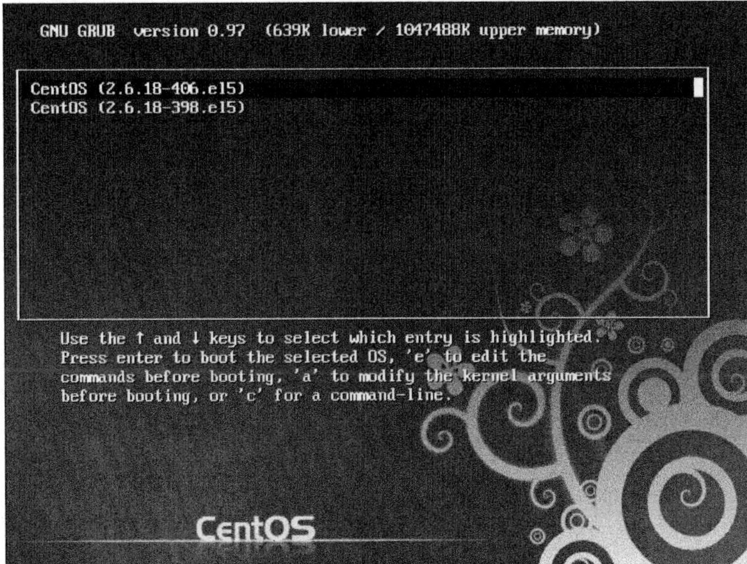

Figure 28-1 *Legacy GRUB Title Screen*

There are two ways to modify the parameters for a title. One technique is to use the **e** command to edit the titles before booting. Most often you are changing the kernel line, so the other technique, using the **a** command to modify the kernel arguments, might be more useful. See Figure 28-2 for an example of editing a title when using the **e** command.

28

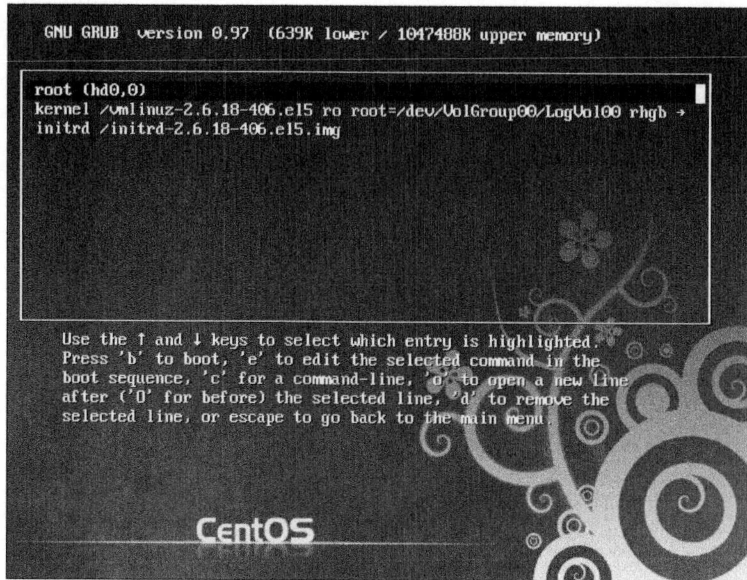

Figure 28-2 *Editing a Legacy GRUB Title*

Note that when you are editing a title, use your arrow keys to move to the line that you want to edit. Once you're on the correct line, use the **e** command to edit the selected line. See Figure 28-3 for an example of editing a line within a title.

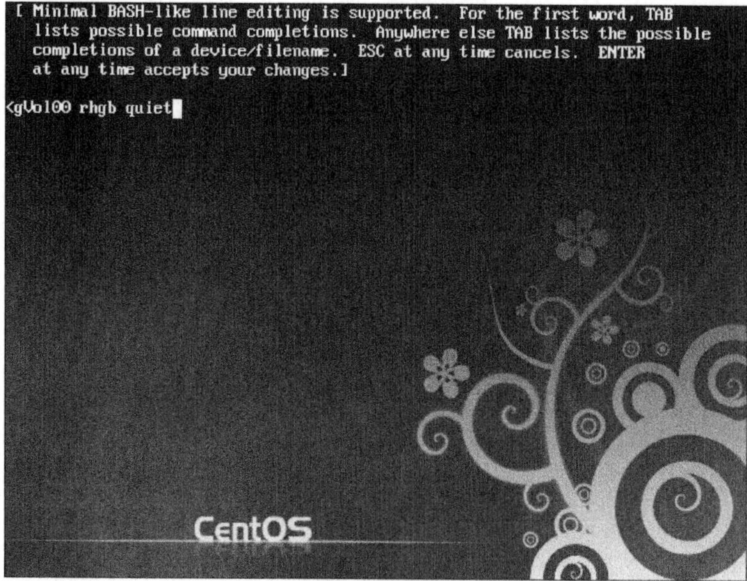

Figure 28-3 *Editing a Legacy GRUB Title Line*

After making your changes, press Enter to return to the previous screen. Pressing the Esc key cancels any changes.

Once back to the previous screen, use the **b** command to boot the system using your customized title parameters.

Finally, you can simply execute GRUB commands by using the **c** command. If you do this, you get a **grub>** prompt where you can execute GRUB commands.

One of the more useful GRUB commands to remember is **help**. This command displays all the possible GRUB commands, as demonstrated in Figure 28-4.

```
    GNU GRUB  version 0.97  (639K lower / 1047488K upper memory)

 [ Minimal BASH-like line editing is supported.  For the first word, TAB
   lists possible command completions.  Anywhere else TAB lists the possible
   completions of a device/filename.  ESC at any time exits.]

grub> help
background RRGGBB                          blocklist FILE
boot                                       cat FILE
chainloader [--force] FILE                 clear
color NORMAL [HIGHLIGHT]                   configfile FILE
displayapm                                 displaymem
find FILENAME                              foreground RRGGBB
geometry DRIVE [CYLINDER HEAD SECTOR [     halt [--no-apm]
help [--all] [PATTERN ...]                 hide PARTITION
initrd FILE [ARG ...]                      kernel [--no-mem-option] [--type=TYPE]
makeactive                                 map TO_DRIVE FROM_DRIVE
md5crypt                                   module FILE [ARG ...]
modulenounzip FILE [ARG ...]               pager [FLAG]
partnew PART TYPE START LEN                parttype PART TYPE
reboot                                     root [DEVICE [HDBIAS]]
rootnoverify [DEVICE [HDBIAS]]             serial [--unit=UNIT] [--port=PORT] [--
setkey [TO_KEY FROM_KEY]                   setup [--prefix=DIR] [--stage2=STAGE2_
splashimage FILE                           terminal [--dumb] [--no-echo] [--no-ed
terminfo [--name=NAME --cursor-address     testvbe MODE
unhide PARTITION                           uppermem KBYTES
vbeprobe [MODE]          CentOS

grub> ▌
```

Figure 28-4 *Getting Help*

Booting to Single-User Mode in Legacy GRUB

Congratulations are in order! Your company's system administrator has moved on to another job and you have been promoted to this position. It is an exciting day for you, and you are eager to impress your boss. Your first task: Update software on your company web server (a task that should have been done months ago).

You sit down at the console for the web server, ready to get to work. And then you realize: When the previous administrator left, he took the knowledge of the root password with him. Your dream promotion has quickly turned into a nightmare.

Fear not, there is a solution. By modifying parameters to GRUB during the boot process, you can recover the root password. The following describes the process:

1. Begin by booting the system and pressing a key on the keyboard once the GRUB menu appears. Now, edit the first title of the GRUB title screen, adding an **s** to the end of the kernel parameters. See Figure 28-5 for an example.

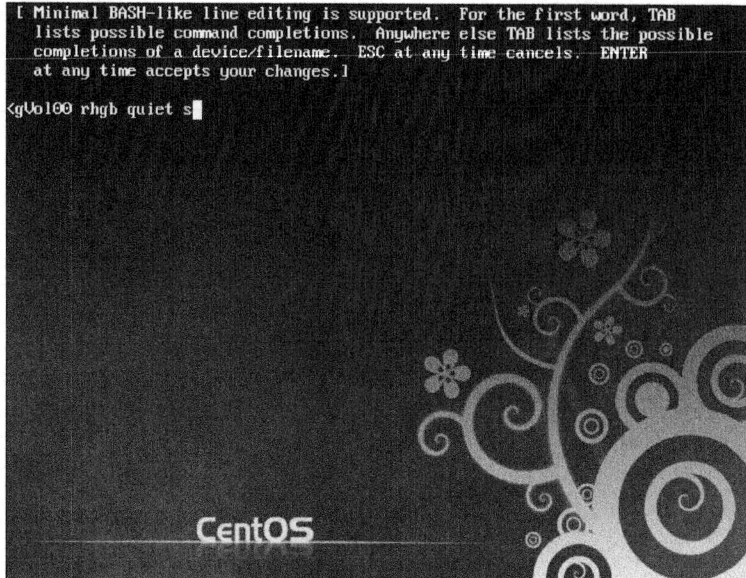

Figure 28-5 *Editing the Kernel Line*

2. Press Enter to accept the changes and then boot the system using the **b** command. The system boots to single-user mode, logging you in as root automatically without asking you for any password.
3. Once you're provided a shell prompt, just execute the **passwd** command to change the root password. See Figure 28-6 for an example.

```
  Found volume group "VolGroup00" using metadata type lvm2
  2 logical volume(s) in volume group "VolGroup00" now active
                Welcome to  CentOS release 5.11 (Final)
                Press 'I' to enter interactive startup.
Setting clock  (utc): Tue Oct 13 21:58:56 PDT 2015         [  OK  ]
Starting udev:                                             [  OK  ]
Loading default keymap (us):                               [  OK  ]
Setting hostname localhost.localdomain:                    [  OK  ]
Setting up Logical Volume Management:   2 logical volume(s) in volume group "Vol
Group00" now active
Kernel alive                                               [  OK  ]
Checking filesystemsg tables up to 100000000 @ 10000-15000
/dev/VolGroup00/LogVol00: clean, 118953/1548288 files, 1019661/1548288 blocks
/boot: clean, 41/26104 files, 23292/104388 blocks
                                                           [  OK  ]
Remounting root filesystem in read-write mode:             [  OK  ]
Mounting local filesystems:                                [  OK  ]
Enabling local filesystem quotas:                          [  OK  ]
Enabling /etc/fstab swaps:                                 [  OK  ]
sh-3.2# passwd
Changing password for user root.
New UNIX password:
Retype new UNIX password:
passwd: all authentication tokens updated successfully.
sh-3.2#
```

Figure 28-6 *Changing the Root Password in Single-User Mode*

4. After changing the root password, you can either reboot the system or press Ctrl+D to continue booting the system to the default runlevel.

> **NOTE** The previous example works on older systems that use Legacy GRUB. Newer systems may require a more complex sequence of commands to reset the root password.

Securing Legacy GRUB

You just cleared your first hurdle as a system administrator! You mentally pat yourself on the back and then you suddenly come to a gut-wrenching realization: Although your web server is physically secure, several other key servers are located in areas that have public access. What prevents someone else from walking up to one of those machines and using the same technique to "recover" the root password?

Fortunately, there is a technique that will prevent someone from accessing single-user mode. You can assign a password to GRUB, which prevents users from modifying titles unless they know the GRUB password.

Step 1 of securing GRUB is to generate an MD5 encrypted password. Although you can use a plain-text password, an encrypted password is more secure. Note the permissions on the Legacy GRUB configuration file:

```
[root@onecoursesource ~]# ls -l /boot/grub/grub.conf
-rw------- 1 root root 760 Oct  9 23:38 /boot/grub/grub.conf
```

The good news is that only the root user can view the contents of this file. The GRUB password goes in this file, so you may consider a plain-text password to be secure enough. However, if you are editing this file, someone could see it on your screen (remember, this system is probably not physically secure). So, an encrypted password really is best.

To create the encrypted password, execute the **grub-md5-crypt** command, as shown here:

```
[root@onecoursesource ~]# grub-md5-crypt
Password:
Retype password:
$1$KGnIT$FU80Xxt31J1qU6FD104QF/
```

Next, add a line like the following to the **/boot/grub/grub.conf** file in the section above the title sections:

```
password --md5     $1$KGnIT$FU80Xxt31J1qU6FD104QF/
```

NOTE If you put the password setting within a title section, it will prevent someone from booting to that title unless they know the password.

28

The **/boot/grub/grub.conf** file should now look something like what's shown in Example 28-2.

Example 28-2 *Revised /boot/grub/grub.conf File*

```
[root@onecoursesource ~]# more /boot/grub/grub.conf
# grub.conf generated by anaconda
#
# Note that you do not have to rerun grub after making changes to this file
# NOTICE:  You have a /boot partition. This means that
#          all kernel and initrd paths are relative to /boot/, eg.
#          root (hd0,0)
#          kernel /vmlinuz-version ro root=/dev/VolGroup00/LogVol00
#          initrd /initrd-version.img
#boot=/dev/sda
default=0
timeout=5
splashimage=(hd0,0)/grub/splash.xpm.gz
hiddenmenu
password --md5 $1$KGnIT$FU80Xxt31J1qU6FD104QF/
title CentOS (2.6.18-406.el5)
        root (hd0,0)
```

```
        kernel /vmlinuz-2.6.18-406.el5 ro root=/dev/VolGroup00/LogVol00 rhgb quiet
        initrd /initrd-2.6.18-406.el5.img
title CentOS (2.6.18-398.el5)
        root (hd0,0)
        kernel /vmlinuz-2.6.18-398.el5 ro root=/dev/VolGroup00/LogVol00 rhgb quiet
        initrd /initrd-2.6.18-398.el5.img
```

Reboot the system to test this new setting. The GRUB title screen should now look different. Note the message below the titles that states you need to enter the **p** command followed by the password to unlock additional features. If you do not know the password, you cannot edit the titles or enter GRUB commands. See Figure 28-7 for a demonstration.

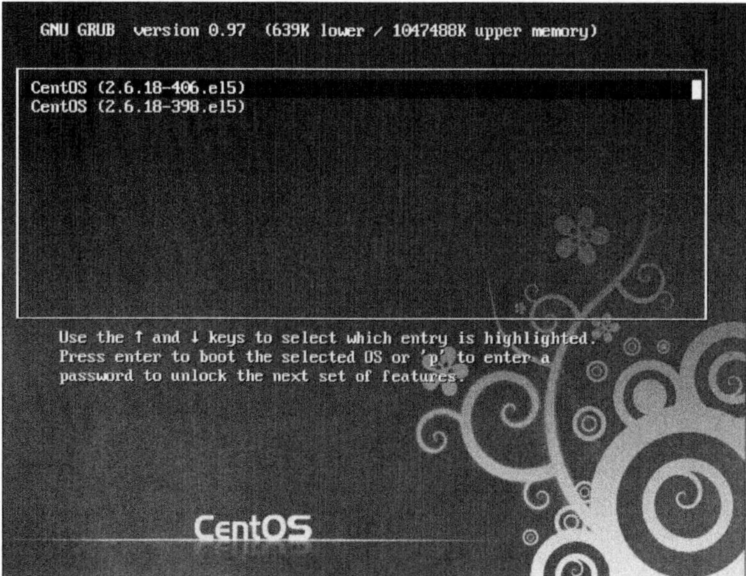

Figure 28-7 *Password Required for Legacy GRUB*

Security Highlight

So, what if you really need to recover the root password, but you do not know the GRUB password? You could boot from a CD-ROM or DVD that has a bootable Linux image, bypassing the hard drive's GRUB program. Once you have done that, you can mount the hard drive and modify the root password.

Clearly, this is another possible security risk. You can limit this risk by removing the CD-ROM/DVD drive, but then someone could also boot from a USB disk. You could modify BIOS to prevent booting from USB devices (and password-protect the BIOS), but then someone could remove the hard drive and take it to another system that has a CD-ROM/DVD drive or allows bootable USB devices.

The point is that no system is entirely secure. Use techniques to limit access and always be prepared for that dreaded hack.

GRUB 2 Configuration

Most modern Linux distributions use GRUB 2. In some ways, GRUB 2 is similar to Legacy GRUB, but there are many differences as well. Perhaps the biggest difference you will notice is how you configure GRUB 2.

On Red Hat–based distributions, the primary configuration file for GRUB 2 is **/boot/grub2/grub.cfg**. On Debian-based distributions, the primary configuration file for GRUB 2 is **/boot/grub/grub.cfg**. However, you should never edit these files directly because each is generated from other configuration files. Instead, edit the **/etc/default/grub** file or files in the **/etc/grub.d** directory.

The file for global GRUB 2 configuration changes is the **/etc/default/grub** file. The files in the **/etc/grub.d** directory are for specific changes, such as for adding a new title. Example 28-3 shows an example of the **/etc/default/grub** file.

Example 28-3 *The/etc/default/grub File*

```
[root@onecoursesource ~]# more /etc/default/grub
# If you change this file, run "'update-grub"' afterwards to update
# /boot/grub/grub.cfg.
# For full documentation of the options in this file, see:
#   info -f grub -n "'Simple configuration"'

GRUB_DEFAULT=0
#GRUB_HIDDEN_TIMEOUT=0
GRUB_HIDDEN_TIMEOUT_QUIET=true
GRUB_TIMEOUT=10
GRUB_DISTRIBUTOR="'lsb_release -i -s 2> /dev/null || echo Debian"'
GRUB_CMDLINE_LINUX_DEFAULT="quiet splash"
GRUB_CMDLINE_LINUX=""

# Uncomment to enable BadRAM filtering, modify to suit your needs
# This works with Linux (no patch required) and with any kernel that obtains
# the memory map information from GRUB (GNU Mach, kernel of FreeBSD ...)
#GRUB_BADRAM="0x01234567,0xfefefefe,0x89abcdef,0xefefefef"

# Uncomment to disable graphical terminal (grub-pc only)
#GRUB_TERMINAL=console

# The resolution used on graphical terminal
# note that you can use only modes which your graphic card supports via VBE
# you can see them in real GRUB with the command "'vbeinfo"'
#GRUB_GFXMODE=640x480

# Uncomment if you don"'t want GRUB to pass "root=UUID=xxx" parameter to Linux
#GRUB_DISABLE_LINUX_UUID=true

# Uncomment to disable generation of recovery mode menu entries
#GRUB_DISABLE_RECOVERY="true"

# Uncomment to get a beep at grub start
#GRUB_INIT_TUNE="480 440 1"
```

This file contains many possible settings in the form of shell variable settings. Table 28-3 describes the common settings you are likely to change in the **/etc/default/grub** file.

Table 28-3 Common **/etc/default/grub** Settings

Setting	Description
GRUB_DEFAULT	This can be set to a number that represents the default title to boot to. The first title is represented by 0, the second by 1, and so on. Using a number can be tricky because the order of titles can vary. This is discussed in more detail later in this chapter. This value can also be set to saved so GRUB will remember the last title chosen. This requires the setting **GRUB_SAVEDEFAULT** to be set as well.
GRUB_SAVEDEFAULT	If set to **true** and if **GRUB_DEFAULT** is set to **saved**, GRUB remembers the last title chosen and marks that as the default for the next boot.
GRUB_TIMEOUT	How many seconds to wait before booting to the default title. A value of -1 will wait indefinitely.
GRUB_TIMEOUT_STYLE	If set to **hidden**, the title menu is not displayed during the timeout countdown.
GRUB_CMDLINE_LINUX	This contains values to add to the kernel line to pass parameters to the kernel (such as **quiet** and **rhgb**). This will be added to every title.
GRUB_CMDLINE_LINUX_DEFAULT	Normally two titles are created for each kernel: a regular title and a recovery title for going to single-user mode. This setting adds kernel parameters to regular titles, not the recovery titles.

Saving GRUB 2 Changes

If you make changes to the **/etc/default/grub** file and reboot the machine, you will note that these changes do not affect GRUB 2 immediately. You first need to run a command that takes the values in the **/etc/default/grub** file (and values from the files in the **/etc/grub.d** directory) and creates a new GRUB 2 configuration file.

On Red Hat–based systems, execute the **grub2-mkconfig** command. On Debian-based systems, execute the **update-grub** command.

NOTE After executing the appropriate command to update the GRUB 2 configuration file, you can see these changes in the **grub.cfg** file (in either the **/boot/grub** or **/boot/grub2** directories). You will notice that this is not a typical Linux configuration, but more like a script. You may be tempted to edit this script, but if you do, then your change will be lost the next time the **grub2-mkconfig** or the **update-grub** command is executed (which could happen when a new kernel is installed, for example).

GRUB 2 Titles

Creating and specifying GRUB 2 titles are a bit tricky. For example, you can set the default title by setting the **GRUB_DEFAULT** parameter in the **/etc/defaults/grub** file to a numeric value. But, how do you determine which title is first, which is second, and so on? You could reboot the machine and look at the order of the titles, but that does not solve another problem: This order could change when your kernel is updated or you manually add additional titles.

When you execute the **grub2-mkconfig** or **update-grub** command, it probes the system for kernels and creates **menuentry** settings in the **grub.cfg** file. An example of one of these entries is shown in the highlighted section of Figure 28-8 for a demonstration.

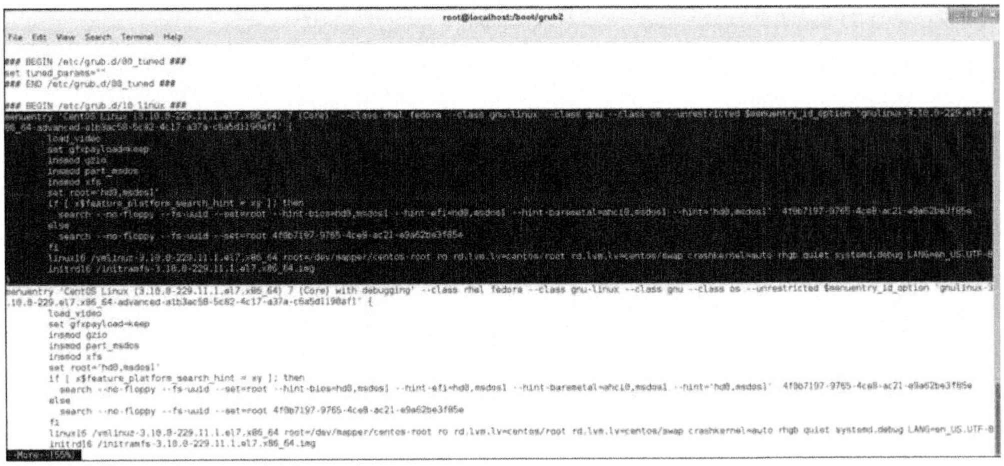

Figure 28-8 *The* ***menuentry*** *Setting in* ***grub.cfg***

Based on the order of the **menuentry** groups in the **grub.cfg** file, you could determine the correct numeric value to assign to **GRUB_DEFAULT**. Just realize that certain changes to the system, such as installing a new kernel, will result in a new order of these **menuentry** groups. So, it might be better to use the name associated with the **menuentry**, for example:

```
GRUB_DEFAULT="'CentOS Linux (3.10.0-229.11.1.e;7.x86.64) 7 (Core)"'
```

If you want to create your own custom title, add an entry in the **/etc/grub.d/40_custom** file. The entry is just like the **menuentry** from the **grub.cfg** file, so you could copy and paste one of those examples to create your own. Remember to run the **grub2-mkconfig** or **update-grub** command after you make changes to the **/etc/grub.d/40_custom** file.

Booting to Single-User Mode in GRUB 2

Earlier in this chapter, you learned how to boot to single-user mode to recover the root password on a system that uses the Legacy GRUB system. If your system is using GRUB 2 for a boot system, the process is going to be different.

Step 1 is the same as with Legacy GRUB: Boot the system and edit the title of your choice by using the **e** command. Next, edit the line that begins with **linux** or **linux16** and add **init=/bin/sh** to the end of that line. Boot the system with Ctlr+x.

Remount the root filesystem as read-write with the following command:

```
mount -o remount,rw /
```

Change the root password by executing the **passwd** command. You will also need to run the following command if you have SELinux enabled on your system (if you do not know if SELinux is enabled, there is no harm to running this command, so it's best to do so):

```
touch /.autorelabel
```

Finally, reboot the machine by executing the following command:

```
exec /sbin/reboot
```

NOTE This process may vary slightly from one distribution to another. Consult the documentation for your distribution before attempting this process.

Securing GRUB 2

Securing Legacy GRUB is straightforward compared to securing GRUB 2. Recall that you want to limit what can be done in the interactive GRUB environment that is provided during the boot process. With Legacy GRUB, you just provide a password in the **/boot/grub/grub.conf** file. With GRUB 2, you provide users and passwords, which allows you to fine-tune the access.

You should create at least one "superuser" account that has full access to all GRUB features during boot. You can do this by adding the following at the bottom of the **/etc/grub.d/01_users** file:

```
cat <<EOF
set superusers="bo"
password bobospassword
EOF
```

To allow for regular users, use the following format:

```
cat <<EOF
set superusers="bo"
password bobospassword
password sarah sarahspassword
EOF
```

Now to assign access to specific users for a specific title, modify the **/etc/grub.d/40_custom** file. In Example 28-4, no restriction is placed on **test1**, so anyone could edit this title. Only the "superuser" and the "sarah" account can edit **test2**. If no option is provided, only the superuser can edit the **menuentry**, so **test3** can only be edited by the superuser.

Example 28-4 *The* ***menuentry*** *Setting*

```
menuentry "'test1"' --unrestricted {
set root=(hd0,1)
linux   /vmlinuz
}
menuentry "'test2"' --users sarah {
set root=(hd0,2)
linux   /vmlinuz
}
menuentry "'test3"' {
set root=(hd0,3)
linux   /vmlinuz
}
```

If you do not want to use plain-text passwords, you can create an encrypted password by executing the **grub2-mkpasswd-pbkdf2** command. The format of the **/etc/grub.d/01_users** file should be changed to the following:

```
cat <<EOF
set superusers="bo"
password_ pbkdf2 bo
grub.pbkdf2.sha512.10000.19074739ED80F115963D984BDCB35AA671C24325755377C3E9B014D862DA6ACC
➥ 77BC110EED41822800A87FD3700C037320E51E9326188D53247EC0722DDF15FC.
C56EC0738911AD86CEA55546139FEBC366A393DF9785A8F44D3E51BF09DB980BAFEF85281CBBC56778D8B19DC
➥ 94833EA8342F7D73E3A1AA30B205091F1015A85
EOF
```

Kernel Components

To understand the Linux kernel, it might be good to start by stating what the kernel is not. The kernel is not one single, massive program. Instead, the kernel consists of a core program and a collection of smaller programs, called kernel modules or LKMs (Loadable Kernel Modules), that can be loaded and unloaded as required.

Recall that the kernel performs several critical system tasks, including managing hardware devices such as hard drives, network cards, and Bluetooth devices. To manage each of these hardware devices, the kernel needs a program (called a driver or a module) to be available in memory. However, there is rarely a case in which all kernel modules need to be stored in memory. As a result, these modules are often only loaded into memory as required.

For example, if you have a desktop machine or a server, it is unlikely that you have a Bluetooth device because these devices are normally only available on laptops. It would serve no purpose to have the Bluetooth module loaded into memory for these systems. Not only would it result in less usable RAM, but booting the system may be much slower if all kernel modules were loaded.

More details about how these modules are loaded and unloaded are provided later in this chapter. However, it is important to understand what modules are before you can start to make changes to the kernel.

Kernel Documentation

If you plan to make changes to the kernel or compile a custom kernel, you really want to have access to the kernel documentation. There are several locations where this can be found:

- **The /usr/src/linux/Documentation directory**: For older versions of the kernel (typically before version 3.0), the documentation is installed with the kernel source files. The kernel source files are what you use when you compile a custom kernel. To obtain the source file (and the documentation), you need to install the **kernel-devel** package.
- **The /usr/share/doc/kernel-doc*/Documentation directory**: For newer versions of the kernel (typically after version 3.0), the documentation files are no longer bundled with the source files. To obtain the documentation, you need to install the **kernel-doc** package.
- **The https://www.kernel.org/doc site**: You can also access kernel documentation from the kernel.org website.

The good news is there is documentation for the Linux kernel! The bad news is it is not very well organized. For example, if you look at the **Documentation** directory, you see a collection of text files with names like **magic-number.txt**, **zorro.txt**, and **bt8xxgpio.txt** (no, we did not make those up). If you are not already comfortable with the **grep** command, it is time take the plunge because that command will be your greatest ally in finding what you need. There is a massive amount of information within the kernel documentation; you just need to be patient to find what you need.

Tweaking the Kernel

In the real world, you need to learn how to make use of kernel documentation. To give you an example of what this information can provide, we are going to introduce a feature that exists in the **/proc/sys** directory.

If you look in the **/proc/sys** directory, you see directories like the following:

```
[root@onecoursesource sys]$ ls
crypto  debug  dev  fs  kernel  net  sunrpc  vm
```

Each one of these directories contains files (and subdirectories) that you can use to modify the behavior of the kernel without having to perform a recompile. For example, if you look in the **/proc/sys/fs** directory, you see a bunch of files, including one named **file-max**:

```
[root@onecoursesource fs]$ ls
aio-max-nr     dir-notify-enable  inode-nr          leases-enable  overflowuid
aio-nr         epoll              inode-state       mqueue         quota
binfmt_misc    file-max           inotify           nr_open        suid_dumpable
dentry-state   file-nr            lease-break-time  overflowgid
[root@onecoursesource fs]$ more file-max
49305
```

You may wonder what this file means. The answer to this question is found within the **/usr/share/doc/kernel-doc-2.6.32/Documentation/sysctl/fs.txt** file:

> "The value in file-max denotes the maximum number of file-handles that the Linux kernel will allocate. When you get lots of error messages about running out of file handles, you might want to increase this limit."

A **file-handle** is an identifier assigned to an open file, for example, when a process opens a file, either for reading or writing. So in the previous example, the maximum number of files that can be opened at any given time for this system is 49,305, the value stored in the **file-max** file. You can temporarily change this value by changing the value in the **file-max** file:

```
[root@onecoursesource fs]$ echo 60000 > file-max
[root@onecoursesource fs]$ more file-max
60000
```

Later in this chapter, you will see how to make this a permanent change.

If you start poking around in the kernel documentation, you are going to discover some discouraging information:

- Not everything is documented.
- Some documentation is out of date. Remember that **zorro.txt** file? If you read it, you will discover that "The Zorro bus is the bus used in the Amiga family of computers." Yes, the Amiga. (Amiga was discontinued in 1996, but who knows, maybe there is still one in your parent's garage?)

Despite these drawbacks, the kernel documentation is still useful. If you make a lot of changes to the kernel, you will explore this documentation frequently.

Kernel Images

By now you should realize that the kernel is really a collection of software pieces that have been merged together. The core of the kernel is a comparatively small software program that does not have a lot of functionality. To be able to perform more advanced tasks, the kernel needs to be augmented by kernel modules.

There are two primary ways that the kernel modules can be merged with the core kernel software. The first method is called LKMs (Loadable Kernel Modules). This is when the kernel modules are in separate files from the kernel and loaded into memory as needed. LKMs can either be loaded into memory during the kernel phase of the boot process or later as needed. LKMs are explored in greater detail later in this chapter.

The second method is to create a kernel that includes the core kernel software as well as necessary kernel modules. The result of merging the kernel with modules is a file called the

kernelimage. There are several different types of kernel images in use in Linux, but here are the two most common:

- **zImage:** On Intel-based hardware architectures, the first 640KB of RAM is referred to as *low memory*. Older systems required that the kernel be stored in low memory, so the **zImage** was a compressed kernel image limited to 512KB (this is the post-compressed image size), so the kernel would fit in low memory.
- **bzImage:** The low memory limitation is rarely a factor anymore because most systems allow the kernel to be stored in *high memory* (memory above 1MB of RAM). This is fortunate because most kernel images are much larger than 512KB in size. The **bzImage** type is designed for kernel images larger than 512KB.

NOTE Some folks will tell you that the "bz" in **bzImage** stands for **bzip2** compression. This is incorrect. Prior to kernel 2.6.30, images were normally compressed using the **gzip** utility, and as of 2.6.30, images are compressed with the **bzip2** utility. The term **bzImage** actually stands for "big zImage."

The kernel image file is typically named with the following format: **vmlinuz-*version.arch***.

The **vmlinuz** just tells you it is a kernel image. It could be either a **zImage** or **bzImage** file. You can tell which type it is by executing the **file** command on the file:

```
[root@onecoursesource ~]# file /boot/vmlinuz-2.6.32-573.el6.x86_64
/boot/vmlinuz-2.6.32-573.el6.x86_64: Linux kernel x86 boot executable
bzImage, version 2.6.32-573.el6.x86_64 (mockbuil, RO-rootFS, swap_dev 0x4,
Normal VGA
```

You could probably also tell by the size of the file that **zImage** files should be smaller than 512KB, so the following is clearly a **bzImage** file because of its size:

```
[root@onecoursesource ~]# ls -lh  /boot/vmlinuz-2.6.32-573.el6.x86_64
-rwxr-xr-x. 1 root root 4.1M Jul 23 09:13 /boot/vmlinuz-2.6.32-573.el6.x86_64
```

The ***version*** part of the image filename typically includes the base kernel version (**2.6.32.573** in this example) and the distribution release (**el6** in this case). The ***arch*** part of the image filename specifies the architecture that the kernel was built for. The value **x86** means Intel 32-bit architecture and compatible architectures, and **x86_64** means Intel 64-bit architecture and compatible architectures.

28

Kernel Modules

In most cases, you will not need to worry about kernel modules because these are normally maintained automatically for you. If a module is needed, it is automatically loaded into memory in almost all cases. And, because modules are small, these rarely need to be unloaded from memory.

Sometimes you may want to adjust how a module is used. Many modules have *parameters* (sometimes called *options*) that can be used to adjust how a module behaves.

Module Files

Modules are stored in the **/lib/modules** directory. Each kernel has its own subdirectory under the **/lib/modules** directory:

```
[root@onecoursesource ~]# ls /lib/modules
2.6.32-573.7.1.el6.x86_64  2.6.32-573.el6.x86_64  2.6.32.68
```

When you're working with modules, it is important to pick the correct subdirectory. This is when the **uname** command is useful because its output tells you which kernel you are currently using:

```
[root@onecoursesource ~]# uname -a
Linux localhost.localdomain 2.6.32-573.7.1.el6.x86_64 #1 SMP Tue Sep 22
22:00:00 UTC 2015 x86_64 x86_64 x86_64 GNU/Linux
```

The contents of a typical **/lib/modules/*kernel_version*** directory look like what's shown in Example 28-5.

Example 28-5 *The **/lib/modules/kernel_version** Directory Contents*

```
[root@onecoursesource 2.6.32-573.7.1.el6.x86_64]# pwd
/lib/modules/2.6.32-573.7.1.el6.x86_64
[root@onecoursesource 2.6.32-573.7.1.el6.x86_64]# ls
build              modules.drm         modules.softdep
extra              modules.ieee1394map modules.symbols
kernel             modules.inputmap    modules.symbols.bin
misc               modules.isapnpmap   modules.usbmap
modules.alias      modules.modesetting source
modules.alias.bin  modules.networking  updates
modules.block      modules.ofmap       vdso
modules.ccwmap     modules.order       weak-updates
modules.dep        modules.pcimap
modules.dep.bin    modules.seriomap
```

You do not need to be concerned about all the files in this directory, but there are a few that you should be aware of. The modules are stored in subdirectories under the **kernel** directory:

```
[root@onecoursesource kernel]# pwd
/lib/modules/2.6.32-573.7.1.el6.x86_64/kernel
[root@onecoursesource kernel]# ls
arch  crypto  drivers  fs  kernel  lib  mm  net  sound
```

These subdirectories provide a means of breaking the modules into categories. For example, all the filesystem modules are located in the **/lib/modules/*kernel_version*/kernel/fs** directory:

```
[root@onecoursesource fs]# pwd
/lib/modules/2.6.32-573.7.1.el6.x86_64/kernel/fs
[root@onecoursesource fs]# ls
autofs4     configfs  exportfs  fat      jbd    mbcache.ko  nls       xfs
btrfs       cramfs    ext2      fscache  jbd2   nfs         squashfs
cachefiles  dlm       ext3      fuse     jffs2  nfs_common  ubifs
cifs        ecryptfs  ext4      gfs2     lockd  nfsd        udf
```

Knowing exactly where the modules are stored is important in the event that you ever need to copy a module manually onto your system. Normally, additional modules are installed via a software management tool, but occasionally you will manually copy these to your system.

After you copy a module, it is critical that you execute the **depmod** command. The **depmod** command probes all the modules under the **/lib/modules/*kernel_version*/kernel** directory and generates the **/lib/modules/*kernel_version*/modules.dep** file and the **/lib/modules/*kernel_version*/*map** files.

The **modules.dep** file is important because it contains a list of all the kernel modules and module dependencies. A *dependency* is when a module requires another module to work successfully. For example, consider the output in Example 28-6.

Example 28-6 *The* ***modules.dep*** *File*

```
[root@onecoursesource 2.6.32-573.7.1.el6.x86_64]# head modules.dep
kernel/arch/x86/kernel/cpu/mcheck/mce-inject.ko:
kernel/arch/x86/kernel/cpu/cpufreq/powernow-k8.ko:
kernel/drivers/cpufreq/freq_table.ko kernel/arch/x86/kernel/cpu/cpufreq/mperf.ko
kernel/arch/x86/kernel/cpu/cpufreq/mperf.ko:
kernel/arch/x86/kernel/cpu/cpufreq/acpi-cpufreq.ko:
kernel/drivers/cpufreq/freq_table.ko kernel/arch/x86/kernel/cpu/cpufreq/mperf.ko
kernel/arch/x86/kernel/cpu/cpufreq/pcc-cpufreq.ko:
kernel/arch/x86/kernel/cpu/cpufreq/speedstep-lib.ko:
kernel/arch/x86/kernel/cpu/cpufreq/p4-clockmod.ko:
kernel/drivers/cpufreq/freq_table.ko kernel/arch/x86/kernel/cpu/cpufreq/speedstep-lib.ko
kernel/arch/x86/kernel/cpu/cpufreq/intel_pstate.ko:
kernel/arch/x86/kernel/test_nx.ko:
kernel/arch/x86/kernel/microcode.ko:
```

The first line lists the module **mce-inject.ko**, which has no dependencies because there is nothing listed after the colon (**:**) character. On the second line, you can see that the **powernow-k8.ko** module depends on the **freq_table.ko** module.

IMPORTANT NOTE The **depmod** command only executes on the current kernel. If you need to have **depmod** create the appropriate files for another kernel, specify the kernel name as an argument:

```
[root@onecoursesource ~]# depmod 2.6.32.68
```

Listing Modules That Are Loaded

When a module is loaded into memory, you can see it in the output of the **lsmod** command. See Example 28-7 for the output of the **lsmod** command.

Example 28-7 *The* ***lsmod*** *Command*

```
[root@onecoursesource ~]# lsmod | head
Module                  Size  Used by
fuse                   79892  2
vboxsf                 37663  0
autofs4                27000  3
8021q                  20362  0
garp                    7152  1 8021q
stp                     2218  1 garp
llc                     5418  2 garp,stp
ipt_REJECT              2351  2
nf_conntrack_ipv4       9154  2
```

There are three columns of output:

- The first column (**Module**) lists the name of the module loaded in memory. Note that the filename of the module is slightly different because the filename includes an extension, such as **.ko**.

28

- The second column (**Size**) is the size of the module in bytes. Typically modules are small and do not take up much memory.
- The last column (**Used by**) is how many "things" are using this module. These things can be processes, other modules, or the kernel itself. If these things are other modules, the output of the **lsmod** command lists those module names. You can only unload a module from memory if the value of this third column is 0, meaning it is currently not being used.

Loading Modules into Memory

Before showing you how to load modules into memory, we first want to show you an example of why you rarely ever need to do this. In most cases, modules are loaded into memory as needed. For example, take a look at the output of the following command:

```
[root@onecoursesource ~]# lsmod | grep fat
[root@onecoursesource ~]#
```

As you can see, there is no module named "fat" loaded into memory. The **fat** module is one of the modules needed to read the FAT (File Allocation Table) filesystem (a Windows-based filesystem that you may find on removable devices like USB drives). None of the currently mounted filesystems are FAT filesystems, so there is no need for this module to be loaded into memory.

In Example 28-8, you can see what happens in the system log file when a USB disk with a FAT filesystem is added to the system.

Example 28-8 *System Log File Entry When Adding a USB Disk*

```
[root@onecoursesource linux-2.6.32.68]# tail /var/log/messages
Nov  9 22:22:04 localhost kernel: USB Mass Storage support registered.
Nov  9 22:22:05 localhost kernel: scsi 7:0:0:0: Direct-Access     Generic  Flash Disk
➥      8.07 PQ: 0 ANSI: 2
Nov  9 22:22:05 localhost kernel: sd 7:0:0:0: Attached scsi generic sg6 type 0
Nov  9 22:22:05 localhost kernel: sd 7:0:0:0: [sdf] 7831552 512-byte logical blocks:
➥ (4.00 GB/3.73 GiB)
Nov  9 22:22:05 localhost kernel: sd 7:0:0:0: [sdf] Write Protect is off
Nov  9 22:22:05 localhost kernel: sd 7:0:0:0: [sdf] Assuming drive cache: write through
Nov  9 22:22:05 localhost kernel: sd 7:0:0:0: [sdf] Assuming drive cache: write through
Nov  9 22:22:05 localhost kernel: sdf: sdf1
Nov  9 22:22:05 localhost kernel: sd 7:0:0:0: [sdf] Assuming drive cache: write through
Nov  9 22:22:05 localhost kernel: sd 7:0:0:0: [sdf] Attached SCSI removable disk
```

The device is recognized by the system and then several actions take place. One action is to create a device file for the USB disk. The USB disk is also automatically mounted. You can see this based on the last line of output of the **mount** command shown in Example 28-9.

Example 28-9 *The **mount** Command*

```
[root@onecoursesource linux-2.6.32.68]# mount
/dev/mapper/VolGroup-lv_root on / type ext4 (rw)
proc on /proc type proc (rw)
sysfs on /sys type sysfs (rw)
devpts on /dev/pts type devpts (rw,gid=5,mode=620)
tmpfs on /dev/shm type tmpfs (rw,rootcontext="system_u:object_r:tmpfs_t:s0")
/dev/sda1 on /boot type ext4 (rw)
none on /proc/sys/fs/binfmt_misc type binfmt_misc (rw)
gvfs-fuse-daemon on /root/.gvfs type fuse.gvfs-fuse-daemon (rw,nosuid,nodev)
/dev/sdf1 on /media/CENTOS63 type vfat
➥ (rw,nosuid,nodev,uhelper=udisks,uid=0,gid=0,shortname=mixed,dmask=0077,utf8=1,flush)
```

Notice the filesystem type: **vfat**. The **vfat** filesystem is one of several variations of the FAT filesystem. How was the kernel able to recognize this filesystem and mount the USB device when the appropriate module was not loaded into memory? Because it was loaded into memory automatically when the kernel tried to mount the filesystem. As you can see from the output of the following command, the **vfat** module is now loaded into memory:

```
[root@onecoursesource ~]# lsmod | grep fat
vfat                    10584  1
fat                     54992  1 vfat
```

The value of 1 in the third column of the **vfat** module indicates one thing is using the module. In this case, that one thing is the mount process itself. Unmount that filesystem and you see this value drop to 0:

```
[root@onecoursesource ~]# umount /media/CENTOS63
[root@onecoursesource ~]# lsmod | grep fat
vfat                    10584  0
fat                     54992  1 vfat
```

As you can see from the previous example, the kernel is normally able to load modules into memory automatically, as required. But, suppose you really want to load the **vfat** module manually. There are two commands you can use: the **insmod** command (the "hard way") and the **modprobe** command (the "easy way").

If you use the **insmod** command, you need to provide a complete pathname to the module (note that before this command is executed, the module is unloaded from memory, a process that will be covered later in this section):

```
[root@onecoursesource ~]# insmod /lib/modules/2.6.32-
➥573.7.1.el6.x86_64/kernel/fs/fat/vfat.ko
insmod: error inserting "'/lib/modules/2.6.32-
➥573.7.1.el6.x86_64/kernel/fs/fat/vfat.ko"': -1 Unknown symbol in module
```

Unfortunately, sometimes the command fails, as you can see from the output of the previous command. This "Unknown symbol in module" error is due to the fact that the **vfat** module has a dependency module. How do you know what this dependency module is? By looking at the **/lib/modules/*kernel-version*/modules.dep** file, like so:

28

```
[root@onecoursesource ~]# grep vfat /lib/modules/2.6.32-
➥573.7.1.el6.x86_64/modules.dep
kernel/fs/fat/vfat.ko: kernel/fs/fat/fat.ko
```

So, if you load the **fat** module first, then you can load the **vfat** module. Of course you first need to check to make sure that the **fat** module doesn't have any dependencies (the first **lsmod** command in the following example is just to verify that these modules are not loaded into memory):

```
[root@onecoursesource ~]# lsmod | grep fat
[root@onecoursesource ~]# grep fat.ko /lib/modules/2.6.32-
➥573.7.1.el6.x86_64/modules.dep
kernel/fs/fat/fat.ko:
kernel/fs/fat/vfat.ko: kernel/fs/fat/fat.ko
kernel/fs/fat/msdos.ko: kernel/fs/fat/fat.ko
[root@onecoursesource ~]# insmod /lib/modules/2.6.32-
➥573.7.1.el6.x86_64/kernel/fs/fat/fat.ko
[root@onecoursesource ~]# insmod /lib/modules/2.6.32-
➥573.7.1.el6.x86_64/kernel/fs/fat/vfat.ko
[root@onecoursesource ~]# lsmod | grep fat
vfat                    10584  0
fat                     54992  1 vfat
```

The **insmod** command is a pain. Not only do you have to load dependency modules, you have to know exactly where the modules are. A much easier command to use is the **modprobe** command:

```
[root@onecoursesource ~]# lsmod | grep fat
[root@onecoursesource ~]# modprobe vfat
[root@onecoursesource ~]# lsmod | grep fat
vfat                   10584  0
fat                    54992  1 vfat
```

The **modprobe** command searches the **modules.dep** file to find the location of the module that you want to load. The command also uses the **modules.dep** file to determine any dependencies that the module has and loads these dependency modules first.

Conversational Learning™—Loading Modules

Gary: Hi, Julia. Do you have much experience with kernel modules?

Julia: A bit… are you having a difficult time with one?

Gary: No, but I have been using **modprobe** to load modules and now I see that the **insmod** command can also load modules. Which one should I use and why?

Julia: I would recommend using **modprobe** in most cases. It does a great job of determining dependency modules, and you don't have to specify the complete path to the module.

Gary: Then I should completely ignore the **insmod** command?

Julia: There are a couple of reasons why you should know about the **insmod** command. To begin with, some older scripts may use **insmod** to load modules.

Gary: Any other reason to know about this command?

Julia: Yes, one advantage of **insmod** is that you can use it to quickly test a new module, as long as it doesn't have any dependencies. With the **modprobe** command, you have to first install the module in the right location, then run the **depmod** command so the **modprobe** command knows where the module is located and what its dependencies are. The **insmod** command doesn't require that, so it can be good for testing a new module—perhaps one that you or another developer in your organization created.

Gary: OK, sounds like I will be mostly using **modprobe**, but there are some use cases for **insmod**. Thanks, Julia.

Unloading Modules from Memory

Before demonstrating how to unload a module from memory, you should consider why you would need to unload a module:

- **The module could cause some sort of conflict or error.** This could be possible for third-party modules, but it is unlikely for any module that comes with the kernel.
- **You can free up memory space by unloading a module.** Keep in mind that modules tend to be small. If you have to free up memory by unloading modules, you really should consider adding more memory to that system.

It is highly unlikely that either of these reasons will be compelling enough to unload modules from memory. Keep in mind that even if you do unload a module, it is going to be reloaded when it is required again. However, on the rare occasion when you do have a need to unload a module from memory, you should be aware of how to accomplish this task.

To unload a module manually, you can use the **rmmod** command:

```
[root@onecoursesource ~]# rmmod fat
ERROR: Module fat is in use by vfat
```

Unfortunately, if the system is using the module, you will receive an error message, as shown in the previous example.

Instead of using the **rmmod** command, consider using the **modprobe -r** command:

```
[root@onecoursesource ~]# rmmod fat
```

This should remove both the **fat** and **vfat** modules from memory (assuming that the **vfat** module is not currently being used). You still get an error if the module is being used by a process or by the kernel.

Listing Module Information

In the real world, you will not load and unload modules from memory often. However, you may find it useful to understand modules—particularly module parameters.

A module parameter is a feature that allows you to modify the behavior of a module. Not all modules have parameters, but for those that do, knowing the parameters can help you customize how your system behaves.

To view a module's parameters (and additional information), execute the **modinfo** command, as shown in Example 28-10.

Example 28-10 *The modinfo Command*

```
[root@onecoursesource ~]# modinfo cdrom
filename:       /lib/modules/2.6.32-573.7.1.el6.x86_64/kernel/drivers/cdrom/cdrom.ko
license:        GPL
srcversion:     6C1B1032B5BB33E30110371
depends:
vermagic:       2.6.32-573.7.1.el6.x86_64 SMP mod_unload modversions
parm:           debug:bool
parm:           autoclose:bool
parm:           autoeject:bool
parm:           lockdoor:bool
parm:           check_media_type:bool
parm:           mrw_format_restart:bool
```

This is the module that allows the kernel to utilize the CD-ROM drive. The lines that start with **parm** are the parameters. For example, you are probably used to the fact that the CD-ROM drive door is locked on Linux systems when a CD-ROM disc is inserted and mounted. This can be controlled by the **lockdoor** parameter for the **cdrom** module.

One way of setting this parameter is to load the module with the **modprobe** command, passing the parameter as an argument:

```
[root@onecoursesource ~]# modprobe cdrom lockdoor=0
```

Because **lockdoor** is a bool (Boolean) type, it can be set to either 1 (lock the door) or 0 (don't lock the door).

The **modprobe** technique is only temporary and requires you to unload and reload the module. If you reboot the system, the parameter will be set to the default. Later in this chapter, you see another way to change the parameter without having to unload the module and a different method to make the change persistent across reboots.

Remember the **modinfo** command; it is a useful way to gather information about a module, including the parameters it supports.

The /proc/sys Filesystem

Earlier in this chapter, the **/proc/sys** directory structure was introduced. This directory is part of the memory-based filesystem that is mounted under the **/proc** mount point. Everything under the **/proc** mount point is information related to the kernel, including kernel modules. This information is not stored on the hard drive, but rather in RAM.

Kernel parameters can be modified on the fly by changing files in the **/proc/sys** directory. Recall the earlier example that demonstrated how you can temporarily change the number of file handles by modifying the value in the **/proc/sys/fs/file-max** file:

```
[student@localhost fs]$ echo 60000 > file-max
[student@localhost fs]$ more file-max
60000
```

Modules can also be modified by changing files in the **/proc/sys** directory structure. For example, consider the output of the following commands:

```
[root@onecoursesource ~]# ls /proc/sys/dev/cdrom
autoclose  autoeject  check_media  debug  info  lock
[root@onecoursesource ~]# modinfo cdrom | grep parm
parm:           debug:bool
parm:           autoclose:bool
parm:           autoeject:bool
parm:           lockdoor:bool
parm:           check_media_type:bool
parm:           mrw_format_restart:bool
```

Note that most of the **parm** values have corresponding files in the **/proc/sys/dev/cdrom** directory (although why the file for the **lockdoor** parameter is called **lock** and not "**lockdoor**" is a bit of a mystery). By changing the value of a file, you can change the behavior of the module without having to unload and reload the module:

```
[root@onecoursesource ~]# cat /proc/sys/dev/cdrom/lock
1
[root@onecoursesource ~]# echo "0" > /proc/sys/dev/cdrom/lock
[root@onecoursesource ~]# cat /proc/sys/dev/cdrom/lock
0
```

Security Highlight

There are over a thousand kernel parameters. Some are designed to provide better security to the system. For example, setting the contents of the **/proc/sys/net/ipv4/icmp_echo_ignore_all** file to a value of 1 will result in the system ignoring requests from commands like the **ping** command. The security advantage of this is that a flood of **ping** requests can result in a denial of service (DoS) as the system attempts to keep up on the responses to a large number of **ping** requests. Take some time to explore other kernel parameters to learn more about how you can better secure the system.

You can also view and change parameters by using the **sysctl** command. For example, to view all the kernel and kernel module parameters, execute the **sysctl** command with the **-a** option, as shown in Example 28-11.

Example 28-11 *The sysctl -a Command*

```
[root@onecoursesource ~]# sysctl -a | head
kernel.sched_child_runs_first = 0
kernel.sched_min_granularity_ns = 1000000
kernel.sched_latency_ns = 5000000
kernel.sched_wakeup_granularity_ns = 1000000
kernel.sched_tunable_scaling = 1
kernel.sched_features = 3183
kernel.sched_migration_cost = 500000
kernel.sched_nr_migrate = 32
kernel.sched_time_avg = 1000
kernel.sched_shares_window = 10000000
```

The name of the parameter (**kernel.sched_child_runs_first**, for example) is a relative pathname that starts from **/proc/sys** and has a dot (**.**) character between the directory and filename rather than a slash (**/**) character. For example, the **/proc/sys/dev/cdrom/lock** file is named the **dev.cdrom.lock** parameter:

```
[root@onecoursesource ~]# sysctl -a | grep dev.cdrom.lock
dev.cdrom.lock = 1
```

You can change the value of this parameter by using the **sysctl** command:

```
[root@onecoursesource ~]# sysctl dev.cdrom.lock=0
dev.cdrom.lock = 0
[root@onecoursesource ~]# sysctl -a | grep dev.cdrom.lock
dev.cdrom.lock = 0
```

It is actually safer to use the **sysctl** command rather than modifying the file directly because the **sysctl** command knows which values for the parameter are valid and which ones are not:

```
[root@onecoursesource ~]# sysctl dev.cdrom.lock="abc"
error: "Invalid argument" setting key "dev.cdrom.lock"
```

The **sysctl** command knows which parameter values are valid because it can look at the **modinfo** output. For example, the value of the **lock** file must be a Boolean (0 or 1) according to the output of the **modinfo** command:

```
[root@onecoursesource ~]# modinfo cdrom | grep lock
parm:           lockdoor:bool
```

If you modify the file directly or use the **sysctl** command, the changes are temporary. When the system is rebooted, the values go back to the defaults, unless you make changes in the **/etc/sysctl.conf** file; see Example 28-12 for a sample of this file.

Example 28-12 *The /etc/sysctl.conf File*

```
[root@onecoursesource ~]#head /etc/sysctl.conf
# Kernel sysctl configuration file for Red Hat Linux
#
# For binary values, 0 is disabled, 1 is enabled. See sysctl(8) and
# sysctl.conf(5) for more details.
```

28

```
# Controls IP packet forwarding
net.ipv4-ip_forward = 0

# Controls source route verification
net.ipv4.conf.default.rp_filter = 1
```

To disable CD-ROM locking across reboots, add the following line to the **/etc/sysctl.conf** file:

```
dev.cdrom.lock=0
```

On some distributions, you can make a file in the **/etc/sysctl.d** directory and provide customized kernel and kernel module parameters. Check your **sysctl** man pages to see whether your distribution supports this method.

The init Phase

As previously mentioned, once the kernel has finished, the init phase is started. Historically there have been several different init phase technologies:

- **SysVinit**: An older method that originated in Unix. Although this method was used for many years, it is rare to come across a modern Linux distribution that uses SysVinit. As a result, this method will not be covered in this book.
- **Upstart**: Designed as a replacement for SysVinit, Upstart has been used in distributions like Debian, Ubuntu, Fedora, and SUSE. However, almost all distributions have migrated to the newest init phase software: systemd. As a result, Upstart will not be covered in this book.
- **systemd**: Although more complex than SysVinit and Upstart, systemd has become the standard init phase technology and will be the focus in this chapter.

Security Highlight

If you are experiencing problems during the boot process, consider viewing the **/var/log/boot.log file**. This file should contain the messages that appear on the screen during the boot process. This information can help you troubleshoot boot issues.

Configuring Systemd

By itself, **systemd** is a fairly large topic. At its core, **systemd** is a process for managing what processes (also called "services") are started during system boot, but it also provides other features, such as the logging tool **journald**. The focus of this chapter is on understanding the essentials of **systemd** and learning how to change the boot process.

One of the core features of **systemd** is the unit, and there are many different types of units available. The following unit types are the most critical to understand for system booting:

- **Service**: A service unit is used to describe a process to start (or stop). For example, the Apache web service is considered a service unit for **systemd**. Service units are described in files that end in **.service**. The exact location of these service files depends on other factors, but you can search for them using the **find** or **locate** command.
- **Target**: A target unit is a collection of other units. One of the purposes of a target unit is to build a "boot level" that defines all the services to start when the system is taken to the defined boot level. These boot levels used to be referred to as "runlevels" in SysVinit and Upstart, so you may see mention of that term in some documentation.

Using Service Units

A service file is used to describe different elements of a service unit. Typically these files are provided when you install the software package for the utility, so you do not need to know how to make them from scratch. However, it can be useful to know some of the features of this file. For a demonstration, view the output of Example 28-13.

Example 28-13 *A Service Unit File*

```
[root@onecoursesource:~ ]# more /etc/systemd/system/sshd.service
[Unit]
Description=OpenBSD Secure Shell server
After=network.target auditd.service
ConditionPathExists=!/etc/ssh/sshd_not_to_be_run

[Service]
EnvironmentFile=-/etc/default/ssh
ExecStart=/usr/sbin/sshd -D $SSHD_OPTS
ExecReload=/bin/kill -HUP $MAINPID
KillMode=process
Restart=on-failure

[Install]
WantedBy=multi-user.target
Alias=sshd.service
```

The key settings for the service file are described in Table 28-4.

Table 28-4 Key Settings of a Service Unit File

Setting	Description
After	Indicates that this service should be started after all the services in the target units listed. See more about target units later in this chapter.
ExecStart	The command to execute to start the service. This is one of the settings that you may modify to change the behavior of the service.
WantedBy	This setting is used to indicate which target *to associate with this service*. For example, **WantedBy=multi-user.target** means "this service is part of the multiuser target." The result of this setting is a symbolic link file created in the directory that defines the target and the service unit file.

Although you can modify the service file to change how the service is started, you can also start, stop, and view the status of the service manually using the **systemctl** command, as demonstrated in Example 28-14.

Example 28-14 *The* ***systemctl*** *Command*

```
[root@onecoursesource ~]# systemctl start sshd
[root@onecoursesource ~]# systemctl status sshd
● sshd.service - OpenSSH server daemon
   Loaded: loaded (/usr/lib/systemd/system/sshd.service; disabled;
   Active: active (running) since Mon 2018-12-11 20:32:46 PST; 6s
     Docs: man:sshd(8)
           man:sshd_config(5)
 Main PID: 13698 (sshd)
```

```
     Tasks: 1 (limit: 4915)
    CGroup: /system.slice/sshd.service
            └─13698 /usr/sbin/sshd -D

Dec 11 20:32:46 localhost.localdomain systemd[1]: Starting OpenSSH
Dec 11 20:32:46 localhost.localdomain sshd[13698]: Server listening
Dec 11 20:32:46 localhost.localdomain sshd[13698]: Server listening
Dec 11 20:32:46 localhost.localdomain systemd[1]: Started OpenSSH
[root@onecoursesource ~]# systemctl stop sshd
[root@onecoursesource ~]# systemctl status sshd
● sshd.service - OpenSSH server daemon
   Loaded: loaded (/usr/lib/systemd/system/sshd.service; disabled;
   Active: inactive (dead)
     Docs: man:sshd(8)
           man:sshd_config(5)

Dec 11 20:32:46 localhost.localdomain systemd[1]: Starting OpenSSH
Dec 11 20:32:46 localhost.localdomain sshd[13698]: Server listening
Dec 11 20:32:46 localhost.localdomain sshd[13698]: Server listening
Dec 11 20:32:46 localhost.localdomain systemd[1]: Started OpenSSH
Dec 11 21:10:26 localhost.localdomain sshd[13698]: Received signal
Dec 11 21:10:26 localhost.localdomain systemd[1]: Stopping OpenSSH
Dec 11 21:10:26 localhost.localdomain systemd[1]: Stopped OpenSSH
```

Other **systemctl** options include **restart** (to stop and start the service) and **reload** (to have a service reload its configuration files without stopping the service).

Using Target Units

Recall that a target unit is a collection of other units (typically service units). You can list all the different target units by executing the **systemctl list-unit-files --type=target** command, as demonstrated in Example 28-15.

Example 28-15 *Listing Targets*

```
[root@onecoursesource ~]# systemctl list-unit-files --type=target | head
UNIT FILE                  STATE
anaconda.target            static
basic.target               static
bluetooth.target           static
busnames.target            static
cryptsetup-pre.target      static
cryptsetup.target          static
ctrl-alt-del.target        disabled
default.target             enabled
emergency.target           static
```

There are dozens of defined targets on a typical system. For the purposes of understanding the boot process, the following targets are the most important:

- **default.target**: The standard set of services needed to boot the system. Normally this target has core software pieces, but full functionality requires additional services provided by other targets.

- **multi-user.target**: The set of services that provide a fully functional system (not including a GUI). The **default.target** unit is a requisite of the **multi-user.target** unit.
- **graphical.target**: The set of services that provides a GUI.

To get a good idea of all of the currently enabled targets (and corresponding services), execute the **systemctl list-dependencies** command as demonstrated in Example 28-16.

Example 28-16 *Listing Target Dependencies*

```
[root@onecoursesource~]# systemctl list-dependencies | head
default.target
● ├─accounts-daemon.service
● ├─gdm.service
● ├─livesys-late.service
● ├─livesys.service
● ├─rtkit-daemon.service
● ├─switcheroo-control.service
● ├─systemd-update-utmp-runlevel.service
● └─multi-user.target
●   ├─abrt-journal-core.service
```

Security Highlight

Spend some time learning about what each of these services is designed to do. The more services you have running on a system, the more potential vulnerabilities. Carefully consider each service to determine which you can disable to make the system more secure.

You can add a service to a target by using the **systemctl enable** command:

```
[root@onecoursesource ~]# systemctl list-dependencies | grep sshd
[root@onecoursesource ~]# systemctl enable sshd
Created symlink /etc/systemd/system/multi-user.target.wants/sshd.service → /usr/
➥ lib/systemd/system/sshd.service.
[root@onecoursesource ~]# systemctl list-dependencies | grep sshd
●   ├─sshd.service
```

The target that the service is added to is based on the **WantedBy** setting in the service's configuration file:

```
[root@onecoursesource:~ ]#grep WantedBy /etc/systemd/system/sshd.service
WantedBy=multi-user.target
```

Summary

The boot-up process for a Linux operating system is a multistep process. In this chapter, you learned some of the areas you can modify to change the boot behavior as well as make the system more secure.

Key Terms

Firmware, BIOS, UEFI, bootloader, MBR, LILO, GRUB, UUID, splashimage, LKM, kernel image file, unit

Review Questions

1. The _____ command is used to create a new **initramfs** file.
2. Which device name is valid in a Legacy GRUB configuration file?
   - A. **hd0,0**
   - B. **(hd0,0)**
   - C. **(hd0.0)**
   - D. **(hd0:0)**
3. The _____ command is used to create a GRUB2 encrypted password.
4. Which commands can load kernel modules into memory? (Choose two.)
   - A. **lsmod**
   - B. **insmod**
   - C. **ldmod**
   - D. **modprobe**
5. The _____ command is used to change **systemd** units, such as start and enable a service.

Develop a Software Management Security Policy

In Chapter 26, "Red Hat-Based Software Management," and Chapter 27, "Debian-Based Software Management," you learned how to install software on Red Hat and Debian systems, respectively. Installing software comes with a responsibility: to ensure that the software placed on your systems does not pose a security risk. In this chapter, you learn how to discover possible security risks that software poses.

You also learned in Chapter 28, "System Booting," how to configure a system to boot, including controlling what services and processes were started during the system boot. Each service has a separate configuration for security, much of which you have learned throughout this book. In this chapter, you explore another method of configuring and securing legacy services using a procedure known as **xinetd**.

After reading this chapter and completing the exercises, you will be able to do the following:

Read Common Vulnerabilities and Exposures (CVE) to discover possible security vulnerabilities

Utilize distribution resources to better secure your systems

Configure and secure legacy services

Ensuring Software Security

Because of how easy it is to install software, security experts might overlook the importance of creating a security policy for software. This section focuses on key elements of creating a security policy that should be followed when managing software on a Linux distribution.

Keep Packages Up to Date

In some ways, keeping all software packages up to date can be a double-edged sword. Many software updates include fixes to bugs or security holes, so installing these updates is critical. On the other hand, software updates that provide more features or functions may introduce a security hole that did not exist in previous versions.

It is a good practice to install any software update that fixes a bug or security vulnerability. Normally, installing software that provides new features is also a good idea, but you should consider exploring the update before installing it. You might not be able to determine if the update introduces a new security hole, but you should be able to determine if the update is really necessary.

It is also important to keep a log of software updates. This may seem like a lot of extra "paperwork," but any time you opt to not install an update, the reason should be clearly stated in a log entry. Otherwise, another administrator might decide to install the update without knowing the reason why the update was omitted.

It is also fairly common to perform updates automatically via a **crontab** job on workstation systems. However, this is normally not a good idea for mission-critical servers because an update could cause problems, especially an update to core operating system software or the kernel. For mission-critical servers, it is normally better to have a lab system that is identical (or as identical as possible) to the mission-critical server and perform updates on the lab system. After the lab system is tested to ensure no problems arise, the software updates should be safe to install on the mission-critical system.

You should also be prepared to undo (back out of) updates in the event that the new updates cause a problem. This isn't something that is always immediately noticeable, so systems with updates should be monitored routinely for faulty software.

Lastly, realize that you do not need to reboot the system after installing a software package (with the exception of the kernel); however, you may need to restart a server program. This is not always the case because many developers include this restart process in the software package's post-installation tasks.

Consider Removing Unnecessary Packages

This may be a challenge at first, but it is very important that you only have necessary software installed on the system. The challenge of determining which packages are necessary is that a typical default Linux installation includes thousands of software packages. For example, a default installation of Kali Linux has almost 3000 packages, as shown here:

```
root@kali:~# dpkg -l | wc -l
2801
```

You might be asking, "do I really need to decide which packages should be installed on each system by reviewing each package one at a time?" The answer is that you should explore what each package in a distribution provides and then create rules for different kinds of systems. For example, what belongs on a typical user workstation and what belongs on a web server?

In fact, you should create three categories:

- The software that should be installed by default.
- Software considered optional (okay to install, but not installed by default).
- Potentially risky or problematic software that should never be installed on any system.

You go through the process of determining if a package should be installed by exploring the package. For example, you might first look at the package to determine what is does, as shown on a Fedora system in Listing 29-1.

Listing 29-1 *Viewing Package Information*

```
[root@onecoursesource ~]#rpm -qi zsh
Name        : zsh
Version     : 5.0.7
Release     : 8.fc20
Architecture: x86_64
Install Date: Mon 10 Mar 2019 03:24:10 PM PDT
Group       : System Environment/Shells
Size        : 6188121
License     : MIT
Signature   : RSA/SHA256, Fri 22 May 2015 11:23:12 AM PDT, Key ID 2eb161fa246110c1
Source RPM  : zsh-5.0.7-8.fc20.src.rpm
Build Date  : Fri 22 May 2015 06:27:34 AM PDT
Build Host  : buildhw-12.phx2.fedoraproject.org
```

```
Relocations : (not relocatable)
Packager    : Fedora Project
Vendor      : Fedora Project
URL         : http://zsh.sourceforge.net/
Summary     : Powerful interactive shell
Description :
The zsh shell is a command interpreter usable as an interactive login
shell and as a shell script command processor.  Zsh resembles the ksh
shell (the Korn shell), but includes many enhancements.  Zsh supports
command line editing, built-in spelling correction, programmable
command completion, shell functions (with autoloading), a history
mechanism, and more.
```

Based on the information provided by the command in Listing 29-1, you may be able to determine this package should not be installed on the system. Perhaps it is because you do not want to support another shell and only want to support BASH on this system. Or you may consider this package unnecessary since a good shell already exists. If you are considering the installation, which requires an additional shell, be sure to investigate the implications and ramifications of running a second shell on the system prior to installation.

If you decide this might be a good package, then before approving it, you should also look at the files it provides, particularly the executable programs (which are typically located in a **/bin** directory, such as **/usr/bin** and **/bin**, but could also be located under **/sbin** or **/usr/sbin**):

```
[root@onecoursesource ~]# rpm -ql zsh | grep /bin/
/usr/bin/zsh
[root@onecoursesource ~]# ls -l /usr/bin/zsh
-rwxr-xr-x 1 root root 726032 May 22  2015 /usr/bin/zsh
```

Look at the documentation (man pages) for these executable programs and look closely at the permissions and ownership of the files. Ask yourself questions like, "does this program provide elevated privileges because of a SUID or SGID permission?"

Lastly, note that the commands demonstrated in this section were performed on a system that already had the software installed. You should be vetting software packages on a test system where you can safely install packages without any concern of impacting a critical system. This system should not even be attached to the network. This allows you to run the commands and test each one before deciding if the software is safe to install on "real" systems in your organization.

Ensure You Install from Trusted Sources

Many administrators rely on the **yum**, **dnf**, and **apt-get** commands to download and install software programs. As long as these tools are configured to download from trusted sources, this is not a bad practice. However, your security policy should include a process in which the source location of packages is confirmed before installing packages in this manner.

This means you should include a review of the configuration files that point the **yum**, **dnf**, and **apt-get** commands to repository servers:

- **For yum and dnf**: The **/etc/yum.conf** file and files in the **/etc/yum.repos.d** directory
- **For apt-get**: The **/etc/apt/sources.list** file or files located in the **/etc/apt/sources.list.d** directory

Also, you should take great care when getting software directly from another source, such as downloading a software package from a website or receiving one via email. Very carefully consider whether such a package should be installed and review it very closely if you choose to move forward with the installation.

CVE

The Common Vulnerabilities and Exposures (CVE) is a system designed to provide a single location where you can learn about security-related software issues. The system is maintained by the MITRE Corporation and accessible via http://cve.mitre.org, as shown in Figure 29-1.

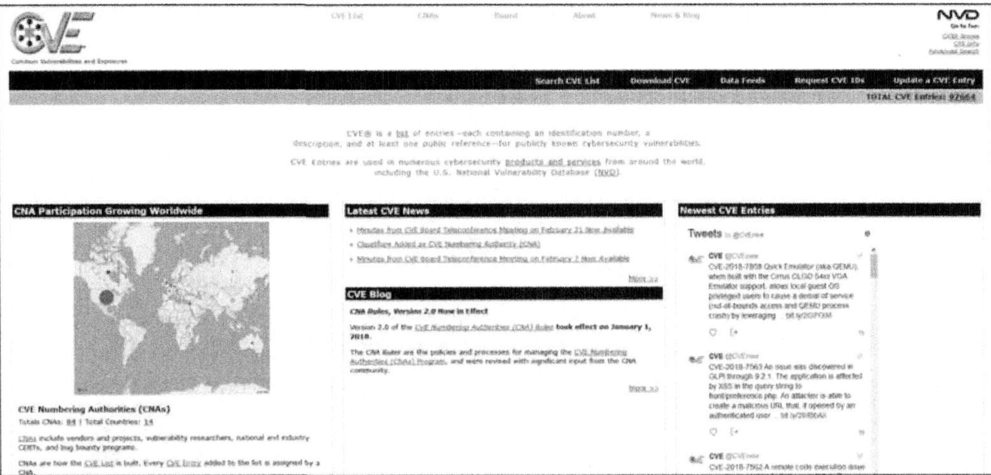

Figure 29-1 *CVE Website*

When a vulnerability is discovered and reported to MITRE, it is assigned a unique ID, regardless of the distribution where the vulnerability was discovered. As a result, each vulnerability can be referred to using this unique ID, making it easier to keep track of it when working in an environment that supports many different distributions.

The CVE data is free to anyone. This is great for administrators because they are provided with details to vulnerabilities, but it also means that hackers can use this information against your system if you do not keep your system updated.

Your security policy should include a practice of reviewing relevant CVEs on a regular basis to determine possible security holes. You can download all of the CVEs and use the **grep** command to find the ones that are related to the software installed on your system. You can also make use of the 29
search tool on the CVE website. Figure 29-2 demonstrates the search results for zsh (the Z shell).

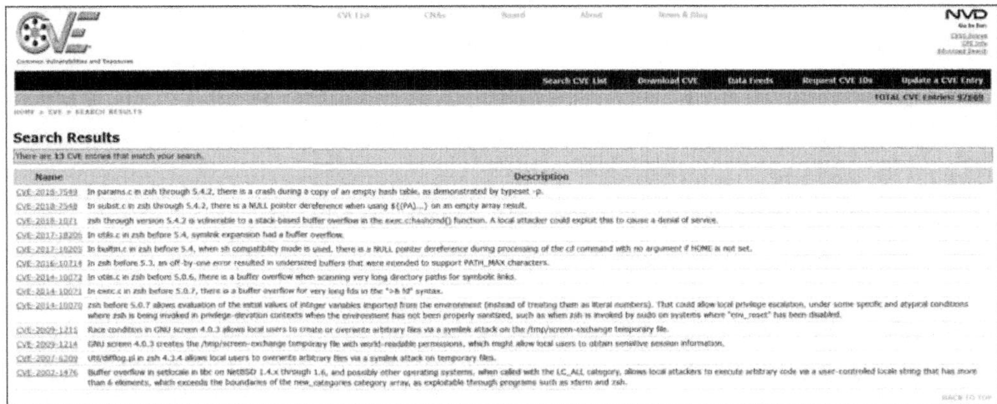

Figure 29-2 *CVE Search Results*

You should consider making use of the "Data Feeds," a feature on the website that lets you learn about CVEs via Twitter or email. If you do choose email, keep in mind that this could result in many emails, so consider using a specific email address such as a general department or admin-only address just for these security alerts, especially if multiple administrators will review the information and make decisions, such as if a different admin is responsible for each shift.

The information provided in a CVE is very well defined and includes the following:

- A unique CVE ID.
- A brief description of the issue.
- References to additional information.
- Organization that assigned the CVE a unique ID.
- The date the CVE was created. This is a very important field because older CVEs are likely not an issue on modern versions of software. Software vendors typically release patches that close any hole that has been reported as a CVE.

See Figure 29-3 for an example of a CVE.

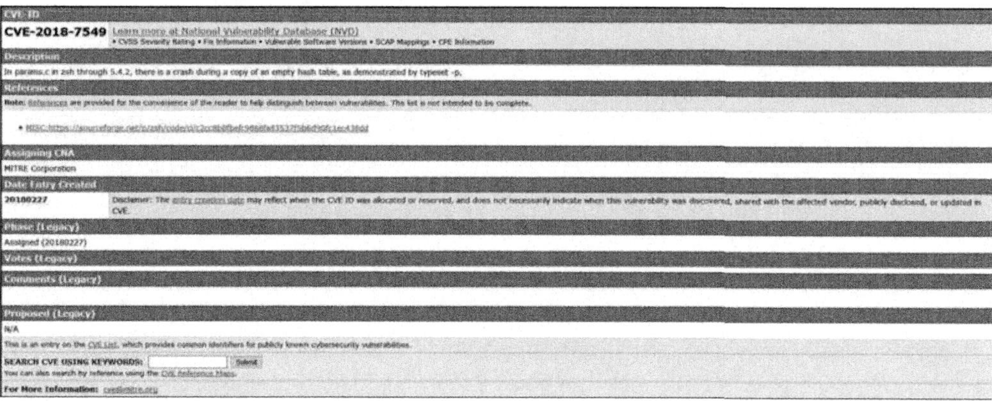

Figure 29-3 *CVE Example*

Distribution-Specific Security Alerts

Each distribution will normally have its own security alerts. This is because part of building a distro is the customization of the software provided by other open source projects. For example, the Z shell may be modified to provide additional features for the distribution that you have installed on your systems.

This is also one of the reasons why many organizations only install and support one or two distributions. More distributions in an environment means more work to properly secure each system. Your security plan should include a regular review of CVEs as well as a review of the distribution's security alerts.

As an example, consider Red Hat Enterprise Linux (RHEL). Red Hat uses Red Hat Security Advisories (RHSAs) to inform security personnel of any potential vulnerabilities. Red Hat also makes references to CVEs when appropriate so you are aware that this is a problem on all distributions, not just RHEL.

RHSAs clearly indicate which versions of the distribution may be affected. This is important because you do not want to investigate a vulnerability that does not affect your current distributions. See Figure 29-4 for an example of an RHSA.

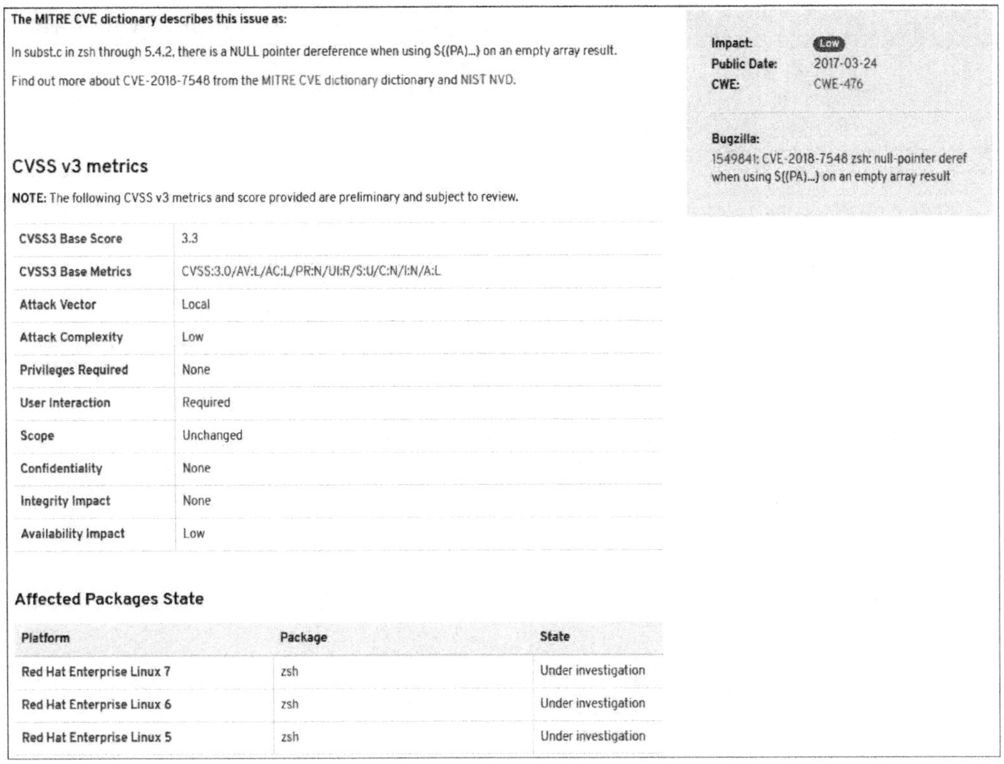

The MITRE CVE dictionary describes this issue as:

In subst.c in zsh through 5.4.2, there is a NULL pointer dereference when using ${(PA)...} on an empty array result.

Find out more about CVE-2018-7548 from the MITRE CVE dictionary dictionary and NIST NVD.

Impact: Low
Public Date: 2017-03-24
CWE: CWE-476

Bugzilla:
1549841: CVE-2018-7548 zsh: null-pointer deref when using ${(PA)...} on an empty array result

CVSS v3 metrics

NOTE: The following CVSS v3 metrics and score provided are preliminary and subject to review.

CVSS3 Base Score	3.3
CVSS3 Base Metrics	CVSS:3.0/AV:L/AC:L/PR:N/UI:R/S:U/C:N/I:N/A:L
Attack Vector	Local
Attack Complexity	Low
Privileges Required	None
User Interaction	Required
Scope	Unchanged
Confidentiality	None
Integrity Impact	None
Availability Impact	Low

Affected Packages State

Platform	Package	State
Red Hat Enterprise Linux 7	zsh	Under investigation
Red Hat Enterprise Linux 6	zsh	Under investigation
Red Hat Enterprise Linux 5	zsh	Under investigation

Figure 29-4 *RHSA Example*

xinetd

xinetd is a collection of older services, normally referred to as "legacy services," that your organization may need to use. For example, in Chapter 22, "Connecting to Remote Systems," the Secure Shell server was introduced as a service that allows a user to remotely log in to a system. The Secure Shell was designed to replace an older service called telnet. The telnet service has security issues; for example, when someone logs in to a system using the telnet service, all data (including user name and password) is sent across the network in plain-text format. This means anyone who is able to "sniff" (watch network traffic) the network will see all user and password data.

In most cases, the telnet service should be avoided, but that is not always possible. There are situations where you need to provide access to a system via telnet, which is why the software is still available on Linux (although not normally installed or configured by default).

The **xinetd** daemon is referred to as the "super daemon" because it will start other daemons (services) as needed and stop each one when it is no longer needed. The primary configuration file for the **xinetd** daemon is the **/etc/xinetd.conf** file.

Table 29-1 describes common settings in the **/etc/xinetd.conf** file.

Table 29-1 Common Settings in the **/etc/xinetd.conf** File

Setting	Description
cps	Used to limit how many connection attempts are made to avoid a denial-of-service attack. Two arguments are given (for example, **cpu 50 10**). The first value is how many connections per second are permitted. The second value is how long to disable the service if the connections per section are exceeded (10 seconds in this example).

Setting	Description
instances	How many concurrent connections are allowed. This is important for security because you do not want a large number of connections to a legacy service to result in a denial of service.
per_source	How many concurrent connections from a specific host are allowed.
includedir	The directory where additional rules can be included.

The files in the **/etc/xinetd.d** directory are used to override and supplement settings from the **/etc/xinetd.conf** file. The one shown in Example 29-2 is for the telnet service.

Listing 29-2 *Sample* ***xinetd*** *Configuration File*

```
[root@onecoursesource ~]# cat /etc/xinetd.d/telnet
# default: on
# description: The telnet server serves telnet sessions; it uses \
#       unencrypted username/password pairs for authentication.
service telnet
{
        flags           = REUSE
        socket_type     = stream
        wait            = no
        user            = root
        server          = /usr/sbin/in.telnetd
        log_on_failure  += USERID
        disable         = yes
}
```

Table 29-2 describes common settings of files in the **/etc/xinetd.d** directory.

Table 29-2 Common Setting in the **/etc/xinetd.d** Directory

Setting	Description
user	The service will run as this user.
server	The executable file for the service.
log_on_failure	What data to store in the log entry if a failed login attempt occurs.
disable	When **disable** is set to **yes**, the service is not enabled; when it is set to **no**, the service is enabled.

Summary

In this chapter, you explored some of the key components of making a software management security policy. You learned about where you can find possible vulnerabilities that software packages may pose. You also discovered how to implement legacy services, like the telnet service.

Key Terms

CVE, RHSA, sniff, xinetd

Review Questions

1. The _____ option to the **dpkg** command can be used to list all packages on a Debian-based system.

2. Which locations are used to determine which repositories are used with the **apt-get** command? (Choose two.)

   A. **/etc/apt/list**

   B. **/etc/apt/sources.list**

   C. **/etc/apt/list.d/***

   D. **/etc/apt/sources.list.d/***

3. _____ is a system designed to provide a single location where you can learn about security-related software issues.

4. The _____ option in the **/etc/xinetd.conf** file limits how many connections are permitted from a specific host.

   A. **per_host**

   B. **per_system**

   C. **per_source**

   D. **per_ip**

5. The _____ daemon is referred to as the "super daemon" because it will start other daemons (services) as needed and stop them when they are no longer needed.

Throughout this book you have been introduced to a large number of Linux security features. Although the focus of each chapter is on a particular Linux topic, security is always kept in the picture.

The next four chapters are designed to focus on Linux security. Yes, there is much more to learn about Linux security!

Part VIII

Security Tasks

In this part of this book, you will be introduced to some important Linux topics:

- Chapter 30, "Footprinting," covers the techniques that hackers use to discover information about systems. By learning about these techniques, you should be able to form a better security plan.
- Chapter 31, "Firewalls," explores how to configure software that protects your systems from network-based attacks.
- Chapter 32, "Intrusion Detection," provides you with an understanding of tools and techniques for determining whether someone has successfully compromised the security of your systems.
- Chapter 33, "Additional Security Tasks," covers a variety of additional Linux security features, including the fail2ban service, virtual private networks, and file encryption.

Footprinting

Footprinting, or reconnaissance, is the process of discovering information about a network or system with the intent to use this information to compromise security measures. A large variety of footprinting techniques and tools can provide useful information. This information is then used in conjunction with other hacking tactics to gain unauthorized access to a network or system.

In this chapter, you learn about a variety of tools that perform footprinting operations.

After reading this chapter and completing the exercises, you will be able to do the following:

Use probing tools, such as nmap

Scan the local network

Understanding Footprinting

You may be wondering why you should learn about footprinting because it certainly sounds like something that only a hacker should do. The fact that footprinting is something that a hacker would use to attack your systems is exactly why you want to learn how to perform these tasks.

Think of it this way: You have decided to make your house as secure as possible, and part of that goal is to make sure all doors leading to the outside have very secure locks. You research different locks and discover three that are considered by experts to be difficult to compromise. But, which of these three is the best? One way of determining this is to find someone who knows how to bypass locks and have them test out each one. You could learn this skill yourself, but it does not make sense for this specific situation.

However, what if you had to choose door locks on a regular basis? Perhaps you were responsible for the security of several office buildings. In that case, it may benefit you to learn more about the art of bypassing the security of locked doors. Not because you want to break into buildings, but because you want to be able to test each lock to determine the best one to use in any given situation.

The security of your systems is much like the security of a building, but much more complex. Consider that most systems already have "open doors" that allow users to access the system. For example, a web server has an open door provided by the network ports where the web server is listening. Not only do you need to know how to close these doors to unauthorized users (which will be covered in Chapter 31, "Firewalls"), but you also need to know how to determine if someone can gain information that will allow them to circumvent your security measures.

A hacker first needs information in order to begin the process of bypassing your security tactics. If a hacker can gain useful information, such as a user account name or password, then all of your efforts to secure the system may become worthless.

How do you know if a hacker can discover this information? You learn how to perform footprinting operations and use these methods on your own systems. Think like a hacker and use the same tools they use in order to probe for weaknesses in your systems.

Security Highlight

Always make sure you have written consent to perform footprinting actions on any system in an organization. Just because you work for a company does not mean you are authorized to perform these actions. In most countries, the act of performing footprinting actions is illegal, and many organizations have prosecuted their own employees who were not authorized to perform these actions.

Common Footprinting Tools

The tools covered in this section are well-known utilities that are typically used for generic reconnaissance. Note that some footprinting commands were covered in previous chapters. For example, the **ping** and **traceroute** commands are useful to determine which systems are active and the routers that are used to connect to the systems. Because routers often act as firewalls, this information could tell a hacker which systems to focus on to access more systems within your network.

The nmap Command

The **nmap** command is used to probe a remote system to determine which network ports are reachable from the local system. This is useful for many reasons:

- Determining what services are available on the remote system.
- Testing security features on the remote system, such as TCP wrappers.
- If the **nmap** command is executed from a remote network, the output could verify the effectiveness of your network's firewall.

To use the **nmap** command, provide either the IP address or hostname of the system you want to scan. For example, see the output in Example 30-1 for a scan performed on a router.

Example 30-1 *The **nmap** Command*

```
root@onecoursesource ~]# nmap 192.168.1.1
Starting Nmap 5.51 ( http://nmap.org ) at 2019-10-31 23:22 PDT
Nmap scan report for 192.168.1.1
Host is up (2.9s latency).
Not shown: 987 closed ports
PORT     STATE SERVICE
23/tcp   open  telnet
25/tcp   open  smtp
53/tcp   open  domain
80/tcp   open  http
110/tcp  open  pop3
119/tcp  open  nntp
143/tcp  open  imap
465/tcp  open  smtps
563/tcp  open  snews
587/tcp  open  submission
993/tcp  open  imaps
995/tcp  open  pop3s
5000/tcp open  upnp
Nmap done: 1 IP address (1 host up) scanned in 4.89 seconds
```

The lines that describe the open ports start with the port number/protocol (**23/tcp**, for example) and end with the corresponding service (**telnet**, for example).

By default, only TCP (Transmission Control Protocol) ports are scanned. To scan UDP (User Datagram Protocol) ports, use the **-sU** option combination, as demonstrated in Example 30-2.

Example 30-2 *Scanning UDP Ports*

```
[root@onecoursesource ~]# nmap -sU 192.168.1.1
Starting Nmap 5.51 ( http://nmap.org ) at 2019-10-31  23:36 PDT
Nmap scan report for 192.168.1.1
Host is up (0.0011s latency).
Not shown: 999 open|filtered ports
PORT   STATE SERVICE
53/udp open  domain
Nmap done: 1 IP address (1 host up) scanned in 4.09 seconds
```

By default, only certain common ports (about 2000) are scanned. To scan all ports, use the command shown in Example 30-3 (and then take a coffee break, because this could take a while).

Example 30-3 *Scanning All Ports*

```
[root@onecoursesource ~]# nmap -p 1-65535 192.168.1.1
Starting Nmap 5.51 ( http://nmap.org ) at 2015-11-01 00:26 PDT
Nmap scan report for 192.168.1.1
Host is up (1.0s latency).
Not shown: 65521 closed ports
PORT     STATE SERVICE
23/tcp   open  telnet
25/tcp   open  smtp
53/tcp   open  domain
80/tcp   open  http
110/tcp  open  pop3
119/tcp  open  nntp
143/tcp  open  imap
465/tcp  open  smtps
563/tcp  open  snews
587/tcp  open  submission
993/tcp  open  imaps
995/tcp  open  pop3s
1780/tcp open  unknown
5000/tcp open  upnp
Nmap done: 1 IP address (1 host up) scanned in 5731.44 seconds
```

Typically a port has an associated local service. The **nmap** command can also probe these services to determine what version of the service is available. This feature is not available for all services, but for those that it is available for, it can provide useful information. Use the **-sV** option combination to see service version information, as shown in Example 30-4.

Example 30-4 *Scanning Service Version Information*

```
[root@onecoursesource ~]# nmap -sV 192.168.1.1
Starting Nmap 5.51 ( http://nmap.org ) at 2019-11-01 09:41 PST
Nmap scan report for 192.168.1.1
Host is up (1.0s latency).
Not shown: 987 closed ports
PORT     STATE SERVICE     VERSION
```

```
23/tcp   open  telnet?
25/tcp   open  smtp?
53/tcp   open  domain        dnsmasq 2.15-OpenDNS-1
###Remaining output omitted
```

You discover a machine with an IP address of 192.168.1.11 on your network, but you do not know what sort of system it is. One of the benefits of the **nmap** command is it might provide a clue as to what sort of system this is by probing it. For example, executing the **nmap** command on that IP address can provide you with an idea of what sort of system a machine is, as demonstrated in Example 30-5.

Example 30-5 *Probing a Machine*

```
[root@onecoursesource ~]# nmap -sU 192.168.1.11
Starting Nmap 5.51 ( http://nmap.org ) at 2019-10-31  23:38 PDT
Nmap scan report for 192.168.1.11
Host is up (0.00045s latency).
Not shown: 992 filtered ports
PORT      STATE         SERVICE
67/udp    open|filtered dhcps
137/udp   open          netbios-ns
138/udp   open|filtered netbios-dgm
443/udp   open|filtered https
1900/udp open|filtered upnp
4500/udp open|filtered nat-t-ike
5353/udp open|filtered zeroconf
5355/udp open|filtered llmnr
Nmap done: 1 IP address (1 host up) scanned in 52.23 seconds
```

Given that **netbios-ns** and some of the other services listed are Microsoft Windows–based services, it is likely that the operating system of this unknown system is a version of Microsoft Windows.

In some cases, you might be able to use the **-O** option to determine the operating system type, but this is not always successful, as demonstrated next:

```
[root@onecoursesource ~]# nmap -O 192.168.1.11
###Output omitted
Aggressive OS guesses: QEMU user mode network gateway (91%), Bay Networks
BayStack 450 switch (software version 3.1.0.22) (85%), Bay Networks
BayStack 450 switch (software version 4.2.0.16) (85%), Cabletron ELS100-
24TXM Switch or Icom IC-7800 radio transceiver (85%), Cisco Catalyst 1900
switch or RAD IPMUX-1 TDM-over-IP multiplexer (85%), Sanyo PLC-XU88
digital video projector (85%), 3Com SuperStack 3 Switch 4300, Dell
PowerEdge 2650 remote access controller, Samsung ML-2571N or 6555N
printer, or Xerox Phaser 3125N printer (85%), Dell 1815dn printer (85%)
No exact OS matches for host (test conditions non-ideal).
OS detection performed. Please report any incorrect results at
http://nmap.org/submit/ .
Nmap done: 1 IP address (1 host up) scanned in 15.37 seconds
```

So, how did you discover that a system with an IP address of 192.168.1.11 existed in the first place? Another useful feature of the **nmap** command is its capability to scan an entire network to determine which IP addresses are in use. To perform this operation, use the **-sP** option combination, as demonstrated in Example 30-6.

30

Example 30-6 *Probing a Network*

```
[root@onecoursesource ~]# nmap -sP 192.168.1.0/24
Starting Nmap 5.51 ( http://nmap.org ) at 2019-10-31  23:51 PDT
Nmap scan report for 192.168.1.0
Host is up (0.00043s latency).
Nmap scan report for 192.168.1.1
Host is up (0.0026s latency).
Nmap scan report for 192.168.1.2
Host is up (0.70s latency).
Nmap scan report for 192.168.1.3
Host is up (0.045s latency).
Nmap scan report for 192.168.1.4
Host is up (0.043s latency).
Nmap scan report for 192.168.1.7
Host is up (0.00011s latency).
Nmap scan report for 192.168.1.11
Host is up (0.0020s latency).
Nmap scan report for 192.168.1.12
Host is up (0.00013s latency).
Nmap scan report for 192.168.1.14
Host is up (3.7s latency).
Nmap scan report for 192.168.1.16
Host is up (0.00088s latency).
```

You can see information about your own system, including a list of network interfaces and the routing table, by using the **--iflist** option, as shown in Example 30-7.

Example 30-7 *Listing Network Interfaces*

```
[root@onecoursesource ~]# nmap --iflist

Starting Nmap 5.51 ( http://nmap.org ) at 2019-11-01 09:39 PST
************************INTERFACES************************
DEV  (SHORT) IP/MASK      TYPE     UP MTU   MAC
lo   (lo)    127.0.0.1/8  loopback up 65536
eth0 (eth0)  10.0.2.15/24 ethernet up 1500  08:00:27:E0:E2:DE

**************************ROUTES**************************
DST/MASK     DEV  GATEWAY
10.0.2.0/24 eth0
0.0.0.0/0    eth0 10.0.2.2
```

The netstat Command

The **netstat** command can be used to view activity of local network information, as opposed to scanning remote network ports with the **nmap** command.

Security Highlight

To run the **netstat** command, the user first needs to gain local access to the system; however, this access can be a regular user account (root access is not required). This highlights the need to make sure regular accounts are secure.

For example, the **netstat -s** command displays a summary of network packet information broken down by protocol, as shown in Example 30-8.

Example 30-8 *The netstat -s Command*

```
[root@onecoursesource ~]# netstat -s
Ip:
    170277 total packets received
    2 with invalid addresses
    0 forwarded
    0 incoming packets discarded
    168563 incoming packets delivered
    370967 requests sent out
    293 dropped because of missing route
Icmp:
    9223 ICMP messages received
    1000 input ICMP message failed.
    ICMP input histogram:
        destination unreachable: 1231
        echo replies: 7992
    10072 ICMP messages sent
    0 ICMP messages failed
    ICMP output histogram:
        destination unreachable: 1507
        echo request: 8001
IcmpMsg:
        InType0: 7992
        InType3: 1231
        OutType3: 1507
        OutType8: 8001
        OutType69: 564
Tcp:
    348 active connections openings
    1 passive connection openings
    8 failed connection attempts
    0 connection resets received
    2 connections established
    158566 segments received
    80619 segments send out
    552 segments retransmited
    0 bad segments received.
    96 resets sent
Udp:
    774 packets received
    6 packets to unknown port received.
    0 packet receive errors
    903 packets sent
UdpLite:
TcpExt:
    130 TCP sockets finished time wait in fast timer
    107 delayed acks sent
    5 delayed acks further delayed because of locked socket
    30284 packets header predicted
```

30

```
    272 acknowledgments not containing data received
    51589 predicted acknowledgments
    0 TCP data loss events
    69 other TCP timeouts
    69 connections aborted due to timeout
IpExt:
    InOctets: 17393378
    OutOctets: 17585203
```

The **netstat** command can also display the routing table, similar to the **route** command:

```
[root@onecoursesource ~]# netstat -r
Kernel IP routing table
Destination     Gateway         Genmask         Flags   MSS Window  irtt Iface
10.0.2.0        *               255.255.255.0   U         0 0          0 eth0
default         10.0.2.2        0.0.0.0         UG        0 0          0 eth0
```

There will be times when you want to see network statistics for each interface. Using the **netstat -i** command, you can see data broken down in this manner:

```
[root@onecoursesource ~]# netstat -i
Kernel Interface table
Iface    MTU Met   RX-OK RX-ERR RX-DRP RX-OVR    TX-OK TX-ERR TX-DRP TX-OVR Flg
eth0    1500   0   93957      0      0      0   294652      0      0      0 BMRU
lo     65536   0   77198      0      0      0    77198      0      0      0 LRU
```

The output of the **netstat -i** command includes many columns of information (which is common for most of the **netstat** command options). Here are the important columns for this command:

- **RX-OK and TX-OK**: Received and transmitted packets with no error
- **RX-ERR and TX-ERR**: Received and transmitted packets that had an error
- **RX-DRP and TX-DRP**: Received and transmitted packets that were dropped
- **RX-OVR and TX-OVR**: Received and transmitted packets that were not receivable by this interface

Normally the **RX-OK** and **TX-OK** values are considerably higher than the rest. If the other values appear to be too high when compared to the **OK** values, there could be a problem with your network. It may be useful to watch these values as they change over time. It is useful to include this information with the baselines for the network for future comparison. This can be accomplished by using the **-c** option: **netstat -ci**.

The **netstat** command has a huge number of options. Table 30-1 provides details about some of the more useful ones.

Table 30-1 Useful **netstat** Options

Option	Description
-at	Only display TCP ports.
-au	Only display UDP ports.
-e	Display extended information. This provides more detailed output, and you can use **-ee** for even more output.
-l	List all listening sockets.

Option	Description
-n	Provide numeric values instead of names. For example, instead of listing port ssh, it would list port 22.
-p	Display the PID (Process ID) of the service associated to the socket/port.

NOTE If you look at the man page for the **netstat** command on most modern Linux distributions, you will likely see a message like the following:

```
NOTE
       This  program is obsolete. Replacement for netstat is ss.
Replacement for netstat -r is ip route. Replacement for net-stat -i
is ip -s link. Replacement for netstat -g is ip maddr.
```

As a result, you may wonder why the authors of this book chose to describe the **netstat** command instead of the **ip** or **ss** command. There are a few reasons:

- Although the **ip** and **ss** commands are very useful tools, the **netstat** command provides many of the same features.
- Many existing shell scripts make use of the **netstat** command, and the assumption here is that you will explore these scripts, so you should understand what this command does.
- Although **netstat** may be listed as obsolete, it still exists on just about all Linux distributions by default. In fact, is has been listed as obsolete for many years now and yet it is still used on a regular basis by many administrators. In other words, it is highly unlikely that it will be "going away" any time soon.

The lsof Command

The **lsof** command is designed to list open files. When you first learned about Linux, you were likely told that everything in Linux is a file. This is definitely true because network sockets are files from the kernel's perspective.

Conversational Learning™—Port vs. Socket

Gary: Hey, Julia. I have a question about ports and sockets.

Julia: OK, what's the question?

Gary: I am having a hard time understanding the difference between the two. The two terms are often used interchangeably, but are they actually two different things?

Julia: Yes, they are. A port is like a door. If a door is open, you can enter a room. If the door is locked, you can't enter the room. So, if port 22 is open on a remote system, you can "enter that room," meaning you can establish a connection via SSH to the remote system.

Gary: So, what is a socket?

Julia: The socket is part of the connection. There are two sockets per connection; these are the endpoints of the connection on each system. A socket is partly defined by the port because that is the "door" that the communication must travel through, but they are not the same thing. A socket is also associated with a process that is handling the connection on the software side of the equation.

Gary: Hmm… I'm not sure I am getting it.

Julia: Here's another way to think about it: Your system can have an open port but can't have a corresponding socket if there is no active connection. You can't have a socket without an open port.

Gary: OK, so having a port is like having a telephone number. But, just because my phone has a telephone number, doesn't mean I am always making a call.

Julia: Right, but when you make or receive a call...

Gary: Then I have created a socket for my telephone!

Julia: You got it!

To list open network sockets with the **lsof** command, use the **-i** option, as shown in Example 30-9.

Example 30-9 *The **lsof -i** Command*

```
[root@onecoursesource ~]# lsof -i
COMMAND     PID     USER    FD    TYPE DEVICE SIZE/OFF NODE NAME
iscsid      1303     root    8u   IPv4  22642      0t0  TCP localhost:48897->localhost:
➥ iscsi-target (ESTABLISHED)
rpcbind     1559      rpc    6u   IPv4  12739      0t0  UDP *:sunrpc
rpcbind     1559      rpc    7u   IPv4  12741      0t0  UDP *:iclcnet-locate
rpcbind     1559      rpc    8u   IPv4  12742      0t0  TCP *:sunrpc (LISTEN)
rpcbind     1559      rpc    9u   IPv6  12744      0t0  UDP *:sunrpc
rpcbind     1559      rpc   10u   IPv6  12746      0t0  UDP *:iclcnet-locate
rpcbind     1559      rpc   11u   IPv6  12747      0t0  TCP *:sunrpc (LISTEN)
rpc.statd 1616 rpcuser     5u   IPv4  12988      0t0  UDP localhost:944
rpc.statd 1616 rpcuser     8u   IPv4  12994      0t0  UDP *:51463
rpc.statd 1616 rpcuser     9u   IPv4  12998      0t0  TCP *:45982 (LISTEN)
rpc.statd 1616 rpcuser    10u   IPv6  13002      0t0  UDP *:41413
rpc.statd 1616 rpcuser    11u   IPv6  13006      0t0  TCP *:46716 (LISTEN)
cupsd       1656     root    6u   IPv6  13155      0t0  TCP localhost:ipp (LISTEN)
cupsd       1656     root    7u   IPv4  13156      0t0  TCP localhost:ipp (LISTEN)
cupsd       1656     root    9u   IPv4  13159      0t0  UDP *:ipp
tgtd        1939     root    4u   IPv4  14111      0t0  TCP *:iscsi-target (LISTEN)
tgtd        1939     root    5u   IPv6  14112      0t0  TCP *:iscsi-target (LISTEN)
tgtd        1939     root   10u   IPv4  22647      0t0  TCP localhost:iscsi-target->
➥ localhost:48897 (ESTABLISHED)
tgtd        1942     root    4u   IPv4  14111      0t0  TCP *:iscsi-target (LISTEN)
tgtd        1942     root    5u   IPv6  14112      0t0  TCP *:iscsi-target (LISTEN)
sshd        1993     root    3u   IPv4  15292      0t0  TCP *:ssh (LISTEN)
sshd        1993     root    4u   IPv6  15303      0t0  TCP *:ssh (LISTEN)
clock-app 2703       root   22w   IPv4  62027      0t0  TCP localhost:54295->
➥ 184.180.124.66:http (ESTABLISHED)
dhclient  2922       root    6u   IPv4  22552      0t0  UDP *:bootpc
```

There are several ways to limit the output, including by port number (**lsof -i:22**), by service name (**lsof -i:ssh**), and by host (**lsof -i @onecoursesource.com**).

Here are two options to the **lsof** command that can speed up the command:

- **-n**: This option tells the **lsof** command to not resolve IP addresses to hostnames.
- **-P**: This option tells the **lsof** command to not resolve port numbers to port names.

The nc Command

The man page of the **nc** command provides an excellent summary of the **nc** command:

> "The nc (or netcat) utility is used for just about anything under the sun involving TCP or UDP. It can open TCP connections, send UDP packets, listen on arbitrary TCP and UDP ports, do

port scanning, and deal with both IPv4 and IPv6. Unlike telnet(1), nc scripts nicely, and separates error messages onto standard error instead of sending them to standard output, as telnet(1) does with some."

There are quite a few uses for the **nc** command. For example, suppose you want to know if a specific port was being blocked by your company firewall before you bring a service online that makes use of this port. On the internal server, you can have the **nc** command listen for connections on that port:

```
[root@server ~]# nc -l 3333
```

The result should be a blank line below the **nc** command. Next, on a remote system outside your network, you could run the following **nc** command to connect (replace ***server*** with the resolvable hostname or IP address of the local system):

```
[root@client Desktop]# nc server 3333
```

If the connection is established, you see a blank line under the **nc** command line. If you type something on this blank line and press the Enter key, then what you typed appears below the **nc** command on the server. Actually, the communication works both ways: What you type on the server below the **nc** command appears on the client as well.

Here are some useful options to the **nc** command:

- **-w**: This option is used on the client side to close a connection automatically after a timeout value is reached. For example, **nc -w 30 server 333** closes the connection 30 seconds after it has been established.
- **-6**: Use this option to enable IPv6 connections.
- **-k**: Use this option to keep server processes active, even after the client disconnects. The default behavior is to stop the server process when the client disconnects.
- **-u**: Use UDP connections rather than TCP connections (the default). This is important for correctly testing firewall configurations as a UDP port might not be blocked while the TCP port is blocked.

You can also use the **nc** command to display open ports, similar to the **netstat** command:

```
[root@onecoursesource Desktop]# nc -z localhost 1000-4000
Connection to localhost 3260 port [tcp/iscsi-target] succeeded!
Connection to localhost 3333 port [tcp/dec-notes] succeeded!
```

The **-z** option can also be used to port-scan a remote host.

30

There is one feature of the **nc** command that is a useful technique to transfer all sorts of data. The format that you use, assuming the transfer is from the client to the server, is shown here (replace ***cmd*** with an actual command):

- On the server: **nc -l 3333 | *cmd***
- On the client: ***cmd* | nc server 3333**

For example, you can transfer an entire **/home** directory structure from the client to the server using the **tar** command by first executing the following on the server:

```
nc -l 333 | tar xvf -
```

Then on the client, execute the following command:

```
tar cvf - /home | nc server 333
```

The client merges the contents of the **/home** directory structure into a tar ball. The **-** tells the **tar** command to send this output to standard output. The data is sent to the server via the client's **nc** command, and then the server's **nc** command sends this data to the **tar** command. The result is the **/home** directory from the client is now copied into the current directory of the server.

Security Highlight

This is just one technique of many that uses this powerful feature of the **nc** command. It also highlights how a hacker could use the **nc** command to transfer data, even if you have blocked other network ports and disabled file sharing software such as Secure Shell and FTP. Remember that all of the tools covered in this chapter are tools used by hackers to compromise systems.

The tcpdump Command

When you're troubleshooting network issues or performing network security audits, it can be helpful to view the network traffic, including traffic that is not related to the local machine. The **tcpdump** command is a "packet sniffer" that allows you to view local network traffic.

By default, the **tcpdump** command displays all network traffic to standard output until you terminate the command. This could result in a dizzying amount of data flying by on your screen. You can limit the output to a specific number of network packets by using the **-c** option, as shown in Example 30-10.

Example 30-10 *The tcpdump Command*

```
[root@onecoursesource ~]# tcpdump -c 5
tcpdump: verbose output suppressed, use -v or -vv for full protocol decode
listening on eth0, link-type EN10MB (Ethernet), capture size 65535 bytes
11:32:59.630873 IP localhost.43066 > 192.168.1.1.domain: 16227+ A? onecoursesource.com.
➥ (37)
11:32:59.631272 IP localhost.59247 > 192.168.1.1.domain: 2117+ PTR? 1.1.168.192.in-addr.
➥ arpa. (42)
11:32:59.631387 IP localhost.43066 > 192.168.1.1.domain: 19647+ AAAA? onecoursesource.com.
➥ (37)
11:32:59.647932 IP 192.168.1.1.domain > localhost.59247: 2117 NXDomain* 0/1/0 (97)
11:32:59.717499 IP 192.168.1.1.domain > localhost.43066: 16227 1/0/0 A 38.89.136.109 (53)
5 packets captured
5 packets received by filter
0 packets dropped by kernel
```

More likely you want to capture the output based on some sort of criteria. For example, you can have the **tcpdump** command only capture packets available on a specific interface by using the **-i** option:

```
[root@onecoursesource ~]# tcpdump -i eth0
```

To limit packets to only a specific protocol, indicate the protocol name as an argument:

```
[root@onecoursesource ~]# tcpdump -i eth0 tcp
```

To only display packets associated with a specific port, use the **port** argument:

```
[root@onecoursesource ~]# tcpdump -i eth0 port 80
```

You can also limit the packets based on the source IP or destination IP:

```
[root@onecoursesource ~]# tcpdump -i src 192.168.1.100
[root@onecoursesource ~]# tcpdump -i dst 192.168.1.100
```

In many case, you will likely want to leave the **tcpdump** command running for a short period of time and view the data at some later date. In this case, it is best to use the **-c** option to limit the output and place the data into a file by using the **-w** option:

```
[root@onecoursesource ~]# tcpdump -c 5000 -w output-tcpdump
```

This file contains binary data. To read its contents, use the **-r** option to the **tcpdump** command:

```
[root@onecoursesource ~]# tcpdump -r output-tcpdump
```

Additional Utilities

We have just started to scratch the surface when it comes to commonly used footprinting tools. Here are some additional utilities you should consider exploring:

- **ping**: The **ping** command is discussed in Chapter 19, "Network Configuration," and is used to determine if a system is reachable via the network.
- **traceroute**: The **traceroute** command is also discussed in Chapter 19. It is used to see the routers used to "get to" a system.
- **whois**: The **whois** command provides information about domain registration. Hackers will use this information to gather intelligence about the register, including names, email addresses, addresses, and phone numbers. This information may then be used to perform additional exploits.
- **nslookup and dig**: These commands are discussed in Chapter 19. They are used to perform queries on DNS servers to discover systems that might be exploited. For example, a DNS query could return the IP address and hostname of a domain's mail server, providing a hacker with the ability to execute attacks designed to work on email servers.

Kali Linux Utilities

Kali Linux has a large selection of footprinting-based tools—well over 60 tools. Some are designed to probe specific types of software, such as Samba or mail servers. In some cases, these tools will provide easier-to-use frontend interfaces to utilities or commands that we have previously discussed. For example, the SPARTA tool uses the **nmap** command to probe systems and generate reports.

Other utilities provide similar functions (although normally with more features) to commands we have already covered. For example, the **fping** utility sends ICMP echo requests to hosts like the **ping** command, but it has more features than the **ping** command provides.

There are so many footprinting tools on Kali Linux that it is impossible to cover all of them in this book. Instead of providing specifics of each of these utilities, this section focuses on providing an overview of some of the categories of tools so that you can explore them on your own.

Essential Information Gathering

While in Kali Linux, click **Applications** and then point to **01 – Information Gathering**. The list provided should be similar to Figure 30-1.

The tools in this category are primarily used to perform basic scans on systems.

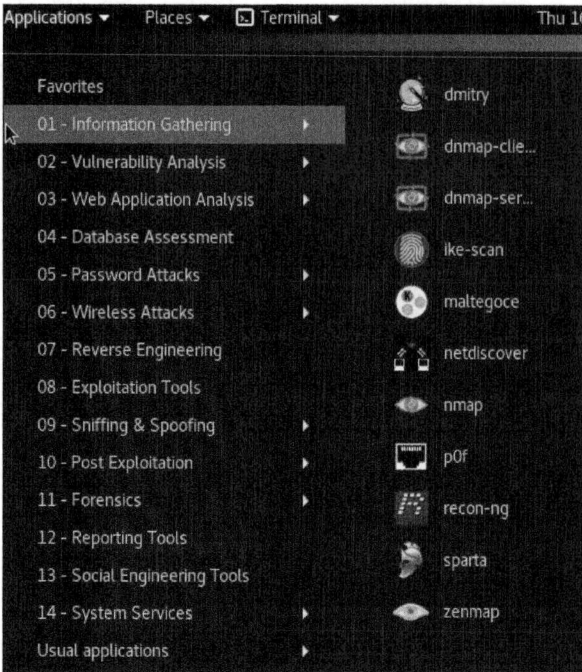

Figure 30-1 *Information-Gathering Tools*

DNS Analysis Tools

While in Kali Linux, click **Applications**, click **01 – Information Gathering**, and then point to **DNS Analysis**. The list provided should be similar to Figure 30-2.

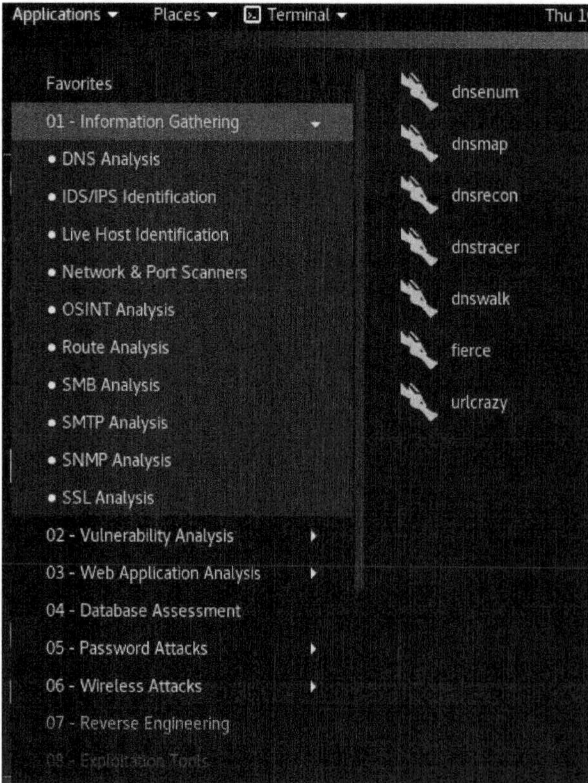

Figure 30-2 *DNS Analysis Tools*

The tools in this category are primarily used to gather DNS information, much like the **nslookup** and **dig** commands, but with more options and features.

Host Identification Tools

While in Kali Linux, click **Applications**, click **01 – Information Gathering**, and then point to **Live Host Identification**. The list provided should be similar to Figure 30-3.

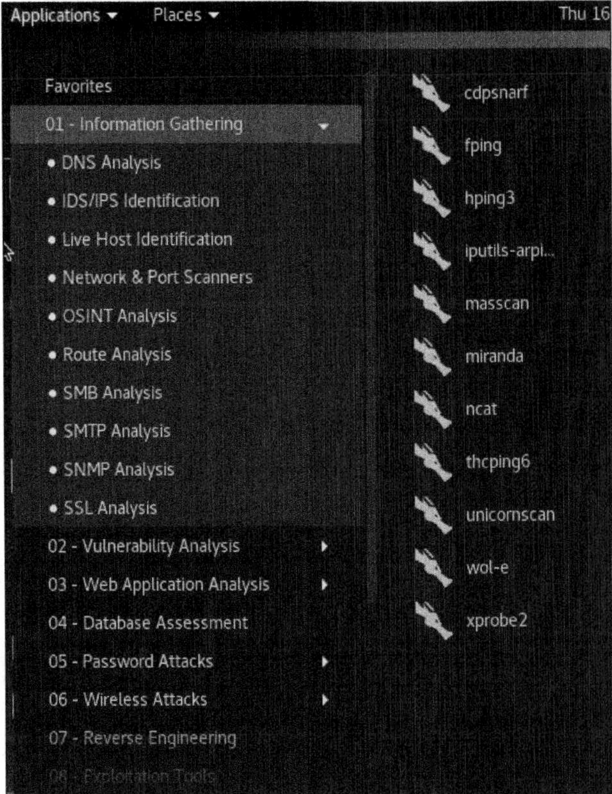

Figure 30-3 *Host Identification*

The tools in this category are primarily used to probe systems to determine if the systems are currently "alive" and reachable via the network.

OSINT Tools

While in Kali Linux, click **Applications**, click **01 – Information Gathering**, and then point to **OSINT Analysis**. The list provided should be similar to Figure 30-4.

The tools in this category primarily use OSINT techniques to gather intelligence about a target. OSINT stands for *open source intelligence*, which refers to using data that is publicly available (hence the term "open") about organizations and systems, similar to the **whois** command.

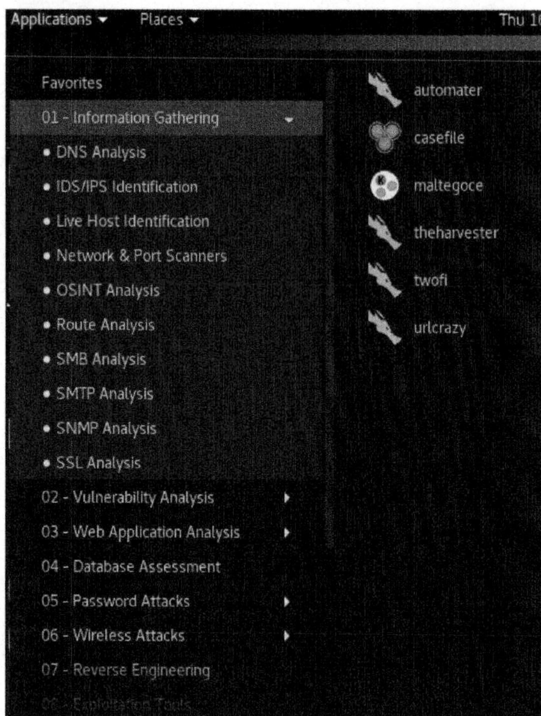

Figure 30-4 *OSINT Analysis*

Route Analysis Tools

While in Kali Linux, click **Applications**, click **01 – Information Gathering**, and then point to **Route Analysis**. The list provided should be similar to Figure 30-5.

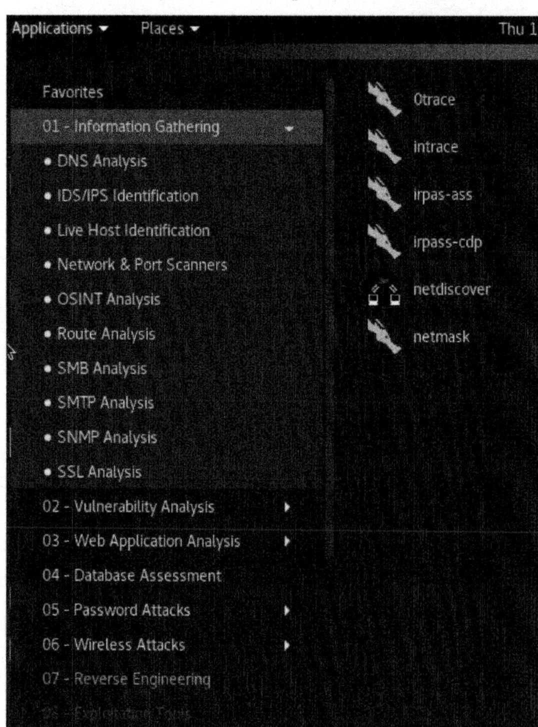

Figure 30-5 *Route Analysis*

The tools in this category are designed to determine the route that is taken to get to a specific host or network, similar to the **traceroute** command.

Summary

In this chapter, you learned about several different techniques for performing footprinting analysis. This included probing systems and networks for critical information.

Key Terms

Footprinting, port scanner, socket, packet sniffer

Review Questions

1. To only scan for open UDP ports using the **nmap** command, what option or options would you use?

   A. **-sP**

   B. **-sU**

   C. **-sT**

   D. **-sD**

2. The _____ option to the **nmap** command attempts to determine the operating system type of a remote system.

3. Which option to the **netstat** command displays the routing table?

   A. **-r**

   B. **-n**

   C. **-t**

   D. None of the above

4. Which option to the **netstat** command displays numeric values instead of names?

   A. **-r**

   B. **-n**

   C. **-t**

   D. None of the above

5. The _____ command lists open files on the local system.

6. The endpoint of a network communication is called a _____.

7. You can open an arbitrary TCP or UDP connection to a remote system by using which command?

   A. **netstat**

   B. **lsof**

   C. **ping**

   D. **nc**

8. The _____ option to the **tcpdump** command limits the display to include packets available only on a specific interface.

Firewalls

One of the major components of securing a system or network is keeping the "bad guys" out while letting the "good guys" have the access they need. This means you need to make sure that network access to your systems is secure and stable.

Creating firewalls gives you the ability to allow or block network connections. A firewall can inspect each network packet and determine if the packet should be allowed in. In this chapter, you learn the essentials to creating firewalls.

After reading this chapter and completing the exercises, you will be able to do the following:

Identify the essential components of a firewall

Create a firewall to control access to a system or network

Block access to external systems

Configure NAT (Network Address Translation)

Introduction to Firewalls

A *firewall* is a network appliance that is designed to either allow or block network traffic. Firewalls can be implemented on a variety of devices, including routers, network servers, and users' systems.

A large variety of firewall software is available within the IT industry. Any organization that creates router devices will have some form of firewall software available. This includes wireless accesses devices such as your home wireless router.

Even within Linux, there are several choices when it comes to firewall software. Dozens of open source and commercial software packages are available. Having so many choices can complicate matters, both in terms of the content within this book and in real-world implementation of firewalls.

For the purposes of learning firewalls, this chapter focuses on iptables, a firewall that is normally available by default on most Linux distributions. In a real-world scenario, iptables is a good solution and is commonly used. However, you should also consider exploring other firewall software, as the requirements for your environment may necessitate a different solution.

Essentials of the iptables Command

To create firewall rules on a system, you can use the **iptables** command. This command allows you to create rules that provide one or more of the following functions:

- Block network packets.
- Forward network packets to another system. In this case, the local system would act as both a firewall for another network and a router.

- Perform NAT (Network Address Translation) operations. NAT offers a method to provide hosts within a private network access to the Internet.
- Mangle (modify) network packets. Although this can be a useful feature, it is beyond the scope of this book.

WHAT COULD GO WRONG? Keep in mind that when you use the **iptables** command to create firewall rules, the rules take effect immediately. This can be an issue if you are remotely logged in to a system and create a rule that ends up immediately blocking access to your own session.

Overview of Filtering Packets

Before you start creating rules with the **iptables** command, you should understand how the firewall service works. Start by reviewing Figure 31-1 to see how packets that are sent to the system are filtered.

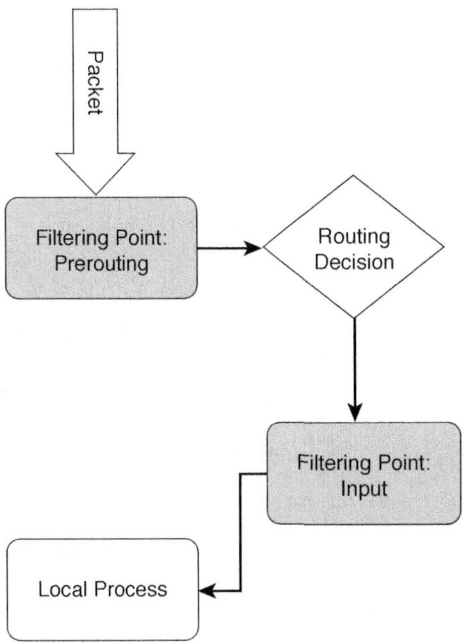

Figure 31-1 *Packet Filtering—Incoming Packets*

In Figure 31-1, the process starts in the upper-left corner when the packet is sent to the system. The iptables service uses sets of rules to determine what to do with this packet. The first set of rules takes place on the PREROUTING filtering point. These rules can be used either to allow the packet to continue to the next step or to block the packet.

If the packet is allowed to continue past the PREROUTING filtering point, the kernel determines if the packet is designed to be sent to the local system or if it should be passed to another network (in other words, routed to another network). Figure 31-1 does not include what happens to the packet if it is routed to another network, but this is included in a figure later in this chapter.

For packets destined for the local system, another filtering point is used to determine if the packets are allowed or blocked. The INPUT filtering point rules are applied to these packets.

You may be wondering why there are two sets of rules (so far—there will be more). Consider this: There may be some packets you want to entirely block, regardless of whether they are destined for the local system or will be routed to a different network. You can place rules to block these packets on the PREROUTING filtering point. But, if you only want to block some packets that will be sent to the local system, then you can place rules on the INPUT filtering point.

Figure 31-2 demonstrates what happens with a packet that's routed to another network.

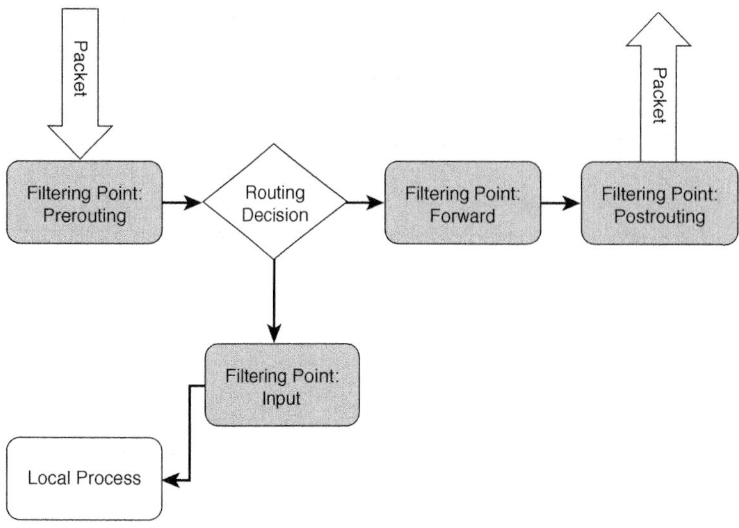

Figure 31-2 *Packet Filtering—Routed Packets*

Packets that are routed to another network first must pass through a set of rules on the FORWARD filtering point. This allows you to create a set of rules that will only apply to packets that are routed to another network.

Conversational Learning™—Configuring a Router

Gary: Hey, Julia. I am setting up a firewall that also needs to act as a router. I know how to create the firewall, but how do I get the system to act as a router?

Julia: Hi, Gary. That is a feature of the kernel. Take a look at contents of the file **/proc/sys/net/ipv4/ip_forward**.

Gary: It contains a 0.

Julia: Right, 0 means "this system isn't a router," and 1 means "this system is a router." Of course, you also need to have two network interfaces defined as well.

Gary: Do I just change this number directly?

Julia: You can use this command to make the change**: echo 1 > /proc/sys/net/ipv4/ip_forward**. However, if the system is rebooted, it will revert back to a 0.

Gary: Can I make this a permanent change?

Julia: Yes, edit the **/etc/sysconf.conf** file and set **net.ipv4.ip_forward = 1**.

Gary: OK. Thanks again, Julia.

Note that after the FORWARD filtering point, the packets are sent to another filtering point (POSTROUTING). It may seem strange to have two filtering points with two separate sets of rules, but the reason for this is shown in Figure 31-3.

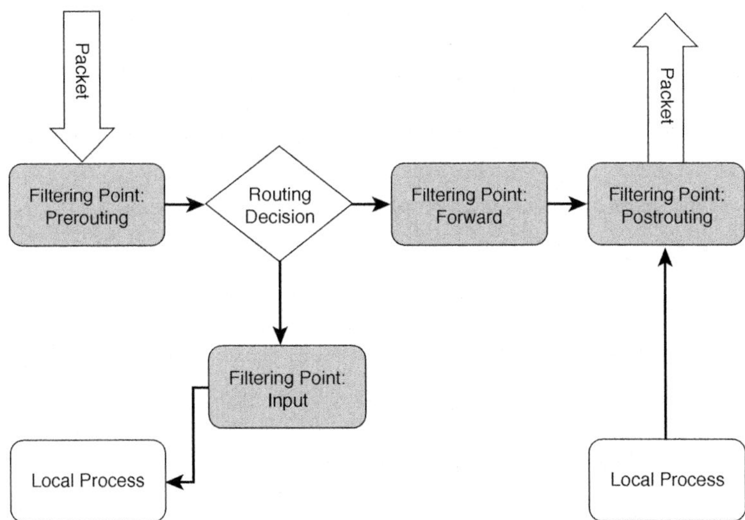

Figure 31-3 *Packet Filtering—Outbound Packets*

Packets are not only subject to filtering when they are sent to a host, but also when packets are sent from the host. Rules can be applied on the OUTPUT filtering point for any packet that originates from a process that is running on the local system. If you want to have a rule that applies to all outbound packets (both routed packets and packets that originate from the local system), then place rules on the POSTROUTING filtering point.

Important Terms

In the previous section, you were introduced to the term *filtering point*. Types of rules, referred to as a *table*, can be placed on a filtering point. A filtering point can have one or more sets of rules because iptables performs multiple functions: either filter (block or allow) the data, perform a NAT operation on the packet, or mangle the packet. The combination of the filtering point plus the table (filter, nat, or mangle) is combined into a single set of rules called a *chain*.

Consider a chain to be a set of *rules* that determines what actions to take on a specific packet. For example, a rule on the "filter INPUT" chain could block an incoming packet based on the source IP address. Another rule could be used to allow packets destined for a specific network port.

The order of the rules is also important. Once a matching rule is found, an action (called a *target*) takes place and additional rules are ignored (with one exception, as noted next). Here are the different types of targets:

- **ACCEPT**: Allow the packet to continue to the next step (filtering point, routing decision, and so on).
- **DROP**: Do not allow the packet to continue to the next step; just discard it.
- **REJECT**: Do not allow the packet to continue to the next step but send a response message to the origin of the packet informing it of the rejection. This is different than DROP because with DROP the origin of the packet is never informed of what happens with the packet.
- **LOG**: Create a log entry. Note that a target of ACCEPT, DROP, or REJECT results in no further rules being evaluated, but LOG will result in creating the log entry and then continuing to evaluate additional rules. So, you can create a rule to log a connection attempt and then DROP or REJECT the attempt with another rule.

31

Security Highlight

Typically DROP is considered a more secure method than REJECT because hackers will use REJECT responses as a means to probe a system or network. Even a negative response provides the hacker with useful information. For example, a REJECT could indicate that the destination machine might be worth hacking into (why secure an unimportant system), or it could indicate that some ports are blocked but others are allowed.

Each chain also has a *default chain policy*. If you have not edited a chain, this should be set to ACCEPT. This means that if a packet does not match any DROP or REJECT rules in the chain, the default policy of ACCEPT will allow it to continue to the next step.

On systems where security is paramount, you might want to change this default rule to DROP. This means that the only packets that are allowed to move to the next step in the process are those that match an ACCEPT rule in the chain.

All of these terms (filtering point, table, chain, rule, and default chain policy) will become clearer as examples are provided during this chapter. So, if some of these terms are a bit fuzzy now, they should make more sense as you explore using the **iptables** command to implement firewall rules.

NOTE The firewall created by iptables can be very complex, well beyond the scope of this book. For example, besides filter, nat, and mangle, there is a table called "raw" that will not be covered in this book. Also, filter points can have multiple rules—for example, a set of rules for OUTPUT-filter, one for OUTPUT-nat, and one for OUTPUT-mangle. However, not every table can be used to create rules (for example, you cannot have a PREROUTING-filter rule). While these complex situations would belong in a book that focuses purely on firewalls, the discussion in this book will include specific scenarios of firewalls.

Lastly, consider a situation in which multiple rule sets appear at one filter point. Clearly, one rule set must be applied first, then another, and so on. An excellent diagram by Jan Engelhardt describes this process. It can be found at the following link: https://upload.wikimedia.org/wikipedia/commons/3/37/Netfilter-packet-flow.svg.

Using iptables to Filter Incoming Packets

A common firewall task involves configuring a system to either allow or block incoming packets. This is something that could be applied to a single host or an entire network (if the current system also acts as a router). To perform this task, you place rules on the INPUT-filter chain.

WHAT COULD GO WRONG? Keep in mind that iptables is not the only possible firewall solution. There could be another solution already installed and enabled on your system. You should only have one firewall service active on a segment of the system at a time. As a result, you may need to disable an existing firewall.

For example, many Red Hat–based distributions have firewalld instead of iptables enabled by default. This can be disabled on modern distributions by executing the **systemctl disable firewalld** command.

The examples in this chapter were performed on an Ubuntu system that uses iptables by default. Consult the documentation for your distribution to determine if another firewall solution is used by default.

It is fairly common on modern Linux distributions to include some default firewall rules. You can see the current rules by executing the following command:

```
root@onecoursesource:~# iptables -t filter -L INPUT
Chain INPUT (policy ACCEPT)
target     prot opt source               destination
ACCEPT     udp  --  anywhere             anywhere   udp dpt:domain
ACCEPT     tcp  --  anywhere             anywhere   tcp dpt:domain
ACCEPT     udp  --  anywhere             anywhere   udp dpt:bootps
ACCEPT     tcp  --  anywhere             anywhere   tcp dpt:bootps
```

At this point, we are not going to worry about what these rules do; they will be described later. To take these rules out of the chain, you could delete them individually. For example, the following command deletes the first rule in the INPUT-filter chain (note that you do not need to include **-t filter** because filter is the default table):

```
root@onecoursesource:~# iptables -D INPUT 1
root@onecoursesource:~# iptables -L INPUT
Chain INPUT (policy ACCEPT)
target     prot opt source               destination
ACCEPT     tcp  --  anywhere             anywhere   tcp dpt:domain
ACCEPT     udp  --  anywhere             anywhere   udp dpt:bootps
ACCEPT     tcp  --  anywhere             anywhere   tcp dpt:bootps
```

You can also remove all rules in a chain by using the **-F** option (F stands for *flush*):

```
root@onecoursesource:~# iptables -F INPUT
root@onecoursesource:~# iptables -L INPUT
Chain INPUT (policy ACCEPT)
target     prot opt source               destination
```

To block all network packets that originate from a specific host, use the following command:

```
root@onecoursesource:~# iptables -A INPUT -s 192.168.10.100 -j DROP
root@onecoursesource:~# iptables -L INPUT
Chain INPUT (policy ACCEPT)
target     prot opt source               destination
DROP       all  --  192.168.10.100        anywhere
```

The **-s** option stands for "source." This value can either be an IP address or a network:

```
root@onecoursesource:~# iptables -A INPUT -s 192.168.20.0/24 -j DROP
root@onecoursesource:~# iptables -L INPUT
Chain INPUT (policy ACCEPT)
target     prot opt source               destination
DROP       all  --  192.168.10.100       anywhere
DROP       all  --  192.168.20.0/24      anywhere
```

Using the **-A** option will place the new rule at the end of the chain. Recall that this is important because the rules are evaluated in order. Suppose you want to allow one machine in the 192.168.20.0/24 network access to this system. Use the **-I** option to insert a new rule above the rule that blocks that network; for example, **-I INPUT 2** states "insert this rule as Rule 2 and move all remaining rules down by one":

```
root@onecoursesource:~# iptables -I INPUT 2 -s 192.168.20.125 -j ACCEPT
root@onecoursesource:~# iptables -L INPUT
Chain INPUT (policy ACCEPT)
target     prot opt source               destination
DROP       all  --  192.168.10.100       anywhere
```

```
ACCEPT     all  --  192.168.20.125       anywhere
DROP       all  --  192.168.20.0/24      anywhere
```

Filtering by Protocol

It is common to filter packets by the protocol. This could either be a protocol like ICMP, TCP, or UDP, or a protocol associated with a specific port (like telnet, which uses port 22). To block a protocol like ICMP, use a command like the following (the first command flushes previous rules so you can focus on the rule being discussed):

```
root@onecoursesource:~# iptables -F INPUT
root@onecoursesource:~# iptables -A INPUT -p icmp -j DROP
root@onecoursesource:~# iptables -L INPUT
Chain INPUT (policy ACCEPT)
target     prot opt source               destination
DROP       icmp --  anywhere             anywhere
```

See the **/etc/protocols** file for a list of protocols that can be used in conjunction with the **-p** option.

To block a specific port, you need to provide the **-m** option and either **--sport** (source port) or **--dport** (destination port). For incoming packets, you typically use the **--dport** option because you are concerned about connections established on a specific port on the local system:

```
root@onecoursesource:~# iptables -A INPUT -m tcp -p tcp --dport 23 -j DROP
root@onecoursesource:~# iptables -L INPUT
Chain INPUT (policy ACCEPT)
target     prot opt source               destination
DROP       icmp --  anywhere             anywhere
DROP       tcp  --  anywhere             anywhere  tcp dpt:telnet
```

The **-m** option is required for iptables to make use of an extension module, an optional add-on feature for iptables. In the previous example, the TCP match extension module was used. See Figure 31-4 for information about iptables extensions.

NOTE You can also specify a range of ports: **--dport 1:1024**

The output of the **iptables -L** command automatically converts port numbers into names (for example, 23 is converted to "telnet"). It also converts IP addresses into hostnames if it can perform a DNS lookup. To avoid these conversations, use the **-n** option:

```
root@onecoursesource:~# iptables -L INPUT -n
Chain INPUT (policy ACCEPT)
target     prot opt source               destination
DROP       icmp --  anywhere             anywhere
DROP       tcp  --  anywhere             anywhere  tcp dpt:23
```

Remember that you can also look up port numbers in the **/etc/services** file.

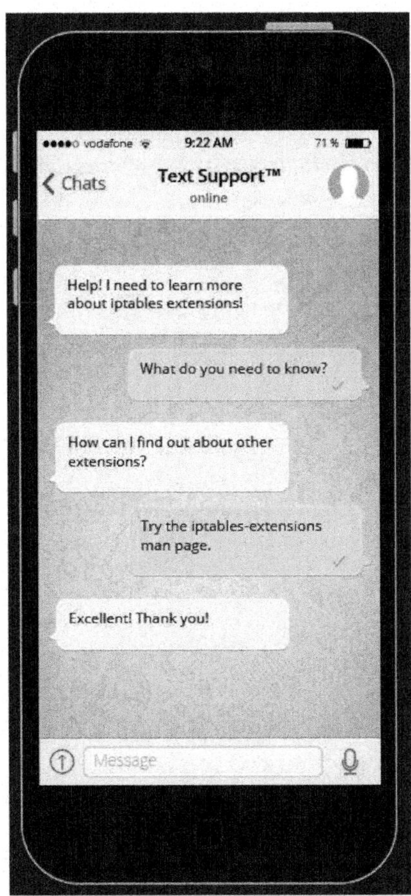

Figure 31-4 *Text Support™—Extensions for iptables*

Multiple Criteria

You can combine multiple criteria to create a more complex rule. For the rule to match, all the criteria must match. For example, suppose you want to create a rule that matches both a protocol and a source IP address. The following rule would perform this task:

```
root@onecoursesource:~# iptables -A INPUT -p icmp -s 192.168.125.125 -j DROP
root@onecoursesource:~# iptables -L INPUT
Chain INPUT (policy ACCEPT)
target     prot opt source               destination
DROP       icmp --  anywhere             anywhere
DROP       tcp  --  anywhere             anywhere    tcp dpt:telnet
DROP       icmp --  192.168.125.125      anywhere
```

The rule added in this example states "drop any ICMP packet that originates from the 192.168.125.125 host."

Filtering Based on Destination

If you look at the output of the **iptables -L INPUT** command, you will see that there is a "destination" column:

```
root@onecoursesource:~# iptables -L INPUT
Chain INPUT (policy ACCEPT)
target     prot opt source               destination
```

```
DROP       icmp --  anywhere             anywhere
DROP       tcp  --  anywhere             anywhere    tcp dpt:telnet
DROP       icmp --  192.168.125.125      anywhere
```

In situations where you have multiple network cards or multiple IP addresses for a network card, you may want to create different rules for different network interfaces. In a situation where each network card has a single IP address, you can create different rules for each network interface:

```
root@onecoursesource:~# iptables -F INPUT
root@onecoursesource:~# iptables -A INPUT -i eth0 -s 192.168.100.0/24 -j DROP
root@onecoursesource:~# iptables -A INPUT -i eth1 -s 192.168.200.0/24 -j DROP
root@onecoursesource:~# iptables -L INPUT
Chain INPUT (policy ACCEPT)
target     prot opt source               destination
DROP       all  --  192.168.100.0/24     anywhere
DROP       all  --  192.168.200.0/24     anywhere
```

The output of the previous **iptables -L INPUT** command does not display the different network ports. To see them, you have to use the **-v** option (for "verbose"):

```
root@onecoursesource:~# iptables -L INPUT -v
Chain INPUT (policy ACCEPT 2 packets, 144 bytes)
 pkts bytes target     prot opt in     out    source               destination
    0     0 DROP       all  --  eth0   any    192.168.100.0/24     anywhere
    0     0 DROP       all  --  eth1   any    192.168.200.0/24     anywhere
```

The **-v** option provides more information, including hope that many network packets have matched the specified rule. This can be useful while testing the firewall rules.

In a situation where an interface is assigned multiple IP addresses, use the **-d** option to indicate the rule applies to a destination address:

```
root@onecoursesource:~# iptables -F INPUT
root@onecoursesource:~# iptables -A INPUT -d 192.168.50.1 -s 192.168.200.0/24 -j DROP
root@onecoursesource:~# iptables -L INPUT
Chain INPUT (policy ACCEPT)
target     prot opt source               destination
DROP       all  --  192.168.200.0/24     192.168.50.1
```

Changing the Default Policy

A more common use of a firewall is to allow specific packets and deny all others by default. This can be accomplished by changing the default policy. For example, suppose the current system is on an internal network and you want to make sure only a handful of systems can access it. The following rules would perform that task:

```
root@onecoursesource:~# iptables -F INPUT
root@onecoursesource:~# iptables -A INPUT -s 10.0.2.0/24 -j ACCEPT
root@onecoursesource:~# iptables -P INPUT DROP
root@onecoursesource:~# iptables -L INPUT
Chain INPUT (policy DROP)
target     prot opt source               destination
ACCEPT     all  --  10.0.2.0/24          anywhere
```

WHAT COULD GO WRONG? Be very careful when setting the default policy to DROP. If you are remotely logged in to the system and you did not create a rule that allows your login session's packets to "get through," your new default policy could end up blocking your access to the system.

Revisiting the Original Rules

Now that you have learned some of the basics of creating firewall rules, recall from earlier in this chapter that the system has some rules in place by default:

```
root@onecoursesource:~# iptables -t filter -L INPUT
Chain INPUT (policy ACCEPT)
target     prot opt source               destination
ACCEPT     udp  --  anywhere             anywhere   udp dpt:domain
ACCEPT     tcp  --  anywhere             anywhere   tcp dpt:domain
ACCEPT     udp  --  anywhere             anywhere   udp dpt:bootps
ACCEPT     tcp  --  anywhere             anywhere   tcp dpt:bootps
```

Part of knowing firewalls is not just writing rules, but also understanding how the rules apply. For example, if you review the rules from the previous output, you will see that several ports ("domain," which is port 53, and "bootps," which is port 67) are allowed to pass through the INPUT filtering point because the target is ACCEPT. This really has no impact on the firewall because the default policy for the chain is also ACCEPT. If the policy was changed to DROP, then the rules would have an impact on which packets are allowed and which are blocked.

Saving the Rules

Up until now, all changes that have been made only affect the currently running firewall. If the system was rebooted, all changes made using the **iptables** command would be lost and the rules would revert back to the default.

You can save the rules into a file by using the **iptables-save** command. Normally the output of this command is sent to the screen, but you can redirect the output to a file:

```
root@onecoursesource:~# iptables-save > /etc/iptables.rules
```

Where exactly you should save the rules and how these are loaded automatically is dependent on your distribution. Some distributions make use of front-end utilities, such as firewalld on Red Hat Enterprise Linux or UFW (uncomplicated firewall) on Ubuntu. These utilities are not only used to configure firewall rules (running **iptables** commands on your behalf), but they also save rules. The rules are also automatically restored during a system reboot.

NOTE Because there are so many of these "iptables helper" utilities (including GUI-based utilities), the authors decided to just cover the **iptables** command. You can always use this command to implement a firewall, and you are welcome to explore the "iptables helper" utilities for the distribution you are working on by consulting the documentation.

If you are not using one of these utilities, there may be another solution enabled on your system. If not, you can just create a shell script that restores the rules from the saved file by using the following command:

```
root@onecoursesource:~# iptables-restore> /etc/iptables.rules
```

Then you would use the techniques covered in Chapter 28, "System Booting," to execute the script during the boot process.

Using iptables to Filter Outgoing Packets

You may wonder why you would want to block outgoing packets. Consider that in many organizations, one of the biggest security concerns is users who visit Internet sites that could result in compromising security. For example, suppose there is a file-sharing site that your organization does not permit users to access because it lacks the proper security restrictions. To prevent this access, you can create a firewall rule on the OUTPUT-filter chain:

```
root@onecoursesource:~# iptables -F OUTPUT
root@onecoursesource:~# iptables -A OUTPUT -m tcp -p tcp -d 10.10.10.10
➥--dport 80 -j DROP
root@onecoursesource:~# iptables -L OUTPUT
Chain OUTPUT (policy ACCEPT)
target     prot opt source               destination
DROP       tcp  --  anywhere             10.10.10.10 tcp dpt:http
```

If you are going to disallow access to a remote system, it might be considered more "user friendly" to use the REJECT target rather than the DROP target. Recall that with DROP, no response is returned to the origin of the packet. Therefore, if a user goes to a website and the DROP target is used, it appears that the website is just hanging. However, a REJECT target would respond with an error message, so the web browser would display an error message to the user.

Perhaps you want to allow this access but create a log entry so you can determine what systems are attempting to access the remote system:

```
root@onecoursesource:~# iptables -F OUTPUT
root@onecoursesource:~# iptables -A OUTPUT -m tcp -p tcp -d 10.10.10.10
➥--dport 80 -j LOG
root@onecoursesource:~# iptables -L OUTPUT
Chain OUTPUT (policy ACCEPT)
target     prot opt source               destination
LOG        tcp  --  anywhere             10.10.10.10
➥ tcp dpt:http LOG level warning
```

Implementing NAT

There are several different forms of NAT:

- **DNAT**: Destination NAT; used when you want to place servers behind a firewall and still provide access from an external network. DNAT rules are placed on the PREROUTING filtering point. Further discussion of this topic is beyond the scope of this book.
- **SNAT**: Source NAT; used when you have an internal network with *statically assigned* private IP addresses. Using SNAT, you can funnel access to the Internet via a single machine that has a live IP address (an address that is routable on the Internet). This system is configured with SNAT, which is used to map internal addresses with external communication. SNAT rules are placed on the POSTROUTING filtering point. Further discussion of this topic is beyond the scope of this book.
- **MASQUERADE**: Used when you have an internal network with *dynamically assigned* private IP addresses (for example, using DHCP). Using MASQUERADE, you can funnel access to the Internet via a single machine that has a live IP address (an address that is routable on the Internet). This system is configured with MASQUERADE, which is used to map internal addresses with external communication. MASQUERADE rules are placed on the POSTROUTING filtering point.

Because most internal networks use DHCP to assign IP addresses, MASQUERADE is more common than SNAT. It is also easier to configure because SNAT requires you to create rules for each internal system. With MASQUERADE, a single command handles all the internal systems:

```
root@onecoursesource:~# iptables -t nat -A POSTROUTING -j MASQUERADE
```

Summary

The focus of this chapter was firewalls, specifically iptables. You learned how to secure a system or network from hackers by creating rules on the INPUT-filter chain. You also learned how to block access to external hosts by creating rules on the OUTPUT-filter chain. Lastly, you learned how to configure NAT to allow internal private systems access to the Internet.

Key Terms

Firewall, NAT, mangle, filtering point, table, chain, target, default chain policy, firewalld, UFW, router, rule

Review Questions

1. If no iptables rules match, the _____ target is used.
2. Which of the following is not a valid iptables target?
   - **A.** REFUSE
   - **B.** REJECT
   - **C.** ACCEPT
   - **D.** LOG
3. The _____ option to the **iptables** command will display current firewall rules.
4. Which of the following options need to be used to create a rule that will filter based on a destination port? (Choose two.)
   - **A.** -p
   - **B.** --dport
   - **C.** -d
   - **D.** -m
5. To view port numbers and IP addresses instead of names, use the _____ option.

Intrusion Detection

You might want to consider this chapter to be an introduction to intrusion detection tools because it is a very large topic, and a complete discussion of this topic is beyond the scope of this book. Intrusion detection incorporates a collection of tools and commands that are designed to allow you to determine if your system or network has been compromised.

The goal of this chapter is to introduce some of these tools, including repurposing tools that you have learned in previous chapters. With the knowledge that you gain in this chapter, you can begin the process of creating an intrusion detection procedure that is customized to your environment.

After reading this chapter and completing the exercises, you will be able to do the following:

Use tools to determine if the network has been compromised

Determine if key system files have been compromised

Explore additional IDS (intrusion detection system) tools and techniques

Introduction to Intrusion Detection Tools

In an ideal world, security measures would prevent all intruders. Unfortunately, we do not live in an ideal world, so you must plan for the possibility that intruders will breach your security. In terms of identifying intruders, the two primary areas on which you should focus are determining if a breach has occurred and what action should be taken.

Determining If a Security Breach Has Occurred

Discovering security compromises can be a challenge because hackers find holes that you are unaware of. Think about it this way: you have a problem with ants invading your house, so you plug every hole you can find. Within a week, they are back again, having found a hole that you were unaware existed.

Sometimes hackers, like ants, leave a trail so you can discover how they got into your systems or network. Unfortunately, some hackers are very clever about covering their tracks and will often escape notice for a significant period of time (like ants who find their way into the back of a food cabinet; you might not discover them for several days).

It is important to emphasize how critical it is to discover security breaches as quickly as possible. To illustrate, consider some of the major hacks that have happened within the last few years:

- **The Target hack of 2013**: The data of more than 40 million credit cards was compromised in this hack, which was discovered several weeks after the security measures were successfully breached.
- **The eBay hack of 2013–2014**: Account details of 145 million users, including passwords (in encrypted format), birth dates, names, and addresses, were compromised. The breach occurred when hackers were able to use employee credentials of three individuals. However, the breach was not discovered immediately. The hackers had access to the system for 229 days before the breach was discovered.

- **The Equifax hack of 2017**: More than 140 million customers' data was compromised in this hack, including social security numbers, addresses, birth dates, and other details. Although this hack was discovered on July 29, Equifax stated that their systems were likely compromised mid-May, meaning the hackers had approximately 45 days to steal data.

Although the previous examples are some of the largest hacks, there are many smaller security compromises similar to these. Note that in all cases, the hackers had weeks, sometimes months, of unabated system access. Sometimes, a good hacker needs only a short amount of time to steal data or cause damage, so the sooner you find them, the better off you will be. If the hacker steals information slowly over a long period of time, they are less likely to be noticed because large amounts of data are not being transferred and you might become familiar with seeing the traffic and not question it.

Intrusion detection tools are used to discover security breaches. As you will discover in this chapter, there are many of these tools available for Linux distributions.

Taking Action

Although you might not want to admit it, your best security plans might be compromised. When that happens, you must have a plan within your security policy that describes what actions to take to limit the loss or damage.

This, by itself, is a huge topic, and a complete discussion of the actions to take is beyond the scope of this book. The following list provides just some of the topics you should include in a "recovery" plan:

- There should be a plan in place to bring the compromised system(s) offline (no longer connected to the network). It is important that you quickly identify every system affected by the compromise so you can effectively stop the attack and the access of the attacker.
- There should be a list of people who need to be notified, in a specific order. The list should also include what information should be provided to each person on the list.
- If it is a mission-critical system, a plan should be in place to bring a replacement server back online *after* the security hole that was used in the compromise has been plugged. Never bring the original server back online because there might still be undiscovered backdoors placed by the hacker.
- A full diagnostic should be performed on the server(s).
- A plan should be put in place to notify customers, clients, the board of directors, government agencies, and the public. Include specific individuals, not departments, who are responsible and empowered to make these notifications. The plan should clearly state no one else is authorized to speak to the public on behalf of the organization.

This is far from a complete list. It is simply provided as a starting point for what you should think about when putting together a "recovery" plan.

Intrusion Detection Network Tools

Several intrusion detection tools are installed by default on most Linux distributions. Consider running these tools on a regular basis to determine if you have any intruders. One way of doing this is to create scripts and then run them on a regular basis using **crontab**.

The netstat Command

The **netstat** command was introduced in Chapter 19, "Network Configuration." Recall that you can use this command to display all active TCP connections:

```
[root@onecoursesource ~]# netstat -ta
Active Internet connections (servers and established)
Proto Recv-Q Send-Q Local Address           Foreign Address         State
tcp        0      0 192.168.122.1:domain    0.0.0.0:*               LISTEN
tcp        0      0 0.0.0.0:ssh             0.0.0.0:*               LISTEN
tcp        0      0 localhost:ipp           0.0.0.0:*               LISTEN
tcp        0      0 localhost:smtp          0.0.0.0:*               LISTEN
tcp6       0      0 [::]:ssh                [::]:*                  LISTEN
tcp6       0      0 localhost:ipp           [::]:*                  LISTEN
tcp6       0      0 localhost:smtp          [::]:*
```

A hacker who has unauthorized access to your system very likely has an established network connection. Probing your system on a regular basis can help you determine if an unauthorized user is accessing your system. Look for any unusual connections, and pay attention to where these connections originate (the "Foreign Address" column).

Another **netstat** command you should consider running on a regular basis is the **netstat -taupe** command, as shown in Example 32-1. This command displays all open ports, which is important because hackers often will open new ports to create more backdoors into the system. You should be aware of what ports should be open on each system in your network, and routinely verify that the correct ports are open and that no additional ports are open on each system.

Example 32-1 *The /etc/passwd File*

```
root@onecoursesource:~# netstat -taupe
Active Internet connections (servers and established)
Proto  Recv-Q  Send-Q  Local Address        Foreign Address  State   User   Inode  PID/Program name
tcp    0       0  10.8.0.1:domain      *:*              LISTEN  bind   24592  1388/named
tcp    0       0  192.168.122.1:domain *:*              LISTEN  root   16122  2611/dnsmasq
tcp    0       0  10.0.2.15:domain     *:*              LISTEN  bind   11652  1388/named
tcp    0       0  localhost:domain     *:*              LISTEN  bind   11650  1388/named
tcp    0       0  *:ftp                *:*              LISTEN  root   10612  990/vsftpd
tcp    0       0  *:ssh                *:*              LISTEN  root   11521  1342/sshd
tcp    0       0  localhost:ipp        *:*              LISTEN  root   15866  2527/cupsd
tcp    0       0  localhost:smtp       *:*              LISTEN  root   13427  1938/master
udp    0       0  *:42052              *:*                      avahi  9597   575/avahi-daemon: r
udp    0       0  *:openvpn            *:*                      root   12202  1576/openvpn
udp    0       0  *:mdns               *:*                      avahi  9595   575/avahi-daemon: r
udp    0       0  192.168.122.1:domain *:*                      bind   24593  1388/named
udp    0       0  10.8.0.1:domain      *:*                      bind   24591  1388/named
udp    0       0  192.168.122.1:domain *:*                      root   16121  2611/dnsmasq
udp    0       0  10.0.2.15:domain     *:*                      bind   11651  1388/named
udp    0       0  localhost:domain     *:*                      bind   11649  1388/named
```

The nmap Command

The problem with the **netstat** command is that a skilled hacker can fool you with false information. For example, they could modify the source code for the command, recompile, and replace the **netstat** command with the modified version that will provide false information. Or, more simply, they could replace the **netstat** command will a shell script that provides false information. This is not to suggest that you should not use the **netstat** command—just realize that it should not be the only way you test for open network ports.

You should also consider routinely running the **nmap** command, which was covered in detail in Chapter 30, "Footprinting." The **nmap** command is not as vulnerable to hackers replacing it because you run this command from a different system than the potentially hacked system (conceivably your entire system could be hacked, but that is less likely than a single system being hacked).

Because the **nmap** command is well covered in Chapter 30, it will not be reviewed again here. However, you should consider it part of your IDS game plan.

The tcpdump Command

Another useful intrusion detection tool covered in Chapter 30 is the **tcpdump** command. This tool allows you to probe network traffic, searching for any suspicious activity. As discussed in Chapter 30, this tool is used by hackers performing footprinting activities. For your purposes, you should use the command within your intrusion detection game plan to warn you of any rogue access points or other unauthorized hardware.

Because the **tcpdump** command is well covered in Chapter 30, it will not be reviewed again here. However, you should consider installing Wireshark, a tool that provides a GUI-based front end to the **tcpdump** command (see Figure 32-1).

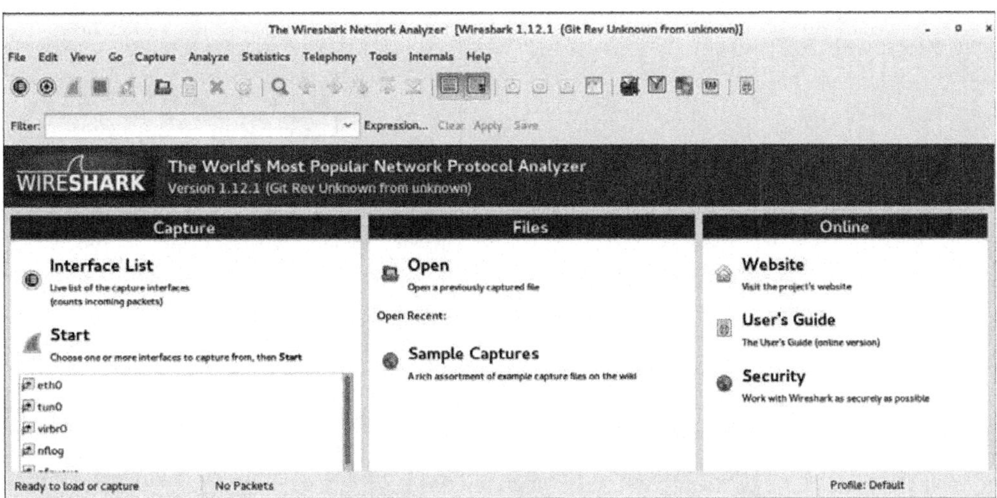

Figure 32-1 *Using Wireshark*

Keep in mind while Wireshark is great for interactive use, you still want to use **tcpdump** to automate network activity. As with the **netstat** command, a good way of using **tcpdump** to monitor the network is with shell scripts and **crontab** entries.

Intrusion Detection File Tools

A common task for hackers who gain unauthorized access to a system is to make changes to key files in order to create backdoors. This section provides two examples of how this may be accomplished as well as discusses incorporating file-change tools in your intrusion detection plan.

Modifying the /etc/passwd and /etc/shadow Files to Create a Backdoor

Assume for a moment that a hacker gains access to the system as the root user. This individual knows that eventually this unauthorized access will be noticed. To create a backdoor, the hacker adds the following entry to the **/etc/passwd** file (highlighted in bold):

```
lp:x:7:7:lp:/var/spool/lpd:/usr/sbin/nologin
mail:x:8:8:mail:/var/mail:/usr/sbin/nologin
news:x:9:9:news:/var/spool/news:/usr/sbin/nologin
uucp:x:10:10:uucp:/var/spool/uucp:/usr/sbin/nologin
nncp:x:0:0:root:/root:/bin/bash
proxy:x:13:13:proxy:/bin:/usr/sbin/nologin
www-data:x:33:33:www-data:/var/www:/usr/sbin/nologin
backup:x:34:34:backup:/var/backups:/usr/sbin/nologin
```

Recall that what provides a user account the superuser privileges is not the user's name, but rather the UID (user ID). Any account that has a UID of 0 has full administrative rights, so the "nncp" user in the previous output is a superuser. The hacker would just now need to add the following bolded line in **/etc/shadow** to allow logins for the nncp user account:

```
lp:*:16484:0:99999:7:::
mail:*:16484:0:99999:7:::
news:*:16484:0:99999:7:::
uucp:*:16484:0:99999:7:::
nncp::1745:7:0:99999:7:::
proxy:*:16484:0:99999:7:::
www-data:*:16484:0:99999:7:::
backup:*:16484:0:99999:7:::
```

Note that the password field for the nncp account is empty, which allows someone to log in with this user name and not have to provide a password. A hacker might also assign a regular password to the account.

Why does this method work so well? To begin with, the user name that was chosen and the placement with the **/etc/passwd** and **/etc/shadow** files allow the hacker to hide this account as if it were a daemon account. Many administrators are unaware of all the daemon accounts on the system, and because new software might install new daemon accounts, this new account will often escape notice.

Creating an SUID Program to Create a Backdoor

Again, assume a hacker gains access to the system as the administrator. Suppose the hacker runs the following **chmod** command:

```
root@onecoursesource:~# ls -l /usr/bin/vim
-rwxr-xr-x 1 root root 2191736 Jan  2  2020 /usr/bin/vim
root@onecoursesource:~# chmod u+s /usr/bin/vim
root@onecoursesource:~# ls -l /usr/bin/vim
-rwxr-xr-x 1 root root 2191736 Jan  2  2020 /usr/bin/vim
```

What this now means is that as long as the hacker can gain access to the system as a regular user, they can run the **vim** editor as the root user, which provides them with the ability to modify any file on the system (including removing the root password from the **/etc/shadow** file to gain full root access again). You might think, "Well, the hacker still needs access to a regular user account," but consider the following:

- The hacker might already have access to a compromised regular user account that you are not aware of.
- The hacker might be an internal employee who just wants to reclaim superuser access.
- The hacker might have left a background process running that runs as a regular user and provides access without having to log in as a regular user.

Incorporating File-Change Tools in the Intrusion Detection Plan

Your IDS plan should incorporate several tools that detect changes in files, including the following:

- Package management tools that determine if a file has changed since it was installed (for example, the **rpm -V** command, which was discussed in Chapter 26, "Red Hat–Based Software Management").
- Commands that compare differences in files, such as the **cmp** and **diff** commands. The **cmp** command is a good way to determine if two text or binary files are different, and the **diff** command can show how two text files are different. These commands require access to the original files, which might be available on a backup device.
- An MD5 checksum is a unique key based on a file's attributes and contents used to create a one-way hash value. This provides a "digital fingerprint" that can be used to determine if a file has been modified. If you create an MD5 checksum of the original, untampered file, you can later verify a suspicious file. See an example of this technique following this list.

To create an MD5 checksum, use the following command:

```
root@onecoursesource:~# md5sum /etc/passwd > passwd.md5
root@onecoursesource:~# cat passwd.md5
7459f689813d3c422bbd71d5363ba60b  /etc/passwd
```

You can use this file later to verify that no changes have been made:

```
root@onecoursesource:~# md5sum -c passwd.md5
/etc/passwd: OK
root@onecoursesource:~# useradd test
root@onecoursesource:~# md5sum -c passwd.md5
/etc/passwd: FAILED
md5sum: WARNING: 1 computed checksum did NOT match
```

Here are a couple notes regarding using the techniques in this section:

- Never trust any file on a system that has been compromised. For example, the database used by **rpm -V** could have been compromised by the hacker to avoid providing information about changes to files. Always make sure you have a clean copy of this database from another system. For the **cmp** and **diff** commands, make sure you store original files on another system. Your MD5 checksums should also be stored on a different system. Be paranoid and never trust anything on a potentially compromised system.

Security Highlight

It is best to always assume systems and data are compromised and then work from that position. Too often security experts assume that the system hasn't been fully compromised and use tools to attempt to fix problems, only later to discover that the tools themselves have been compromised.

- Research other tools that provide similar features. For example, instead of using the **md5sum** command, you may want to use the **sha1sum** command (or one of its varieties, like **sha256sum** or **sha512sum**).

Additional Intrusion Detection Tools

The tools discussed in this chapter just begin to scratch the surface of the large number of intrusion detection tools available for Linux. A complete discussion of these tools could fill an entire book. The following list highlights just some of the intrusion detection system (IDS) categories available:

- **Passive IDS**: An IDS that detects possible intrusions and then notifies administrators
- **Reactive or Active IDS**: An IDS that attempts to automatically react or respond to intrusions
- **NIDS**: Network-based IDS, designed to discover intrusions or attempts by monitoring key networks
- **HIDS**: Host-based IDS, which runs on a specific system to determine if an intrusion attempt has occurred

There are additional categories (research signature-based IDS, for example). IDS is a huge topic!

In terms of what additional tools you should consider researching, consider the following:

- Kali Linux has some useful tools. In particular, focus on categories 09, 10, and 11 in Figure 32-2.

Figure 32-2 *Kali Linux IDS Tools*

- Security Onion is a distribution that primarily focuses on IDS tools. It includes, by default, many of the other tools in this list.
- Tripwire is a tool that is designed to report when key system files have been changed. Both a commercial version and an open source (free) version are available.
- Snort is an IDS tool that has been available for more than 20 years. It is used to provide real-time analysis of traffic and can also be used to log network packets.
- AIDE (Advanced Intrusion Detection Environment), like Tripwire, is used to determine if changes have been made to the filesystem.

Keep in mind that this is nowhere close to a complete list! This list is simply designed to provide you with a starting point for further exploration.

Summary

In this chapter, you were introduced to some techniques you can use to perform intrusion detection. You discovered how to use some of the tools you learned about in previous chapters, and you were also introduced to some new commands and tools.

Key Terms

Intrusion detection, IDS, passive IDS, reactive or active IDS, NIDS, HIDS

Review Questions

1. The _____ command can be used to display all active network connections on the local system.
2. Which of the following commands can be used to probe open network ports on a remote system?
   - A. **netstat**
   - B. **tcpdump**
   - C. **nmap**
   - D. **md5sum**
3. The _____ tool allows you to probe network traffic, searching for any suspicious activity.
4. Which option for the **rpm** command can be used to display changes in files since the file was installed?
   - A. **--verifyfiles**
   - B. **--verify**
   - C. **-V**
   - D. **-v**
5. A _____ IDS detects possible intrusions and then notifies administrators.

Additional Security Tasks

As you have likely learned by now, security on Linux is a huge topic. There is really so much more you can learn and so much more we could have included in this book.

Consider this final chapter a collection of different security features that we, the authors, wanted to cover but that just did not fit logically anywhere else in the book. In this chapter, you learn how to use the fail2ban service to temporarily block access to a system. You also learn how to set up a basic VPN (virtual private network) and secure files using the **gpg** utility. Lastly, you learn about security sites that provide useful alerts.

After reading this chapter and completing the exercises, you will be able to do the following:

Configure the fail2ban service

Set up a virtual private network

Encrypt files using gpg

Use security sites to become informed about security issues

The fail2ban Service

The **fail2ban** daemon scans specific log files, searching for IP addresses of systems that attempt to breach a system via repeated connection attempts. This service is not typically installed by default on most distributions, so you will need to install it with either the **yum** or **apt-get** command.

After installing the utility, you will have a new configuration directory: **/etc/fail2ban**. The primary configuration file is **/etc/fail2ban/jail.conf**. However, if you look at this file, you will likely see the message displayed in Example 33-1.

Example 33-1 *The fail2ban Configuration File Warning*

```
# HOW TO ACTIVATE JAILS:
#
# YOU SHOULD NOT MODIFY THIS FILE.
#
# It will probably be overwritten or improved in a distribution update.
#
# Provide customizations in a jail.local file or a jail.d/customisation.local.
# For example to change the default bantime for all jails and to enable the
# ssh-iptables jail the following (uncommented) would appear in the .local file.
# See man 5 jail.conf for details.
```

The problem that you run into in modifying this file directly is that updates to the fail2ban software package could result in overwriting this file. As the warning in this file recommends, you can create **.local** files with customizations.

The file is called **jail.conf** because remote hosts are placed in a "jail" due to suspicious activity. As with a real jail, the intent is to let the hosts out of jail after a specific period of time.

Some key settings in this file are described in Table 33-1.

Table 33-1 Key fail2ban Configuration Settings

Setting	Description
bantime	How long in seconds that a host is banned.
maxretry	The number of failures in connecting within the "**findtime**" before a host is banned.
findtime	The period of time, in seconds, that the **maxretry** entry uses. For example, suppose the following settings are applied: **bantime = 600** **findtime = 600** **maxretry = 5** In this case, five failures within 600 seconds would result in a ban for 600 seconds.
enabled	If set to **true**, this setting indicates that the jail is enabled. This is a very important setting because the default value for this setting in the **jail.conf** file is **false**. Only specific sections should be enabled (the ones you want to use).
ignoreip	Allows you to create "white lists" of IP addresses to never ban.

In addition to the global settings described in Table 33-1, there are sections for different "jails." For example, you can have a section related to SSH connections, like the following:

```
[sshd]
enabled = true
maxretry = 3
```

This is a very simple example, and there are many other possible features you can use in the section. For example, you could create a custom action rule, including sending someone an email in the event the rule is used to block an IP address:

```
[sshd]
enabled = true
maxretry = 3
action   = iptables[name=SSH, port=ssh, protocol=tcp]
           sendmail-whois[name=SSH, dest=root, sender=fail2ban@example.com]
```

The action setting tells the **fail2ban** daemon what actions to take. The actions are normally defined in the **/etc/fail2ban/action.d/iptables.conf** file, which you can review to determine more about what these actions are designed to do.

OpenVPN

Consider an organization that is geographically located in a single building in San Diego, California. This organization provides its employees access to sensitive data from a locally administered database. By keeping all of the data transfer of this sensitive data within the company's physical network (on the local area network, or LAN), the company enjoys a higher level of security than if the data were transmitted over the Internet (a wide area network, or WAN).

However, as the company grows, this method of providing access to the data becomes a hindrance. Employees who need to travel to meet clients cannot access this important data. The company is also considering expanding by acquiring a company based in New York City, but there are concerns as to how the data would be shared.

You are the system administrator for the company and it is your responsibility to develop a viable (and secure) solution. Fortunately for you, there is virtual private network (VPN). With this VPN, you can securely transfer data between a VPN server and a VPN client. This feature is much like how Secure Shell (SSH) provides secure data transfer; it makes use of public and private keys to encrypt and decrypt the data. All of the routers between the VPN server and VPN client only see encrypted data.

Several different VPN-based software packages are available for Linux; one of the most common VPN solutions is called OpenVPN. This is an open source variation of VPN software.

Most likely your distribution does not include OpenVPN by default. You will likely need to install **openvpn** and perhaps some additional software. For example, on an Ubuntu system, you should install the following:

```
root@onecoursesource:~# apt-get install openvpn easy-rsa
```

In order to configure OpenVPN, you must perform five primary steps:

- Configure a Certificate Authority (CA).
- Generate the VPN Server certificate.
- Generate the VPN Client certificate.
- Configure the VPN server.
- Configure the VPN client.

Configuring the Certificate Authority

The first step in setting up the CA is to create a directory and copy some files from the **/usr/share/easy-rsa** directory:

```
root@onecoursesource:~# mkdir /etc/openvpn/easy-rsa
root@onecoursesource:~# cp -r /usr/share/easy-rsa/* /etc/openvpn/easy-rsa
```

The **/usr/share/easy-rsa** directory contains configuration files and scripts that are used to generate the CA. Before you execute the scripts, you should edit the following settings in the **/etc/openvpn/easy-rsa/vars** file:

```
export KEY_COUNTRY="US"
export KEY_PROVINCE="CA"
export KEY_CITY="SanDiego"
export KEY_ORG="One-Course-Source"
export KEY_EMAIL="bo@onecoursesource.com"
export KEY_OU="MyOrg"
export KEY_ALTNAMES="OCS"
```

Of course, use the values that make the most sense for your organization. The next step is to change the directory to **/etc/openvpn/easy-rsa** (using the **cd** command) and execute the following three commands:

```
source vars
./clean-all
./build-ca
```

These steps are demonstrated in Example 33-2. Note that you will be asked questions that have default values that you provided in the **/etc/openvpn/easy-rsa/vars** file. Just press the Enter key to accept these defaults.

Example 33-2 *Creating the CA*

```
root@onecoursesource:~# cd /etc/openvpn/easy-rsa
root@onecoursesource:/etc/openvpn/easy-rsa# source vars
NOTE: If you run ./clean-all, I will be doing a rm -rf on /etc/openvpn/easy-rsa/keys
root@onecoursesource:/etc/openvpn/easy-rsa# ./clean-all
root@onecoursesource:/etc/openvpn/easy-rsa# ./build-ca
Generating a 2048 bit RSA private key
..................+++
.....+++
writing new private key to 'ca.key'
-----
You are about to be asked to enter information that will be incorporated
into your certificate request.
What you are about to enter is what is called a Distinguished Name or a DN.
There are quite a few fields but you can leave some blank
For some fields there will be a default value,
If you enter '.', the field will be left blank.
-----
Country Name (2 letter code) [US]:
State or Province Name (full name) [CA]:
Locality Name (eg, city) [SanDiego]:
Organization Name (eg, company) [One-Course-Source]:
Organizational Unit Name (eg, section) [MyVPN]:
Common Name (eg, your name or your server's hostname) [MyVPN]:
Name [MyVPN]:
Email Address [bo@onecoursesource.com]:
root@onecoursesource:/etc/openvpn/easy-rsa#
```

NOTE The **source** command is just the shell **source** command that will read the variable settings from the **vars** file and create these variables in the current shell. This is needed because the **./build-ca** script does not read the variables from the **vars** file, but rather from the current shell variables.

Generating the VPN Server Certificate

The next step in this process is to create the certificates for the specific client and the server. To create the server certificate, execute the **./build-key-server** script followed by the name you want to give your server, as demonstrated in Example 33-3. You will be asked several questions, and you can just accept the default for most of them by pressing the Enter key. However, you must answer **y** for two questions:

```
Sign the certificate? [y/n]:
```

and

```
1 out of 1 certificate requests certified, commit? [y/n]
```

Example 33-3 *Creating the Server Certificate*

```
root@onecoursesource:/etc/openvpn/easy-rsa# ./build-key-server ocs-server
Generating a 2048 bit RSA private key
.......................................+++
................................+++
writing new private key to 'ocs-server.key'
-----
You are about to be asked to enter information that will be incorporated
into your certificate request.
What you are about to enter is what is called a Distinguished Name or a DN.
There are quite a few fields but you can leave some blank
For some fields there will be a default value,
If you enter '.', the field will be left blank.
-----
Country Name (2 letter code) [US]:
State or Province Name (full name) [CA]:
Locality Name (eg, city) [SanDiego]:
Organization Name (eg, company) [One-Course-Source]:
Organizational Unit Name (eg, section) [MyVPN]:
Common Name (eg, your name or your server's hostname) [ocs-server]:
Name [MyVPN]:
Email Address [bo@onecoursesource.com]:

Please enter the following 'extra' attributes
to be sent with your certificate request
A challenge password []:
An optional company name []:
Using configuration from /etc/openvpn/easy-rsa/openssl-1.0.0.cnf
Check that the request matches the signature
Signature ok
The Subject's Distinguished Name is as follows
countryName           :PRINTABLE:'US'
stateOrProvinceName   :PRINTABLE:'CA'
localityName          :PRINTABLE:'SanDiego'
organizationName      :PRINTABLE:'One-Course-Source'
organizationalUnitName:PRINTABLE:'MyVPN'
commonName            :PRINTABLE:'ocs-server'
name                  :PRINTABLE:'MyVPN'
emailAddress          :IA5STRING:'bo@onecoursesource.com'
Certificate is to be certified until Jan 16 23:39:58 2026 GMT (3650 days)
Sign the certificate? [y/n]:y


1 out of 1 certificate requests certified, commit? [y/n]y
Write out database with 1 new entries
Data Base Updated
```

Next, you need to execute the following script to generate the **dh** (Diffie-Hellman key exchange method) parameters:

```
root@onecoursesource:/etc/openvpn/easy-rsa# ./build-dh
Generating DH parameters, 2048 bit long safe prime, generator 2
```

```
This is going to take a long time
.........................................+............................
```

As you can see from the output of the previous command, it takes a while to execute, and you will see a lot more dots and plus signs than we have included in the previous output.

The result now should be a set of keys in the **/etc/openvpn/easy-rsa/keys** directory:

```
root@onecoursesource:/etc/openvpn/easy-rsa# ls keys
01.pem  ca.key      index.txt       index.txt.old   ocs-server.csr  serial
ca.crt  dh2048.pem  index.txt.attr  ocs-server.crt  ocs-server.key  serial.old
```

The new key should be placed in the **/etc/openvpn** directory, assuming that the current machine is the VPN server:

```
root@onecoursesource:/etc/openvpn/easy-rsa# cd keys
root@onecoursesource:/etc/openvpn/easy-rsa/keys# cp ocs-server.crt
➥ocs-server.key ca.crt dh2048.pem /etc/openvpn
```

Generating the VPN Client Certificate

The process for creating a VPN client certificate is similar to creating a server certificate. Each client system needs a certificate, so you may perform these steps several times.

Return to the **/etc/openvpn/easy-rsa** directory and execute the **./build-key** script, providing the name of the client as an argument. See Example 33-4 for a demonstration.

Example 33-4 *Creating the Client Certificate*

```
root@onecoursesource:/etc/openvpn/easy-rsa/keys# cd /etc/openvpn/easy-rsa
root@onecoursesource:/etc/openvpn/easy-rsa# ./build-key vpnclient1
Generating a 2048 bit RSA private key
........................+++
.....+++
writing new private key to 'vpnclient1.key'
-----
You are about to be asked to enter information that will be incorporated
into your certificate request.
What you are about to enter is what is called a Distinguished Name or a DN.
There are quite a few fields but you can leave some blank
For some fields there will be a default value,
If you enter '.', the field will be left blank.
-----
Country Name (2 letter code) [US]:
State or Province Name (full name) [CA]:
Locality Name (eg, city) [SanDiego]:
Organization Name (eg, company) [One-Course-Source]:
Organizational Unit Name (eg, section) [MyVPN]:
Common Name (eg, your name or your server's hostname) [vpnclient1]:
Name [MyVPN]:
Email Address [bo@onecoursesource.com]:

Please enter the following 'extra' attributes
to be sent with your certificate request
A challenge password []:
An optional company name []:
Using configuration from /etc/openvpn/easy-rsa/openssl-1.0.0.cnf
```

```
Check that the request matches the signature
Signature ok
The Subject's Distinguished Name is as follows
countryName           :PRINTABLE:'US'
stateOrProvinceName   :PRINTABLE:'CA'
localityName          :PRINTABLE:'SanDiego'
organizationName      :PRINTABLE:'One-Course-Source'
organizationalUnitName:PRINTABLE:'MyVPN'
commonName            :PRINTABLE:'vpnclient1'
name                  :PRINTABLE:'MyVPN'
emailAddress          :IA5STRING:'bo@onecoursesource.com'
Certificate is to be certified until Jan 17 00:01:30 2027 GMT (3650 days)
Sign the certificate? [y/n]:y


1 out of 1 certificate requests certified, commit? [y/n]y
Write out database with 1 new entries
Data Base Updated
```

There will be new keys in the **/etc/openvpn/easy-rsa/keys** directory:

```
root@onecoursesource:/etc/openvpn/easy-rsa# ls keys
01.pem  dh2048.pem          index.txt.old   serial           vpnclient1.key
02.pem  index.txt           ocs-server.crt  serial.old
ca.crt  index.txt.attr      ocs-server.csr  vpnclient1.crt
ca.key  index.txt.attr.old  ocs-server.key  vpnclient1.csr
```

These keys need to be copied to the VPN client: the **ca.crt**, **vpnclient1.crt**, and **vpnclient1.key** files.

Setting Up the Basic Server

The OpenVPN software package comes with some sample configuration files. On a typical Ubuntu system, these files are located in the following directory:

```
root@onecoursesource:~# ls /usr/share/doc/openvpn/examples/sample-config-files
client.conf      loopback-server      README              tls-home.conf
firewall.sh      office.up            server.conf.gz      tls-office.conf
home.up          openvpn-shutdown.sh  static-home.conf    xinetd-client-config
loopback-client  openvpn-startup.sh   static-office.conf  xinetd-server-config
```

Copy the **server.conf.gz** file to the **/etc/openvpn** directory and extract the contents with the **gunzip** command:

```
root@onecoursesource:~# cp /usr/share/doc/openvpn/examples/sample-
➥config-files/server.conf.gz /etc/openvpn
root@onecoursesource:~# gunzip /etc/openvpn/server.conf.gz
```

Change the following settings to match the files on your system:

```
# OpenVPN can also use a PKCS #12 formatted key file
# (see "pkcs12" directive in man page).
ca ca.crt
cert server.crt
key server.key  # This file should be kept secret
```

```
# Diffie hellman parameters.
# Generate your own with:
#   openssl dhparam -out dh1024.pem 1024
# Substitute 2048 for 1024 if you are using
# 2048 bit keys.
dh dh1024.pem
```

For example, these settings might be as follows:

```
ca ca.crt
cert ocs-server.crt
key ocs-server.key  # This file should be kept secret
dh dh2048.pem
```

Now, start the **openvpm** service and test the configuration by viewing the new network interface, **tun0**:

```
root@onecoursesource:~# ifconfig tun0
tun0      Link encap:UNSPEC  HWaddr 00-00-00-00-00-00-00-00-00-00-00-00-00-00-00-00
          inet addr:10.8.0.1  P-t-P:10.8.0.2  Mask:255.255.255.255
          UP POINTOPOINT RUNNING NOARP MULTICAST  MTU:1500  Metric:1
          RX packets:0 errors:0 dropped:0 overruns:0 frame:0
          TX packets:0 errors:0 dropped:0 overruns:0 carrier:0
          collisions:0 txqueuelen:100
          RX bytes:0 (0.0 B)  TX bytes:0 (0.0 B)
```

Setting Up the Basic Client

For the client setup, first make sure the **openvpn** software is installed. Then copy the client configuration file to the **/etc/openvpn** directory:

```
root@onecoursesource:~# cp /usr/share/doc/openvpn/
➥examples/sample-config-files/client.conf /etc/openvpn
```

Also make sure you copy over the following files from the VPN server system and put these in the **/etc/openvpn** directory (remember the client filenames may differ, but be sure to copy over the **.crt** and **.key** files only):

- **ca.crt**
- **vpnclient1.crt**
- **vpnclient1.key**

Edit the **/etc/openvpn/client.conf** file and make sure the following settings are correct:

```
ca ca.crt
cert vpnclient1.crt
key vpnclient1.key
```

In the **/etc/openvpn/client.conf** file, you'll see a setting similar to the following:

```
remote my-server-1 1194
```

Here, **my-server-1** must be changed to the hostname of the VPN server. The value 1194 is the port number; 1194 is the standard VPN port. Also, you must include the **client** setting. Here's an example:

```
client
remote vpnserver.onecoursesource.com 1194
```

Next, start the **openvpm** service and test the configuration by viewing the new network interface, **tun0**:

```
root@onecoursesource:~# ifconfig tun0
tun0      Link encap:UNSPEC  HWaddr 00-00-00-00-00-00-00-00-00-00-00-00-00-00-00-00
          inet addr:10.8.0.6  P-t-P:10.8.0.5  Mask:255.255.255.255
          UP POINTOPOINT RUNNING NOARP MULTICAST  MTU:1500  Metric:1
          RX packets:0 errors:0 dropped:0 overruns:0 frame:0
          TX packets:0 errors:0 dropped:0 overruns:0 carrier:0
          collisions:0 txqueuelen:100
          RX bytes:0 (0.0 B)  TX bytes:0 (0.0 B)
```

Now, how can you tell that this really works? Notice that the **tun0** interface is in a completely different network than your local network:

```
root@ubuntu:/etc/openvpn# ifconfig eth0
eth0      Link encap:Ethernet  HWaddr 08:00:27:ca:89:f1
          inet addr:192.168.1.25  Bcast:192.168.1.255  Mask:255.255.255.0
          inet6 addr: fe80::a00:27ff:feca:89f1/64 Scope:Link
          UP BROADCAST RUNNING MULTICAST  MTU:1500  Metric:1
          RX packets:785 errors:0 dropped:0 overruns:0 frame:0
          TX packets:307 errors:0 dropped:0 overruns:0 carrier:0
          collisions:0 txqueuelen:1000
          RX bytes:88796 (88.7 KB)  TX bytes:39865 (39.8 KB)
```

In fact, your new **tun0** interface is not directly routable outside of the current network. However, if you did everything right, the following should work:

```
root@onecoursesource:~# ping -c 4 10.8.0.1
PING 10.8.0.1 (10.8.0.1) 56(84) bytes of data.
64 bytes from 10.8.0.1: icmp_seq=1 ttl=64 time=0.732 ms
64 bytes from 10.8.0.1: icmp_seq=2 ttl=64 time=1.68 ms
64 bytes from 10.8.0.1: icmp_seq=3 ttl=64 time=1.76 ms
64 bytes from 10.8.0.1: icmp_seq=4 ttl=64 time=0.826 ms

--- 10.8.0.1 ping statistics ---
4 packets transmitted, 4 received, 0% packet loss, time 3003ms
rtt min/avg/max/mdev = 0.732/1.253/1.768/0.477 ms
```

That IP address that you just "pinged" is the VPN server IP address (note that it may be different from this example; double-check the **tun0** interface on the server when you test this).

How does this work? Any attempt to connect to 10.8.0.1 will result in the local OpenVPN capturing the network packet, encrypting it, and then sending it to the correct "real IP" address of the server.

But, how does it "capture" the packet? It essentially sets itself up as a router for the network associated with the **tun0** interface. You can see this by executing the **route** command:

```
root@onecoursesource:~# route
Kernel IP routing table
Destination     Gateway         Genmask         Flags Metric Ref    Use Iface
default         192.168.1.1     0.0.0.0         UG    0      0        0 eth0
10.8.0.1        10.8.0.5        255.255.255.255 UGH   0      0        0 tun0
10.8.0.5        *               255.255.255.255 UH    0      0        0 tun0
```

```
192.168.1.0     *               255.255.255.0   U     0      0        0 eth0
192.168.122.0   *               255.255.255.0   U     0      0        0 virbr0
```

One last note: there are a lot of "moving parts" when it comes to a VPN. If you follow all the steps carefully, it should work for you. However, if you make a mistake, first look at the VPN log. For example, suppose you forgot to copy the client files to the **/etc/openvpn** directory, causing the VPN client service to fail to start. A quick look at the log file (and an obligatory slap on the forehead) is all you should need to determine where the problem resides (see Example 33-5).

Example 33-5 *Viewing the VPN Log File*

```
root@onecoursesource:~# grep -i vpn /var/log/syslog
Jan 19 16:47:18 ubuntu NetworkManager[1148]: <info> VPN: loaded org.freedesktop.Network
➥ Manager.pptp
Jan 19 17:09:02 ubuntu NetworkManager[1304]: <info> VPN: loaded org.freedesktop.
➥ NetworkManager.pptp
Jan 19 17:09:03 ubuntu ovpn-client[1407]: Options error: --ca fails with 'ca.crt': No such
➥ file or directory
Jan 19 17:09:03 ubuntu ovpn-client[1407]: Options error: --cert fails with 'client.crt':
➥ No such file or directory
Jan 19 17:09:03 ubuntu ovpn-client[1407]: Options error: --key fails with 'client.key': No
➥ such file or directory
Jan 19 17:09:03 ubuntu ovpn-client[1407]: Options error: Please correct these errors.
Jan 19 17:09:03 ubuntu ovpn-client[1407]: Use --help for more information.
Jan 19 17:45:15 ubuntu ovpn-client[3389]: Options error: --ca fails with 'ca.crt': No such
➥ file or directory
Jan 19 17:45:15 ubuntu ovpn-client[3389]: Options error: --cert fails with 'vpnclient1.
➥ crt': No such file or directory
Jan 19 17:45:15 ubuntu ovpn-client[3389]: Options error: --key fails with 'vpnclient1.
➥ key': No such file or directory
Jan 19 17:45:15 ubuntu ovpn-client[3389]: Options error: Please correct these errors.
Jan 19 17:45:15 ubuntu ovpn-client[3389]: Use --help for more information.
```

gpg

The GNU Privacy Guard utility, **gpg**, can be used to create public and private encryption keys. These keys can be used for several features, including encrypting a file so the data in the file is more secure when transported to another system.

The first step is to create the encryption keys by using **the gpg --gen-key** command. The result of this command will be a collection of files in the **~/.gnupg** directory that can be used to encrypt data or digitally sign messages. See Example 33-6 for an example.

Example 33-6 *The **gpg --gen-key** Command*

```
root@onecoursesource:~# gpg --gen-key
gpg (GnuPG) 1.4.16; Copyright (C) 2013 Free Software Foundation, Inc.
This is free software: you are free to change and redistribute it.
There is NO WARRANTY, to the extent permitted by law.

Please select what kind of key you want:
   (1) RSA and RSA (default)
   (2) DSA and Elgamal
   (3) DSA (sign only)
   (4) RSA (sign only)
Your selection? 1
RSA keys may be between 1024 and 4096 bits long.
```

33

```
What keysize do you want? (2048)
Requested keysize is 2048 bits
Please specify how long the key should be valid.
         0 = key does not expire
<n>  = key expires in n days
<n>w = key expires in n weeks
<n>m = key expires in n months
<n>y = key expires in n years
Key is valid for? (0)
Key does not expire at all
Is this correct? (y/N) y
You need a user ID to identify your key; the software constructs the user ID
from the Real Name, Comment and Email Address in this form:
    "Heinrich Heine (Der Dichter) <heinrichh@duesseldorf.de>"

Real name: June Jones
Email address: june@jones.com
Comment: Test
You selected this USER-ID:
    "June Jones (Test) <june@jones.com>"

Change (N)ame, (C)omment, (E)mail or (O)kay/(Q)uit?O
You need a Passphrase to protect your secret key.

We need to generate a lot of random bytes. It is a good idea to perform
some other action (type on the keyboard, move the mouse, utilize the
disks) during the prime generation; this gives the random number
generator a better chance to gain enough entropy.
gpg: key 1946B1F2 marked as ultimately trusted
public and secret key created and signed.

gpg: checking the trustdb
gpg: 3 marginal(s) needed, 1 complete(s) needed, PGP trust model
gpg: depth: 0  valid:   1  signed:   0  trust: 0-, 0q, 0n, 0m, 0f, 1u
pub   2048R/1946B1F2 2017-06-05
      Key fingerprint = 1D6A D774 A540 F98C EBF0  2E93 49D5 711C 1946 B1F2
uid                  June Jones (Test) <june@jones.com>
sub   2048R/FED22A14 2019-06-05
```

WHAT COULD GO WRONG? If you get the message "Not enough random bytes available. Please do some other work to give the OS a chance to collect more entropy!", then continue working on your system, and it will eventually generate enough random bytes. *This error occurs because the system generates the encryption key from random items in the system's random access memory (RAM), which fills based on system operations.* If you are impatient, try running a system-intensive command, such as **sudo find / -type f | xargs grep blahblahblah > /dev/null**.

In order for a user to encrypt data to send to you, they need your public key. To send this public key to a user, first execute the following command to create a public key file:

```
gpg --output pub_key_file  --export 'June Jones'
```

The **--output** option is used to specify the name of the public key file. The **--export** option is used to specify the key that you want to send.

After sending the public key, the receiving user imports the key into their GPG database by executing the following command (**pub_key_file** is the file they received from you):

```
gpg --import pub_key_file
```

Then the user can encrypt a file using the following command:

```
gpg --encrypt --recipient june@jones.com data.txt
```

After the file has been encrypted, the only way it can be decrypted is with the private key on your system using the **gpg --decrypt** command.

Security Alert Services

Security alert services provide timely information about current security issues, vulnerabilities, and exploits. Several services are available that are designed to provide you with important security alerts. Here are a few of these services:

- **BugTraq**: This service is an email-based program that is sponsored by Security Focus (www.securityfocus.com). Per the website, "BugTraq is a full disclosure moderated mailing list for the *detailed* discussion and announcement of computer security vulnerabilities: what they are, how to exploit them, and how to fix them." To subscribe to the list, visit the following link: http://www.securityfocus.com/archive/1/description#0.3.1.
- **CERT**: Generically, the term CERT stands for Computer Emergency Response Teams. In this case, however, there is a specific CERT that this refers to: The CERT Coordination Center (CERT-CC) at Carnegie Mellon University (CMU). This organization is a component of a larger organization at CMU called the Software Engineering Institute (SEI). CERT provides a variety of features, including vulnerability analysis tools, a knowledgebase of vulnerability notes, and coordination with private and governmental organizations regarding security issues. Visit www.cert.org to learn more about this organization.
- **US-CERT**: The United States CERT (www.us-cert.gov). The National Cybersecurity and Communications Center (NCCIC) is found at this site. Per the website, US-CERT is "the Nation's flagship cyber defense, incident response, and operational integration center," and its mission is "to reduce the Nation's risk of systematic cybersecurity and communications challenges."

Summary

When it comes to security, you will find that there is always more to learn. This chapter covered some additional security topics that did not fit logically in other chapters of this book. You discovered how you can secure files for transport by encrypting them with the **gpg** utility. You also learned how to configure fail2ban and OpenVPN. Lastly, you learned about security websites that can provide you with important information regarding security issues.

Key Terms

CERT, VPN, certificate, public key, private key, RSA

Review Questions

1. The primary configuration file for the fail2ban utility is the **/etc/fail2ban/**_____ file.

2. Which of the following settings of the fail2ban configuration file will allow you to "white list" IP addresses?

   A. **white-list**

   B. **ignoreip**

   C. **allowip**

   D. **white-ip-list**

3. Which of following is the correct way to specify a section called "sshd" in a fail2ban configuration file?

   A. **"sshd"**

   B. **<sshd>**

   C. **[sshd]**

   D. **{sshd}**

4. Before you create an OpenVPN CA, you should execute the following command: _____ **vars**.

5. Which of the following scripts will create an OpenVPN CA when executed in the **/etc/openvpn/easy-rsa** directory?

   A. **./create-ca**

   B. **./set-ca**

   C. **./generate-ca**

   D. **./build-ca**

6. To generate the Diffie-Hellman parameters, execute the **build-dh** script in the **/etc/openvpn/**_____ directory.

Appendix A

Answers to Review Questions

Chapter 1

1. A *file system* is a structure that is used to organize files and directories in an operating system.
2. C
3. D
4. A *shell* program provides a command-line interface to the Linux operating system.
5. A *virtual machine* is an operating system that thinks it is installed natively, but it is actually sharing a system with a host operating system.

Chapter 2

1. The **rm -r** command can be used to delete a directory and all its contents.
2. A and D
3. A
4. The **-l** option to the **ls** command will display a file's permissions.
5. The **file** command will tell you what sort of contents a file contains.

Chapter 3

1. The **/** character can be used while viewing a man page in order to search for a term in the document.
2. C
3. B and D
4. The **help** command provides information about built-in shell commands.
5. The **b** key will move you to the previous node while viewing an info page.

Chapter 4

1. The *last line* or *ex* mode allows you to enter complex operations while working in the vi editor.
2. B
3. C
4. The **yy** command will copy an entire line in the vi editor.
5. The **/** command will allow you to search for text forward from the current position while using the vi editor.

Chapter 5

1. The **/etc/issue** file is displayed prior to local command-line login attempts.
2. The **/etc/issue.net** file is displayed prior to telnet login attempts.
3. The **/etc/motd** file is displayed after a successful login.
4. A and D
5. The **-c** option to the **shutdown** command is used to cancel a shutdown operation.

Chapter 6

1. Every user is a member of at least *one* group(s).
2. A and D
3. C and D
4. Special groups are groups with GID numbers typically under the numeric value of *1000*.
5. If the system is using UPG, the group name of the user account named jake should be *jake*.

Chapter 7

1. User passwords and password aging data is stored in the **/etc/*shadow*** file.
2. A
3. D
4. The **/etc/default/*useradd*** file contains default values used by the **useradd** command.
5. PAM configuration files are stored in the **/etc/*pam.d*** directory.

Chapter 8

1. Fill in the missing option so the user of the bob account can't change his password: **passwd -m 99999 -M 99998 bob**
2. B
3. The **psattc** package provides process accounting.
4. A
5. D

Chapter 9

1. The **-l** option to the **ls** command will display basic file permissions.
2. C
3. C
4. The **umask** command is used to specify which default permissions to mask (not include) when creating a new file or directory.
5. Fill in the blank to set the SGID permission set for the **/data** directory: **chmod g+s /data**.

Chapter 10

1. B and C
2. The **umount** command is used to unmount a filesystem.
3. C and D
4. C
5. D
6. The **swapoff** command removes a swap device from current use.
7. C
8. D
9. Fill in the blank to make an ext4 filesystem: **mkfs -t ext4 /dev/sdb1**
10. The **-m** option to the **tune2fs** command allows you to change the percentage of the filesystem reserved for the superuser.

Chapter 11

1. The **vgcreate** command is used to create volume groups.
2. C
3. C
4. The **pvdisplay** command displays information about a physical volume.
5. D
6. D
7. D
8. The **resize2fs** command is used to change the size of an ext4 filesystem.

Chapter 12

1. The SAMBA-client software package provides SAMBA client utilities.
2. A and C
3. D
4. The **[homes]** section of the **smb.conf** file is used to share a SAMBA user's home directories by default.
5. C
6. C
7. Fill in the missing setting for the following SAMBA printer share:

```
[hp-101]
        path = /var/spool/SAMBA/
        browseable = yes
        printable = yes
        printer name = hp-101
```

8. Starting the SAMBA server results in two server processes starting: **smbd** and **nmbd**.

9. B
10. The **map** setting can be used to match Windows account names to local user accounts when placed in the **[global]** section of the **smb.conf** file.
11. The **portmap** service provides the functionality of RPC.
12. C and D
13. D
14. The **async** share option results in better performance but has the potential for data loss.
15. D
16. A and D
17. The **rpc.mountd** process handles the NFS client mount requests.
18. You can see RPC port information on the system by executing the **rpcinfo** command.
19. B and D
20. The **soft** mount option attempts to mount the share once and then stops trying.
21. B
22. The **scsi_id** command is used by the **udev** daemon to map an iSCSI target to a local device file.

Chapter 13

1. For tools that use numbers to specify full and incremental backups, the number **0** specifies a full backup.
2. C and D
3. B and C
4. The **rsync** command is used to remotely back up data; by default, it only backs up data that has changed since the last time the command was used.
5. C
6. D
7. The "no rewind" device name for the first tape device on the system is **/dev/nst0**.
8. B
9. The **-e** option to the **rsync** command is used to enable data transfer via SSH.

Chapter 14

1. The **-r** option to the **crontab** command will remove all entries in the current user's **crontab**.
2. D
3. A and D
4. The **/etc/crontab** file is used by the system administrator to execute system-critical processes at specific intervals.
5. The **atq** command will display the current user's **at** jobs.

Chapter 15

1. The **execute** permission must be added to a script before it can be run like a program.
2. D
3. A and D
4. The **-le** operator is used to determine if one integer is less than or equal to another integer.
5. The **read** command gathers user input and stores the value that the user types into a variable.

Chapter 16

1. The **logrotate** script rotates, compresses, and mails system logs.
2. C and D
3. D
4. The **nl** command displays files, including line numbers.
5. In coding terms, a **repository** is a location where people share programs.

Chapter 17

1. The permissions for the **/var/spool/cron** directory should be **drwx------**.
2. C
3. BASH scripts should never have the SUID and SGID permissions set.
4. C
5. A

Chapter 18

1. A **protocol** is a well-defined standard for network communications between two hosts.
2. C
3. D
4. The **/etc/services** file contains traditional service-to-port mappings.
5. The **DNS** protocol is used to translate hostnames to IP addresses.

Chapter 19

1. Based on the output of the **ifconfig** command shown next, **192.168.1.16** is the IPv4 address for the **eth0** device.
2. C
3. The **arp** command displays information about the table that contains IP-address-to-MAC-address translation.
4. C and D
5. Fill in the blank in the following command to add a gateway for the 192.168.2.0/255.255.255.0 network:

```
route add -net 192.168.2.0 netmask 255.255.255.0 gw 192.168.1.100
```

6. The **ip** command is the replacement command for the **ifconfig**, **arp**, and **route** commands.
7. D

Chapter 20

1. B
2. C
3. A zone file is used to store IP-address-to-domain-name translation information (also called "records").
4. Fill in the blank to create a master DNS server entry in the **/etc/named.conf** file:

```
zone "onecoursesource.com" {
type master;
file "named.onecoursesource.com";
};
```

5. A and C
6. D
7. C
8. The **subnet** directive is used to define a network that the DHCP server provides IP information for.
9. D
10. B

Chapter 21

1. The directive used to specify the directory that contains the web files that will be served by the Apache Web Server is the **DocumentRoot** directive.
2. C
3. D
4. B
5. The HTTPS protocol is used when a web browser communicates with an Apache Web Server using SSL.
6. A, B, and D
7. Fill in the blank for the following command to generate an RSA key file:

```
opensslgenrsa -des3 -out server.key 1024
```

8. A tunneling proxy server acts as a gateway between two networks.
9. The configuration file for Squid is **/etc/squid/squid.conf**.
10. D

Chapter 22

1. An attribute is a component of an object.
2. C

3. B
4. The permissions of the OpenLDAP database directory should be set to **700**. (Provide an octal value.)
5. The **slaptest** command can be used to test the OpenLDAP configuration file before starting the server.
6. D
7. B
8. The **anonymous_enable** directive in the **vsftpd.conf** file is used to allow anonymous FTP connections.
9. A, B, and D
10. The **ListenAddress** setting in the **/etc/ssh/sshd_config** file is used to specify which interfaces to accept SSH connections on.
11. The **AllowUsers** setting of the **/etc/ssh/sshd_config** file is used to specify which users can connect to the SSH server.

Chapter 23

1. The primary configuration file for kernel parameters is the **/etc/sysctl.conf** file.
2. A and D
3. The **libwrap** library is used to implement TCP wrappers.
4. C and D
5. The **ntpq** command allows you to perform queries on NTP servers.

Chapter 24

1. The **ps** command is used to display all processes running on the system.
2. C
3. The highest CPU priority for a process is specified by the nice value of **-20**.
4. C and D
5. The **nohup** command can be used to prevent a process from terminating if its parent process stops running.

Chapter 25

1. The **/etc/rsyslog.conf** file is the primary configuration file for the **rsyslogd** daemon.
2. C
3. Log entries that are generated by the kernel are typically stored in the **/var/log/kern.log** file.
4. D
5. The **logger** command can be used to send a log entry to the **syslogd** daemon.

Chapter 26

1. The RPM databases that contain metadata about software packages are stored in the **/var/lib/rpm** directory.
2. C
3. The **createrepo** command will make a repository in the specified directory.
4. D
5. The **search** feature of the **yum** command will match a glob pattern in package names and summaries.

Chapter 27

1. The **-I** option to the **dpkg** command is used to display information about a package file.
2. C
3. The **apt-scanpackages** command is used to create a source repository for APT.
4. C and D
5. The **–installed** option to the **apt list** command will only display packages that are currently installed on the system.

Chapter 28

1. The **dracut** command is used to create a new **initramfs** file.
2. B
3. The **grub2-mkpasswd-pbkdf2** command is used to create a GRUB2 encrypted password.
4. B and D
5. The **systemctl** command is used to change **systemd** units, such as start and enable a service.

Chapter 29

1. The **-l** option to the **dpkg** command can be used to list all packages on a Debian-based system.
2. B and D
3. Common Vulnerabilities and Exposures (or CVE) is a system designed to provide a single location where you can learn about security-related software issues.
4. C
5. The **xinetd** daemon is referred to as the "super daemon" because it will start other daemons (services) as needed and stop them when they are no longer needed.

Chapter 30

1. B
2. The **-O** option to the **nmap** command attempts to determine the operating system type of a remote system.
3. A
4. B

5. The **lsof** command lists open files on the local system.
6. The end point of a network communication is called a socket.
7. D
8. The **-i** option to the **tcpdump** command limits the display to include packets available only on a specific interface.

Chapter 31

1. If no iptables rules match, the default chain policy target is used.
2. A
3. The **-L** option to the **iptables** command will display current firewall rules.
4. B and D
5. To view port numbers and IP addresses instead of names, use the **-n** option.

Chapter 32

1. The **netstat** command can be used to display all active network connections on the local system.
2. C
3. The **tcpdump** tool allows you to probe network traffic, searching for any suspicious activity.
4. C
5. A **passive** IDS detects possible intrusions and then notifies administrators.

Chapter 33

1. The primary configuration file for the fail2ban utility is the **/etc/fail2ban/jail.conf** file.
2. B
3. C
4. Before you create an OpenVPN CA, you should execute the following command: **source vars**.
5. D
6. To generate the Diffie-Hellman parameters, execute the **build-dh** script in the **/etc/openvpn/easy-rsa** directory.

Resource Guide

Resources by Chapter

Part I: Introducing Linux

Chapter 1: Distributions and Key Components

- **Distro Watch (www.distrowatch.com)** Reviews Linux distributions, keeps track of which distros are popular, and provides links to distribution websites.
- **What is Linux? (https://www.linux.com/what-is-linux)** A tutorial that provides useful information about the components that make up the Linux OS.
- **Techradar Pro (https://www.techradar.com/news/best-linux-distro)** Evaluation of several distributions to aid in user selection.
- **Linux.com (https://www.linux.com/blog/learn/intro-to-linux/2018/1/best-linux-distributions-2018)** Identifies the "best" Linux distributions for 2018.
- **Penguin Tutor (http://www.penguintutor.com/linux/basic-shell-reference)** Linux basic shell reference guide.

Chapter 2: Working on the Command Line

- **FOSSBYTES (https://fossbytes.com/a-z-list-linux-command-line-reference/)** A huge list of Linux commands with a brief summary of each command.
- **Regular Expressions Tutorial (https://www.regular-expressions.info/tutorial.html)** A tutorial for regular expressions.
- **RegExr (https://regexr.com/)** A regular expression testing tool.
- **Regex Crossword (https://regexcrossword.com/)** A regular expression game.

Chapter 3: Getting Help

- **die.net (https://linux.die.net/man/)** Linux man pages available online. Sometimes easier to search for or filter the command help you are searching for.
- **The Linux Documentation Project (https://www.tldp.org/)** A variety of Linux documents, how-to's, and guides. Although some of these guides are out of date, there are some very good resources as well. The "Advanced Bash-Scripting Guide" is a great reference.
- **Linux Forums (http://www.linuxforums.org)** A place where you can ask questions and experienced Linux users will provide answers.
- **GNU Software Foundation (https://www.gnu.org/software/gzip/manual/gzip.html)** An excellent user guide for GNU software.
- **How-To Geek (https://www.howtogeek.com/108890/how-to-get-help-with-a-command-from-the-linux-terminal-8-tricks-for-beginners-pros-alike/)** Tips for beginners and pros to find help with the Linux terminal.
- **Computer Hope (https://www.computerhope.com/unix/uhelp.htm)** Linux help command in depth.
- **Linux.com (https://www.linux.com/learn/intro-to-linux/2017/10/3-tools-help-you-remember-linux-commands)** Three tools to help you remember Linux commands.

Chapter 4: Editing Files

- **The vi Lovers Home Page (http://thomer.com/vi/vi.html)** A source for vi and vim manuals, tutorials, and cheat sheets.
- **Vi Reference Card (https://pangea.stanford.edu/computing/unix/editing/viquickref.pdf)** A printable reference card for using vi editor.
- **Glaciated (http://glaciated.org/vi/)** A no-frills reference to the commands in vi.
- **GNU Emacs Manuals Online (https://www.gnu.org/software/emacs/manual/)** A series of emacs user guides.
- **gedit Text Editor (https://help.gnome.org/users/gedit/stable/)** Documentation for the gedit editor.
- **The KWrite Handbook (https://docs.kde.org/trunk5/en/applications/kwrite/index.html)** Documentation for the kwrite editor.
- **Joe's Own Editor (https://joe-editor.sourceforge.io/4.5/man.html)** The primary site for the joe editor.

Chapter 5: When Things Go Wrong

- **Bugzilla (www.bugzilla.org)** A site that is used to track issues or problems on your systems.

Part II: User and Group Accounts

Chapter 6: Managing Group Accounts

- **Arch Linux (Users and Groups; https://wiki.archlinux.org/index.php/users_and_groups)** A good overview of Linux users and groups.
- **linode (Linux Users and Groups; https://www.linode.com/docs/tools-reference/linux-users-and-groups/)** A good article that covers accounts and basic permissions.
- **User Private Groups (https://access.redhat.com/documentation/en-US/Red_Hat_Enterprise_Linux/4/html/Reference_Guide/s1-users-groups-private-groups.html)** A discussion about user private groups (UPGs).
- **YoLinux (http://www.yolinux.com/TUTORIALS/LinuxTutorialManagingGroups.html)** Managing group access.

Chapter 7: Managing User Accounts

- **Arch Linux (Users and Groups; https://wiki.archlinux.org/index.php/users_and_groups)** A good overview of Linux users and groups.
- **linode (Linux Users and Groups; https://www.linode.com/docs/tools-reference/linux-users-and-groups/)** A good article that covers accounts and basic permissions.
- **The Linux-PAM Guides (http://www.linux-pam.org/Linux-PAM-html/)** Documentation for Pluggable Authentication Modules.
- **YoLinux (http://www.yolinux.com/TUTORIALS/LinuxTutorialManagingGroups.html)** Managing group access.

Chapter 8: Develop an Account Security Policy

- **Ubuntu (User Management; https://help.ubuntu.com/lts/serverguide/user-management.html)** Contains some essential security considerations for user and group accounts.
- **UpCloud (Managing Linux User Account Security; https://www.upcloud.com/support/managing-linux-user-account-security/)** A good tutorial that includes some key security policies and features.

- **Sans.org (https://www.sans.org/reading-room/whitepapers/policyissues/preparation-guide-information-security-policies-503)** A preparation guide to information security policies.

Part III: File and Data Storage

Chapter 9: File Permissions

- **Archlinux (File permissions and attributes; https://wiki.archlinux.org/index.php/File_permissions_and_attributes)** A good overview of Linux permissions.
- **SELinux (https://wiki.centos.org/HowTos/SELinux)** A how-to guide on SELinux.

Chapter 10: Manage Local Storage: Essentials

- **Archlinux (File systems; https://wiki.archlinux.org/index.php/file_systems)** A good overview of Linux filesystems.
- **Archlinux (Partitioning; https://wiki.archlinux.org/index.php/partitioning)** A guide on Linux partitions.
- **An Introduction to Storage Terminology and Concepts in Linux (https://www.digitalocean.com/community/tutorials/an-introduction-to-storage-terminology-and-concepts-in-linux)** Article on Linux storage devices.
- **An Introduction to Linux Filesystems (https://opensource.com/life/16/10/introduction-linux-filesystems)** An article on Linux filesystems.
- **Learn IT Guide (http://www.learnitguide.net/2016/05/disk-management-in-linux-basic-concepts.html)** Disk management in Linux; understanding basic concepts.

Chapter 11: Manage Local Storage: Advanced Features

- **How to Add a New Disk to an Existing Linux Server (https://www.tecmint.com/add-new-disk-to-an-existing-linux/)** A quick step-by-step guide.
- **A Beginner's Guide to LVM (https://www.howtoforge.com/linux_lvm)** A quick guide to logical volume management.
- **Funtoo (https://www.funtoo.org/Learning_Linux_LVM,_Part_1)** Learning Linux logical volume management.

Chapter 12: Manage Network Storage

- **Samba Documentation (https://www.samba.org/samba/docs/)** The main website for Samba documentation.
- **Network File System (NFS; https://help.ubuntu.com/lts/serverguide/network-file-system.html)** User guide for NFS on Ubuntu.
- **iSCSI Storage: A Beginner's Guide (http://blog.open-e.com/iscsi-storage-a-beginners-guide/)** A good overview of iSCSI.

Chapter 13: Develop a Storage Security Policy

- **Linux Backup Types and Tools Explored (https://blog.storagecraft.com/linux-backup-types-tools-explored/)** Describes different backup types and available tools.
- **Sans.org (https://www.sans.org/reading-room/whitepapers/policyissues/preparation-guide-information-security-policies-503)** A preparation guide to information security policies.

Part IV: Automation

Chapter 14: Crontab and At

- **Linux Cron Guide (https://linuxconfig.org/linux-cron-guide)** A guide for using and administering cron.
- **CronHowto (https://help.ubuntu.com/community/CronHowto)** A how-to guide for cron on Ubuntu.
- **Admin's Choice (http://www.adminschoice.com/crontab-quick-reference)** Crontab quick reference.
- **Computer Hope (https://www.computerhope.com/unix/ucrontab.htm)** Linux crontab command.

Chapter 15: Scripting

- **Advanced Bash-Scripting Guide (http://tldp.org/LDP/abs/html/)** A great guide for scripting.
- **Linux Command (http://linuxcommand.org/lc3_resources.php)** A collection of tools, tips, and templates for BASH shell scripts.
- **TecMint (https://www.tecmint.com/command-line-tools-to-monitor-linux-performance/)** Twenty command-line tools to monitor Linux performance.
- **Make Tech Easier (https://www.maketecheasier.com/online-resources-for-learning-the-command-line/)** A collection of online resources for learning the command line.

Chapter 16: Common Automation Tasks

- **Singer'sScripts (ftp://ftp.cs.duke.edu/pub/des/scripts/INDEX.html)** A collection of useful scripts.
- **John Chambers' directory of useful tools (http://trillian.mit.edu/~jc/sh/)** A collection of useful scripts.
- **Cameron Simpson's Scripts (https://cskk.ezoshosting.com/cs/css/)** A collection of useful scripts.
- **Carlos J. G. Duarte's Scripts (http://cgd.sdf-eu.org/a_scripts.html)** A collection of useful scripts.
- **Linux Academy (https://linuxacademy.com/howtoguides/posts/show/topic/14343-automating-common-tasks-with-scripts)** Automating common tasks with scripts.
- **TecMint (https://www.tecmint.com/using-shell-script-to-automate-linux-system-maintenance-tasks/)** Using shell scripts to automate Linux system maintenance.

Chapter 17: Develop an Automation Security Policy

- **Google's Shell Style Guide (https://google.github.io/styleguide/shell.xml)** A good guide to show you how to style your scripts.
- **Sans.org (https://www.sans.org/reading-room/whitepapers/policyissues/preparation-guide-information-security-policies-503)** A preparation guide to information security policies.

Part V: Networking

Chapter 18: Networking Basics

- **Request For Comments (https://www.rfc-editor.org)** Description of RFCs.
- **Subnet calculator (https://www.adminsub.net/ipv4-subnet-calculator)** A subnet calculator.

- **The Internet Protocol Stack (https://www.w3.org/People/Frystyk/thesis/TcpIp.html)** A description of the primary protocols.
- **Commotion (https://commotionwireless.net/docs/cck/networking/learn-networking-basics/)** Learning network basics.

Chapter 19: Network Configuration

- **Network setup (https://www.debian.org/doc/manuals/debian-reference/ch05)** A guide for setting up networking on Debian-based systems.
- **Configure IP Networking (https://access.redhat.com/documentation/en-us/red_hat_enterprise_linux/7/html/networking_guide/ch-configure_ip_networking)** A guide for setting up networking on Red Hat–based systems.
- **Open Source (https://opensource.com/life/16/6/how-configure-networking-linux)** How to configure networking in Linux.

Chapter 20: Network Service Configuration: Essential Services

- **The BIND 9 Administrator Reference Manuals (https://www.isc.org/downloads/bind/doc/)** The main website for BIND documentation.
- **Postfix Documentation (http://www.postfix.org/documentation.html)** The main website for Postfix documentation.
- **Procmail Documentation Project (http://pm-doc.sourceforge.net/)** Provides links to Procmail documentation.
- **Dovecot Documentation (https://www.dovecot.org/documentation.html)** The main website for Dovecot documentation.
- **Linode (https://www.linode.com/docs/tools-reference/linux-system-administration-basics/)** Linux administration basics.

Chapter 21: Network Service Configuration: Web Services

- **Apache HTTP Server Documentation (https://httpd.apache.org/docs/)** The main website for Apache HTTP documentation.
- **Squid Documentation (http://www.squid-cache.org/Doc/)** The primary website for Squid Proxy server documentation.
- **Digital Ocean (https://www.digitalocean.com/community/tutorials/how-to-configure-the-apache-web-server-on-an-ubuntu-or-debian-vps)** How to configure Apache Web Server on an Ubuntu or Debian VPS.
- **Apache HTTP Server project (https://httpd.apache.org/docs/trunk/getting-started.html)** A "getting started" tutorial.

Chapter 22: Connecting to Remote Systems

- **Open LDAP documentation (http://www.openldap.org/doc/)** The primary website for Open LDAP documentation.
- **vsftpd (https://help.ubuntu.com/community/vsftpd)** Ubuntu's documentation page for the vsftpd server.
- **Open SSH (https://www.openssh.com/)** The main web page for the Open SSH project.
- **Colorado State University (https://www.engr.colostate.edu/ens/how/connect/serverlog-in-linux.html)** How to connect to a remote Linux server.

Chapter 23: Develop a Network Security Policy

- **Kernel parameters (https://www.kernel.org/doc/Documentation/admin-guide/kernel-parameters.txt)** A text document that provides a list of kernel parameters along with brief descriptions.
- **TCP Wrappers (https://www.centos.org/docs/5/html/Deployment_Guide-en-US/ch-tcpwrappers.html)** A tutorial on how to implement TCP Wrappers and xinetd; created for CentOS 5, but content is still valid.
- **NTP documentation (http://www.ntp.org/documentation.html)** The main site for all documentation related to the Network Time Protocol.
- **Sans.org (https://www.sans.org/reading-room/whitepapers/policyissues/preparation-guide-information-security-policies-503)** A preparation guide to information security policies.

Part VI: Process and Log Administration

Chapter 24: Process Control

- **How to Manage Processes from the Linux Terminal: 10 Commands You Need to Know (https://www.howtogeek.com/107217/how-to-manage-processes-from-the-linux-terminal-10-commands-you-need-to-know/)** An introduction to processes on Linux.
- **30 Useful 'ps Command' Examples for Linux Process Monitoring (https://www.tecmint.com/ps-command-examples-for-linux-process-monitoring/)** An article that provides more details about using the **ps** command.
- **Geeks for geeks (https://www.geeksforgeeks.org/process-control-commands-unix-linux/)** Process control commands in Unix and Linux.

Chapter 25: System Logging

- **Overview of Syslog (https://www.gnu.org/software/libc/manual/html_node/Overview-of-Syslog.html)** Syslog essentials.
- **systemd-journald.service (https://www.freedesktop.org/software/systemd/man/systemd-journald.service.html)** Describes the journald service.
- **Tutorials Point (https://www.tutorialspoint.com/unix/unix-system-logging.htm)** Unix and Linux system logging.

Part VII: Software Management

Chapter 26: Red Hat–Based Software Management

- **Installing and Managing Software (https://access.redhat.com/documentation/en-us/red_hat_enterprise_linux/7/html/system_administrators_guide/part-installing_and_managing_software)** The official Red Hat manual for installing and managing software.

Chapter 27: Debian-Based Software Management

- **Debian Package Management (https://wiki.debian.org/DebianPackageManagement)** A resource for managing packages on Debian-based systems.

Chapter 28: System Booting

- **Kernel documentation (https://www.kernel.org/doc)** A source for information about kernel parameters used during the boot process.
- **GRUB Documentation (https://www.gnu.org/software/grub/grub-documentation.html)** Official GRUB documentation.

- **systemd System and Service Manager (https://www.freedesktop.org/wiki/Software/systemd/)** A page that contains links to many useful resources for **systemd**.

Chapter 29: Develop a Software Management Security Policy

- **Common Vulnerabilities and Exposures (CVE; http://cve.mitre.org)** A system designed to provide a single location where you can learn about security-related software issues.
- **Red Hat Security Advisories (https://access.redhat.com/security/updates/advisory)** Site that provides information from Red Hat about security issues.
- **Sans.org (https://www.sans.org/reading-room/whitepapers/policyissues/preparation-guide-information-security-policies-503)** A preparation guide for information security policies.

Part VIII: Security Tasks

Chapter 30: Footprinting

- **Nmap documentation (https://nmap.org/docs.html)** A reference that provides a lot of uses of the nmap utility.
- **Ehacking (https://www.ehacking.net/2011/03/footprinting-information-gathering.html)** Footprinting and information-gathering tutorial.
- **Nmap (https://nmap.org/)** Free network scanner nmap.

Chapter 31: Firewalls

- **Archlinux (iptables; https://wiki.archlinux.org/index.php/iptables)** A guide for configuring iptables.
- **TecMint (https://www.tecmint.com/open-source-security-firewalls-for-linux-systems/)** Ten useful open source firewalls for Linux.

Chapter 32: Intrusion Detection Systems

- **The Best Open Source Network Intrusion Detection Tools (https://opensourceforu.com/2017/04/best-open-source-network-intrusion-detection-tools/)** An article that provides an overview of intrusion detection as well as descriptions of several tools.
- **SNORT (https://www.snort.org)** Snort free download and documentation.

Chapter 33: Additional Security Tasks

- **BugTraq (www.securityfocus.com)** This service is an email-based program that is sponsored by Security Focus.
- **Computer Emergency Response Teams (www.cert.org)** Provides a variety of features, including vulnerability analysis tools, a knowledgebase of vulnerability notes, and coordination with private and governmental organizations regarding security issues.
- **US-CERT (www.us-cert.gov)** U.S.-specific CERT.

absolute path Directions provided to a file or directory from the root directory.

access control lists ACLs are used to grant permissions to specific users or groups.

Active Directory A Microsoft Windows product based on the LDAP protocol. Designed to store information and provide this data for various purposes, such as user authentication.

active FTP mode In this mode, the FTP server initiates the data connection.

alias A shell feature that allows a collection of commands to be executed by issuing a single "command."

Amanda A third-party backup utility.

anonymous FTP An FTP feature where a special account (anonymous or ftp) can be used to connect to an FTP server without the need of a password or access to a local user account.

Apache A common way to refer to the Apache Web Server (the formal name is Apache Hypertext Transfer Protocol Server).

argument A parameter provided to a command that tells the command what thing (file, user, and so on) to perform an action on.

ARP Address Resolution Protocol; a protocol that defines how IP addresses are translated into MAC addresses.

ARP table A memory-based table that contains IP addresses and corresponding MAC addresses.

asymmetric cryptography An encryption technique in which one key (the public key) is used to encrypt data, and another key (the private key) is used to decrypt data. Also referred to as PKC (public key cryptography).

at A system for scheduling one or more commands to be executed at one specific time in the future.

attribute A component of an object.

authoritative name server A name server that returns results based on the records stored locally on the system. Also see *name server*.

autofs A system designed to automatically mount filesystems on demand.

background process A process that runs without impacting the ability of the parent process to execute additional programs.

Bacula A third-party backup utility.

Berkeley Internet Name Domain (BIND) The DNS software that is most widely used on the Internet.

BIOS Basic Input/Output System; firmware that starts the process of booting a system.

bootloader A software program provided by the operating system that is designed to access files on the hard drive (specifically the kernel) and start the booting of the operating system.

CA Certificate Authority; a system designed to digitally sign certificates to authenticate another system's identity. CAs have a hierarchy, and the top-level CA is called the *root CA*.

caching name server A name server that returns results based on information obtained from another name server, such as an authoritative name server.

CERT Computer Emergency Response Teams; the original is the CERT Coordination Center (CERT-CC) at Carnegie Mellon University (CMU).

certificate For SSH, certificates are used to allow for password-less authentication.

chain A set of firewall rules that includes both the type and the filtering point.

child directory See *subdirectory*.

CIDR Classless Inter-Domain Routing; like VLSM, CIDR provides a subnet mask, but by specifying how many bytes of the IPv4 address are reserved for the network.

CIFS Common Internet File System; an SMB-based protocol made popular on Microsoft Windows systems.

CLI Command-line interface; a means to communicate with an operating system via commands typed within a shell program.

CN Common name; the relative name of an object.

component In terms of Debian package configuration, this is a feature used to categorize packages. Common components include Main Restricted, Universe, and Multiverse.

conditional expression A programming term that means to perform a statement based on the outcome of a true or false test.

crontab A system for scheduling processes to execute at specific times in the future.

current directory The directory that the shell is currently in.

CVE Common Vulnerabilities and Exposures; a system designed to provide a single location where security personnel can learn about security-related software issues.

daemon A program that runs in the background, performing specific system tasks.

DDoS attack Distributed denial of service; when packets are sent from multiple systems to overwhelm a host.

default chain policy The target to use when no rule in a chain is matched.

dependency In terms of software packages, a dependency is a feature that a package requires to function correctly.

DFS Distributed File System; a technique of sharing files and directories across a network.

DHCP Dynamic Host Configuration Protocol; provides administrators with the ability to dynamically assign network-related information to client systems.

digital signature A unique "key" that an organization can place on a software package to provide the means to verify the origin of the package.

distribution A specific implementation of a Linux operating system.

distro See *distribution*.

DN Distinguished name; the full name of an object.

DNS Domain Name Service; used to translate hostnames to IP addresses.

DNS forwarder A DNS server designed to take DNS queries from an Internet network and send the queries to an external DNS server.

DNS master The DNS server where changes to the zone files are made.

DNS slave A DNS server that holds a copy of the zone files from the DNS master.

Domain Name Service (DNS) A protocol that allows for hostname-to-IP-address resolution.

DoS attack Denial of service; when a large number of network packets are sent to a system, making it difficult for the system to handle all the data and thus rendering the system unresponsive.

dotted decimal notation A 32-bit number divided into four octets that is used to define an IPv4 address or subnet mask.

environment variable A variable that is passed from the current shell into any program or command that is invoked from the shell.

ESMTP Extended SMTP. See *SMTP*.

ESSID Extended Service Set Identification; a name given to a wireless router to distinguish it from other wireless routers.

eth0 The primary Ethernet device name.

Ethernet A technology that allows hosts to form a network—the physical lines of connection between the hosts.

exit status A numeric value returned by a command or program to the calling process (shell). A value of 0 means success whereas a value of 1 means failure.

extension module In terms of iptables, an extension module is an optional feature.

facility In terms of system logging, the facility is the service that is sending the system log.

fiber optic A high-speed technology that allows hosts to form a network—the physical lines of connection between the hosts.

file glob A symbol that is used to match a filename pattern when specifying files on the command line.

file system A structure that is used to organize files and directories on an operating system.

Filesystem Hierarchy Standard A standard that specifies in which directories specific files should be stored.

filtering point A component of a firewall where rules are placed.

firewall A network appliance that is designed to either allow or block network traffic.

firewalld A front-end utility designed to make the process of configuring firewalls with iptables easier.

firmware A program embedded within hardware.

footprinting Also called *reconnaissance*; the process of discovering information about a network or system with the intent to use this information to compromise security measures.

foreground process A process that prevents the parent process from executing any additional programs until the foreground process has terminated.

forward DNS lookup When a query provides a domain name and the DNS server provides the corresponding IP address for that domain name.

forward lookup The process of translating an IP address into a domain name.

FTP File Transfer Protocol; used for transferring files between hosts.

fully qualified domain name (FQDN) The domain name of a host starting from the top of the DNS structure.

gateway A network device that connects two networks. Also called a router.

GECOS General Comprehensive Operating System; a feature that makes use of specific commands to populate and view the comment field of the **/etc/passwd** file.

GID See *group ID*.

group account An account that users can be assigned to in order to provide additional system access.

group ID A unique numeric value assigned to a group account.

GRUB The Grand Unified Boot Loader; the most commonly used boot loader on modern Linux distributions.

GUI Graphical user interface; a means to communicate with an operating system via a window-based environment using a mouse and keyboard.

hexadecimal notation A 128-bit number divided into eight equal parts that is used to define an IPv6 address.

HIDS Host-based IDS; an intrusion detection system that runs on a specific system to determine if an intrusion attempt has occurred.

host A device that communicates on a network.

HTML Hypertext Markup Language; a language used to develop web pages.

HTTP Hypertext Transfer Protocol (or simply *hypertext*); a protocol that has been a standard for web pages since the 1990s.

HTTPS HTTP Secure or HTTP SSL; a secure version of HTTPS that uses SSL. (See also SSL.)

HUP A signal sent to processes when the parent process terminates.

ICMP Internet Control Message Protocol; a protocol used primarily to send error messages and for determining the status of network devices.

IDS Intrusion detection system; a suite of tools used to discover security breaches.

IMAP Internet Message Access Protocol; a protocol used by MUAs to retrieve email.

IMAPS Internet Message Access Protocol, Secured; used to retrieve email via encrypted connections.

info page A document that describes a command or configuration file and provides hyperlinks to additional information related to the topic.

initialization file A file that is executed when a shell starts in order to customize the environment for the user.

initiator In terms of iSCSI, this is the client that connects to the target.

inode A component of a filesystem that stores metadata about a file, including the file ownership, file permissions, and timestamps.

intrusion detection The process of identifying unauthorized access to system and network resources.

IP Internet Protocol; A protocol that's responsible for delivering network packets between hosts.

IP address A unique, numeric-based value used for network communications. Each host has a unique IP address.

IP source routing A feature that enables the sender of a packet to specify the network route that should be taken.

iSCSI Internet Small Computer System Interface; a network storage solution based on the communication protocol provided by SCSI.

job A process started from a shell.

journal A filesystem feature designed to make the **fsck** command perform more quickly.

kernel A software program that controls the operating system.

kernel image file A file that contains a collection of kernel modules and is used during the boot process to provide more kernel features that are required to properly boot the system.

kernel module A software component that provides more features to the kernel.

kill A term used when stopping a program

label A name assigned to a filesystem to make it easier to mount the filesystem.

LAN local area network; this network describes all the hosts that communicate directly with other hosts on the same network.

LDAP Lightweight Directory Access Protocol; provides user and group account data, as well as other data that can be defined by the LDAP administrator. Often used for network-based authentication.

LDAPS Lightweight Directory Access Protocol, Secured; Used to provide network-based information via encryption, such as network account information.

LDIF LDAP Data Interchange Format; a file format used to create LDAP objects.

LE logical extent; a small partition of a logical volume.

libraries A collection of software that is used by other programs to perform specific tasks.

libwrap A library that uses the **/etc/hosts.allow** and **/etc/hosts.deny** files to control access to specific services.

LILO Linux Loader; an older bootloader rarely used on modern Linux distributions.

LKM Loadable Kernel Module; *see* kernel module.

lo The local loopback network address.

local variable A variable that only exists in the current shell.

log A location where actions or issues are described.

login shell A shell that is open when the user initially logs in to the system.

LUKS Linux Unified Key Setup; a filesystem encryption specification.

LUN Logical Unit Number; this is a value used by the target to identify a iSCSI device.

LV logical volume; a device that can act as a partition but has the flexibility to be resized.

LVM Logical Volume Manager; a storage method alternative to traditional partitions.

MAC Media Access Control; a unique address assigned to a network device.

mail spool The location where email messages are placed by the MTA or procmail.

Maildir A format for storing mail spools in different directories.

man page A document that describes a command or configuration file.

man-in-the-middle attack When a system interjects itself between a client and server's communications.

mangle A firewall feature that modifies a network packet.

mask A technique to block default values, such as the **umask** setting that blocks default maximum file and directory permissions.

mbox A format for storing mail spools in a single file for each user.

MBR Master Boot Record; a reserved location at the beginning of the hard disk designed for the bootloader software.

MDA Mail delivery agent; a server that takes the message from the MTA and sends it to the local mail spool.

metadata Information about the software and its dependencies.

mirror In terms of servers, a mirror is a server that provides a copy of data from another server.

mount point A directory used to provide access to the files stored on a physical filesystem.

mounting The process of placing a physical filesystem within the virtual filesystem.

MSA Mail submission agent; a program that accepts an email message from the MUA and communicates with an MTA.

MTA Mail transfer agent; a server responsible for accepting the email message from the MUA and sending it the correct receiving mail server.

MUA Mail user agent; the client program that the user employs to create email messages.

name server A system that responds to DNS client requests.

NAT Network Address Translation; An IPv4 feature that allows for a host with an Internet-accessible IP address to provide access to multiple hosts with internal, private IP addresses.

NetBIOS Network Basic Input/Output System; a set of software that allows different operating systems to communicate.

network A collection of devices that have the means to communicate with other devices sharing that connection.

network packet A well-defined message that includes the data and metadata (called the packet header).

NFS Network File System; a method for sharing files across the network.

NIDS Network-based IDS; an intrusion detection system designed to discover intrusions or attempts by monitoring key networks.

NIS Network Information Service; a limited network-based authentication service.

non-login shell A shell that is open after the user logs in to the system.

NSS Name Service Switch; a service that determines which location to search for system data, including user and group account data.

NTP Network Time Protocol; a protocol that allows a host's system time to be updated from a set of centralized servers.

object Also called an *entry* or *record*; a single item within the LDAP directory.

OpenLDAP An open source server that provides LDAP functionality.

option A predefined value that modifies the behavior of a command.

package Also called a software package; a file that contains a collection of files that make up a software program. The package also includes metadata.

packet header The part of a network packet that provides information about how the network packet is to reach its destination.

packet sniffer A tool that displays local network traffic.

PAM Pluggable Authentication Modules; a Linux feature that allows an administrator to modify the manner in which user accounts are authenticated.

parent directory A directory that holds other directories (called *subdirectories*).

passive FTP mode In this mode, the FTP client initiates the data connection.

passive IDS An IDS that detects possible intrusions and then notifies administrators.

PE physical extent; a small portion of a physical volume.

Perl A scripting language often used on Linux distributions and known for its flexible programming style.

permission A feature that allows or blocks access to a file or directory.

PHP A language commonly used to create dynamic web pages. PHP originally stood for Personal Home Page.

physical filesystem A filesystem placed on a device, such as a partition or logical volume.

PID Process ID; a unique number that is used to control a process.

piping Sending the output of a command as input to the next command.

PKC See *asymmetric cryptography*.

plug-in A component of a utility or server that adds more features. You can add or remove the features by turning the plug-in on or off.

POP Post Office Protocol; a protocol used by MUAs to retrieve email.

POP3 Post Office Protocol; Used to retrieve email.

POP3S Post Office Protocol, Secured; Used to retrieve email via encrypted connections.

port scanner A tool that probes a system for open network ports.

primary group The group that, by default, a user account's new files belong to.

priority In terms of system logging, the priority is the level of the message.

private IP address An IPv4 address that can't be connected directly to the Internet. *Also see* NAT.

private key A key used by the system to decrypt data that has been encrypted with a corresponding public key.

process A program that is running on the system.

promiscuous mode A network mode that has the local network device listen to all network traffic instead of traffic only intended for that network device.

protocol A well-defined standard for network communications between two hosts.

proxy server A system that serves to facilitate the communications between a client and a server.

public key A key used by other systems to encrypt data.

pull server In email terminology, a server that waits for a client to initiate the transfer of data.

push server In email terminology, a server that initiates the transfer of data.

PV physical volume; a storage device used as the base of LVM.

Python A scripting language often used on Linux distributions and known for its rigid programming style.

reactive or active IDS An IDS that attempts to automatically react or respond to intrusions.

record Within the zone file, a record is an entry that defines one IP-address-to-domain-name translation.

recursive acronym An acronym that has the acronym as part of the definition.

redirection Taking the input or output of a command and sending it to an alternative location.

regular expressions Special characters that are used to match the pattern of text from a file's contents or the output of a command.

relative path Providing directions to a file or directory from the current directory.

repository Also called repo; a location, typically network accessible, that contains RPM packages and a small database that describes the relationship between these packages. In coding terms, a repository is a location where people share programs.

reverse DNS lookup When a query provides an IP address and the DNS server provides the corresponding domain name for that IP address.

reverse lookup The process of translating a domain name into an IP address.

RHSA Red Hat Security Advisory; a Red Hat technique to inform security personnel of any potential vulnerabilities.

root directory The top-level directory of the Linux filesystem.

root servers The DNS servers at the very top of the DNS hierarchy. These servers are aware of the IP address of the top-level domain DNS servers.

route The path from one network to another.

router A system that forwards network packets between networks.

routing How network packets are moved from one network to another.

RPC Remote Procedure Call; a service that acts as a go-between for a client and a server.

RPM RPM Package Manager; a tool for managing software packages.

RSA Rivest-Shamir-Adleman; an encryption system that uses private and public keys.

Samba A service that provides authentication and file-sharing features.

schema Used to define the attributes and objects in an LDAP directory.

secondary group An additional group that the user belongs to, providing the user with access to more system resources.

self-signing When a system acts as the root CA for its own certificate.

SELinux Security Enhanced Linux; a security method that adds a layer of security to files and directory access.

SGID Set group ID; a method to give default group ownership to files created within a specific directory.

shell A software program that provides a command-line interface to the operating system.

skel directory A directory used to populate a user's home directory when the user account is created.

SMB Server Message Block; a protocol invented in the mid-1980s by IBM for the purpose of sharing directories between hosts on a local area network (LAN).

SMTP Simple Mail Transfer Protocol; the standard protocol for email exchange.

SMTPS Simple Mail Transfer Protocol, Secured; used to send encrypted email messages.

snapshot A technique to make a filesystem appear to be static to perform an accurate backup.

sniff To watch network traffic.

SNMP Simple Network Management Protocol; Used to gather information about network devices.

socket Part of a network connection between two systems, associated with a specific network port.

source For package management, this is the term used for repositories on Debian-based systems.

source repository In terms of Debian packages, this is the location from which packages are downloaded when the **apt** commands are used.

sourcing Executing the code from a separate file as if it was code embedded in the current shell or script. This is often used to create variables in the current shell or script.

special groups Groups that are either part of the default Linux installation or created when software is added to the system. These groups normally provide special access to the system for system processes or software.

splashimage A graphic displayed when the Legacy GRUB boot menu is displayed.

SSH Secure Shell; Used for connecting to remote systems and executing commands.

SSL Secure Sockets Layer; a cryptographic protocol used to secure data transfer and authenticate systems.

SSSD System Security Services Daemon; a daemon that interacts with directory structures to provide authentication services.

static host A host that is provided the same network information from a DHCP server each time the host requests an IP address. Also called a *reservation*.

Sticky bit A permission set that modifies the write permissions on directories.

subcommand A command that is executed on another (primary) command's argument list. The output of the subcommand is passed as an argument to the primary command.

subdirectory A directory under another directory (the parent directory of the subdirectory).

subdomain Any domain that is a component of a larger domain.

subnet A network feature that, when combined with an IP address, defines the network of a host.

SUID Set user ID; a method to grant additional access to files when a process is run.

swap space Hard drive space used in place of RAM when available RAM runs low.

SYN flood attack A DoS attack where SYN requests are used to make a system unresponsive.

syncing The process of writing data being stored in memory to the hard drive.

syslog Used to send system log messages to remote systems.

table A type of firewall rule, such as filter, nat, or mangle.

tape device A device that allows you to back up filesystem data to tape.

tar ball A file that is the result of merging files together using the **tar** command.

target In terms of iSCSI, the target describes the storage device, which resides on a remote server.

target The action to be taken when a rule is matched.

TCP Transmission Control Protocol; A protocol that is designed to ensure that the network packages arrive in a reliable and ordered manner.

TCP Wrappers A library used by some servers to allow or deny access to the service.

telnet Used for connecting to remote systems and executing commands.

terminal A place where a user is provided command-line access to the system. This could be a physical terminal machine connected to the system or a virtual terminal, such as a GUI terminal window or an SSH connection.

time to live How long a caching DNS server should hold data obtained from a master or slave DNS server.

TLS Transport Layer Security; a cryptographic protocol used to secure data transfer and authenticate systems. Designed to replace SSL, TLS is often generically called SSL.

Tower of Hanoi A backup strategy based on a mathematical puzzle.

TTL See *time to live*.

TTY Represents a terminal; a unique name of a physical or virtual terminal.

UDP User Datagram Protocol; A protocol designed to allow for the transportation of packages in a connectionless manner.

UEFI Unified Extensible Firmware Interface; software designed to replace BIOS (*also see* BIOS).

UFW Uncomplicated firewall; a front-end utility designed to make the process of configuring firewalls with iptables easier.

UID See *user ID*.

unit One of the core features of a system.

UPG See *User Private Group*.

URI (uniform resource identifier) In terms of Debian package configuration, a URI is used to define the path to a source repository.

user ID A unique numeric value assigned to a user account.

user ID mapping The mapping of one user name or group name on an NFS client to a user name or group name on an NFS server.

User Private Group A group account created for a specific user.

UUID Universally Unique Identifier; a unique value used to designate a disk device.

variable A way to store a value in the shell or in a programming language.

VG volume group; a collection of physical volumes used to create logical volumes.

vi mode A feature of the vi editor; the mode you are in allows you to perform specific operations.

virtual filesystem The collection of physical filesystems merged together via mount points.

virtual host When an Apache Web Server serves up web pages for more than one website.

virtual machine An operating system that thinks it is installed natively but is actually sharing a system with a host operating system.

VLSM Variable-Length Subnet Mask; A 32-bit number divided into four octets that is used to define an IPv4 subnet mask.

VM See *virtual machine.*

VPN Virtual private network; a virtual network that provides the privacy normally only available on a physical network.

WAN Wide area network; this network describes a collection of LANs that communicate through a series of routers or switches.

WAP Wi-Fi Protected Access; an encryption specification used to secure the wireless router from unauthorized users.

WEP Wireless Encryption Protocol; an old encryption specification used to secure the wireless router from unauthorized users.

white pages A schema designed to provide information about users.

wildcard See *file glob.*

WWID World Wide Identifier; in terms of iSCSI, this is an identifier guaranteed to be unique throughout the world.

xinetd Known as the "super daemon" because it will start other daemons (services) as needed and stop each one when it is no longer needed.

zone transfer The process of copying new DNS zone information from the master server to the slave server.

Symbols

A

B

C

D

E

F

G

H

I

J

K

L

M

N

O

P

Q

R

S

T

U

V

W

X

Z